The Best of Bible Pathway

Presented to

____

on this __________ of ________________________

____

____

____

____

____

____

By

____

____

THE BEST OF BIBLE PATHWAY

THRU THE BIBLE IN ONE YEAR READING 15 MINUTES A DAY

366 DAILY DEVOTIONS
GENESIS THROUGH REVELATION

JOHN A. HASH

Published By

BIBLE PATHWAY MINISTRIES
INTERNATIONAL

P. O. Box 20123
Murfreesboro, Tennessee 37129

Printed in the United States of America

ISBN 1-879595-34-6

Bible Pathway is a Christ-centered through-the-Bible devotional commentary and not a theological exposition.

The devotional thought reveals how each day's Bible reading relates to our personal relationship with God and our fellow man, as well as our own spiritual needs.

Recommended by leaders in all major denominations and educators throughout the world.

The world's most-widely-read through-the-Bible devotional commentary

Bible Pathway Ministries International
PO Box 20123
Murfreesboro TN 37129

Table of Contents

Introductions To The Books Of The Old Testament Maps & Charts

Introductions To The Books Of The New Testament
Maps & Charts

NOTE 1: The references given in the devotions often include more verses than the ones actually quoted to give the reader a more complete overall thought.

NOTE 2: When given consecutive Scripture references from the same book, the name of the book is only mentioned with the first reference.

Acknowledgments

I ESPECIALLY WANT TO THANK Karen Hawkins, Barbara Ann Bivens, Benjamin Wallace, and Ken Sharp, whose help with research and writing was invaluable to the creation of this book. I am very appreciative of Clarence Rathbone for his insight and editing; Jé French for her skills in preparing the maps, charts, and illustrations; Mary Kay Wagner for proofreading; Rita Guerra, Barbara Jean Jackson, and Wanda Baker for their editorial assistance; and sincere appreciation to Gina Lesnefsky, chief typesetter, and her assistant Charity Ryan; and the other invaluable team members for their significant contributions: George Kopchak, Jim Ryan, Pam Pendergrast, and Clarence Chauncey.

WE ARE INDEBTED TO LifeWay Christian Resources' president, James T. Draper, Jr., for his encouragement to compile *The Best of Bible Pathway*; to Holman Bible Publishers for the use of the *Holman Christian Standard Bible*; to Sam Gantt at Holman Bible Publishers; and to Greg Webster of the The Gregory Group.

THERE IS ONE PERSON more than any other who is unequaled: my precious wife, Letha, whose spiritual insight, patience, and advice has been priceless, and whom I admire with unequaled esteem. We have experienced 59 years together sharing the abundant love of God – *above all that we ask or think* (Ephesians 3:20).

– In Memory of –

I AM DEEPLY GRATEFUL for the loving concern of my mother, Iva Ann Hash McElroy, who faithfully taught me to be loyal to Christ and His Word; an old preacher, Ted Hutchins, who was the first to tell me, as a teenager, that I ought to read through the Bible; Gerald Heskett, a preacher friend, who spent many days and weeks with me fasting and praying for God to have first place in our lives; and for M.E. Harding, a blind lady who gave me much spiritual insight 60 years ago. A few of her poems have been included in this book.

If *The Best of Bible Pathway* leads you to see more clearly that *all Scripture . . . is profitable*, then praise the Lord and give Him all the glory.

John A Hash

Foreword

God gives every generation of believers a select group of saints whose unique gifts and insights help keep His people on the right track. During the past half century, the Body of Christ has been blessed by the energetic yet unassuming work of Dr. John Hash.

I was still a boy when, the year after the close of World War II, Pastor Hash began a brilliant work among the people the Lord had given into his charge. Because knowing God's Word is the key to life for any Christian, Dr. Hash made it his top ministry priority to teach every member of his congregation how to keep the Bible at the center of their lives. He developed a tightly organized reading plan to guide people through the entire Bible each year. Week by week, he assembled the readings, handed out mimeographed copies of the program, and preached from the selected Scriptures each Sunday.

The result? A congregation in love with the Bible and the Lord to which the Word of God points.

Years later, after Dr. Hash's faithful weekly lessons blossomed into Bible Pathway Ministries, I had the privilege of meeting him personally. At the time, I was serving as president of the Southern Baptist Convention and so was in a position to see a remarkable variety of approaches faithful pastors and teachers could take to help people draw nearer to God. But I said to Dr. Hash, in all sincerity, that there is nothing more valuable anyone can do than to establish a daily commitment simply to read God's Word itself. For that reason, I cannot praise highly enough the vision and purpose of Bible Pathway. Its sole focus is to encourage believers to read the Bible and facilitate their understanding of Scripture.

As I reviewed the manuscript for this book, it was everything I would have expected from Dr. Hash – and a great deal more! It's ripe with some of the most helpful charts, maps, and illustrations available, and Dr. Hash offers sensitive insights into pressing issues that face today's church. Yet he always keeps foremost in mind the need of individual believers to maintain a vital, growing relationship with Jesus Christ.

Read the Scriptures outlined for you in *The Best of Bible Pathway*, and take to heart Dr. Hash's nurturing words. If you've never read the Bible through in a year, you're in for a wonderful experience, and if you have, then you know the richness that awaits you as you do it again.

The Lord promised in Matthew 5:6 – *Blessed are those who hunger and thirst for righteousness, because they will be filled.* There is truly no better way to be filled with the righteousness for which you thirst than to drink deeply of His Word.

May God bless your journey along the path toward Him!

– James T. Draper, Jr., President
LifeWay Christian Resources

Introduction

Know what you believe. Know why you believe it. Then live it!

That's the theme of every Greek and Hebrew language class I've ever taught. It is also the theme of one man whose ministry stands tall among those who are raised up by God to advance His Kingdom.

More than half a century ago, Dr. John Hash first grasped what should be to all of us the obvious connection between reading Scripture and knowing what you believe. All that we as Christians believe is revealed in the written Word of God. Unless you know what that Word says, you cannot know what you believe. And unless you know what you believe, you cannot know how to live it.

This book presents the wisdom Dr. Hash has gained through his years of repeated study of God's Word, and it offers direction and encouragement in a highly refined presentation of scriptural truths. The approach is essentially the same as when Dr. Hash first introduced his congregation to the idea of reading the entire Bible: *If you spend just fifteen minutes reading Scripture every day following this guide, you will read through the entire Bible in one year.*

You will find in the pages that follow, a guide to tell you which passage of Scripture to read each day. In addition, Dr. Hash explains background information about biblical history, culture, geography, and other details which bring the Bible into clearer focus. Three invaluable features deliver these insights:

(1) Each book of the Bible is introduced with an overview of the message and summary of the biblical narrative. From the outset, you will see how the message of Genesis ties to the message of the Gospel of John or the book of Hebrews or Paul's letter to the Corinthians. You will glimpse how each book of the Bible fits into the whole of God's revelation, and you will understand the impact of the events in each account on the people involved. Consequently, you will better apprehend its relevance for your own life.

(2) Every day's Scripture reading is headed by a summary statement that encapsulates what you will learn that day. For example, on Day 73 when you are to read Joshua 1-3, the summary says: "God speaks to Joshua; spies sent to Jericho; pledge between the spies and Rahab; Israel crosses the Jordan River." The day's commentary shows you the significance of Joshua's faith and of Rahab's role in the ongoing revelation of God (she's part of the genealogy of Jesus!). A "Thought

for Today" ties the threads together and helps you grasp the scripture's implication for your life.

(3) Maps of biblical lands and charts explaining time lines as well as other pertinent information pepper the book. Just when you need it, you'll find a map of the Exodus from Egypt or of the boundaries of David's Kingdom; you'll review a list of the fifteen judges of Israel or study a diagram of the desert tabernacle.

Since the focus of *The Best of Bible Pathway* is Scripture itself, each devotional references several key verses relevant to the focal passage of the day. In the *The Best of Bible Pathway*, these Scriptures are cited from the *Holman Christian Standard Bible*®. Dr. Hash has used this new translation because its translators are committed to reflect the original wording of Scripture accurately, yet readably, in modern English. You'll no doubt be reading each day's recommended passage in the translation of your choice, but be sure to pay close attention to scriptures cited in the book and soak in the meaning of these key verses.

Finally, let me encourage you to avoid thinking of yourself in terms of "success" or "failure." You may be tempted to think you've failed if you miss a day, or on the other extreme, become so obsessed with "succeeding" in reading the whole Bible in 365 days, that you lose sight of each day's opportunity to experience God's peace and receive His message in His timing. If you miss a day, never mind! Pick up the next day and move on. Read two days' worth, if you can, but whatever you do, don't give up!

There may be days when the clarity of a particular truth sets you on the mountaintop. Yet there may be other periods when God communicates His direction gradually over several days, or maybe even weeks. But be assured that He does have a message for you, and you will hear Him speak it in a way that you will understand. Your part is to be faithful in reading His Book.

Remember: Fifteen minutes a day is all you have to invest. Just make sure that once you read it and know it, you live it!

– Samuel J. Gantt, III
Holman Bible Publishers, Nashville, Tennessee
Former Director of Biblical Language Instruction
Fuller Theological Seminary, Pasadena, California

Thy Word Have I Hid in My Heart
From Psalm 119
Adapted by Ernest O. Sellers, 1869-1952
Ernest O. Sellers, 1869-1952
1. Thy Word is a lamp to my feet, A light to my path al - way,
2. For - ev - er, O Lord, is Thy Word Es - tab-lished and fixed on high;
3. At morn - ing, at noon, and at night I ev - er will give Thee praise;
4. Thro' Him whom Thy Word hath foretold, The Sav-iour and Morn-ing Star,
To guide and to save me from sin, And show me the heav'n-ly way.
Thy faith-ful-ness un - to all men A - bid-eth for - ev - er nigh.
For Thou art my por - tion, O Lord, And shall be thro' all my days!
Sal - va - tion and peace have been bro't To those who have strayed a - far.
Refrain
Thy Word have I hid in my heart (in my heart), That I might not
sin a-gainst Thee (a - gainst Thee); That I might not sin, that
I might not sin, Thy Word have I hid in my heart.
Copyright, 1908. Renewal, 1936. Broadman Press, owner. Used by permission

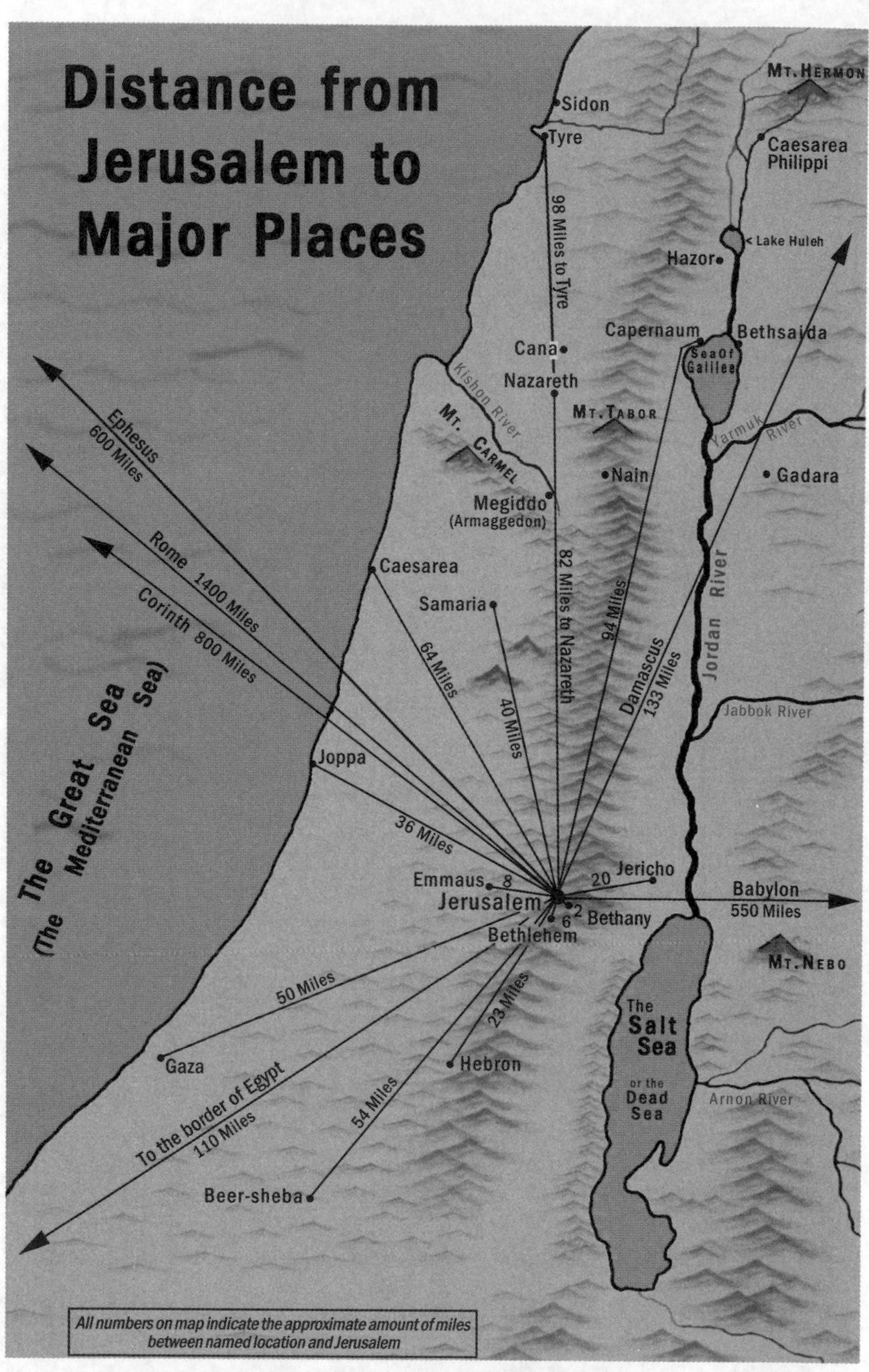

You will be My witnesses in Jerusalem, in all Judea and Samaria, and to the ends of the earth (Acts 1:8)

THE POWER OF GOD'S WORD

Jesus Christ set the example of how important the Old Testament was to Him and should be to us. His emphasis started with the first recorded words of our Lord following His baptism. After 40 days of fasting, He was tempted of the Devil, who said: *If You are the Son of God, tell these stones to become bread. But He answered, It is written, Man must not live by bread alone* [physical necessities], *but on every word that comes from the mouth of God* [spiritual necessities] [Matthew 4:3-4; compare Deuteronomy 8:3]. By quoting this Old Testament Scripture, our Lord revealed the "Key to Victory" over satanic deceptions. We can have that same victory over Satan as we become familiar with *every word that comes from the mouth of God.*

ASHAMED

II Timothy 2:15 — *Be diligent to present yourself approved to God, a worker who doesn't need to be ashamed, correctly teaching the word of truth.*

COMFORT

John 14:26 — *But the Counselor, the Holy Spirit . . . will teach you.*

John 15:11 — *I have spoken these things to you so that My joy may be in you and your joy may be complete.*

I Thess. 4:18 — *Therefore encourage one another with these words.*

Psalms 119:50 — *This is my comfort in my affliction: Your promise has given me life.*

Psalms 119:28 — *I am weary from grief; strengthen me through Your word.*

DISCIPLESHIP

John 8:31-32 — *So Jesus said to the Jews who had believed Him, If you continue in My word, you really are My disciples. You will know the truth, and the truth will set you free.*

John 8:51 — *I assure you: If anyone keeps My word, he will never see death – ever!*

Psalms 1:2 — *Instead, his delight is in the LORD's instruction, and he meditates on it day and night.*

ENDURES FOREVER

Psalms 119:160 — *The entirety of Your word is truth, and all Your righteous judgments endure forever.*

I Peter 1:25 — *But the word of the Lord endures forever. And this is the word that was preached as the gospel to you.*

Matthew 24:35 — *Heaven and earth will pass away, but My words will never pass away.*

Enlightens

Psalms 119:130	*The revelation of Your words brings light and gives understanding to the inexperienced.*

Faith

Romans 10:17	*So faith comes from what is heard, and what is heard comes through the message about Christ.*

Fire

Jeremiah 20:9	*If I say, I will not mention Him, nor speak any longer in His name, His message becomes a fire burning in my heart, shut up in my bones. I become tired of holding it in, and I cannot prevail.*

Food

Matthew 4:4	*But He answered, It is written: Man must not live on bread alone, but on every word that comes from the mouth of God.* (You can't live by *every word* if you have never read it.)
Jeremiah 15:16	*Your words were found, and I ate them. Your words became a delight to me and the joy of my heart. For I am called by Your name, O LORD, God of Hosts.*
Job 23:12	*As for the command of His lips – there, too, I have not turned away: I have treasured up the words of His mouth more than my daily food.*
I Peter 2:2	*Like newborn infants, desire the unadulterated spiritual milk, so that you may grow by it in your salvation.* (The strength of our spiritual life and our ability to please the Lord will be in exact proportion to the time we set aside to read through the Bible.)

God's Word Ignored

Hosea 4:6	*My people are destroyed for lack of knowledge! Because you have rejected knowledge, I will reject you from serving as My priest. Since you have forgotten the law of your God, I, on My part, will forget your children.*
Proverbs 13:13	*The one who has contempt for instruction will pay the penalty, but the one who respects a command will be rewarded.*

Guide

Psalms 119:105	*Your word is a lamp for my feet and a light on my path.*

Hammer

Jeremiah 23:29	*Is not My word like fire, says the LORD, and like a sledgehammer that pulverizes rock?*

Helmet

Ephesians 6:17	*Take the helmet of salvation, and the sword of the Spirit, which is God's word.*

Instructs

II Tim. 3:16-17	*All Scripture is inspired by God and is profitable for teaching, for rebuking, for correcting, for training in righteousness, so that the man of God may be complete, equipped for every good work.*

Judge

John 12:47-48	*If anyone hears My words and doesn't keep them, I do not judge him; for I did not come to judge the world, but to save the world. The one who rejects Me and doesn't accept My sayings has this as his judge: the word I have spoken will judge him on the last day.*
Rev. 22:18-19	*I testify to everyone who hears the prophetic words of this book: If anyone adds to them, God will add to him the plagues that are written in this book. And if anyone takes away from the words of this prophetic book, God will take away his share of the tree of life and the holy city, written in this book.*

Life

James 1:18	*By His own choice, He gave us a new birth by the message of truth so that we would be the firstfruits of His creatures.*
I Peter 1:23	*Since you have been born again – not of perishable seed but of imperishable – through the living and enduring word of God.*

Neglect

Jeremiah 2:13	*For My people have committed a double evil: They have abandoned Me, the fountain of living water, to dig cisterns for themselves, cracked cisterns that can hold no water.*

Peace

John 16:33	*I have told you these things so that in Me you may have peace. In the world you have suffering. But take courage! I have conquered the world.*
Psalms 119:165	*Abundant peace belongs to those who love Your instruction; nothing makes them stumble.*

Perfects

I John 2:5 — *But whoever keeps His word, truly in him the love of God is perfected. This is how we know we are in Him.*

Prayer Answered

John 15:7 — *If you remain in Me and My words remain in you, ask whatever you want and it will be done for you.*

I John 3:21-22 — *We have confidence before God, and can receive whatever we ask from Him because we keep His commands and do what is pleasing in His sight.*

John 15:10 — *If you keep My commandments you will remain in My love, just as I have kept My Father's commandments*

Prayers That Are Detestable

I Corinthians 2:14 — *But the natural man does not welcome what comes from God's Spirit, because it is foolishness to him; he is not able to know it since it is evaluated spiritually* (speaking about the *Spirit of God* giving understanding of His Word).

Proverbs 28:9 — *Anyone who turns his ear away from hearing the law – even his prayer is detestable.*

Sanctification

John 17:17 — *Sanctify them by the truth; Your word is truth.*

I Peter 1:22 — *By obedience to the truth, having purified* [sanctified] *yourselves for sincere love of the brothers, love one another earnestly from a pure heart.*

Strengthen

Hebrews 5:14 — *But solid food is for the mature – for those whose senses have been trained to distinguish between good and evil.*

Success

Joshua 1:8 — *This book of the law must not depart from your mouth; you must recite it day and night, so that you may keep observing all that is written in it. For then you will make your way prosperous and will succeed.*

I Kings 2:3 — *Keep your obligation to the LORD your God to walk in His ways and to keep His statutes, His commandments, His judgments, and His testimonies, as is written in the Law of Moses, so that you may have success* (do wisely) *in everything you do and wherever you turn.*

Sustains

Philippians 2:16	*Hold firmly the message of life. Then I can boast in the day of Christ that I didn't run in vain or labor for nothing.*
Psalms 119:92	*If Your instruction had not been my delight, I would have died in my affliction.*

Sword

Ephesians 6:17	*Take the helmet of salvation, and the sword of the Spirit, which is God's word.*
Hebrews 4:12	*For the word of God is living and effective and sharper than any two-edged sword, penetrating as far as to divide soul, spirit, joints, and marrow; it is a judge of the ideas and thoughts of the heart.*

Treasure

Psalms 19:9-10	*The ordinances of the Lord. . . . They are more desirable than gold – than an abundance of pure gold; and sweeter than honey – than honey dripping from the comb.*

Truth

John 16:13	*When the Spirit of truth comes, He will guide you into all the truth.* (We are all dependent upon the Holy Spirit to reveal His will as we read His word. But the Holy Spirit will not reveal what we refuse or neglect to read.)
Hebrews 4:12	*The word of God is living and effective and sharper than any two-edged sword, penetrating as far as to divide soul, spirit, joints, and marrow; it is a judge of the ideas and thoughts of the heart.*

Will Not Return Empty

Isaiah 55:11	*So is My word that goes out from My mouth. It will not return to Me empty, but will accomplish what I please, and will prosper in what I send it to do.*

Wisdom

Colossians 3:16	*Let the message about the Messiah dwell richly among you, teaching and admonishing one another in all wisdom, and singing psalms, hymns, and spiritual songs, with gratitude in your hearts to God.*
II Timothy 3:15	*And that from childhood you have known the sacred Scriptures, which are able to instruct you for salvation through faith in Christ Jesus.*

THE JEWISH CALENDAR

Civil Calendar - Official calendar of kings, childbirth, and contracts **Sacred Calendar** - Used to compute festivals

Month Sacred/Civil	Days in Month	Pre-Exile Name	Post Exile Name	Present-day Equivalent	Biblical References	Season	Day Festivals
1/7	30	Abib	Nisan	March/April	Exodus 12:2; Nehemiah 2:1	Spring Latter rains Barley harvest	14th Passover (Ex. 12:18) 15-21st Unleavened Bread (Lev. 23:6) Firstfruits (Lev. 23:10)
2/8	29	Ziv (Zif)	Iyyar	April/May	I Kings 6:1,37	Dry season begins	
3/9	30		Sivan	May/June	Esther 8:9	Wheat harvest Early figs ripen	Festival of Weeks (Pentecost) Harvest (Lev. 23:15-21)
4/10	29		Tammuz	June/July		Hot season; Grape harvest	
5/11	30		AB (AV)	July/August		Olive harvest	9th Fast, Destruction of Temple
6/12	29		Elul	August/September	Nehemiah 6:15	Dates & Summer figs	
7/1	30	Ethanim	Tishri	September/October	I Kings 8:2	Early (former) rains, plowing time	1st Trumpets (Nu. 29:1) 10th Day of Atonement (Lev. 26:27) 15-21st Tabernacles (Lev. 23:34) 22nd Solemn Assembly (Lev. 23:36)
8/2	29	Bul	Cheshvan or Marcheshvan	October/November	I Kings 6:38	Wheat & Barley sown Winter figs	
9/3	30		Chislev (Chisleu) or Kisleu	November/December	Nehemiah 1:1	Winter rains, sowing	25th 8 Day Dedication (Jn. 10:22) added in between Old & New Testaments
10/4	29		Tebeth (Tevet)	December/January	Esther 2:16	Winter rains	
11/5	30		Shebat (Shevat)	January/February	Zechariah 1:7	Almond trees blossom	
12/6	29		Adar	February/March	Ezra 6:15	Latter rains, citrus harvest	13-15th Purim - began with Queen Esther (Esth. 9:15-19)

*The Hebrew year had 354 days based on a lunar cycle. Months were alternately 30 and 29 days long. An extra 29-day month, Veadar, was added between Adar and Nisan about every 3 years.

The Jewish day was from sunset to sunset, in 8 equal parts:

FIRST WATCH .... Sunset to 9 P.M.
SECOND WATCH .. 9 P.M. to Midnight
THIRD WATCH ...... Midnight to 3 A.M.
FOURTH WATCH ... 3 A.M. to Sunrise

FIRST HOUR .... Sunrise to 9 A.M.
THIRD HOUR .... 9 A.M. to Noon
SIXTH HOUR .... Noon to 3 P.M.
NINTH HOUR ....3 P.M. to Sunset

Annual Bible-Reading Check List

JANUARY

		Check this column as you read each day
1	Genesis 1-3	
2	Genesis 4-6	
3	Genesis 7-9	
4	Genesis 10-12	
5	Genesis 13-15	
6	Genesis 16-18	
7	Genesis 19-21	
8	Genesis 22-24	
9	Genesis 25-27	
10	Genesis 28-30	
11	Genesis 31-33	
12	Genesis 34-36	
13	Genesis 37-39	
14	Genesis 40-42	
15	Genesis 43-45	
16	Genesis 46-48	
17	Gen. 49-Exodus 1	
18	Exodus 2-4	
19	Exodus 5-7	
20	Exodus 8-10	
21	Exodus 11-13	
22	Exodus 14-16	
23	Exodus 17-19	
24	Exodus 20-22	
25	Exodus 23-25	
26	Exodus 26-28	
27	Exodus 29-31	
28	Exodus 32-34	
29	Exodus 35-37	
30	Exodus 38-39	
31	Exodus 40	

FEBRUARY

		Check this column as you read each day
1	Leviticus 1-3	
2	Leviticus 4-6	
3	Leviticus 7-8	
4	Leviticus 9-10	
5	Leviticus 11-13	
6	Leviticus 14-15	
7	Leviticus 16-18	
8	Leviticus 19-21	
9	Leviticus 22-23	
10	Leviticus 24-25	
11	Leviticus 26-27	
12	Numbers 1-2	
13	Numbers 3-4	
14	Numbers 5-6	
15	Numbers 7	
16	Numbers 8-9	
17	Numbers 10-11	
18	Numbers 12-13	
19	Numbers 14-15	
20	Numbers 16-18	
21	Numbers 19-20	
22	Numbers 21-22	
23	Numbers 23-25	
24	Numbers 26-27	
25	Numbers 28-29	
26	Numbers 30-31	
27	Numbers 32-33	
28	Numbers 34-35	
29	Numbers 36	

MARCH

		Check this column as you read each day
1	Deut. 1-2	
2	Deut. 3-4	
3	Deut. 5-7	
4	Deut. 8-10	
5	Deut. 11-13	
6	Deut. 14-16	
7	Deut. 17-20	
8	Deut. 21-23	
9	Deut. 24-27	
10	Deut. 28	
11	Deut. 29-31	
12	Deut. 32-34	
13	Joshua 1-3	
14	Joshua 4-6	
15	Joshua 7-8	
16	Joshua 9-10	
17	Joshua 11-13	
18	Joshua 14-16	
19	Joshua 17-19	
20	Joshua 20-21	
21	Joshua 22-24	
22	Judges 1-2	
23	Judges 3-5	
24	Judges 6-7	
25	Judges 8-9	
26	Judges 10-11	
27	Judges 12-14	
28	Judges 15-17	
29	Judges 18-19	
30	Judges 20-21	
31	Ruth 1-4	

APRIL

		Check this column as you read each day
1	I Samuel 1-3	
2	I Samuel 4-7	
3	I Samuel 8-11	
4	I Sam. 12-14:23	
5	I Sam. 14:24-16	
6	I Samuel 17-18	
7	I Samuel 19-21	
8	I Samuel 22-24	
9	I Samuel 25-27	
10	I Samuel 28-31	
11	II Samuel 1-2	
12	II Samuel 3-5	
13	II Samuel 6-9	
14	II Samuel 10-12	
15	II Samuel 13-14	
16	II Samuel 15-16	
17	II Samuel 17-18	
18	II Samuel 19-20	
19	II Samuel 21-22	
20	II Samuel 23-24	
21	I Kings 1-2:25	
22	I Kings 2:26-4	
23	I Kings 5-7	
24	I Kings 8	
25	I Kings 9-11	
26	I Kings 12-13	
27	I Kings 14-15	
28	I Kings 16-18	
29	I Kings 19-20	
30	I Kings 21-22	

MAY

		Check this column as you read each day
1	II Kings 1-3	
2	II Kings 4-5	
3	II Kings 6-8	
4	II Kings 9-10	
5	II Kings 11-13	
6	II Kings 14-15	
7	II Kings 16-17	
8	II Kings 18-20	
9	II Kings 21-23:20	
10	II Kings 23:21-25	
11	I Chron. 1-2	
12	I Chron. 3-5	
13	I Chron. 6-7	
14	I Chron. 8-10	
15	I Chron. 11-13	
16	I Chron. 14-16	
17	I Chron. 17-20	
18	I Chron. 21-23	
19	I Chron. 24-26	
20	I Chron. 27-29	
21	II Chron. 1-3	
22	II Chron. 4-6	
23	II Chron. 7-9	
24	II Chron. 10-13	
25	II Chron. 14-17	
26	II Chron. 18-20	
27	II Chron. 21-24	
28	II Chron. 25-27	
29	II Chron. 28-30	
30	II Chron. 31-33	
31	II Chron. 34-36	

JUNE

		Check this column as you read each day
1	Ezra 1-2	
2	Ezra 3-5	
3	Ezra 6-7	
4	Ezra 8-9	
5	Ezra 10	
6	Neh. 1-3	
7	Neh. 4-6	
8	Neh. 7-8	
9	Neh. 9-10	
10	Neh. 11-12	
11	Neh. 13	
12	Esther 1-3	
13	Esther 4-7	
14	Esther 8-10	
15	Job 1-4	
16	Job 5-8	
17	Job 9-12	
18	Job 13-16	
19	Job 17-20	
20	Job 21-24	
21	Job 25-29	
22	Job 30-33	
23	Job 34-37	
24	Job 38-40	
25	Job 41-42	
26	Psalms 1-9	
27	Psalms 10-17	
28	Psalms 18-22	
29	Psalms 23-30	
30	Psalms 31-35	

JULY

		Check this column as you read each day
1	Psalms 36-39	
2	Psalms 40-45	
3	Psalms 46-51	
4	Psalms 52-59	
5	Psalms 60-66	
6	Psalms 67-71	
7	Psalms 72-77	
8	Psalms 78-80	
9	Psalms 81-87	
10	Psalms 88-91	
11	Psalms 92-100	
12	Psalms 101-105	
13	Psalms 106-107	
14	Psalms 108-118	
15	Psalm 119	
16	Psalms 120-131	
17	Psalms 132-138	
18	Psalms 139-143	
19	Psalms 144-150	
20	Proverbs 1-3	
21	Proverbs 4-7	
22	Proverbs 8-11	
23	Proverbs 12-15	
24	Proverbs 16-19	
25	Proverbs 20-22	
26	Proverbs 23-26	
27	Proverbs 27-31	
28	Eccles. 1-4	
29	Eccles. 5-8	
30	Eccles. 9-12	
31	Song of Sol. 1-8	

AUGUST

		Check this column as you read each day
1	Isaiah 1-4	
2	Isaiah 5-9	
3	Isaiah 10-14	
4	Isaiah 15-21	
5	Isaiah 22-26	
6	Isaiah 27-31	
7	Isaiah 32-37	
8	Isaiah 38-42	
9	Isaiah 43-46	
10	Isaiah 47-51	
11	Isaiah 52-57	
12	Isaiah 58-63	
13	Isaiah 64-66	
14	Jer. 1-3	
15	Jer. 4-6	
16	Jer. 7-10	
17	Jer. 11-14	
18	Jer. 15-18	
19	Jer. 19-22	
20	Jer. 23-25	
21	Jer. 26-28	
22	Jer. 29-31	
23	Jer. 32-33	
24	Jer. 34-36	
25	Jer. 37-40	
26	Jer. 41-44	
27	Jer. 45-48	
28	Jer. 49-50	
29	Jer. 51-52	
30	Lam. 1-2	
31	Lam. 3-5	

SEPTEMBER

		Check this column as you read each day
1	Ezek. 1-4	
2	Ezek. 5-9	
3	Ezek. 10-13	
4	Ezek. 14-16	
5	Ezek. 17-19	
6	Ezek. 20-21	
7	Ezek. 22-24	
8	Ezek. 25-28	
9	Ezek. 29-32	
10	Ezek. 33-36	
11	Ezek. 37-39	
12	Ezek. 40-42	
13	Ezek. 43-45	
14	Ezek. 46-48	
15	Daniel 1-3	
16	Daniel 4-6	
17	Daniel 7-9	
18	Daniel 10-12	
19	Hosea 1-6	
20	Hosea 7-14	
21	Joel 1-3	
22	Amos 1-5	
23	Amos 6-9	
	Obadiah 1	
24	Jonah 1-4	
25	Micah 1-7	
26	Nahum 1-3	
	Habak. 1-3	
27	Zeph. 1-3	
	Haggai 1-2	
28	Zech. 1-7	
29	Zech. 8-14	
30	Malachi 1-4	

OCTOBER

		Check this column as you read each day
1	Matthew 1-3	
2	Matthew 4-6	
3	Matthew 7-9	
4	Matthew 10-11	
5	Matthew 12	
6	Matthew 13-14	
7	Matthew 15-17	
8	Matthew 18-20	
9	Matthew 21-22	
10	Matthew 23-24	
11	Matthew 25-26	
12	Matthew 27-28	
13	Mark 1-3	
14	Mark 4-5	
15	Mark 6-7	
16	Mark 8-9	
17	Mark 10-11	
18	Mark 12-13	
19	Mark 14-16	
20	Luke 1	
21	Luke 2-3	
22	Luke 4-5	
23	Luke 6-7	
24	Luke 8-9	
25	Luke 10-11	
26	Luke 12-13	
27	Luke 14-16	
28	Luke 17-18	
29	Luke 19-20	
30	Luke 21-22	
31	Luke 23-24	

NOVEMBER

		Check this column as you read each day
1	John 1-3	
2	John 4-5	
3	John 6-8	
4	John 9-10	
5	John 11-12	
6	John 13-16	
7	John 17-18	
8	John 19-21	
9	Acts 1-3	
10	Acts 4-6	
11	Acts 7-8	
12	Acts 9-10	
13	Acts 11-13	
14	Acts 14-16	
15	Acts 17-19	
16	Acts 20-22	
17	Acts 23-25	
18	Acts 26-28	
19	Romans 1-3	
20	Romans 4-7	
21	Romans 8-10	
22	Romans 11-13	
23	Romans 14-16	
24	I Cor. 1-4	
25	I Cor. 5-9	
26	I Cor. 10-13	
27	I Cor. 14-16	
28	II Cor. 1-4	
29	II Cor. 5-8	
30	II Cor. 9-13	

DECEMBER

		Check this column as you read each day
1	Galatians 1-3	
2	Galatians 4-6	
3	Ephesians 1-3	
4	Ephesians 4-6	
5	Philippians 1-4	
6	Colossians 1-4	
7	I Thess. 1-5	
8	II Thess. 1-3	
9	I Timothy 1-6	
10	II Timothy 1-4	
11	Titus 1-3	
	Philemon 1	
12	Hebrews 1-4	
13	Hebrews 5-7	
14	Hebrews 8-10	
15	Hebrews 11-13	
16	James 1-5	
17	I Peter 1-2	
18	I Peter 3-5	
19	II Peter 1-3	
20	I John 1-3	
21	I John 4-5	
22	II John	
	III John	
	Jude	
23	Rev. 1-2	
24	Rev. 3-5	
25	Rev. 6-8	
26	Rev. 9-11	
27	Rev. 12-13	
28	Rev. 14-16	
29	Rev. 17-18	
30	Rev. 19-20	
31	Rev. 21-22	

Upon completion of one year's reading, send your name and address for a Certificate of Recognition.

Introduction To The Book Of Genesis

The book of Genesis is the first of the five books that God inspired Moses to write, except for the Ten Commandments which were written on *two . . . stone tablets inscribed by the finger of God* (Exodus 31:18). This points out how exceedingly important the Ten Commandments are and to ignore them is an offense to God.

Evidence of the life-giving power of His word can be seen prior to each creative act, as we read: *Then God said* and at that moment it was created (Genesis 1:3,6,9,11,14,20,24,26,29). *For the word of God is living and effective* (Hebrews 4:12).

Genesis is an accurate account of the origin of the universe, the creation of man, marriage, the family, sin, and the origin of the Hebrew nation. The first sentence in the Bible states: *In the beginning God created the heavens and the earth* (Genesis 1:1). This makes it clear that God is a living, personal Being who is the Creator of all things and the Absolute Sovereign over all that He created (John 1:1-3; Colossians 1:16-17).

The word God used here in Genesis 1 is the Hebrew plural noun *Elohim*, even though the singular noun *Eloah* would have been used if God did not include the Son and the Holy Spirit (Deuteronomy 32:15,17; Habakkuk 3:3). The first chapter of Genesis also states: *Let Us make man in Our image and according to Our likeness* (Genesis 1:26). By recognizing the plurality of the Hebrew noun *Elohim* and the plural English pronouns *Us* and *Our*, as well as the reference to *the Spirit of God* (1:2), we have a clear revelation that the one true God is Triune and exists as God the Father, God the Son, and God the Holy Spirit.

Jesus also made the Trinity clear when He said: *When the Counselor comes, whom I will send to you . . . the Spirit of Truth . . . He will testify about Me. . . . He will not speak on His own. . . . I am leaving the world and going to the Father* (John 15:26; 16:13,28).

It is of utmost importance that believers acknowledge the Lord Jesus Christ as coequal and coeternal with God the Father and God the Holy Spirit and give Him His rightful exalted place in their hearts.

The historical reliability of Genesis also becomes apparent in the gospel of Matthew when Jesus refers to Sodom and Gomorrah as actual cities that were destroyed by fire from God, and to Noah as a man who lived at the time of the flood (Matthew 10:15; 24:37-38; Genesis 6:5,13;

7:6-23; 19:24-25). Furthermore, when Jesus was questioned by His critics concerning divorce, He confirmed the validity of creation when He said: *Haven't you read . . . that He who created them in the beginning made them male and female, and He also said: For this reason a man will leave his father and mother and be joined to his wife, and the two will become one flesh?* (Matthew 19:4-6; Genesis 1:27; 2:24).

Of all creation, only man has a *spirit, soul, and body* (I Thessalonians 5:23). It is in His image that Adam was created like God. *God is Spirit, and those who worship Him must worship Him in spirit and truth* (John 4:24). No animal has a spirit, a God consciousness, or the ability to worship God.

Genesis explains how Satan deceived Eve, who then, with Adam, decided not to obey their Creator. Because of sin, mankind inherited a sin nature and became destined for both physical and spiritual death (Genesis 3:1-7,16-19). *Just as in Adam all die, so also in Christ all will be made alive* (I Corinthians 15:22). God prepared the way for repentant sinners to receive eternal life with the first promise of a Savior (Genesis 3:15). The woman would have a Son. The Son (Jesus Christ) would destroy Satan and provide eternal life *to all who did receive Him . . . who were born . . . of God. . . . Unless someone is born again, he cannot see the kingdom of God* (John 1:12-13; 3:3). To illustrate how the Lord Jesus, as the Lamb of God, would die for sin that we might be clothed with the righteousness of God in Him, God Himself killed animals and *made coats of skins, and clothed them* (Adam and Eve) (Genesis 3:21; see also Hebrews 9:22; I Corinthians 1:30; I Peter 2:24; II Peter 1:1).

Chapters 1 – 11 record the first 2,000 years* of man's history. During that time, six major events took place: [1] the creation of all things; [2] the sin of Adam and Eve; [3] some 1600 years* later, the building of an ark by Noah; [4] the great flood; [5] 200 years* later, the building of the Tower of Babel; and [6] the diversification of tongues and scattering of people across the earth.

Chapters 12 – 50 cover the next 500 years* and focus on four men chosen by God to bless the world – Abraham, Isaac, Jacob, and Joseph. Through these men we see the love of God for His creation and His willingness to protect and provide for those who are obedient to His revealed word.

*Note: *Dates are approximate time periods and unimportant or God would have included them in the Bible.*

In Today's Reading

Creation of all things; creation of Adam and Eve; temptation by Satan; Adam and Eve rebel against God and forfeit Garden of Eden.

God made mankind in His image and His likeness. He made us different from every animal that He created in that each of us is a triune being – body, soul, and spirit. *God is Spirit, and those who worship Him must worship in spirit and truth* (John 4:24). No animal has a spirit, a God consciousness or is capable of worshiping God.

The LORD God took the man and placed him in the garden of Eden to work it and watch over it – not to own it (Genesis 2:15). Man's responsibility was to obey the word of God and to take care of His garden. However, God allowed his love, loyalty, and obedience to be tested.

In Eden, we are introduced to Satan, the one who came in the guise of *the serpent* (3:1). He is also called *the Devil. . . . the enemy. . . . your adversary . . . the accuser* (Revelation 20:2; see also Isaiah 14:12; Matthew 13:39; I Peter 5:8; Revelation 12:10). He did not reveal himself as the enemy of God or as a wicked deceiver intent on destroying every enjoyment of mankind. His intent was, and still is, to prevent man from obeying his Creator. First, Satan tried to create doubt concerning the truth of what God had said. He implied that God was withholding the best enjoyments in life from Adam and Eve. He asked: *Did God really say, You cannot eat from any tree in the garden* (Genesis 3:1)? This was followed by Satan's partial truth, which was a lie: *God knows that when you eat of it your eyes will be opened and you will be like God, knowing good and evil* (3:5). At that moment, Eve chose to trust self rather than God, began to "covet" what belonged only to God and dis-regarded His ownership and authority. She saw *that the tree was good for food and delightful to look at, and that it was desirable for obtaining wisdom,* so she chose to trespass on God's property and *took . . . its fruit and ate* (3:6).

Eve yielded to lust when she coveted what God had reserved for Himself. On that day, Adam and Eve, the father and mother of all mankind, chose to eat the forbidden fruit. They sinned and died spiritually. From that moment on, all of Adam's descendants inherited his sinful nature. *In this way death spread to all men* (Romans 5:12).

Thought for Today: The only means to heaven is through Jesus Christ.

In Today's Reading

Sacrifices of Cain and Abel; Cain murders Abel; genealogy from Adam to Noah; Noah's ark.

The physical, spiritual, and eternal consequences of sin are staggering and irreversible. It did not take long for Adam and Eve's sin nature to become evident. Their firstborn son Cain became jealous of his brother Abel and angry with God because his sacrifice was unacceptable.

Abel . . . presented . . . the firstborn of his flock. . . . The LORD had regard for Abel and his offering (received it with favor), *but He did not have regard for Cain and his offering* (Genesis 4:4-5). The Lord approached Cain in love and offered him an opportunity to repent of his sin: *If you do right, won't you be accepted? But if you do not do right, sin is crouching at the door* (4:6-7). While Cain's offering of the firstfruits of the ground recognized God as Creator, it did not recognize Cain as a sinner. *Without the shedding of blood there is no forgiveness* (Hebrews 9:22). *By faith Abel offered to God a better sacrifice than Cain. . . . he was approved as a righteous man, because God approved his gifts* (11:4). Abel brought the best as a thanksgiving offering, but recognized himself as a sinner when he *presented . . . the firstborn of his flock* (Genesis 4:4), which means he offered a blood sacrifice of a lamb for atonement of his sins.

The genealogy of *the sons of God* (6:2,4) continued through Adam and Eve's third son Seth (5:3), through whose lineage Jesus would come (Luke 3:38).What often happens today is exactly what happened then: *The sons of God saw that the daughters of men* (the people who lived in disobedience to God) *were beautiful; and . . . they chose wives for themselves* (Genesis 6:2). It is often assumed that marriage of believers with nonbelievers may be an advantage. The heart could swell with pride that these mixed marriages produced brilliant men. *They were powerful men of old, the famous men* (6:4). But, they were not men who lived in obedience to God.

From the beginning, the biblical principle has always been: *Do not be mismatched with unbelievers* (II Corinthians 6:14).

Thought for Today: Jesus is the Way that leads from where we are, as a sinner, to where God is.

In Today's Reading

Noah, his family, seven pairs clean and one pair unclean, of every living creature enter the ark as *God had commanded* (Gen. 7:2,9); the great flood; the Rainbow Covenant.

The LORD said to Noah, Enter the ark, you and all your household (Genesis 7:1). Noah was able to save his family and preserve mankind because his faith in the spoken word of God led him to build the ark. During the many years spent in constructing the ark, he was also known as *a preacher of righteousness* in an ungodly world (II Peter 2:5). This illustrates the New Testament truth that *faith without works is dead* (meaningless) (James 2:26). The ark was a secure refuge from certain death; it was also a type of Christ, who provides spiritual refuge for believers. Christ, our spiritual Ark, is calling to the lost today: *Come to Me . . . and I will give you rest* (Matthew 11:28).

For Noah and his family, there came a day, prior to the flood, when they were told to enter the ark, *and the LORD shut him in* (Genesis 7:16). This is a reminder that *now is the day of salvation* (II Corinthians 6:2). All who wait for a more convenient time to be saved need to realize that no one knows on what day his door of opportunity will be shut forever. *Therefore be alert, because you don't know either the day or the hour* (Matthew 25:13).

Just as Noah was able to rest within the ark, secure from the waters of death, so we can be assured of spiritual rest, for our lives are *hidden with the Messiah in God* (Colossians 3:3). As soon as he was once more on dry land, *Noah built an altar to the LORD . . . and offered burnt offerings on the altar* (Genesis 8:20). The obedience of faith and the worship of God go hand in hand. Just as Noah was not given an exact day when the flood would come, neither do we know the day of our Lord's return.

As the days of Noah were, so the coming of the Son of Man will be. For in those days before the flood they were eating and drinking, marrying and giving in marriage, until the day Noah boarded the ark. They didn't know until the flood came and swept them all away. So this is the way the coming of the Son of Man will be. . . . This is why you also should get ready (Matthew 24:36-39,44).

Thought for Today: We don't know the day that our lives will end – be prepared.

The Journeys of Abraham, Sarah, & Lot

1. Ur of Chaldees

2. Haran *(Genesis 11:27-31)*
   Distance: 600 miles
   - Reason for leaving Ur: Called by God *(Acts 7:2-4; Hebrews 11:8)*
   - Death of Abraham's father *(Genesis 11:32)*

3. Shechem *(Genesis 12:1-7)*
   Distance: about 400 miles, Age: 75
   - Crossing the Jordan River at Succoth
   - First altar built; Abram worshiped God

4. Bethel *(Genesis 12:8)*
   Distance: 20 miles
   - Second altar built; prayer offered
   - Famine in Canaan

5. Egypt *(Genesis 12:9-20)*
   Distance: about 225 miles
   - Abram denied that Sarai was his wife; she was taken into Pharaoh's house

6. Bethel *(Genesis 13:1-5)*
   - Abram called on the name of the Lord
   - Lot's selfish decision and separation from Abram

7. Mamre/Hebron *(Genesis 13:14-18)*
   Distance: 35 miles
   - Third altar built
   - Abram promised the whole land by God

8. Hobah [North of Damascus] *(Genesis 14:1-17)*
   Distance:160 miles
   - Battle of the Canaanite kings
   - Lot taken captive *(Genesis 14:1-12)*
   - Abram rescued Lot

9. Mamre/Hebron *(Genesis 14:18-20)*
   - Abram gave tithes to Melchizedek at Jerusalem
   - Promise of a son renewed *(15:1-5)* – Covenant renewed *(15:6-18)* – Ishmael born when Abram was 86 *(16:15-16)* – Circumcision at 99 *(17:1-27)* – Names changed *(17:5-15)* – Isaac to be born *(18:1-19)* – Sodom destroyed/Lot rescued *(19:1-38)*

10. Gerar *(Genesis 20:1)*
    Distance: 40 miles
    - Covenant fulfilled
    - Isaac born when Abraham was 100 *(Genesis 21:1-8; Hebrews 11:11)*
    - Hagar and Ismael cast out *(Genesis 21:9-21)*

11. Beer-sheba *(Genesis 21:27-34)*
    - Covenant with Abimelech
    - Abraham called on the name of the Lord

12. Mount Moriah (Jerusalem) *(Genesis 22:1-14; Hebrews 11:17-19)*
    Distance: About 70 miles
    - Altar built
    - Isaac prepared to be offered as a sacrifice – a type of God offering Jesus, His only Son, on same site 2,000 years later
    - God renewed covenant with Abraham *(Genesis 22:15-18)*

13. Beer-sheba *(Genesis 22:19)*
    - Death of Sarah *(Genesis 23:1-20)*
    - Abraham sent servant to Mesopotamia to get a wife for Isaac *(Genesis 24:1-67)*

14. Hebron *(Genesis 25:1-4)*
    Distance: About 30 miles
    - Abraham married Keturah
    - Abraham's death and burial in cave of Machpelah at age 175 *(Genesis 25:7-10)*

In Today's Reading

Descendants of Noah; Babel; origin of languages; God's call and covenant with Abram; his journey to Canaan and Egypt.

Nimrod is the first king mentioned in the Bible: *His kingdom started with Babylon* (Genesis 10:10). Nimrod means "rebel." *He was a powerful hunter in the sight of the LORD* (10:9). Later we read: *Nimrod . . . was the first to become a great warrior on the earth* (I Chronicles 1:10).

With Nimrod as their leader, the people united to *build a city and a tower with its top in the sky* (Genesis 11:4). They said: *Let us make* ***a name for ourselves****; otherwise, we will be scattered over the face of the whole earth.* The words *make us a name* revealed their desire for power. The human heart seeks a name for itself and has no desire to glorify God.

The *powerful* Nimrod established the first world empire and ruled it. His ambition to build a tower *with its top in the sky* did not mean he expected to reach the throne of the Almighty God – his desire was to make himself and his followers *powerful* enough to rule the world. Nimrod was a *hunter* – probably meaning a *hunter* of men who would support his ambitions. *In the sight of the LORD* means that this rebel pursued his own ambitious plans in defiance of God, who commanded Adam: *Multiply and fill the earth* (1:28); and to Noah: *Multiply and fill the earth* (9:1).

Just as in the days of Nimrod, today there is a worldwide movement to unite and control all people and all religions into a one-world government and one church. The only assurance of not being deceived in this age of lawlessness is knowing the word of God. It alone exposes the actions of leaders in world affairs.

In striking contrast to Abram, who symbolizes submission to God, Nimrod is a symbol of self-seeking independence. The call of God came to Abram: *Go from your country . . . to the land that I will show you. . . . all the people on earth will be blessed through you. So Abram went* (12:1-4).

The call of God demands that we make a choice. Even the closest ties of human loyalty or affection must be cut when they conflict with our submission to Christ and what is written in His word. *Whoever doesn't take up his cross and follow Me is not worthy of Me* (Matthew 10:38).

Thought for Today: Nothing is more important than obeying God's word.

In Today's Reading

Abram and Lot separate; Abram moves to Hebron, builds an altar; Lot rescued; Melchizedek blesses Abram; God's covenant with Abram.

The testing of Abram's faith began after he and Lot left Ur of the Chaldees on their journey of about 1000 miles to the promised land. Upon arrival, he discovered there was a famine and they traveled south near Sodom where the pastureland was best. Abram and Lot both had large flocks. Soon *there was quarreling between the herdsmen of Abram's livestock and the herdsmen of Lot's livestock* (Genesis 13:7). Abram could have taken the best for himself since he was older than his nephew, as well as being the spiritual leader. Instead, he graciously said to Lot: *Please, let's not have quarreling between you and me . . . since we are relatives. Isn't the whole land before you? Separate from me: if to the left, I will go to the right* (13:8-9). Lot selfishly took advantage of Abram and chose all the well-watered plain near Sodom.

It was after this experience that Abram received a promise from the Lord that He would make Abram's *offspring* (descendants) as numerous as *the dust of the earth* (13:16). Abram went north *to live beside the oaks of Mamre at Hebron* (a mountain region), *where he built an altar for the LORD* (13:18).

Lot decided to ignore his spiritual need to be in fellowship with Abram. Instead, he made friends with the people of Sodom, who were *sinning greatly against the LORD* (13:10-13).

Lot was typical of many Christians today who deplore our wicked society but who make decisions based on their material advantages. Only a few listen seriously to their Savior, who said: *No servant can be the slave of two masters* (Luke 16:13). Satan wants us to doubt that, when we obey the Lord, we have chosen the best in life.

Paul wrote: *We are pressured in every way . . . perplexed but not in despair . . . persecuted . . . struck down but not destroyed. . . . we do not give up. . . . our momentary light affliction is producing for us an absolutely incomparable eternal weight of glory* (II Corinthians 4:8-17).

Thought for Today: The trials we face now will one day seem insignificant compared to what God was able to accomplish through them.

In Today's Reading

Ishmael; Abram's name changed; covenant of circumcision; Sarai's name changed; Isaac promised to Abraham and Sarah; Abraham's prayer for Sodom.

Abram and Sarai were childless. Although God had promised Abram a son, he still had no son when he was 85 years old. At that time, *Sarai said to Abram . . . the LORD has prevented me from bearing children, go to my slave* (Hagar)*; perhaps I can have children through her* (Genesis 16:2). At the age of 86, Abram did receive a son, Ishmael, by Hagar.

Thirteen years passed after the birth of Ishmael (16:16; 17:1). Then God again spoke to Abram: *I am God Almighty. . . . Your name will be Abraham. . . . I will keep My covenant between Me and you, and your offspring. . . . I will confirm my covenant with Isaac, whom Sarah will bear to you at this time next year* (17:1-21).

Abraham was now 99 years old and Sarah was 90. At her age, it was humanly impossible for Sarah to have a child. But God revealed to Abraham: *I am the Almighty God,* meaning the One who is all-sufficient. Through Abraham, God would teach us how our faith can be strengthened when He said: *I have chosen him . . . he will command his children and his house after him to keep the way of the LORD by doing what is right . . . in order that the LORD may bring about for Abraham what He has promised him* (18:19).

One of the great tests of our faith is waiting upon the Lord. It may take two weeks, two years, or, as in Abraham's situation, 25 years. The Holy Spirit led the apostle Paul to write concerning Abraham's faith that he *was fully convinced that what He* (God) *had promised He was also able to perform. Therefore, it was credited to him for righteousness* (Romans 4:21-22).

God had said to Abraham: *Live before Me and be devout,* meaning devoted to God (Genesis 17:1). We too have a responsibility in our covenant relationship with God. *Let us approach the throne of grace with boldness, so that we may receive mercy and find grace to help us at the proper time* (Hebrews 4:16).

Thought for Today: The greatest test of our faith is waiting upon the Lord, but the outcome is always His best.

In Today's Reading

Sodom destroyed; Lot and his daughters; birth of Isaac; Hagar and Ishmael; agreement between Abraham and Abimelech.

Lot soon had a prominent position in Sodom since he was *sitting at Sodom's gate* where business and legal matters were conducted (Genesis 19:1). Lot associated with the people of Sodom even though he was *distressed by* (their) *unrestrained . . . immoral . . . deeds he saw* (II Peter 2:7).

The Scriptures denounce homosexuality for which Sodom was known. Since homosexuality is so detestable in the eyes of God, we should pray for the sinner that he will repent and forsake sin (I Corinthians 9:11). The law grouped homosexuality with incest and bestiality (Leviticus 18:22-30; 20:13; Romans 1:24-27).

Sarah became pregnant and bore a son to Abraham in his old age, at the appointed time God had told him (Genesis 21:2).

Isaac, the miracle child of promise, entered the family life of Abraham, Sarah, and Hagar the bondwoman. Hagar's son Ishmael soon revealed his true character through his contempt for Isaac. In the New Testament we read that *Abraham had two sons. . . . the women represent . . . two covenants. One is from Mount Sinai and bears children into slavery – this is Hagar. . . . Now you, brothers, like Isaac, are children of promise. But just as then the child born according to the flesh persecuted the one born according to the Spirit, so also now* (Galatians 4:22,24,28-29).

These two sons, Ishmael and Isaac, illustrate the nature of our lives. We are first *born of the flesh* (John 3:6), symbolized by Ishmael. When the people on the day of Pentecost asked: "What do we do?" Peter said to them: *Repent . . . and be baptized . . . and you will receive the gift of the Holy Spirit* (Acts 2:38). The believer then becomes the possessor of the nature of God and the new life in Christ which is symbolized by Isaac, the child of faith (Romans 10:9-10; I John 3:1-2; 4:15).

Ishmael's hatred for Isaac is symbolic of the world and its hatred of Christ and His followers. *Those who belong to Christ Jesus have crucified the flesh with its passions and desires* (Galatians 5:24).

Thought for Today: God will guide those who read His word.

In Today's Reading

Abraham's willingness to offer Isaac; God's covenant renewed; Sarah's death; Rebekah's marriage to Isaac.

After 25 years of waiting for the promised son, God said to Abraham: *Sarah will bear you a son . . . you will name him Isaac. I will confirm My covenant with him* (Genesis 17:19). *After these things God . . . said to . . . Abraham! . . . Take . . . your only son Isaac, whom you love, go to the land of Moriah, and there offer him as a burnt offering* (22:1-2).

Isaac was a young man when this final test came to Abraham's faith. A burnt offering sacrifice was always to be a male animal, was the best the offerer had, and was to be wholly consumed by fire. It was an expression of dedication to God. Abraham knew that Isaac must live since God had said: *I will confirm My covenant with him* (17:9); yet, now the command of God was to offer Isaac as a sacrifice. Obediently, *Abraham got up . . . and took . . . his son Isaac. He split wood for a burnt offering and set out to go to the place God had told him about* (22:3). With unquestioned faith in God, *Abraham said to his young men, Stay here . . . The boy and I will go over there to worship; then we'll come back to you* (22:5).

On Mount Moriah, Abraham built an altar. When Isaac inquired how they could offer a sacrifice without a sacrificial animal, Abraham responded: *God Himself will provide the lamb for the burnt offering, my son* (22:8). Abraham's many years of trusting in the Lord gave him faith in God. This is an amazing testimony of how Abraham's faith had grown over the years until he knew that God never makes a mistake and he believed *God to be able even to raise someone from the dead* (Hebrews 11:19).

Abraham . . . took the knife to slaughter his son. But the angel of the LORD . . . said, Abraham . . . Do not lay a hand on the boy or do anything to him. For now I know that you fear God . . . Abraham looked up and saw a ram caught by its horns in the thicket. So Abraham went and took the ram and offered it as a burnt offering instead of his son (Genesis 22:10-13).

Through trials and suffering, the Lord develops our faith. *He will not allow you to be tempted beyond what you are able, but with the temptation He will also provide a way of escape* (I Corinthians 10:13).

Thought for Today: Our faith is strengthened through stressful situations, even though they are painful.

In Today's Reading

Abraham's death; birth of Jacob and Esau; Esau sells his birthright; Isaac blesses Jacob with the Abrahamic Covenant.

Esau returned from *the field, exhausted . . .* and *said to Jacob, Let me eat some of that red stuff, because I'm exhausted.* Jacob, knowing the character of his brother, replied: *First sell me your birthright* (Genesis 25:29-31). Esau had no interest in spiritual things so he agreed, saying: *I'm about to die, so what good is a birthright to me?*(25:32-34). Esau could not have been *at the point of death* by missing one meal.

Though much maligned by Esau and others, the fact is, Jacob purchased the birthright for what Esau thought it was worth. More importantly, God had told Rebekah that *the older will serve the younger* (25:23).

Esau and Jacob were twin brothers, but Esau was born first and fell legal heir to the family birthright which included, among other things, being heir to the covenant between God and Abraham. The birthright was a link in the line of descent through which the Messiah was to come (Numbers 24:17-19). In contrast with Esau, *Jacob was a quiet* (plain) *man who stayed at home* (Genesis 25:27). The Hebrew word for *quiet* is the same word translated in other Scripture as *perfect, upright, undefiled;* so the word *quiet* refers to Jacob's character – a man of God. God records His highest praise and blessing for Jacob: *The LORD has chosen Jacob for Himself* (Psalms 135:4). It appears that Isaac's admiration for his worldly-minded son Esau caused him to ignore the prophecy that God had revealed to Rebekah before the twins' birth (Genesis 25:23), and he chose to disregard Esau's sale of his birthright to Jacob (25:34).

The moment Isaac realized that Rebekah had thwarted his evil scheme, he quickly and openly conferred the Abrahamic covenant upon Jacob, an obvious admission of how terribly wrong he had been (28:3-4). There is no hint that Isaac thought that Rebekah did wrong. The Hebrew word *Yaacov* (Jacob) is translated "supplanter." One of the definitions of supplant in Webster's Dictionary is "to take the place of and serve as a substitute for, especially by reason of superior excellence."

See that there isn't any immoral or irreverent person like Esau, who sold his birthright in exchange for one meal (Hebrews 12:16).

Thought for Today: How prone we are to blame others for our failures!

In Today's Reading

Abrahamic Covenant conferred upon Jacob; vision of Jacob's ladder; journey to Paddan-aram; Jacob's marriages to Leah and Rachel.

When Isaac realized that God had overruled his scheme to confer the God-ordained birthright of Jacob upon Esau, he *began to tremble uncontrollably* (Genesis 27:33). He quickly conferred with Rebekah, not to accuse her of any wrongdoing, but to decide how best to plan for Jacob's future. If Jacob violated the word of God in marrying an idol-worshiping woman, as Esau had done, Rebekah asked: *What good is my life?* (27:46). *Isaac summoned Jacob, blessed him, and commanded him: Don't take a wife from the Canaanite women. Go at once to Paddan-aram. . . . Marry one of the daughters of Laban, your mother's brother. May God Almighty bless you and make you fruitful and . . . give you and your offspring the blessing of Abraham* (28:1-4). This was an obvious admission of how wrong Isaac had been in his attempt to defraud Jacob.

However, Esau was quick to blame Jacob for his trouble, saying: *He* (Jacob) *has taken my blessing* (27:36). Esau is typical of sinners who irresponsibly blame someone else for their failures.

Isaac lived 43 years after his attempt to thwart God's plan, but there is no record of him being used again of God. For Jacob, however, his remarkable blessings began on his first night away from home.

Without map or companion, but according to the exact plan of God, Jacob left home on his journey of more than 500 miles and arrived safely in Paddan-aram. God marvelously guided him to Rachel and the home of his *mother's father*, where he was received with a warm welcome (28:2).

Just as it is with everyone who lives to please the Lord, Jacob's life was set apart for a purpose. When Christians realize this truth, their attitude toward their marriage partners, workplace, physical limitations, and hardships will be seen as in the will of God.

At a much later date, Jacob's son Joseph would be sold as a slave by his brothers. But, 20 years later he could say to them: *You planned evil against me; God planned it for good* (Genesis 50:20).

Thought for Today: Eternal treasures are reserved for those who forsake earthly pleasures to do the will of God.

In Today's Reading

Laban's jealousy; Jacob flees; Jacob wrestles with the angel of God; his name changed to Israel; peace between Jacob and Esau.

The greed of Laban and his sons resulted in a hostile attitude toward Jacob, the servant of God. *The LORD said . . . Go back to the land of your fathers . . . and I will be with you . . . I am the God of Bethel . . . where you made a solemn vow to Me* (Genesis 31:3,13).

After 20 years, Jacob was returning home with his two wives, two concubines, 11 sons and one daughter, servants, and flocks. Esau, who had threatened to kill Jacob (27:41-45), was approaching with 400 men; *Jacob was greatly afraid* (32:3,6-7). He hastily divided his wives, children, and flocks into two groups, reasoning that if Esau should come upon one camp and destroy it, the remaining camp would escape in the opposite direction. In the dark of night, Jacob was then left alone. He earnestly prayed and reminded the Lord that He had said: *Go back to your land and to your family, and I will make things go well for you* (32:9). We need to learn a lesson from Jacob: first to know what God has said and then to remind the Lord that we are relying on His promises.

Jacob was also praying for the future fulfillment of the covenant promise.

This godly and humble servant of the Lord spent the night alone, agonizing in prayer, until he was conferred with the highest honor given by God to any man in Old Testament history: *Your name will no longer be Jacob . . . It will be Israel because you have struggled with God and with men and have prevailed* (32:28). Through the centuries, the people of God would be called by his name – Israelites. Through his son Judah, Jesus the Messiah was promised (49:10).

We too are in a covenant relationship with God through Jesus Christ our Savior and our Mediator, who declared that the Christian life requires struggle: *Make every effort to enter through the narrow door, because I tell you, many will try to enter and won't be able* (Luke 13:24).

Thought for Today: The more we love the word of God, the more we will love the God of the word.

In Today's Reading

Dinah, daughter of Jacob and Leah, was raped; Simeon and Levi's revenge; Jacob's return to Bethel and Abrahamic covenant renewed.

Jacob continued on toward Bethel, since the Lord had said: *I am the God of Bethel . . . return to your native land* (Genesis 31:13). But, just a short distance from Bethel, Jacob discovered the beautiful valleys and opportunities for financial gain near *the Canaanite city of Shechem* near the promised land (33:18).

For ten years Jacob's stay seemed to be successful. Then we read the tragedy of his daughter Dinah. When *Shechem . . . a prince of the region, saw her, he took her, slept with her, and forced her* (34:2). In revenge for their sister Dinah's rape, Simeon and Levi slew all the men of Shechem.

Godly parents often become so involved with achieving material goals that they neglect to *train up a child in the way he should go* (Proverbs 22:6). This often results in worldly attractions gaining control of their children's hearts, leading to heartbreaking consequences.

Surely, we can learn from Jacob that material success is no assurance that we are in the will of God. But the greatest lesson we can learn from Jacob's tragedies is that he didn't give up when his situation looked hopeless. Instead, he turned to the Lord, who said: *Get up! Go to Bethel and settle there. Build an altar there to the God who appeared to you when you fled from your brother Esau* (Genesis 35:1). At this time of renewal, Jacob instructed his family to *get rid of the foreign gods. . . . Purify yourselves and change your clothes. We must get up and go to Bethel. I will build an altar there to the God who . . . has been with me everywhere I have gone* (35:2-3).

Three things Jacob said to his family have a parallel for Christians. He first said: *Get rid of the foreign gods* – a reminder that old habits of sin must be forsaken; the second: *Purify yourselves and change your clothes* – a reminder to *pursue . . . holiness – without it no one will see the Lord* (Hebrews 12:14). Thirdly, we are to worship only God: *You shall worship the LORD your God, and Him alone you shall serve* (Luke 4:8).

Participation in church worship is a very important way in which God can speak to us, through Bible School, Bible study, and sermons. *Christ loved the church and gave Himself for her, to make her holy, cleansing her in the washing of water by the word* (Ephesians 5:25-26).

Thought for Today: Compromise always results in disappointments.

In Today's Reading

Joseph's dreams; Joseph sold into slavery; the cruel lies of Potiphar's wife; Joseph imprisoned.

Joseph was the only one of Jacob's 12 sons who expressed interest in spiritual things. Joseph was deeply troubled about his older brothers' evil conduct while away from home. *At 17 years of age, Joseph tended sheep with his brothers* and reported to his father the evil things they were doing (Genesis 37:2). The fact that Joseph *was a son born to him* (Jacob) *in his old age* (37:3), and probably his concern for his brothers' spiritual well-being, influenced Jacob to love him *more than his other sons* (37:4).

Some people discourage exposing wrongdoing, and others say they do not want to become involved. But Joseph possessed spiritual integrity and was willing to face abuse from his brothers for exposing their evil ways. Their envy turned to hatred when Joseph shared his prophetic dreams with them (37:5-7). His brothers scoffed, saying: *Are you really going to reign over us? . . . So they hated him even more because of his dream* (37:8).

Joseph's brothers *had gone to pasture their father's flocks at Shechem,* which was a considerable distance from their home (37:12). Some time later, Jacob, concerned about his sons' welfare, sent Joseph to see if everything was all right with them (37:14). After a long search, Joseph found his brothers near the village of Dothan (37:17).

When his brothers saw Joseph coming, they plotted to *kill him . . . and . . . say* (lie to their father) *that a vicious animal ate him* (37:18-20). Shocking as it must have been to the poor teenager, *they stripped off his . . . robe of many colors . . . and threw him into the pit* (37:23-24). Joseph was sold as a slave to Ishmaelites, who sold him in the slave market to Potiphar, the captain of the royal guard (37:27-28,36; 39:1). Their last memories of their terrified brother were of him pleading for his life (42:21).

God used the experiences of Joseph in Egypt to prepare him to be the preserver of God's people and, thus, the lineage of the coming Messiah, Jesus Christ. *All things work together for the good of those who love God: those who are called according to His purpose* (Romans 8:28).

Thought for Today: Faith is strengthened when trials are accepted with patience.

In Today's Reading

Dreams interpreted by Joseph; Joseph made a ruler of Egypt; his brothers buy corn and bow down to him; Simeon detained.

Thirteen years had passed since Joseph's brothers sold him into slavery. Following that horrifying ordeal, he experienced many pitiful disappointments. Consider his many lonely nights suffering as an innocent prisoner. *They hurt his feet with shackles; his neck was put in an iron collar* (Psalms 105:18). Joseph spent many years as a slave but never became bitter. He remained faithful to the Lord.

At the age of 30, Joseph was called to interpret Pharaoh's dreams. *Joseph answered Pharaoh, God will give Pharaoh a favorable answer* (Genesis 41:16). Because the Lord interpreted the dreams through Joseph, Pharaoh acknowledged him as the wisest man in Egypt. This former outcast then received Pharaoh's own ring as a sign of his new authority as second ruler over all the land of Egypt (41:39-44). The dreams that Joseph experienced many years before were becoming a reality.

We may endure months, or even years, when it may appear that God either does not care about us or cannot do anything about our circumstances. The faithless critic blames God for his problems and complains: "Why me?" God has amazing ways of developing our talents, maturing us spiritually, and honoring all who remain faithful to Him.

All of us have known someone who seemed so promising for future service for the Lord but who succumbed to Satan's temptation, such as his assistant of whom the apostle Paul wrote: *Demas has deserted me, because he loved this present world* (II Timothy 4:10). This does not imply that Demas had rejected what Paul was preaching. By today's standards, he wanted future security, better pay, less work, and retirement benefits. Demas left the Lord's ministry for secular benefits that are often disappointing and seldom satisfying. Even at best, they only last for this short lifetime but then the awful regret for all eternity. All of us need to seriously consider that Jesus said: *Don't worry about your life. . . . The Gentiles* (worldly-minded) *eagerly seek . . . things. . . . But seek first the kingdom of God and His righteousness* (Matthew 6:25-33).

Thought for Today: Adverse circumstances cannot defeat the faithful.

In Today's Reading

Jacob's sons return to Egypt for food; Judah offers to take the place of Benjamin; Joseph makes himself known to his brothers.

Because of the great famine, Jacob was forced to send his sons to Egypt to buy food. As the second most powerful ruler of Egypt spoke to them through an interpreter, they were unaware that he was their brother Joseph, whom they had sold into slavery about 20 years earlier.

After questioning them about their family, Joseph had his brothers imprisoned for three days (Genesis 42:17). During their stay in prison, they recalled how their younger brother Joseph had pleaded with them not to sell him as a slave to the Ishmaelite traders on their way to Egypt. Now, in an Egyptian prison, they humbly confessed what a terrible act of cruelty they had committed and *said to each other, It is plain that we are being punished for what we did to our brother. We saw his deep distress when he pleaded with us, but we would not listen. That is why this trouble has come to us* (42:21). Simeon was then held hostage in Egypt until they brought their youngest brother to Egypt (42:24).

When Joseph's brothers returned home without Simeon, Jacob heard of the ruler's demand to bring his youngest son Benjamin to Egypt before they could buy any more food. He was deeply distressed, and said: *My son will not go down with you* (42:38). However, as the famine continued, Jacob had no choice but to let Benjamin return with his brothers to Egypt.

Joseph demanded that his brothers come to his home. Imagine their shock when he said, in their Hebrew language: *I am Joseph, your brother . . . the one whom you sold into Egypt* (45:4). To their amazement, he lovingly added: *Don't be . . . angry with yourselves for selling me here, because God sent me ahead of you to preserve life* (45:5).

For years, Joseph's brothers had deceived their father and had escaped all accountability for their cruel sin against Joseph. Now they were forced to face their brother. Joseph explained: *You sold me*; but *God sent me*. Although God used their wickedness to fulfill His will, this did not lessen their guilt. But, regardless of how cruel someone has been, *if you don't forgive people, your Father will not forgive your wrongdoing* (Matthew 6:14-15).

Thought for Today: Don't wait until the difficulty is past to praise God.

In Today's Reading

Jacob's vision at Beersheba; the journey to Egypt; Joseph and the famine; the best land given to Jacob; Joseph's sons blessed.

Jacob knew that God had planned for his people to live in Canaan, not in Egypt, so he did not rush to Egypt for a grand reunion with his precious son Joseph. Since the will of God remained uppermost in Jacob's heart, he needed assurance from God concerning his journey to Egypt. After Jacob left Hebron, he journeyed about 25 miles *to Beersheba, and he offered sacrifices to the God of his father Isaac. Then God spoke to Israel that night in a vision: Jacob, Jacob! . . . And Jacob replied, Here I am. . . . God said. . . . Do not be afraid to go down to Egypt, for I will make you a great nation there. . . . I will . . . bring you back* (Genesis 46:1-4).

The Lord assured Jacob that their sojourn in Egypt was not to be a permanent one, but that it would be a time of preparing his family to become *a great nation*. Earthly life is a time of preparation for eternity (Luke 12:20-21). What gets priority, and how we live, is an expression of our preparation for eternity. Our eyes should not be set on worldly securities and achievements, but foremost on being the person God wants us to be in order to accomplish the purpose for which He created us.

The life of Jacob gives the believer insight into the sovereignty of God, who protects, directs, and provides for the needs of all who are faithful to Him. As the years in Egypt passed, Jacob could see how God had been directing, protecting, and providing for him all his life.

This remarkable man of God received so much abuse throughout his life, but God conferred more blessings on Jacob than any other man in Old Testament history. The name of Abraham, the father of the faithful, appears over 300 times in Scripture. The name of Isaac appears only 131 times, and many times only in conjunction with Abraham and Jacob. Jacob, however, is mentioned over 370 times, and his new name Israel, referring to both himself and his descendants, appears over 2500 times. It is a serious thing to criticize one whom God has chosen to esteem, as He clearly said: *Jacob I have loved, but Esau I have hated* (Romans 9:13; Malachi 1:2-3).

Thought for Today: Christians are to forgive regardless of circumstances.

Introduction To The Book Of Exodus

The word *Exodus* means "exit, departure, the way out" (Hebrews 11:22). This book continues the history of the descendants of Jacob's 12 sons. In the first chapter of Exodus, just two short verses, 11 and 12, cover the time to which God referred when He said: *Your offspring will be strangers in a land that does not belong to them; they will serve them and will be oppressed 400 years* (Genesis 15:13; Acts 7:6).

Chapters 1:1 – 11:10 cover the period when the Israelites first settled in the most fertile land in Egypt until the time when they became slaves to the Egyptians and endured much suffering. God directed Moses to pronounce a series of ten plagues upon Egypt.

Chapters 12:1 – 14:18 At the time chosen by Him, God said: *I will execute judgments against all the gods of Egypt: I am the LORD* (Exodus 12:12). The Israelites' miraculous deliverance from Egypt was made possible by their obedience to the word of God as they, by faith, applied the blood of an innocent lamb to their doorposts. God had also required them to *eat the meat that night; they should eat it, roasted over the fire, along with unleavened bread. . . . your loins girded, your sandals on your feet, and your staff in your hand* (12:7-11). Only after they obeyed all that God commanded were they prepared to leave Egypt.

Chapters 14:19 – 15:27 detail the account of Israel's victorious deliverance from Egypt and Moses' song of praise to the Lord for redeeming them. At the time they were delivered from slavery, there were about 600,000 Israelite men in addition to the women and children. Also there was a mixed multitude who were probably the result of intermarriage (12:37-38).

Chapters 16:1 – 18:27 provide an account of the Israelites' journey from Elim, along the Red Sea to Mount Sinai, which took about three months.

Chapters 19:1 – 40:38 begin in the third month of the Exodus and record the Israelites' stay at Mount Sinai, which lasted about 11 months. During this time, the covenant relationship between God and the Israelites as a nation was established. God said *to the Israelites . . . if you will fully obey Me and keep My covenant, you will be My special possession out of all the people* (Exodus 19:3-5).

The book of Exodus reveals how God faithfully protected and provided for His people in the midst of great difficulties and fierce enemies.

In Today's Reading

Jacob's prophecies; deaths of Jacob and Joseph; the Hebrews oppressed in Egypt.

After Joseph's death, the prestige the Israelites had enjoyed in Egypt gradually disappeared. *A new king came to power in Egypt,* who felt no obligation to the descendants of Joseph (Exodus 1:8). He was fearful of the Israelites' growing numbers and said to his administrators: *Look, the Israelite people are more numerous . . . than we are! . . . they may join our enemies, fight against us, and leave the country. So the Egyptians assigned taskmasters over them to oppress them with forced labor . . . But the more they oppressed them, the more they multiplied and spread so that the Egyptians came to dread the Israelites* (1:9-12). The word *dread* ex-presses a mixture of hatred and fear.

Desperate for an answer to his dilemma, Pharaoh demanded of *the Hebrew midwives* (concerning the birth of a child) . . . *If it is a son, kill him* (1:15-16). Sometime after this horrifying edict was issued, *a man from the family of Levi married a Levite woman. The woman . . . gave birth to a son* (Moses), *and . . . she hid him for three months* (2:1-2). But then, fearful of being discovered, she prepared *a papyrus basket for him and . . . placed the child in it and set it among the reeds by the bank of the Nile* (2:3).

If it had not been for Pharaoh's cruel edict, Moses would never have been rescued by Pharaoh's daughter and given all the advantages of the world's greatest empire of that time. God was preparing Moses to lead the Israelites to the promised land.

We too may face suffering where we seem to be under the control of a situation where we are as powerless as the Israelites were. It could be that death has left you without a parent or spouse. You may feel defeated following the breakup of your family or have received a terminal diagnosis from a doctor. We all will face many unforeseen sorrows.

Every Christian can say with the apostle Paul: *I am persuaded that neither . . . rulers, nor things present, nor things to come, nor powers . . . nor any other created thing will have the power to separate us from the love of God* (Romans 8:38-39).

Thought for Today: The all-sufficient God doesn't show favoritism.

In Today's Reading

Early life of Moses; his flight into Midian; the burning bush; his commission to free the nation of Israel; his return to Egypt.

Moses, the son of Israelite slaves, enjoyed the luxury of the Egyptian palace! *After Moses had grown up, he went out to his own people and observed their forced labor. He saw an Egyptian beating a Hebrew, one of his countrymen. Looking all around and seeing no one, he struck the Egyptian dead and hid him in the sand* (Exodus 2:11-12).

Moses was 40 years old when he executed the cruel Egyptian. This was Moses' legal right, since he was of the royal household and possibly second only to Pharaoh in administering justice. Moses was in the prime of his life and, from a natural point of view, it would seem to be the ideal time for God to use him to set His people free from their suffering.

But Moses fled Egypt. This was followed by 40 years of loneliness as a shepherd. It must have seemed to Moses a waste of 40 years to do nothing of importance. But, with the Lord, such time is never wasted. It was in the desert that the Angel of the Lord appeared and said: *Do not come closer! He said, Remove the sandals from your feet, for the place where you are standing is holy ground* (3:5). Moses could never have learned humility or been able to *come closer* to God in an Egyptian palace. He was too busy and too important. But both experiences were vital in preparing him to be the person God could use to lead His people out of Egypt, through the desert, and on to the borders of the promised land.

The wisdom of the world cannot qualify us to make right decisions in life. We must be taught by the Holy Spirit through reading His word. It is the Holy Spirit's anointing on what we do and say that makes our lives worthwhile. Like Moses, our most basic need is the removal of self-sufficiency. It was spiritually necessary for Moses to tend sheep on *the far side of the wilderness* to eliminate self-will and fully yield to God's will (3:1).

The highly-educated apostle Paul wrote: *Not that we are competent in ourselves to consider anything as coming from ourselves* (to decide anything by our human wisdom), *but our competence is from God* (II Corinthians 3:5).

Thought for Today: You are a vital part of God's plan to reach others.

In Today's Reading

Moses' demands to Pharaoh; Aaron to speak for Moses; Moses' rod turned into a snake; plague of blood.

God commanded Moses to face the Pharaoh of Egypt, who referred to himself as a god, and say: *The God of Israel, says: Let My people go, that they may hold a festival* (offer a sacrifice) *for Me in the wilderness. But Pharaoh responded, who is the LORD that I should obey Him? . . . I do not know the LORD, and . . . I will not let Israel go* (Exodus 5:1-2).

Moses' immediate reaction was to blame God, saying: *LORD, why have You caused trouble for this people? And why did You ever send me* (to Pharaoh)*? Ever since I went in to Pharaoh to speak in Your name, he has caused trouble for this people, and You haven't delivered Your people* (5:22-23). How often in life our questions far outnumber our answers: "Why have I been diagnosed with cancer? Why did my husband divorce me? Why did my child become a drug addict? Why was my child born with handicaps? Why did I lose my job? Why?" God didn't answer Moses' questions, and seldom does He answer us in the way we expect.

When Moses cried out: *Why, LORD?* God merely reminded him who He was. What is important for us to know is that God is the unchangeable, almighty, loving God of truth. He said: *I will bring you out from under the forced labor of the Egyptians and free you from slavery. . . I will take you as My people, and I will be your God* (6:6-8). Before He spoke the first *I will,* God said: *I am Yahweh,* meaning: "I am the only One who knows what is best and I am altogether sufficient to meet your needs" (6:2); and after the seventh *I will,* He repeated for emphasis: *I am the LORD* (the only self-existent One) (6:8). God has never once failed to keep His word; but, seldom are His promises fulfilled as soon as we expect, and almost never in the way we think would be best.

Pharaoh persisted in keeping the Israelites under his cruel authority. However, as had been foretold, the judgment of God was poured forth on each false Egyptian deity, on every household of the Egyptians, on Pharaoh's son, and eventually on Pharaoh himself and his armies.

Today . . . hear His voice, do not harden your hearts (Hebrews 3:7-8).

Thought for Today: Some are more concerned over present problems than being submissive to His purpose.

In Today's Reading

Plagues of frogs, lice, flies, death of cattle, boils, hail, locusts, and darkness.

While God was in the process of delivering the Israelites, the Egyptians suffered through each of the ten plagues which did not affect the Hebrews. Even Pharaoh's magicians recognized who was in control of the plagues. They said to Pharaoh: *This is the finger of God . . . But Pharaoh's heart was hard, and he would not listen to them* (Exodus 8:19). Following the hail that destroyed *everything in the field, both man and beast . . . Pharaoh sent for Moses and Aaron. I have sinned. . . . The LORD is the righteous One, and I and my people are the guilty ones* (9:25,27).

Pharaoh assured Moses that the Israelites could go free the moment the hail ceased. But, again Pharaoh changed his mind and hardened his heart against the will of God. Without a doubt, *Pharaoh's heart was hard* each time he decided to reject the word of God (7:13-14,22; 8:15,19,32; 9:7). But, the time arrived when *the LORD hardened Pharaoh's heart* (9:12).

Eventually, Pharaoh agreed to Moses' request, saying: *Go, worship the LORD your God . . . but . . . who will be going? Moses replied, We will go with our young and our old; we will go with our sons and daughters and with our flocks and herds because we must hold the LORD's festival* (10:8-9) – meaning that everyone from the youngest child to the most elderly person must worship the Lord. However, Pharaoh insisted that the Israelite slaves must worship on his terms. His own advisers withstood him, saying: *Let the men go, that they may worship the LORD their God. Don't you realize yet that Egypt is devastated?*(10:7). Disregarding his advisers, Moses and Aaron *were driven out of Pharaoh's presence* (10:8-11).

The person who is most deceived is the one who believes he can worship the Lord on his own terms. Others who are equally deceived say they will live for Jesus later in life and, like Pharaoh, refuse to give up control of their lives. But there comes a day when the time for repentance is past. God alone decides how long He will be insulted.

Depart from evil, and do good, and dwell there forever. For the LORD loves justice, and will not abandon His faithful ones (Psalms 37:27-28).

Thought for Today: The real issue is: "Who is in control of your life?"

In Today's Reading

Death of the firstborn; the Lord's Passover; the Exodus; pillar of cloud and pillar of fire.

With each miraculous plague, God proved that Egypt's gods were false deities and that He was the one true God who controls His creation. The final plague of judgment was death. God spoke to Moses: *About midnight I will go throughout Egypt and every firstborn male in the land of Egypt will die, from the firstborn of Pharaoh . . . to the firstborn of the servant girl* (Exodus 11:4-5). However, God lovingly provided a way for all of the Israelites who were obedient to save their firstborn from death. The sentence of death would not fall on them, but upon *an unblemished animal . . . take some of the blood and put it on the two doorposts and the lintel of the houses in which. . . . They are to eat the meat that night; they should eat it, roasted over the fire, along with unleavened bread and bitter herbs . . . you must eat it: with your loins girded, your sandals on your feet, and your staff in your hand. You are to eat it quickly; it is the LORD's Passover* (12:5,7-11).

The Hebrew word translated *atonement* carries the idea of covering something, thereby removing it from God's sight. However, even though an innocent lamb made a temporary atonement, sin was not fully eradicated. Even though there were numerous daily, weekly, and monthly sin offerings, the Israelites were still required to annually observe a full Day of Atonement.

The sin offering, the trespass offering, and the Day of Atonement as the supreme act of national atonement for sins were offered. They were only substitute offerings until Jesus, the one true Sacrifice, died for the sins of the world.

Since God is holy, He cannot fellowship with man in his sinful state. But God has provided His sinless Son as the perfect and complete substitute to die for our sins. *How much more will the blood of the Messiah, who through the eternal Spirit offered Himself without blemish to God, cleanse our consciences from dead works to serve the living God?* (Hebrews 9:14).

Thought for Today: The cross that ended the earthly life of Jesus forever ended the power of Satan to control the Christian.

In Today's Reading

Crossing the Red Sea; song of Moses; the waters of Marah; murmurings; manna and quail.

Freed from slavery in Egypt, the Israelites were on their way to the promised land. They had traveled only a short distance when they saw all the chariots of Pharaoh's army rushing toward them in a desperate effort to recover his slaves and *chased after them and caught up with them. . . . The Israelites became very afraid and cried out to the LORD for help. They said to Moses: Is it because there are no graves in Egypt that you took us to die in the wilderness?* (Exodus 14:7-11). When the Israelites *cried out to the LORD,* it was not in faith, but in fear, hostility, and criticism toward Moses.

The Israelites had seen the miracles in Egypt that had set them free; yet, they chose not to trust God and His ability to provide for them. Although Moses could not see how the Lord would save them, he confidently declared: *Don't be afraid. Stand firm and see the LORD's salvation* (14:13). In a spectacular display of His power, *the LORD hurled the Egyptians into the sea. The waters came back and covered the chariots and horsemen, the entire army of Pharaoh* (14:27-28).

Although God met that need miraculously, just three days later He led the Israelites to Marah, where they could not drink the bitter water. *And the people complained to Moses* (15:24). *So . . . the LORD showed him* (Moses) *a tree. When he threw it into the water, the water became sweet* (15:25).

The children of Israel's lack of trust in God was again evident when their food supply was exhausted. *In the wilderness the whole Israelite community complained about Moses and Aaron . . .* and *said to them, If only we had died by the LORD's hand in the land of Egypt . . . Instead, you brought us out into this wilderness to make this whole assembly die of hunger! Then the LORD said to Moses, I am going to rain bread from heaven . . . so that I can test them to see whether or not they will follow My instruction. . . . The household of Israel named the substance manna. . . . They gathered it every morning* (16:2-4,15,31,21).

Jesus declared Himself to be *the true bread . . . who comes down from heaven and gives life to the world. . . . I am the bread of life* (John 6:32-35).

Thought for Today: A heart filled with faith in God has no room for fear.

In Today's Reading

Thirst causes murmuring against Moses; water from the rock; Amalek defeated; Jethro's advice; God speaks at Mount Sinai.

As they continued their journey toward the promised land, the Israelites faced another test of their dependence upon God. *The whole Israelite community traveled . . . according to the LORD's command. They camped at Rephidim, but there was no water for the people to drink. . . . But the people were thirsty for water there, and complained to Moses. They said, Why did you ever bring us up out of Egypt, to kill us . . . with thirst? . . . And he named the place Massah and Meribah because the Israelites argued, and because they tested the LORD, saying, Is the LORD among us or not?* (Exodus 17:1,3,7). The Lord knew that there was no water there and yet He directed the Israelites to that very place.

The wilderness journeys exposed the Israelites' refusal to trust the Lord. God has warned us: *Do not harden your hearts as in the rebellion, on the day of testing in the desert, where your fathers tested Me, tried Me, and saw My works for forty years. Therefore I was provoked with this generation and said, They always go astray in their hearts* (Hebrews 3:8-10).

Israel's release from bondage and the wilderness journey is symbolic of the Christian's pilgrimage through life. From their experiences, we should learn to trust God even when anticipated resources are not available. Just as the Israelites blamed Moses, we are tempted to blame others. Frustration on the job, emotional stress, discontent, finding fault with our uncomfortable situation, hate, jealousy, fits of anger – these are all evidence of the selfish life demanding its own way. Even more serious, it is an expression of distrust in the wisdom, competence, and goodness of God.

The Christian's faith is not based on favorable circumstances, but on our all-wise Creator. The key to peace of mind and overcoming all life's problems is confidence in His word. The Christian is admonished to express faith when *distressed by various trials so that the genuineness of your faith – more valuable than gold, which perishes though refined by fire – may result in praise, glory, and honor at the revelation of Jesus Christ* (I Peter 1:6-7).

Thought for Today: To complain exposes a lack of faith.

In Today's Reading

Ten Commandments and other laws and regulations given.

The Ten Commandments are very sacred because they were written *by the finger of God* (Exodus 31:18). It is no surprise that pagans hate to see them displayed. They are an expression of the spiritual and moral conduct of the people of God. Eight are expressed negatively: *You shall not.* Six present requirements for our relationship with others. Four reveal the perfection of the holy, one true God, who alone is to be worshiped.

Then God spoke all these words: I am the LORD your God. . . . You shall have no other gods before Me. You shall not make an idol for yourself, whether in the shape of anything in the heavens . . . or on the earth . . . for I, the LORD your God, am a jealous God . . . showing faithful love to . . . those who love Me and keep My commandments. You shall not misuse the name of the LORD your God, because the LORD will not leave anyone unpunished who misuses His name. Observe the Sabbath day by keeping it holy. . . . Honor your father and your mother. . . . You shall not murder . . . commit adultery . . . steal . . . give false testimony against your neighbor . . . or *covet* (20:1-17).

We are warned that it is wrong to steal – wrong whether it is done by shoplifting, cheating on income tax, or failing to give an employer a full day's work. It is wrong to bear false witness against a neighbor, and it is wrong to commit adultery. *The . . . unbelievers, vile, murderers, sexually immoral, sorcerers, idolaters, and all liars – their share will be in the lake that burns with fire* (Revelation 21:8). We are also warned against practices of witchcraft, sorcery, bestiality, and sacrificing *to any gods, except the LORD alone* (Exodus 22:18-20). All who were guilty of these sins were to be put to death immediately. Obedience should come from the heart. If I have love toward my neighbor, I will not steal his property, or commit adultery with his wife, or commit fornication with his daughter. I will protect and respect his loved ones because they are the property of God.

The law is a mirror that reveals what we should be with absolute accuracy. The apostle Paul said: *I would not have known sin if it were not for the law. For example, I would not have known what it is to covet if the law had not said, You shall not covet* (Romans 7:7).

Thought for Today: We enjoy the peace of God when our desire is: "Whatever pleases you, Lord, pleases me."

In Today's Reading

Laws instituted; three feasts which must be kept; angel promised for a guide; instructions for tabernacle furnishings.

The Israelites were commanded: *Serve the* LORD *your God* (Exodus 23:25). This was followed by 14 blessings which God promised the Israelites for their obedience, including the assurance: *I will place the inhabitants of the land under your control, and you will drive them out before you* (23:31). Then a warning concerning the Canaanites followed: *You must not make a covenant with them or their gods* (23:32). The people responded, saying: *We will do everything that the* LORD *has commanded* (24:3).

God alone determines what is acceptable conduct as well as worship to Him. Thus, He gave Moses detailed instructions for building the tabernacle where He would accept their worship.

The tabernacle provided a way for man to maintain a right relationship with God and a place for man to worship the Lord. But, most importantly, it was a place for God to dwell among His people. In outward appearance, covered with *rams' skins* (26:14), it was unattractive, like Jesus, of whom Isaiah prophesied: *He had no form or splendor that we should look at Him, no appearance that we should desire Him* (Isaiah 53:2). But, like Jesus, nothing could be more inspiring from within, for it was the only place on earth where God met with His people. The court of the tabernacle was a rectangular enclosure with only one entrance through which sinful man could approach God (Exodus 26:36; 27:16-18).

The white linen wall of separation was symbolic of the holiness of God and excluded all Gentiles. Consequently, they could not so much as look over the curtain fence to observe what was going on inside the courtyard, or they would *be put to death* (Numbers 1:51). This linen curtain illustrates that sin has separated sinful man from the holy presence of God.

The Bible says: *For the law was given through Moses; grace and truth came through Jesus Christ. . . . Here is the Lamb of God, who takes away the sin of the world!* Our Lord Jesus said: *I am the door. If anyone enters by Me, he will be saved* (John 1:17,29; 10:9).

Thought for Today: Unless you have something good to say about someone, it's best not to say anything.

Continued on page 34

The Tabernacle

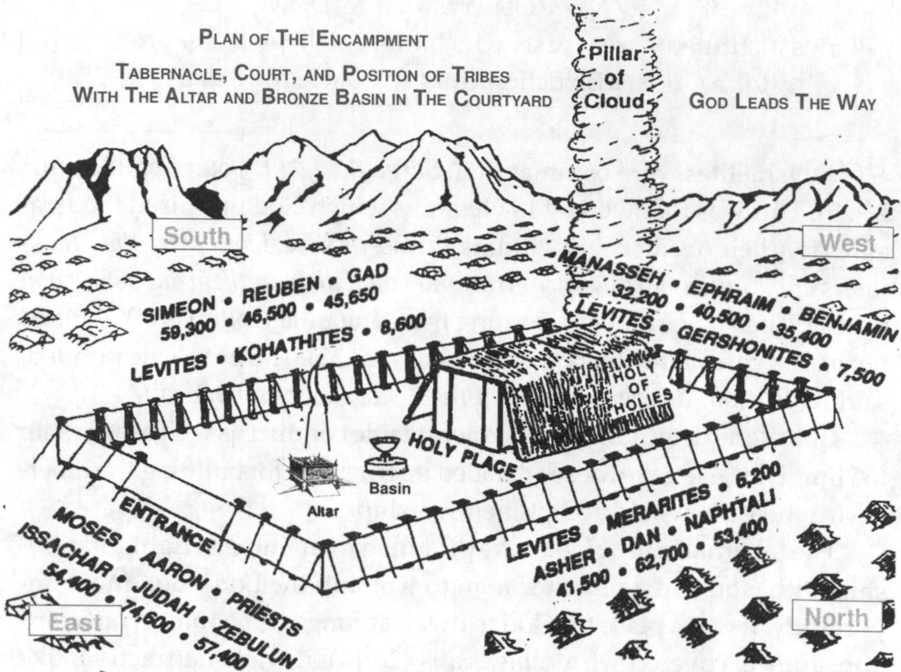

Be careful to make them according to the design . . .
you have been shown on the mountain (Exodus 25:40).

The Fenced Enclosure Bronze Altar Bronze Basin The Tabernacle
The Holy Place Lamp Stand Table of the Presence Gold Altar
Holy of Holies The Ark of the Lord's Covenant and the Mercy Seat

Everything according to the pattern (Hebrews 8:5).

THE TABERNACLE

The tabernacle was a rectangular structure, about 45 feet long and 15 feet wide, and was set up in the center of the encampment of the 12 tribes. It was protected by an enclosure that was about 150 feet long and 75 feet wide. Nothing was left to human opinion.

Sixty posts, 7½ feet high, were equally spaced around the tabernacle. This wall separated the unbeliever from the worshiper and was symbolic of the righteousness of God that bars the sinner from His presence.

There was only one entrance through which sinful man could approach God (Exodus 26:36). It was symbolic of Christ, who said: *I am the door. If anyone enters by Me, he will be saved, and will come in and go out and find pasture* (John 10:9).

PILLAR OF CLOUD
GOD LEADS THE WAY
MOSES, AARON, PRIESTS
JUDAH, ISSACHAR, ZEBULUN
GERSHONITES
WITH TWO WAGONS CARRYING
THE TENT, CURTAINS, COVERINGS
HANGINGS, GATE, DOOR AND CORDS
MERARITES
WITH FOUR WAGONS CARRYING
THE BOARDS, BARS, PILLARS,
SOCKETS, COURT PILLARS,
COURT SOCKETS,
PINS, AND CORDS
REUBEN, SIMEON, GAD

KOHATHITES
BEARING THE
ARK – GOD IN THE MIDST
TABLE
PURE GOLD LAMPSTAND
BRONZE ALTAR
GOLD ALTAR
VESSELS
BRONZE BASIN
EPHRAIM, MANASSEH, BENJAMIN,
DAN, ASHER, NAPHTALI

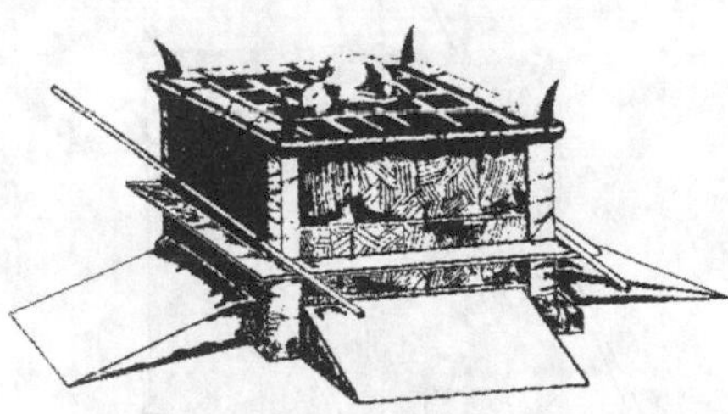

THE BRONZE ALTAR

(Exodus 38:1-7)

After passing through the gate into the fenced enclosure, the worshiper approached the bronze altar, also called the altar of burnt offering. It was about 7½ square feet and 4½ feet high, with a grill in the center.

At this altar the worshiper received covering for his sin through offering the sin and compensation sacrifices.

All sacrifices were offered on the bronze altar with the exception of the sin offering which was burned outside the camp, except for its fat which was burned on the bronze altar. The blood of the sin offering was sprinkled upon the gold altar and the remainder poured out at the bronze altar (Lev. 4:4-12). Our Lord was both *the Lamb of God, who takes away the sin of the world* (John 1:29), and our High Priest. *We have this kind of high priest . . . at the right hand of the throne of the Majesty in the heavens* (see Hebrews 8:1; 9:11-14; Eph. 2:13; I Pet. 2:24).

THE BRONZE BASIN

(Exodus 29:4; 30:18-21; 38:8)

After the priest offered the sacrifice, he approached the bronze basin that contained water for the priests to cleanse their hands and feet before ministering in the holy place. It was symbolic of the word of God that reveals our sins and is the cleansing power in our lives (see John 15:3; Titus 3:5; James 1:23,25).

TABLE OF THE PRESENCE

(Exodus 25:23-30; 37:10-16)

After the priest washed his hands and feet at the bronze basin, he proceeded toward the tabernacle, passing through the linen veil, the only door to the holy place. Inside the holy place on the right was the table of the Presence, made of shittim (acacia) wood and overlaid with pure gold. Twelve loaves of unleavened bread sprinkled with incense were placed in two rows of six upon the table. They were eaten only by the priests in the holy place. Its name "bread of the Presence" meant more than physical nourishment; it indicated gaining spiritual insight that was not obtainable in any other way.

The Holy Spirit is able to do something beyond our ability to explain. He enlightens, empowers, and then transforms the lives of those who prayerfully continue to read the word of God with a desire to do His will. Jesus said: *I am the living bread that came down from heaven. If anyone eats of this bread he will live forever* (John 6:51; see also 6:29-38; 12:24-33).

THE PURE GOLD LAMPSTAND

(Exodus 37:17-24)

Inside the holy place on the left was the seven-branched pure gold lamp-stand that provided the only source of light. Without this light, the room would have been in total darkness. The lampstand represents Christ, the *light of the world*, who makes Himself known through His word (compare John 8:12 and Revelation 1:12-20).

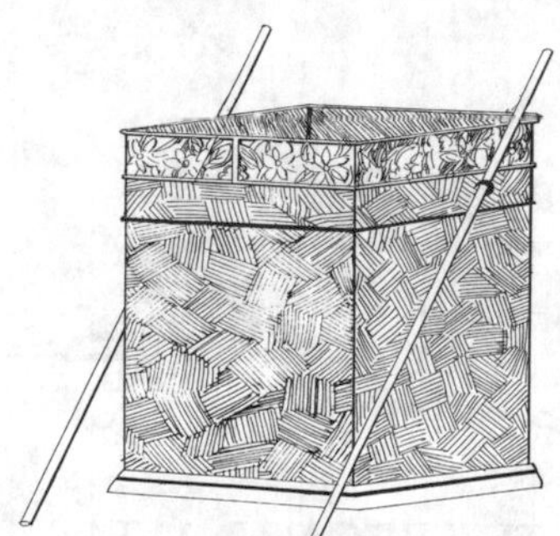

THE GOLD ALTAR

(Exodus 30:1-10; 37:25-28; 40:5; Leviticus 16:12-13)

Just in front of the veil leading to the holy of holies was a gold altar called the gold altar of incense (see I Kings 6:22; Hebrews 9:4). This altar was about 3 feet high, 1½ feet wide, and 1½ feet deep. It was made of acacia (shittim) wood overlaid with pure gold.

The gold altar was used exclusively to burn incense morning and evening. A coal of fire from the bronze altar was placed on this altar each morning and incense put on it. Only the high priest was permitted to offer incense, a type of intercessory prayer that ascended toward heaven day and night.

The gold altar was the smallest piece of furniture in the tabernacle and, as such, may seem insignificant. But it was symbolic of Christ as our intercessor (John 17:1-26; Hebrews 7:25). It is through Him that the praise as well as the prayers of undeserving people become precious to God (Hebrews 13:15).

THE ARK OF THE LORD'S COVENANT and THE MERCY SEAT

(Exodus 37:1-9; Numbers 10:33)

The Ark of the Lord's Covenant was also known as the ark of the testimony (Exodus 25:22). It was made of acacia (shittim) wood, covered within and without with pure gold. The ark contained Aaron's rod that budded, a golden pot of manna, and the two tables of stone on which were written the Ten Commandments (see Exodus 16:33; 31:18; 34:29; Numbers 17:10; Deuteronomy 10:5; Hebrews 9:4).

The mercy seat, or lid of the ark, was made of pure gold. On this lid were two gold cherubim with outstretched wings, facing each other, but looking down on the mercy seat. Between the cherubim dwelt the manifestation of the presence of God, which lighted the holy of holies.

Only one man, the high priest, symbolic of Christ, could enter the holy of holies. Once each year, on the Day of Atonement, he sprinkled the blood of the sacrificed animal on the mercy seat and then before it seven times, symbolic of the perfect and complete salvation and forgiveness of sins made possible by Jesus Christ.

Christ, our High Priest, presented His blood as His sacrifice so that we might be acceptable to God (see Hebrews 9:11-15; 10:19).

Continued from page 29

In Today's Reading

Directions given for constructing the tabernacle, court, furniture, and enclosure; plans for altar; Aaron's priestly garments; ephod.

Just inside the courtyard surrounding the tabernacle stood the bronze altar (Exodus 27:1-8), also called *the altar of burnt offering* (30:28). God had said to Moses: *You are to construct the altar of acacia wood. . . . Overlay it with bronze* (27:1-2). Throughout the Bible, bronze is a symbol of the judgment of God on sin (compare Numbers 21:6-9; John 3:14-16). All sacrifices were offered on the bronze altar, with its fire which was kindled by an act of God and which was never to go out (Leviticus 6:13).

In offering an unblemished sacrificial animal, the Israelite understood that the animal's life was being forfeited in his place because of sins he had committed. He knew that it was only through the sinless animal being slain on his behalf that he could regain a right relationship with God. The worshiper entered the one door into the outer court and approached the bronze altar. Then he placed his hands upon his sacrifice to signify his guilt being transferred to the innocent animal.

Between the altar and the tabernacle was the large bronze basin made out of many bronze mirrors which the women of the camp had provided (Exodus 38:8). Each day after the priest had offered a sacrifice, he approached the *bronze basin* (30:17-19) and washed his hands and feet before ministering in the holy place. The water and mirrors were symbolic of the word of God which both reveals our sins and is the cleansing power to remove sin in our lives (Titus 3:5; James 1:23,25).

God used the Romans to destroy Herod's temple with its bronze altar, bronze basin, pure gold lampstand, table of the Presence, and gold altar of incense. The ark of the Lord's covenant, with its mercy seat, had been missing since the Babylonian captivity. All were symbolic of Christ, who fulfilled them (Hebrews 9:1 – 10:22; 13:10-12). Since the crucifixion, bodily resurrection, and ascension of Christ, both Jews and Gentiles have but one God-appointed means of cleansing from sin.

Christ gave Himself for the church *to make her holy, cleansing her in the washing of water by the word* (Ephesians 5:26). Jesus also said: *You are already clean because of the word I have spoken to you* (John 15:3).

Thought for Today: Will what I do today honor the Lord?

IN TODAY'S READING

The rules and sacrifices for the priests; continual burnt offering; gold altar (of incense); the ransom of souls; the holy anointing oil; Sabbath regulations; Moses receives two tablets of stone.

The priests, who ministered in the tabernacle, had to be cleansed before entering. So, *the LORD spoke to Moses: Make a bronze basin for washing and a bronze stand for it. Set it between the tent of meeting and the altar, and put water in it. Aaron and his sons must wash their hands and feet with water from it* (Exodus 30:17-19). After a priest had washed his hands and feet at the basin, which provided cleansing from the activities of life, he then was qualified to enter the tabernacle through a heavy linen veil which was the only entrance into the holy place.

On the right was the table of the Presence with its 12 loaves of unleavened bread sprinkled with incense. The name bread of the Presence suggests more than just bodily nourishment. It implies spiritual insight that is not obtainable anywhere else. The bread is symbolic of Christ, who said: *I am the bread of life. . . . the living bread that came down from heaven. If anyone eats of this bread* (makes it a vital part of his life), *he will live forever* (John 6:48,51; 6:29-38; 12:24). Just as physical food is assimilated to sustain our physical lives, in like manner, as we continue to read the word of God, which is the bread of life, the Holy Spirit enlightens and then transforms our lives. *So rid yourselves of all wickedness, all deceit, hypocrisy, envy, and all slander. Like newborn infants, desire the unadulterated spiritual milk, so that you may grow* (I Peter 2:1-2).

On the left, across from the table of the Presence, was the seven-branched lampstand made of solid, beaten gold. Its seven lamps burned with pure olive oil. It provided the only source of light in the holy place (Leviticus 24:2-4).

God has provided just one book – the holy Bible – as the source of *light* for understanding His will (Psalms 119:105,130; Proverbs 6:23).

Christ said: *I am the light of the world. Anyone who follows Me will never walk in the darkness, but will have the light of life* (John 8:12).

Thought for Today: Ignoring God's word always leads to deception.

In Today's Reading

Moses on Mount Sinai; Aaron's golden calf; its destruction; death of 3,000 Israelites; law renewed; God's covenant; three festivals.

Moses was on Mount Sinai when God *gave him the two tablets of the testimony, stone tablets inscribed by the finger of God* (Exodus 31:18). At the same time, something tragic was taking place at the base of the mountain. *When the people saw that Moses delayed coming down from the mountain, they assembled before Aaron and said to him, Come, make us gods who will go before us because this Moses, the man who brought us up from the land of Egypt – we don't know what has happened to him!* (32:1). It didn't take Aaron long to make a golden calf and *he built an altar before it. . . . Early the next morning they arose, offered burnt offerings, and presented fellowship offerings* (32:2-6).

A true burnt offering was a delight to the Lord since it symbolized full surrender to Him; but these idolatrous sacrifices were hypocrisy.

Returning to the camp, Moses saw how quickly the Israelites had *acted corruptly* (32:7). Did they think that a golden calf, which they could see, was a better reminder of whom they worshiped than the invisible, yet ever present God? Or had they turned to Apis, an Egyptian god in the form of a bull? Only six weeks before, the whole congregation had sworn: *All that the LORD has spoken we will do* (19:8).

False worship leads to irresponsible moral conduct. Let us compare the Israelites' sins with our own 21st-century behavior. Most of us would reject man-made idols; but think how easily money, possessions, talents, hobbies, and success become idols for many. The apostle Paul reminds us that, although *they knew God, they did not glorify Him as God or show gratitude. Instead, their thinking became nonsense, and their senseless minds were darkened* (Romans 1:21).

The golden calf stands as a symbol of human intellect which devises its own system of worship apart from, or added to, the word of God. The world admires the independent person who is determined to be in control. They *were celebrating what their hands had made* (Acts 7:41).

Thought for Today: Following the opinions of people instead of listening to God results in disaster.

In Today's Reading

Freewill offerings for the tabernacle; construction of the tabernacle; the ark of the testimony; mercy seat; table of the Presence; lampstand; gold altar (of incense).

The gold altar was *made . . . out of acacia wood. . . . and . . .* (had) *a gold molding . . . all around . . . also* (Moses was instructed to make) *the holy anointing oil and the pure fragrant incense* (Exodus 35:15; 37:25-26,29). He was also directed to *place the altar in front of the veil that is by the ark of the testimony, in front of the mercy seat which is over the testimony, where I will meet with you. Aaron must burn fragrant incense on it; he must burn it every morning . . . as a regular incense offering before the* L*ORD* (Exodus 30:6-8).

The priests were permitted in the holy place, but only the high priest could enter the holy of holies, once a year on the Day of Atonement. In front of the veil was a gold altar. This altar was much smaller than the bronze altar, but was far more costly since it was covered with pure gold. The bronze altar, where burnt offerings were made, dealt with the judgment of sin and it was located near the entrance in the outer courtyard.

The gold altar was symbolic of Christ as our Intercessor (John 17:1-26; Heb. 7:25). Each morning, Aaron the high priest would refill the lamps with pure olive oil and burn incense upon the altar. He would take a coal of fire from the bronze altar and place it on the gold altar and then place the incense on it as a sweet fragrance that ascended toward heaven day and night. God alone was the source of fire on this altar.

Only Jesus Christ can make it possible for us to approach the heavenly Father in prayer. *Christ Jesus is the One who died, but even more, has been raised; He also is at the right hand of God and intercedes for us* (Romans 8:34). In Hebrews, we read: *He is always able to save those who come to God through Him, since He always lives to intercede for them* (Hebrews 7:25). Christ our High Priest is interceding for us each time we pray. We are encouraged to *in everything, through prayer . . . with thanksgiving, let your requests be made known to God* (Philippians 4:6-7).

Thought for Today: It is through Christ that the prayers of undeserving people become precious to God.

In Today's Reading

Bronze altar of burnt offering; tabernacle courtyard; priest's garments.

At Mount Sinai, the tabernacle was completed according to the instructions the Lord commanded Moses: *All the work for the tabernacle . . . was finished. . . . with all its furnishings . . . the ark of the testimony . . . and the mercy seat* (Exodus 39:32-35). *The ark of the testimony* (25:22; Numbers 10:33) contained the covenant between God and His people Israel. It was a wooden chest overlaid with gold, both inside and out. The ark was a type of Jesus the Messiah, the Son of God, who alone can atone for sin. The wood represented His human nature, as foretold by Isaiah: *He grew up like a young plant before Him, and like a root out of dry ground* (Isaiah 53:2). The gold represented His divine nature, for He is both fully God and fully man. The ark was made from the wood of the acacia tree which grew in the deserts, symbols of the world system of things.

The "lid" of the ark was made of pure gold and was called the *mercy seat*. It covered the law that had been placed in the ark. All men are sinners, but Christ, the perfect, sinless Son of God became our High Priest. By His perfect atonement for our sins, He provided us with mercy and salvation represented by the *mercy seat*.

The ark was behind the veil, inside the holy of holies. Without the Presence of the Lord above the ark, all the services of the tabernacle would have been meaningless. You can be sure that, as you prayerfully read the word of God daily and worship the Lord, His indwelling presence will bring meaning to your life.

On the Day of Atonement, the high priest sprinkled the blood of an innocent goat on the *mercy seat* and then in front of it seven times (Leviticus 16:14). The number seven is symbolic of the perfect and complete salvation and forgiveness of sins which would be made possible by Jesus Christ.

The law provides the "knowledge" of sin, but not the "forgiveness" of sin (Galatians 2:16; 3:11). *The law was given through Moses; grace and truth came through Jesus Christ* (John 1:17). Jesus is the One *in whom we have redemption, the forgiveness of sins* (Colossians 1:14).

Thought for Today: The more we recognize our unworthiness, the more we will appreciate His mercy in saving us.

In Today's Reading

Tabernacle completed and erected; furnishings arranged; consecration of Aaron and sons; glory of the Lord fills the tabernacle.

On Mount Sinai, God instructed Moses: *Make a sanctuary for Me so that I may dwell among them. . . . according to all that I show you* (Exodus 25: 8-9). After nine months, the building of the tabernacle was completed (39:32; compare 19:1; 40:2). Moses did *just as the LORD had commanded him* (40:16). This phrase emphasizes the supreme importance of obedience to the will of God (40:16-32). Moses' obedience was complete in every detail for making about 40 different items, including the tent, altars, vessels, bronze basin, garments, tent pegs, bronze bases, loops, posts, and furniture (25:40; 26:30; 39:42-43).

The first thing to be placed within the tabernacle was the ark of the testimony which contained the Ten Commandments of God: *On the first day of the first month you are to erect the tabernacle, the tent of meeting. Put the ark of the testimony there . . . Moses took the testimony and placed it in the ark . . . He brought the ark into the tabernacle . . . just as the LORD had commanded* (40:2-3,20-21).

God's word provides all the wisdom, spiritual guidance, and strength necessary to live for Him. It is vital that we, like Moses, do all that *the LORD had commanded.*

After the tabernacle was constructed, the cloud of His Presence (Exodus 13:21) and the tabernacle were inseparable throughout the Israelites' journeys. If the cloud lifted and moved forward, the tabernacle and the people then followed; if the cloud stopped, the people remained until it moved again (40:36-37).

Soon, the glorious presence of God will again be seen on earth, as the apostle John revealed while imprisoned on Patmos, when he wrote: *I also saw the Holy City, new Jerusalem, coming down out of heaven from God, prepared like a bride adorned for her husband. Then I heard a loud voice from the throne: Look! God's dwelling is with men, and He will live with them. They will be His people, and God Himself will be with them and be their God* (Revelation 21:2-3).

Thought for Today: Allow Christ to take charge of the affairs of your life. You will be so glad you did.

Introduction To The Book Of Leviticus

The purpose of this book was to explain how the Israelites could have a personal relationship with God. The first seven chapters are occupied with the five sacrifices. Chapters 8 – 10 cover the priesthood; chapters 11 – 16 express the qualifications for sanctification and explain the Day of Atonement; and chapter 17 emphasizes the bronze altar as the place where sacrifices were to be offered. All five of the Levitical sacrifices were necessary to give a complete understanding of the death of *our Lord Jesus Christ, who gave Himself for our sins to rescue us from this present evil age* (Galatians 1:3-4).

Chapters 18 – 27 reveal how fellowship with God is maintained. The basic principle is the same today, *for it is written, Be holy, because I am holy* (I Peter 1:16; Leviticus 11:44-45; 19:2; 20:7). Chapters 18 – 22 express God's standard of holiness and the regulations of sanctification for the priests. Chapters 23 – 27 are concerning *the LORD's appointed times for the Israelites* to maintain fellowship with a holy God (Leviticus 23:44).

The seven festivals were timed so that, after they had settled in the promised land the men could go to Jerusalem. *Three times a year all your males are to appear before the Lord GOD* (Exodus 23:17).

The first journey to Jerusalem was to be in the first month of the religious year. Three festivals were celebrated in this month. The Passover Festival began on the 14th and lasted 7 days; the Festival of Unleavened Bread was celebrated on the 15th; and the Festival of Firstfruits began *on the day after the Sabbath* of the Passover week, which was always on a Sunday (Leviticus 23:1-14). Jesus Christ is the perfect Passover Lamb, as well as the Unleavened Bread, who arose on Sunday, the first day of Firstfruits: *But now Christ has been raised from the dead, the firstfruits of those who have fallen asleep* (I Corinthians 15:20).

The second journey was seven weeks later. It commemorated the early harvest and was called the Festival of Weeks. It also occurred on a Sunday, the first day of the week (Leviticus 23:16).

The third group of festivals was during the seventh month of the religious year. Included were the Festival of Trumpets (beginning of their civil year) on the first day, the Day of Atonement on the 10th day, and the Festival of Tabernacles from the 15th through the 21st.

The Sabbaths were occasions free from work. They were times to teach the word of God and worship Him (23:2-4, 7-8, 21, 24, 27, 35-37).

In Today's Reading

Burnt offering; meat (meal) offering; fellowship sacrifice.

The first three offerings mentioned in the first three chapters of Leviticus are called *pleasing aroma offerings,* which means they were voluntary and pleasing to God. *Speak to the Israelites and tell them: When any of you presents an offering to the LORD from the livestock, you may present your offerings from the herd or the flock. If his gift is a burnt offering from the herd, he is to present an unblemished male. He must present it at the entrance to the tent of meeting that he may be accepted before the LORD. He should lay his hand on the head of the burnt offering so it can be accepted on his behalf to make atonement for him* (Leviticus 1:2-4,9).

The first offering mentioned is called *the burnt offering.* It symbolized the offerer giving his own life in full submission to God and without a selfish motive. The offering was to be a bull, lamb, goat, turtledove, or pigeon, according to the financial ability of the offerer (1:3, 10,14). If the offerer owned a herd, then he offered a bull. If, however, the offerer possessed only flocks, then his offering would be a lamb or a goat; for either of these men to offer a pigeon would have been offensive to God. But, if the offerer were so poor that he did not own a herd or a flock, then an acceptable offering could be the less-expensive turtledove or young pigeon. This was the offering made by Joseph and Mary, the mother of Jesus, which points out how very poor they were before the wise men arrived with their expensive gifts (Luke 2:22-24; Matthew 2:11; see Leviticus 12:2-8).

The procedure for the offering was for the offerer to lay his hands heavily upon the head of the animal, symbolizing the transfer of sin from the guilty to the sinless to atone for his sin. Next, the priest had to *slaughter the bull before the LORD, and Aaron's sons, the priests, are to present the blood and sprinkle it against all sides of the altar* (1:5). The blood offered to God indicated that a life had been given as a substitute for the one who had sinned. This was a foreshadowing of the crucifixion of Jesus Christ, who *gave Himself for us to redeem us from all lawlessness and to cleanse for Himself a special people, eager to do good works* (Titus 2:13-14).

Thought for Today: It's the spirit of giving that counts most.

In Today's Reading

Sin offering; compensation offering; further directions concerning burnt, meat (meal), and sin offerings.

The *grain offering* is also translated cereal or meat offering. It could be brought with either the burnt offering or the fellowship sacrifice; but it was never to be brought with the sin or compensation (trespass) offering. *Now this is the law of the grain offering: Aaron's sons will present it before the LORD. . . . It is to be eaten as unleavened bread. . . . in the courtyard of the tent of meeting. It must not be baked with leaven. . . . It is most holy, like the sin offering and the compensation offering* (Leviticus 6:14-17).

The Hebrew word for *grain offering* is *minchah,* "a gift" given by an inferior to a superior, in the sense of a required tribute paid to a king by a peasant. The Lord's portion was burned on the altar, signifying that the offerer was now in a right relationship with the Most High God.

The fine flour reminded the people that God gave them their food and that they, in turn, owed Him their lives. The grain was usually crushed and ground into fine flour which was sometimes mixed with oil and/or frankincense, but always with salt, and then baked. Frankincense, as it burned with the offering, gave forth a satisfying odor symbolizing that the prayers and intercessions of all who are in covenant relationship with God are satisfying to Him.

While the *burnt offering* expressed a consecration of self, the *grain offering* was a consecration of service. It also illustrates the life of Christ, the sinless Savior, who laid aside His glory as the God of creation to be crushed as a grain of wheat by the mill of humiliation. *He was pierced through because of our transgressions, crushed because of our iniquities* (Isaiah 53:5). He endured beatings and intense suffering, was crowned with thorns in mockery, and was finally put to death on the cross for the sins of all repentant sinners who receive Him as their Savior and Lord. The atonement of Christ secured for the sinner the benefits of forgiveness from God and peace and fellowship with Him. *The Son of Man did not come to be served, but to serve, and to give His life – a ransom for many* (Matthew 20:28).

Thought for Today: Loyalty and dependability are of far more value than outstanding abilities.

The Five Offerings

The Offering	Purpose	Meaning for Today
Sin Offering [Required First] Lev. 4:1-35; 6:24-30 Bulls, goats, lambs were acceptable -- the whole animal was burned outside the camp. The poor could bring two young pigeons or two turtledoves.	This offering provided atonement for the convicted sinner who was separated from God by sin. It was the first offering, because *all have sinned, and fall short of the glory of God* [Romans 3:23]; no one was exempt. It was offered for all the people on feast days. It was a type of Christ crucified outside Jerusalem.	Christ, the perfect, sinless Son of God, gave Himself as the final sacrifice for our sins. *He made the One who did not know sin to be sin for us* [II Cor. 5:20-21; Gal. 1:4; Heb. 10:3-4; 13:12], thereby providing a cleansing from sin and reconciliation with God for all who accept Christ as Savior [John 1:12].
Compensation Offering [Required] Similar to Sin Offering Lev. 5:1-19; 6:1-7; 14:12-18	The sinner was required to *make restitution for his sin* [Lev. 5:16], whether the sin was against another or against God.	The injured person was compensated. Restitution included an additional 20% of the value restored. Fellowship with the wronged person and with God also was restored.
Grain Offering **Meal, Cereal** **(sometimes translated meat)** Lev. 2:1-16; 6:14-23; 7:9-10 "Fine" flour, unleavened bread, cakes, wafers, and grain were offered – always with salt and oil, and with frankincense. This always followed the morning and evening burnt offerings.	This freewill offering was an expression of thanksgiving: *A pleasing aroma to the Lord* [Lev. 2:2]. Grain ground into fine flour signifies Christ's brokenness by His crucifixion on our behalf. Jesus was wholly devoted to His Father's will. *The Messiah also loved us and gave Himself for us, a sacrificial and fragrant offering to God* [Ephesians 5:2].	The individual grains being ground into fine flour and mixed with oil symbolize our need to lose our identity to become part of the Body of Christ. Our unreserved submission to God's will, under the guidance of the Holy Spirit, today arises as *a pleasing aroma to the Lord* [Leviticus 2:2]. *For to God we are the fragrance of Christ among those who are being saved and among those who are perishing* [II Corinthians 2:15].
Burnt Offering [Voluntary] Lev. 1:1-17; 5:7; 6:8-13 Based on financial ability: bull for the rich; two turtledoves or young pigeons for the poor.	After sin, compensation, and grain offerings, the offerer, was now reconciled to God and came to worship Him. A bull, ram, goat, turtledove, or young pigeons were completely burned to ashes on the altar. This was a freewill offering.	This offering illustrates the complete act of self-surrender [Matt. 22:37]. We too are to present our bodies to God as *a living sacrifice* [Rom. 12:1-2] – this means the best of our time, talents, and possessions.
Fellowship Offering [Voluntary, Last] Lev. 3:1-17; 7:11-36 *From the herd . . . flock . . . the priest will burn it on the altar* [3:1,6,11].	This is the only offering shared in fellowship with God, the priests, and families, expressing praise to God. It was a symbol of enjoyment and unity and was always a joyful occasion [Eph. 2:14-15; 5:2; see also 1:2; Col. 1:20; 3:12-16].	Christ is "our fellowship offering." He alone makes possible true peace and fellowship between God and believers. His prayer was: *May they all be one* [John 17:22]. Jesus promised: *Peace I leave with you, My peace I give to you* [14:27].

In Today's Reading

Regulations concerning offerings; consecration of Aaron and his sons for the priesthood, and the priests' offerings.

The *fellowship* (peace) *offering* was the only offering shared by three parties. First: *The priest is to burn the fat on the altar, but the breast belongs to Aaron and his sons. The right thigh you are to give to the priest as a contribution from your fellowship sacrifices* (Leviticus 7:31-32) and all that was left was eaten by the offerer and his family. The sacrifice for the *fellowship offering* was to be an ox and a ram (9:3-4). But birds were not acceptable for a *fellowship offering.* The animal had to be unblemished, characteristic of the perfect, sinless Christ.

The *fellowship offering* could be brought for answered prayer, in connection with a vow, or as an act of thanksgiving. It was not required, but strict regulations had to be followed. To offer a *fellowship offering,* the offerer *should lay his hand on the head of his offering and slaughter it at the entrance to the tent of meeting. Then Aaron's sons, the priests, will sprinkle the blood against the altar on all sides* (Leviticus 3:2). The priest burned the fat on the altar. The fat was always God's portion and was never to be eaten by man: *If anyone eats the fat of an animal from which an offering by fire may be presented to the LORD, the person who eats must be cut off from his people* (7:25).

In all the offerings, the Lord's portion was presented first. We are never to give the Lord only whatever is left over after every other desire is met. He is to be given His tithe first from all income. Furthermore, a right relationship with God results in love and peace in fellowship with other believers. *Therefore, since we have been declared righteous by faith, we have peace with God through our Lord Jesus Christ* (Romans 5:1).

The *fellowship offering* expressed a peaceful relationship with God, as well as with others. It was a time of sharing, and friendship, a perfect illustration which foreshadowed the church, a reminder that we are not to stay *away from our meetings, as some habitually do, but* (encourage) *each other, and all the more as you can see the day drawing near* (Hebrews 10:25).

Thought for Today: Pride and jealousy are deadly to health, happiness, fellowship with others, and peace with God.

In Today's Reading

First offerings of Aaron; offerings for the people; sin and deaths of Nadab and Abihu; restrictions for the priesthood.

The *sin offering* and the *compensation offering* (Leviticus 5:6-7) were mandatory and were the first two *offerings* to be presented. They were required to restore the broken relationship between God and sinful man. *Moses said to Aaron . . . sacrifice your sin offering and your burnt offering; make atonement for yourself and the people* (9:7).

Then the LORD spoke to Moses: Tell the Israelites: When someone unintentionally sins regarding any of the LORD's commandments about things not to be done and does one of them – If the anointed priest sins, bringing guilt on the people, he is to present to the LORD a young, unblemished bull as a sin offering for the sin he has committed. He must bring the bull before the LORD to the entrance of the tent of meeting, lay his hand on the bull's head, and slaughter the bull before the LORD (4:1-4). This also served as a reminder that the innocent animal died in the sinner's place. The animal's body was then taken outside the camp for burning.

Scripture points out that ignorance is not an excuse for failing to obey the laws of God (Romans 2:12-16). Disobedience to the will of God is an inexcusable sin and must be repented of and atoned for.

No animal could be an absolute substitute for a sinner, but could only provide a temporary covering for sin. Christ is our sin offering. *God sent His Son, born of a woman, born under the law* (Galatians 4:4); Jesus died in the sinner's place for the sins of all mankind. *He* (God) *made the One* (Christ) *who did not know sin to be sin for us, so that we might become the righteousness of God in Him* (II Corinthians 5:21).

Christ is also our *compensation offering*. *When you were dead in trespasses and in the uncircumcision of your flesh, He made you alive with Him and forgave us all our trespasses. He erased the certificate of debt, with its obligations, that was against us . . . and has taken it out of the way by nailing it to the cross* (Colossians 2:13-14), so that we have *escaped the world's impurity through the knowledge of our Lord and Savior Jesus Christ* (II Peter 2:20).

Thought for Today: We cheat ourselves when we give less than our best to the Lord.

In Today's Reading

Health and dietary laws; the cleansing (purification) of women after childbirth; signs and laws concerning leprosy.

Over 40 times in Leviticus we read: *I am the LORD* or *I am the LORD your God*; and more than six times the Lord demands: *You shall be holy; for I am holy*. Both inward and outward, morally and spiritually, we must separate ourselves from all that defiles: *For I am the LORD your God, so you must consecrate yourselves and be holy because I am holy* (Leviticus 11:44). The Israelites were to eat clean food (chapter 11); have clean bodies (chapter 12-13), clean clothes (13:47-59), clean houses (14:33-57), and clean personal hygiene (chapter 15); and be a clean nation (chapter 16).

The word *unclean* is used about 100 times in chapters 11 through 16, showing us that God required every unclean thing to be removed from their lives. God also required that the Israelites separate themselves from heathens, idolatry, immorality, and even unsanitary habits. The people of God were not to intermarry with gentile unbelievers. The many sacrifices, rules, and regulations concerning what is *clean* and *unclean* (what defiles a person), lead us to understand how sin separates us from God.

This is also a daily reminder to every New Testament (covenant) Christian that *whether you eat or drink, or whatever you do, do everything for God's glory* (I Corinthians 10:31).

The Holy Spirit led the apostle Paul to write: *Therefore, brothers, by the mercies of God, I urge you to present your bodies as a living sacrifice, holy and pleasing to God; this is your spiritual worship* (Romans 12:1). And, to the church at Corinth, he wrote: *Don't you know that you are God's sanctuary and that the Spirit of God lives in you? If anyone ruins God's sanctuary, God will ruin him; for God's sanctuary is holy, and that is what you are* (I Corinthians 3:16-17). To the Ephesians, he wrote: *Be holy and blameless in His sight* (Ephesians 1:4). *God has not called us to impurity, but to sanctification* (I Thessalonians 4:7). And it is also written: *Pursue peace with everyone, and holiness – without it no one will see the Lord* (Hebrews 12:14).

Thought for Today: The worldly-minded person never perceives what God reveals to those who are *pure in heart* (Matthew 5:8).

In Today's Reading

Purification after having skin diseases; signs of leprosy; uncleanness of men and women; sacrifice for cleansing from defilements.

When an Israelite was pronounced a leper, God said: *The priest must pronounce him unclean. . . . his clothes must be torn, his hair must be disheveled, he must cover his mouth, and he must cry out, Unclean! Unclean! . . . He must live . . . outside the camp* (Leviticus 13:44-46). To express his extreme grief and deep humiliation, this poor, wretched person had to pass through the camp for one last time, crying: *Unclean! Unclean!*

When leprosy first appears, it seems harmless – just a small white or pink spot on the skin and, in its earliest stages, it is totally painless. The spot might remain for months or even years before it begins to develop further. Eventually, leprosy produces an extremely repulsive disfigurement of the entire body, including spongy tumor-like swellings on the face and head. The movement of joints causes deep, painful, bleeding fissures. The fingers and toes become misshapen, rough, and ragged. The fingernails swell, curl up, and fall off. And, as leprosy progresses, the flesh develops offensive, running sores, and the gums begin to bleed. Eventually, the body's extremities fall away. As the years pass, the leper becomes thin and weak, plagued with diarrhea, an incessant thirst, and burning fever.

Leprosy illustrates how insignificant a sin may first appear, but how dreadful, loathsome, and fatal it finally becomes. Sin immediately separates us from God, for we are "unclean." People controlled by sin exist in a state of living death, unless they turn to Christ, truly repent, and forsake their sins. During the ministry of Jesus many lepers were healed, which attested to His deity. *Though your sins are like scarlet, they will be as white as snow; though they are as red as crimson, they will be like wool* (Isaiah 1:18). *How happy is the man whom the Lord will never charge with sin!* (Romans 4:8).

Before Jesus came, only two recorded cases of leprosy were ever healed – Miriam (Numbers 12:10-16) and Naaman the Syrian (II Kings 5:1-14), both of whom were sovereignly healed by God. *The blood of Jesus . . . cleanses us from all sin* (I John 1:7).

Thought for Today: The lust of the flesh and the eye are never satisfied.

In Today's Reading

Day of Atonement; the scapegoat; the eating of blood forbidden; civil and religious laws; immorality forbidden.

On the annual Day of Atonement, Aaron the high priest was first required to present a young bull as sacrifice for his own sins before he could proceed with the sin offering for the people. God had said that *only in this way may Aaron enter the most holy place: with a young bull for a sin offering and a ram for a burnt offering. . . . Next he will take the two goats and place them before the LORD at the entrance to the tent of meeting. . . . He slaughters the male goat for the people's sin offering and . . . blood: he is to sprinkle it against the mercy seat and in front of it. . . . Aaron will lay both his hands on the head of the live goat and confess over it all the Israelites' . . . sins. So he is to put them on the goat's head and send it away into the wilderness. . . . The goat will carry all their wrongdoings. . . . On this day, atonement will be made for you* (Leviticus 16:3-30).

Two goats were necessary to express our Lord's twofold atonement. One goat was sacrificed upon the altar for a *sin offering*. Then Aaron laid his hands upon the head of the remaining goat, the scapegoat, and confessed the sins of the congregation, thereby transferring their sins to the scapegoat which was led away *into a desolate land, and the man will release it* (16:22) where it disappeared from sight, a symbol that *as far as the east is from the west, so far has He removed our transgressions from us* (Psalms 103:12). There was no justification but merely a "covering" of another year's sins for the Israelites. But Christ, our great High Priest, did not need to present a sacrifice for Himself, for He is *holy. . . . He doesn't need to offer sacrifices every day, as high priests do – first for their own sins, then for those of the people. He did this once for all when He offered Himself* (Hebrews 7:26-27).

The scapegoat has an added application for all of us, for we should both forgive and choose not to remember offenses against ourselves. Therefore, *all bitterness, anger and wrath, insult and slander must be removed from you. . . . And be kind and compassionate to one another, forgiving one another, just as God also forgave you in Christ* (Ephesians 4:31-32).

Thought for Today: We should never condemn ourselves or others over sins confessed and forsaken – because God has forgiven them.

In Today's Reading

Laws of holiness and justice for the people and priests; penalties for idolatry and immorality; laws regarding defilement of priests.

The priests were to represent the Lord God at all times. They were also to represent Him in their own personal lives and family relationships, lest the sanctuary of God be profaned. *The LORD said to Moses: Speak to the priests, the sons of Aaron and tell them: A priest may not make himself ceremonially unclean for a dead person among his relatives. . . . As a husband, he is not to make himself unclean among his relatives by marriage and so defile himself. . . . They are to be holy to their God and not profane the name of their God. For they present the fire offerings to the LORD, the food of their God, so they must be holy. They must not marry a woman defiled by promiscuity or marry a woman divorced by her husband, for the priest is holy to his God* (Leviticus 21:1,4,6-7; Ezekiel 44:22). The marriage status of a priest was so important that God repeated: *He is not to marry these: a widow, a divorcée, or a woman defiled by promiscuity. He may only take a virgin from his own people as a wife* (Leviticus 21:14). The priest represented the Most High God. Surely a higher standard of conduct should be required of an elder, minister, pastor, or priest today (Titus 1:6-7; I Timothy 3:12).

The priest's right ear, right thumb, and big toe of his right foot were to be anointed with blood. The blood-anointed ear was a reminder to listen to the voice of God above all others; the blood-anointed hand was a reminder of the priests' privilege to serve in the tabernacle; and the blood-anointed foot was a reminder to live in obedience to the word of God.

Since he was the spiritual leader among his people, the sacrifice for the sins of a priest required a young bull, the most highly valued animal. In comparison, this was the same sacrifice required for all the sins of the congregation. The priest was a spiritual role model who could influence the entire congregation to sin (Leviticus 4:3,22-23). As representatives of God, a priest who disregards the qualifications for service *will be cut off from My presence* (put to death): *I am the LORD* (22:3-7).

As Christians we must set the example and abstain from any conduct that may influence others to be less than their best for Christ. He has *made us a kingdom, priests to His God and Father* (Revelation 1:6).

Thought for Today: A Christian represents the Lord God at all times.

The Annual Festivals All Men Were Required To Attend

Festivals	Significance to Israel	Meaning Today
Passover 1 Day Nisan 14 [March/April] And	Beginning of the religious year [Lev. 23:5-8].The Passover commemorated their deliverance from death by placing the lamb's blood on the door post, eating the lamb, and preparation for the exodus.	Our deliverance from the death penalty of sin by Christ, the Lamb of God, who died in our place [John 1:29; I Cor. 5:7; I Pet. 1:18-19].
Unleavened Bread Nisan 15-21 [March/April] **Firstfruits** [Day After Sabbath of Passover Week] [March/April]	Leaven is symbolic of sin and was prohibited during this week. This day involved careful house cleaning, including ceilings, walls, floors, and every piece of furniture. All cooking utensils were boiled in water. It was a reminder that they were a holy people, a people separated unto the Lord. A sheaf of the firstfruits of the barley harvest was presented as a wave offering, indicating the beginning of harvest.	Unleavened bread illustrates the sinlessness of Christ, the *Bread of Life. Therefore, come out from among them and be separate, says the Lord; do not touch any unclean thing, and I will welcome you* [II Cor. 2:17].
Pentecost [or Festival of Weeks] 1 Day Sivan [May/June]	Celebrated 7 weeks after [50 days]. Thanksgiving for the harvest [Lev. 23:15-22; Deut. 16:9-12]. It included presenting two loaves of leavened bread from the firstfruits of the wheat harvest commemorating the end of the summer harvest.	The outpouring of the Holy Spirit took place at Pentecost, 50 days after the resurrection of Christ [Acts 2]. Pentecost means 50th in Greek. Two loaves of leavened bread illustrate the sinful nature of both Jew and Gentile.
Trumpets 1 Day Tishri 1 [September/October]	Beginning of the civil year. Symbolic of the voice of God. Special sacrifices were brought [Lev. 23: 23-25; Num. 29:1-6].	The word of God preached is His trumpet. [See II Tim. 4:1-2; compare Rev. 4:1.]
Day of Atonement 1 Day Tishri 10 [September/October]	The high priest made atonement for the nation's sins of the past year. He first offered a sacrifice, then sprinkled the blood on the Mercy Seat and at the base of the Bronze Altar. Two goats were also selected for a Sin Offering – one by death and the other by confessing over it the sins of the people and taking it into the wilderness [Lev. 23:26-32].	Christ, our High Priest, gave Himself as the perfect sacrifice. He did this not only by dying on the cross for our sins, but also by removing the guilt and consequences of sin. They are never to be remembered. [Heb. 7:27; 8:12; 10:17; I John 1:7-9].
Tabernacles [or Booths or Festival of Ingathering] 7 Days Tishri 15-21 [September/October]	During this Festival they lived in temporary shelters in commemoration of God's gracious provisions during the 40 years in the wilderness [Ex. 23:16; Lev. 23:36; Num. 29:12-34; Deut. 16:13-15].	Jesus revealed Himself as the source of living Water at this Festival [John 7:37-39], and prior to this, the *True Bread from heaven* [John 6:31-35].

In Today's Reading

Death penalty for defiled priests who eat holy things; acceptable offerings; Sabbath, Passover, festivals, and other requirements.

The Passover was the first festival of the religious year. *The Passover to the LORD comes in the first month, at twilight on the fourteenth day of the month, and the Festival of Unleavened Bread to the LORD is on the fifteenth day of the same month. For seven days you must eat unleavened bread* (Leviticus 23:5-6). The *Festival of Unleavened Bread* lasted seven days during which unleavened bread was the only bread eaten (Exodus 34:18-19). Unleavened bread represents the sinless nature of Christ. *Jesus said to them, I assure you: Moses didn't give you the bread from heaven, but My Father gives you the true bread from heaven. For the bread of God is the One who comes down from heaven and gives life to the world* (John 6:32-33). Israel's abstinence from leaven for seven days was a reminder that they were a holy people separated unto their Lord God.

It took seven weeks to harvest all the crops, beginning with the barley crop that ripened in the spring. After that came the harvest of olives and the vineyards, followed by wheat, the final summer harvest. Just as there was a day of Firstfruits in the spring to indicate faith in the coming harvests, the Festival of Weeks, also known as the Festival of Harvest, expressed thankfulness for the completion of the summer harvest (Exodus 23:16). It was also called *Pentecost* because *pente* in Greek means 50, and this festival took place on the 50th day after the one sheaf offering of the Festival of Firstfruits (Leviticus 23:15-16).

In contrast to the unleavened bread required for Passover were the *two wave loaves* that were to be baked with leaven for the *Festival of Weeks* (Pentecost) (23:17). Leaven is symbolic of our sin nature and was required in the *two wave loaves* because they were symbolic of both Jewish and Gentile believers within the church.

Clean out the old yeast so that you may be a new batch, since you are unleavened. For Christ our Passover has been sacrificed. Therefore, let us observe the feast, not with old yeast, or with the yeast of malice and evil, but with the unleavened bread of sincerity and truth (I Corinthians 5:7-8).

Thought for Today: The Christian has a desire to please the Lord and be clean in mind, body and spirit.

In Today's Reading

The tabernacle, lampstand, bread of the Presence; blasphemy; year of jubilee; laws concerning redemption of property and the poor.

Following the *command* for *the Israelites to bring . . . pure oil of beaten olives, in order to light the lamp regularly* (Leviticus 24:2), they were given detailed instructions for making the bread of the Presence. *Also take fine flour and bake it into 12 cakes of bread. . . . Set them in two stacks, six to a stack, on the pure gold table before the LORD. . . . Regularly each Sabbath the bread must be set out before the LORD as a perpetual covenant obligation on the part of the Israelites* (24:5-9).

The term bread of the Presence literally means "bread of the face" and "Presence of God," signifying that He and His word alone sustained their very lives. When the priests ate the bread, it ratified Israel's dependence upon Him. The loaves were made of *fine flour* – coarse flour could not be used, for these loaves represented Christ, the perfect One, *holy, innocent, undefiled, separated from sinners, and exalted above the heavens* (Hebrews 7:26).

The aromatic frankincense that was required to be placed on the loaves is symbolic of praise to God as well as a reminder that Christ, as *the bread of life,* provides true satisfaction; yes, *how sweet Your word is to my taste sweeter than honey to my mouth* (Psalms 119:103).

The loaves also picture Christ, who faced the fierce oven of affliction and crucifixion to come forth as *the bread of life.* Jesus declared: *No one who comes to Me will ever be hungry, and no one who believes in Me will ever be thirsty again* (John 6:35). The 12 identical loaves were a reminder that the Lord was the satisfier and sustainer of all 12 tribes.

Light is a revealer of truth, and this lampstand shone upon the sacred showbread that typified Christ. *For the bread of God is the One who comes down from heaven and gives life to the world* (6:33). As we read His word, the Holy Spirit, who indwells believers, provides light on the moral and spiritual values of life. This light enables Christians to fulfill one of their essential missions to the world: *Let your light shine before men, so that they may see your good works and give glory to your Father in heaven* (Matthew 5:16).

Thought for Today: Everything we possess is a gift from God.

In Today's Reading

Blessings for obedience; judgment for disobedience; redeeming persons and property; tithes shall be holy to the Lord.

The Lord warns His people: *You must not make idols for yourselves . . . to worship before it, since I am the LORD your God. You must keep My Sabbaths and revere My sanctuary: I am the LORD. . . . Keep My commandments. . . . And you will be My people. . . . But if you do not obey Me and observe all these commandments. . . . I will set My face against you so that you will be defeated by your enemies. . . . I will scatter you among the nations* (Leviticus 26:1-33). The Israelites were reminded that the first and fourth of the Ten Commandments are the foundation of a right relationship with our Creator and for all true worship.

Numerous blessings were recorded as benefits of obedience to the word of God (26:3-13). Also recorded were clear warnings regarding sin and disobedience to His word which later were fulfilled (26:14-39).

Although the book of Leviticus was written to Israelites, its basic truths are just as relevant for us today. The God of holiness is *the same yesterday, today, and forever* (Hebrews 13:8).

Despite their continued rejection of Jesus as the Messiah, the Jews will eventually recognize their spiritual blindness, repent, and worship their Messiah Jesus, the true source of eternal peace. Just as God foretold: *I will . . . return them to this land. . . . because they will return to Me with all their heart* (Jeremiah 24:6-7). The times of the gentiles that began with King Nebuchadnezzar will soon end and Jesus Christ, the King of kings, will rightfully rule the world from Jerusalem.

The marvelous compassion and love of God is seen in His desire to forgive and restore the sinner to Himself. However, no one can escape the tragic losses of a wasted lifetime. Sins can be forgiven; but we cannot relive or restore our lives. Recognizing the eternal consequences of sin, confession is of utmost importance. *If we confess our sins, He is faithful and righteous to forgive us our sins and to cleanse us from all unrighteousness* (I John 1:9).

Thought for Today: The tragic losses of a wasted lifetime cannot be relived or restored, but they can be forgiven.

Introduction To The Book Of Numbers

The book of Numbers continues the history of the Israelites where the book of Exodus left off. Just one month had passed between the completion of the tabernacle (Exodus 40:17) and the command of God to number the people (Numbers 1:1-2). During that time, the instructions in the book of Leviticus were given. The first census of all men 20 years old and older records that 603,550 men were qualified to serve in the army of Israel (1:1– 10:10).

On the twentieth day of the second month in the second year, the cloud was lifted from above the tabernacle of the testimony (10:11), and the Israelites followed the cloud as it moved toward Kadesh-barnea, about 160 miles to the north (10:11 – 14:45). It was not long, however, before the people complained and then rebelled.

After the Israelites arrived at Kadesh-barnea, 12 spies were sent out to investigate the land (Numbers 13 – 14; Deuteronomy 1:22-40). When they returned 40 days later, *Caleb . . . said, We should certainly go up and take possession of the land because we will surely win the victory over it* (Numbers 13:30). Ten of the spies strongly protested, saying: *We can't go up against the people: they're stronger than we are* (13:31). However, Joshua and Caleb pleaded: *The LORD is with us. Don't be afraid of them.* But the people agreed with the ten disbelieving spies (14:1-45). Because of their unbelief God pronounced His judgment of death upon that generation (14:26-45).

Thus, they wasted 38 years wandering in the wilderness until all the people from the first generation who were 20 years old or older at the first census had died (15:1 – 21:35).

Later, the Lord commanded Moses and Eleazar, Aaron's son and successor, to take a second census of the new generation of men 20 years old and older, whose parents had left Egypt (26:1-65). This second numbering took place almost 40 years after the first census, in the 10th month of the 40th year (1:19; 26:4; compare Exodus 1:1-5; Deuteronomy 1:3).

Only Joshua and Caleb, the two men of faith from the first generation of Israelites, lived to enter the promised land. The new generation was estimated to be more than two million people. They gathered on the Plains of Moab, north of the Dead Sea and east of the Jordan River, across from Jericho, ready to take the land their parents had refused.

In Today's Reading

First numbering (census) of the Israelites for military purposes and encampment location of each tribe in relation to the tabernacle.

About 70 times in the book of Numbers, we read: *The LORD said* or *the LORD spoke to Moses*. These were the words of our heavenly Father speaking to His children. The desire of God was to have a people that would love, obey, and follow Him without reservation. He, in turn, would be their God, and lead them into the promised land. While the Israelites remained at Mount Sinai, it was twice said of them: *They did everything just as the LORD commanded Moses* (Numbers 1:54; 2:34). As long as the Israelites were neither accomplishing anything for the Lord nor going anywhere, but were just talking about it, they were satisfied. But, just days after *they moved out from the mountain of the LORD . . . to seek out a resting place for them. . . . The people began complaining. . . . Who will feed us meat? . . . We're wasting away, and there's nothing to look at but this manna!* (10:33; 11:1,4,6). Rather than see their difficulties as an opportunity to believe that God would continue to meet their needs and lead them to the promised land, they chose to be dissatisfied with their circumstances.

In much the same way, our lives are also a wilderness journey, a march each day through unfamiliar territory. Let us not forget that, from the time the Israelites were led to move forward in obedience to God's word, Satan was there to create discontent.

When Christians find fault and complain about their hardships, as the Israelites did, they too disqualify themselves from the Lord's best.

Only a faithful few, like Caleb, Joshua, and Moses, recognize that God is in control and has arranged His plan for our lives. We all can avoid wasted years. As we faithfully read the Bible with an unreserved desire to be all that He would have us be, and to do all that He would have us do, then His indwelling Holy Spirit enlightens our minds and stirs our hearts to pray. *The intense prayer of the righteous is very powerful* (James 5:16).

Thought for Today: Don't disqualify yourself from the Lord's best blessings because of faultfinding and dissatisfaction with your circumstances.

In Today's Reading

Census and duties of the Levites: the Kohathites, the Gershonites, and the Merarites; the redemption of the firstborn.

Nadab and Abihu, Aaron's two oldest sons, had been greatly honored by being included with Moses and 73 others on Mount Sinai to hear the voice of God (Exodus 24:1,9). They had been given national recognition and God-ordained spiritual leadership. But, all this did not protect them from the consequences of their disobedience. The newly-ordained priests *Nadab and Abihu died in the LORD's presence when they presented unauthorized fire in the LORD's presence in the wilderness of Sinai* (Numbers 3:4). They presumed to burn incense, symbolic of the prayers of the people, with unauthorized fire, not kindled by God on the bronze altar (Leviticus 9:23-24; 10:1-2).

Their unauthorized fire underlined the seriousness of departing from the commandments of God. It points out that no one becomes so important or popular as a "spiritual" leader that God will overlook disobedience of His word. To be a minister, or even to become a member of a church, with no intent to submit one's life to please Christ, is hypocrisy.

The decision to ignore any command of God is sin. We are not to use circumstances to justify an exception to His word. Neither is there a choice of what part of His word we can neglect or reject, for all is God-breathed (inspired). The word of God is the source of meeting the needs of the human heart; it is the final and only source of absolute truth.

All Scripture (Old and New Testament) *is . . . profitable* (II Timothy 3:16). All New Testament doctrine is based on Old Testament principles. *If we deliberately sin after receiving the knowledge of the truth, there no longer remains a sacrifice for sins, but a terrifying expectation of judgment. . . . If anyone disregards Moses' law, he dies without mercy, based on the testimony of two or three witnesses. How much worse punishment, do you think one will deserve who has trampled on the Son of God, regarded as profane the blood of the covenant by which he was sanctified, and insulted the Spirit of grace?* (Hebrews 10:26-29).

Thought for Today: No Christian is worthy, but we have been accepted by our Savior because of God's forgiving love and grace.

In Today's Reading

Laws concerning cleansing, confession and restitution, jealousy; the Nazirite vow.

The Nazirite vow committed an individual to a life set apart to God for a specific period of time or even for life. The Nazirite vow prohibited *drinking any grape juice or eating fresh grapes or raisins. . . . The Nazirite is never to go near a dead body. . . . During the period of consecration, the Nazirite is holy to the LORD* (Numbers 6:2-8).

The Nazirite's separation unto God was expressed in several ways: (1) By abstaining from grape juice and even eating fresh grapes or raisins, representative of physical satisfaction; (2) by refusing to be defiled with the dead, representative of spiritual deadness (vss 6-12). However, the Nazirite was still responsible for offering all the usual sacrifices, such as the sin offering. This points out that even in doing our very best to separate ourselves from the world we still fall far short of being free from all spiritual defilement.

Only two people in the Old Testament are recorded as lifelong Nazirites. One was Samson (Judges 13:7), who failed in his separation from the world and consequently did not fulfill his opportunities to lead the Israelites to victory over the Philistines. In contrast Samuel's dedication (I Samuel 1:28) to the Lord led him to free the nation from Philistine domination and unite the tribes in preparation for a united kingdom. Although the Nazirite vow no longer applies, our personal consecration and dedication is vital to fulfilling the will of God.

There was nothing sinful about eating grapes, for God created the fruit of the vine; but often, even the "good" can take the place of Christ. Those who have a desire to dedicate their lives to Christ will abstain from pleasures that interfere with serving Him and also *stay away from every form of evil* (I Thessalonians 5:22).

The apostle Paul was led to write: *I urge you to present your bodies as a living sacrifice, holy and pleasing to God; this is your spiritual worship. Do not be conformed to this age, but be transformed by the renewing of your mind, so that you may discern what is the good, pleasing, and perfect will of God* (Romans 12:1-2).

Thought for Today: Dedication often requires self-denial, even of things which in themselves may not be sinful.

In Today's Reading

The princes' offerings for the dedication of the tabernacle.

When Moses finished setting up the tabernacle, he anointed and consecrated it and all its equipment. At the same time he anointed and consecrated the altar and all its equipment. The chiefs of Israel – the patriarchal family heads – presented offerings. . . . They brought their offerings before the LORD – six covered carts and 12 oxen: a cart for every two chiefs and an ox for each one – and presented them in front of the tabernacle. The LORD said to Moses, Take these carts and oxen from them, as they will be used in the transportation of the tent of meeting. Give them to the Levites, to each according to his transportation work (Numbers 7:1-5).

These gifts were not equally divided among the Levites. The family of the Gershonites received two carts and four oxen for their duties (compare Numbers 4:25-26; 7:7). The Merarites, who had much heavier burdens to bear (4:31-32; 7:8), received four carts and eight oxen. But the Kohathites received none. They were required to carry the tabernacle furniture, but Moses *did not give any to the Kohathites because the transportation of the holy objects was* (to be) *carried . . . on their shoulders,* including the pure gold lampstand, table of the Presence, gold altar of incense, bronze basin, bronze altar, and mercy seat on the ark of the Lord's covenant. These were all symbolic of Jesus Christ (4:1-5; 3:31; 7:9).

Although all the gifts were identical, each prince was recognized for his gift. From this we learn that every gift and act of service to our Lord is faithfully remembered. Mount Sinai is often associated with the severity of the law. But the tabernacle that was built there illustrates the loving concern of God to communicate and fellowship with His people, and to direct them through life. All the princes revealed their gratitude through their generous freewill gifts. All responded equally to the need.

Giving always benefits the giver. Your gift to missions can lift burdens, provide happiness, answer prayers, and save a soul from eternal hell. God has said: *Give, and it will be given to you; a good measure . . . running over will be poured into your lap. For with the measure that you use, it will be measured back to you* (Luke 6:38).

Thought for Today: When our thoughts are to please God, not self, we enjoy peace of mind.

In Today's Reading

Cleansing of the Levites; observance of the second Passover; the Lord's guiding presence in the cloud and the fire over the tabernacle.

The Israelites gained their freedom from Egypt after they observed the first Passover. The blood was placed on the doorpost but, equally impor-tant, they were commanded to eat the lamb.

Freedom from Egypt did not mean that they were free to do as they pleased. In Egypt they were under the heartless slavery of Pharaoh; now they were free to follow the leadership of the one true God.

In the first month of the second year after their departure from . . . Egypt, the LORD told Moses . . . The Israelites are to observe the Passover at its appointed time. . . . On the fourteenth day of this month at twilight at its appointed time. You are to observe it according to all its statutes and ordinances (Numbers 9:1-3).

The Passover was a reminder of how the Israelites gained their freedom. Not only were they to partake of the Passover Festival, but they were also required to bring *the LORD's offering: But the person who fails to observe the Passover even though he is ceremonially clean* (and) *is not on a journey must be cut off from his people* (punished with death) *because he did not present the LORD's offering at its designated time* (9:13).

Our observance of the Lord's Supper is a reminder that, because of Jesus' atoning death, we were made free from sin, became children of God, and are prepared for our wilderness journey through life. *For Christ our Passover has been sacrificed* (I Corinthians 5:7). It was Jesus who said: *As often as you eat this bread and drink the cup, you proclaim the Lord's death until He comes* (11:26).

Just as the Lord determined the journey of the Israelite tribes, He has a plan for you as you journey through life. Our supreme aim should be to accomplish His purpose for creating us. When God is our Guide, what is there to fear? He has provided a reliable threefold Guide for direction – His perfect word, the indwelling Holy Spirit, and the power of prayer: *For it is God who is working among you both the willing and the working for His good purpose* (Philippians 2:13).

Thought for Today: Our objective in life should be to accomplish His purpose for creating us.

In Today's Reading

Two silver trumpets; the Israelites leave Sinai; complaint of the people; the 70 elders chosen; the Lord sends a plague.

It was the responsibility of the priest to *make yourself two silver trumpets; you are to make them of hammered silver. Use them to summon the community together and to break camp* (Numbers 10:2). The trumpets were long, straight tubes of silver with bell-shaped mouths. They could not be made from inferior metal, nor from silver fragments; instead they were to be fashioned from one whole piece of silver. Regardless of how far away one was from the tabernacle, the clear tones of the silver trumpets would communicate various messages: *They are to sound a signal for moving out. When calling the assembly together, you are to sound the trumpet. . . . When you enter into battle against an adversary who is oppressing you in your own land, sound the signal on the trumpets. You will be remembered before the LORD your God, and you will be delivered from your enemies. Also on joyous occasions such as your designated feasts and New Moon festivals, you are to sound the trumpets over your burnt offerings and over your fellowship sacrifices. They will be a memorial for you in the presence of your God* (10:6-10; Leviticus 23:24; II Chronicles 5:12-14; 7:6; 29:26-29; Ezra 3:10; Nehemiah 12:35,41).

Whether they worshiped, went to war, or journeyed, every move of the people was to be in obedience to the various sounds of the trumpets. The two silver trumpets represent the truth of God's word and remind us that both the Old and the New Testaments are each a part of the whole word of God.

God's people are to be fully dependent upon and subject to the will of God as revealed in His word. If our hearts are accustomed to hearing the true silver trumpet, His voice through His word, we will then be in harmony with the Holy Spirit's prompting as to what we should or should not do. His word will keep us from missing the will of God.

Our Lord assures us that, *when the Spirit of truth comes, He will guide you into all the truth. For He will not speak on His own, but He will speak whatever He hears. He will also declare to you what is to come* (John 16:13).

Thought for Today: The most insignificant person is important to Christ.

In Today's Reading

Miriam and Aaron speak against Moses; Miriam stricken with leprosy; Moses prays; 12 spies sent to Canaan; their report.

Miriam was the sister of Moses and of Aaron the high priest. She was honored above all the women of Israel, had a prophetic anointing, and was gifted in music and singing (Exodus 15:20; Micah 6:4).

Miriam and Aaron criticized Moses because of the Ethiopian (Cushite) *woman he had married. . . . They said, does the LORD speak only with Moses? Does He not also speak with us? The LORD heard* (Numbers 12:1-2).

Suddenly, the Lord demanded to meet with Miriam, Aaron, and Moses. Miriam may have been delighted, thinking that God was just as displeased with Moses as she was and would agree with her criticism. Undoubtedly, she experienced an overwhelming shock when God said to her: *One on one I speak with him. . . . So why were you so brazen to speak against My servant Moses? The LORD's anger blazed forth against them* (12:8-9). To her horror, Aaron turned and said: *Look! Miriam has a horrible skin disease* (leprosy). *. . . Aaron said to Moses, O, my lord, don't hold this sin against us who have made fools of ourselves* (12:10-11).

Covetousness and pride are never satisfied. Even the possession of spiritual gifts can lead to pride which, in turn, can lead to jealousy if others with similar spiritual gifts appear to be competitors. When someone we have known as less qualified is promoted above us in our office or given recognition, we may be tempted to fall into Miriam's sin of criticizing. Pride takes many forms. It can be based on physical beauty, wealth, education, or talents; but pride is a self-destructive and self-deceptive sin.

Miriam succeeded, as many others have, in making it appear that her concern came from a "spiritual" motive. But God saw through her jealousy, envy, pride, and hurt feelings. It was the God-ordained leadership of Moses, not his choice of a wife or what he was teaching, that was being questioned. God has clearly declared: *Do not touch My anointed ones; do not harm My prophets* (I Chronicles 16:22; Psalms 105:15).

Thought for Today: Covetous people never get enough money, proud people never get enough praise, and self-centered people never get enough attention.

In Today's Reading

Moses interceded in prayer for the Israelites; Israel's wasted life; laws concerning offerings, sins, and the Sabbath.

Leaving the wilderness of Sinai, the Israelites were led northward until they reached Kadesh-barnea, where, for the first time, the people could actually see the promised land lying before them. The march from Egypt, including the 12-month stay at Mount Sinai (Horeb), had taken about 16 months. Now they stood on the threshold of that glorious promised land. A leader from each tribe had taken 40 days to spy out the land. When they returned, the Israelites were assured by all of them that Canaan *really is flowing with milk and honey – here is some of its fruit!* (Numbers 13:27). This was a confirmation of its extraordinary fruitfulness. Caleb, one of the 12, was quick to say: *We should certainly go up and take possession of the land because we will surely win the victory* (13:30). How-ever, ten of the spies discouraged the people, saying: *The people living in the land are strong; the cities are very heavily fortified* (13:28,31). *The whole community broke out in loud cries; the people wept all through the night. . . . The whole community moaned, If only we had died in the land of Egypt* (14:1-2). This marked the end of their journey to the land of promise and the beginning of 38 years of wilderness wanderings.

The Israelites who *wept all through the night* remind us of Esau who had grown up disregarding his holy calling and had sold his birthright. *For you know that later, when he wanted to inherit the blessing, he was rejected because he didn't find any opportunity for repentance, though he sought it* (earnestly) *with tears* (Hebrews 12:17); but his prayers were not heard. His only interest had been in what he had to gain, not in how he could be used by the Lord.

Satan's objective is that your decisions be like the unbelieving Israelites and not like Caleb's. Satan seeks to divert a Christian's thoughts from trust in the Lord. Such diversion is in opposition to the single eye that takes God at His word, that puts the Lord first and foremost above all other considerations. *Let us draw near with a true heart in full assurance of faith* (Hebrews 10:22).

Thought for Today: *He who calls you is faithful, who also will do it* (I Thessalonians 5:24).

Israel's Unbelief

The Lord responded (to Moses) . . . Not one of the men who saw My glory and the signs I performed in Egypt and in the wilderness and yet tested Me these 10 times – refusing to obey My voice – will ever see the land I promised to their forefathers under oath (Numbers 14:20-23).

PLACE	REBELLION	GOD'S MERCY REVEALED	KEY THOUGHT
RED SEA Ex. 14:10-12	Israelites murmuring against Moses at the sight of Egyptian chariots	In destroying their enemies and providing a way of deliverance (Ex. 14:21-31)	There is a great temptation for a person to desire the things of his sinful past (I John 2:15-17).
MARAH Ex. 15:23-24	Grumbling because God took them to bitter water	By sweetening the water (15:25-27)	Disappointments provide opportunities to exercise faith (II Cor. 4:16-17).
DESERT Ex. 16:2-3	Grumbling – they feared starvation	By providing manna (16:14-15)	God always supplies all our needs (Phil. 4:19).
DESERT Ex. 16:20	Disbelieving God by keeping manna overnight	Provision continued for 40 years (16:35)	God's word is essential and must be obeyed (II Tim. 3:16-17).
DESERT Ex. 16:26-27	Ignoring God and searching for manna on the Sabbath	In still providing a day of rest (16:28-30)	We must show proper respect for the Lord's day (Heb. 10:25).
REPHIDIM Ex. 17:1-3	Quarreling with Moses over the lack of water	In providing water from the rock (17:6)	Christians must depend on God (Matt. 6:33).
HOREB Ex. 32:1-10	Worshiping the golden calf	In sparing those who did not sin (32:32-33)	Satan will provide opportunities for us to return to sin (II Tim. 4:10).
TABERAH Num. 11:1	Complaining against God about adversity	Answering Moses' prayer (11:2-3)	Remedy for sin is loving obedience (John 14:21).
KIBROTH-HATTAAVAH Num. 11:10-15,34	Weeping for a variety of food with the people of the world	By providing quail in abundance (11:31-32)	Discontentment is a lack of trust in the love of God (I Tim. 6:8; Phil. 4:11; Heb 13:5).
KADESH-BARNEA Num. 14:2-10	Refusing to believe God and enter the promised land	In sparing Joshua, Caleb, and the children (14:20-31)	God always rewards the faithful (Heb. 11:6).

In Today's Reading

Korah leads a rebellion against Moses and Aaron; plague sent by God; Aaron's rod; duties for priests; the tithe offering.

Korah, Dathan, and Abiram *rebelled against Moses. With them were 250 Israelite men of good reputation who were chiefs in the community and had been called out as national assembly members. . . . Korah assembled the whole community* (in a conspiracy to overthrow Moses as their leader) (Numbers 16:2,19).

Once again, Moses was confronted with opposition, this time from his own cousins and the key leaders of the 12 tribes. Two hundred fifty of the leading men of Israel were influenced by Korah, Dathan, and Abiram and rebelled against Moses and Aaron. They accused Moses and Aaron of assuming too much authority, and their argument seemed very convincing: *They gathered against Moses and Aaron and accused them, You've assumed too much authority! Indeed, the entire community, every one of them, is holy, and the LORD is in their midst. Why, then, do you elevate yourselves above the LORD's assembly?* (16:3). They refused to recognize that Moses and Aaron were appointed by God to lead the people and that they were actually *uniting together against the LORD* (16:11).

Korah did not just make a mistake, but committed a serious sin, as recorded by Jude, who wrote: *Now I want to remind you . . . the Lord, having first of all saved a people out of Egypt, later destroyed those who did not believe. . . . Woe to them! For they have traveled in the way of Cain, have abandoned themselves to the error of Balaam for profit, and have perished in Korah's rebellion* (Jude 1:5,11).

Korah was a believer in God from the chosen tribe of Levi. He was assigned to lead the people in worship and teach the will of God. However, it appears that Korah would serve the Lord only if it resulted in bringing recognition to himself.

Some self-willed and self-pleasing people refuse to submit to authority or to a life of holiness. It is comforting to know that *no condemnation now exists for those in Christ Jesus* (Footnote: Other mss add *who do not walk according to the flesh but according to the Spirit)* (Romans 8:1).

Thought for Today: Let us live as if we were to meet Christ today.

In Today's Reading

Red heifer sacrifice; Miriam's death; Moses strikes the rock twice; Edom refuses Israel passage; Aaron's death.

The red heifer sacrifice was instituted in the wilderness of Paran at a time when all Israel was under the sentence of death. The law required that *anyone who touches a corpse – the body of a person who has died – and does not purify himself defiles the tabernacle of the LORD* (Numbers 19:13).

The blood of the red heifer was burned with the carcass, and its ashes were mixed with running water and sprinkled upon the defiled ones in order to restore them to a holy God. The Hebrew word for "running" also means "living" – implying not only cleansing from sin, but renewal of life. The water of purification was made from the ashes of just one heifer, which was sufficient for all the people.

Through the red heifer ordinance, God gave a new revelation of the importance of cleansing from defilement – whether it be through our thoughts, our conversations, the books we read, our associations with unbelievers, or whatever we may do that defiles our minds or bodies. God has said: *Be holy, because I am holy* (I Peter 1:16).

The red heifer sacrifice is symbolic of Christ. Through His death on the cross, *He has given us very great and precious promises, so that through them you may share in the divine nature, escaping the corruption that is in the world because of evil desires* (II Peter 1:4). It is the plan of God that Christ's own life be reproduced in Christians.

Since humility is a means of overcoming pride, jealousy, greed, and envy, some assume we should pray for humility; but the real need is to pray that Christ be magnified in our lives. God does not give humility or patience or love as separate gifts of His grace. The indwelling Christ is the answer to every need. As we pray for Him to live out His life in us, we will express humility, patience, love, and everything else that reveals His character. Paul said: *I no longer live, but Christ lives in me. The life I now live in the flesh, I live by faith in the Son of God, who loved me and gave Himself for me* (Galatians 2:20).

Thought for Today: When we try to impress others with our importance, the Lord will not be glorified.

In Today's Reading

Poisonous snakes; bronze snake; Israel defeats King Arad, Amorites, Moabites; Balaam hired to curse the Israelites.

The Israelites were near their last encampment and would soon cross the Jordan River to enter into the promised land. Some of these people were children when, with their parents, they had left Egypt; others had been born in the wilderness. *The people became impatient on the way. . . .* (and) *complained . . . Why have you brought us up from Egypt to die in this wilderness? There is no bread and no water. We loathe this miserable food!* (Numbers 21:4-5). At this point, *the LORD sent poisonous snakes. . . . And many Israelites died* (21:6). *Moses interceded for the people* (21:7).

The response to Moses' *prayer* was immediate. *The LORD told Moses, Make for yourself a poisonous snake* (of bronze) *and mount it on a pole. Anyone who was bitten may look at it and live* (21:8). The bronze snake was a symbol both of God's judgment against their sin and of His mercy and love for all who repented and truly believed in Him.

Many centuries later, in His conversation with *Nicodemus, a ruler of the Jews* (John 3:1-21), Jesus said that the *snake* which had been lifted up by Moses in the wilderness illustrated Himself as the One to *be lifted up* on the cross as the only way for sinners to be saved from eternal death (3:14; 12:32). Jesus did not tell Nicodemus how he should live to have eternal life, rather He told him how to be made alive. Jesus replied to Nicodemus: *I assure you: Unless someone is born of water and the Spirit, he cannot enter the kingdom of God* (3:5). This is far more than changing one's way of life, giving up bad habits, or turning over a new leaf. All mankind, with one exception, *were dead in our trespasses and sins* (Ephesians 2:1). Each of us was born with our parents' human nature and, when we receive Christ as our Savior, we are "born again" and receive His spiritual nature: *To all who did receive Him, He gave them the right to be children of God, to those who believe in His name* (John 1:12).

As children of our heavenly Father, we are reminded: *Therefore do not let sin reign in your mortal body, so that you obey its desires. . . . But . . . offer yourselves to God* (Romans 6:12-13).

Thought for Today: It is impossible to have a right attitude toward God while maintaining a wrong attitude toward delegated authority.

In Today's Reading

Prophecies of Balaam; Israel sins; the plague stopped because of the intercession of Phinehas.

The last encampment of the Israelites on the eastern side of the Jordan River was on the Plains of Moab just northeast of the Dead Sea near Mount Nebo, a few miles south of today's Amman, Jordan (Numbers 33:49; Joshua 2:1; 3:1). Everything seemed peaceful, with no apparent dangers. However, upon seeing this vast multitude of Israelites who had defied Pharaoh, left Egypt, and conquered everyone who opposed them on their way to Canaan, the Moabites, who lived nearby, were fearful that they too would soon be destroyed. This fear led King Balak to form an alliance with his Midianite neighbors against Israel (Numbers 22:4-7). Even then, believing they could never defeat Israel in battle, Balak sent for the prophet Balaam to put a curse on Israel. He lived in Pethor, a city of northern Mesopotamia (modern Iraq). This was in the vicinity where Abraham had lived. *God said to Balaam, You must not go with them! You must not curse these people, because they are blessed* (22:12).

Knowing the judgment of God would come upon Israel if he could cause the Israelites to sin, and coveting the king's rewards, Balaam wickedly suggested that the Moabite women make friends with the men of Israel. The friendliness of the Moabite women quickly led the Israelite men to become involved in sexual immorality and idol worship, thus breaking their covenant vow of allegiance to the one true God.

Disobedience resulted in a plague of death that swept through the tribes of Israel and *24,000 died in the plague* (25:9).

Some will say that we should not be judgmental, that we should be tolerant of the immoral (alternative) lifestyles that are growing in popularity. But sexual sins are still an outrage against God: *Do you not know that your bodies are the members of Christ? So should I take the members of Christ and make them members of a prostitute? Absolutely not! . . . The person who is sexually immoral sins against his own body. Do you not know that your body is a sanctuary of the Holy Spirit who is in you, whom you have from God? You are not your own, for you were bought at a price; therefore glorify God in your body* (I Corinthians 6:15-20).

Thought for Today: Covetousness is always self-defeating.

In Today's Reading

Second numbering (census) of the Israelites;
law of inheritance; Joshua to succeed Moses.

Almost 40 years had passed since the exodus of the Israelites from Egypt. All the 603,550 men included in that first census, except Joshua, Caleb and Moses had died. This second generation was now near the promised land. *The LORD told Moses and Eleazar son of Aaron the priest, Take a census of the entire* (male) *Israelite community, those 20 years old and above, by their patriarchal families, everyone who marches in Israel's army* (Numbers 26:1-2). This took place *in the plains of Moab by the Jordan* (River) *across from Jericho* (26:3).

Another major event was to take place before the Israelites could enter the promised land. *The LORD said to Moses, Ascend this Abarim mountain range* (Mount Nebo) *and view the land that I have given to the Israelites. When you have seen it, you will be gathered to your people, even you, just as Aaron your brother was. For at the waters in the wilderness of Zin as the community quarreled, both of you rebelled against My command to treat Me as holy in their sight. Those were the waters of Meribah of Kadesh in the wilderness of Zin. Moses requested of the LORD, May the LORD, the God of the spirits of all flesh, appoint a man over the community. . . . The LORD replied to Moses, Take Joshua son of Nun, a man in whom is the Spirit. Lay your hand on him* (27:12-16,18).

Despite his rebuke and his great disappointment in not being allowed to enter the promised land, *Moses did just as the LORD had commanded him. He took Joshua and had him stand before Eleazar the priest and the entire community* (27:22). And, without hesitation, he stepped down from leadership and announced that his helper, Joshua, would become his successor to lead the Lord's people (27:23). Moses blessed Joshua and *laid his hands on him,* symbolic of transferring his leadership.

God has said that Moses was the meekest man on earth (12:3). One test of meekness is to yield our prominent position to another. As a follower of Christ, we are taught to *do nothing out of rivalry or conceit, but in humility consider others as more important than yourselves* (Philippians 2:3).

Thought for Today: Remain faithful to serving the Lord -- even when you must step down and release your position.

In Today's Reading

The daily and weekly offerings (sacrifices), Sabbath and monthly offerings (sacrifices), and the offerings (sacrifices) at the appointed festivals.

The Israelites' civil year began in the fall with the Festival of Trumpets: *The first day of the seventh month will be a sacred assembly for you; do not do any regular* (daily) *work. It will be a day for you to sound the horn* (Numbers 29:1). This joyous day of blowing the trumpets was followed 10 days later by the solemn Day of Atonement. This was followed by the Festival of Tabernacles (Booths), which was also called the Festival of Ingathering because the work in the fields was finished and the time had come for the people to rest from their labors. It was a time of great rejoicing and lasted for seven days, from the 15th through the 21st of Tishri (Sept/Oct) (Exodus 23:16; 34:22; Leviticus 23:33-44). It was followed by an eighth day of holy convocation on the 22nd which, though closely connected with the Festival of Tabernacles, was not a part of that festival for the people no longer lived in "booths."

The Festival of Tabernacles was the last festival of the religious year. For seven days, all the residents of Israel dwelt in temporary booths (shelters) as an annual reminder of the time when they dwelt in tents during the 40 years in the wilderness. The trees used for these temporary dwellings also had symbolic meanings. The fig tree provided shade, as well as reminding the people of the Lord's protection and provision. The palm tree was the emblem of victory and the olive tree was a symbol of peace and God's presence (Nehemiah 8:15). The willow tree of the brook signified a thriving and blessed people, a reminder that *he is like a tree planted beside streams of water that bears its fruit in season and whose leaf does not wither. Whatever he does prospers* (Psalms 1:3).

The life of a Christian is a journey much like that of the Israelites through the wilderness. It should be a great adventure of going on with the Lord into deeper experiences and greater faith. With the apostle Paul, let us each say: *I pursue as my goal the prize promised by God's heavenly call in Christ Jesus* (Philippians 3:14).

Thought for Today: It is impossible to gain God's best when our hearts are obsessed with gaining more and more things of the world.

The Exodus Out of Egypt & Route to the Promised Land

1. **Rameses** – (Numbers 33:3)
2. **Succoth** – (Numbers 33:5)
3. **Etham** – (Numbers 33:6)
4. **Migdol / Pi-Hahiroth** – (Numbers 33:7-8)

Scholars do not agree on the exact route, but it is located near the vicinities shown.

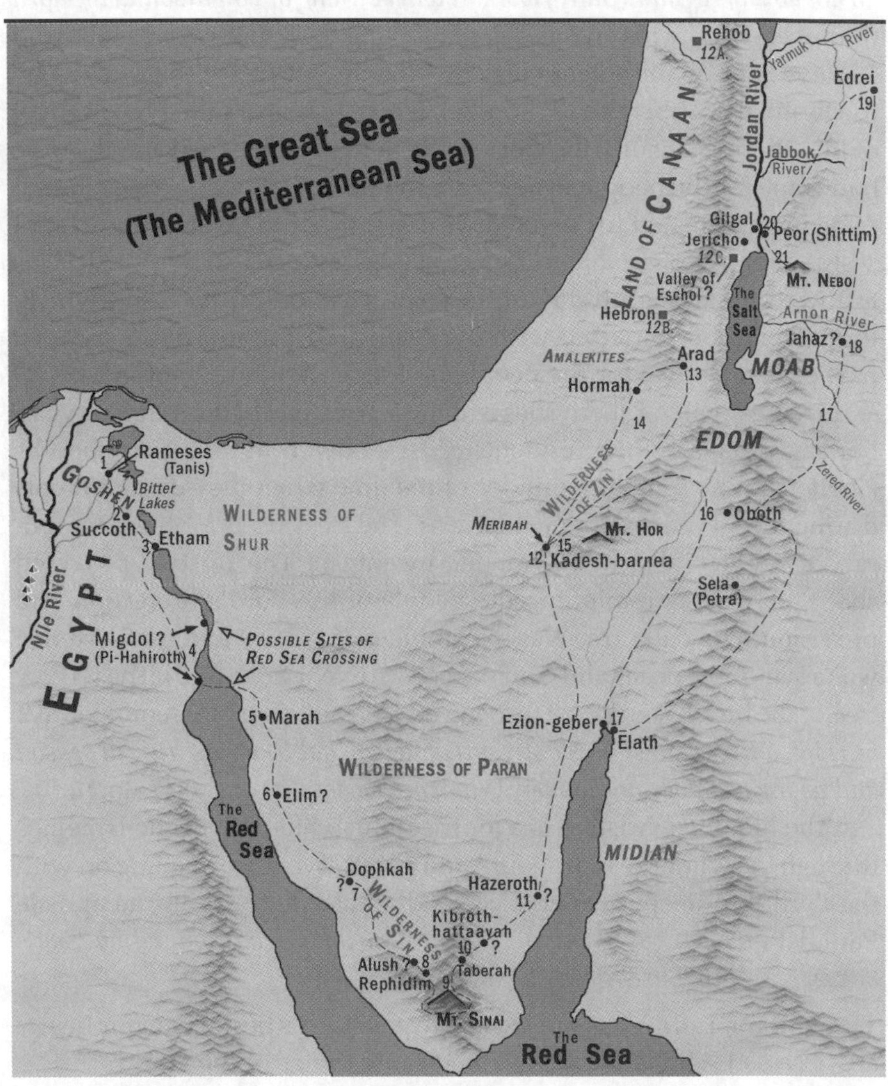

5. **Marah** – (Numbers 33:8)
6. **Elim** – (Numbers 33:9)
7. **Wilderness of Sin and Dophkah** – (Numbers 33:11)
8. **Rephidim** – (Numbers 33:14) – People complain of thirst, Moses speaks to the rock in Horeb and brings forth water (Exodus 17:1-7); Victory over Amalekites (17:8-16)
9. **Wilderness at the base of Mount Sinai** – (Numbers 33:15; Exodus 19:1 – 40:38) – Moses receives 10 Commandments (Exodus 20:1-17); Golden calf worshiped; Moses intercedes; People repent; Moses prays; covenant is renewed (32:1 – 34:35); Moses receives instructions for building the tabernacle (25:1 – 31:18); tabernacle is built (35:1 – 40:38); First Passover is observed outside Egypt at Sinai (Numbers 9:1-14)
10. **Kibroth-hattaavah** – 3 days' journey from Mount Sinai (Numbers 10:33; 33:16-17); People murmur and then die from eating too much quail (11:31-35)
11. **Hazeroth** – (Numbers 33:17) – Miriam and Aaron rebel against Moses; Miriam becomes a leper; Moses intercedes for Miriam and she is restored (12:1-16)
12. **Kadesh-barnea** (Rithmah ?) – (Numbers 33:18) – Spies sent out to: A. Rehob (North end of Jordan Valley) B. Hebron C. Valley of Eschol; The people refuse to believe Joshua and Caleb's good report (14:6-10); Rebellion against God; God's judgment was that they would die in the wilderness (14:11-38)
13. **Arad** – People attempt to enter the promised land (Numbers 14:40-42)
14. **Hormah** – Amalekites and Canaanites defeat Israel even unto Hormah (Numbers 14:44-45); Israelites return to Kadesh-barnea

WILDERNESS WANDERINGS FOR 38 YEARS – Miriam dies at Kadesh-barnea

15. **Meribah** – No water; People complain; Moses sins by striking rock (Numbers 20:2-13); Refused passage through Edom(20:14-21); Aaron dies on Mount Hor in 40th year (20:22-29); Victory over king of Arad at Hormah(21:1-3)
16. **Oboth** – Between Kadesh-barnea and Oboth, sin results in poisonous snakes; God has Moses make a bronze snake to save those who would look upon it (Numbers 21:4-10)

VARIOUS OTHER UNIDENTIFIED LOCATIONS – (Numbers 33:12-47; 21:10-20)

17. **Plains of Moab** – From Kadesh-barnea to the plains of Moab via Elath and Ezion-geber (Numbers 33:37-49; Deuteronomy 2:8)
18. **Jahaz** – The Amorite king, Sihon, refuses Israel passage through his territory; Israel defeats him at Jahaz (Numbers 21:21-32)
19. **Edrei** – After defeating the Amorites, they defeat Og, the king of Bashan (Numbers 21:33-35); King Balak, a Moabite, hires Balaam to curse Israel (22:1 – 24:25)
20. **Peor (near Shittim)** – (Numbers 25:1-18) – Israelites' apostasy with the Midianites; Second Census (26:1-65)
21. **Mount Nebo** (Pisgah in Abarim mountain range) – (Numbers 27:12-23; Deuteronomy 34:1-4) - Moses appoints Joshua his successor (Numbers 27:12-23); Israelites defeat Midianites and kill 5 kings and the prophet Balaam (31:1-8); Moses ascends to the top of Mount Pisgah (Mount Nebo) and views the promised land; Moses dies there and God Himself buries Moses (Deuteronomy 34:5-6)

JOSHUA ASSUMES LEADERSHIP OF THE ISRAELITES – (Deuteronomy 34:8-9; Joshua 1:1-2)

In Today's Reading

Law concerning vows; Midianites conquered; division of booty; officers and captains bring an offering to the Lord.

The Midianites were descendants of Abraham through his second wife Keturah, whom he married after Sarah died (Genesis 25:1-2). The Midianites had devastated Israel, not as enemies who had won a war but as friendly idol worshipers who seduced the Israelites into committing spiritual adultery. Israel became involved in the worship of their pagan deity Baal-peor followed by physical adultery with their women. This had resulted in the death of 24,000 Israelites (Numbers 25:9). Some time later, God spoke to Moses, saying: *Pay the Midianites back for what they did to the Israelites* (31:2).

In this war, *Moses sent . . . 1,000 from each tribe along with Phinehas son of Eleazar the priest who had the sacred vessels and the signal trumpets in his hand* (31:6) to execute the judgment of God upon the Midianites. The *trumpets* were symbols of truth and God's direction. Not one Israelite died in this battle which resulted in the deaths of all five kings of the con-federation and every Midianite male (31:7-9,15-17). *Along with the other casualties, they killed the five kings of Midian. . . . They also killed* (the prominent prophet) *Balaam . . . with the sword* (31:8). It was not incidental that Balaam had chosen to live in luxury among the Midianites while enjoying the esteem of the king and the people.

Balaam was from Mesopotamia which included Ur of the Chaldees, where Abraham had lived before his call from God (Deuteronomy 23:4; see also Genesis 15:7; Acts 7:2). Balak had said to Balaam: *Come! Curse Jacob for me! Come! Bring doom on Israel!* (Numbers 23:7). Like Balaam, how easy it is to say: *Everything the LORD speaks I must do* (compare 22:18, 38; 23:26; 24:13). *Let me die the death of the upright; let my end be like theirs* (Numbers 23:10). But, like Balaam, greed and compromise have deceived many who did not *die the death of the upright*. Their destiny is eternal hell. *But you, dear friends, building yourselves up in your most holy faith and praying in the Holy Spirit, keep yourselves in the love of God, expecting the mercy of our LORD Jesus Christ for eternal life* (Jude 20-21).

Thought for Today: All earthly treasures cannot compare to an eternal inheritance.

In Today's Reading

Reuben, Gad, and half the tribe of Manasseh settle east of the Jordan; a summary of Israel's 40 years in the wilderness.

More than 40 years had passed since Moses, while still in Egypt, foretold that God would lead the Israelites to the land He had promised to Abraham, Isaac, and Jacob. While moving with great anticipation toward the fulfillment of that promise, and almost in view of the promised land, two of the twelve tribes, those of Reuben and Gad, who *had abundant herds of livestock,* decided not to go on (Numbers 32:1). Believing they would be financially better off if they remained on the eastern side of the Jordan, they said to Moses: *The land the LORD struck down before the Israelite community – is suited for livestock, and your servants own livestock. They said . . . let this land be given to your servants as a possession. Don't make us cross the Jordan* (32:4-5). Moses replied: *Why would you discourage the hearts of the Israelites from crossing into the land the LORD has given them* (32:7)? The leaders of the two tribes were joined by half the tribe of Manasseh. Humanly speaking, it was a wise financial decision; but it was an act of compromise. The unity of the nation and being near the tabernacle and the presence of God should have been uppermost in their desires.

These two and a half tribes typify self-indulgent "Christians" who foolishly allow physical advantages to compromise fulfilling the will of God. They stand as a warning to those whose business interests, social advancements, or attainment of prominence are chosen over how they can best serve the Lord. Some who claim to be Christians are consumed with worldly pursuits that keep them from giving their time and/or tithes to the Lord. Their spiritual indifference often causes their children to follow their example until the opportunity to influence them to live for the Lord is forever past.

The Lord's instructions concerning His will are also for us today. *These things I am commanding you today are to be in your heart. Repeat them to your children, speak of them when you are at home and when you go on a journey, when you lie down and when you get up. Bind them on your hand as a sign, and let them be like a symbol on your forehead. Write them on the doorposts of your house, and on your gates* (Deuteronomy 6:6-9).

Thought for Today: Men of faith find ways to obey God and please Him – others settle for excuses.

In Today's Reading

Dividing the land of Canaan; inheritance of the Levites.

Unlike the other tribes, the tribe of Levi, which included the priests, did not have a separate inheritance in the land. They were to depend on the people's tithes, as God had commanded. Forty-eight cities and pasturelands scattered throughout the other tribes were assigned to them as permanent residences (Joshua 21:1-42). Of their 48 cities, six were assigned as cities of refuge, which were easily accessible throughout the 12 tribes. For those suspected of manslaughter, these cities were vitally important as places of safety until a trial could determine their guilt or innocence (Numbers 35:11).

Our Creator demands that, *when anyone strikes a person dead* (intentionally), *the murderer is to be murdered* (executed) *upon the word of witnesses. However, a lone witness is not sufficient testimony against a person to put him to death. Do not accept a ransom for the life of a murderer who is guilty of a capital crime. He must surely be put to death. . . . Do not defile the land you are in, because blood defiles the land and because for the land there can be no atonement from the blood that is shed in it except by the blood of the person who shed it* (35:30-31,33).

When it was proven to the satisfaction of the congregation that the accused person was guilty of murder, he had to be put to death, regardless of age or whether it was a man or a woman. There was to be no consideration of being sentenced to time in prison, the possibility of parole, rehabilitation, or any kind of financial settlement.

Without a doubt, the prosecution and execution of criminals is an exceedingly painful situation that everyone would prefer to avoid; yet it is necessary to maintain justice and order, the welfare of our society, and, most importantly, the approval of God. *Blessed are those who wash their robes, so that they may have the right to the tree of life and may enter the city by the gates. Outside are the dogs, the sorcerers, the sexually immoral, the murderers, the idolaters, and everyone who loves and practices lying* (Revelation 22:14-15).

Thought for Today: God demands the highest respect for human life, for He created man in His image.

In Today's Reading

Laws concerning female inheritance within their patriarchal tribe.

Five of *the daughters of Zelophehad approached* (Moses). . . . *He was a member of the clans of Manasseh, the son of Joseph. His daughters. . . . stood before Moses, Eleazar the priest, the chiefs, and the entire community at the entrance to the tent of meeting* (Numbers 27:1-2), awaiting a decision concerning their tribal territory after they married. *Moses brought their case before the LORD* (27:5). The Lord declared through Moses: *This is the word the LORD commanded concerning Zelophehad's daughters: They may marry anyone they like except that they must marry within the clan of their father's tribe. . . . because each of the sons of Israel is to cling to the inheritance of his patriarchal tribe* (36:6-7).

Although they had the legal right to *marry anyone they like,* they were to consider the responsibility that rested on their actions. To marry someone from another tribe would forfeit their father's inheritance. The decision involved an important principle of denying one's own personal satisfaction and remaining faithful to fulfilling the will of God. *The daughters of Zelophehad did just what the LORD commanded Moses* (36:10).

No one should overlook how perfectly the request of the five *daughters of Zelophehad* corresponds to our relationship with Christ. We too are often faced with personal satisfaction that is not sinful, but which can cause us to relinquish other spiritual opportunities.

In contrast, no one who remains true to Christ forfeits the best in life. A commitment to God's word preserves and enhances, rather than hinders, the enjoyment of one's life. Our enemy Satan often appears as an angel of light, seeking our consent to yield, just once, so that he can gain a foothold, and then he gradually takes control of one's life.

The book of Hebrews continues the warning of God: *Do not harden your hearts as in the rebellion, on the day of testing in the desert. Watch out, brothers, so that there won't be in any of you an evil, unbelieving heart that departs from the living God. But encourage each other daily, while it is still called today, so that none of you is hardened by sin's deception* (Hebrews 3:8,12-13; see also Psalms 95:8).

Thought for Today: We always miss God's best when we neglect His word.

Introduction To The Book Of Deuteronomy

The events of the book of Deuteronomy took place in the 40th year after the Israelites left Egypt, in the final weeks of Moses' life. At that time, Moses reviewed the 40 years in the wilderness and the reason their parents had failed to enter the promised land (Numbers 14:22-24; Deuteronomy 1:22-36). The first generation of adults, except for Joshua, Caleb, and Moses, had all died because of their unbelief that led to disobedience. Now the new generation of Israelites was camped on the Plains of Moab, about to enter the promised land (29:1-5).

From Genesis through Numbers, the love of God was never mentioned; but now, four times Moses revealed: *He loved your fathers, He chose their descendants. . . . and redeemed you from the place of slavery* (4:37; 7:7-8; 10:15; 23:5). *So that He might take us and give us the land which He swore to our fathers* (6:21,23).

Moses stated that the Lord had made a covenant with their parents at Horeb (Mount Sinai), but they continually failed to keep it. After giving the Mosaic law to the new generation, Moses stressed the importance of obedience to God's word and of teaching it to their children (4:9,44; 5:31-33; 11:19). *However, if you . . . go after other gods, to serve and worship them . . . you will surely be destroyed* (8:19).

Moses reminded them of the importance of their loyalty to God, saying: *And now, Israel, what does the LORD your God ask of you? Just this: to fear the LORD your God by walking in all His ways, and to love and serve Him . . . for your good* (10:12-13; 27:1 – 29:1; 30:20). The two key words *for your good* are *obey* and *do* which occur more than 170 times in this book. This key to success is the central message of Deuteronomy as well as the entire Bible.

Instructions were also given concerning the importance of tithes and offerings. Of particular significance is the revelation that *the LORD will raise up for you a prophet like me from among you, from among your brothers. You must listen to him* (18:15). Fifteen hundred years later, Peter applied this prophecy to Jesus (Acts 3:22-23), as did Stephen and the apostle Philip (7:37; John 1:45).

The book of Deuteronomy ends with the death of Moses after his commission of Joshua, a man *filled with a spirit of wisdom* to lead the Israelites into the promised land (Deuteronomy 34:1-9).

In Today's Reading

Moses' review of Israel's past 40 years; command to leave Mount Sinai; refusal to enter the promised land; 38 years of wanderings.

In his first message to the new generation (Deuteronomy 1:1 – 4:43), Moses reminded them that *it is* (only) *an 11 days' journey from Horeb* (Mount Sinai) *to Kadesh-barnea* (about 165 miles) (1:2). This message was given *in the fortieth year* after leaving Egypt (1:3). Despite their miraculous deliverance from Egypt, the older generation sinned against the Lord by not believing that He would give them victory over the Canaanites. By faith, the promised land could have been theirs.

The generation of adult Israelites who had left Egypt did not recognize that their hardships were designed to test their faith in His word. As a consequence of their sin of unbelief, that first generation failed to accomplish the will of God and wasted their lives wandering in the wilderness until they all died. Now, the new generation would also be tested. Would they take God at His word?

We too have a choice. We can choose to be like the many Israelites who found fault with everything, or choose to be like Caleb and Joshua whose faith in God's word overcame all fears and frustrations.

It can truly be said of some believers today that, although they accepted Christ as their Savior, they have made little spiritual progress since they first believed. They do as little as possible, for they have not made Him Lord of their lives. It is our responsibility to *be doers of the word and not hearers only* (James 1:22).

Loving submission to the Lord develops our faith in His ability to guide, protect, and provide for our every need. Just as God had a plan for Israel, so He has a plan for each of us.

In the midst of "giant" problems, the Holy Spirit is available to all who, like Caleb and Joshua, do not trust in themselves to overcome their giants. God's word is our only infallible Guide. *We are His making, created in Christ Jesus for good works, which God prepared ahead of time so that we should walk in them* (Ephesians 2:10).

Thought for Today: In the midst of "giant" problems, strength to be an overcomer through the Holy Spirit is available to all who trust in Him.

In Today's Reading

Division of the land east of Jordan; Moses' prayer; cities of refuge established east of Jordan.

Moses reminded the new generation of Israelites that living according to God's word would bring lasting fulfillment. He began to explain the law that God had given their parents 40 years earlier at Mount Sinai (Deuteronomy 1:5). *To explain this law* meant more than merely "repeating" the law; it meant to "explain its meaning." Moses' first message highlighted the importance of keeping all the word of God, *that you may . . . take possession of the land. . . . Keep the commands of the LORD your God. . . . follow them, for this will show your wisdom and understanding. . . . For what great nation is there whose gods are near it in the way the LORD our God is near us* (4:1-7).

That you may live (4:1) meant that the Israelites would enjoy the best in life. The one essential requirement for remaining in the land of promise was obedience to God's word. He warned them that when you *do what is evil in the LORD's sight . . . you will surely be destroyed* (4:25-26). God has also said to *seek after Him with all your heart and soul* (4:29).

Obedience to the one true God would have enabled Israel to be successful, and morally and spiritually unique among all other nations.

We too need a daily reminder to *take heed, watch yourselves carefully, lest you forget the things you have seen, so that they do not depart from your mind. . . . Teach them to your children and your grandchildren* (4:9).

Children begin developing respect for God by first being taught to behave in a respectful way toward their parents. Unfortunately, unless children learn respect for their parents, they seldom learn to respect and obey God, who said: *Teach a youth about the way he should go; even when he is old he will not depart from it* (Proverbs 22:6).

The Bible provides our only source of knowing the will and character of our Creator. *Keep His statutes and commands which I am giving you this day, so that it will go well for you and your children after you* (Deuteronomy 4:40).

Thought for Today: It is our faith in God – not our strength or wisdom – that leads to victory.

In Today's Reading

Review of the covenant made on Horeb (Mount Sinai); chosen to be a holy people; command to destroy idol worship.

Moses reminded the Israelites that *the LORD our God . . . is One* (Deuteronomy 6:4-5).

The Hebrew word translated *our God* is *Elohenu,* meaning "our Gods." This, then, is what Moses said: *Hear, Israel, the LORD* (the self-existent One) *our God . . . is One* (6:4). The word *One* (echad) expresses "one" in the collective sense. It signifies a compound unity. The *one LORD* is a glorious revelation of the one true God as being one, yet three distinct persons: Father, Son, and Holy Spirit. *Let Us make man in Our Image* (Genesis 1:26); *like one of Us* (3:22); *Let Us go* (11:7); and *Who will go for Us?* (Isaiah 6:8).

The same Hebrew word *echad* is used in Genesis 2:24 where man and woman became *one flesh* and, even with numerous children, they are still called "one" family, and soldiers became *a single unit* (II Samuel 2:25).

The Hebrew word for "one" in the sense of absolute oneness is the word *yacheed,* meaning an "absolute one." It is never used in reference to the Godhead. Moses had the word *yacheed* available to him; but obviously God led Moses to accurately refer to Himself by the word *echad,* meaning a compound unity. This fact reveals that those who reject Jesus as fully God, as well as fully Man, are rejecting the true revelation of God the Father, God the Son, and God the Holy Spirit. It is of utmost importance that we understand that worshipers of any other "gods" are deceived.

In the beginning was the Word; and the Word was with God, and the Word was God. He was with God in the beginning. All things were created through Him, and apart from Him not one thing was created that has been created. . . . The Word became flesh and took up residence among us (John 1:1-3,14).

For there is one God and one mediator between God and man, a man, Christ Jesus (I Timothy 2:5).

Thought for Today: Rejoice! Jesus will soon return to rule the world as King of kings.

In Today's Reading

Keep the commandments; reminder of parents' rebellion, golden calf; the second tablets of stone.

Jesus began His earthly ministry by quoting from Deuteronomy: *Man must not live on bread alone, but on every word that comes from the mouth of God* (Matthew 4:4; compare Deuteronomy 8:3). He responded to Satan, who tempted Him to make bread for Himself from stones after His 40-day fast. Satan had said: *If You are the Son of God, tell these stones to become bread* (Matthew 4:3), meaning: "Why should You, of all people, go hungry? If You are the Son of God, why not use Your powers to satisfy Your hunger."

Satan the tempter quoted Scripture, but he misapplied its meaning. Jesus again quoted Deuteronomy at the second temptation, saying: *You must not tempt the LORD your God* (4:7; Deuteronomy 6:16). Jesus did not compromise even once – a lesson some Christians need to learn. At the third temptation, Jesus once again quoted Deuteronomy: *It is written: You must worship the LORD your God, and you must serve Him only* (Matthew 4:10; Deuteronomy 6:13). A vital key to overcoming Satan is knowing God's word with which we are empowered to be overcomers. *For the word of God is living and effective* (Hebrews 4:12), the only weapon needed to defeat Satan. As we read all of God's word, the Holy Spirit brings it to our minds when needed.

We need to remember Moses' warning to Israel: *Be careful, lest you forget the LORD your God, failing to keep His commands. . . . Then you will be likely to think, My strength and my own work have created this wealth for me. But remember the LORD your God, for it is He who gives you strength to create wealth* (Deuteronomy 8:11,17-18).

After reviewing the commandments, Moses added: *What does the LORD your God ask of you? Just this: to fear the LORD your God by walking in all His ways, and to love and serve Him with all your heart and with all your being, by keeping the LORD's commandments and decrees which I am commanding you today for your good* (10:12-13).

Jesus not only quoted these verses as applying to His followers, but said that *the one who has My commandments and keeps them is the one who loves Me: If anyone loves Me, he will keep My word* (John 14:21-23).

Thought for Today: Does Jesus get credit for your achievements?

In Today's Reading

Israel is to love and obey God; warning against false gods and adding to or taking away anything from His word.

To perpetuate loyalty and love to God in future generations, the word of God was to dominate every Israelite's life. To accomplish this God said: *Teach them to your children* (Deuteronomy 11:19). Our first concern every day should be to teach our children to love the Lord and be obedient to Him. They should have no doubt that we also truly love the Lord and are obedient to Him. If our hearts are filled with the word of God, it will overflow from our lives: *When you stay in your house and when you go on a journey, when you lie down and when you get up* (11:19).

Moses repeated to the new generation what the Lord said to their parents, reminding them of how important it is to *faithfully keep this entire command which I* (God) *am giving you to follow, by loving the LORD your God, walking in all His ways, and holding fast to Him* (11:22).

God has said: *You will . . . rejoice along with your household over every undertaking of yours in which the LORD your God has blessed you* (12:7).

What our children will be is usually dependent upon what they learn about our values in life. What we are in great measure is what our children will be. That is why it is so important that parents of young children devote their time to molding their rapidly developing minds. It is of utmost importance that parents guide even the youngest children to reverence God, to worship Him, to pray, and to recognize the Bible as the voice of God speaking to them.

Influences outside the home often send strong messages to our children that are contrary to the values we desire them to live by. It becomes increasingly important for parents in this time of moral chaos to provide our children with a strong spiritual environment.

Children need to fear (have a reverential attitude of deep concern to be obedient) God and to know that He said: *Honor your father and mother – which is the first commandment with a promise – that it may go well with you and that you may have a long life in the land* (Ephesians 6:2-3).

Thought for Today: Christian parents are responsible to teach their children the way they should live (Proverbs 22:6).

In Today's Reading

Clean and unclean food; the law of the tithe; dedication of the firstborn; three festivals to be observed; judges and justice.

The prosperity of Israel in the promised land did not depend on advanced agricultural techniques, but on obedience to the word of God (Deuteronomy 11:10-15). The Israelites were taught: *Be sure to set aside a tithe of all your crops . . . year by year. . . . Then you will learn to fear the LORD your God always* (14:22-23).

Tithing reminded the people that they, as well as the land, belonged to the Lord, who should occupy first place in their lives. Since all they possessed was the result of His loving provision, before all other considerations, their tithes to the Lord were to be given first. Furthermore, no Israelite could come before the Lord without an offering commensurate with his income. To merely bring leftovers or a small pittance of one's income would be an expression of disobedience and ingratitude.

The command was clear: *No one is to present himself before the LORD empty-handed. Each shall come with a gift in his hand, according to the blessing of the LORD your God which He has bestowed on you* (16:16-17).

The Israelites were not only taught to bring their tithes to the Lord as a spiritual and moral obligation, but they were to "rejoice" with a heartfelt appreciation for the privilege of honoring God with their tithes and offerings; *then the LORD your God will bless you* (14:29).

Five hundred years before the law was given to Moses, Abraham, father of the faithful (Romans 4:11), paid a tenth (tithe) as an acceptable offering to the Lord. That principle continued throughout the Old Testament, and includes all believers today who are called *Abraham's sons* (Galatians 3:7). Today, the Lord's ministries, missionaries, churches, Bible schools, Bible publishers, translators, and other agencies are being sustained through the tithes and offerings of His people. Unexpected expenses test the sincerity of our faith. All of us were born selfish and self-centered, desiring to keep everything for self. However, all of what we call our possessions, even ourselves, belongs to God. Jesus said: *Therefore, give back to Caesar the things that are Caesar's, and to God the things that are God's* (Matthew 22:21).

Thought for Today: Tithing is ackowledgment of God's ownership.

In Today's Reading

Idolaters and obedience to authority; offerings due priests and Levites; heathen practices; prophecy concerning the coming of Christ; cities of refuge.

Moses foretold: *The LORD will raise up for you a Prophet* (Jesus) *like me from among you, from among your brothers. You must listen to Him. . . . The LORD said to me . . . I* (God) *will place My words in His mouth, and He will say to them everything I command Him. . . . Whoever does not listen to My words which He will speak . . . I will hold to account* (Deuteronomy 18:15,17-19). The prophet Jeremiah foretold that, in the end times, God would make a new covenant with His people (Jeremiah 31:31-34).

In conversing with His critics, Jesus said that Moses and the Scriptures bore witness of Him: *For if you believed Moses, you would believe Me, because he wrote about Me. But if you don't believe his writings, how will you believe My words* (John 5:46-47)?

Jesus declared to Pilate: *My Kingdom is not of this world,* meaning it has no earthly origin, but is a spiritual kingdom without end (18:36). On the Day of Pentecost, Peter boldly proclaimed that Jesus fulfilled the prophecy of Moses, who said: *The LORD your God will raise up for you a Prophet like me from among your brothers. You must listen to Him in everything He will say to you. And it will be that everyone who will not listen to that Prophet will be completely cut off from the people. In addition, all the prophets who have spoken, from Samuel and those after him, have also announced these days* (Acts 3:22-24; Deuteronomy 18:19). The Prophet whom Moses foretold is Jesus, who said: *Anyone who follows Me will never walk in the darkness* (John 8:12).

The writer of the book of Hebrews wrote: *If anyone disregards Moses' law, he dies without mercy. . . . How much worse punishment, do you think one will deserve who has trampled on the Son of God, regarded as profane the blood of the covenant by which he was sanctified, and insulted the Spirit of grace?* (Hebrews 10:28-29).

Thought for Today: Christ makes intercession for all who come to the Father through Him.

In Today's Reading

Laws concerning murders; female war captives; marriage; divorce; another's property; sanitation and human relations.

The Israelites had been taught that everything belonged to God and they were only caretakers of His possessions. Because of their covenant relationship with the Lord, they even were responsible for the welfare of their neighbor's property: *If you see your brother's ox or sheep wandering, you must not ignore them: make sure you return them to your brother* (Deuteronomy 22:1-4).

Under the laws of our country, we may not be held legally responsible for failing to prevent someone else's financial loss. But our stewardship responsibility to God requires that we respond to another's needs in a spirit of Christlike love.

In our Lord's Sermon on the Mount, He taught His followers to go far beyond merely helping preserve the property of a neighbor. As His disciples, we must *love your enemies, and pray for those who persecute you, so that you may be sons of your Father in heaven* (Matthew 5:44-45).

The person we help may or may not appreciate or deserve the kindness shown. Our responsibility, however, is not to the person who needs our help, but to the Lord, who is the true Owner of all creation, and who provides opportunities for us to express His love.

Jesus illustrated this by saying: *A man was going down from Jerusalem to Jericho and fell into the hands of robbers. . . . leaving him half dead. A priest. . . .* (and) *a Levite* (the official minister of the temple) *. . . saw him* (and) *passed by* (perhaps they had completed their religious responsibilities in Jerusalem and were on their way home to Jericho, the city of palm trees, where many of the temple priests lived. To stop and help this man could have defiled them and made them ceremonially unclean). *. . . But a Samaritan* (wasn't looking for excuses as to whether the hurting man was deserving of being helped) *had compassion. . . . and took care of him* (Luke 10:30-34).

The apostle John was led to remind us: *We must not love in word or speech, but in deed and truth* (I John 3:18).

Thought for Today: We should take advantage of every opportunity to express Christ's love to those around us.

In Today's Reading

Divorce; domestic relations; firstfruits and tithes; the law on Mount Ebal; an altar on Mount Gerizim.

Moses, the lawgiver and prophet, placed great emphasis on the necessity of honesty and truthfulness in all areas of life. In his second message, he warned against taking advantage of others. He illustrated this by the merchant who had two sets of weights and measures – one for buying and the other for selling: *You must not have two different ephahs in your house, a larger and a smaller. You must have a full and fair weight, and you must have a full and fair ephah . . . that you may live long in the land the LORD your God is giving you. For everyone who . . . acts crookedly, is detestable to the LORD your God* (Deuteronomy 25:14-16).

God hates lying and bribery. Each of us has the opportunity to exercise the principles of justice and equity or to take advantage of others, which may take some form of dishonesty such as wasting time on the job, taking what doesn't belong to us, unethical business transactions, lies, fraud, or any other dishonest act.

Our relationship with others goes much deeper than either word or deed; it goes to the hidden motives of our hearts and reveals what we truly are. This means that the thoughts of a Christian should always be the expression of what would Jesus do.

The attitude of fairness and consideration for others' well-being applies to a Christian's daily conduct. The self-centered "I" must give way to Christ and His control.

It is possible to have bitter thoughts while doing kind deeds and to say loving words while having wrong attitudes and motives. But, our Adamic nature and its self-serving conduct can be overcome by the Christ-centered nature that He has bestowed within us.

Abraham, the father of the faithful (Romans 4:11), exemplified this as he gave up his right to the possession of the best land to his nephew Lot in order to settle a dispute.

Demolish arguments (mental warfare) *and every high-minded thing that is raised up against the knowledge of God, taking every thought captive to the obedience of Christ* (II Cor. 10:4-5; see also Gen. 13:8-9).

Thought for Today: A Christian should resist all temptation to lie, cheat, or steal. These evils will result in the judgment of God.

In Today's Reading

Blessings for obedience; consequences for disobedience.

Moses related to the Israelites the blessings the people would receive: *If you faithfully obey the* LORD *your God, being careful to follow all His commands which I am giving you today . . . The* LORD *will open . . . the heavens, for you, to provide the rain for your land in due time, and to bless all the work of your hands* (Deuteronomy 28:1,12). The Israelites could choose either to live as His word directed and enjoy the Lord's blessings or to reject His word, as their parents had done, and suffer the consequences. Moses further warned: *The* LORD *will pursue you with plague until He has completely removed you from the land which you are entering to possess. The* LORD *will afflict you . . . with sword . . . and you will not prosper in your endeavors. Surely you will be oppressed and plundered forever, and there will be no deliverer* (28: 21-22,29).

Almost four times as many verses warn of the curses resulting from disobedience. The obvious conclusion of God's word is that each sin has a consequence – and it definitely does. However, this fact can also be misapplied, as in the case when Jesus' *disciples questioned Him: Rabbi, who sinned, this man or his parents, that he was born blind? Neither this man sinned nor his parents, Jesus answered. This came about so that God's works might be displayed in him* (John 9:2-3). What seemed to be a curse, became a blessing, for it brought this man to His Savior.

This points out that not all misfortunes are the result of sin, and that not all wealth and good health are necessarily a blessing from God. Consider the rich young ruler who chose to keep his wealth but it kept him from denying self and becoming a follower of Jesus.

Victory over our present-day Canaanite giants – *the lust of the flesh, the lust of the eyes, and the pride in one's lifestyle* (I John 2:16) – is achieved, not because of our abilities, but through our commitment to do the will of God. Overcoming power is found in cooperating with the Spirit of Christ, who dwells within us. As the apostle Paul revealed: *I am able to do all things through Him who strengthens me* (Philippians 4:13).

Thought for Today: God takes note of every thought of the heart.

In Today's Reading

New generation covenant; warnings against disobedience; Joshua, Moses' successor; Moses' last counsel.

The Creator chose the small Israelite nation as the people through whom He would reveal Himself as the one true self-existent God. *So observe the words of this covenant and follow them, so that you may succeed* (do wisely) *in all that you do. . . . So that He may establish you this day as His people, and that He may be your God as He has promised you, and as He swore to your fathers, to Abraham, Isaac, and Jacob* (Deuteronomy 29:9,13). Moses continued to warn the people of the consequences of disregarding their covenant responsibilities: *Be careful lest there* (be) *a man, woman, clan or tribe among you whose heart is turning today away from the LORD our God, to go and serve the gods of these nations. Be careful that there is no root among you bearing poison and bitterness when he hears the words of this oath* (29:18-19).

A covenant is a binding agreement between two or more parties to do or refrain from doing certain acts in which they voluntarily accept the terms of the agreement. The Israelites ignored their covenant relationship with the Lord and consequently suffered the loss of their land.

When the Israelites entered the promised land, they were surrounded by influences that would test their loyalty to the one true God. They were faced with people who seemed to have "advantages" such as chariots for war and an "attractive" religious system with images they could see and feel. The Israelites were tempted to depart from loyalty to their God. In Joshua's last message, he proclaimed: *If you . . . serve other gods . . . the LORD's anger will burn against you, and you will quickly disappear from this good land* (Joshua 23:16).

As the nations of the world become our near neighbors, some will be tempted to believe that their false gods are also the one true God just called by another name and that their faith is but one of many ways to worship our almighty God. But all worshipers of false gods reject *the blessed hope and the appearing of our great God and Savior, Jesus Christ* (Titus 2:13).

Thought for Today: Our love for the Lord is the same as our love for God's word.

In Today's Reading

The song of Moses; Moses blessed the 12 tribes; death of Moses on Mount Nebo; Joshua succeeds Moses.

The Israelites were to proclaim *greatness to our God. . . . for all His ways are just; a faithful God . . . righteous and upright*. The almighty Rock will never forsake the faithful. *The Rock, His work is perfect, for all His ways are . . . without injustice, He is righteous* (Deuteronomy 32:3-4). Moses foretold of the blessings and happiness that could be theirs if they would live in obedience to the word of God (33:6-29).

After conferring spiritual blessings upon each of the tribes, Moses concluded with praise to God: *The eternal God is a dwelling-place, and underneath are the everlasting arms. He drives the enemy from before you* (33:27). Although it is written: *No other prophet like Moses has arisen in Israel, whom the LORD knew face to face* (34:10), Moses forfeited the privilege of leading Israel into Canaan because of his sin (32:48-52; compare Numbers 20:1-13). Thus Moses became an example for all Israel that God is holy and cannot allow His law to be broken without consequences. Moses' life had been almost perfect. However, even though he had been the Lord's lawgiver, he had also broken the law once, and the law did not permit exceptions. Moses is last seen alone, climbing one of the most prominent mountain peaks in Moab from which he was allowed to view the promised land, though he could not enter it. Moses' penalty illustrates that even forgiveness of sin does not remove its earthly consequences (James 2:10).

Centuries later, Moses, symbolizing God's law, stood on Mount Hermon in the promised land with Elijah, who symbolized the prophets of God. Together they talked with Jesus as *He was transformed in front of them, and His face shone like the sun. Even His clothes became as white as the light . . . .While he was still speaking, suddenly a bright cloud covered them, and a voice from the cloud said: This is My beloved Son. I take delight in Him. Listen to Him!* (Matthew 17:2,5).

Thought for Today: Express the same patience to others that you expect to re-ceive from the Lord.

Introduction To The Book Of Joshua

The book of Joshua covers a period of about 25 years and is a continuation of the history of Israel recorded in Numbers.

Through Moses God spoke to Joshua, saying: *This book of the law must not depart from your mouth; you must recite it day and night, so that you may keep observing all that is written in it. For then you will make your way prosperous and will succeed* (Joshua 1:8).

Major events in the book of Joshua:

1. Two men spy out the land and make a covenant with Rahab (2:1-24).
2. The Israelites move from Shittim to the eastern bank of the Jordan River and remain three days to *sanctify* themselves (3:5).
3. The flood waters of the Jordan are miraculously parted (3:9-16).
4. Crossing the Jordan. *Joshua also set up 12 stones in the middle of the Jordan* (4:9,24).
5. In the promised land, the people first camped at Gilgal, near the banks of the Jordan, where *the LORD said to Joshua, Make flint knives and circumcise the sons of Israel* (5:2,5). A second memorial was built at Gilgal (4:20).
6. Observance of the first Passover in the promised land (5:10).
7. Conquest of Jericho and Ai (6:1 – 8:29).
8. Joshua offered a burnt sacrifice and fellowship offering on Mount Ebal, near Jacob's Well. *There, Joshua copied on the stones the law of Moses, which he had written in the presence of the Israelites* (8:32).
9. Deception by the Gibeonites followed by a peace treaty (9:1-27).
10. War declared by kings in the south. Joshua conquered them through the miraculous intervention of the Lord (10:1-4,11-14).
11. The defeat of all the kings in the land with their armies (11:1-23). The key to conquering the Canaanites is clear: *Just as the LORD had commanded His servant Moses . . . Joshua did . . . leaving nothing undone of all that the LORD . . . commanded Moses* (11:15).
12. Territory assigned to the tribes (13:1 – 22:34), except the tribe of Levi (21:41) which was given 48 cities throughout all the tribes. *None of the . . . promises that the LORD . . . made to the house of Israel failed. Everything was fulfilled* (21:43-45; 1:1-6).
13. Joshua's farewell message: *Continue obeying all that is written in the book of the law . . . do not turn from it to the right or to the left* (23:6).

A Prayer

In Jesus' Name, Oh Lord, I pray
That Thou wilt guide me day by day
Keep my heart set on things Above
And fill me with Thy gracious love.

Do Thou my Stay and Comfort be
My Strength, my All--I trust in Thee--
Then shall communion be complete
My life and service for Thee--meet.

Live out Thy life, Oh Christ, each day
In this poor body made of clay,
Reveal again, through me, dear Lord
The mighty power of Thine own Word.

- M. E. H.

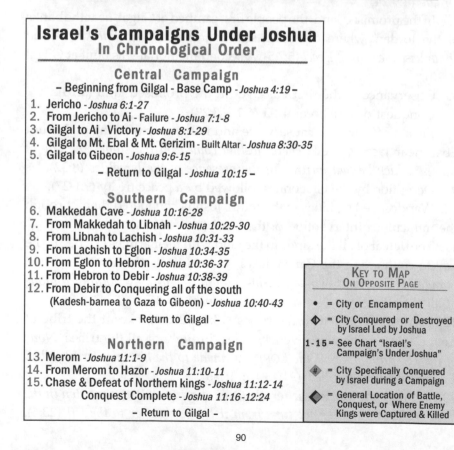

Israel's Campaigns Under Joshua
In Chronological Order

Central Campaign

– Beginning from Gilgal - Base Camp - *Joshua 4:19* –

1. Jericho - *Joshua 6:1-27*
2. From Jericho to Ai - Failure - *Joshua 7:1-8*
3. Gilgal to Ai - Victory - *Joshua 8:1-29*
4. Gilgal to Mt. Ebal & Mt. Gerizim - Built Altar - *Joshua 8:30-35*
5. Gilgal to Gibeon - *Joshua 9:6-15*

– Return to Gilgal - *Joshua 10:15* –

Southern Campaign

6. Makkedah Cave - *Joshua 10:16-28*
7. From Makkedah to Libnah - *Joshua 10:29-30*
8. From Libnah to Lachish - *Joshua 10:31-33*
9. From Lachish to Eglon - *Joshua 10:34-35*
10. From Eglon to Hebron - *Joshua 10:36-37*
11. From Hebron to Debir - *Joshua 10:38-39*
12. From Debir to Conquering all of the south (Kadesh-barnea to Gaza to Gibeon) - *Joshua 10:40-43*

– Return to Gilgal –

Northern Campaign

13. Merom - *Joshua 11:1-9*
14. From Merom to Hazor - *Joshua 11:10-11*
15. Chase & Defeat of Northern kings - *Joshua 11:12-14*

Conquest Complete - *Joshua 11:16-12:24*

– Return to Gilgal –

Key to Map On Opposite Page

- • = City or Encampment
- ◆ = City Conquered or Destroyed by Israel Led by Joshua
- 1-15 = See Chart "Israel's Campaign's Under Joshua"
- # = City Specifically Conquered by Israel during a Campaign
- ◆ = General Location of Battle, Conquest, or Where Enemy Kings were Captured & Killed

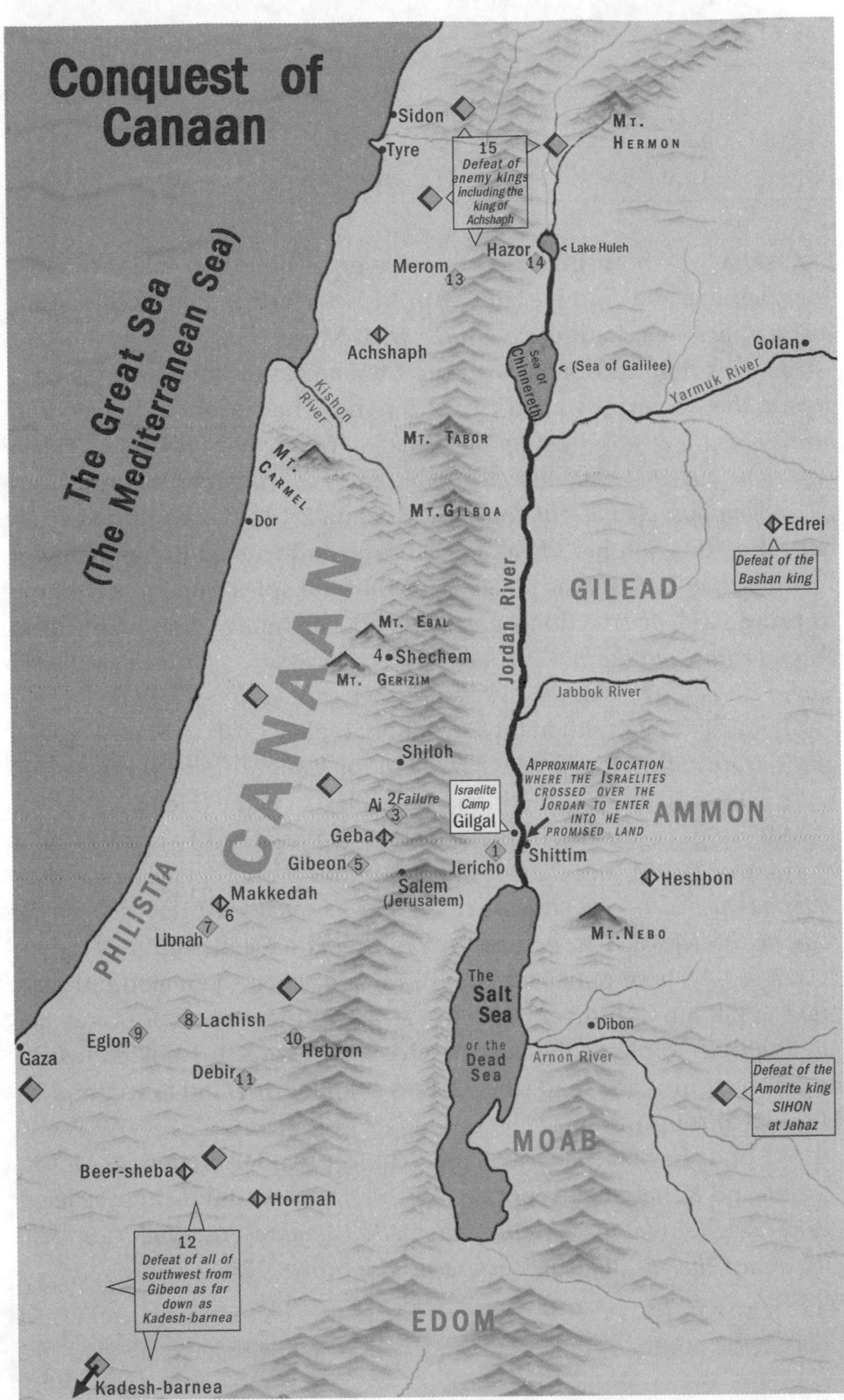

Conquest of Canaan
The Great Sea (The Mediterranean Sea)
Sidon
Tyre
15 Defeat of enemy kings including the king of Achshaph
MT. HERMON
Hazor
Lake Huleh
14
Merom
13
Achshaph
Sea of Chinnereth
(Sea of Galilee)
Golan
Yarmuk River
Kishon River
MT. TABOR
MT. CARMEL
MT. GILBOA
Dor
Edrei
Defeat of the Bashan king
GILEAD
CANAAN
Jordan River
MT. EBAL
4 Shechem
MT. GERIZIM
Jabbok River
Shiloh
APPROXIMATE LOCATION WHERE THE ISRAELITES CROSSED OVER THE JORDAN TO ENTER INTO HE PROMISED LAND
Ai
2 Failure
3
Israelite Camp
Gilgal
AMMON
Geba
1
Shittim
Gibeon
5
Jericho
Heshbon
Salem (Jerusalem)
Makkedah
6
7
Libnah
MT. NEBO
PHILISTIA
The Salt Sea or the Dead Sea
8 Lachish
Dibon
Eglon
9
10
Hebron
Gaza
Arnon River
Debir
11
Defeat of the Amorite king SIHON at Jahaz
MOAB
Beer-sheba
Hormah
12 Defeat of all of southwest from Gibeon as far down as Kadesh-barnea
EDOM
Kadesh-barnea

In Today's Reading

God speaks to Joshua; spies sent to Jericho; pledge between the spies and Rahab; Israel crosses the Jordan River.

Joshua was born into Egyptian slavery. While the majority were complaining and finding fault with Moses during their desert trials, Joshua became a faithful coworker with Moses.

Israel's first encounter with the Canaanites in the promised land was at the powerful walled city of Jericho. The people of Jericho had *heard how the LORD dried up the waters of the Red Sea before you when you came out of Egypt, and what you did to . . . the two Amorite kings . . . whom you completely destroyed* (Joshua 2:10). Rahab turned from her false gods, left her life as a prostitute, and trusted in the mercy of the one true God. It was no accident that the spies came to her home to bring God's protection upon her and her family. She had *said to them, I know that the LORD has given you this land . . . for the LORD your God—He is God in heaven above and on earth below* (2:9,11).

Because of her faith in the Lord, Rahab gave birth to Boaz, David's great-grandfather in the Messianic line of Jesus Christ (Matthew 1:5; Luke 3:32), and she is listed in the Faith Hall of Fame (Hebrews 11:31).

Moses gave up life in the palace and possibly his right to be a Pharaoh of Egypt, *and chose to suffer with the people of God rather than to enjoy the short-lived pleasure of sin. For he considered reproach for the sake of the Messiah to be greater wealth than the treasures of Egypt* (11:25-26). Joshua, remained faithful to God when the majority threatened to kill him (Numbers 14:6-10). A prostitute, Rahab, forsakes her sin and lives to please the Lord. Each of these three forsook the world and its pleasures and made themselves available for God to accomplish His will through them.

All of us have faced, or will face, choices similar to those of Moses, Joshua and Rahab. Let us not be like the majority, but: *Let us lay aside every weight and the sin that so easily ensnares us, and run with endurance the race that lies before us* (Hebrews 12:1).

Thought for Today: Most of us will pass into eternity with unfinished goals; but if our life's work is of God, it will continue to bless others.

In Today's Reading

Memorial at Gilgal; circumcision; Passover at Gilgal; manna ceases; Jericho besieged and destroyed.

God said: *I have given the land to you to possess it* (Numbers 33:53); but, the promises of God always include personal responsibilities. Before going further, *the LORD said to Joshua . . . circumcise the sons of Israel* (Joshua 5:2-5).

The rite of circumcision had been instituted by the Lord with Abraham, the father of the faithful, as a visible sign of the people's covenant relationship with Him (Genesis 17:9-14). It was required before anyone could eat the Passover (Exodus 12:48).

After being circumcised, the new generation became identified as the Lord's covenant people and qualified to keep the Passover (Joshua 5:8,10). The Passover commemorated the Lord's deliverance of His people from Egypt and pointed the way to the messianic Deliverer (I Corinthians 5:7). Circumcision and the Passover foreshadowed the ordinances of believer's baptism and the Lord's supper.

At His last Passover supper, our Lord Jesus revealed that His death on the cross would fulfill and replace the Passover. Paul spoke of this new covenant, saying: *On the night when He was betrayed, the Lord Jesus took bread, gave thanks, broke it, and said, This is My body, which is for you. Do this in remembrance of Me. In the same way He also took the cup, after supper, and said, This cup is the new covenant in My blood. Do this, as often as you drink it, in remembrance of Me. For as often as you eat this bread and drink the cup, you proclaim the Lord's death until He comes* (I Corinthians 11:23-26).

The Christian's circumcision is also explained by Paul: *In Him you were also circumcised with a circumcision not done with hands, by putting off the body of flesh, in the circumcision . . . Having been buried with Him in baptism, you were also raised with Him through faith in the working of God, who raised Him from the dead. And when you were dead in trespasses and in the uncircumcision of your flesh, He made you alive with Him and forgave us all our trespasses* (Col. 2:6,11-13).

Thought for Today: The Holy Spirit through the word of God enables us to rise above temptations.

In Today's Reading

Sin of Achan; Israel defeated by Ai; judgment of Achan; Ai defeated; altar on Mount Ebal; covenant renewed; law read.

The Lord held back the waters of the Jordan River at the time of year when the Jordan River overflowed its banks and all the Israelites *crossed on dry ground* into Canaan (Joshua 3:6-17). After the victory over Jericho, the Israelites were rejoicing. However, without seeking direction from God the Israelites attacked the city of Ai. *The men of Ai struck down some thirty-six of them and chased them from outside the gate as far as the crevices, striking them down on the descent* (7:5).

Nine times in the first six chapters of this book it is said that the Lord had directed Joshua (1:1; 3:7; 4:1,8,10,15; 5:2,15; 6:2). By not consulting the Lord, Israel's defeat was inevitable (7:2-5). Joshua had momentarily failed to consider that the Lord Himself was their Commander-in-Chief, that He alone could issue orders that would result in success (1:5). First, the evil sin by Achan had to be judged. Then, Joshua called on the Lord who directed him in the complete victory over Ai.

The Israelites' reasoning that led to their defeat at Ai has been repeated by most of us. When no serious problems seem to exist, we become overconfident, seemingly self-sufficient, and assume the Lord expects us to use "our own good judgment." However, apart from our submission to the indwelling presence of the Holy Spirit, the smallest temptation will prove to be too powerful for us. He alone imparts discernment as we desire to read and obey the word of God.

Many begin their Christian lives in prayer and daily Bible reading but eventually become self-confident and forget that *pride comes before destruction, and an arrogant spirit before a fall* (Proverbs 16:18). The truth here is we don't win our victories because we are Christians any more than Joshua won the battle at Ai because he was an Israelite.

The word of God is living and effective and sharper than any two-edged sword, penetrating as far as to divide soul, spirit, joints, and marrow; it is a judge of the ideas and thoughts of the heart (Hebrews 4:12).

Thought for Today: Any of our accomplishments that are worthwhile are the result of God working through us.

In Today's Reading

Israel's treaty with Gibeon; Gibeon attacked; God intervenes, causing the sun and moon to stand still; Amorite kings defeated.

After Joshua's victories over Jericho and Ai, five kings united to fight the Israelites. However, the Gibeonites, located between the land of the Canaanite kings and the encampment of Israel (Joshua 9:17), decided their chances of survival would be greater by making a league with the Israelites than by joining with the Canaanite kings in their war with Israel. They told Joshua: *Your servants have come from a very distant land because of the reputation of the LORD your God. For we have heard of His fame, and all that He did in Egypt. . . . So our elders and all the inhabitants of our land told us, Take provisions with you for the journey, and go meet them and say, We are your servants. Therefore make a treaty with us. . . . Then the men of Israel took some of their provisions, but did not seek the LORD's counsel. So Joshua established peace with them and made a treaty to let them live* (9:9-11,14-15) – a violation of the law (see Exodus 23:32-33; 34:12). This points out that ignorance of God's word does not nullify the results.

This league with the Gibeonites should impress upon us the enemy's skill in deception. We should also learn how fallible our human reasoning is. If Joshua had prayed for the Lord's guidance, the league never would have been agreed to.

The Israelites did not break their oath, even though the Gibeonites deceived them. However, over 400 years later, King Saul broke this covenant and it resulted in a 3-year famine in Israel (II Samuel 21:1). Through this, the Lord teaches us that the wrong done by another does not give us the right to do a similar wrong. One sin never justifies another. The characteristic of the children of God that distinguishes us from all other people is that we *conquer evil with good* (Romans 12:21). God wants us to learn from the Gibeonite covenant how important it is to have personal integrity and keep our commitments.

The moldy bread seemed to be visible proof of the strangers' words (Joshua 9:12-13). Too often we are foolish in making decisions based on what we see or think. *Trust in the LORD with all your heart, and do not rely on your own understanding . . . and He will guide you* (Prov. 3:5-6).

Thought for Today: Faith dispels fear of the future.

In Today's Reading

Conquest of the northern kings; Joshua's obedience; conquered kings; 2-1/2 tribes settle on the east side of the Jordan River.

Everyone in Jericho knew the reputation of Israel's God as did Rahab who confessed: *When we heard this, we lost heart, and everyone's courage failed because of you; for the LORD your God—He is God in heaven above and on earth below* (Joshua 2:11). Rahab alone put her faith in the God of the Hebrews and was not only saved but was included in the genealogy of Jesus (Matthew 1:5; Hebrews 11:31; James 2:25). The Canaanite kings had known what the Gibeonites knew, but they decided to defend their heathen gods against the true God.

News of Joshua's invasion quickly spread throughout Canaan. Jabin, King of Hazor in the north, enlisted the kings and their soldiers from farther into the northern mountains (Joshua 11:1-2,8).

Joshua's comparatively small army received a report that they were facing *a multitude as numerous as the sand on the seashore – along with a vast number of horses and chariots. All these kings joined forces. . . . Do not be afraid of them, the LORD said to Joshua, for at this time tomorrow I will hand all of them over to Israel – dead. . . . So Joshua and his whole military force surprised them at the waters of Merom. . . . They struck them down, leaving no survivors* (11:4-8).

So Joshua took the entire land, in keeping with all that the LORD had told Moses. . . . After this, the land had rest from war (11:23). Thirty-one kings (12:24) had been defeated. Joshua established military control over all of the promised land. The individual tribes were to complete the destruction of the Canaanites (Exodus 23:29-30; Deut. 7:22).

The judgment of the Canaanites foreshadows the final judgment of all who continue in their sins. *This will take place at the revelation of the Lord Jesus from heaven with His powerful angels, taking vengeance with flaming fire on those who don't know God and on those who don't obey the gospel of our Lord Jesus. These will pay the penalty of everlasting destruction, away from the Lord's presence and from His glorious strength* (II Thessalonians 1:7-9).

Thought for Today: Obedience to God's word is the key to victory.

In Today's Reading

Canaan divided among the tribes; territories given to Judah, Caleb, Ephraim, and Manasseh.

The Anakim had been driven out of Hebron by Joshua, perhaps five years before this time (Joshua 10:2-11; 11:21-22). Now they were back and in control of the territory – undoubtedly, with a much greater determination to retain the land promised to Caleb.

At Caleb's "retirement" age of 85, he recounted to the younger generation how God had brought him that far: *I was 40 years old when Moses the LORD's servant sent me from Kadesh-barnea to scout the land, and I brought back an honest report. My brothers caused the people's heart to melt with fear, but I remained loyal to the LORD my God* (14:7-8). Caleb's unshakable faith can be seen in his report as a spy: *I brought back an honest report.* He spoke his convictions as he faced the opposition of the other spies and the people. He stood alone with Joshua.We are sometimes afraid to speak about our faith when our convictions are unpopular; but the person blessed of God speaks what is in his heart on spiritual issues.

Caleb boldly said: *I remained loyal to the LORD.* His decision was unaffected by what others said or did. The loyal few who have their hearts fixed on the Lord and trust in His word are not afraid to speak out or move forward to accomplish the Lord's will regardless of what others say or do.

Caleb's courageous spirit not only inspires us, but reminds us that *those who hope in the LORD will renew their strength; they will spread out their wings like eagles; they will run and not become weary; they will walk and not faint* (Isaiah 40:31). The truly blessed are faithful to God.

Yes, most of us will face giant "Canaanite" difficulties in life as well as friends who attempt to discourage us. Surely our faith ought to exceed Caleb's, inasmuch as *Christ Jesus is . . . at the right hand of God and intercedes for us. Who can separate us from the love of Christ? Can affliction or anguish or persecution or famine or nakedness or danger or sword? . . . No, in all these things we are more than victorious through Him who loved us* (Romans 8:34-35,37).

Thought for Today: God honors faith that is established in His word.

In Today's Reading

Distribution of land to all the tribes; Manasseh fails to drive out Canaanites; tabernacle set up at Shiloh; Joshua's inheritance.

The conquest of Canaan was completed and the land was divided, not by majority vote, but by the Lord. When *the entire Israelite community assembled at Shiloh and set up the tent of meeting there; the land had been subdued by them. . . . Joshua cast lots for them at Shiloh in the presence of the LORD; there he distributed the land to the Israelites* (Joshua 18:1,10).

Although they had received some of the best territory in the promised land, the tribes of Manasseh and Ephraim complained that they should have more territory given to them because of their great numbers and what they perceived as their prominent position among the tribes (17:14-18). The Ephraimites were proud of their history as descendants of Joseph, and that Joshua, the victorious commander who led in the conquest of Canaan, was also from their tribe.

Sadly, these two tribes chose the easy way of compromise with the Canaanites. The blessings of God often depend upon faith: *Foolish man! Are you willing to learn that faith without works is useless* (James 2:20)? It is wise to refuse to help those who will not help themselves.

When we have our priorities centered upon the Lord, we need not fear losing our share of anything. In fact, we gladly accept less to maintain peace with others. True men of God do not expect others to serve or praise them.

In a striking contrast to the tribes of Manasseh and Ephraim, Joshua chose to be the last to lay claim to any territory (Joshua 19:49). As captain, we could expect him to be first and take the best for himself. Instead, he chose last. His choice was a very small area near Shiloh where the tabernacle was erected and where he could best worship and serve the Lord. It was there, in the nearness of the Lord's presence, that Joshua built his small city. Joshua illustrates the importance to *be fervent in spirit; serve the LORD. . . . Therefore, submit to God. But resist the Devil, and he will flee from you. . . . Humble yourselves before the LORD, and He will exalt you* (Romans 12:11; James 4:7,10).

Thought for Today: Meekness is not weakness.

In Today's Reading

Six Cities of Refuge appointed; 48 cities given to the Levites; the Israelites possessed the land.

Unlike all the other tribes of Israel, the tribe of Levi was given no separate territory (Joshua 14:3). *But to the tribe of Levi, Moses did not give a portion. The LORD Himself, the God of Israel, was their inheritance, just as He had promised them* (13:33). *But the Levites among you do not get a portion . . . their inheritance is the priesthood of the LORD* (18:7).

The Levites were divided into three groups according to the descendants of Levi's three sons, Gershon, Kohath, and Merari. But only those Israelites who were descendants of Levi through Kohath's grandson Aaron, could be priests and serve in the tabernacle. However, even some of these descendants were physically disqualified to be ministers at the altar because of disabilities and defects; and some were spiritually disqualified because of violating one or more of the commandments (Leviticus 21:1-23). The priests were responsible for preserving, transcribing, teaching, and interpreting the law. They were also the civil officers responsible for the administration of the law (Deuteronomy 17:9-12; 31:9,11-12,26). All the Levites, not merely the ones who were responsible for the worship at the tabernacle, were to receive an equal share of the tithes from the other tribes. Each tribe was to provide for the physical welfare of the priests within its own territory. This was not left up to the goodwill of the people, but was a command from God.

God devoted 42 of the 45 verses in Joshua 21 to emphasizing the Israelites' obligation to support the ministers of His word. No one is too poor or exempt from giving his tithe which is a tenth of his income and, thus, proportionately equal for all. When Israel was faithful in this, God mightily blessed them. When they failed, they suffered.

The apostle Paul illustrated this saying: *For it is written . . . Do not muzzle an ox while it treads out the grain. Is God really concerned with oxen? Or isn't He really saying it for us? Yes, this is written for us. . . . If we have sown spiritual things for you, is it too much if we reap material things from you? . . . the Lord has commanded that those who preach the gospel should earn their living by the gospel* (I Corinthians 9:9-12,14).

Thought for Today: Nothing is too hard for God!

In Today's Reading

Two and one-half tribes build an altar, then return east of the Jordan; civil war averted; Joshua's final proclamation.

When God told Joshua: *I have given you every place where you set foot, just as I promised Moses* (Joshua 1:3), Joshua did not merely "trust the Lord" that He would force the Canaanites to voluntarily give up their land. The fact is, the Israelites received their inheritance by faith; but they were to fight for every foot of land that God had promised them.

After about seven years, the Israelites under the leadership of Joshua had conquered Canaan. *The LORD gave them rest on every side according to all He had sworn to their fathers. None of their enemies could withstand them, for the LORD delivered all their enemies into their hands* (21:44).

The Israelites' greatest danger was yet to be faced. *Joshua told the people. . . . If you forsake the LORD and serve foreign gods, He will . . . completely destroy you, after He has been good to you. . . . Now then, get rid of the foreign gods that are among you and offer your hearts to the LORD, the God of Israel* (24:19-20,23).

Jesus, our "Joshua," freed us from sin by His substitutionary death on the cross and His triumphant physical resurrection.

We too need to be reminded daily to *offer* (our) *hearts to the LORD.* What a tragedy that so many people assume that, once a person has accepted Jesus Christ as Savior, he has nothing to do but "just leave everything up to the Lord." The truth is, the Lord has left it up to us. *This is why* ***you*** *must take up the full armor of God, so that* ***you*** *may be able to resist in the evil day, and having prepared everything, to take* ***your*** *stand. Stand, therefore, with truth like a belt around* ***your*** *waist, righteousness like armor on* ***your*** *chest, and* ***your*** *feet sandaled with the readiness of the gospel of peace. In every situation take the shield of faith, and with it* ***you*** *will be able to extinguish the flaming arrows of the evil one. Take the helmet of salvation, and the sword of the Spirit, which is God's word* (Ephesians 6:13-17).

Thought for Today: Every day serve only the Lord.

Introduction To The Book Of Judges

The book of Judges relates fragments of Israel's history from the death of Joshua to the beginning of Samuel's ministry.

The key to the conquest of Canaan is clear: *The people served the LORD all the days of Joshua and all the days of the elders who outlived Joshua and who had seen all the great deeds of the LORD, which He had done for Israel* (Judges 2:7). After Joshua's death there was no God-appointed national leader, and each tribe acted independently (1:1 – 2:23).

Most of the Israelite tribes disregarded the Lord's command to drive out all the Canaanites who remained in their territories. Instead, they compromised by gradually enslaving them. This compromise led to intermarriage with the Canaanites and, ultimately, to Israel's worship of their false gods.

The reason for this failure is obvious: *All of that generation was also gathered to their fathers, and another generation arose after them who did not know the LORD nor the deeds He had done for Israel. . . . They abandoned the LORD and served Baal* (the chief god of the Canaanites) (2:10,13). Without a central leader or government, a time of spiritual failure and confusion prevailed.

Seven major apostasies are recorded when *the sons of Israel did evil in the LORD's sight and served the Baals* (2:11; 3:7,12; 4:1; 6:1; 10:6; 13:1). In each case, the Israelites were overcome by their enemies, lost their freedom, and were greatly impoverished; but, when the people prayed, God delivered them from their oppression. These judges acted under the authority of God, who was Israel's invisible King. Each successive judge exalted God, and this provided a period of peace and prosperity.

Chapters 17 – 21 are not a continuation of Israel's history, but contain insight into the Israelites' moral and spiritual degradation that prevailed preceding the time when Samuel became a prophet of God and their judge. The book of Judges reveals that disobedience to the word of God inevitably results in defeat. In contrast, obedience to God and His word assures blessings in all areas of life.

Judges of the Israelites (Judges – I Samuel 7)

Judge	From the Tribe of	Text	Oppressor	Oppressed Years	Peace Years
Othniel	Judah	Judges 3:7-11	Mesopotamians	8	40
Ehud	Benjamin	Judges 3:12-30	Moabites, Ammonites, Amalekites	18	80
Shamgar	Judah	Judges 3:31	Philistines		
Deborah	Ephraim	Judges 4:1-5:31	Canaanites	20	40
Gideon	Manasseh	Judges 6:1-8:32	Midianites, Amalekites	7	40
Abimelech (A Usurper)	Ephraim	Judges 8:33-9:57	No Peace, Only chaos		
Tola	Issachar	Judges 10:1-2			23
Jair	Manasseh	Judges 10:3-5			22
Jephthah	Manasseh (East of the Jordan River)	Judges 11:1-12:7	Ammonites	18	6
Ibzan	Judah	Judges 12:8-10			7
Elon	Zebulun	Judges 12:11-12			10
Abdon	Ephraim	Judges 12:13-15			8
Samson	Dan	Judges 13:24-16:31	Philistines	40	20
Eli	Ephraim	I Samuel 4:18	Philistines	40	40
Samuel	Ephraim	I Samuel 1:20-7:17	Philistines		About 40

The Six Cities of Refuge (See Map on opposite page)

Kedesh – located about 15 miles north of the Sea of Galilee in the mountains bordering the west side of the Huleh Valley in the territory of Naphtali

Shechem - located in the valley between Mount Ebal and Mount Gerizim in the mountains of Ephraim

Hebron (Kiriath-arba) – located in Judah about 20 miles south of Jerusalem

Bezer – located east of the Jordan River in the tribe of Reuben

Ramoth-gilead – located about 50 miles north of Bezer in the highlands of Gilead in the tribe of Gad

Golan – located in the highlands of the tribe of Manasseh, east of the Jordan River

Since the Law required a near relative of the one killed to become an avenger of blood (Deuteronomy 19:6,12), the cities of refuge provided a sanctuary for those who had been killed by accident. Under the law, the slayers had to remain in the city until after the death of the high priest.

The law did not provide for any sacrifice for the manslayer. The guilt of the man who killed accidentally was removed only by the death of the high priest. He could not pay a fine or be set free any sooner.

There is a sharp distinction between an accidental death and a willful murder. God demands that a murderer be put to death. The Levites and the elders in each city were designated to investigate if the death was accidental or a willful murder.

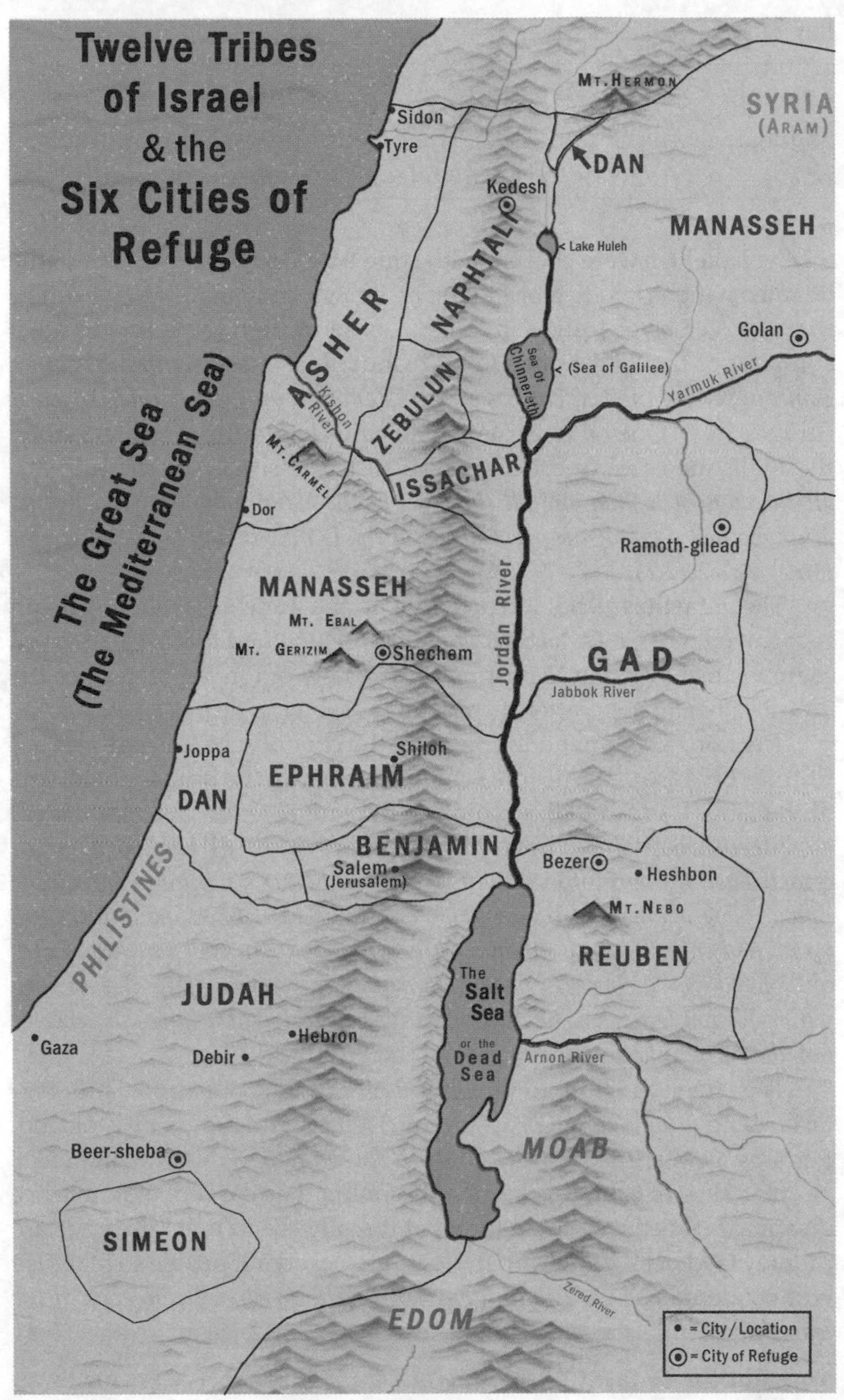

Twelve Tribes of Israel & the Six Cities of Refuge
The Great Sea (The Mediterranean Sea)
Mt. Hermon
SYRIA (Aram)
Sidon
Tyre
DAN
Kedesh
MANASSEH
Lake Huleh
NAPHTALI
ASHER
Golan
Sea of Chinnereth
(Sea of Galilee)
Yarmuk River
ZEBULUN
Kishon River
Mt. Carmel
ISSACHAR
Dor
Ramoth-gilead
MANASSEH
Jordan River
Mt. Ebal
Mt. Gerizim
Shechem
GAD
Jabbok River
Joppa
Shiloh
EPHRAIM
DAN
BENJAMIN
Salem (Jerusalem)
Bezer
Heshbon
Mt. Nebo
PHILISTINES
REUBEN
The Salt Sea or the Dead Sea
JUDAH
Gaza
Hebron
Debir
Arnon River
MOAB
Beer-sheba
SIMEON
Zered River
EDOM
• = City/Location
⊙ = City of Refuge

In Today's Reading

Judah chosen to lead wars; Israel fails to drive Canaanites out; Angel of the Lord's rebuke; Joshua's death.

The Israelites were chosen by the one true God to reveal Him to the heathen nations and to glorify Him by being obedient to His word. The first few verses of Judges give us a sense of high hope for the total conquest of the land as begun by Joshua: *Judah went with his brother Simeon, struck the Canaanites . . . in Zephath, and utterly destroyed it* (Judges 1:17). One by one, Canaanite cities fell to the Israelites – then the Philistine cities (see 1:10-11,13,17-18). *The people served the LORD all the days of Joshua and all the days of the elders who outlived Joshua and who had seen all the great deeds of the LORD, which he had done for Israel* (1:1-2; 2:7).

The Israelites who were living at the time of Joshua's death recognized that God was their captain and king and that He had given them victory over the Canaanites. But a new era in the history of the 12 tribes began soon after the death of Joshua.

The Lord's command to complete the conquest of Canaan was not fulfilled because of the people's compromise with the pagan inhabitants of the land. It is more disappointing to read: *Another generation arose after them who did not know the LORD nor the deeds He had done for Israel. Then the sons of Israel did evil in the LORD's sight and served the Baals. They abandoned the LORD. . . . So the LORD became angry with Israel and said, Because this nation has violated My covenant . . . I also will no longer dispossess from before them anyone among the nations which Joshua left when he died. This was to test Israel, to see whether or not they would keep the way of the LORD* (2:10-22).

The Israelites chose to do what they thought was more "humanitarian" and would create peaceful coexistence with the enemies of God. Perhaps they argued: "How could a God of love destroy 'innocent' people? This, of course, is human reasoning. The concept of innocence disappears when we see sin for what it really is and that false gods are robbing God of love and worship, and are deceiving people so that they will be eternally lost. *And anyone not found written in the book of life was thrown into the lake of fire* (Revelation 20:12,15).

Thought for Today: Considering our guilt God's mercy is amazing.

In Today's Reading

Israel intermarries with Canaanites, worships false gods, is defeated; the Lord raises up judges to deliver Israel; Deborah and Barak

The Lord had left certain groups of Canaanite people in the land. *They were left to test Israel, to see if they would keep the commandments of the LORD, which He had commanded their fathers* (Judges 3:4).

The first major step in the downfall of the Israelites was their disregard for *the commandments of the LORD*. The next step was that they *lived among the Canaanites, Hittites, Amorites, Perizzites, Hivites, and Jebusites* (3:5). The third step in their decline soon followed: *They took their daughters to themselves for wives, gave their own daughters to their sons; and served their gods* (3:6). The fourth step was inevitable, because the Israelites' heathen wives, who worshiped idols, would not teach their children to worship the one and only true God. Sadly the final step was: *The sons of Israel did evil in the sight of the LORD . . . and served the Baals and the Asheroth* (3:7). The outcome was certain; sin separates the sinner from the protective hand of God. However, *the sons of Israel cried out to the LORD. So the LORD raised up a deliverer for the sons of Israel and delivered them by means of Othniel, the son of Kenaz, Caleb's youngest brother* (3:9,15; 4:3). There was a ray of hope as the Lord again provided a deliverer. But the Israelites developed a pattern of recurring apostasy. *Ehud had died – so the LORD sold them into the hand of Jabin, king of Canaan. . . . Jabin had 900 iron chariots and had harshly oppressed . . . Israel for 20 years* (4:1-3).

From Deborah we learn that success in accomplishing the will of God does not depend upon age or gender. And we also learn from Israel's history that, regardless of how far we have backslidden and drifted away from the Lord, our merciful Father in heaven always hears the prayers of those who confess their sins and commit their lives to Him. However, the wasted years of opportunity cannot be relived.

Who is the one who condemns? Christ Jesus is the One who died, but even more, has been raised; He also is at the right hand of God and intercedes for us (Romans 8:34).

Thought for Today: Wealth and pleasures can be deceptive snares to keep the believer from accomplishing God's eternal purposes.

In Today's Reading

Israel forsakes God; Midianites oppress Israel for seven years; Israel prays; God sends a prophet; Gideon destroys altar of Baal.

Once more the Israelites were enslaved, this time by the Midianites. *The sons of Israel did evil in the sight of the LORD. So the LORD gave them into the hand of Midian for seven years. . . . Israel became poverty stricken . . . the sons of Israel cried out to the LORD* (Judges 6:1,6). The answer to their prayers began with reproof: *The LORD sent a prophet . . .* (who) *said to them, Thus says the LORD God of Israel: I Myself brought you up from Egypt. . . . and from the hand of all who oppressed you. . . . I gave you their land. . . . but you did not obey Me* (6:8-10). There was no word of comfort, only reproof. The people were left with the consciousness of their sins and with no hope of relief. They needed to recognize that their miserable suffering was the direct result of their disregarding the word of God.

It would appear that this unnamed prophet may have had only one convert – Gideon: *Then the Angel of the LORD appeared to him and said . . . The LORD is with you, O mighty warrior. . . . Go in this strength of yours and deliver Israel from the hand of Midian* (6:12,14).

Gideon was deeply conscious of his poverty and inability, and confessed: *LORD, how can I deliver Israel? Indeed, my family is the weakest in Manasseh, and I am the youngest in my father's house* (6:15). We tend to think that the only people God can use are those who have influence in their communities. But, often these people are too busy, want to do it their way, or would rather compromise than lose their popularity. Gideon was truly a man of inexperience and uncertainty, but he unconditionally obeyed the Lord without fear of the opposition. Gideon was ready to worship the God of Israel and *built an altar to the LORD there and called it The LORD is Peace* (6:24). We too must get our eyes off of circumstances and fix our faith on the word of God. *Listen, my dear brothers: Didn't God choose the poor in this world to be rich in faith and heirs of the kingdom that He has promised to those who love Him* (James 2:5)?

Thought for Today: Faith in God, not our wisdom, brings success.

In Today's Reading

Gideon makes an ephod; his death; Gideon's son Abimelech murders 70 of his brothers; Abimelech's accidental death.

Gideon was called of God to deliver the Israelites from the Midianites. Thirty-two thousand men responded to Gideon's call to war; but God chose to use just 300 men to defeat the Midianites. The other Israelites were sent home and with only 300 men, 135,000 Midianite soldiers were defeated in battle. *The land enjoyed peace for 40 years during the days of Gideon* (Judges 8:28). This illustrates a wonderful principle. God would not act without man's cooperation, and man could not overcome without the wisdom and power of God.

The Israelites urged Gideon to be their king. It was an appeal to his pride. But Gideon knew that it was not he who had saved his people, but God who was the true King. So *Gideon said to them: I . . . will not rule over you . . . the LORD shall rule over you* (8:23). Gideon knew that, as a judge of Israel, he would need God to guide him.

The Israelites soon forgot that God was the One who had miraculously delivered them from the Midianites.

After Gideon's death, with an appetite for power, his cruel and crafty son Abimelech negotiated a large sum of money from the Baal temple treasury to pay men to murder his 70 brothers. *But Jotham, the youngest son of Jerubbaal survived, because he hid himself* (9:5). Following the execution of his competition, *all the lords of Shechem . . . made Abimelech king* (9:6). However, at the moment of Abimelech's proudest achievements, Jotham, the son of Gideon who escaped execution, warned that they would soon discover that this self-made king would bring suffering and death upon them as well as himself (9:7-21). As Jotham had foretold, they soon brought about their own destruction (9:22-57).

Abimelech is an example of a person controlled by the deceptive and destructive forces of pride and ambition, one who is determined to gain selfish ends regardless of whom he hurts. He is a reminder of what Jesus said to the church of Ephesus and the church of Smyrna: *Remember then how far you have fallen; repent, and do the works you did at first. . . . Anyone who has an ear should listen to what the Spirit says to the churches* (Revelation 2:5,11).

Thought for Today: Surrender to God ensures victory.

In Today's Reading

Israel forsakes the Lord and worships idols; Israel oppressed by Ammonites for 18 years; Jephthah's daughter dedicated to God.

After suffering because they worshiped false gods (Judges 10:8), *the sons of Israel said, We have sinned. . . . So they put away the foreign gods from their midst and served the LORD* (10:15-16). *So when the Ammonites made war with Israel, the elders of Gilead. . . . said to Jephthah . . . be our leader and let's fight against the Ammonites* (11:5-6).

Jephthah prayed: *Give the Ammonites into my hand, then whatever comes out of the doors of my house to greet me when I return in peace . . . it shall belong to the LORD* (11:30-31). God arranged that Jephthah's daughter should be the first to meet him. It was as if God were saying: "I have given you all you asked; now I ask you to give Me your best" (11:30-40). This could not have meant human sacrifice. Jephthah knew the Scriptures well and human sacrifices were condemned by God (Leviticus 20:2-5; Deuteronomy 12:29-31; 18:10-12). How could one imagine he would cut the throat of his daughter to offer her as a burnt offering? To do that would have made God, as well as this man of faith, responsible for a vile murder, since it was *the Spirit of the LORD* who gave Jephthah his victory (Judges 11:29,32).

How he fulfilled his vow becomes clear as we consider all the facts. *She was his only child; he had neither son nor daughter besides her* (11:34). The Lord declared that the firstborn were to be "sanctified" – not sacrificed: *It is Mine* (Exodus 13:2; Numbers 3:13). And his daughter's response to Jephthah's vow made the outcome unmistakably clear. She asked for *two months* to go up and down the valleys to *weep over my virginity* (Judges 11:37) – meaning to "bewail that I will never marry." *She returned to her father, and he completed his vow* (11:39). She was dedicated to serve the Lord in lifelong chastity, even as Hannah dedicated Samuel as a "spiritual" burnt offering unto the Lord. Undoubtedly, she became one of the servants of God in the tabernacle.

Jephthah became one of the heroes of faith: *And what more can I say? Time is too short for me to tell about Gideon, Barak, Samson, Jephthah. . . . who by faith conquered kingdoms, administered justice, obtained promises* (Hebrews 11:32-33).

Thought for Today: Trust and obey . . . for there's no other way.

In Today's Reading

Jephthah's victory over the Ephraimites; Israel under Philistine control; Samson's Philistine wife in Timnath.

In the area of Dan and Ephraim, the Israelites were oppressed by the Philistines for 40 years. During that time, Samson was born. Unlike Jephthah, Samson had a godly mother and father who desired to train him to do what the Angel of the Lord had instructed. Samson's mother was deeply concerned that her son be fully dedicated to the Lord (Judges 13:3-21; compare I Samuel 1:11).

From time to time, the Spirit of God came upon Samson and *began to stir him* (Judges 13:25). Eventually, Samson ruled as judge. Early in his life, we see his disregard for his holy calling. His first act of unfaithfulness was friendship with the enemies of God. It seemed that Samson was easily distracted with his own physical desires and satisfactions, as in Timnath, when he fell in love with a Philistine woman. *He then went up and told his father and his mother, and said . . . get her for me as a wife. . . . at that time the Philistines were ruling over Israel* (14:1-4).

Samson ignored Israel's covenant relationship with the Lord. Samson's life typified the spiritual condition of Israel during that period of the Judges and revealed how a self-willed life results in sorrow and suffering for self and others.

All of us are tempted to please ourselves. Self-pleasing comes in many forms: pride, jealousy, theft, refusing to tithe, sexual sins, hate, avoidance of responsibility, using drugs or alcohol, and a host of other things. Every day that we continue in willful sin, Satan's hold becomes stronger, and our chances of deliverance become less likely. Perhaps the greatest deceptive sin is that of presuming that the mercy and long-suffering of God will continue indefinitely.

As a Nazarite, Samson was meant to be an example before all Israel of loyal commitment to God. We too are called upon to be separated from the world with a desire to fulfill the Lord's will. *The night is nearly over, and the daylight is near, so let us discard the deeds of darkness and put on the armor of light* (Romans 13:12).

Thought for Today: A person's conscience can only be a safe guide when it is guided by God's word.

In Today's Reading

Samson loses his wife; 1,000 Philistines slain; Delilah; Samson defeated, blinded, dies with the Philistines; Micah's idols.

The early life of Samson is recorded in chapters 13, 14, and 15 of the book of Judges. Then it appears that many years passed for which we have no record until we read the tragic events in chapter 16.

There is no record that Samson ever expressed a desire to be used by the Lord to deliver the Israelites from the Philistine's oppression. So it is not a surprise that he neither prayed for guidance nor protection. He chose the enemies of God for his friends.

Early in life, Samson disregarded the spiritual significance of his Nazarite dedication by marrying a Philistine woman. He became deeply involved in sin as he made friends with Delilah, a Philistine woman. And, as always, with each person who presumptuously believes that God's mercy and long-suffering will continue indefinitely, we see Samson yield to Delilah's treachery. *Then she said, Samson! The Philistines are upon you. When he awoke from his sleep he said, I will go out as at other times and shake myself free. (But he didn't know that the LORD had turned from him.)* (Judges 16:20).

When Samson saw Delilah, he should have thought of his sacred Nazarite vow and his high calling as a judge. But sin had blinded him to his high calling and to the reason he was gifted with great strength. Consequently, *the Philistines seized him and gouged out his eyes. They brought him down to Gaza and bound him in bronze shackles, and he ground grain in the prison* (16:21). Not only did he suffer the gruesome torture of having his eyes gouged out, but he was forced to take the place of an animal and spend his time turning the mill to grind corn into meal (16:21).

The story of Samson should send a strong message to every Christian who has fallen into the treacherous web of sinful pleasures. Samson is not the only servant of God who ever lost his power through worldliness and self-indulgence (16:19).

In contrast, *by faith Moses . . . chose to suffer with the people of God rather than to enjoy the short-lived pleasure of sin* (Hebrews 11:24-25).

Thought for Today: Oh, the high cost of lust and its treachery.

In Today's Reading

Danites force Micah's Levite to be their priest, attack Laish, then occupy it; a concubine victimized.

Israel continued to ignore God's word. Consequently, we read: *In those days there was no king in Israel; everyone did what was right in his own eyes* (Judges 18:1; 19:1; 21:25). This means doing whatever seemed most gratifying.

To illustrate the deplorable moral condition that existed at that time, a Levite, representing spiritual leadership, and his concubine are introduced. We are disappointed to read of the violation of the law by his relationship with his concubine who *was unfaithful to him and went away from him to her father's house in Bethlehem* (19:2; Leviticus 21:7). But, after *four months,* the Levite decided that he wanted her back, so he went to her father's house. *When the girl's father saw him, he gladly welcomed him* (Judges 19:2-3).

When the Levite decided to return home several days later, it was too late to complete their journey before nightfall, so they stopped in Gibeah (19:14). An old man offered them hospitality in his house, which they accepted. *While they were enjoying themselves, suddenly the men of the city—perverted men—surrounded the house beating on the door. They said to . . . the old man, Bring out the man who came to your house so that we may have sex with him* (19:22). After much pleading, the old man offered his own virgin daughter as well as the Levite's concubine to the demanding men. Although to do so was a very sinful act, homosexuality was far more wicked by comparison. So the old man said: *Here's my virgin daughter and his concubine. . . . but to this man, do not do this foolish thing!* (19:24). The vileness of this sin is confirmed in the New Testament where we read: *This is why God delivered them over to degrading passions. For even their females exchanged natural sexual intercourse for what is unnatural. The males in the same way also left natural sexual intercourse with females and were inflamed in their lust for one another. Males committed shameless acts with males and received in their own persons the appropriate penalty for their perversion* (Romans 1:26-27).

Thought for Today: The morally perverted need our prayers.

In Today's Reading

Civil war between Benjamites and other tribes; Benjamites defeated; wives provided for few remaining Benjamites.

The tribe of Benjamin refused to allow justice to be done to the homosexual mob that gang-raped a defenseless Israelite woman, causing her death (Judges 20:13). All the tribes of Israel united to execute judgment against them and *came to Bethel. There they wept and sat before the LORD, and they fasted that day until evening. Then they offered burnt offerings and fellowship offerings before the LORD* (20:26). In deep humility, they committed themselves to the Lord.

It was only after they had built an altar and offered the sacrifices for their own need that *the LORD said, Go up, for tomorrow I'll give them into your hand* (20:28). The tribe of Benjamin was almost destroyed before the consequences of this wicked sin had been meted out.

There is growing indifference to immorality in our society similar to what existed in the tribe of Benjamin. We have redefined sin. *Adultery* is now called "having an affair." *Homosexuality* is replaced with "gay and lesbian," or "alternative lifestyles." *Fornication* is referred to as "live-in lovers." The purpose is to remove the sense of guilt for violating God's moral law and make the sinner feel comfortable, as they did when *in those days. . . . everyone did what was right in his own eyes* (21:25). However, while hating and exposing sin, we must also show mercy and kindness as we pray for and lovingly entreat the sinner to come to Christ and allow him to change their lives.

All sin is abominable to our holy God; however, all sin that is truly repented of and forsaken is forgiven through the atoning blood of Jesus Christ. The apostle Paul reminded the Corinthians that some of them had been delivered from sexual sins when he wrote: *Do you not know that the unjust will not inherit God's kingdom? Do not be deceived: no sexually immoral people, idolaters, adulterers, male prostitutes, homosexuals . . . will inherit God's kingdom. Some of you were like this; but you were washed, you were sanctified, you were justified in the name of the Lord Jesus Christ and by the Spirit of our God* (I Corinthians 6:9-11).

Thought for Today: We cheat ourselves when withholding what we should give to God.

Introduction To The Book Of Ruth

The events of the book of Ruth occurred when the judges ruled (Ruth 1:1). *In those days there was no king in Israel; everyone did what was right in his own eyes* (did as he pleased) (Judges 21:25). The book of Ruth provides insight on faithfulness to God during the lawless period of the judges. The purpose of the book is to reveal how the mercy and providential care of God extends to both Jew and Gentile.

The book of Ruth highlights our Lord's loving-kindness in selecting a Moabite woman to be included in His covenant with Israel, and to be one of only two women after whom books of the Bible are named. Ruth was also one of only four women mentioned in the genealogy of Jesus (Matthew 1:5-6,16), demonstrating the love of God for all mankind.

The law provided for Boaz, as a kinsman-redeemer, to reclaim the deceased Elimelech's inheritance, to marry Ruth, and to raise a child to continue the lineage of Elimelech. An unnamed near kinsman (symbolic of the law) had the first legal right to redeem Elimelech's lost inheritance. He refused, saying that to marry Ruth, a Moabite, would *. . . ruin my own inheritance! . . . I can't redeem it!* (Ruth 4:6). The law excluded Moabites from living among the Israelites: *An Ammonite or a Moabite may not enter the LORD's assembly . . . even down to the tenth generation* (Deuteronomy 23:3). The law cannot forgive or make exceptions; it can only expose our sins and condemn us. But, Ruth had forsaken her false gods, confessing her faith in the God of Israel.

Boaz, a type of Christ who assumed the right of "kinsman-redeemer," purchased the property inheritance for Naomi and took Ruth as his wife. After making the necessary arrangements, *Boaz said to the elders . . . You are witnesses today that here and now I buy back everything belonging to Elimelech . . . for Naomi. I also acquire Ruth the Moabi-tess, Mahlon's widow, as my own wife, in order to raise up the deceased man's name on his inheritance, that the name of the deceased man may not disappear* (Ruth 4:9-10; Leviticus 25:25-34,47-48; Deut. 25:5-10).

Through the marriage of Boaz and Ruth, for the third time God united both Jew and Gentile in the ancestry of David and of our Lord Jesus, the Messiah (Matthew 1:5-6; Luke 3:31-32). *There is no Jew or Greek, slave or free, male or female; for you are all one in Christ Jesus. And if you are Christ's, then you are Abraham's seed, heirs according to the promise* (Galatians 3:28-29).

In Today's Reading

Famine; Elimelech and Naomi move from Bethlehem to Moab; Naomi and Ruth return to Bethlehem; marriage of Boaz and Ruth.

Bethlehem, the land of promise was experiencing a severe famine. All Israel knew the Lord's warning: *If you reject . . . My commandments. . . . Your land will not yield its produce, and the trees of the land will not bear their fruit* (Leviticus 26:15-16,19-20).

Perhaps, while standing in their unproductive fields in the Judean hills, Elimelech, his wife Naomi, and their sons Mahlon and Chilion looked down on Moab, where it was reported that all was prosperous. They decided to abandon their God-given inheritance in Bethlehem, and *sojourn in the fields of Moab* (Ruth 1:1-2).

However, unforeseen tragedy struck in the idol-worshiping country of Moab (1:3-5). Elimelech died, then his sons ignored their covenant relationship with God and married Ruth and Orpah, who were Moabite women. Sometime later, Mahlon and Chilion also died. The three childless widows were left without a means of support. *Then* (Naomi) *arose, with her daughters-in-law . . . they went on their way to return to the land of Judah* (1:6-7).

Soon Orpah returned to her earthly securities, *to her people, and to her* (pagan) *gods* (1:15). But Ruth was no longer a Moabite in her heart, for she had forsaken the gods of Moab and confessed her loyalty to the God of Israel, saying: *Your God will be my God* (1:16).

Ruth and Naomi arrived in Bethlehem where Ruth married Boaz.

Ruth became the mother of *Obed. He was the father of Jesse, the father of David* (4:17). The book of Ruth highlights our Lord's lovingkindness in selecting a Moabite woman to become the great-grandmother of David. Ruth is one of three Gentile women mentioned in the genealogy of Jesus (Matthew 1:3,5-6). These historical facts illustrate the love of God for all mankind.

A person is not a Jew who is one outwardly . . . a person is a Jew who is one inwardly, and circumcision is of the heart—by the Spirit, not the letter (Romans 2:28-29).

Thought for Today: We cheat ourselves if we fail to give God our best.

Introduction To The Books Of I & II Samuel

The first book of Samuel covers about 125 years from the birth of Samuel, the last judge of Israel, through the forty-year reign of Saul, the first king. It continues the book of Judges during the transition from a loose federation of the 12 tribes under the rule of judges to a united kingdom.

Samuel grew up in the home of Eli who was judge of Israel and in charge of the tabernacle at Shiloh, the center of Israel's worship.

All Israel from Dan to Beer-sheba knew that Samuel was a faithful prophet of the LORD (I Samuel 3:20; compare Acts 3:24). When Samuel assumed both civil and spiritual leadership, the Israelites were entrenched in apostasy and were politically fragmented. Through his loyalty to the word of God, Samuel restored the nation's moral and spiritual condition to the highest level since the days of Joshua.

Samuel founded the first school of the prophets, faithfully teaching God's word (I Samuel 10:5; 19:20). Because Samuel was a man of prayer and obedient to the word of God (7:5-9; 8:6; 12:17-18,23; 15:11), he was able to unite the tribes of Israel into one nation.

God directed Samuel to anoint as king, Saul, *an impressive young man* (9:2).

II Samuel opens with a brief report of the events surrounding the death of Saul. The tribe of Judah immediately anointed David as their king. However, Abner, captain of Saul's army as well as Saul's cousin (I Samuel 14:50), influenced the other tribes to accept Ish-bosheth, Saul's son, as their king.

After seven years , Joab, David's nephew and military commander, killed Abner. Ish-bosheth was assassinated by two of his own captains. *So all . . . Israel . . . anointed David king over Israel* (II Samuel 5:3).

David . . . reigned. . . . In Hebron . . . over Judah seven years and six months, and . . . 33 years over all Israel and Judah (5:4-5).

David's first conquest as king of the united kingdom was the fortress of Jebus. *David did capture the stronghold of Zion, that is, the city of David* (5:7). The Messianic covenant was then foretold to David by the prophet Nathan: *I will establish the throne of his kingdom forever* (7:13). Later the prophet Isaiah foretold: *The dominion will be vast, and its prosperity will never end. He will reign on the throne of David and over His kingdom to establish it and sustain it with justice and righteousness from now on and forever* (Isaiah 9:7; 11:1; Jeremiah 23:5-6; Ezekiel 37:25).

In Today's Reading

Samuel, the last judge; his mother and her sorrow; her song; Samuel hears the voice of God; all Israel knows Samuel as a prophet.

Near the end of the period of the Judges, we are introduced to Hannah, a godly woman who had lived many years in deep sorrow and humiliation because she could not have children. Since the Hebrew culture considered this a disgrace, *every year . . . she went up to the LORD's house, her rival taunted her . . . Hannah wept and wouldn't eat. . . . Making a vow she pleaded, O LORD of Hosts, if You will take notice of Your handmaid's affliction and remember me and not forget me and give Your handmaid a son, then I will give him to the LORD all the days of his life* (I Samuel 1:7,11). Although Hannah had prayed for a son for many years, she did not give up. *While she was praying in the LORD's presence, Eli* (the priest and judge) *watched her mouth. Hannah was speaking in her heart, and although her lips were moving, her voice couldn't be heard, so Eli concluded that she was drunk. . . . Eli scolded her* (1:12-14). Although she was wrongfully accused, Hannah did not become angry, but graciously and humbly answered Eli: *Oh no, my lord . . . I'm a woman whose spirit is troubled. I haven't had any wine or beer; I've been pouring out my soul before the LORD. Don't think of me as a wicked woman; I've been praying from the depth of my anguish and provocation* (1:15-16).

It was Eli's responsibility to rebuke those who did evil. In this case, Eli's misjudgment was truly a test of the genuineness of Hannah's humility. Had she reacted in indignation and anger toward Eli for being so judgmental, she would have returned home with a bitter attitude. However, instead of being angry, she entreated Eli, telling him of her sorrow. *Eli responded, Go in peace and may the God of Israel grant the petition that you've requested from Him* (1:17). Hannah returned home rejoicing.

Hannah lived centuries before the New Testament experience of being filled with the Holy Spirit; and yet we see her maintaining a godly attitude. The acceptance of an undeserved rebuke in a right spirit often brings an answer to our prayer.

Therefore, God's chosen ones, holy and loved, put on heartfelt compassion, kindness, humility, gentleness, and patience (Colossians 3:12).

Thought for Today: Children are not likely to worship the Lord if their parents are not living in obedience to the will of God.

In Today's Reading

Consequences of sin; death of Eli; ark of the covenant taken; Israel defeated; ark is returned.

The Philistines lived on the coastal plains of the Mediterranean Sea, on the Israelites' southwestern border. They were a hostile people who declared war. *As the battle intensified, Israel was defeated by the Philistines* (I Samuel 4:2). In desperation, *the elders of Israel asked, Why did the LORD defeat us today ? . . . Let's bring the ark of the LORD's covenant from Shiloh. Then He will go with us and save us from the hand of our enemies* (4:3-5).

Because of a lack of spiritual insight, the Israelites' hopes were on the ark, not on God who alone has power to save (Exodus 25:10-22). The Israelites marched into battle against the Philistines, confident of victory. But the two sons of Eli who carried the ark were evil men (I Samuel 2:12).

Eli was old and blind and sat near the tabernacle anxious to hear the outcome of the battle. A messenger returned and reported: *Israel has fled from the Philistines, and there was a great slaughter. . . . Also . . . Hophni and Phinehas, died, and the ark of God has been taken! When the messenger mentioned the ark of God, Eli fell backward . . . and he died* (4:17-18).

With the death of Eli, Samuel came to the forefront of both Israel's civil and spiritual life. *Samuel told them . . . set your hearts on the LORD, and serve only Him. Then, He will rescue you from the hand of the Philistines. . . . Samuel then said, Gather all Israel at Mizpah, and I'll pray to the LORD on your behalf. . . . They confessed, We've sinned against the LORD* (7:3,5-6). When the Philistines learned that the Israelites were worshiping God, they assumed it was an opportune time to attack. *Samuel was still offering the burnt offering when the Philistines drew near to fight against Israel. The LORD thundered with a powerful blast against the Philistines that day and . . . they were defeated by Israel* (7:10-13).

The satisfying truth is that God works through men and women of faith, like Samuel, who display their trust in Him by their obedience to His word. *Let us hold on to the confession of our hope without wavering, for He who promised is faithful* (Hebrews 10:23).

Thought for Today: The most profitable part of our day is the time we spend in God's presence, praying and reading His word.

In Today's Reading

Samuel's evil sons; Israel demands a king; Saul chosen; Saul begins as a humble ruler, defeats the Ammonites, and delivers Jabesh-gilead.

During the history of the judges, Samuel accomplished more as a spiritual leader than any other judge. *When Samuel grew old, he appointed his sons as judges . . . . However, his sons . . . took bribes, and perverted justice* (I Samuel 8:1-3). Eventually, *all the elders of Israel . . . went to Samuel . . . . They said . . . you're old, and your sons haven't lived according to your ways. Therefore, appoint a king for us, like all . . . nations. . . . Samuel considered their demand evil* (8:4-6). *However, the LORD* said: *It isn't you they have rejected* (but)*they have rejected Me as their king* (8:7). Samuel anointed Saul king in Ramah as the Lord had directed him. After a brief time, *Samuel summoned the people to the LORD at Mizpah. He said . . . You have rejected your God, the One who saves you from all your dilemmas* (10:17-19). He then presented Saul to them as *the one whom the LORD has chosen. . . . And all the people shouted, Long live the king!* (10:24).

The first test of the new king came when Saul was told that Nahash the Ammonite king had put his army in position to attack. The Ammonites had not attacked the Israelites since Jephthah, a hero of faith (Hebrews 11:32), had defeated them many years before (Deuteronomy 2:19; 23:3-4; Judges 3:13; 10:7; 11:5). Responding to this threat, Saul called together men from all the tribes of Israel to be his soldiers.

Saul led the Israelites in a spectacular victory. As he finished his first battle, he shouted: *Today the LORD has provided deliverance in Israel* (I Samuel 11:13).

Saul had a good beginning, but pride and self-will soon became his way of life that resulted in a succession of failures. This illustrates the temptation that often follows success, the deception of pride that inevitably leads to a self-centered life (Matthew 16:24). The assumption that we have the ability to make decisions as to what is best for our lives and no longer need to pray for guidance is a reminder that Jesus said: *You can do nothing* (that has eternal value) *without Me* (John 15:5).

Thought for Today: There are many ways in which God works in our lives, but most often it is simply through ordinary circumstances.

In Today's Reading

The people have their king; other battles with the Philistines; priest's office usurped by Saul.

Saul, the first king of Israel, was a man of great ability, but he had a fatal flaw. Perhaps three years after Saul became king, his first great failure occurred when he trusted his own judgment and not the Lord. *The Philistines had gathered to fight against Israel* (with) *30,000 chariots, 6,000 horsemen, and troops as numerous as the sand on the seashore* (I Samuel 13:5). The Israelites were greatly outnumbered and, humanly speaking, they appeared doomed to defeat.

Realizing the military might of the Philistines, the majority of Saul's army *hid themselves in caves. . . . Saul registered the troops who were with him about 600 men* (13:6,15). Saul realized that their only hope was in God. *He waited seven days . . . but Samuel didn't come. . . . So Saul. . . . offered the burnt offering. Just as he finished . . . Samuel arrived* (13:8-10). Saul's decision to assume the role of priest violated the word of God. Saul first made an excuse: *When I saw that the troops were deserting me . . . I thought, the Philistines will now descend on me . . . and I haven't sought the LORD's favor. So I forced myself to offer the burnt offering* (13:11-12).

The burnt offering symbolized surrender to God; but, when Saul assumed the position of priest, the sacrifice became an abomination to the Lord (15:22-23; see Numbers 16; Proverbs 21:27).What seemed to Saul a tardiness in Samuel's arrival was, in reality, a test of Saul's obedience to God. Samuel spoke bluntly to *Saul, You've been foolish. You have not kept the command which the LORD your God gave you* (I Samuel 13:13-14).

Though we may consider Saul's disobedience of little consequence, the Lord said that what Saul did was a sin in the sight of the Lord. How easily we can deceive ourselves into believing that God will be pleased with our accomplishments "for Him" even though we obey only what pleases us.

We are all tempted at times to disregard what the Bible states is wrong, assuming that circumstances justify it. Saul's presumption demonstrates the importance of always obeying God's word. *For the LORD gives wisdom; from His mouth come knowledge and understanding* (Proverbs 2:6).

Thought for Today: A true servant of the Lord willingly follows his Master's instructions without exception.

In Today's Reading

Saul's foolish oath; Saul commanded to destroy all Amalekites; he sins by sparing the enemy king; David anointed king; Saul rejected as king.

Few kings in biblical history were blessed with as many advantages as Saul. But he soon forgot the source of his success. He became more concerned with impressing the people than with pleasing the Lord. It was not long before Saul exposed his true character when Samuel came to him and said: *The LORD of Hosts says: I witnessed what the Amalekites did to the Israelites . . . as they were coming up from Egypt. . . .* (You must) *completely destroy everything they have. . . . Kill men and women, children and infants, oxen and sheep, camels and donkeys* (I Samuel 15:2-3).

Saul defeated the Amalekites and then erected a memorial to himself at Carmel to commemorate his victory (15:12). He then returned. When Samuel met him, *Saul responded to Samuel . . . I brought back Agag, king of Amalek, and I completely destroyed the Amalekites* (15:20). Although there had been a great victory, Saul had disobeyed the command of God by "sparing" the Amalekite king. He tried to shift the blame by saying: *The troops took sheep and cattle . . . to sacrifice to the LORD your God at Gilgal* (15:21). Saul seemed blind to his own disobedience. To *utterly destroy* would have been a true burnt offering to God. But, when people kept the best, it was for themselves to eat at their next festival.

Saul was more concerned about his public image before the elders of Israel than with his right relationship with God. *Then Samuel said, Does the LORD take pleasure in . . . sacrifices as much as in obeying the LORD ? Know this: to obey is better than a sacrifice, to pay attention is better than the fat of rams. . . . You have rejected the word of the LORD, He has rejected you as king* (15:22-23). Saul finally confessed his partial obedience, saying: *I was afraid of the people, I obeyed them. . . . I have sinned. Please honor me now before the elders . . . and before Israel* (15:24,30).

There is nothing so deceitful to one's heart than acknowledging Christ as Savior and Lord, while continuing a self-centered life of sin.

Jesus said . . . If you continue in My word, you really are My disciples (John 8:31).

Thought for Today: We form opinions about people, but only God knows their hearts.

In Today's Reading

David kills Goliath; Saul appoints David captain of his guard; he marries Saul's daughter Michal; Jonathan's loyalty to David.

The Philistines continually threatened the kingdom of Israel. *The conflict with the Philistines was fierce all of Saul's days, so whenever Saul saw any strong or valiant man, he enlisted him* (I Samuel 14:52). Early in Saul's reign, the giant warrior Goliath challenged the Israelite army to send a man to fight him and let the outcome of their fight decide who won the war. Apparently Saul was unwilling to accept his challenge.

But, when young David came into the camp and heard Goliath's taunts, he agreed to fight him and *said to the Philistine, You come against me with a sword, a spear, and a javelin, but I come against you in the name of the LORD of Hosts, the God of Israel's armies, whom you have defied. This very day the LORD will hand you over to me. Today, I'll strike you down. . . . Then all the world will know that Israel has a God* (17:45-46).

Following his spectacular victory over Goliath, David was welcomed into the palace of King Saul, was made his trusted captain of the guard, and soon became his son-in-law by marrying the king's daughter Michal (18:27). We are not told how much time passed after David was welcomed into the king's court until Saul was determined to destroy him. But, when Saul heard women singing David's praises, he became exceedingly jealous and attempted to kill David by throwing a javelin at him as he was playing his harp (18:10-11).

David fled and escaped with the help of his wife Michal. *He went to Samuel at Ramah and told him everything Saul had done to him* (19:12,18). He once enjoyed acceptance in the king's palace but now was reduced to hiding in caves. The difficulties, handicaps, and suffering in life are permitted by the Lord to develop godly character and enable us to accomplish His purposes. Like David, we are put to the test to see if we will remain faithful and prove worthy of our high calling. We each are accountable for the effect trials, suffering, or handicaps will have on us. They can be used to develop faith in the Lord, or we can become bitter and revengeful, blaming God and others for our troubles. *It is necessary to pass through many troubles on our way into the kingdom of God* (Acts 14:22).

Thought for Today: Faith is developed as we trust the Lord when we face difficult disappointments.

In Today's Reading

Saul attempts to kill David; Jonathan's covenant with David; David's flight to Nob; David flees for his life to Gath in Philistine territory.

David became a national hero and, as time passed, King Saul became increasingly jealous of his popularity. *Saul ordered his son Jonathan and all his servants to kill David. Saul's son Jonathan, however, liked David very much so he told David: My father Saul is seeking to kill you. . . . Stay in a secret place and hide yourself* (I Samuel 19:1-2).

Prior to this, Saul had manipulated circumstances to expose David to the Philistines, hoping they would kill him (18:25). *Jonathan spoke well of David to his father Saul. The king shouldn't sin against his servant. . . . He took his life in his hands when he struck down the Philistine, and the LORD performed a great act of deliverance for all Israel. You saw it and rejoiced. So why would you sin against innocent blood by killing David for no reason?* (19:4-5).

Saul had become violent, with an uncontrolled temper. He considered any opposition as treason. Jonathan revealed remarkable spiritual insight and courage when he confronted his father the king in defense of David. The risk was very real and, in a fit of rage, Saul denounced his son and, on another occasion, he attempted to kill Jonathan (20:33).

Jonathan could have avoided any risk to himself if he had decided not to get involved in defending David. To defend an innocent person from slander or harm's way, whatever the cost to self, is to remain faithful to biblical principles and do what is morally right.

We too may find ourselves in situations where people whom we know are being threatened, accused, maligned, intimidated, or taken advantage of. We are then faced with the decision of whether or not to get involved. We dare not be an accomplice to their evil by remaining silent, but must act as Jonathan did. There is a direct connection between what we truly believe and how we behave. We need to *be doers of the word and not hearers only, deceiving yourselves* (James 1:22).

I tell you, love your enemies, and pray for those who persecute you, so that you may be sons of your Father in heaven (Matthew 5:44-45).

Thought for Today: The Bible was not given to merely inform us, but to transform us.

In Today's Reading

David's escape; Saul murders the priests of Nob; David protects the Israelites in Keilah; David will not kill Saul.

After Saul's third attempt to murder David (I Samuel 18:10-17; 19:10), *he also struck down Nob, the city of the priests, with the sword both men and women, children and infants, oxen, donkeys, and sheep, with the sword* (22:19). It was located just northeast of Jerusalem, where the sacred vessels had been kept by the priests since the destruction of Shiloh. Ahimelech the priest had given David food and allowed him to take the sword that had belonged to Goliath.This was reported to Saul in Gibeah by Doeg, an Edomite servant. In a rage of anger, *the king sent messengers to summon Ahimelech the priest . . . and his father's whole family, who were priests in Nob. All of them came to the king* (22:11). Then Saul accused Ahimelech of conspiracy. *In reply, Ahimelech asked the king, Who among all your servants is as faithful as David? He is the king's son-in-law, captain of your bodyguard, and honored in your house* (22:14).

Blinded by jealous hate, Saul ordered the execution of all the priests and their families. *Then the king said to the guards standing by him, Turn and kill the priests of the LORD because they sided with David. For they knew he was fleeing, but they didn't tell me. But the king's servants wouldn't lift their hands to execute the priests of the LORD* (22:17). Without hesitation, *Doeg the Edomite . . . killed 85 men who wore linen ephods. . . . However, one . . . escaped. His name was Abiathar, and he fled to David* (22:18-20).

There are times in the lives of most Christians when everything seems hopeless, as it must have for David who was in hiding for many years. In fact, we all experience times when we need to be encouraged about ourselves, our gifts and talents, our work, our children, or even our relationship with the Lord.

This was also true of David, who received spiritual direction and comfort from Abiathar and prophets such as Gad (22:5).

The angel of the LORD encamps around those who fear Him, and rescues them (Psalms 34:7).

Thought for Today: Loving our enemies means sharing God's love with those who need it most.

In Today's Reading

Death of Samuel; Nabal, a wicked landowner, dies;
David marries his widow Abigail; Saul's pursuit of David.

Samuel was one of the greatest spiritual giants in Israel's history and is listed as one of the heroes of the faith (Hebrews 11:32), but just one sentence records the death of this grand, old prophet. The all-wise God, who controls the universe, knew what was best at this treacherous time in Israel's history. *Samuel died, and all Israel gathered together to mourn for him; they buried him by his home in Ramah.* Because of Saul, David could not attend the funeral, but he *went down to the Wilderness of Paran* (I Samuel 25:1).

We are tempted at times to think that death has come to the wrong person or has come at the wrong time, especially when a child is left without a mother, or when children die at a young age. Familiar as we are with death, the ways of God regarding it may seem strange to us. But, without a doubt, God never abandons His children. He leads us to look beyond our grief and trust in His wisdom and His tender love to comfort our broken spirit, and He said: *Your heart must not be troubled. Believe in God; believe also in Me* (John 14:1).

At times we all need comfort. This is especially true during experiences of distress and grief when a loved one dies. Those of us who have lost loved ones know what a word of compassion can mean. As we see others suffering, let us also remember that our heavenly Father has said: *Comfort, comfort My people! says your God* (Isaiah 40:1).

Last, but not least, the death of loved ones makes heaven all the more desirable for us who remain. *In the sight of the LORD the death of His faithful ones is precious* (Psalms 116:15).

Death for the Christian is a promotion from this world's suffering, and a welcome home by our wonderful Lord. Soon, *He will wipe away every tear from their eyes. Death will exist no longer; grief, crying, and pain will exist no longer, because the previous things have passed away* (Revelation 21:4).

Thought for Today: At this moment, pray for someone you know who seems discouraged.

In Today's Reading

David stays in Philistine territory; Saul is troubled over the Philistine army and consults a witch who claims to contact the dead.

After Samuel became judge, the Philistines were so badly defeated because of his prayer meeting at Mizpah that they *did not venture into Israel's territory. . . . The LORD's hand was against the Philistines all of Samuel's days* (I Samuel 7:13). But, *the conflict with the Philistines was fierce all of Saul's days* (14:52).

In the final year of Saul's reign, *the Philistines brought all their military units together at Aphek* (29:1). Saul panicked when he realized the size and power of the Philistine armies that were ready to attack. Could Saul forget that Samuel had said: *Because you have rejected the word of the LORD, He has rejected you as king* (15:23)? Out of jealousy, Saul also had attempted to kill David and forced him into exile. Saul was desperate and *inquired of the LORD* (28:6). Since he had murdered the priests of God, how could he expect an answer ? How pathetic it is to see Saul riding through the night, frantically seeking counsel from a fortune-teller in Endor. He knew that mediums, spiritualists, witches, and fortune-tellers are *detestable to the LORD* (Deuteronomy 18:10-12). In fact, Saul had banished them from the land (I Samuel 28:3). However, the fortune-teller was no help. Instead his fears increased even more after the appearance of Samuel, who said: *The LORD has turned away from you and has become your enemy, why are you inquiring of me?* (28:16). The next day Saul, along with Jonathan and his brothers, was killed in battle. Saul reaped what he had sown.

Saul's worst enemy was himself. He had lived a self-serving life. Power, wealth, popularity, and talents are often great hindrances to a spiritual life. Some seek guidance from psychics, fortune-tellers, palm readers, and other demon-controlled people, rather than crying out to the Lord in times of great distress and relying upon Him.

True success is the result of seeking the Lord's will through reading His word, while at the same time praying to the Lord for guidance. *He does not withhold the good from those who live with integrity* (Psalms 84:11).

Thought for Today: Ignoring God's word leads to deception.

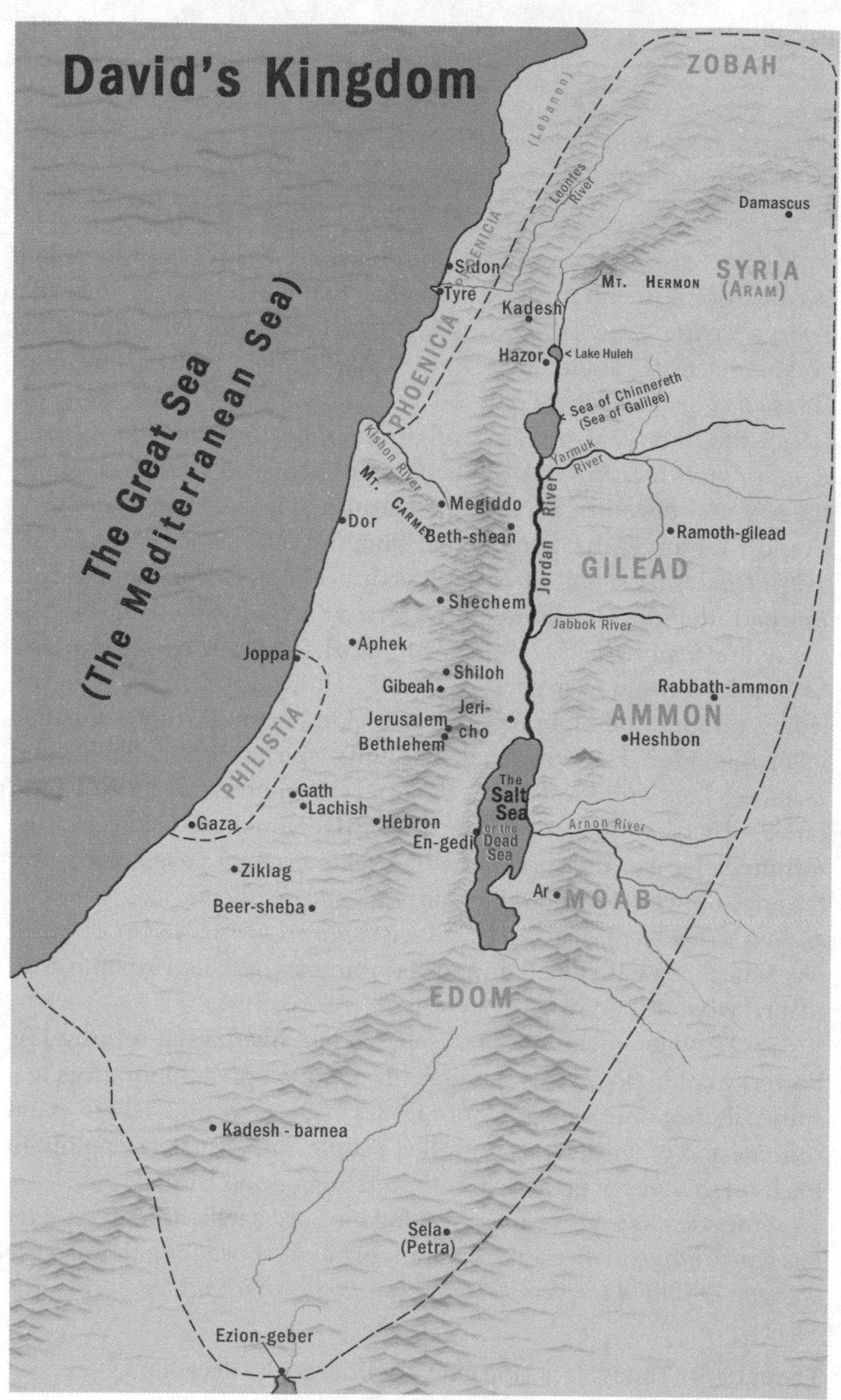
David's Kingdom
The Great Sea
(The Mediterranean Sea)
ZOBAH
(Lebanon)
Leontes River
Damascus
PHOENICIA
Sidon
Tyre
MT. HERMON
SYRIA
(ARAM)
Kadesh
Hazor
< Lake Huleh
Sea of Chinnereth
(Sea of Galilee)
Yarmuk River
Kishon River
MT. CARMEL
Megiddo
Dor
Beth-shean
Jordan River
Ramoth-gilead
GILEAD
Shechem
Jabbok River
Aphek
Joppa
Shiloh
Gibeah
Rabbath-ammon
Jeri-
cho
Jerusalem
Bethlehem
AMMON
Heshbon
PHILISTIA
The
Salt
Sea
or the
Dead
Sea
Gath
Lachish
Hebron
En-gedi
Gaza
Arnon River
Ziklag
Ar
MOAB
Beer-sheba
EDOM
Kadesh - barnea
Sela
(Petra)
Ezion-geber

In Today's Reading

Saul killed in battle; David mourns the deaths of Saul and Jonathan; David crowned king of Judah; Ish-bosheth made king of Israel.

Saul had driven David from his family, his wife, and his friends, and into exile as a fugitive far from the palace. An Amalekite nomad, who carried in his hand the crown of Saul, mistakenly thought David would be pleased that he had executed him. The Amalekite could not conceive of David not rejoicing in the death of such an enemy. But, David *mourned, wept, and fasted until the evening for those who had fallen by the sword. . . .* (saying) *The beauty of Israel lies slain upon your heights. How the mighty have fallen! Don't tell it in Gath; don't announce it in the streets of Ashkelon. Or the daughters of the Philistines will rejoice* (II Samuel 1:12,19-20).

The world delights in the failures of Christians. Surely no Christian should ever be involved in gossip about the failures of fellow Christians. *If anyone thinks he is religious, without controlling his tongue but deceiving his heart, his religion is useless* (James 1:26).

Now that Saul was dead, who would reign in his place? Israel was without a king. David had been anointed long ago by Samuel the prophet to be the next king of Israel (I Samuel 16:13). However, Abner, Saul's cousin and the powerful commander of Saul's army, was determined to retain his position. He persuaded the elders of Israel to put Saul's son Ish-bosheth on the throne over the 10 tribes. David could have felt justified to face Abner in battle for his right as God's chosen successor. Instead, *David inquired of the LORD, Should I go up to one of the towns of Judah? The LORD answered him, Go. Then David asked, Where should I go? To Hebron, the LORD directed. . . . Then the men of Judah came, and there they anointed David king over the house of Judah* (II Samuel 2:1,4).

How prone we are to jump at opportunities for personal advancement rather than seek God for His plan for our lives. But we need not fight for our rights. David prayed for God's will to be done in His way and at His time. It is comforting for Christians to know that: *Abundant peace belongs to those who love Your instruction; nothing makes them stumble* (Psalms 119:165).

Thought for Today: Spiritual victory is not dependent on human strength or reasoning, but on submission to the Holy Spirit.

In Today's Reading

Abner deserts Ish-bosheth to join David; Abner murdered by Joab; Ish-bosheth murdered; David declared King of all Israel; the city of Jebus (Jerusalem) is captured.

Following the death of Saul, Abner, the powerful commander of Saul's armies, proclaimed Saul's son Ish-bosheth king of Israel. He then controlled the puppet-king and his kingdom.

About seven years later, there was a fierce quarrel between Abner and Ish-bosheth (II Samuel 3:6-11). Because of this, *Abner sent messengers as his representatives to say to David . . . Make your covenant with me, and you may be certain I'll side with you to turn all Israel over to you* (3:12-16). Abner contacted the elders of Israel, reminding them: *Concerning David, the LORD has spoken, Through My servant David I will save My people Israel from the hand of the Philistines and from the hand of all their enemies* (3:18). A short time after Abner met with David, he was murdered by Joab, the commander of David's army, and Ish-bosheth was assassinated by two of his own guards.

The elders of Israel came to the king at Hebron. . . . and . . . anointed David king over Israel (5:3). The time had come for David to move his capital from Hebron to the central location where the Jebusites held a stronghold in the heart of the promised land. *The king and his men marched to Jerusalem . . . and. . . . David did capture . . . Zion . . . the City of David* (5:6-7).

There could never have been a temple for the dwelling place of God in the place that He had chosen until the Jebusites, who held the central position in the promised land, were cast out. This *stronghold of Zion* is symbolic of strongholds which lie deep within our minds and which may not be known to anyone, either by our conduct or in our conversation. They depict secret thoughts that keep Christ from becoming Lord of our lives. The secret strongholds may not conflict with giving the Lord our time, talents, or tithes. The *fleshly mind* (Colossians 2:18), with its physical impulses subtly demands to remain within our hearts. As we read God's word daily, we will be filled with *the knowledge of His will in all wisdom and spiritual understanding* (Colossians 1:9).

Thought for Today: Genuine devotion to God brings eternal rewards.

In Today's Reading

David brings the ark of God into Jerusalem; covenant of God with David; David's prayer of thanksgiving; his victories; David's kindness to Mephibosheth.

David was now king of the united kingdom. He desired to honor God by bringing the ark of the covenant, the dwelling place of God, to Jerusalem. It would be the religious and political capital of David's kingdom. For about 75 years, during most of Samuel's leadership and during Saul's 40-year reign, the ark had remained with Abinadab at Kirjath-jearim.

David assembled all the choice men in Israel, 30,000 in all. . . . to bring . . . the ark of God (to Jerusalem). . . . *They set the ark of God on a new cart* as the Philistines had done many years before, and proceeded toward Jerusalem with great rejoicing. . . . *Uzzah and Ahio, sons of Abinadab, were guiding the new cart* (II Samuel 6:1-4). David made the procession a national day of rejoicing to impress all Israel with the importance of putting God in the center of their nation.

David often *inquired of the LORD* about what to do (II Samuel 2:1), but he saw no need to pray about moving the ark to Jerusalem.

Uzzah, attempting to keep the ark from toppling off the cart, *reached out to the ark of God and took hold of it because the oxen had stumbled. . . . and God struck him down. . . . He died there alongside the ark of God* (6:6-7). Undoubtedly, David was humiliated (6:8). Why would God allow this to happen? David had overlooked two very important instructions in the word of God: The ark must be carried by poles on the shoulders of the priests, and the penalty for touching the ark was death (Exodus 25:10-15; Numbers 3:30-31; 4:15; 7:9; I Kings 8:7-8).

This incident should teach us that it is a serious error to believe that, as long as a person is sincere, it makes no difference what he believes or does. It should also teach us the importance of knowing God's word: *Be diligent to present yourself approved to God, a worker who doesn't need to be ashamed, correctly teaching the word of truth* (II Timothy 2:15).

Finally, pray for us, brothers, that the Lord's message may spread rapidly and be honored, just as it was with you (II Thessalonians 3:1).

Thought for Today: Is your chief concern that God be honored? Then tell your friends to read His directions.

In Today's Reading

The Ammonites and the Syrians are defeated; Bathsheba and David; Nathan's parable and David's repentance; birth of Solomon.

David, King of Israel, had never lost a war and had grown accustomed to getting what he wanted. *In the spring when kings march out to war, David sent Joab out with his officers and the troops of all Israel. . . . but David remained in Jerusalem* (II Samuel 11:1). Satan always has something or someone to attract us when we are in a position to gratify our fleshly desires. He always presents sin as both attractive and satisfying.

For David, his spiritual defeat began with a look of lust at beautiful Bathsheba. David knew that adultery was a wicked sin against God and was punishable by death (Leviticus 20:10). But, *David sent messengers to get her, and when she came to him, he lay with her. . . . Afterwards, she returned home* (II Samuel 11:4). One sin usually leads to unforeseen complications and to other evils.

From the moment David first lusted after Bathsheba until their marriage, no one interfered with their pleasure. However, about one year later, Nathan the prophet boldly confronted David: *Why . . . have you despised the word of the LORD by doing . . . evil?* (12:9). Because of David's adultery, Nathan foretold: *Now, therefore, the sword will never depart from your house because you despised Me and took the wife of Uriah the Hittite to be your own wife. This is what the LORD says, I am about to cause trouble to rise up against you from your own household: I will take your wives before your very eyes and give them to another, and he will lie with them openly* (12:10-11). Brokenhearted in his spirit, David confessed: *I have sinned against the LORD. Then Nathan replied to David, The LORD has taken away your sin; you won't die* (12:13).

For the entire last half of his reign, until his death, David's sorrows and sufferings never ceased from just one night of yielding to his lust.

In addition to facing God on Judgment Day, no one can avoid the bitter consequences of yielding to the temptation of lust. Because of David's sincere repentance, as recorded in Psalm 51, God forgave him. But forgiveness does not remove the results: *Don't be deceived: God is not mocked. For whatever a man sows he will also reap* (Galatians 6:7).

Thought for Today: We must live in the world, but we don't have to live by its standards.

In Today's Reading

Rape, incest, and murder occur amidst David's children;
Absalom flees to Geshur in Syria (Aram); Absalom's return.

Absalom's sister Tamar was the beautiful daughter of King David. David's oldest son Amnon was about 20 years of age when he pretended to be sick and asked his father David to send his half-sister Tamar to prepare him a meal (I Samuel 25:43; II Samuel 3:2; I Chronicles 3:1).

When she approached him so he could eat, he grabbed her and said to her, Come lie with me, my sister! . . . she replied, Don't humiliate me – such a thing should never be done in Israel! Don't commit this outrage! . . . he overpowered her and lay with her. Afterwards, Amnon hated Tamar with intense hatred. . . . He said to her, Get up! Get out! (II Samuel 13:11-15). After his brief moment of lustful gratification, he forced her out of his home and locked the door, *so Tamar lived as a desolate woman in the house of her brother Absalom* (13:20).

When David learned of Amnon's deception and wicked sin against his daughter, *he was furious. Absalom didn't say anything to Amnon.* But he *hated Amnon for having disgraced his sister Tamar* (13:21-22). Amnon was David's firstborn son and heir to the throne. David took no legal action, even though the law of God demanded the death sentence for rape (Leviticus 20:17).

Two full years later . . . Absalom invited all the king's sons to a great feast. *Now Absalom commanded his young men . . . When I order you, Strike Amnon! then kill him. . . . So Absalom's young men did to Amnon just as Absalom had commanded* (II Samuel 13:23-29). We should note that, with Amnon's death, he no longer stood in the way of Absalom becoming the next king. Absalom fled for safety to Syria (Aram) where he lived with his grandfather for three years (13:37-38).

A parent can experience no greater suffering than to see his own sin repeated in his children's lives. We cannot undo past sins, failures, and wasted time, but Christians are assured that, *if anyone does sin, we have an advocate with the Father – Jesus Christ the righteous One* (I John 2:1).

Thought for Today: *Sin is a disgrace to any people* (Proverbs 14:34).

In Today's Reading

Absalom wins over national leaders; he leads a revolt and overthrow of David; David flees in fear of his son; Absalom's death.

After Absalom had been in exile three years (II Samuel 13:34-38), Joab, commander-in-chief of David's army, initiated a clever plan which persuaded David to bring Absalom home.

About two years after Absalom had returned from exile (14:28), with an arrogant, shameless, and defiant attitude, he demanded that Joab arrange to have the king see him. David forgave Absalom, who then began an ambitious and deceptive scheme to take over his father's throne: *Absalom provided himself with a chariot, horses, and 50 men to run before him. He would rise early and stand beside the road leading to the city gate.When anyone had a grievance to bring before the king* he pretended a deep concern. *Absalom would say to him, Look, your claims are good and right, but the king doesn't have a deputy justice to listen to you. . . . If only someone would appoint me judge in the land . . . anyone who had a grievance or dispute could come to me, and I would make sure he received justice* (15:1-4).

Soon the shocking news reached David that *the hearts of the men of Israel are with Absalom!* (15:13). During this time, he had no thought of self-pity, bitterness, or revenge. David was confident that his life and the destiny of Jerusalem were in the sovereign control of God.

It is sad to read that David, the brokenhearted old king, left Jerusalem, running barefoot down the rocky, rugged hills to the Brook Kidron and up the Mount of Olives, weeping, fleeing Jerusalem in fear of his own beloved son (15:30).

Committing himself to God, David prayed: *O LORD . . . please, turn the counsel of Ahithophel into foolishness!* (15:31). Then, he sent Hushai his longtime friend (15:37; I Chronicles 27:33) back to Jerusalem with instructions as to how he could become Absalom's adviser, and thus refute Ahithophel's counsel (II Samuel 15:33-35).

Wicked men are often used by our holy God to correct those whom He loves. David later confessed: *Before I was afflicted I went astray, but now I keep Your word* (Psalms 119:67).

Thought for Today: In contrast to the accepted immoral principles of the world, the word of God reveals the vileness of sin.

In Today's Reading

Absalom follows advice of Hushai; David's troops battle Absalom and his followers; Absalom killed by Joab; David weeps in bitter grief.

David's adviser Ahithophel was far from being the person David believed him to be. It often takes a crisis to reveal who our true friends are. Ahithophel was invited by Absalom to join his conspiracy. *The conspiracy grew strong, and the number of people supporting Absalom continued to increase* (II Samuel 15:12). Since David was old, Ahithophel deserted him and joined Absalom. He revealed his true character with the words "me" and "I." *Let **me** choose 12,000 men, and **I'll** set out in pursuit of David . . . . **I'll** hit his camp. . . . **I'll** strike down only the king, and **I'll** bring all the people back to you. . . .* Then *all the people will be at peace* (17:1-3). At first, *Absalom and all the elders of Israel thought this proposal seemed good* (17:4). Apparently, Absalom realized that he would be in a secondary position to Ahithophel. David had prayed: *O LORD . . . turn the counsel of Ahithophel into foolishness!* (15:31).

David had sent his friend Hushai to join Absalom. Undoubtedly, his coming appealed to Absalom's ego, for he now had gained his father's two top advisers. Ahithophel assumed Absalom would accept his plan. But it offended Absalom as well as Amasa. This led them to consider the counsel of Hushai, who reminded Absalom that *all Israel knows that your father and the valiant men with him are warriors* (17:10).

As Absalom considered the possibility of losing his first battle, he realized this could produce panic and the loss of his followers. Hushai advised *that all Israel, from Dan to Beer-sheba . . . be wholly gathered to you* (Absalom) *and that you personally go into battle* (17:8-11). This appealed to Absalom, and gave David and his men time to prepare for the battle that led to Absalom's death. The Bible clearly warns that *pride comes before destruction, and an arrogant spirit before a fall* (Proverbs 16:18). Undoubtedly, Hushai's advice was an answer to David's prayer.

Pity the ignorant who are unaware of the "Unseen Presence" of God, who defends those who trust in Him (Hebrews 4:13; Psalms 40:17).

Exaltation does not come from the east, the west, or the desert, for God is the judge: He brings down one and exalts another (Psalms 75:6-7).

Thought for Today: No one can defeat God's purposes for you.

In Today's Reading

Joab rebukes David; he returns; Sheba revolts and is killed.

Absalom was a traitor who was determined to destroy his father, so that he could be king. The battle ended when Joab killed Absalom.

David's soldiers returned expecting a celebration; instead they heard the king weeping: *O Absalom, my son, my son!* (II Samuel 19:4). In deep sorrow, David ignored his loyal followers who had defended him. The victory that day was turned into mourning and the soldiers slipped away *like people . . . humiliated for having fled in battle* (19:3).

David had faced many sorrows throughout his life. When Bathsheba's first child became sick, David prayed and fasted. Then, when he received word the child had died, David confidently said: *I'll go to him, but he'll never return to me* (12:23). David knew heaven would be all the more precious because his child was with the Lord. But David expressed no hope that he would see Absalom in heaven.

David probably felt that, if Joab had only given Absalom one more chance, perhaps he would have turned from his wicked ways. But, had he lived, he would have been in fierce competition with Solomon, God's choice to take David's place as king.

All of us, at times, are responsible for the adversities and sorrows we experience. It is also natural to condemn ourselves for our faults and failures, or even to blame others for the things that "happen."

All of us also go through experiences beyond our control. Like David, we can grieve too long over what might have been. If we are out of the will of God, we need to repent of our sins, ask God to forgive us, and be like Paul, who said: *Forgetting what is behind. . . . I pursue as my goal the prize promised by God's heavenly call* (Philippians 3:13-14).

In our darkest moments, we all need friends to remind us to trust the Lord. We need to be a friend who can share comforting words with the despondent sufferer. By God's grace, we should encourage them to become involved in a local church where others can help deepen and nurture their faith in the love of God *since we are members of His body. . . . I am talking about Christ and the church* (Ephesians 5:30,32).

Thought for Today: Christ heals the brokenhearted who trust Him.

In Today's Reading

God punishes Israel with a 3-year famine; seven members of Saul's family put to death; victories over Philistine giants.

The days of harvest had once again come, but there was nothing to eat because *there was a famine for three successive years* (II Samuel 21:1). The famine expressed the judgment of God: *If you do not obey the LORD your God by keeping and following all His commands. . . . The heavens above your head will be bronze, and the earth beneath you will be iron* (Deuteronomy 28:15,23).

It is assumed that this three-year famine occurred during the early years of David's reign, even though it is recorded here more than 25 years later. Recognizing the famine as the judgment of God, *David inquired of the LORD. The LORD answered, It is on account of Saul . . . because he killed the Gibeonites* (II Samuel 21:1). Saul had violated the covenant that Israel had made with the Gibeonites 400 years earlier. That treaty was still sacred because the covenant had been sworn to in the name of God (Joshua 9:3,15-27).

The surviving Gibeonites did not ask David for silver or gold to compensate for the murder of loved ones or for the loss of their property (II Samuel 21:4). From their many years of association with the Israelites, the Gibeonites knew the commandment of God. *Do not accept a ransom for the life of a murderer who is guilty of a capital crime. He must surely be put to death* (Numbers 35:31). Disobedience to this command meant Israel had been defiled. The Gibeonites asked permission to hang seven men who were descendants of Saul.

Therefore, David was responsible before God to deliver the seven men to the Gibeonites. An exception was made for the crippled son of Jonathan, Mephibosheth (II Samuel 21:7; I Samuel 20:14-17; 23:16-18).

Throughout the Old Testament, we learn the value God has placed on keeping our promises. Let us recognize the danger of disregarding our moral and spiritual responsibilities. In God's eyes, not even the king of a nation is above its laws. *The LORD watches over the way of the righteous, but the way of the wicked leads to ruin* (Psalms 1:1-6).

Thought for Today: God expects us to keep our promises. Can you be trusted to fulfill what you said you would do?

In Today's Reading

The last words of David; David's last recorded sin; David builds an altar; his sacrifice; the three-day plague.

David never lost a battle in his 40-year reign. Although he had often prayed for the Lord's direction during his early years of conquest, his desire at this time to take a census of his army was obviously not based on any threat by invaders. When we begin feeling proud, Satan is quick to suggest wrong thoughts, as he did with David. *Satan stood up against Israel and incited David to count the people* (I Chronicles 21:1). The Chronicles passage further explains the incident in II Samuel. From the standpoint of the absolute sovereignty of God over everything, including Satan, we read: *Again the LORD's anger burned against Israel. He incited David against them by instructing: Go, count . . . Israel and Judah! . . .* Then *David's conscience troubled him after he had numbered the troops. He said to the LORD, I've sinned greatly in what I've done. Now, O LORD, because I've been very foolish, please take away your servant's guilt. . . . Then the LORD answered prayer on behalf of the land, and the plague on Israel was halted* (II Samuel 24:1,10,25).

It would be inconceivable for God to actually force David to commit this sin and then, before the census was completed, to destroy 70,000 people because of it (24:15; I Chronicles 27:24). The Holy Spirit directed the writing of II Samuel to let us see that everyone is under the sovereign will of God, who allows us to stubbornly go our own way, for He will not violate our free will.

There is no record that taking a census was prohibited. But the law did state: *When you take a census of the Israelites . . . each of the men must pay a ransom for himself to the LORD as they are registered. Then no plague will come on them . . . the registered group must pay . . . half a shekel as a contribution to the LORD* (Exodus 30:12-13).

Because of this violation, a plague spread over the land. This tragic experience of David is a reminder of how important it is that we pray one for another that: *The God of peace . . . equip you with all that is good to do His will, working in us what is pleasing in His sight, through Jesus Christ* (Hebrews 13:20-21).

Thought for Today: The weapons of our spiritual warfare are mighty.

Introduction To The Books Of I & II Kings

All the kings of Judah and Israel are recorded in I & II Kings except for Saul.

The purpose of I & II Kings is to illustrate the blessings that result from faithfulness and obedience to the Lord and His judgment upon unfaithfulness and disobedience. The first 11 chapters of I Kings focus attention primarily on the reign of Solomon. Chapters 12 – 22 cover about the first 80-100 years of the divided kingdom. During that time, four kings reigned over the southern kingdom and nine over the northern kingdom.

David's final words to Solomon were: *Keep your obligation to the* LORD *your God to walk in His ways and to keep . . . His commandments . . . that you may have success in everything you do* (I Kings 2:3; see Joshua 1:7). But Solomon ignored David's advice. His reign resulted in a divided kingdom after his son came to the throne.

The first 17 chapters of II Kings focus on the prophets Elijah and Elisha as well as record the decline of both the southern and northern kingdoms. Nineteen kings ruled the northern kingdom of Israel during its approximately 210-year history as a divided kingdom. Chapter 17 ends with the conquest and removal of the people of the northern kingdom of Israel by the Assyrians. Most of the Israelites were scattered throughout the Assyrian Empire, while captives from other nations were brought into Samaria. These pagans intermarried with the few remaining Israelites. Their descendants became known as Samaritans, a people despised by Jews. The smaller southern kingdom of Judah remained independent for another 135 years, existing for a total of about 500 years. Including the 120 years of the united kingdom, Judah had 19 kings and one usurper, Queen Athaliah (II Kings 18 – 25). The remaining eight chapters are devoted to the southern kingdom of Judah.

By the end of the last chapter, we read that Jerusalem was destroyed and Solomon's temple burned by the Babylonians. Most of Judah's population was taken captive and dispersed throughout Babylonia.

The prophets Elijah and Elisha prophesied in Israel, as did Amos, Hosea, and Jonah. Obadiah, Joel, Isaiah, Micah, Nahum, Habakkuk, Zephaniah, and Jeremiah prophesied during this time in Judah. These men of God exposed the nation's sins and appealed to the people to reject their idols and repent or experience defeat and judgment.

In Today's Reading

David's son, Adonijah, revolts; Joab defects; Abiathar defects; King David charges Solomon to be obedient to God's word.

As we grow old, all of us want to remain useful; but increasing age continues to diminish our strength and narrow our options. *Now King David was old and getting on in years* (I Kings 1:1). Just like everyone else, the beloved king became feeble. But his spiritual insight had grown even stronger. Spiritual alertness is maintained as we continue to take in and share God's word with others.

David's last words to Solomon express his heartfelt desire for his son: *As for me, I am going the way of all of the earth. Now be strong, be a man* (stand firm against all pressure to compromise), *and keep your obligation to the LORD* (2:2-4). Compromise for us could include active involvement in secular organizations that rob us of time that could be invested in Christ-centered goals with the church and other ministries. These goals include influencing friends, neighbors, business associates, and others to give priority to eternal values. David said nothing to Solomon about amassing wealth or enlarging his kingdom. Instead, he stressed the true, lasting values of living in obedience to the one true King of Israel.

Solomon was probably 20 years of age when he became King of Israel. God had commanded that Israel's king must not *make the people return to Egypt in order to acquire large numbers of horses, seeing that the LORD has told you, You will never go back that way again* (Deuteronomy 17:16). But, sadly, Solomon ignored God's word and his first years as king were occupied in accumulating 40,000 horses for himself (I Kings 4:26).

God had also commanded all the kings to intimately know His word: *He must write a copy of this law for himself on a scroll like . . . the Levitical priests. It will remain with him, and he will read from it all the days of his life, in order that he may . . .* (follow) *them* (Deuteronomy 17:18-20). The division and eventual destruction of the kingdom of Israel, can be attributed to the sins of Solomon. He failed in *observing all the requirements of this law . . . and following them*. Let us *not focus on what is seen, but on what is unseen; for what is seen is temporary, but what is unseen is eternal* (II Corinthians 4:18).

Thought for Today: You are precious to the Lord.

In Today's Reading

Abiathar banished from priesthood; Joab put to death; Shimei executed; Solomon's control of the kingdom becomes secure.

Soon after Solomon became king, we read: *Solomon loved the LORD, walking in the statutes of his father David, he also used to sacrifice and burn incense at the high places* (I Kings 3:3). The tabernacle and the altar of burnt offerings were still located at Gibeon, about six miles northwest of Jerusalem (I Chronicles 16:37-40; 21:29). The last major event to take place at Gibeon was Solomon's great dedication service as king (II Chronicles 1:1-13; 7:8). On the night of that great sacrifice, Solomon had a remarkable dream in which he asked God for *an obedient heart to judge Your people, discerning between good and evil* (I Kings 3:9). God was trying to get Solomon's attention through a dream to remind him that he needed to meditate upon the Scripture, *discerning between good and evil* (3:7-9). . . . *Then Solomon awoke and discovered that it had been a dream* (3:14-15). But this remarkable dream had no lasting effect on his life.

Solomon ignored God's word concerning the kings of Israel: *He must not acquire large numbers of horses. . . . He must not acquire large numbers of wives. . . . Silver and gold, too, he must not acquire in very large amounts* (Deuteronomy 17:16-17). He not only turned to Egypt for horses, but also *married the Pharaoh's daughter* (I Kings 3:1).

Solomon offered enormous sacrifices to God, built the world famous temple, and offered the longest recorded prayer in the Bible; but his disregard for God's word, his marriages to pagan wives, and his worship at the Canaanite *high places* were all acts of rebellion against God. These actions eventually led to his apostasy.

Solomon refused to follow his godly father's advice to *keep your obligation to the LORD your God . . . keep . . . His commandments* (2:3). He is typical of the brilliant, multitalented people who compromise biblical principles, assuming that God is pleased since they are successful and popular. But compromise is the first foothold of sin that sooner or later destroys one's spiritual usefulness and influence for Christ.

Solomon eventually confessed: *I saw all the accomplishments . . . under the sun. . . . Every one is futile, a chasing after the wind* (Ecclesiastes 1:14). He wrote: *Fear God and obey His commandments* (Ecclesiastes 12:13).

Thought for Today: Surely the highest of all wisdom is to obey the Lord.

In Today's Reading
Solomon builds the temple;
furnishings of the temple and his own palace.

Solomon's temple was twice the size of the tabernacle, but it was still comparatively small, only 90 feet long, 30 feet wide, and 45 feet tall. The interior was divided into two rooms. The first room was called the holy place and was 60 by 30 feet; the second room was called the holy of holies and was 30 feet square.

In the four hundred eightieth year after the Israelites came out from the land of Egypt, in the fourth year of Solomon's reign over Israel, in the month of Ziv the second month he built the temple for the LORD (I Kings 6:1). No other building in the world compared with Solomon's temple. The most costly materials and treasures were lavished upon it. But the world observed only the external beauty of the temple; its true glory was in the presence of God who chose to dwell within the holy of holies.

The temple was built without the noise of craftsmen since the stones were shaped in the quarry and made ready to fit together on Mount Moriah (6:7). This should remind us not to mistake noise for spiritual progress. We are transformed into His glorious likeness, not by noisy human efforts, but silently by the power of the Holy Spirit, as day by day He perfects His temple within every believer (Zechariah 4:6).

Every child of God is more precious to our heavenly Father than Solomon's temple. *You are God's sanctuary. . . . we are . . . created in Christ Jesus* (born anew) *for good works, which God prepared ahead of time* (I Corinthians 3:16-17; Ephesians 2:10), we are His workmanship.

Every day is a sacred trust that becomes more meaningful with the awareness that the God of heaven lives within every believer. The miracle of the new birth and the indwelling Holy Spirit are the differences between the true Christian and the "religious world." Jesus said: *I am the way, the truth, and the life. No one comes to the Father except through Me* (John 14:6). The apostle Peter attested: *There is salvation in no one else, for there is no other name . . . by which we must be saved* (Acts 4:12).

You were bought at a price (made His own)*; therefore glorify God* (bring honor to Him) *in your body* (I Corinthians 6:20).

Thought for Today: The beauty of the Christian is the presence of God who dwells within and radiates without.

In Today's Reading

Glory of the Lord filling the temple; ark brought into the temple; Solomon's sermon, prayer, and dedication.

The day had arrived for the dedication of the glorious temple on Mount Moriah in Jerusalem. *Solomon assembled . . . at Jerusalem the elders of Israel . . . in order to bring up the ark of the covenant of the LORD from the city of David, that is, Zion. . . . The priests brought the ark of the covenant of the LORD to its place . . . the holy of holies* (I Kings 8:1,6). The ark is where the presence of God dwelt above the mercy seat. Now *nothing was in the ark except the two stone tablets that Moses had deposited there at Horeb. . . . and the glory of the LORD filled the LORD's temple* (8:9-11).

The people stood in the courtyard and worshiped the Lord at the dedication of the temple.

The Israelites were chosen to let the world know there is only one true God, *that all the people of the earth may know Your name, to fear You as Your people Israel do. . . . that He may incline our hearts to Him to walk in all His ways and to keep His commands. . . . so that all the peoples of the earth may know that the LORD is God . . . no other!* (8:43,57-58,60). Buddha, Allah, and all other "gods" are false gods.

The one true God includes all three persons of the Trinity: God the Father, Jesus, who is God the Son, and God the Holy Spirit. Each person's daily conversation and conduct should express our love and loyalty to the one true God.

Solomon offered a sacrifice . . . to the LORD (of) *22,000 cattle and 120,000 sheep. Thus the king and all the Israelites dedicated the LORD's temple* (8:61-63). The word "sacrifice" does not mean "a great loss." A sacrifice to the Lord is never a deprivation, but is a gift of something dedicated to the Lord. However, sacrifices are an abomination if they don't represent an expression of our true inner devotion to the Lord.

Solomon prayed the longest recorded prayer in the Bible and stressed the faithfulness of God, *keeping the covenant and mercy to Your servants, who walk before You with their whole heart* (I Kings 8:22-23).

Thought for Today: The holiness of God reveals the vileness of sin.

In Today's Reading

Warning to Solomon; alliance with King Hiram of Tyre;
Solomon's riches and wisdom.

The Lord gave Solomon special privileges far exceeding those of other kings. But the Lord's continued blessings are conditional, as He said to Solomon: *If you walk before Me as your father David walked, with integrity of heart and in uprightness, to do . . . what I have commanded . . . then I will establish your royal throne over Israel forever* (I Kings 9:4-7).

Did Solomon assume that building the most sacred temple in history, praying the longest prayer, and offering the most sacrifices meant that God would overlook his sins? In disregard for the word of God, Solomon amassed thousands of horses and chariots, and lived in an atmosphere of unparalleled luxury. He also violated the command of God by accumulating 700 wives and 300 concubines (Deuteronomy 17: 16-17). Did Solomon deceive himself into thinking that, as king, he could ignore the word of God in his personal life?

Solomon not only chose daughters of foreign kings for his wives, but he encouraged them to worship their idols. This had been expressly forbidden in the law (18:9-12). There is no indication that Solomon made an effort to encourage any of his wives to worship the one true God.To do this would have interfered with his political agenda, since his foreign wives were daughters of kings who would insure peace with their countries. His power, prestige, and wealth eventually became his undoing. We are shocked to read that Solomon eventually *went after Ashtoreth, the goddess of the Sidonians, and after Milcom, the abominable idol of the Ammonites. . . . So the LORD was angry with Solomon because his heart had turned from the LORD God of Israel, who had appeared to him twice* (I Kings 11:5,7,9).

What happened to Solomon can happen to all who allow an abundance of "things" to crowd out one's loyalty to the Lord.

How solemn is the warning: *The love of money is a root of all kinds of evil, and by craving it, some have wandered away from the faith and pierced themselves with many pains* (I Timothy 6:10).

Thought for Today: God's word has solutions to all of life's problems.

In Today's Reading

Solomon's death; ten tribes revolt; Jeroboam rebuked by an unnamed prophet; death of the disobedient prophet.

King Solomon *was buried in the city of his father David* (I Kings 11:43). His son Rehoboam inherited power and a treasury full of wealth. However, Solomon left the kingdom morally and spiritually bankrupt.

Jeroboam and all the assembly of Israel came and spoke with Rehoboam, and said: Your father made our yoke burdensome. . . . lighten . . . the heavy yoke that he put on us, and we will serve you (12:3-4).

King Rehoboam consulted with the elders . . . (and) *said: How do you advise me? . . . they spoke to him, saying, If today you . . .* (speak) *good words to them, then they will be your servants forever. But he rejected the advice of the elders who had advised him, and he consulted with the young men who had grown up with him, who served him* (12:6-8).

Note that Rehoboam said to the wise old men: *How do **you** advise?* But, he said to his newly-appointed cabinet of young friends: *What message do you advise **we** send back to this people who spoke to me saying, Lighten the yoke that your father put on us?* (12:9). Taking the young men's counsel, Rehoboam foolishly threatened the nation with additional taxes and even more cruel treatment. This blunder caused the people to rebel: *So . . . . They made him* (Jeroboam) *king* (12:19-20).

Jeroboam provided his new kingdom with two "more convenient" places of worship located at Bethel in the south and Dan in the north. This violated the word of God that clearly commanded that all worship sacrifices must be conducted at the temple in Jerusalem. *The LORD. . . . will give Israel up because of Jeroboam's sins that he committed and that he caused Israel to commit* (14:15-16).

A similar departure from the fundamental doctrines of the word of God is prevalent today. Pitiful as this is, some people neglect to read His word and simply do not know the difference. *Beware of false prophets who come to you in sheep's clothing, but inwardly are ravaging wolves. . . . Not everyone who says to Me, Lord, Lord! will enter the kingdom of heaven, but the one who does the will of My Father in heaven* (Matthew 7:15,21).

Thought for Today: Pity the one who compromises the word of God.

In Today's Reading

Ahijah's prophecy; reign and death of Rehoboam;
Abijam's wicked reign and Asa's good reign in Judah.

After the division of the united kingdom of Israel, Jeroboam set up worship centers at Bethel and at Dan. The southern kingdom of Judah was greatly influenced to worship the Lord when *the Levites* (in the northern kingdom) *left their . . . possessions and went to . . . Jerusalem. . . . Rehoboam son of Solomon . . . walked in the way of David . . . for three years* (II Chronicles 11:14,17).

In the fifth year of Rehoboam's reign in Jerusalem, *Rehoboam . . . forsook the law of the LORD* (12:1-2). Rehoboam followed the policy of his father Solomon in being "broad-minded" and "tolerant" of other religions. This could be expected of Rehoboam since *his mother's name was Naamah the* (idol-worshiping) *Ammonite* (I Kings 14:21-24).

Although the kingdom of Judah did not forsake the prescribed order of the temple services, *Judah did what was evil in the LORD's eyes. They provoked Him to jealous anger. . . . Also male shrine prostitutes were in the land. They imitated all the abominations of the nations that the LORD had dispossessed before the Israelites* (14:22-24). God has declared: *There must be no shrine prostitute among the daughters of Israel, and no male shrine prostitute among the sons of Israel* (Deuteronomy 23:17).

God withdrew His blessings and protection from Judah. *In the fifth year of King Rehoboam, Shishak king of Egypt went to war against Jerusalem. He seized the treasuries of the LORD's temple and the treasuries of the royal palace. He took everything* (I Kings 14:25-26). The kingdom was not only emptied of all its wealth but now was under the control of Egypt.

In his later years, Solomon encouraged the worship of false gods and it continued to gain popularity during the reign of his son Rehoboam. Once cults and false worship become acceptable in a nation, they are followed by the acceptance of homosexuals and lesbians.

For God's wrath is revealed from heaven against all godlessness and unrighteousness of people who . . . suppress the truth (Romans 1:18).

Thought for Today: *Blessed are the pure in heart* (Matthew 5:8).

In Today's Reading

Evil kings of Israel; Elijah's pronouncement of drought; Elijah fed by ravens and the widow; raises the widow's son; contest with prophets of Baal.

Ahab became the most wicked king to reign over the northern kingdom. He promoted Baal worship as a result of his marriage to Jezebel. Israelite worshipers of God hid in caves in fear for their lives. Then the prophet Elijah boldly declared to Ahab: *As the LORD God of Israel lives, before whom I stand, there shull be no dew or rain during these years except at my word!* (I Kings 17:1). Elijah's faith was in God, who said: *Be careful lest you . . . turn aside and serve and worship other gods. Then the LORD will . . . dry up the skies. There will then be no rain* (Deuteronomy 11:16-17).

After three-and-one-half years of no rain, Elijah boldly faced Ahab. After informing the king that Israel's drought was the result of rejecting *the LORD's commandments. . . .* (He said) *gather all Israel to me at Mount Carmel, along with the 450 prophets of Baal and the 400 prophets of Asherah* (I Kings 18:18-19). Ahab, desperate for rain, immediately responded.

Elijah challenged the 850 false prophets to *call on the name of your god* to consume your sacrifice (18:25). After a full day of Jezebel's prophets frantically praying, Elijah called the people to *come near to me. . . . Then he repaired the altar of the LORD that had been torn down* (18:30), and prayed: *O LORD God . . . today let it be known that You are God in Israel and I am Your servant and that at Your word I have done all these things. . . . Then the fire of the LORD fell and consumed the burnt offering, the wood, the stones, and the dust. . . . When all the people saw it, they fell on their faces and said, The LORD, He is God! The LORD, He is God!* (18:36-39).

Elijah then demanded that all 850 false prophets be executed according to the word of God: *If . . . a prophet . . . says . . . Let us follow other gods . . . . he must be put to death* (Deuteronomy 13:1-5). After their execution, *Elijah said to Ahab . . . there is the sound of a rainstorm* (I Kings 18:41).

Elijah illustrates how the power of God is released when we pray and are obedient to His word. Therefore, *pray at all times in the Spirit . . . with all perseverance and intercession for all the saints* (Ephesians 6:18).

Thought for Today: Through difficulties, exercise faith in the Lord.

In Today's Reading

Jezebel's threat against Elijah; Elijah's flight; the call of Elisha; Ahab's death foretold.

Apparently, Elijah believed that the miraculous fire from heaven and the end of the drought would prove Baal to be a false god, and it would result in Ahab and Jezebel's conversion to the one true God.

Ahab headed toward his palace to tell Jezebel what had happened. Responding immediately, *Jezebel sent a messenger to Elijah, saying, May the gods punish me and do so severely if by this time tomorrow I don't make your life like the life of one of them! Then he became afraid and immediately fled for his life* (I Kings 19:2-3). Avoiding the ruthless Jezebel was not weakness, but wisdom. However, feeling defeated and discouraged, he prayed: *O LORD, Take my life, for I'm no better than my fathers* (19:4).

There is no indication that Elijah contemplated suicide; he believed that God was the Creator and Lord of life and only He had the right to take life. What he meant was: "I'm a failure. I have not achieved my mission, and there seems to be no hope of restoring the nation to worship You as the one true God." However, God lovingly provided Elijah's physical needs by sending an angel to supply nourishment after his long journey (19:5-6). Often our mountaintop spiritual victories will be quickly followed by opposition or desert testing.

When we stand before the Lord, each person's work shall be judged, not by how spectacular it was, but by its true eternal worth. All of us have moments of disappointment when it seems we have failed. Often our estimation of what we should achieve and God's estimation are far apart. We are not called to be successful, but to be available and to remain faithful to God (I Corinthians 1:9).

Although he did not know it, Elijah did accomplish what God wanted him to do. One of his great successes was that the leaders in Ahab's kingdom went home with a renewed conviction that *the LORD, He is God* (I Kings 18:39). Elijah has given encouragement to millions of believers that: *The LORD is near all who call out to Him, all who call out to Him with integrity. . . . The LORD guards all those who love Him, but He destroys all the wicked* (Psalms 145:18,20).

Thought for Today: God has a purpose for disappointments we face.

In Today's Reading

The covetousness of Ahab leads Jezebel to murder Naboth; death of Ahab and Jezebel foretold.

Ahab ruled the northern kingdom of Israel. His capital was at Samaria. His life is summed up in just a few words: *Surely there was no one like Ahab, who sold himself to do what was evil in the LORD's eyes because his wife Jezebel incited him. He behaved very abhorrently by going after idols* (I Kings 21:25-26).

Ahab invited Jehoshaphat, his daughter's father-in-law and King of Judah, to join him in a war to regain Ramoth-gilead, a strategic fortress on the Syrian border. Four hundred of Ahab's paid prophets unanimously assured the two kings of a great victory. But godly Jehoshaphat must have felt uneasy and asked Ahab: *Isn't there a prophet of the LORD here anymore? Let's inquire of him!* (22:7). Reluctantly, Ahab replied: *There's still one man from whom to inquire of the LORD . . . but I hate him because he doesn't prophesy good about me, but only disaster* (22:8).

The messenger who was sent to bring Micaiah from prison *said to him. . . . let your words be like the word of one of them, and speak favorably. But Micaiah said, As the LORD lives, whatever the LORD says to me, that I will speak!* (22:13-14). If Micaiah had cooperated, no doubt he would have immediately gained his freedom. But Micaiah knew that obedience to God was far more important than his freedom, and he courageously proclaimed: *I saw all Israel scattering to the hills like sheep that have no shepherd* (22:17).

Micaiah had bluntly foretold Ahab's death. *So the king of Israel said to Jehoshaphat, Didn't I tell you he wouldn't prophesy anything good about me, but only disaster?* (22:18). He then ordered Micaiah to be taken back to prison.

Ahab was killed on the first day of battle (22:34,37).

The tragic consequences of Ahab's disregard for the word of God should be a warning to all who are making the same fatal mistake. In contrast, a follower of Christ can express unlimited peace of mind with the psalmist: *I keep the LORD in mind always. Because He is at my right hand, I will not be defeated* (Psalms 16:8).

Thought for Today: All who do God's will receive eternal rewards.

In Today's Reading

Death of Ahaziah King of Israel; Elijah taken up by a whirlwind; Elisha purifies Jericho's water; Elisha mocked by the children.

Ten years before Elijah's departure in a "chariot of fire," the *LORD* said to him: *You are to anoint Jehu . . . as king over Israel, and Elisha . . . you are to anoint as prophet in your place. . . . So he left there and found Elisha. . . . He was plowing; twelve teams of oxen were in front of him, and he was with the twelfth team. Elijah passed by him and threw his mantle over him* (I Kings 19:16,19), designating Elisha to replace him. At the time Elijah called Elisha to join him, Elisha was a prosperous young farmer. To accept Elijah's calling to be his servant would mean that Elisha would have to forsake his family and friends as well as financial securities. His friends probably thought that to be the servant of a prophet would be a lonely, menial occupation. But, Elisha knew the true values of life and immediately converted his plows into firewood and *took the team of oxen, and slaughtered them. With the oxen's wooden yoke and plow he boiled their flesh and gave it to the people, and they ate. Then he set out and went after Elijah and ministered to him* (19:21). Elisha's actions demonstrate that the key to one's usefulness in the kingdom of God is to immediately respond to our opportunities to serve the Lord, regardless of how great or how insignificant the task may appear.

Just prior to Elijah's translation into heaven, Elisha again revealed his spiritual discernment and loyalty to God, which qualified him to be Elijah's successor: *Elijah said to Elisha, Stay here; the LORD is sending me on to Bethel. But Elisha replied, As surely as the LORD lives . . . I will not leave you. So they went down to Bethel* (II Kings 2:2). Elisha was determined to continue with Elijah on his journey from Gilgal to Bethel, on to Jericho, and then across the Jordan River (2:3-8).

Like Elisha, circumstances have placed each of us where we are today to determine the sincerity of our commitment to the Lord. *Therefore, my dear brothers, be steadfast . . . always abounding in the Lord's work, knowing that your labor in the Lord is not in vain* (I Corinthians 15:58).

Thought for Today: The Lord is present in every circumstance, and His grace is sufficient to meet every need.

In Today's Reading

Widow's oil; Elisha and the Shunammite woman; Elisha's miracles; Elisha feeds 100 men; Naaman cured of leprosy; Gehazi's leprosy.

Desperate to be healed of his leprosy, Naaman appeared before King Jehoram in Israel *with . . . 750 pounds of silver, 150 pounds of gold, and 10 changes of clothes* and a letter from King Ben-hadad of Syria (Aram) that read: *I have sent you my servant Naaman for you to cure him of his leprosy* (II Kings 5:2-6). Jehoram had no faith in God and thought that King Ben-hadad was seeking an excuse to declare war. *When Elisha the man of God heard . . . he sent a message to the king. . . . Have him come to me, and he'll know there's a prophet in Israel* (5:8). When Naaman obeyed the words of the *prophet*, he was miraculously healed.

Elisha refused the huge reward that Naaman offered him. But his greedy servant Gehazi persuaded himself that God had blessed him with the opportunity to be wealthy. He probably did not think it was much of a sin to gain wealth that he didn't deserve from someone who was ungodly and didn't need it.

When Naaman saw someone running after him . . . he *asked, Is everything all right?* (5:21). Gehazi then told him this lie: *My master has sent me to say . . . two young men from the sons of the prophets have come to me. . . . Please give them 75 pounds of silver and two changes of clothes* (5:22). The schemer thought he could rush back before Elisha discovered he was missing. After Gehazi's return, Elisha said: *Where did you go, Gehazi?. . .*(I) *didn't go anywhere, he replied. But Elisha* (said) *. . . Is it a time to accept money and clothes, olive orchards and vineyards, sheep and oxen, and male and female slaves? Therefore, Naaman's leprosy shall cling to you. . . . So Gehazi went out from his presence a leper* (5:25-26).

Gehazi forfeited his opportunity to be the next honored prophet of God. Instead, he became a leper! When Gehazi was tested, he exposed his true character as a covetous hypocrite.

Ask yourself the question Elisha asked Gehazi: *Is it a time to accept* (make) *money?* – meaning: "What is your goal in life?" How will you respond to Christ, who said: *Seek first the kingdom of God* (Matthew 6:33)?

Thought for Today: Remain faithful in your trials; God has His purposes.

In Today's Reading

The ax head made to float; Syrians (Arameans) attack Israel; famine in Samaria; Elisha's prophecy fulfilled.

Ben-hadad, the King of Syria (Aram), could not have "forgotten" that, when the Aramean (Syrian) soldiers had attempted to capture the prophet Elisha, they had been miraculously blinded and were then led by Elisha inside the walls of the capital city of Samaria. The soldiers then were trapped and at the mercy of the king of Israel. However, at Elisha's command, the king *prepared a great feast for them. When they had eaten and drunk, he sent them away, and they went to their master. The Aramean raiders did not come into Israel's land again* (II Kings 6:23). Yet, *some time later, King Ben-hadad of Aram brought all his military units together and marched up to besiege Samaria* (6:24-25).

The once-powerful, luxurious, fortress-city of Samaria was faced with all the horrors of an extended famine. To surrender to Syria (Aram) meant death for King Jehoram (Joram) and slavery for his people. But, remaining within the walls eventually reduced the people to starvation, even resorting to cannibalism. These appalling conditions were the result of Israel's disobedience as God had forewarned (Leviticus 26:14-29).

When it appeared there was no hope, the Lord again brought Jehoram face to face with Elisha, who proclaimed: *Hear the word of the LORD! . . . About this time tomorrow at the gate of Samaria, six quarts of fine meal will sell for a shekel and twelve quarts of barley will sell for a shekel* (II Kings 7:1). One of the king's officials ridiculed him, saying: *If the LORD were to make windows in heaven, could this thing really happen? You will in fact see it with your own eyes, Elisha insisted, but you won't eat any of it* (7:2). The prophecy was miraculously fulfilled when God, in His great mercy, sent fear into the hearts of the Syrian army and they hurriedly abandoned their camp and their food was in abundance for the Israelites. The king's official was trampled to death in the rush for food (7:17).

Obedient Christians need not fear for tomorrow! Instead, we can rejoice in the promises of God, who *will supply all your needs according to His riches in glory in Christ Jesus* (Philippians 4:19).

Thought for Today: The answers to our prayers are sometimes postponed because God has a better plan.

In Today's Reading

Jehu anointed King of Israel; Jehu kills Joram (Jehoram) and Ahaziah; Jezebel killed; Ahab's family killed; Baal worshipers executed.

After Ahab's death, his son Ahaziah reigned over Israel for two years, followed by the 12-year reign of his brother, Jehoram (also known as Joram). These two kings zealously promoted Baal worship, which had been initiated by their wicked mother Jezebel. Baal worship had also become popular in the southern kingdom of Judah due to its king, who was also named Jehoram. He had married Jezebel's daughter Athaliah, and their son Ahaziah was equally wicked.

During this time of spiritual decline, the Lord was preparing Jehu, the military commander of the armies of the northern kingdom, as His instrument of judgment. God had earlier revealed to Elijah that Jehu would become King of Israel (I Kings 19:16). Perhaps 20 years passed before the Lord directed Elisha to send a young prophet east of the Jordan River to Ramoth-gilead, where Jehu was stationed with his army. The prophet anointed Jehu as King of Israel and the God-appointed executioner of Israel's evil King Jehoram and all the descendants of Ahab.

Jehu drove his chariots furiously to Jezreel where he executed Joram (Jehoram), King of Israel, and then Ahaziah, King of Judah. Then Jehu had Jezebel thrown out of a window and he trampled her with his horse. And, as foretold by Elijah, the dogs ate her body (II Kings 9:33-37).

Jehu zealously executed all the family of Ahab in Samaria. However, Athaliah (I Kings 21:17-24), the daughter of Jezebel, continued to promote Baal worship as queen in Judah. Jehu had bragged to Jehonadab: *Come with me and see my zeal for the LORD!* (II Kings 10:16). But Jehu's *zeal for the LORD* was just enough to achieve his own selfish ends. *Jehu was not careful to follow with all his heart the law of the LORD God of Israel. He did not turn from the sins that Jeroboam had caused Israel to commit* (10:31-32). This illustrates that it is possible for one to be used by God and yet never be in submission to Christ as Lord of one's life. Hypocrites serve the Lord for their own self-interests. *So that each of you knows how to possess his own vessel in sanctification and honor. . . God has not called us to impurity, but to sanctification* (I Thessalonians 4:4,7).

Thought for Today: God may cut short a life that is disobedient to Him.

In Today's Reading

Athaliah reigns; David's descendants murdered; Joash crowned king; he repairs the temple; worship restored; evil reign of Jehoahaz.

When Athaliah, daughter of Jezebel, received word that her son, King Ahaziah, was dead, she seized the throne of Judah and proclaimed herself queen. To make sure she had no competition, she ruthlessly murdered her own grandsons. She thought she had killed all of David's descendants (II Kings 11:1; II Chronicles 22:10).

However, God intervened and saved the one-year-old Joash (Jehoash), the sole link that preserved the dynasty of David and the lineage of Jesus Christ (II Kings 11:2-3; II Chronicles 22:11-12). *While Athaliah ruled over the land, he was hiding with Jehosheba in the LORD's temple for six years* (II Kings 11:3).

Joash was in the care of Jehoiada the high priest. When Joash was about seven years old, Jehoiada *brought out the king's son, put the crown on him, gave him the testimony, and made him king. Anointing him, they clapped their hands and cried, Long live the king!* (11:12). The excited shouts caught the attention of Athaliah, who ran into the temple court just in time to hear Jehoiada the high priest command the captains of the guard to execute her. *Then Jehoiada made a covenant between the LORD, the king, and the people that they would be the LORD's people* (11:17-18).

Throughout the time that Jehoiada the priest instructed him, Joash did what was right in the LORD's eyes (12:2; II Chronicles 24:2). *However, after Jehoiada died, the rulers of Judah came and paid homage to the king. Then the king listened to them, and they forsook the temple of the LORD God of their fathers and served . . . idols. So there was wrath against Judah and Jerusalem for this their guilt. Nevertheless, He sent them prophets . . . but they wouldn't listen. . . . Joash's servants conspired against him and killed him* (24:17-18,20,25; II Kings 12:20). The account of Joash illustrates that to forsake the word of God results in untold miseries: *They perish because they did not accept the love of the truth in order to be saved* (II Thessalonians 2:10).

Thought for Today: What a privilege to trust God for guidance!

In Today's Reading

Reigns of Amaziah, Azariah (Uzziah), and Jotham over Judah; reigns of five of last six kings over Israel.

Following the death of his father Jehoash, Jeroboam II ruled the northern kingdom of Israel in Samaria for 41 years (II Kings 14:16-29). However: *He did what was evil in the LORD's eyes. He did not turn away from all the sins that Jeroboam son of Nebat had caused Israel to commit* (14:24). Immorality and idolatry flourished during the reign of Jeroboam II. Finally, God commanded the prophet Amos, from the southern kingdom of Judah, to go to Bethel and prophesy the destruction of Jeroboam's kingdom (Amos 7:9). Both Hosea and Amos spoke out against the sweeping religious and moral decay during Jeroboam's reign (Hosea 6:4-10; 10:1-15; Amos 2:6-8; 3:13 – 5:27). For about 30 years the nation enjoyed peace, prosperity, and political prestige unparalleled since the days of David and Solomon. Jeroboam *restored Israel's border from Lebo-hamath (Hamath) as far as the Sea of the Arabah, according to the word which the LORD, the God of Israel, had spoken through His servant, the prophet Jonah* (II Kings 14:25).

Sadly, Israel's prosperity did not cause the people to worship the Lord. It appears that they attributed their prosperity to idols. Thus, immorality and violence continued to permeate the nation (17:13-17).

After Jeroboam's death, anarchy prevailed and Israel rapidly degenerated. Jeroboam was succeeded by his son Zechariah (14:29) who reigned only six months (15:8). This was the fourth and last generation of the house of Jehu (15:12).

About 30 years after Jeroboam's death, the words of the prophets were fulfilled. The northern kingdom was destroyed and its people taken captive by the Assyrians (17:1-18). Material success is often deceptive, as it was for King Jeroboam II. We cannot measure men's character by the length of their lives, nor by their material prosperity.

Surely the goodness of God should lead us, in gratitude, to do the will of Jesus Christ our *LORD. He has rescued us from the domain of darkness and transferred us into the kingdom of the Son He loves* (Colossians 1:13).

Thought for Today: We forfeit His best when we fail to keep His word.

In Today's Reading

Ahaz reigns in Judah, defiles the temple; Hoshea reigns in Israel; fall of Samaria; captivity and deportations of Israel.

Fearing the growing power of Assyria, Pekah, King of Israel, made an alliance with Rezin, King of Syria (Aram) (II Kings 15:37). Together, they attempted to force Ahaz, King of Judah, to join them. When Ahaz refused, Aram's King Rezin and Israel's King Pekah came up to wage war against Jerusalem. *They besieged Ahaz but were not able to conquer him* (16:5). In retaliation, Ahaz made an alliance with Tiglath-pileser, King of Assyria, to attack Syria (Aram) and Israel. This cost Ahaz all *the silver and the gold that were found in the LORD's temple and in the treasuries of the king's palace* (as payment) . . . *to the king of Assyria* (16:8). By this time, the king of the Assyrian Empire had conquered the small kingdom of Syria (Aram) and killed Rezin, its king (16:9). Tiglath-pileser also defeated the tribes of Reuben and Gad and the half-tribe of Manasseh on the eastern side of the Jordan. He then took control of the northern part of the Jordan Valley, making Galilee and Gilead into Assyrian provinces (15:29; compare Isaiah 9:1). All that was left of the ten-tribe northern kingdom of Israel was the capital city of Samaria and the surrounding hill country of Ephraim.

The captivity and dispersion of the northern kingdom throughout Assyria took place because the Israelites *served idols, concerning which the LORD had told them, You shall not do this. Still, the LORD warned Israel and Judah through every prophet and every seer, saying, Turn from your evil ways and keep My commandments and statutes according to all the law that I commanded your fathers and that I sent to you through My servants the prophets. However, they would not listen* (II Kings 17:12-23).

They lived as if God did not exist. We must remember, whoever or whatever gets our loyalty becomes our idol, be it a person, purpose, or possession.

Jesus said: *How narrow is the gate and difficult the road that leads to life; and few find it* (Matthew 7:14).

Thought for Today: Compromise is a characteristic of the double-minded person.

In Today's Reading

Hezekiah's reign; Assyria invades Judah; Hezekiah and Isaiah pray; Hezekiah's miraculous healing.

Hezekiah son of Ahaz became king of Judah. He was 25 years old when he became king; he reigned 29 years in Jerusalem.... He did what was right in the LORD's eyes just as his forefather David had done (II Kings 18:1-3). When Hezekiah became king, he did not follow the ways of his evil father Ahaz; instead, he believed the prophets of God, including the unpopular Micah. Hezekiah not only benefited from the ministry of Micah, but he also gained spiritual encouragement from the prophet Isaiah. *He removed the high places and shattered the sacred pillars and cut down the Asherah poles.... Hezekiah trusted in the LORD God of Israel; not one of the kings of Judah was like him: neither those who came after him nor those who came before him. He held fast to the LORD. He did not turn aside from following Him but kept the commandments that the LORD had commanded Moses* (18:4-6).

Hezekiah led the nation to keep the Passover and renew its covenant with the Lord. *The rejoicing was great in Jerusalem* (II Chronicles 30:26-27). Hezekiah's spiritual reformation was followed by a radical reorganization of the entire administration of both the secular and religious affairs of the kingdom. We learn from Hezekiah that people will be blessed, and prayers will be answered, when the word of God is obeyed.

The greatest opposition to Isaiah, Micah, and Hezekiah's reformation did not come from the pagan nations around Judah, but from the false prophets within their own country, as well as those who worshiped the idols which had been introduced earlier by King Solomon.

Some popular religious leaders today seem to do nothing to encourage people to forsake their sins, live godly lives, and read the Bible. But, instead, they preach what appeals to man's physical desires. Others cry out: "Cooperate with the majority, compromise, be tolerant, avoid the extreme right, keep up with the times, don't offend anyone but let everyone believe what he wishes." Still, there are always the faithful few who desire to *be blameless . . . children of God . . . in a crooked and perverted generation* (Philippians 2:15-16).

Thought for Today: It is not enough merely to be traveling; we must be on the narrow road that leads to heaven.

In Today's Reading

Evil reigns of Manasseh and Amon; Josiah's good reign; book of the law discovered; true worship restored; idolatry destroyed.

Hezekiah was one of the best kings in the history of Judah; but his son Manasseh was even more wicked than his grandfather Ahaz, who had closed the temple (II Chronicles 28:24). Manasseh *did . . . evil in the LORD's eyes, imitating the abominations of the nations. . . . He built altars to the whole heavenly host in both courtyards of the LORD 's temple. He passed his son through the fire. . . . He did . . . evil in the LORD's eyes, provoking Him to anger* (II Kings 21:2-6).

Manasseh's wickedness resulted in his being defeated. The fierce Assyrians *captured Manasseh with hooks, bound him . . . and took him to Babylon. When they confined him, he sought favor from the LORD his God . . . earnestly humbled himself before . . . God. . . . He prayed . . . so He granted his request . . . and brought him back to Jerusalem and to his kingdom. So Manasseh came to know that the LORD is God.* The Lord permitted him to return to Jerusalem and be reinstated as king (II Chronicles 33:10-13). This was an answer to Manasseh's prayers for mercy and forgiveness, as well as to the prayers of his godly father Hezekiah many years before. God forgives even the most evil of sinners when they truly repent and pray for forgiveness. Upon being restored as king, Manasseh immediately destroyed the false gods and altars he had previously built and rebuilt the altar and returned to true worship to the Lord.

But Manasseh could not relive the wasted years of his wicked rule or even convince his own son to reject idols and worship the Lord. This points out the irreversible law of nature: *Don't be deceived. . . . Whatever a man sows he will also reap . . . the one who sows to his flesh will reap corruption . . . but the one who sows to the Spirit will reap eternal life* (Galatians 6:7-8). After Manasseh's death, his son Amon reinstated all the wicked, idolatrous practices of his father's earlier reign (II Chronicles 33:22). *He . . . served . . . idols . . . and . . . worshiped them* (II Kings 21:21).

He Himself is the propitiation (personal atonement) *for our sins, and not only for ours, but also for those of the whole world* (I John 2:2).

Thought for Today: The measure of a person's surrender determines his usefulness to God.

In Today's Reading

Passover restored; destruction of Jerusalem and temple foretold; death of Josiah; fall of Jerusalem; captivity of Judah.

Josiah was the last godly king of Judah before the destruction of Jerusalem. *He did what was right in the LORD's eyes and walked in all the ways of his forefather David* (II Kings 22:2; II Chronicles 34:2). He destroyed all the idolatrous practices in Jerusalem and Judah. *Then the king went up to the LORD's temple. . . . He read . . . all the words of . . . the covenant that had been found in the LORD's temple. Next the king . . . made a covenant . . . to follow the LORD and to keep His commandments. . . . He also tore down the houses of the male shrine prostitutes* (II Kings 23:2-3,7).

Josiah went beyond Judah, into the Assyrian-controlled former northern kingdom, to Bethel, where Jeroboam had built one of the golden calves. *He broke the sacred pillars. . . . He sent someone to take the bones out of the tombs, and . . . burned them on the altar. . . . according to the word of the LORD* prophesied almost 300 years before (23:14-16; I Kings 13:1-3).

The king commanded . . . Keep the Passover of the LORD . . . as written in the . . . covenant. . . . Josiah removed the . . . household idols . . . and all the detestable things that were . . . in . . . Judah and . . . Jerusalem. . . . in order to carry out the words of the law . . . found in the LORD's temple (II Kings 23:21,24).

The last four kings who followed Josiah were all evil, puppet rulers, appointed by and subject to first Egypt and then to Babylon.

Finally, Nebuchadnezzar marched his army into Judah and surrounded Jerusalem, eventually reducing its people to starvation. The Babylonians forced King Zedekiah to watch as *they slaughtered Zedekiah's sons before his very eyes. Finally, the king of Babylon blinded Zedekiah's eyes, bound him in bronze shackles, and took him to Babylon* (25:7).

The destruction of the once-glorious kingdom of Judah and Solomon's temple reminds us that even the greatest present-day nation on earth, with all its wealth, military might, and nuclear defense, cannot survive – regardless of how much the people may pray – if they continue to ignore the word of God (23:25-27). *Anyone who turns his ear away from hearing the law – even his prayer is detestable* (Proverbs 28:9).

Thought for Today: A nation is successful when it is faithful to God.

Introduction To The Books Of I & II Chronicles

The books of II Samuel and I & II Kings cover about the same period in history as I & II Chronicles. Kings primarily focus on the political history of Israel and Judah, while Chronicles primarily present the religious history of Judah, Jerusalem, and the temple as it relates to the Davidic Covenant.The northern tribes are of little significance in Chronicles.

I Chronicles opens with the longest genealogical history in the Bible and covers approximately 3,500 years (chapters 1 – 9). Its second chapter is devoted to the descendants of Judah because the promised Messiah would descend from this tribe (Genesis 49:8-12). The record begins with Adam (I Chronicles 1:1); then to Abraham, Isaac, and Jacob; then Judah; and on to David, through whom the Messiah would come. These families are the vital links connecting the legal genealogy of Christ through Joseph, who was His legal, but not His biological, father (Matthew 1:1-17; II Samuel 7:12-13; Psalms 89:3-4; 132:11; Isaiah 11:1; Jeremiah 23:5). The rightful Heir to the throne of David is the Messiah Jesus, who was born through the virgin Mary, as recorded in Luke 2:7,11; 3:23-38. The Messianic lineage passed from David to Nathan, Solomon's brother (II Samuel 5:14; I Chronicles 3:5; 14:4; Luke 3:31). The line of Solomon was eliminated (Jeremiah 22:22-30). While Abraham and David were ancestors of both Joseph and Mary, the royal Davidic lineage of Jesus as the Messiah is traced to Joseph in Matthew and the actual human blood line is traced through Mary in Luke.

Saul's last battle and death are mentioned in chapter ten of I Chronicles. Chapters 11 – 29 cover the 40-year reign of David.

II Chronicles continues with the reign of Solomon. It records the division of the kingdom, and covers the history of Judah until the exile of the people to Babylon. The last verses contain the proclamation of the Persian King Cyrus for their return to Jerusalem, according to the prophecy of Jeremiah (II Chronicles 36:22-23; Jeremiah 29:10-14).

The first seven chapters of II Chronicles record the building of the temple on Mount Moriah in Jerusalem after the pattern of the tabernacle. The temple was completed and dedicated to God in the 11th year of Solomon's reign (chapter 5; compare I Kings 6:38). II Chronicles ends with the fall of Jerusalem and the destruction of Solomon's temple in 586 B.C. (chapters 10 – 36).

In Today's Reading

Jesus' lineage through Adam, Noah, Abraham, Israel (Jacob), and Judah.

The first nine chapters of I Chronicles may first appear to be an unimportant list of names. But, this ancient genealogy reveals the exact plan and choices of our Creator in selecting the people who qualified to serve Him, beginning with *Adam, Seth, Enosh . . . Noah. . . . Abraham . . . . Isaac. . . . and Israel* (I Chronicles 1:1,3-4,28,34; compare Genesis 5:1-32). Here Jacob is called by his God-given name *Israel* (compare 35:9-12).

This genealogy was exceedingly important after the Israelites' captivity. It showed how God continued to protect the family line of the coming Messiah, whose descent was traced from Adam through Abraham and David. In Luke 3:23-38, we see the genealogy of the second Adam, Jesus Christ (I Corinthians 15:22,45), traced through the very names recorded in Chronicles. Unless a man's name had been included in this genealogy, he could not minister in the temple.

Our Lord is now drawing to Himself *a holy nation, a people for His possession* (I Peter 2:9), united not by a human genealogical bloodline that dates back to Adam, but united by a spiritual rebirth into the family of God through the blood of the second Adam, Jesus Christ.

Christ is Lord of our lives and oversees every detail. You can be sure that things that happen to believers are never "accidents"; they are allowed by our Lord, the Master Engineer, to prepare us to be the person He can use to accomplish the purpose for which He created us. As we prayerfully read all His word, He continually reveals His will to us. Although we do not understand many of the things that God allows a Christian to suffer, His word makes it clear that He has an eternal purpose for them and this new life in Christ is only the beginning.

This genealogy is a reminder that soon the final books in heaven will be opened. *The victor will be dressed in white clothes, and I will never erase his name from the book of life, but will acknowledge his name before My Father and before His angels* (Revelation 3:5).

Thought for Today: There are no "accidents" with God's children.

In Today's Reading

Descendants of David, Solomon, Judah, Simeon, Reuben, Gad and Manasseh (east).

God compares the small tribe of Simeon that chose to live in the promised land to the much larger tribe of Reuben that chose not to settle in the promised land. *From these sons of Simeon 500 men . . . went to Mount Seir. They* ***struck down*** *the remnant of the* ***Amalekites*** *that had escaped, and they* ***still live there today*** (I Chronicles 4:42-43). What a contrast this is to the more powerful *sons of Reuben. . . .* (who) *were unfaithful to the God of their fathers. They prostituted themselves to the gods of the people of the land whom God had destroyed before them. So the God of Israel stirred up the . . . king of Assyria . . . who took the* ***Reubenites . . . into exile. . . . where they are still today*** (5:1,25-26).

The Reubenites chose to live in the fertile lands outside the promised land on the eastern side of the Jordan, even though it was far from the tabernacle, which was the only place God had chosen to worship Him (Numbers 32). They chose what they believed would bring them greater material success rather than spiritual direction and protection.

Jacob's prophecy regarding Reuben truly came to pass. By birthright, the descendants of the firstborn son should have had preeminence over all the other tribes. But Jacob prophesied: *Reuben, you are . . . excelling in power. . . .* (but) *turbulent as water, you will no longer excel, because you got into the bed of your father and you defiled it* (Genesis 49:3-4). Water is a good illustration, because it naturally flows to the lowest possible level. Water is also unstable in that it can be driven by the winds as well as evaporate with the heat. The Reubenites are an example of some today who become so involved in the things of the world that little time is left for serving the Lord and for reading His word. They too consider the plan of God for their lives less important than satisfying personal ambitions and pleasures. We need not fear that we are not talented enough, strong enough, or good enough. Everything God wants us to be or to do He makes possible. *I know, O LORD, that a man's way of life is not his own; no one who walks determines his own steps* (Jeremiah 10:23).

Thought for Today: Those who entrust their all to God receive His best.

In Today's Reading

Descendants of Levi; temple singers and keepers appointed; descendants of Aaron; cities of the Levites; numerous genealogies.

The long and seemingly uninteresting genealogy in these chapters reveals that God does not look on mankind as just a multitude of human beings who populate the earth. The name of every individual priest and Levite, along with the family and tribe he belonged to, was carefully registered. However, in gratitude for their spiritual leadership, the other tribes were given the responsibility of sustaining the Levites who lived within their communities through their tithes and offerings. We see a striking contrast in the character of the men mentioned in these chapters. Some were devoted to their God-given responsibilities, while others profaned their holy calling.

Of first consideration in this listing was the high priest, who was to be chosen only from the family of Aaron (I Chronicles 6:3). Aaron, Eleazar, and Ithamar were devoted to their calling as priests, but Aaron's two oldest sons Nadab and Abihu were struck dead when they ignored the commandments of God. Samuel was a godly judge, but *the sons of Samuel: Joel his firstborn, and Abijah his second son* (6:28) were evil. For years, Abiathar was a dedicated high priest, but later he became a traitor to David (I Kings 1:5-7; 2:26-27).

As we look around us, we see some who, at first, seemed to be blessed with remarkable spiritual gifts like these five men; but, when tested, they forfeited their spiritual positions and opportunities.

God is just as concerned with each of us today as He was with the Israelites then. *The doorkeeper opens it for him, and the sheep hear his voice. He calls his own sheep by name and leads them out* (John 10:3). Every Israelite returning from the Babylonian captivity was individually and carefully registered to ensure his participation in worship at the temple (Ezra 2:2-63). To serve the Lord in eternity our names must be written in the book of life. *Nothing profane will ever enter it: no one who does what is vile or false, but only those written in the Lamb's book of life* (Revelation 21:27).

Thought for Today: Your name is recorded in the book of life when you receive Christ as your Savior.

In Today's Reading

Descendants of Benjamin; priests and Levites in Jerusalem and their responsibilities; genealogy of Saul; tragic deaths of Saul and his sons.

Only a small minority of Israelites were willing to leave the comforts of the new Persian kingdom and return to Jerusalem to rebuild the temple.

The first to live again on their own holdings in their towns were Israelites, priests, Levites, and temple servants (I Chronicles 9:2-3; Nehemiah 11:3). The work of *the Nethinims* (temple servants) may seem rather insignificant, but it was essential work that needed to be done for the Lord. Loyalty to their heavenly King made them willing to work and to serve wherever needed. Of the Levites, *some of them were in charge of the utensils used in worship; they would count them when they brought them in and when they took them out* (I Chronicles 9:28). This responsibility appears to be of little importance. Some were overseers, *others . . . were put in charge of the furnishings and all the utensils of the sanctuary, as well as the fine flour, the wine, the oil, the incense, and the spices* (9:29-30), which perhaps required a little more skill; still others were responsible for *making the bread-wafers* (9:31). All were ordinary laborers and, to us, may seem hardly worth mentioning. But God esteemed each responsibility as indispensable and worthy of recording and, collectively, all tasks were necessary to fulfill the service to the Lord.

Now there are different gifts, but the same Spirit. . . . But one and the same Spirit is active in all these, distributing to each one as He will and not necessarily as we prefer (I Corinthians 12:4,11). Regardless of the seeming importance or insignificance of our abilities, they are a sacred trust from God. The Lord does not expect the person who is given one talent to fulfill the responsibility of the person who has five talents (Matthew 25:24-28). But, the person who fails to respond to his opportunities will hear on judgment day: *You evil, lazy slave! . . . you knew that I reap where I haven't sown and gather where I haven't scattered* (25:26).

We are required to be faithful stewards (managers) of our lives and the abilities and opportunities that God has entrusted to us. *Whatever you do, do it enthusiastically, as something done for the Lord and not for men* (Colossians 3:23).

Thought for Today: Faith becomes stronger as we read God's word.

In Today's Reading

David made king over Judah; Israel anoints David king;
He reigns in Jebus (Jerusalem).

David did not see any possibility that he could ever be King of Israel when Saul, the first anointed king of Israel, with all his authority and other resources, was determined to kill him. Saul was also far from being an old man, and he had sons who were the expected heirs to the throne. Moreover, how could David expect that the large and jealous tribe of Ephraim would agree that David, from the tribe of Judah, should rule over them? How would Saul's tribe, the Benjamites, permit the monarchy to be taken from them? David suffered under very difficult circumstances for years until it seemed he must flee to the land of the Philistines. But then, Saul died a violent death and God fulfilled His word, and the leaders of *all Israel gathered together around David at Hebron and said, Here we are, your own flesh and blood. . . . Furthermore, the LORD your God said to you, You will shepherd My people Israel and be a ruler over My people Israel. . . . and they anointed David king over Israel, in accordance with the LORD's word through Samuel* (I Chronicles 11:1-3).

In many respects, David's problems parallel situations that some of us face today. Just as surely as the Lord gives us a desire to accomplish something for His honor, obstacles will appear. It may be a financial situation that seems hopeless, or simply a feeling of inability to cope with problems. For some, not much opposition is needed before they feel there is no use in trying. Whatever the case, overcoming these difficulties may seem as impossible as it was of David ever becoming king. The Lord never promised an easy road for any of His followers. In fact, Jesus said: *If anyone wants to come with Me, he must deny himself, take up his cross daily, and follow Me* (Luke 9:23). The way of the cross is often long and lonely and it is never popular. Once we recognize the authority of Christ over our lives, we will patiently look to Him for direction and strength. *The one who looks intently into the perfect law of freedom and perseveres in it, and is not a forgetful hearer but a doer who acts – this person will be blessed in what he does* (James 1:25).

Thought for Today: We never build ourselves up by putting others down.

In Today's Reading

King Hiram's kindness to David; Philistines defeated; Ark brought to Jerusalem; David's psalm of thanksgiving.

Soon after establishing his capital in Jerusalem, David united the nation for a glorious time of praising the Lord while bringing the ark of God from the house of Obed-edom to Jerusalem. To demonstrate his reverence for God, and in recognition that God was the Supreme Ruler, David humbly laid aside his kingly garments and dressed in a plain linen ephod, a garment the priests wore when ministering before the Lord. In doing this, David was publicly acknowledging his submission to the authority of the supreme King and expressing adoration and praise to his Lord as Almighty God and the true King of Israel.

On that day, David provided an inspiring psalm for his choir to sing. It still lifts our spirits as we worship our wonderful Lord. David proclaimed to the world: *Give thanks to the LORD; call on His name; proclaim His deeds among the people* (I Chronicles 16:8-9). *Sing praise to Him; tell about all His wonderful works! . . . Rejoice. . . . Remember His covenant forever— the promise He ordained for a thousand generations . . . . Declare His glory among the nations. . . . For the LORD is great and is highly praised . . . . bring an offering and come before Him. Worship the LORD in His holy majesty. . . . The LORD is King!* (16:9-31). Is it any surprise that David was a man after God's own heart (I Samuel 13:14; Acts 13:22)? Yes, the Lord reigns. He is still Sovereign and the world needs to hear us praise the Lord and to talk of all His wondrous works (Acts 16:9).

David also stands out as a man of prayer; thus, we see the often-repeated phrase: *David inquired of God, Should I* (I Chronicles 14:10,14; note: I Samuel 23:2,4; 30:8; II Samuel 2:1; 5:19,23; 21:1). As a result of these basic, God-honoring characteristics, *David's fame spread through all the lands, and the LORD caused all the nations to fear him* (I Chronicles 14:17).

When we complain, it is truly a victory for Satan and an insult to God.

It is good to praise the LORD, to sing praise to Your name, Most High, . . . to declare Your faithful love in the morning and Your faithfulness at night (Psalms 92:1-2).

Thought for Today: People who complain can't sing praises to the Lord.

In Today's Reading

David forbidden to build the temple; covenant of God with David; his prayer; extends his kingdom; administered justice to his people.

Prayer and praise to God were distinguishing characteristics in the life of David. It is often recorded: *David inquired of the LORD* (I Samuel 23:2,4; 30:8; II Samuel 2:1; 5:19,23; 21:1; I Chronicles 14:10,14).

David's prayer life was often words of praise. David prayed: *LORD, there is no one like You, and there is no God besides You, which is confirmed by all that we have heard with our own ears* (17:20). Although almost everyone is aware of the importance of prayer, few make it a vital part of their lives. But prayer has led many Christians to make the right decisions.

As we pray, we are speaking to our Father, and as we read His word, He is speaking to us. That is "open communication" in the family of God. Prayer and knowing God's word are vital links in releasing heaven's power to answer prayer.

There is no other how-to-pray manual nor any better reading plan than beginning in Genesis and ending with Revelation. It is an attitude of foolish pride to believe we are qualified to choose what not to read when He clearly said: *All Scripture is . . . profitable* (II Timothy 3:16). If it is *all . . . profitable* and we don't read all of it, then we fail to gain the best preparation for prayer that God has provided. When we recognize the Bible as His unique prayer manual for us, we will give it priority far above all other "important matters" in our daily schedules.

Let us open our Bibles reverently, daily, praying *that the God of our Lord Jesus Christ, the glorious Father, would give you a spirit of wisdom and revelation in the knowledge of Him. I pray that the eyes of your heart may be enlightened so you may know what is the hope of His calling, what are the glorious riches of His inheritance among the saints, and what is the immeasurable greatness of His power to us who believe, according to the working of His vast strength* (Ephesians 1:17-19).

Let the dominating motive in all our reading of God's word be *that you may walk worthy of the Lord, fully pleasing to Him, bearing fruit in every good work and growing in the knowledge of God* (Colossians 1:10).

Thought for Today: A problem? Pray, then trust God for the outcome!

In Today's Reading

David's sin in taking a military census; his preparation for building the temple and instructions to Solomon; duties of the Levites.

Solomon was about 20 years of age when he was anointed king. Since young people do not have the years of experience that their elders do, they often underestimate the things that are of greatest importance. Consequently, David was not satisfied with just providing Solomon with the materials needed to build the temple. *Above all, may the LORD give you insight and understanding when He puts you in charge of Israel so that you may keep the law of the LORD your God. Then you will succeed if you carefully follow the statutes and ordinances that the LORD commanded Moses for Israel. . . . Now set your heart and soul on seeking the LORD your God. Get started building the LORD God's sanctuary so that you may bring the ark of the covenant of the LORD and the holy vessels of God to the temple that is to be built for the name of the LORD* (I Chronicles 22:12-13,18-19).

David's accumulation of materials for the temple were now in the possession of his son. But Solomon ignored the spiritual advice of his father David to *set* (his) *heart . . . on seeking the LORD. . . . Get started building the . . . sanctuary.* Building the temple should have been his first priority, but Solomon put personal interests first and did not begin building the temple until the fourth year of his reign. Instead, he began to amass chariots and horses (II Chronicles 1:14; 3:1-2). This was in violation of the law for the kings of Israel (Deuteronomy 17:16-18; I Kings 10:26 – 11:4).

David's appeal to Solomon is still the need of every Christian. True faith is demonstrated by our commitment and obedience to the word of God and our dependency upon Him to answer prayer while we do all we can to bring it to pass. We should not assume that we can just "leave it up to the Lord and do nothing." The Lord expects our participation in all that we can do. Christ calls every believer to *seek first the kingdom of God and His righteousness, and all these things will be provided for you* (Matthew 6:33). Then consider this fact: *Wasn't Abraham our father justified by works when he offered Isaac his son on the altar? You see that faith was active together with his works, and by works, faith was perfected* (James 2:21-22).

Thought for Today: Satan will tempt you to sin, but by God's grace you can resist him.

In Today's Reading

Duties assigned to priests; musicians and singers; divisions of the porters (gatekeepers); treasurers and other officials.

David . . . appointed priests, singers, porters (gatekeepers), treasurers, and other workers (I Chronicles 25:1; 9:22-29) of the temple who were entrusted with responsibilities for temple worship. The gatekeepers were called *capable men . . . for the work* (26:8). They were the Korahites and Merarites, descendants of Levi (Genesis 46:11). Twenty-four gatekeepers guarded the entrances day and night lest an unqualified person attempted to enter (I Chronicles 26:17-18).

Every position was equally important to maintain worship in the temple as ordered by the Lord. Today, everything that needs to be done in the church and in ministries dedicated to fulfilling the great commission is also a sacred responsibility from God.

Earlier, David had planned to make Jerusalem the religious center of Israel by bringing the ark of the covenant there. After Uzzah was struck dead for touching the ark, it was taken to the home of Obed-edom. When Obed-edom received the ark, he received more than the word of God; he received the very presence of God (Exodus 25:22; I Samuel 4:4; II Samuel 6:2). The presence of the Lord brought blessing on the home of Obed-edom. In like manner, the presence of the Lord will also bless our families and homes when the word of God is prominent in our lives.

Some people ignore the Master's ownership rights to their lives and do not recognize their position as His managers of their talents, time, and even the Lord's tithe. All these are meant to be used for His purpose rather than for our own pleasures and personal interests. Each day is given to us as a trust that we may become like Christ and glorify Him. What God has entrusted to us can become multiplied blessings to others; but, when kept for selfish purposes, it can become a curse.

In our family devotions, let us thank our heavenly Father for each of our children and help them to know their importance to Him. *Whoever is faithful in very little is also faithful in much. . . . So if you have not been faithful with the unrighteous money, who will trust you with what is genuine?* (Luke 16:10-11).

Thought for Today: Uppermost in our thoughts should be Christ and His word.

In Today's Reading

Solomon encouraged to build the temple; David's gifts for the temple; his thanks and prayer; Solomon made king; David's death.

David had reigned *over Israel . . . 40 years,* 33 years in Jerusalem, 7 years in Hebron (I Chronicles 29:27). Now his life was almost over. In his last year, David assembled all the tribal princes and military captains. He told them how God had chosen Solomon to build His temple and the greatest concern should be to *seek after all the commandments of the LORD your God* (28:8). Then David charged Solomon: *Know the God of your father, and serve Him with a whole heart . . . for the LORD searches every heart and understands the intention of every thought. If you seek Him, He will be found by you, but if you forsake Him, He will reject you forever* (28:9).

David then offered one of the most inspiring prayers recorded in the Scriptures. *David said, Blessed are You, O LORD God of our father Israel . . . Yours, LORD, is the greatness and the power and the glory and the splendor and the majesty, for everything in the heavens and on earth belongs to You. Yours, LORD, is the kingdom, and You are exalted . . . . In Your hand are power and might . . . to make great and to give strength to all. Now . . . our God, we give You thanks and praise Your glorious name* (29:10-13).

David's heartfelt prayer is a reminder to all of us that prayer should be a time of praising, adoring, and worshiping Him with thanksgiving for who He is, as well as for what He has given us. As we recognize our total dependence upon God for everything, we will praise Him for His provision.When we neglect to praise the Lord daily, our worship often becomes a mere ritual. Every day, under every circumstance, *Give thanks in everything* (I Thessalonians 5:18). To grumble about our circumstances is to express dissatisfaction with God and to question His wisdom and His love for us.

Kneeling, bowing the head, and stretching forth hands are all expressions of worship. David was inspired by the Holy Spirit to write: *Lift up your hands in the holy place, and praise the LORD!* (Psalms 134:2). *Therefore I want the men in every place to pray, lifting up holy hands without anger or argument* (I Timothy 2:8).

Thought for Today: Let us freely offer praise to God *today*.

In Today's Reading

Solomon's sacrifices; his dream; his accumulation of chariots and horsemen; Solomon builds the temple.

King Solomon began his reign in submission to *the LORD his God* (II Chronicles 1:1). *Solomon and the whole assembly with him went to . . . the tent of meeting of God, which . . . Moses had made in the wilderness. . . . and offered 1,000 burnt offerings. . . . That night God appeared to Solomon and said . . . Ask! What should I give you?* (1:3-7). In I Kings we have more complete details of this event. *At Gibeon the LORD appeared to Solomon in* ***a dream*** *at night; God said, Ask! What should I give you? . . . Then Solomon awoke and discovered that* ***it had been a dream!*** (I Kings 3:5,15). In this dream, *Solomon said to God. . . . grant me wisdom and knowledge . . . for who can judge this great people of Yours?* (II Chronicles 1:8-12). Through this dream the Lord was revealing to Solomon that his greatest need was to be obedient to His word.

Following the sacrifices at Gibeon, Solomon began accumulating massive numbers of *chariots and horsemen* (II Chronicles 1:14; 9:25; I Kings 4:26). However, God had commanded that the king *must not . . . make the people return to Egypt in order to acquire large numbers of horses . . . the LORD has told you . . . never go back that way again* (Deuteronomy 17:16). But he even married the daughter of Pharaoh (I Kings 11:1). He again defied God, who said that *he must not acquire large numbers of wives for then his heart will . . . go astray. Silver and gold, too, he must not acquire in very large amounts* (Deuteronomy 17:16-17). Solomon ignored all three of these commandments. But his most serious neglect was his indifference toward the fourth commandment to Israel's kings: *He must write a copy of this law for himself on a scroll like that in the possession of the Levitical priests. . . .he will read from it all the days of his life . . . observing all the requirements of this law* (17:18-19).

It makes little difference whether or not we become famous, powerful, or wealthy. But, it is most important for us to recognize that God has first claim on our wisdom and our abilities, and on our use of them. *For His divine power has given us everything required for life and godliness, through the knowledge of Him who called us by His own glory and goodness* (II Peter 1:3).

Thought for Today: God is the one true source of wisdom.

In Today's Reading

The temple's furnishings; the ark brought into the temple; the cloud of the Lord fills the temple; Solomon's prayer of dedication.

The Israelites gathered around Solomon as he *stood before the altar of the LORD. . . . He spread out his hands. For Solomon had made a bronze platform and. . . . knelt on his knees before the entire congregation of Israel, and spread out his hands toward heaven* (II Chronicles 6:12-13). It was not uncommon for the people of God to lift their hands in prayer and praise (Psalms 63:3-4). Hands lifted toward heaven are a sign of wholehearted submission and worship. Surely it is natural to lift up our hands or to kneel in humility before the living God.

Solomon began his prayer, saying: *LORD God of Israel, there is no God like You in heaven or on earth, keeping the covenant and mercy to Your servants, who walk before You with their whole heart. . . . that all the people of the earth may know Your name, to fear You as Your people Israel do, and that they may know that this temple I have built is called by Your name* (II Chronicles 6:14,16,33). Sadly, his talk didn't match his conduct.

Solomon also had prayed: *When Your people . . . have sinned . . . and they repent . . . and they pray . . . forgive the sin of Your people Israel. . . . that all the peoples of the earth may know Your name, to fear You* (6:24-25,33). It is pathetic to realize there is no record that Solomon repented of his sins.

Somewhere, at this moment, on a hospital bed or in a prison cell, facing unemployment or the cruel experiences of family problems, there are people repenting of their sins, reading God's word for direction, being restored to Him, and coming forth stronger in their faith. It is wonderful to know how much the Lord loves us. *When we are judged, we are disciplined by the Lord, so that we may not be condemned with the world* (I Corinthians 11:32). The best years of our lives can be the outcome of failure, heartbreak, or loneliness that lead to a true commitment to Christ as Lord of our lives. We can become the people God meant us to be. Suffering could be caused by God, Satan, or foolish decisions; but it can be used of God, if we have faith to turn to Him. *For I consider that the sufferings of this present time are not worth comparing with the glory that is going to be revealed to us* (Romans 8:18).

Thought for Today: Are we so occupied expecting recognition that we fail to praise God?

In Today's Reading

Solomon's sacrifices; glory of the Lord; God appears to Solomon; Queen of Sheba visits Solomon; his riches and fame; his death.

When Solomon finished praying, fire descended from heaven and consumed the burnt offering and the sacrifices. The glory of the LORD filled the temple (II Chronicles 7:1).

After that great dedication, the Lord again appeared to Solomon by night, saying: *If I close the sky so there is no rain, or if I command the grasshopper to consume the land, or if I send pestilence on My people, and My people who are called by My name humble themselves, pray and seek My face, and turn from their evil ways, then I will hear from heaven, forgive their sin, and heal their land* (7:13-14).

Carefully consider the qualifications for God to *heal their land*. First, He is speaking of *My people*. This implies our need to receive Christ according to His word. Then, to *humble* ourselves means, first and foremost, a confession of our sin of neglecting His word, as if we could live by our own good judgment and do not need His advice. To humble one's self also includes acknowledgment of sin, a sorrow for sin, and genuine repentance. God alone can, and does, forgive and cleanse us from all confessed sin (I John 1:9).

When God said: *Seek My face,* He means for us to seek Him in His word daily that we may know what life is all about. As we read His word, the Holy Spirit not only enlightens our understanding of how to know His will, but He empowers us to live it. God has warned: *Anyone who turns his ear away from hearing the law – even his prayer is detestable* (Proverbs 28:9).

We need to consider and ask ourselves: "Will what I'm seeking in prayer bring honor to the Father or merely benefit me?"

Our great need is to prayerfully read all His word. Jesus said: *If anyone does not remain in Me, he is thrown aside like a branch and he withers. They gather them, throw them into the fire, and they are burned. If you remain in Me and My words remain in you, ask whatever you want and it will be done for you* (John 15:6-7).

Thought for Today: *The LORD is near all who call out to Him* (Psa. 145:18).

The Divided Kingdom (During the ministries of Elijah & Elisha)

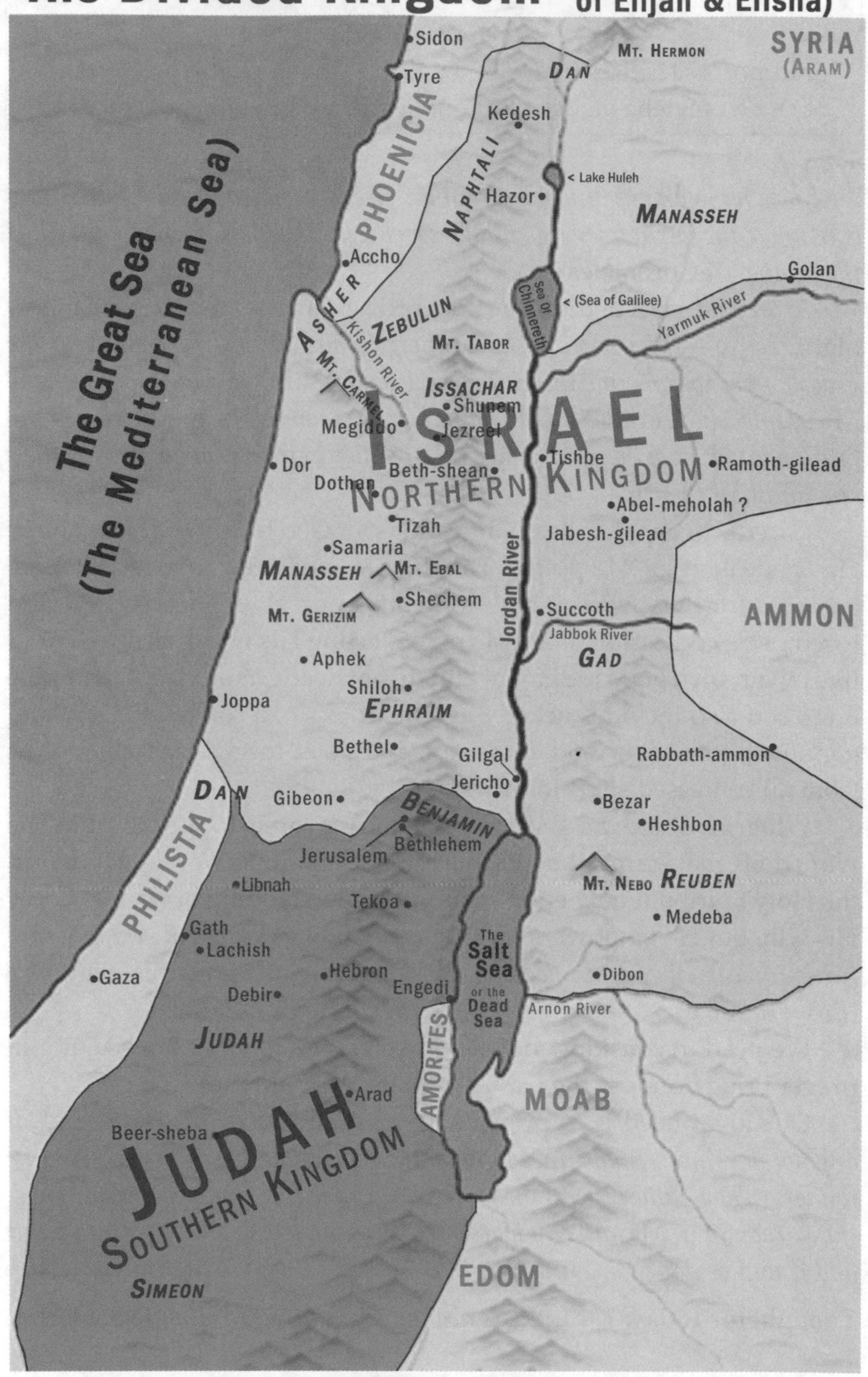

In Today's Reading

Rehoboam succeeds Solomon; Jeroboam leads revolt of the 10 tribes; Rehoboam forsakes *the law* of God; Shishak invades Judah.

When Solomon was made king, David urged him: *Keep your obligation to the LORD your God to walk in His ways and to keep . . . His commandments . . . as is written in the law of Moses, so that you may have success in everything you do* (I Kings 2:3). Sadly, however, there is no record of Solomon urging his own son Rehoboam to read God's word and remain faithful to the Lord.

Neither is there any mention that Rehoboam began his reign with altar sacrifices and prayer as his father did. What we do read is that, three years after Rehoboam became king, *he forsook the law of the LORD he and all Israel with him. . . . he did evil because he did not set his heart to seek the LORD* (II Chronicles 11:17; 12:1-14).

The leaders of Israel met with Rehoboam with a reasonable request – that he ease the excessive taxes that his father had imposed upon them. They also asked that he discontinue the forced labor which had persisted since they first began building the gorgeous palaces, stables, and chariot houses, luxurious parks, and other spectacular structures within Solomon's famous kingdom. If Rehoboam would consent, the leaders agreed to pledge their loyalty to him.

Rehoboam's first decision as king was a major blunder. His intolerance led most of the tribes to secede and form the northern kingdom. Rehoboam was left with only a small part of the original promised land. Only the tribes of Judah and Benjamin remained. But, how could he have made wise choices since he *did not set his heart to seek the LORD* (12:14)?

Notice that it does not say to "serve the Lord." It was not better service that the Lord expected, but for Rehoboam to *seek the LORD*. The same spiritual principles hold true today. Though we may be unaware of it, if we humbly seek the Lord, our lives will be guided by His Spirit to accomplish His perfect will and purpose. *But He gives greater grace. Therefore He says: God resists the proud, but gives grace to the humble* (James 4:6).

Thought for Today: Without God, the most clever strategy of the wisest counselors is worthless.

In Today's Reading

King Asa's reforms; his covenant with God; his treaty with Syria (Aram); Asa rebuked by Hanani; Asa's death; Jehoshaphat succeeds Asa.

King Asa was the grandson of Rehoboam and the great-grandson of Solomon. But Asa rejected their pagan idols. Asa was greatly encouraged by *Azariah son of Oded* (II Chronicles 15:1). When Azariah spoke: *Asa . . . took courage and removed the detestable idols from the whole land of Judah and Benjamin and from the cities he had taken in the hill country of Ephraim. He repaired the altar of the LORD that was in front of the vestibule of the LORD's temple. Then he gathered all Judah and Benjamin, as well as those from the tribes of Ephraim, Manasseh, and Simeon who had settled among them, for they had defected to him from Israel in great numbers when they saw that the LORD his God was with him. . . . Then they entered into a covenant to seek the LORD God of their fathers with all their heart and all their soul. . . . So the LORD gave them rest* (from war for 10 years) (14:1-7; 15:8-9,12,15-16).

Asa left no room for compromise. *He banished the male shrine prostitutes from the land, and removed all of the idols that his fathers had made* (I Kings 15:12). He even removed his own grandmother Maachah *from being queen-mother, because she had made a detestable image of Asherah. And Asa chopped down her detestable image and burned it in the Kidron Valley* (15:13; II Chronicles 15:16).

You can be sure that, when anyone takes a firm stand for moral and spiritual values, Satan will instigate opposition and then seek to bring about a compromise in that person's positive declaration of faith.

As his wealth and power increased, Asa's dependence upon God decreased. *Hanani the seer came to King Asa . . .* and rebuked him: *Because you depended on the king of Aram* (Syria) *and have not depended on the LORD . . . the army of the king of Aram has escaped from your hand* (16:7).

Hanani was put in prison for his faithful witness. But his words have imparted immeasurable faith and boldness to all of us to remain faithful in the midst of a hostile world: *For the eyes of the LORD range to and fro throughout the earth to show Himself strong for those whose heart is at perfect peace with Him* (II Chronicles 16:9).

Thought for Today: Only the unsaved are powerless against Satan.

In Today's Reading

Jehoshaphat allied himself with Ahab; defeat of Jehoshaphat; death of Ahab; Jehoshaphat's national reformation; death of Jehoshaphat.

Jehoshaphat was one of the most godly kings in the history of Judah. He appointed Levites throughout the country to read and instruct people in the law of God. He forced the Baal and Ashtoreth cult followers, as well as the male prostitutes (homosexuals), out of his country (II Chronicles 17:3-9).

Jehoshaphat made a serious mistake when he associated with Ahab, the idol-worshiping king of the northern kingdom. Their friendship led to the marriage of Jehoshaphat's son Jehoram to Ahab's daughter Athaliah (18:1; 21:1,6). Ahab then asked Jehoshaphat to join him in a battle with Syria (Aram) to regain his border city of Ramoth-gilead (18:3). Can you imagine godly Jehoshaphat feasting with Ahab and Jezebel, his Baal-worshiping wife, in Ahab's palace?

Following Jehoshaphat's request for a word from God, a fearless prophet named Micaiah boldly foretold that Ahab would not return alive from that war (18:4,13,16). In disregard of the prophet's warning, Jehoshaphat joined Ahab and almost lost his life. When surrounded by Aramaeans (Syrians), Jehoshaphat *cried out and the LORD helped him, and God drew them away from him* (18:31). *Jehoshaphat king of Judah returned to his home in Jerusalem in peace* (19:1). God sent the prophet Jehu to rebuke him: *Do you love to help the wicked?. . . Because of this, wrath from the LORD's presense is on you* (19:2).

The marriage of Jehoshaphat's son Jehoram to the daughter of Jezebel opened the door to Baal worship in Judah and the massacre of all of Jehoshaphat's sons and grandsons except for one-year-old Jehoash (Joash) who was hidden by the high priest Jehoiada (22:10-12).

No Christian man or woman should have a close relationship with an unsaved person, regardless of how "good" the unsaved person may seem or how "sure" the Christian is that further involvement will not occur. *Do you not know that friendship with the world is hostility toward God? So whoever wants to be the world's friend becomes God's enemy* (James 4:4).

Thought for Today: A marvelous transformation takes place when anyone – even the most wretched sinner – prays for mercy.

In Today's Reading

Jehoram's, Ahaziah's and Athaliah's reigns; prophecy of Elijah; Joash becomes king and repairs the temple; the nation turns to idolatry.

During most of Jehoshaphat's reign, he maintained friendly relations with Ahab, the idol-worshiping king of the northern kingdom. His son's marriage to Ahab's daughter resulted in a heritage of wicked leadership for Judah. Jehoshaphat's life should serve as a warning to those today who say: "I know God said we should not have close relationships with unsaved people, but I don't let them affect me." However, we can see that Jehoshaphat, though it may not have affected him personally, could not control the way it affected his sons and his grandchildren.

After the death of Jehoshaphat, his son Jehoram took control of the kingdom. He proceeded to destroy all the godly influence of his father's reign. He also killed *with the sword all his brothers* . . . and . . . *walked in the way of the kings of Israel . . . for Ahab's daughter was his wife. He did what was evil in the LORD's eyes. . . . and he caused the inhabitants of Jerusalem to prostitute themselves and led Judah astray* (II Chronicles 21:4,6,11).

Although the prophet Elijah lived in the northern kingdom, he sent a letter to the ungodly Jehoram, King of the southern kingdom, and rebuked his evils, saying: *Because you have not walked in the ways of your father Jehoshaphat . . . but have walked in the way of the kings of Israel . . . the LORD is now about to strike your people, your sons, your wives . . . with a horrible affliction. You yourself will be struck with many illnesses . . . and . . . After . . . two full years . . . he died* (21:12-19).

Godly Jehoshaphat could not have realized the tragic consequences that resulted from his friendship with Ahab and his son's marriage to an unbeliever. Some Christian parents' hearts have been broken as a result of permitting a son or daughter to date an unsaved person who seems so desirable in many other ways. Every Christian young man and woman should recognize why there are strong warnings against dating the unsaved. *Therefore, come out from among them and be separate, says the LORD; do not touch any unclean thing, and I will welcome you* (II Corinthians 6:17).

Thought for Today: Neglecting the Bible has caused many to lose their sense of spiritual direction.

In Today's Reading

Amaziah reigns in Judah; war against Edom; Israel defeats Judah; Uzziah reigns in Jerusalem; Uzziah stricken with leprosy.

After Joash was murdered by his servants, his son Amaziah became King of Judah (II Chronicles 24:25-27). As he began his reign, *he did what was right in the LORD's eyes but not wholeheartedly* (25:2; see II Kings 12:21; 14:3-6). The mixed motives in Amaziah's life eventually destroyed him. On one occasion, he hired 100,000 idol worshipers from the northern kingdom of Israel to help him fight against Edom to regain lost territory (II Chronicles 25:6). After *a man of God* rebuked him for not fully trusting in the Lord, who alone has *power to help or to make one stumble* (25:7-8), Amaziah dismissed the Israelite army and was successful in defeating the Edomites. But, instead of praising the Lord for victory, he *brought the gods of the Seirites* (Edom) *and set them up as his gods. He worshiped before them and burned incense to them. So the LORD's wrath was against Amaziah* (25:14-16).

From the time that Amaziah turned from following the LORD, a conspiracy was formed against him in Jerusalem . . . and they put him to death there (25:27). One of the most successful kings in Judah's history was his 16-year-old son Uzziah (26:1). The key to his success was unmistakable: *He sought God throughout the lifetime of Zechariah. . . . So his fame spread even to distant places, for he was marvelously helped until he became strong. But when he became strong. . . . He acted unfaithfully against the LORD his God by going into the LORD's sanctuary to burn incense* (26:5,15-16). Only priests were qualified to offer incense to God; but Uzziah refused to stop even when rebuked by Azariah and 80 other priests (26:17). Consequently, God struck Uzziah with leprosy. Even though he was a great king, God still judged him, for no man is above the law of God. During the last 10 years of his life, because of his leprosy, Uzziah was an outcast from both his own palace as well as the temple.

Few sins are as deceptive and destructive as overestimating one's importance. *For by the grace given to me, I tell everyone among you not to think of himself more highly than he should think. Instead, think sensibly, as God has distributed a measure of faith to each one* (Romans 12:3).

Thought for Today: You glorify Jesus when saying: "Praise the Lord."

In Today's Reading

Ahaz reigns in Judah; Aram (Syria) and Israel defeat Judah; death of Ahaz; Hezekiah's reign; temple worship restored.

Ahaz had the wonderful heritage of a godly father Jotham (II Chronicles 27:6). But Ahaz was one of the most wicked kings in Judah's history, *for he . . . made . . . images of the Baals. He burned incense in the Valley of the Son of Hinnom and burned his children in the fire, imitating the abominations of the nations that the LORD had dispossessed before the Israelites. . . . So the LORD his God handed Ahaz over to the king of Aram (Syria). He attacked him, captured a large number of them, and took them to Damascus. Ahaz was also handed over to the king of Israel, who struck him with a severe blow* (28:2-3,5).

Because of the great wickedness of King Ahaz, the Kingdom of Judah continued to suffer serious losses of territory. The Edomites gained their independence from Judah on the southeast. The Philistines raided the cities in the southwest and occupied them (28:17-18). Thousands of his people were taken as slaves into other countries (28:5-17).

Regrettably, the many defeats of Ahaz never caused him to humble himself and repent. He fiercely rejected the Lord and *sacrificed to the gods of Damascus* (28:23). *Then Ahaz gathered up the utensils of God's temple, cut them into pieces, shut the doors of the LORD's temple, and made himself altars on every street corner in Jerusalem. In each and every city of Judah he made high places to offer incense to other gods, and he provoked the God of his fathers to anger* (28:24-25). In this tragic account of Ahaz, King of Judah, the Lord is warning us of the awful fate of those who turn from Him. Just as Ahaz attempted to suppress the worship of the one true God, the unsaved world, with all of its deceptive attractions, attempts to suppress our loyalty and obedience to the Lord. To overcome these hindrances and remain faithful we need to pray each day: *Help me understand Your instruction, and I will obey it and follow it with all my heart. Help me stay on the path of Your commands, for I take pleasure in it. Turn my heart to Your decrees and not to material gain. Turn my eyes from looking at what is worthless; give me life in Your ways* (Psalms 119:34-37).

Thought for Today: Someone today needs to hear how the Lord answers prayer.

In Today's Reading

Hezekiah destroys idols; firstfruits and tithes; Assyria invades Judah; Hezekiah's death; Manasseh's reign; Amon's reign.

After the death of wicked King Ahaz, his godly son Hezekiah became king and assumed leadership of a nation where idol worship was both popular and prevalent. Furthermore, his father had placed the kingdom of Judah in subjection to Assyria, which was fast becoming the world's most powerful kingdom. Its seemingly invincible armies had seized control of both Syria (Aram) and the northern kingdom of Israel. In addition, Sennacherib, King of Assyria, had jurisdiction over 46 walled cities inside the kingdom of Judah.

Hezekiah could have mourned over the mess he inherited, either hating his father or blaming God for the wretched moral and economic conditions that prevailed throughout the nation. Instead, he *appointed the divisions of the priests. . . . The king contributed from his own possessions for the . . . burnt offerings. . . . He told the people . . . to give a contribution for the priests. . . .* (and) *the LORD . . . blessed* (II Chronicles 31:2-10).

Hezekiah observed the Passover (30:1-11). He reopened the temple which his wicked, idol-worshiping father had desecrated, and restored worship of the true God.

As with Hezekiah, who inherited serious problems because his father was evil, we too may be the victim of other people's sins. But never fear the future or "unfortunate circumstances" of the past. We should not be concerned about our parents' mistakes, which we may have inherited, or other situations over which we have no control. Christian counselors agree that dwelling on one's past mistakes, or those of others, never provides helpful solutions, and can create depression, suspicion, self-hatred, and hatred of others. How encouraging it is to know that, when Hezekiah and Isaiah prayed with no hint of ill will, the Lord protected them.

With Paul, let us say: *One thing I do: forgetting what is behind and reaching forward to what is ahead, I pursue as my goal the prize promised by God's heavenly call in Christ Jesus* (Philippians 3:13-14).

Thought for Today: Don't give up. Even the vilest sinner can be saved.

In Today's Reading

Josiah's reign; book of the law found; fall of Jerusalem; captivity of Judah; decree of Cyrus to rebuild the temple.

One of the highest honors ever attributed to a king was given to Josiah, who *did what was right in the LORD's eyes and walked in the ways of his forefather David; he did not turn aside to the right or the left. . . . He read in their hearing all the words of the book of the covenant that had been found in the LORD's temple* (II Chronicles 34:2,30).

But the last four kings of Judah – Jehoahaz, Jehoiakim, Jehoiachin, and Zedekiah – were all evil, and led the nation in a descending course morally, politically, and spiritually to its disastrous end. During his reign of 11 years (36:11), Zedekiah (Mattaniah), the youngest son of Josiah, *did what was evil in the eyes of the LORD* (36:12), and rebelled against Babylon's domination because he thought he had the support of Egypt. This time, the Lord left the Israelites to their ruin. Nebuchadnezzar showed no mercy and surrounded Jerusalem until *the people of the land had no food* (II Kings 25:3). The horrors of the starving defenders of Jerusalem are recorded in Lamentations 2:19; 4:3-10 and Ezekiel 5:10.

Nebuchadnezzar's soldiers eventually broke through the north wall and mercilessly butchered both young and old. Then they *burned God's temple. They tore down Jerusalem's wall, burned down all its palaces, and destroyed all its valuable utensils* (II Chronicles 36:17-19; II Kings 25:4-11; Jeremiah 52:5-11).

Most of those who had escaped the massacre were driven off as slaves to become exiles in a foreign land (II Chronicles 36:20-21).

Because of His great love for Israel and His covenants with Abraham, Isaac, Jacob, and David, the Lord made a precious promise to the Jewish people that is fast approaching fulfillment. They will soon recognize Jesus of Nazareth as their Messiah. *A partial hardening has come to Israel until the full number of the Gentiles has come in. And in this way all Israel will be saved, as it is written: The Liberator will come from Zion; He will turn away godlessness from Jacob. And this will be My covenant with them, when I take away their sins* (Romans 11:25-27).

Thought for Today: Can others depend upon what you say?

Introduction To The Book Of Ezra

The book of Ezra begins with the history of the Jews from the time Cyrus of Persia released them from Babylonian exile, permitting them to return to Jerusalem to rebuild the temple under the leadership of Zerubbabel.

Most of the older generation of Israelites who had been taken into captivity by Nebuchadnezzar had died. The majority of the new generation did not desire to return to a homeland they had never seen.

Ezra records that the first expedition was made up of 42,360 Jews and 7,337 of their servants (Ezra 2:64-65) led by Zerubbabel, who was appointed governor by king Cyrus (5:14; Haggai 1:1,14; 2:2,21).

The original temple, built by King Solomon, had been destroyed by King Nebuchadnezzar of Babylon in 586 B.C. After arriving in Jerusalem with Zerubbabel, the returned exiles built an altar and observed the Festival of Tabernacles (Booths) which commemorates the Israelites' 40 years in the wilderness. Ezra records that, *in the second month of the second year after they arrived at God's house in Jerusalem, Zerubbabel . . . began to build . . . to supervise the work on the LORD's house* (Ezra 3:8; 5:16). It took about two years to complete the foundation, after which the work ceased because of opposition from adversaries (chapters 3 – 4).

About 15 years later, stirred by the preaching of the word of God by the prophets Haggai and Zechariah, the Israelites *began to rebuild God's house* (5:2). They completed it in about five years despite intense opposition (chapters 5 – 6). Between chapters 6 and 7 there is an interval of about 60 years. During this time, Zerubbabel, Haggai, and Zechariah died and the events in the book of Esther probably took place.

Perhaps 78 years after Zerubbabel's expedition (7:1-10:44), Ezra, a descendant of Aaron the first high priest, received a letter of authority from the king to lead another expedition to Jerusalem, *according to the law of your God . . . . Whatever is commanded . . . must be done diligently* (7:11-14,23). At that time, Ezra led about 5,000 people, from the Persian capital of Babylon to Jerusalem (7:28 – 8:31). The book of Ezra reveals how God controls the destiny of all mankind and, thus, the book of Ezra is a message of God's continuing covenant grace.

In Today's Reading

Cyrus' proclamation to rebuild the temple;
list of the Jews who returned from captivity.

About 200 years before the time of Ezra, Isaiah had prophesied that Babylon would be overthrown by a man named Cyrus. The Lord said of this heathen king of Persia: *He will fulfill all My pleasure, saying to Jerusalem, She will be built, and of the temple, its foundation will be laid. . . . and will set My exiles free* (Isaiah 44:28; 45:13). These prophecies reassured the Israelites that, following the judgment foretold by Jeremiah of 70 years of captivity due to their sins, God would restore them once again to the promised land (Jeremiah 25:11-12).

To fulfill that prophecy, *the LORD stirred up the spirit of King Cyrus of Persia to issue a proclamation . . . . Whoever is among you from His people, may his God be with him. He may go up to Jerusalem in Judah and build the house of the LORD, the God of Israel – He is the God who is in Jerusalem . . . . Then the heads of the families of Judah and Benjamin, the priests, the Levites – everyone whose spirit God had stirred – prepared to go up to rebuild the LORD's house in Jerusalem* (Ezra 1:1,3,5).

On this journey, there was neither a pillar of fire by night nor a cloud by day to guide the way, and no manna fell from heaven as experienced earlier by their ancestors (Numbers 9:15-16,22-23), but there is not one complaint recorded. This is in sharp contrast to the continual complaints of their ancestors, who had been miraculously released from Egypt (20:24; 27:14; Deuteronomy 1:26,43; 9:23).

When we recognize that our sovereign Creator controls everything that affects our lives, we can truly enjoy the peace of God, regardless of what happens, since *all things work together for the good of those who love God* (Romans 8:28). Believing this will remove all fear, depression, and discouragement, as well as faultfinding, anger, and strife. Our loving Lord is sovereign over all that takes place in our lives, including suffering and pain, and will use whatever happens in our lives to our ultimate advantage. Because of this, we can *be at peace, and the God of love and peace will be with you* (us) (II Corinthians 13:11).

Thought for Today: *Be glad in the LORD, you righteous ones, and praise His holy name* (Psalms 97:12).

The Exiles & Return

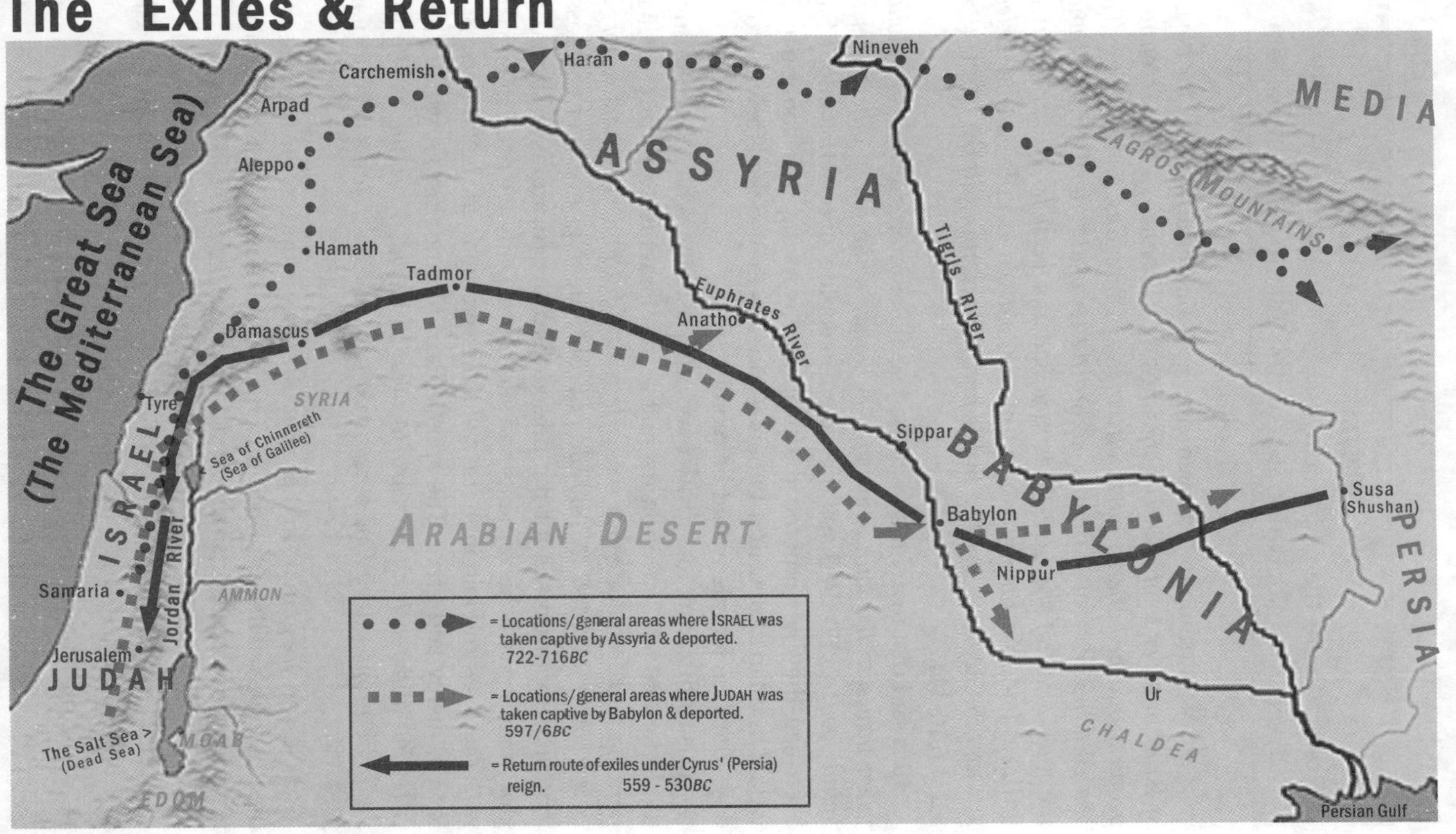

In Today's Reading

Restoration of the altar and worship; rebuilding temple begun; adversaries stop work, it resumes; Tatnai writes to Darius.

After returning to Jerusalem, the Jews first built *the altar for the God of Israel in order to offer burnt offerings. . . . they feared the surrounding peoples, and they offered burnt offerings . . . morning and evening. They observed the Festival of Booths, according to what is written. . . . though the foundation of the LORD's temple had not been laid. . . . When the builders had laid the foundation of the LORD's temple . . . the priests . . . and the Levites . . . sang praise and thanksgiving to the LORD* (Ezra 3:2-4,6,10-11).

It is said that many men who had seen Solomon's temple *wept loudly when they saw the foundation of this house, while many others raised a joyful shout* (3:12). Perhaps they were weeping over what might have been had they not ignored the prophet's warning that continued sin would result in destruction. Others rejoiced as they looked forward to the day when the temple would be rebuilt.

It is right for us to sorrow over our past sins which have brought the judgment of God upon us, just as the Israelites did. But, after repenting and forsaking our sins, *He is faithful and righteous to forgive us our sins* (I John 1:9). We should not continue to grieve over past losses that blur opportunities for the present and the future. Nor should we glory in our past achievements and successes. Daily we need to move on with our lives and join in *praise and thanksgiving to the LORD* (Ezra 3:11) for His mercy and grace. The apostle Paul reminds us: *Forgetting what is behind and reaching forward to what is ahead, I pursue as my goal the prize promised by God's heavenly call in Christ Jesus* (Philippians 3:13-14).

A lesson we gain from these devout Jews is that, as we seek to serve the Lord, we will face opposition. During the rebuilding of the temple's foundation *the people of the land . . . made them afraid to build. . . . Work on the house of God in Jerusalem had stopped* (Ezra 4:4,24).

Let us move ahead with confidence, not in ourselves, but in God *and by His vast strength* (Ephesians 6:10).

Thought for Today: Winners never quit and quitters never win.

In Today's Reading

Darius' decree to complete the temple; dedication of temple; Passover restored.

The prophets Haggai and Zechariah reminded the Israelites in Jerusalem that the real reason the Lord's work went unfinished was because their first interest was in building their own homes. These anointed men boldly preached the word of God and inspired the people to rebuild the temple: *So the elders of the Jews went on successfully with the building under the prophesying of Haggai the prophet and Zechariah . . . according to the command of the God of Israel* (Ezra 6:14).

Nothing is recorded about the Jews in Jerusalem between the time of Haggai and Zechariah's ministry and the coming of Ezra from Persia about 60 years later. Zerubbabel, Haggai, and Zechariah had all died leaving the next generation to grow up without spiritual leadership.

Ezra was born during the Babylonian captivity. He was a descendant of Aaron, Israel's first high priest (7:1-5; I Chronicles 6:3-15). The key to Ezra's great effectiveness in accomplishing the will of God is clear: *For Ezra had determined in his heart to study the law of the LORD, to obey it, and to teach its statutes and ordinances to Israel* (Ezra 7:10). Note carefully the threefold key to Ezra's great success: Ezra *had determined in his heart to study the law of the LORD.*The word *determined* implies a steadfast effort to know all of God's word. The second qualification for the Lord's great blessings upon his life was that Ezra committed himself *to obey* the law. And third, he planned *to teach its statutes and ordinances.*

Ezra was committed to seeking, doing, and teaching God's word. This should be a reminder that, if we want God to bless our lives, we too must set our hearts upon the whole counsel of God. *In every situation take the shield of faith, and with it you will be able to extinguish the flaming arrows of the evil one. Take . . . the sword of the Spirit, which is God's word* (Ephesians 6:16-17).

Ezra is an example of how God will use anyone who will take His word seriously and *be diligent . . . correctly teaching the word of truth* (II Timothy 2:15).

Thought for Today: Living to please the Lord will encourage others to be obedient to Him.

In Today's Reading

Genealogy of Ezra's companions; Ezra proclaims a fast; treasures delivered to the priests; Ezra's prayer and confession.

Ezra knew the Scriptures and decided to be responsible for leading perhaps five thousand men, women, and children on the treacherous, possibly 800-mile journey from Babylon to Jerusalem. Added to this was the responsibility for priceless treasures of *silver, gold, and vessels . . . for the house of God offered by the king* (Ezra 8:25). Ezra was also aware of the danger of bandits who could murder and plunder. The people would face physical and emotional hardships as well.

It would have been easier to remain in Babylon and just pray for the people in Jerusalem. But Ezra decided to do what he could. Furthermore, Ezra did not ask the king for a protective military guard; rather it is recorded that Ezra *proclaimed a fast, so that we might humble ourselves before our God and ask Him for a safe journey. . . . I was ashamed to request infantry . . . from the king to protect us from enemies . . . since we had said to the king, Our God's gracious hand is on all who seek Him for their good* (8:21-22).

Ezra and all his followers arrived safely in Jerusalem about four months after leaving Babylon (7:8-9; 8:31). However, Ezra was grief stricken upon hearing about the low moral and spiritual state of affairs in Jerusalem since the temple had been rebuilt. Ezra was told: *The people of Israel, the priests, and the Levites, have not separated themselves from the surrounding people with their detestable practices* (9:1). Again, he did not say: "It's not my problem, so I'll leave it up to someone else." Instead, he became involved and *everyone who trembled at the words of the God of Israel . . . gathered around me* (9:4). At the evening sacrifice, he fell on his knees and spread out his hands to the Lord, and prayed: *My God, I am ashamed . . . because* (of) *our iniquities . . . . For we have abandoned Your commandments* (9:6,10).

When the word of God is neglected, we too need to be as concerned as Ezra. *Wasn't Abraham our father justified by works when he offered Isaac his son on the altar? You see that faith was active together with his works, and by works, faith was perfected* (James 2:21-22).

Thought for Today: *Faith without works is useless* (James 2:20).

In Today's Reading

Foreign wives and children.

The Israelites had married Canaanites. Consequently, many were worshiping their idols. The law of God, had warned: *Nor shall you intermarry with them . . . for they will turn your children away from Me . . . then the LORD will . . . swiftly destroy you* (Deuteronomy 7:3-4).

As the Israelites listened to Ezra proclaim the word of God, they were convicted of their sins. Shechaniah, spokesman for the offenders, said to Ezra: *We have been unfaithful to our God. . . . Let us . . . make a covenant before our God to send away all the foreign wives* (Ezra 10:2-3).

One by one, each man who had married a Canaanite had to present himself with his wife and children before a court of *the elders and judges of each town* (10:14) to determine if they were involved in idol worship or were worshipers of the true God of Israel. If the only consideration had been the excommunication of all Canaanite wives, it would have been a simple, immediate decision. But, something more than simple separation was being considered in their courts. There was an examination of each family to determine if the Canaanite wives had forsaken their idols and converted to the one true God of Israel. If these men had led their wives to reject their idols and worship the one true God, their wives would have become Israelites and would not have been called *foreign wives*. This precedent had been set by Joshua when he welcomed and protected Rahab, the harlot of Jericho, who had rejected her idols and sinful life to place her trust in the one true God of Israel. Much later, Ruth, a Moabitess, joined with Naomi, confessing: *Your God will be my God* (Ruth 1:16). Ruth rejected her people's idols and became an Israelite. In the providence of God, both she and Rahab became a part of the genealogy of Jesus.

We are prone to underestimate the heartbreak and suffering that results from disobedience to the word of God. The price of sin is much greater than anyone suspects! *The one who sows to his flesh will reap corruption . . . but the one who sows to the Spirit will reap eternal life* (Galatians 6:8).

Thought for Today: Self-denial that honors Christ may result in suffering, but the outcome is peace and satisfaction.

Introduction To The Book Of Nehemiah

The book of Nehemiah is a continuation of the history recorded in the book of Ezra. Nehemiah grew up in Persia among the Jews who had been exiles in Babylon before Cyrus restored their freedom. Nehemiah had the honored position of cupbearer to King Artaxerxes, the son of Xerxes, known as Ahasuerus in the book of Esther. His position was one of great trust and responsibility (I Kings 10:5; II Chronicles 9:4).

Nehemiah was heartbroken when he received a report of the spiritual and physical poverty that existed in Jerusalem. Upon learning of Nehemiah's great concern, the Persian king appointed him governor of Judah and gave him the authority to return to his homeland and rebuild the walls (Nehemiah 2:5-7; 5:14). This was about 100 years after Zerubbabel arrived in Jerusalem.

The walls had remained in ruins since Nebuchadnezzar had completely destroyed Jerusalem about 140 years before (II Kings 25:8-11). The Jewish remnant had no protection against surrounding nations which could easily come in and rob them of their harvests and possessions. Restoring the broken-down walls which had once protected Jerusalem from its enemies was Nehemiah's first major project. Yet some of the leading citizens of Jerusalem who would benefit from those walls refused to cooperate with him (Nehemiah 2:19; 3:5; 4:1-12). Although faced with many problems (4:12-23; 6:2-4,10-13), by continual prayer, fasting, and faith in the word of God, Nehemiah led the people to complete the walls in the short time of 52 days (6:15).

There was great emphasis placed upon hearing the word, as well as understanding and applying it, which led to a revival among the people (8:2-3,7-8,12).

After the walls of Jerusalem were dedicated by Ezra and Nehemiah (12:27-43), Nehemiah continued in Jerusalem as governor of Judah for about 12 years (5:14). He then returned to the Persian court for an indefinite period of time. During Nehemiah's absence from Jerusalem, the word of God was once again disregarded and corruption and immorality gained acceptance (13:6). Nehemiah again obtained leave from the Persian king and returned to Jerusalem. With great fervor, he turned the nation from its sins, reestablished its covenant relationship with God, and restored the people to true worship (13:7-31).

In Today's Reading

Nehemiah's prayer for Jerusalem and his leave of absence; Nehemiah inspects Jerusalem's walls; the builder of the walls.

When Nehemiah's relative Hanani arrived in Persia from Jerusalem, he told Nehemiah of the pitiful conditions that existed there. Nehemiah said: *When I heard these words, I sat down and wept. For a number of days I mourned, fasting and praying before the God of heaven. . . . Both I and my father's house have sinned. . . . and have not kept the commands* (Nehemiah 1:4,6-7). Over a period of about four months, he continued to pray.

When King Artaxerxes asked why he was so sad, Nehemiah told him that it was because *the city of my ancestors' tombs lies in ruins* (2:1-3). The king graciously responded by appointing him governor over Judah and commissioned him to rebuild the walls of Jerusalem. The king even provided some of the materials (2:6-8).

Three basic characteristics made Nehemiah's efforts a success. First, his desire to do the will of God (1:1,11). This led him to leave the luxury and security of living in the king's palace in Persia and to endure the hardships in Jerusalem in order to restore the city of God.

Second, he not only *fasted and prayed*, but he confessed: *We . . . have not kept the commands* (1:4-11). He recognized that obedience to the word of God is essential to answered prayer.

Third, he was determined to persuade his people to join him in rebuilding the walls, regardless of opposition. Sanballat and his crowd expressed their hostility to Nehemiah: *They mocked and despised us* (2:19). Their ridicule then turned to slander: *Are you rebelling against the king* (2:19)? In addition, Judah's *nobles* refused to *help the supervisors* (3:5).

Nehemiah refused to become discouraged and give up. Accomplishing the will of God is dependent upon remembering that He is Sovereign over the affairs of our lives. *Therefore, we may boldly say: The Lord is my helper; I will not be afraid. What can man do to me* (Hebrews 13:6)?

Thought for Today: Much can be accomplished when Christians work together.

In Today's Reading

Builders opposed and ridiculed; Nehemiah's prayer; weapons for the workers; evils corrected; plots of adversaries; walls completed.

Nehemiah determined to rebuild the walls around Jerusalem, even though there was fierce opposition. He armed workers *with their swords, spears, and bows* (Nehemiah 4:13). He also said: *Don't be afraid of them. Remember the great and awe-inspiring LORD. . . . Our God will fight for us! So we continued the work, half of us holding spears from daybreak until the stars came out* (4:14,20-21; compare Numbers 14:9; Exodus 14:13-14). Working about 12 hours a day left little time for anything else. The Israelites' faith had been strengthened through the reading of God's word.

Sanballat again attempted to stop their work, saying: *Come, let's meet together in the villages of the Ono valley* (Nehemiah 6:2), about 28 miles northwest of Jerusalem. Nehemiah replied: *I am doing a great work and cannot come down. Why should the work cease while I leave it and go down to you?* (6:3).

After Sanballat made five attempts to meet with Nehemiah, he then accused him of rebelling against the king of Persia (6:5-7). When this failed, Sanballat hired a prophet to foretell Nehemiah's death.

Eleven times it is recorded that Nehemiah prayed (1:4-11; 2:4; 4:4-5,9; 5:19; 6:9,14; 13:14,22,29,31). He encouraged his workers, saying: *The God of heaven . . . will enable us to succeed. . . . for the people had the will to keep working. . . . The wall was completed in 52 days* (2:20; 4:6; 6:15).

Once we recognize that *the battle is the LORD's* (I Samuel 17:47), and God is the One who allows the opposition, we will not panic. Instead, we will seek to learn what the Lord expects of us in order to qualify to have our prayers answered. People of faith, though a minority, will always find a way to accomplish God's will, while the majority will find excuses to wait for a more convenient time.

In serving the Lord, the greatest problem is not doing our best with what we have. *We must do the works of Him who sent Me while it is day. Night is coming when no one can work* (John 9:4).

Thought for Today: Prayerless Christians weaken their effectiveness.

In Today's Reading

Nehemiah's appointment of leaders; genealogy of returned exiles; Scriptures read and explained; the Festival of Tabernacles (Booths) observed.

The ultimate purpose of God for His people was more than the restoration of His temple and the walls of Jerusalem. These man-made structures were powerless to protect the Israelites from their enemies unless the people knew and obeyed the word of God. The Hebrew language in which *the book of the law* (Nehemiah 8:3) was written was no longer the common language of the people. During their captivity, they spoke Aramaic, which was the international trade language used by the Aramaeans (Syrians), Persians, and Babylonians at that time.

After the wall was completed under Nehemiah's supervision, thousands of Jews assembled in Jerusalem day after day from sunrise until noon to hear Ezra and the Levites read and explain the book of the law. This resulted in a renewal of the covenant relationship of the Israelites with God and the restoration of scriptural worship.

A revival took place, *for all the people were weeping as they heard the words of the law* (8:9).

The most pressing need today is for Christians to become seriously concerned about reading all of God's word because it is *a judge of the ideas and thoughts of the heart* (Hebrews 4:12). God speaks to us through His word and, as we read it, our various acts of disobedience, whether by ignorance, omission or commission, are brought to mind. This will lead to our conviction, confession, and cleansing. We will then become *doers of the word, and not hearers only* (James 1:22).

Furthermore, the guilt which results from sins we have committed should no longer remain after we have confessed and repented. We dare not dig up past confessed and forgiven sins of our own or of others; instead, we should rejoice in the merciful, forgiving love of God through Christ our Savior. In our Lord's parable, the unforgiving servant was delivered to the tormentor. *So My heavenly Father will also do to you if each of you does not forgive his brother from his heart* (Matthew 18:35).

Thought for Today: Obeying God's word prepares our hearts for the Holy Spirit to work in and through us.

In Today's Reading

Fasting and confession of sins; reading of the law; confession of God's goodness; new covenant to keep the law.

Ezra stands out as a godly man because he knew the Scriptures. Not only did Ezra lead in reading from the law, but many Levites *explained the law to the people . . . translating and giving the meaning* (Nehemiah 8:7-8). Teaching the word of God was so important that it is mentioned seven times in one chapter (8:2,3,7,8,9,12,13). This points out how essential it is to read all the Bible from Genesis to Revelation.

The Israelites were taught the meaning of the Festival of Tabernacles, also called Booths or Sukkoth. Sukkoth celebrated the fall (second) harvest and commemorated the 40 years their ancestors dwelt in *booths* (tabernacles) in the wilderness (Leviticus 23:42-43). On the 24th day of Tishri (September/October), *the Israelites assembled, fasting* (Nehemiah 9:1). The Festival of Tabernacles had been observed as required by the law, but there was a movement of the Holy Spirit following the reading of the Scriptures so that *they stood and confessed their sins . . . they read out of the book of the law of the LORD their God for a fourth of the day and spent another fourth of the day in confession and in worship of the LORD their God* (9:2-3). The Levites were led to say to the people: *Stand up! Bless the LORD your God from everlasting to everlasting. Blessed be Your glorious name, and may it be exalted above all blessing and praise* (9:5).

The priests revealed how God, in *great compassion*, had provided His *good Spirit to instruct them . . . they lacked nothing* (9:19-21). It is the same Holy Spirit who still guides believers, as Jesus promised: *When He comes, He will convict the world about sin. . . . When the Spirit of truth comes, He will guide you into all the truth* (John 16:8,13). The Holy Spirit also seeks to guide all Christians into the occupation or position God has chosen for us to most effectively serve Him and to prepare us for our eternal inheritance. The Holy Spirit alone can enlighten our minds, impart conviction of sin, and empower us to live a sanctified (holy) life (I Corinthians 2:16; 6:11).

I pray that He may grant you, according to the riches of His glory, to be strengthened with power through His Spirit in the inner man (Ephesians 3:16).

Thought for Today: If we live by faith, we need not fear.

In Today's Reading

Residents of Jerusalem; priests and Levites with Zerubbabel; dedication of the walls; temple offices restored.

Ordinary people, although not skilled in building walls, willingly went to work under Nehemiah's leadership and did the best they could to rebuild the walls around Jerusalem.

Only a minority of the people who left Persia to rebuild Jerusalem actually lived inside the city's walls. Most of the Jews lived in suburbs where they could grow crops, pasture their animals, and make a living more easily. Because of this, there were not enough people living in Jerusalem to maintain and protect it. *Now the leaders of the people stayed in Jerusalem, and the rest of the people cast lots for one out of ten to come and live in Jerusalem, the holy city* (Nehemiah 11:1).

The Israelites could now assemble within the rebuilt walls of Jerusalem and worship without fear of their enemies. *At the dedication of the wall of Jerusalem, they sent for the Levites wherever they lived and brought them to Jerusalem to celebrate a joyous feast of consecration with thanksgiving and singing. . . . On that day they offered great sacrifices and rejoiced because God had given them great joy. . . . Jerusalem's rejoicing was heard far away* (12:27,43).

The Israelites' worship demonstrated a heartfelt commitment to the Lord in their renewed relationship to Him. Though all true Christians love the Lord, not all are willing to give up personal interests and financial security to do what is needed to accomplish His purposes.

It is no less important for followers of Christ to consider "the walls" that may need to be rebuilt in their own lives where worldly interests have broken through and devastated their zeal for the Lord.

In our Christian walk, we need to be on guard against anything, including good, wholesome activities, which may cause us to divert either our time or our money from their usefulness to God and from becoming *treasures in heaven . . . for where your treasure is, there your heart will be also* (Matthew 6:20-21).

We all will want to hear our Lord say: *Well done, good and faithful slave! You were faithful over a few things; I will put you in charge of many things. Enter your master's joy!* (Matthew 25:21).

Thought for Today: God can use the least servant to fulfill His needs.

In Today's Reading

Reading of the law; separation from the heathen; tithes given; Sabbath-breaking forbidden; mixed marriages condemned.

During Nehemiah's absence, the Israelites' worship of God and the Sabbath observance were neglected. Intermarriage with Canaanite idol worshipers was common. Nehemiah again *asked the king for a leave of absence so that* (he) *could return to Jerusalem* (Nehemiah 13:6-7). He was grieved over the people's disregard of the law and took firm action to return the nation to God. *At that time the book of Moses was read publicly to the people. The command was found written in it that no Ammonite or Moabite should ever enter into the assembly of God* (13:1).

The greatest evils were committed by those who held the highest positions of spiritual leadership. *Eliashib the priest . . . was related to Tobiah* (through marriage). . . . *Even one of the sons of Jehoiada, the son of Eliashib the high priest, was a son-in-law to Sanballat the Horonite* (13:4,28). Other priests had also married Canaanite women.

Added to these sins, Nehemiah *discovered . . . that Eliashib had . . . provided a room for* (Tobiah) *in the courts of God's house* (13:7). This was not only forbidden by . . . God (Deuteronomy 23:3-4), but Tobiah formerly had opposed Nehemiah's work (Nehemiah 2:10,19; 4:3-8; 6:17-19). Nehemiah *threw all of Tobiah's . . . possessions out of the room. . . . and rebuked the officials, saying, Why is the house of God being neglected* (13:8-9,11)? The reasons were: *the nobles of Judah* had transgressed by marrying heathen women, consequently *defiling the priesthood* (13:29).

Nehemiah continued his reformation while facing much opposition. He warned the people concerning marriage with the Canaanites: *You must not give your daughters to their sons or take their daughters for your sons. . . . Didn't king Solomon of Israel sin in things like this? . . . foreign women drew him into sin* (13:25-26). Like Nehemiah we too can make a difference in our world. He was mightily used of God because he knew the Scriptures and refused to compromise.

Draw near to God. . . . and purify your hearts, (you) *double-minded people* (James 4:8)!

Thought for Today: Give all praise to the Lord for all achievements.

Introduction To The Book Of Esther

The book of Esther centers around the descendants of the Israelites who remained in Persia after the 70-year captivity and the Hebrew maiden Hadassah, who was given the Persian name Esther. The events in this book probably took place in the time period between chapters six and seven of the book of Ezra, occurring about 40 years after the temple had been rebuilt (Ezra 3:10; 5:14-15), but about 30 years before the walls of Jerusalem were rebuilt (Nehemiah 6:15). It is quite possible that Esther, who was by then the queen mother, was used of God to prepare the way for her fellow Israelite Nehemiah to become the cupbearer to her Persian stepson King Artaxerxes I. This trusted position and relationship with the king was probably the basis for Nehemiah to receive the king's support for rebuilding the walls in Jerusalem.

Ahasuerus is the Hebrew name and *Xerxes* (Esther 1:1) the Greek name, of Khshayarsha, king of Persia. He *ruled 127 provinces from India to Ethiopia.* It is assumed that, at the banquet which opens the book of Esther, he was planning a battle against Greece which eventually led to his defeat. Ahasuerus reigned in Shushan (Susa) which was located in modern Iran near the eastern border of Iraq. The rule of his son Artaxerxes I is recorded in Ezra 7-10 and Nehemiah 1-13.

The book of Esther, as well as the books of Ezra and Nehemiah, confirm that our Creator can accomplish His perfect will through a helpless minority of faithful servants, even when they are ruled by evil men (Jeremiah 32:27).

I love thee, Lord; I love Thy will.
Do Thou Thy plan through me fulfill
That glory may return to Thee
For time and for eternity.

In natural strength no honor lies;
Thy grace alone sin's power defies,
but Satan's power is nullified
Through all in whom Christ does abide.

- M. E. H.

In Today's Reading

Vashti removed as queen; Esther made queen; Mordecai saves the king's life; Haman's plan to destroy all the Jews.

Hadassah was the Hebrew name for the Jewish orphan whose Persian name was Esther (Star). She was taken to the king's palace along with other maidens, either to be made queen or to become a part of the king's harem. Esther found herself in a situation over which she had no control. She and her faithful, older cousin Mordecai, who had adopted her (Esther 2:7,15), could only trust God for direction and protection. To complicate their situation, the man given the power to enforce the king's commands was the evil and self-serving Haman (3:10, 15; 6:6-10; 7:9). Haman was an Amalekite, a descendant of Esau (Esther 3:1), who hated all Jews (Deuteronomy 25:17-19). When Mordecai refused to bow down in "reverence" (Esther 3:2), Haman was determined to use his authority to destroy Mordecai and all Jews in the kingdom. Haman's plan was declared law with the king's approval and the lot (*Pur*) was cast to determine the best day to execute all Jews (3:7-13). However, Mordecai and Esther used every legal means to defend the interests of the people of God, even risking their own well-being.

God expects us to do all we can to resolve our own health, job, and financial problems. However, we should never doubt that God is in ultimate control to protect us and provide what we can't do. God never makes a mistake and never overlooks one of His children. We should not give in to self-pity and defeat but remain faithful and look to the Lord and His word for guidance and strength. Like Mordecai, we must not bow down to the Hamans of this world who would seek to destroy our loyalty to Christ.

Like Esther, you may feel hopelessly trapped where you are and may long for the time when you would be free to do what you desire. But, Jesus explained the importance of doing your best now with the parable of a *man with two talents. . .* (who) *said, Master, you gave me two talents. Look, I've earned two more talents. His master said to him, Well done, good and faithful slave! You were faithful over a few things; I will put you in charge of many things* (Matthew 25:22-23).

Thought for Today: God does hear and answer your prayers.

In Today's Reading

Fasting among the Jews; Esther's banquet for Haman and the king; Haman forced to honor Mordecai; Haman executed.

About five years after Esther became queen, Haman was promoted *higher than all the other officials* (Esther 2:16-17; 3:1-7). When the decree was proclaimed that all Jews would be destroyed, Mordecai urged Esther *to approach the king . . . to implore his favor and to plead with him personally for her people* (4:8). No one knew that Esther was a Jew because Mordecai had forbidden her to reveal her nationality. Esther was fearful and reminded him that Persian law stated that anyone who approached the king uninvited could be put to death. The risk was real, for she had *not been summoned to appear before the king for 30 days* (4:11). Esther could easily have reasoned: "If the king has lost interest in me or even discovered that I am a Jew, how could I favorably influence him?" But Esther believed that the risk of losing her prestigious position as queen Vashti had done, or even losing her own life, was not as important as doing what she could to save her people.

After three days of fasting, queen Esther *stood in the inner courtyard of the palace* (5:1) and waited to see if she would face life or death. The king welcomed her and offered to grant her request. *If it pleases the king, Esther replied, may the king and Haman come today to the banquet I have prepared for them* (5:4).

The king accepted and then, at a second banquet, he again asked Esther what her request might be. He was shocked to hear her pleading for her own life: *O king . . . may my life be given to me. . . . my people and I have been sold out to . . . extermination. . . . This evil Haman is an . . . enemy* (7:3-6). Angrily, *the king commanded, Hang him . . . . They hanged Haman on the gallows he had prepared for Mordecai* (7:9-10).

Esther is an encouragement to all of us to use whatever talents, position, popularity, or wealth we have been blessed with to tell a lost world that our King gave His life to save them from the eternal torment of hell. *For whoever wants to save his life will lose it, but whoever loses his life because of Me and the gospel will save it* (Mark 8:35).

Thought for Today: Throughout the ages, Satan has tried to destroy God's witnesses, but the Lord guides and guards His children.

In Today's Reading

Esther's plea to reverse Haman's decree; enemies of the Jews destroyed; Festival of Purim instituted; Mordecai promoted to great honor.

Haman's "wise counselors" *had cast Pur* (lot) to determine the most favorable time for the execution of all Jews. Haman's "lucky day" fell on the 13th day of the twelfth month (Esther 3:7-13; 9:1,24). Undoubtedly Haman felt fortunate that the lot had fallen on the last month of the year so that he would have plenty of time to make his evil plans to murder every Jew in the kingdom.

The fixed day of execution, which came to be known as Purim (Lots), was turned from death to deliverance by the intervening providence of God. Haman did not realize that Mordecai's God is in control of the affairs of earth. Even though *the lot is cast into the lap . . . its every decision is from the LORD* (Proverbs 16:33).

Following Haman's execution, the king allowed Mordecai to write a new decree giving the Jews the right to defend themselves.

On the day when the Jews' enemies had hoped to overpower them, just the opposite happened. The Jews overpowered those who hated them (Esther 9:1). The book of Esther demonstrates how God uses faithful servants to change world affairs in order to fulfill His word.

In days of peace and prosperity, we are prone to be less concerned about the presence of God. But, when our situation seems critical, we seek His presence, and when He wonderfully intervenes, we praise Him for His merciful protection and provision.

Esther is a testimony to the fact that, even in a secular society dominated by a heathen power, our God can protect His people. But, He expects us, like Esther, to respond courageously in faith to the threats of the Hamans of this world.

The peace and satisfaction enjoyed by Mordecai and Esther can only be experienced by those who share our Lord's compassion for a lost world. Everyone has a right to know how to be saved. Jesus said: *No one comes to the Father except through Me* (John 14:6).

Thought for Today: No sin works more deceitfully than pride.

Introduction To The Book Of Job

The book of Job opens with a brief history of a godly, praying man named Job, *the greatest of all the people of the east* (Job 1:3). In the first two chapters, we read of Satan's accusations against Job and the ordeal God permitted him to experience to test his faith. Job proved God could trust him to be faithful even through life's most painful experiences.

God said there *was a man in the land of Uz, whose name was Job* (1:1). Uz was a descendant of Noah's third son Shem, through whom the Messiah would come (Genesis 10:22-23). The *land of Uz* (Job 1:1) is not specifically located, but it was situated in the area of the tribes of the Temanites, the Shuhites, and the Naamathites, as well as the Buzites (2:11; 32:2; compare Genesis 22:20-22). It also would have been within raiding distance of the Sabeans and Chaldeans (Job 1:15,17). Jeremiah wrote of *all the kings of the land of Uz; all the kings of the land of the Philistines* (Jeremiah 25:20). Most of these are well-documented places. In Lamentations 4:21 it appears that Uz was located in Edom, just below the Dead Sea: *O Daughter of Edom, that dwells in the land of Uz.* The exact locations are unimportant, but the spiritual insight concerning how we should understand and accept our circumstances and suffering is of utmost importance, relevant, and applicable to every age.

In the book of Job we see the reasonings of God, Job, his wife, his three friends, Elihu the Buzite, and Satan who is exposed as the instigator of all suffering. As you read through each chapter, carefully distinguish between the wisdom of godly Job and the well-meaning, but inaccurate, half-truths and misleading humanistic arguments of his friends. God highly complimented Job as being *perfectly righteous* (Job 1:1,8,22; 2:10) for having spoken the truth, but said that his friends had not spoken the truth about Him (42:7).

Job's friends and Elihu reveal how deceptive and unreliable human reasoning can be. The only satisfying answers to the needs of all of us are found in the infallible, holy word of God.

In each day's reading, note the intensifying of Job's suffering but also the development of his spiritual insight. In the final chapter, God once again removes all doubt concerning Job's righteousness and truthfulness when the Lord said to Eliphaz: *I am angry with you and with your two friends. For you have not spoken what is valid concerning Me, as My servant, Job has* (42:7).

In Today's Reading

Job's wealth and godliness; Satan permitted to afflict Job; critical counsel by Job's wife and his three friends.

Without the holy Scriptures, we would never understand the reason for suffering. Job, the faithful servant of the Lord, was stripped of his family, possessions, reputation, and health. But his suffering was not misfortune or bad luck, nor was it punishment from God for sin as his friends mistakenly assumed. Our Creator, who knows our innermost thoughts, declared that Job *was perfectly righteous, he feared God, and he turned away from evil* (Job 1:1).

Behind all the world's evil is Satan, *touring the earth . . . going to and fro* (1:7) in his continuous effort to destroy all that is good. But Satan is under the constant surveillance of God and can do nothing without His permission.

Satan assumed that, like every self-serving person, Job was faithful only because God would reward him. During his intense suffering and testing, Job's wife even suggested that he *curse God, and die* (2:9). She too had suffered loss, but it seems that her greatest loss was her faith in God. Job realized he was not the owner of all he possessed, not even of his children, but he was merely the Lord's manager of things entrusted to his care. From there, it was just one more step of faith for Job to accept that God, in His infinite wisdom, had the right to reclaim His possessions anytime He chose. Instead of cursing God, Job worshiped Him, saying: *The LORD has given, and the LORD has taken away. May the name of the LORD be blessed* (1:21).

Just as Satan used Job's "friends" to belittle and condemn him, Satan still delights in using family, friends, coworkers, and even fellow church members to do the same today. *Be on the alert! Your adversary the Devil is prowling around like a roaring lion, looking for anyone he can devour* (I Peter 5:8). But Satan is not a *lion*; he only appears like a lion, and his *roaring* is all bluff.

Our God, the Master Planner, is still in full control. *Jesus Christ is the same yesterday, today, and forever* (Hebrews 13:8).

Thought for Today: *It is good to praise the LORD, to sing praise to Your name, Most High* (Psalms 92:1).

In Today's Reading

Eliphaz' rebuke of Job continues; Job's response; Job reproaches his friends; Bildad's theory about Job's affliction.

After one full week of silent contemplation about Job's suffering, Eliphaz, his eldest friend spoke first (Job 2:13). He tried to convince Job to confess his secret sin, saying: *Blessed is the man whom God corrects; therefore, do not reject the discipline of Shaddai* (the Almighty) (5:17). Eliphaz then went on to elaborate on the blessings he could expect if Job would only confess his sin, and he confidently concluded: *We have looked into this thoroughly. It is true! Hear it, and get to know it for yourself* (5:27).

In addition to Job's physical sufferings, his financial loss, the death of his children, and his wife's bitterness toward God, all three of his friends misjudged his integrity and continued to unmercifully harass him day after day. Job felt the bitter sting of Eliphaz's condemnation and his insinuation that Job was a hypocrite. Job did not understand why God had not come to his defense. Even worse, it seemed to him that he had even been struck down by *the arrows of Shaddai* (6:4).

However, Job's sufferings reveal his spiritual insight: *What is mortal man that You magnify him, that You pay attention to him; that You test him every morning—every moment You try him!* (7:17-18).

We too recognize our insignificance in comparison to the eternal, holy, and Almighty God. Although He created us, by nature we are defiled by sin and deserve eternal punishment. But, through the miraculous new birth, we have the joy of being eternally with our loving Creator. However, all who reject Christ as personal Savior and Lord will be *thrown into the lake of fire. This is the second death* (Revelation 20:14-15).

It is not our heavenly Father's will for *any to perish, but all to come to repentance* (II Peter 3:9). However, God *tries* (proves) *us* – either with afflictions or with blessings. Through it all, He is seeking to develop in us a genuine love for and commitment to Him.

All that God does and allows is for our ultimate good. *For it has been given to you on Christ's behalf not only to believe in Him, but also to suffer for Him* (Philippians 1:29).

Thought for Today: Every trial gives us an opportunity to draw closer to God and can make us more the person He wants us to become.

In Today's Reading

Job acknowledges God's justice; his weariness of life; Zophar's accusation; Job's affirmation of faith in God's wisdom.

All of us will benefit by listening carefully to the spiritual discernment of Job, whom God said *was perfectly righteous, he feared God, and he turned away from evil* (Job 1:1).

This man of spiritual insight proclaimed with confidence: *Does not mortal man have hard service on earth? . . . So I have been made heir to months of futility, and nights of trouble have been apportioned for me* (7:1,3). His friend Bildad incorrectly believed that God had *apportioned . . . nights of trouble* of suffering only for sinners, and his response to Job was critical and cynical: *How long will you go on saying these things? . . . If you are pure and upright, even now He will arouse Himself on your behalf and restore your proper household* (8:2,6).

Bildad concluded that those who enjoy good things in this life are righteous and all suffering is the result of sin. But, in a parable given by Jesus, the rich man who built bigger barns for "great blessings" was not one who pleased the Lord (Luke 12:18,20). Another time, Jesus revealed that the man was not born blind because of sin (John 9:2-3).

Job's suffering led him to experience deep, spiritual maturity as he recognized God as far superior to himself and he spoke with confidence, saying: *Recall that You fashioned me like clay . . . You have given me life and loving-kindness, and Your providence has guarded my spirit* (Job 10:9,12). However, Job knew that he and God could not meet on the same level, *for He is not a man like me, that I might answer Him, that we might enter together into judgment.There is no arbitrator between us* (9:32-33). Job expressed the desperate need for a mediator, someone who would stand in the gap between the holy God and sinful man.

Our Lord Jesus Christ is the only Mediator who can restore man's broken fellowship with God (Romans 5:8-10). *For there is one God and one mediator between God and man, a man, Christ Jesus* (I Timothy 2:5). We now have access to the Father through our Mediator Jesus Christ, who has entered *into heaven itself, that He might now appear in the presence of God for us* (Hebrews 9:24).

Thought for Today: Love the person who is unlovely.

In Today's Reading

Job's defense of his integrity; his desire to die; Eliphaz' intensified condemnation; Job's complaint of God's dealing with him.

Satan prompted the attacks on Job by his wife and by his "devoted" friends in an attempt to substantiate his own accusation that Job would curse God if his many blessings were removed.

Job's suffering intensified with days and weeks of sleeplessness and painful, ulcerating boils that would only worsen with no painkillers. It may appear that he wavered at times, but Job always ended his comments on a high note of praise. Job confidently stated: *If He slaughtered me, I would hope in Him.* He could say with the utmost confidence: *I know I will be proven right* (Job 13:15,18).

Although Job gave up hope of recovering his health, wealth, children, or high esteem among the people, he did not become bitter or resentful toward his accusers or toward God. Instead, he looked forward to being with the Lord after his death, saying: *If a man dies, will he revive? All the days of my hard service I will wait until my transformation comes* (14:14), meaning: "After death I shall live again and I will be changed."

How different Job's attitude was from many today who blame fate, circumstances, or others for what goes wrong in their lives. They easily become dissatisfied, bitter, pessimistic, or engulfed in self-pity. Their self-image depends on others' reactions. When others praise them, their self-esteem rises; when they are criticized or their plans fail, they feel defeated. Job didn't need praise from people to maintain his faith since he retained his confidence in the wisdom and justice of his Creator.

Christians can thank God for a perfect Savior and great High Priest who *always lives to intercede for them* (Hebrews 7:25). Having accepted Jesus as Savior and Lord of our lives, we should have a sincere desire to know His will by reading all His word.

Job's unshakable faith in God resulted from his obedience to the revealed word of God. He said: *As for the command of His lips—there, too, I have not turned away: I have treasured up the words of His mouth more than my daily food* (Job 23:12).

Thought for Today: Treasures laid up in heaven pay high dividends.

In Today's Reading

Job's appeal to God; Bildad's cruel accusation; Job's reaffirmation of faith; Zophar refers to Job as a wicked man.

God leads us to see, through Job, that we have no valid excuse for complaining about our suffering, material loss, or being misunderstood by others. Job assumed all hope of recovery was gone when he said: *My spirit is broken. My days are extinguished. A graveyard awaits me. . . . my whole form is like a shadow . . . My days have passed by; my plans have been shredded* (Job 17:1,7,11).

Bildad interrupted this suffering saint with scathing words that were even more cruel and critical than his first speech. He assumed that Job's sufferings exposed him as a sinful hypocrite who was hopelessly condemned: *For he is cast into a net by his own feet. . . . He is driven from light to darkness; he is hounded out of the world* (18:8,18). Bildad went on to say: *Surely these were the dwellings of an evil one, the place of one who knew not God* (18:21). This mistaken accusation from Job's "friend" must have been a bitter blow. Not only was Job facing death, but to die misjudged as a hypocrite when he knew his heart was right with God must have seemed unbearable.

Our hearts are deeply stirred with compassion as this pitiful, lonely man looked beyond his suffering. And, with great spiritual discernment, Job said: *But I know that my Redeemer lives* (19:25).

According to the law, a redeemer was the next of kin who was responsible for redeeming (buying back) an enslaved kinsman or his lost inheritance (Leviticus 25:25). The kinsman-redeemer foreshadowed the coming of Jesus Christ, our Savior-Redeemer. The continuous harassment that Job suffered only drove him closer to the Lord. This revelation of life after death is one of the greatest in the Old Testament and has blessed millions of suffering people throughout the ages.

In contrast to Job are those today with a negative outlook who, when things go wrong, think that nothing good ever happens to them and continue to focus on themselves and their "bad luck."

The LORD redeems the life of His servants, and all who take refuge in Him will not be punished (Psalms 34:22).

Thought for Today: The wise person has discovered that he is never alone; he has a personal, living Savior to guide him.

In Today's Reading

Job declares that wicked men sometimes prosper; Eliphaz accuses Job of sin; Job's desire to plead his case before God.

Few men in Bible history are so highly esteemed by God as Job. God said of him: *There is none like him on earth, a perfectly righteous man, who fears God and turns away from evil* (Job 1:8). His friends mistakenly supposed that all his problems were the result of his secret sins. They assumed that wicked men are miserable and, since Job was exceedingly miserable, he must be very wicked!

It is shocking to read how wrong Eliphaz could be with his blunt, critical, and cruel condemnation of Job, saying: *Come to terms with God and be at peace. . . . Receive instruction from His mouth and . . . put evil far away from your tent* (22:21-23). In striking contrast, God said to Job's friend Eliphaz: *You have not spoken what is valid concerning Me, as My servant, Job has* (42:7).

There are still self-righteous, overbearing, opinionated people like Eliphaz who are quick to pass judgment on anyone who doesn't believe as they do or who experience difficulties or sickness. Job's faith was unshakable because he could truthfully say: *I have kept to His way and not turned aside. As for the command of His lips—there, too, I have not turned away: I have treasured up the words of His mouth more than my daily food* (23:11-12). He believed that, since God was faithful to His Word, He also would be faithful to His obedient servant.

We often do not understand why we face disappointments, sufferings, or being misunderstood. But, we can believe and trust in God since He always gives His best to the one who desires to do His will.

The devotion of Job should be an inspiration to all of us who are not as concerned about knowing the "reason" for our suffering as with knowing God and His word, the only true source of guidance.

It seemed to Job that God was nowhere to be found. But, regardless of this, Job said: *He knows the way I have taken. When He has tried me, I will come forth as gold* (Job 23:10).

Thought for Today: Strength from God's word on a day-to-day basis upholds our faith in Him in times of testing.

In Today's Reading

Bildad's answer; Job's reproof of Bildad; Job's praise to God; Job's truthfulness; source of wisdom; recalling past wealth.

The book of Job is the inspired word of God. Job was not searching for answers when he said: *Wisdom—where can it be found, and where is understanding located? No mortal knows its place nor can it be found in the land of the living. . . . its price cannot be weighed in silver . . . . But where does wisdom come from. . . . It is hidden from the eyes of every living thing* (Job 28:12-13,15,20-21).

God is the Author and Revealer of true wisdom. There is no substitute for reading all of His word to understand His perfect plan for our lives. This means that it is important to read through every book of the Bible, from Genesis to Revelation, with a sincere desire to apply its instruction to our own lives.We can be sure that Satan will attempt to distract us from the true source of wisdom and cause us to make decisions based on circumstances or contemporary standards.

The worldly-minded find fault with God, just as the Israelites did as they journeyed through the wilderness. They complained about their circumstances instead of acknowledging that God was in control. We too can make unwise decisions when we allow ourselves to become frustrated. To illustrate, we may say to someone: "You make me angry." But the fact is, we choose to be angry. Or we may say: "I am depressed today." However, the sad truth is that we have refused to see God in the circumstances He has allowed to take place in our lives. We can be sure that our Lord is far more concerned with our best interests than we are. *So those who suffer according to God's will should, in doing good, entrust themselves to a faithful Creator* (I Peter 4:19). We always have the choice to move above and beyond anger and disappointments by permitting the indwelling Christ to rule our lives. This is the key to experiencing *the peace of God* (Philippians 4:7). *The revelation of Your words brings light and gives understanding to the inexperienced* (Psalms 119:130).

Thought for Today: Our faith in God is revealed by the way we react to both our sorrows and our sufferings.

In Today's Reading

Job's proclamation of his integrity; Elihu's accusations.

No one in biblical history, other than Christ, suffered so much public humiliation and intense physical and emotional pain as Job did. He had held the chief administrative position in his country and had *dwelled as a king* (Job 29:25). *I delivered the poor who cried out, and the orphan who had no helper . . . I was a pair of eyes to the blind and a pair of feet to the lame. I was a father to the needy, and examined the case of the stranger* (29:12,15-16). In chapter 31 he listed 12 common sins that no one could accuse him of committing. Yet, in his time of need, no one expressed compassion or a kind word to him.

For Job, there seemed to be no end to the cruelty of the people who made his suffering even more painful and miserable: *They set a trap for my feet. . . . Terrors are turned against me; my nobility is pursued like the wind, and my prosperity passes by like a cloud. And now my life drains away; days of affliction seize me* (30:12-17). But, by far, the most troubling to Job was that it seemed that God did not care and was not hearing his prayers: *I cry out to You, but You do not answer me* (30:20).

At such times our faith is put to the test, *for we walk by faith* (II Corinthians 5:7) and are not dependent upon "the things that are seen." We are to trust the Lord and the promises of His word. Faith does not originate with us but it is a gift from God (Ephesians 2:8).

Job's three friends mistakenly judged his relationship to God, but he did not allow them to destroy his faith.

As we consider Job, whom God had declared the most perfect man on earth (Job 1:8), should we be surprised when we are falsely criticized? The most devoted Christian often suffers the worst indignities and humiliation from thoughtless, inconsiderate people – even from some who profess to be Christians.

Therefore we ourselves boast about you among God's churches – about your endurance and faith in all the persecutions and afflictions you endure. It is a clear evidence of God's righteous judgment that you will be counted worthy of God's kingdom, for which you also are suffering (II Thessalonians 1:4-5).

Thought for Today: If you are confronted with gossip, immediately turn the conversation to something commendable (Philippians 4:8).

In Today's Reading
Elihu continues his accusations against Job.

Elihu did not speak until Job's three friends had ended their accusations. He condemned Job's three friends but expressed even greater hostility toward Job. Four times in five verses we read variations of the phrase that Elihu's *anger smoldered* (Job 32:1-5).

This young egotist referred to himself by the words "me," "my," and "I" at least 55 times to inform Job that he alone was chosen to intercede on Job's behalf and to speak *as you are before God* (in God's stead) (32:6 – 33:33). Elihu's accusations against Job's testimony are, at best, half-truths and misinterpretations (33:8-13).

One of Elihu's accusations was that Job had claimed to be sinlessly perfect (34:6). The fact is Job acknowledged his imperfection as sin in 7:21 and 13:26. However, the Lord proclaimed Job as *My servant . . . For there is none like him on earth, a perfectly righteous man* (1:8). Elihu falsely stated that Job *has said, It does not profit a man when he tries to find favor with God* (34:9). But Job never said that. Elihu continued his vicious attack on this dear, godly man, saying: *Job has spoken without knowledge; his words are without insight. O that Job might be tested to the uttermost, for responding like wicked men. For he adds rebellion to his sins . . . multiplies his words against God* (34:35-37).

Elihu's conclusions were in direct opposition to the testimony of God who said that Job had *spoken what is valid concerning Me* (42:7-8).

During times of personal afflictions, heartbreaking bereavement, persecution, or financial struggles, we are often tempted to become depressed and even fail to pray. That is when we need someone's loving comfort and assurance that our Lord ultimately controls every situation that comes into our lives. Regardless of how bad it may seem, He wants to use it for our good and for His glory (Romans 8:28; also Genesis 50:20).

Have faith in the wisdom of God, *casting all your care upon Him, because He cares about you* (I Peter 5:7).

Thought for Today: Enjoying fellowship with God, among other things, is dependent upon one's attitude toward others.

In Today's Reading

Elihu's speech interrupted by God; God's challenge to Job; man's weakness and ignorance; Job humbled.

Is it any surprise that God interrupted Elihu's speech and said to *Job from the whirlwind . . . Who is this who obscures counsel with ignorant words* (Job 38:1-2)?

For the first time since his suffering started, Job began hearing words of comfort rather than condemnation. The God of love said: *Gird up your loins like a man* (38:3); He seemed to be saying: "Step out of the ashes; you have suffered long enough; you have proven Satan a liar; get ready to move a little closer to Me. I'm not as far away from you as it seemed when you said: *I do not perceive Him . . . I do not see Him* (23:8-9). I want you to see that I, and I alone, control the vast universe and yet am greatly concerned with even the smallest detail of your life."

The second statement of God to Job was equally comforting: *I shall question you, and you will advise Me* (38:3). The Lord was saying to Job: "You no longer have to listen to the insults of cruel men, for I am in control and will reveal to you the most amazing wisdom concerning the universe ever given to mankind." First, God wanted Job to consider the limitations of his own wisdom compared to the wisdom of the One who created the universe: *Can you fasten the chains of the Pleiades* (38:31)? God asked Job about 60 questions in this first cycle of conversation (38:1 – 40:2), and over 80 questions altogether (38 – 41). The wisest astronomer can't explain or change one star in the marvelous array of Pleiades, one of the most beautiful clusters of stars.

The mighty God who created the universe also created us, cares for us, patiently listens to our prayers, and provides us with what is best for us in the light of our eternal destination. We need to see how unqualified we are to question His wisdom. Nothing is unforeseen and no one is overlooked, slighted, or left out by our heavenly Father. He imparts inner strength and sustains us by His indwelling Holy Spirit.

God's words to the apostle Paul were also for us: *My grace is sufficient for you, for power is perfected in weakness* (II Corinthians 12:9).

Thought for Today: The vastness of the universe reveals God's unlimited resources and matchless wisdom.

In Today's Reading

God's great power reviewed; Job's submission to God; his prayer for his friends; God blesses Job.

Through a series of over 80 questions, God revealed to Job many of the wonders of the universe, some of which have only recently been "discovered" by science. Because of his faith in God and his patience through suffering, Job acknowledged the supreme authority of God compared to how little is known by mankind. It is no surprise to read that Job confessed to God: *I know that You can do all things, and that no plan of Yours can be thwarted . . . I have expounded on matters I did not understand* (Job 42:2-3). By this he meant: "Although I did not understand, I will never again question what God does or what He allows to happen, since His love and wisdom are perfect." All of us need to be reminded that our limited knowledge and ability to cope with life's problems should cause us to realize how foolish, as well as sinful, it is to question the wisdom and love of God for His children. We need to accept, with submissive hearts, the circumstances He allows into our lives, which He will use to fulfill His loving purpose.

During his suffering, Job experienced glorious revelations of the incomparable greatness of God and His ways. Job's spiritual understanding continued to grow as he said: *I had heard of You with my ears, but now my eyes have seen You. Therefore I despise myself, and repent in dust and ashes* (42:5-6). Those who trust in the Lord, as Job did, are not searching for the answers to all of life's problems, nor asking the questions: "Why?" or "Why me?" They are simply trusting our loving, all-wise Father who always knows what we need and will give the best to those who trust Him.

Job's friends must have been astounded to hear the Voice from heaven say to Eliphaz: *I am angry with you and with your two friends. For you have not spoken what is valid concerning Me, as My servant, Job has* (42:7). Job could have become proud after God came to his defense. Instead, he humbly prayed for God to forgive his three friends who had so cruelly misjudged him. Jesus also set an example when He said: *Bless those who curse you, pray for those who mistreat you* (Luke 6:28).

Thought for Today: Can the Lord say to you: *Well done, good and faithful slave* (Matthew 25:21,23)?

Introduction To The Book Of Psalms

The book of Psalms includes songs of praise and thanksgiving. Each of the last five psalms begins and ends with the phrase: *Praise the LORD,* which is the English translation of the Hebrew word *Hallelujah.* It has become a universal word, for it is the same in every language. It is impossible to be praising the Lord while being dissatisfied with our circumstances. The psalms teach us to forgive others, as well as to express gratitude to God for His forgiveness of our many sins and our restoration to fellowship with Him.

The psalms also include prayers seeking mercy and help, as well as expressing confidence. Prominent in the book of Psalms is the high esteem God has given to the Scripture itself. He inspired David to write: *I will . . . give thanks to Your name for Your constant love and faithfulness. You have exalted Your name and Your promise* (Your word) *above everything else* (138:2). Because God has exalted His word above all else, we are made to see that the Scriptures are exceedingly important for our personal well-being. The vital importance of the Scriptures is brought to our attention at least 170 times in Psalm 119.

Although written about a thousand years before the birth of Jesus, many psalms refer to the coming of the Messiah – His birth, life, betrayal, crucifixion, resurrection, and ascension into heaven, as well as His return to reign on earth. In the New Testament, the following psalms are applied to Jesus Christ: 2; 8; 16; 22; 40; 41; 45; 68; 69; 72; 89; 102; 109; 110; 118; and 132. In Psalm 2, the Messiah is God's Son who is to be worshiped; 16:10-11 proclaims His resurrection; chapter 22 His suffering; and chapter 40 His sacrifice. In Psalm 45:6 the Messiah is God; in chapter 89 He is the One promised to fulfill God's covenant with David. In Psalm 110 He is *the LORD* (vs 1), a *mighty scepter* (Ruler) (vs 2), *in holy splendor* (vs 3), *forever, You are a Priest* (vs 4), *He will crush* (be Conqueror of) *kings* (vs 5), *judge the nations* (vs 6).

After His resurrection, Jesus opened the eyes of two of His disciples: *Beginning with Moses and all the Prophets, He interpreted for them in all the Scriptures the things concerning Himself. . . . Then He told them . . . everything written about Me in the Law of Moses, the Prophets, and the Psalms must be fulfilled* (Luke 24:27,44).

In Today's Reading

The blessed and the ungodly; David's confidence in God; prayer for protection, mercy, and deliverance.

The key to receiving a blessing from God begins with three negative statements. The first is: *How happy is the man who does not follow the advice of the wicked* (Psalms 1:1). The *wicked* may live acceptable lifestyles that conform to the basic moral standards of society but live and act as though the Creator God does not exist. Therefore, they assume that any religion, or none at all, is equally acceptable. In doing this, they feel no accountability to God and see no need of a Savior.

The second negative statement is: *Or take the path of sinners*. Sinners speak, act, think, and live to please themselves. They may be honest, upright, and generous in the eyes of the majority of people. They may even believe there is a God and may live a good, moral life. Consequently, they are deceived and see no need to repent of sin because they do not think they are sinners. The Christian life is centered in God, but the sinner's life is centered on himself.

The third negative statement is: *Or join a group of mockers!* The mocker makes known his belittling, antagonistic attitude against God the Father as Creator of all things and against worshiping Jesus Christ as God the Son – *our great God and Savior, Jesus Christ* (Titus 2:13). *The mockers*, for the most part, stand firmly and openly against the Bible and Jesus Christ as the only way to be saved and reach heaven.

The *blessed* person has an attitude of *delight . . . in the LORD's instruction, and he meditates on it day and night* (1:2). If we delight in pleasing Jesus Christ, we will "meditate" upon His word. As we meditate prayerfully *upon His word*, the Holy Spirit speaks to our hearts, revealing the meaning of His word for our lives. Such people have a desire to be led by *the Spirit of Truth* (John 16:13).

One of the great blessings that is imparted to those who meditate upon God's word comes silently and unnoticed, *like a tree planted beside streams of water that bears its fruit in season and whose leaf does not wither. Whatever he does prospers* (Psalms 1:3).

Thought for Today: Only to the extent that we love God will we enjoy obeying His word.

In Today's Reading

Judgment upon the wicked; David's desire for justice; those who shall dwell with God; prayer for protection.

David asked a question that has eternal consequences: *LORD, who can dwell in Your tent? Who can live on Your holy mountain?* (Psalms 15:1). David focused on two of the all-important issues of life when he asked: *Who can dwell?* and *Who can live?* The Holy Spirit provided the answer: *The one who lives honestly, practices righteousness, and acknowledges the truth in his heart* (15:2). To *practice righteousness* can only take place after one becomes a child of God through faith in Christ. Jesus told Nicodemus: *Unless someone is born of water and the Spirit, he cannot enter the kingdom of God* (John 3:5). To *acknowledge the truth in his heart* comes from knowing God's word.

Although the book of Psalms foretells the resurrection of Christ, it also offers assurance that all who believe in Him will rise to share in His resurrection and life eternal. *For the LORD Himself will descend from heaven . . . and the dead in Christ will rise first* (I Thessalonians 4:16). How wonderful to *dwell* in Him and to look forward to *living* in the presence of our Lord forever. Like David, let us rejoice: *I keep the LORD in mind always. Because He is at my right hand, I will not be defeated. Therefore my heart is glad, and my spirit rejoices; my body also rests securely* (Psalms 16:8-9). The Almighty God fulfilled the prophecy of David: *You will not allow Your Faithful One to see the Pit* (16:10). Forty days after His resurrection, Jesus Christ ascended heavenward to take His place at the right hand of the Father as had been prophesied. *You reveal the path of life to me; in Your presence is abundant joy; in Your right hand are eternal pleasures* (16:11).

On the *day of Pentecost,* Peter quoted from this psalm to assure about three thousand people that Jesus was the Christ of whom David had prophesied (Acts 2:1,25-28,31).

The risen Christ is the good news of the gospel upon which our faith is based. *For just as in Adam all die, so also in Christ all will be made alive* (I Corinthians 15:22).

Thought for Today: Christ died to reconcile you to Himself.

In Today's Reading

Thanksgiving for deliverance; creation and covenants of God; a prayer for God's people; cry of anguish and song of praise.

The effects of the word of God are beyond compare, for it was by His word that the worlds were created and by which they are still upheld (Hebrews 1:3). *The heavens declare the glory of God, and the sky proclaims the work of His hands* (Psalms 19:1). Most exciting is the transforming power of Jesus, the Word of God made flesh, upon all who receive Him as Lord: *The instruction of the LORD is perfect, reviving the soul; the testimony of the LORD is trustworthy* (19:7). You can count on it!

The first six verses of Psalm 19 refer to the works of God in the world, and the remaining eight refer to the marvelous influence of His word on the lives of all who love and obey Him.

In this short psalm, six names are used to express the word of God:

1. It is the *instruction of the LORD* and, as such, *is perfect* (19:7). It is as far superior to the words of man as the heavens are above the earth. Then why should anyone settle for less than to *humbly receive the implanted word, which is able to save you* (James 1:21)?
2. It is the *testimony of the LORD* (Psalms 19:7). The apostle Paul confirmed this to Timothy, saying: *You have known the sacred Scriptures, which are able to instruct you for salvation* (II Timothy 3:15).
3. It is the *precepts of the LORD* and, therefore, *right* (Psalms 19:8), because they are founded solely on the righteousness of God. His word reveals what we are, as well as what God has planned for us to be.
4. It is the *commandment of the LORD* (19:8) – not merely suggested alternatives of popular opinion; it is the expression of the holiness of God. His commandments provide a new life free from sin's bondage.
5. It reveals the *fear of the LORD* (19:9), a reverential admiration for His holiness and a fear of offending His majesty.
6. It is the *ordinances of the LORD* (which) *are reliable and altogether righteous* (19:9).

The psalmist expresses well what our feelings should be concerning the word of God. It is *more desirable . . . than an abundance of pure gold; and sweeter than honey* (Psalms 19:10).

Thought for Today: Thank the Lord for His Presence in your life today!

In Today's Reading

The Great Shepherd; King of Glory; prayer for guidance; love for God's house; prayer for God's help; adoration of God's mighty power.

David, the old shepherd-king who saw himself as nothing more than a sheep that needed to be led, was inspired by the Holy Spirit to say: *The LORD is my shepherd; there is nothing I lack. . . . He leads me along the right paths for His name's sake* (Psalms 23:1-3). No other livestock requires more attention than sheep. Left alone, they can easily become separated from the flock and lose their way. Of all domesticated animals, sheep are the most defenseless and helpless.

By nature, we are all like sheep. We may blindly follow the same paths that have ruined the lives of others. Or we can become so caught up in our own affairs that we lose sight of the *Good Shepherd* and find ourselves separated from Him (John 10:11,14).

The trouble with most of us is that many times we try to be our own shepherd. There is something almost terrifying about the consequences of the destructive, self-willed stubbornness of those who refuse to be led in *the right paths*. They are determined to go their own way, even though the path they take will inevitably lead to trouble. It is a fact that without the *Good Shepherd* we are helpless, defenseless sheep. When we recognize this we will fully trust the *Good Shepherd*. We are comforted and encouraged by knowing that *even when I go through the darkest valley, I am not afraid of any danger, for You are with me* (Psalms 23:4).

Even *Your rod and Your staff—they give me comfort* (23:4). We know that *the Lord disciplines the one He loves* (Hebrews 12:6).

The utmost desire of every one of God's sheep should daily be *taking every thought captive to the obedience of Christ* (II Corinthians 10:5). God will guide and provide for every need of the one with a *mind that is dependent on* (Him) (Isaiah 26:3).

We should pray each day: Lord lead *me along the right paths for* (Your) *name's sake* (Psalms 23:3).

Thought for Today: Often God's ways differ from our expectations!

In Today's Reading

David's trust in God; the blessedness of forgiveness; the Lord hears the righteous; David's prayer for safety.

What a privilege we have to join with David and the multitudes since his time, saying: *I will praise the LORD at all times; His praise will always be on my lips. . . . Proclaim with me the LORD's greatness; let us exalt His name together. . . . This poor man cried, and the LORD heard him and saved him from all his troubles. The angel of the LORD encamps around those who fear Him, and rescues them* (Psalms 34:1,3,6-7). Praise in our worship services, at mealtime, and during daily devotions is good and right and fills our hearts with joy. But, the psalmist went beyond the expected times of worship and praise because he was continually expressing love and devotion to the Lord. He wrote: *My tongue will proclaim Your righteousness,Your praise all day long* (35:28).

We are expected to praise the Lord even when everything seems to go wrong, since we know that *many adversities come to the one who is righteous, but the LORD delivers him from them all* (34:19). *We know that all things work together for the good of those who love God* (Romans 8:28). David suffered numerous injustices at the hands of enemies of God. He refers to himself *like broken pottery. . . . they conspired . . . to take my life* (Psalms 31:12-13). He could have become bitter or could have blamed others. Instead, he declared: *I trust in You, LORD,* and confidently said: *The course of my life is in Your power* (31:14-15). Only in yielding our lives to God will we find the assurance, peace, and security we long for. This is not "holding on" to Him, but abiding in Him – trusting that He is holding on to us, for He has promised we are in the heavenly Father's hand (John 10:28-29).

Though, at times, we may not feel like praising God because of some pressing concern or problem, we should remember that God is still on the throne. With David we can *be glad in the LORD and . . . shout for joy* (Psalms 32:11). Yes! Without hesitation, and regardless of circumstances, David said: *I will praise the LORD at all times; His praise will always be on my lips* (Psalms 34:1).

Thought for Today: Unwavering confidence in God brings a spontaneous spirit of gratitude and praise.

In Today's Reading

David's confidence in God; destruction of the wicked; the prayer of a penitent heart; brevity of life.

As David sat watching a fire burning, its bright flames slowly turning to ashes, he was reminded of how life, once bright, soon fades and ends in death. The Holy Spirit moved him to write: *My heart grew hot within me; as I mused, a fire burned* (out) (Psalms 39:3). This was a reminder that regardless of how inspiring and promising life may be, it will soon end. David then prayed: *Let me know how transitory I am. You, indeed, have made my days short in length, and my life span as nothing in Your sight. Yes, every mortal man is only a vapor* (39:4-5). David's prayer points out that the brevity of life is an issue for everyone to consider, not just senior citizens. However, our culture seeks to distract us from realizing that life is short and opportunities for fulfilling the will of God are quickly gone.

Compared to eternity, earthly life is *short* – very brief. Yet, strangely enough, it is easy to be caught up with daily activities and forget that our lives are always just one breath away from death.

In our brief journey on earth, we may sometimes retrace our steps or repeat a task; but, in our journey through life, wasted time can never be recovered. This points out how seriously we need to consider what God would have us do today and take advantage of every opportunity to serve the Lord.

Death will forever separate us from all of the material things that we possess. For the majority of us, death will come unexpectedly, and much sooner than we think. Let us reconsider secular goals that rob us of our opportunities to help reach a lost world with the words of eternal life.

Most of our time and energy is devoted to preparations for earthly securities and pleasures. Many make the fatal mistake of waiting too long for a "convenient time" to serve the Lord. Jesus said: *We must do the works of Him who sent Me while it is day. Night is coming when no one can work* (John 9:4).

Another psalmist prayed: *Teach us to number our days carefully so that we may develop wisdom in our hearts* (Psalms 90:12).

Thought for Today: Side by side with special privileges are temptations to test our willingness to sacrifice in order to gain God's best.

In Today's Reading

Praise for answered prayer; David's enemies; his longing for God's presence; prayer for deliverance from present troubles.

It was foretold by the psalmist that Jesus Christ, our wonderful Lord of lords and King of kings, will *ride* (reign) *triumphantly* (victoriously) *in the cause of truth, humility, and justice. May your right hand show your awe-inspiring deeds. . . . Your throne, God, is forever and ever; the scepter of Your kingdom is a scepter of justice. You love righteousness and hate wickedness; therefore God, your God, has anointed you, more than your companions, with the oil of joy* (Psalms 45:4,6-7). For the most part, kings are known for their tyranny; but the eternal King of kings has the perfect character traits of truth, equity, humility, and righteousness. Here we have a reminder of the words of Jesus to His disciples after His resurrection: *These are My words that I spoke to you while I was still with you, that everything written about Me in the Law of Moses, the Prophets,* ***and the Psalms*** *must be fulfilled* (Luke 24:44).

The apostle Paul quoted from Psalm 45 concerning Christ: *But about the Son: Your throne, O God, is forever and ever, and the scepter of Your kingdom is a scepter of justice. You have loved righteousness and hated lawlessness; this is why God, Your God, has anointed You, rather than Your companions, with the oil of joy* (Hebrews 1:8-9; see Psalms 45:6-7). The love of righteousness and hatred of lawlessness are attributes of Christ. Those who have accepted Jesus Christ as their Lord and Savior have become the Bride of Christ, the King of Kings. *And the king will desire your beauty. Bow down to* (reverence) *him, for he is your lord* (45:11). He must have our undivided allegiance. The Lord has assured us of His loving care over our lives.

In the midst of trying and uncertain circumstances, no Christian needs to fear the outcome. The Lord's *kingdom is a scepter of justice* and righteousness; therefore we have nothing to fear. Because God has taught us to pray: *Father* (a very close family relationship) . . . *give us today our daily bread* (meaning whatever I need) (Matthew 6:9,11). *Therefore don't worry about tomorrow, because tomorrow will worry about itself. Each day has enough trouble of its own* (Matthew 6:34).

Thought for Today: Why worry? God knows what is best.

In Today's Reading

The psalmist's confidence and praise of God; deception of worldly wealth; a prayer for mercy and forgiveness.

By inspiration of God, David wrote: *How happy is the man who does not follow the advice of the wicked, or take the path of sinners. . . . Instead, his delight is in the LORD's instruction, and he meditates on it day and night* (Psalms 1:1-2). Years later, on one occasion, his *delight* was not in the *LORD's instruction,* but in the beautiful wife of his neighbor, Uriah the Hittite, one of his most loyal soldiers. While Uriah was at war, David committed adultery with his wife. Through a planned military maneuver initiated by David, Uriah was killed, allowing David to legally marry Bathsheba.

It appeared to be a happy ending for David and Bathsheba until Nathan, the fearless prophet of God, appeared and denounced the king's selfish and wicked sins, saying: *Why . . . have you despised the word of the LORD by doing . . . evil? You struck down Uriah the Hittite with the sword and took his wife as your own wife* (II Samuel 12:9). Under the law, he deserved to die and he knew it (Leviticus 20:10). He cast himself on the mercy of God as a brokenhearted sinner and prayed: *Be gracious to me, God . . . according to Your abundant compassion, blot out my rebellion. . . . For I am conscious of my rebellion, and my sin is always before me. . . . God, create a clean heart for me and renew a steadfast spirit within me* (Psalms 51: 1,3,10). Because of David's sincere prayers for mercy, God forgave him. But the result of his sin was personal shame and suffering for the rest of his life, as well as many tragic personal and national consequences.

We wish that this blight upon David's life had not happened. But, it was recorded to reveal the deception and never ending wholesale devastation of lust. The Holy Spirit inspired David to record his own cry of sorrow and repentance. It holds out hope to the sinner who truly repents, that he can experience the mercy and forgiving love of God while teaching the inescapable consequences of sin.

As many as I love, I rebuke and discipline. So be committed and repent (Revelation 3:19).

Thought for Today: God does not overlook the sin of anyone.

In Today's Reading

Tendency of corrupt tongue; foolishness of atheism; a prayer for protection; a cry against deceitful friends; the psalmist's trust in God.

God must judge all unconfessed sin. So it is fitting that David, the man after God's own heart (I Samuel 13:14), expressed the exceeding hatred God has for evil. Included in Psalm 59 are the punishments that God will mete out against all evildoers on judgment day. He cannot *show grace to any wicked traitors. . . .* He will *consume them until they are gone* (Psalms 59:5,13).

David wrote: *Let them be erased from the book of life and not be recorded with the righteous* (69:28).

Asaph said: *Those who hate You . . . devise clever schemes against Your people. . . . They say, Come, let us wipe them out as a nation so that Israel's name will no longer be remembered . . . . Let them be put to shame* (83:2-4,17).

The psalmist presents sin as rebellion against God. David identified himself with God, who hates sin: *I hate them with extreme hatred; I consider them my enemies* (139:22). An *extreme hatred* is not one of personal jealousy, spite, envy, or ambition. Instead, it is the expression of a king who recognized that he was the anointed representative of God on earth and was responsible to administer justice on the Lord's behalf.

All mankind has inherited Adam's sinful nature. Consequently, *the heart is more deceitful than anything else* (Jeremiah 17:9). *There is no one righteous, not even one. . . . For all have sinned* (Romans 3:10,23) and are spiritually *dead in your trespasses and sins* (Ephesians 2:1). Because Jesus Christ was the virgin-born Son of God, the sin nature that passed from Adam to all men did not exist in Jesus because He was born sinless (see II Corinthians 5:21). He also lived *without sin* (Hebrews 4:15). His sinless nature qualified Jesus to die in our place and for our sins that we might receive eternal life (I John 5:11). True repentance prepares our hearts to receive Christ as our Savior and to allow Him to become Lord of our lives in obedience to His word (Acts 2:38; 4:12).

Our loving Savior will soon return as King of kings. *In righteousness He judges and makes war. . . . From His mouth came a sharp sword, so that with it He might strike the nations* (Revelation 19:11,15).

Thought for Today: Pleasing Jesus insures where you spend eternity.

In Today's Reading

David's prayer for deliverance from his enemies; his confidence in God's promises; David's exhortation to praise God for His goodness.

Because of Saul's relentless search and effort to kill him, David was forced to flee to a desolate area outside the promised land in exile from his home, his loved ones, and the physical comforts of the palace.

David was overwhelmed with sorrow, even as we would have been, when he prayed: *God, hear my cry; pay attention to my prayer. I call to You from the ends of the earth when my heart is without strength. Lead me to a rock that is high above me, for You have been a refuge for me, a strong tower in the face of the enemy* (Psalms 61:1-3). Although that desolate location seemed like *the ends of the earth,* David knew that his true source of security *in the face of the enemy* was the living God Himself.

Making God our *strong tower* means recognizing that we are in the protective care of the invincible God. Depression and frustration do not exist in the life of one who believes that God is a *strong tower* in the face of the enemy. He has assured us: *He does not withhold the good from those who live with integrity* (84:11). Like David, we can depend upon the Lord for protection and provision, regardless of how helpless we may feel our circumstances to be, for nothing is too hard for the Lord (Jeremiah 32:27).

Although David's difficult circumstances remained the same for many years, he continued to express confidence in the Lord, saying: *He alone is my rock and my salvation, my stronghold. . . . my refuge, is in God.* David then turned his thoughts to others who faced trials and suffering, and continued: *Trust in Him at all times, you people; pour out your hearts before Him. God is our refuge* (Psalms 62:2,6-8). It is a comfort to know that everything we face in life is to better prepare us for eternity.

Who can separate us from the love of Christ? Can affliction or anguish or persecution or famine or nakedness or danger or sword? . . . No, in all these things we are more than victorious through Him who loved us (Romans 8:35,37).

Thought for Today: Our confidence in the Lord's power and protection will be increased as we daily read God's word.

In Today's Reading

The blessings of God upon His people; His judgment upon enemies; David's prayer in time of trouble; prayer of praise and thanksgiving.

Four times in this short psalm we read: *Let the people praise You, God* (Psalms 67:3,5). This is a reminder to worship our wonderful Lord, who has promised His blessing upon genuine, Holy Spirit-inspired praise: *Let the people praise You, God; let all the people praise You* (67:3,5). While we await His return from heaven, *the righteous are glad; they rejoice before God and celebrate with joy. Sing to God! Sing praises to His name* (68:3-4).

The psalmist then foretold the resurrection of Christ, saying: *A great company of women brought the good news. . . . You ascended to the heights, taking away captives. . . . Our God is a God of salvation. . . . Sing to God, you kingdoms of the earth; sing praise to the Lord* (68:11,18,20,32). Paul quoted this psalm, but worded it: *When He ascended on high, He took prisoners into captivity* (Ephesians 4:8). Then he added: *He personally gave some to be apostles, some prophets, some evangelists, some pastors and teachers, for the training of the saints in the work of ministry, to build up the body of Christ* (4:11-12).

Let us join with the psalmist in a proclamation of praise and adoration for Jesus Christ: *Day after day He bears our burdens; God is our salvation. . . . My mouth will tell about Your righteousness and Your salvation all day long, though I cannot sum them up* (Psalms 68:19; 71:15).

During Christ's triumphant reign, all the *kingdoms of the earth;* will *sing praise to the LORD* (68:32). We too need to join with David, saying: *Let all who seek You rejoice and be glad in You; let those who love Your salvation continually say, God is great!* (70:4).

The apostle Paul was inspired to write: *All Scripture* (both Old and New Testaments) *is inspired by God and is profitable for teaching, for rebuking, for correcting, for training in righteousness, so that the man of God may be complete, equipped for every good work* (II Timothy 3:15-17).

Thought for Today: Life is like the uncontrollable sea until we turn to the Lord who imparts His perfect peace.

In Today's Reading

David's prayer for Solomon; mystery of the prosperity of the wicked; the wicked and the proud rebuked; Majesty of God praised.

We give thanks to You, God; we give thanks to You, for Your name is near. People tell about Your wonderful works (Psalms 75:1). The psalmist praised the Lord for the assurance that no effort against the faithful people of God, regardless of how powerful, can hinder His ability to protect and bless them. Praise and thanksgiving lead to a renewed assurance that God controls both the present and the future of His people.

When confronted by problems, we are taught to pray in faith that our almighty God will protect, guide and strengthen us. However, our psalmist was also led to foresee that some precious saints would suffer violence because of their faith and was led to write: *He will redeem them from oppression and violence, for their lives are precious in His sight* (72:14).

Here God is referred to as *the God of Jacob* (75:9); therefore, we will profit by studying why God wonderfully blessed and protected Jacob. Esau had threatened to murder his brother Jacob over the birthright God had foretold would rightfully be Jacob's. God knew that Esau would despise the birthright and that Jacob would cherish it enough to risk his life to secure the final blessing of Isaac, confirming that God had chosen Jacob to be heir to the Abrahamic Covenant.

Twenty years later, when Esau received word that Jacob was returning home, Esau went out to meet him with 400 of his servants (Genesis 32:6). It appeared that Esau would now fulfill his vow to kill Jacob. This threat led Jacob to pray all night. *Jacob was left alone, and a man wrestled with him until daybreak. When the man saw that He could not defeat him, He struck Jacob's hip as they wrestled and dislocated his hip socket. Then He said to Jacob, Let Me go, for the day is breaking. But Jacob said, I will not let You go unless You bless me. What is your name? the man asked. Jacob! he replied. Your name will no longer be Jacob, He said. It will be Israel because you have struggled with God and with men and have prevailed. . . . And He blessed him there* (32:24-29). *Set your minds on what is above, not on what is on the earth* (Colossians 3:2).

Thought for Today: Choose to set your heart on the *narrow . . . gate . . . that leads to life . . . few find it* (Matthew 7:14).

In Today's Reading

His judgment against disobedience; prayer against enemies; prayer for mercy and restoration.

We are reminded of the heartbreaking horror felt by the Israelites following the destruction of the temple and their nation because *they did not keep God's covenant and refused to live by His law* (Psalms 78:10).The psalmist again reminds us of the inevitable results of sin: *The nations have invaded Your inheritance, desecrated Your holy temple, and turned Jerusalem into ruins* (79:1-4).

God had chosen Israel to be a witness to the world, showing how He would bless all who honor Him and His word; but as a nation they failed miserably. The few remaining faithful cried out: *Do not hold past sins against us; let Your compassion come to us quickly, for we have become weak. God of our salvation, help us – for the glory of Your name. Deliver us and atone for our sins, for Your name's sake* (79:8-9).

The blood sacrifices of animals could only temporarily atone (cover) for sins until Jesus, the sinless, perfect Lamb of God, sacrificed His own life's blood for the sins of the world. When John the Baptist *saw Jesus coming toward him* he *said, Here is the Lamb of God, who takes away the sin of the world!* (John 1:29). With Jesus' death, all of the Old Testament sacrifices for sins, which formerly had only temporarily "covered" sin, were removed by His sinless blood. Now, *if we confess our sins, He is faithful and righteous to forgive us our sins and to cleanse us from all unrighteousness* (I John 1:9). The sacrifice of Christ on the cross made it possible for both Jews and Gentiles who truly repent and turn to Jesus as their Savior to be forgiven of their sins (Galatians 3:27-28). Israel's sacrifices and festivals were symbols foreshadowing all that was to be accomplished by Jesus the Messiah. He perfectly fulfills their prophetic meaning.

Thus, God forever destroyed the old sacrificial system under the law and now proclaims: *He is the mediator of a new covenant, so that those who are called might receive the promise of the eternal inheritance, because a death has taken place for redemption from the transgressions committed under the first covenant* (Hebrews 9:15).

Thought for Today: True success in life depends on living in accordance with God's word – not on our well-laid plans.

In Today's Reading

God's goodness and Israel's waywardness; blessedness of living in God's presence; David's desire to walk in truth.

The Holy Spirit guided David to unite the two weapons of our spiritual warfare – prayer and the inspired word of God – in Psalm 86, pointing out the power we have when these two become our way of life.

When David offered his prayer: *Listen, LORD, and answer me, for I am poor and needy* (Psalms 86:1), he was acknowledging his dependence upon God. He saw himself as *poor and needy,* but he stated: *Protect my life, for I am faithful. You are my God; save Your servant who trusts in You* (86:2). He prayed to the Lord daily, not just in times of crisis (86:3). Although David was the king of Israel and never lost a war, when he spoke of himself as *Your servant,* he recognized the lordship of God over his life (86:4).

David prayed: *For You, LORD , are kind and ready to forgive, abundant in faithful love to all who call on You* (86:5). It is a reminder that when we are faced with situations beyond our control, we too should say with David: *I call on You in the day of my distress, for You will answer me. . . . For You are great and perform wonders; You alone are God* (86:7,10).

The supreme desire of every Christian should be this prayer of David: *Teach me your way, LORD, and I will live by Your truth* (86:11). This is a prayer that all of us need to offer each day.

When David prayed: *Give me an undivided mind to fear Your name,* he was declaring a single aim in his life (86:11).

An undivided mind is essential. *For this very reason, make every effort to supplement your faith with goodness . . . knowledge with self-control, self-control with endurance, endurance with godliness, godliness with brotherly affection, and brotherly affection with love. For if these qualities are yours and are increasing, they will keep you from being useless or unfruitful in the knowledge of our Lord Jesus Christ. The person who lacks these things is blind and shortsighted, and has forgotten the cleansing from his past sins. Therefore, brothers, make every effort to confirm your calling and election, because if you do these things you will never stumble* (II Peter 1:5-10).

Thought for Today: God's grace is sufficient for you.

In Today's Reading

A cry for deliverance from death; praise for God's covenant and promises; frailty and brevity of life; the faithful protected.

The one who lives under the protection of the Most High is the one whose heart is set on being obedient to the Lord (Psalms 91:1). To *dwell in the shadow of the Almighty,* there is a need to *draw near to God* (James 4:8). Drawing *near to God* requires that you *cleanse your hands* (of questionable activities) . . . *and purify your hearts* (of sinful thoughts, attitudes, and motives). Be assured that He *will be a protective shield* (assurance of security) (Psalms 91:4).

The psalmist expressed the utmost confidence in the loving care of God when he said: *You will not fear the terror of the night, the arrow that flies by day* (meaning the numerous satanic attacks) (91:5-8). Then he assured the faithful by saying: *Because you have made the LORD . . . your dwelling place* (way of life), *no harm will come to you. . . . For He will give His angels orders concerning you, to protect you in all your ways. They will support you with their hands so that you will not strike your foot against a stone* (91:9-12).

Satan, a fallen angel, quoted these verses to Jesus after His 40-day fast in his attempt to persuade Jesus to leap off the pinnacle of the temple, saying: *If You* (since You) *are the Son of God, throw Yourself down. For it is written: He will give His angels orders concerning you, and, In their hands they will lift you up, so you will not strike your foot against a stone* (Matthew 4:6; Luke 4:9-11; see also Psalms 91:11-12). In tempting our Lord, Satan was like some today who love the promises of God, but fail to consider the conditions of the promises. Our Lord's response to the temptation of Satan was: *It is also written: You must not tempt the Lord your God* (Matthew 4:7; see also Deuteronomy 6:16). We have no assurance that His angels will keep us in "ways" that ignore His word.

Satan has deceived many by saying: "Your situation is an exception" or "Just this one time" or "Be broad-minded, everyone is doing it." He also uses examples of hypocrites to deceive some by pointing out "religious people do these things, so why shouldn't you?" Always remember to *stay away from every form of evil* (I Thessalonians 5:22).

Thought for Today: *Don't be foolish, but understand what the Lord's will is* (Ephesians 5:17).

In Today's Reading

Praise for the loving-kindness of the Lord; appeal for justice; a call to sing, worship, and praise the Lord.

Worship is not a "time" set aside for receiving personal satisfaction or for the enjoyment of a "sermon." Worship should be an active, heartfelt expression of prayer, praise, and adoration, demonstrating our esteem for our heavenly Father and our Savior Jesus Christ. Following this, all else, including the sermon, becomes more meaningful. By the inspiration of the Holy Spirit, the psalmist invites the faithful to *come, let us shout joyfully to the LORD, shout triumphantly to the rock of our salvation! . . . Come, let us worship and bow down; let us kneel before the LORD our Maker. For He is our God, and we are the people of His pasture, the sheep under His care* (Psalms 95:1,6-7). Singing with a heartfelt attitude of gratitude and *thanksgiving* is a vital part of worship. The word *shout* carries with it the thought of expressing great joy and devotion to our Lord.

Praise will lift worship beyond the level of personal needs to the higher plane of love and adoration as we glorify the heavenly Father, our precious Savior Jesus Christ, and the indwelling Holy Spirit. A "self-centered" person assumes the "worship" service was meant for his personal satisfaction. Consequently, we hear such people say: "I didn't get much out of the service." The reason is clear – they didn't put much into it. Some lack spiritual fulfillment because they reflect the mood and attitude of unbelievers when confronted with adverse circumstances, such as the loss of a job, the death of a loved one, a divorce, the betrayal of a friend, or some other painful experience. Deciding to be unhappy and dissatisfied, we deprive ourselves of the joy of an abundant, peaceful life.

Think of all our Lord has done for you, in you, and with you, and all He has promised to you for all eternity and you cannot help but praise, worship, and *serve the LORD with gladness;* (and) *come before Him with joyful songs* (100:2).

Our *gladness* will be in direct proportion to our faith in His unfailing presence and promises. *For the LORD is good, and His love is eternal; His faithfulness endures through all generations* (Psalms 100:5).

Thought for Today: How much of Christ will others see in you today?

In Today's Reading

Personal commitment to the Lord's ways; a cry in distress; gratefulness to God for His mercy; His mighty power; God's providence over Israel.

David was inspired by the Holy Spirit to prophesy beyond the life, death, resurrection and ascension of Jesus to His coming kingdom reign when He will administer equal justice for all the world. Because of this, David declared: *I will live with integrity of heart in my house. I will not set anything godless before my eyes. I hate the doing of transgression* (Psalms 101:2-3). David was testifying that all his personal pleasures as well as business transactions were to please the Lord. To maintain this attitude, David chose his friends wisely saying: *A devious* (deceitful) *heart will be far from me; I will not be involved with evil* (101:4) meaning, I will have nothing to do with anyone that is evil.

A few of the many reasons for praising the Lord are given in Psalm 103, but it is the loving Lord Himself who is our highest reason for praise. First, we praise Him for who He is, the all-powerful, all-wise, righteous Creator. We thankfully praise Him because *He has not dealt with us as our sins deserve or repaid us according to our offenses. For as high as the heavens are above the earth, so great is His faithful love toward those who fear Him* (103:10-11). We never cease to praise Him for His mercy and forgiving love in cleansing us from all our sins. Therefore, it is an act of unbelief on our part, a deception of Satan, and contrary to the nature of our loving Lord, for us to bring up former sins – either ours or those of others. Forgiven means no longer remembered, not only by God, but by us as well (I John 1:9; II Peter 1:9). God has assured us that *as far as the east is from the west, so far has He removed our transgressions from us* (Psalms 103:12).

We are reminded that unlimited forgiveness should characterize every true disciple of Christ, for He said: *Whenever you stand praying, if you have anything against anyone, forgive him, so that your Father in heaven may also forgive your wrongdoing. But if you don't forgive people, your Father will not forgive your wrongdoing* (Mark 11:25-26).

Thought for Today: God often overrules our wishes and plans in order to accomplish His highest purpose in our lives.

In Today's Reading

Israel's rebellion in the wilderness; God's mercies to Israel; exhortation to praise God for His goodness.

Although God had faithfully blessed Israel with a miraculous deliverance from Egyptian slavery, provided the promised land, victory over the Canaanites and great prosperity, *they* (the Israelites) *soon forgot His works and would not wait for His counsel. They . . . tested God in the wilderness* (Psalms 106:13-14). Numerous sins of Israel's faithlessness and past sins are brought to our attention. Among them: *At Horeb they made a* (golden) *calf and worshiped the cast metal image* (vs 19); *forgot God their Savior* (vs 21); *despised the pleasant land* (Canaan) *and did not believe His promise* (vs 24); *grumbled* (complained) *in their tents* (vs 25); *did not destroy the people as the LORD had commanded* (vs 34); *but mingled* (associated) *with the* (idolatrous) *nations and . . . served their idols* (vss 35-36).

The psalmist then points out the inevitable consequences: *Therefore the LORD's anger burned against His people, and He abhorred His own inheritance. He handed them over to the nations, those who hated them ruled them* (vss 40-42). But, judgment is mingled with mercy: *Then they cried out to the LORD in their trouble; He rescued them from their distress. . . . Let them give thanks to the LORD for His faithful love. . . . He sent His word and healed them* (107:6-9,20).

Note carefully that their one method of deliverance is still the same today: *He sent His word and healed them*. The psalmist could have simply said: *The LORD rescued them*. Instead, he chose to say: *He sent His word, and healed them*. His Word is Jesus, for *in the beginning was the Word and the Word was with God, and the Word was God* (John 1:1). His Word, the Written Word, when believed and acted upon, is the means God has chosen to supply and satisfy man's every need.

Let them give thanks to the LORD for His faithful love and His wonderful works for the human race. . . . The upright see it, and rejoice. . . . Let whoever is wise pay attention to these things and consider the LORD's acts of faithful love (Psalms 107:8,15,21,31,42-43).

Thought for Today: How much of the word do you make available for God to use in your life?

In Today's Reading

David's praise to God for His sovereignty over nations; prayer for judgment upon the wicked; exhortation to trust in God, not idols.

When Jesus Christ ascended into heaven, He fulfilled the prophecy which the Holy Spirit had earlier inspired David to write: *The LORD* (God the Father) *declared to my LORD* (God the Son), *Sit at My right hand until I make Your enemies Your footstool* (Psalms 110:1). Jesus quoted this psalm as referring to Himself (Mark 12:36).

Israel, as a nation, rejected their Messiah King. But, *the stone that the builders rejected has become the cornerstone. . . . It is wonderful in our eyes. . . . Blessed is he who comes in the name of the LORD. . . . The LORD is God and has given us light. Bind the festival sacrifice with cords to the horns of the altar. You are my God, and I will give You thanks. . . . I will exalt You. . . . His faithful love endures forever* (Psalms 118:22-23,26-29).

Jesus quoted this psalm, saying: *Then what is the meaning of this Scripture: The stone that the builders rejected, this has become the cornerstone? Everyone who falls on that stone will be broken to pieces, and if it falls on anyone, it will grind him to powder!* (Luke 20:17-18; Mark 12:10-11).

Paul quoted this psalm when he wrote to the Ephesians: *So then you are no longer foreigners and strangers, but fellow citizens with the saints, and members of God's household, built on the foundation of the apostles and prophets, with Christ Jesus Himself as the cornerstone. The whole building is being fitted together in Him and is growing into a holy sanctuary in the Lord* (Ephesians 2:19-21).

After a miracle of healing, *Peter was filled with the Holy Spirit and said to them, Rulers of the people and elders . . . let it be known to all of you and to all the people of Israel, that by the name of Jesus Christ the Nazarene – whom you crucified and whom God raised from the dead – by Him this man is standing here before you healthy. This Jesus is The stone despised by you builders, who has become the cornerstone. There is salvation in no one else, for there is no other name under heaven given to people by which we must be saved* (Acts 4:8,10-12).

Thought for Today: Fears vanish as we daily trust God.

In Today's Reading

The greatness, power, and perfection of God's word.

The purpose of the longest chapter in the Bible is to focus our attention on the only Infallible Guide to Life given by our Creator. In it, God has provided everything we need to be the person He planned for us to be and to accomplish the purpose for which He created us. Equally indispensable is knowing our Creator, Savior, and coming Messiah King. It opens with: *How happy are those whose way is blameless, who live according to the law of the LORD! . . . and seek Him with all their heart* (Psalms 119:1-2). This means much more than just avoiding sin or living a good life. We are blessed as we diligently seek God Himself.

All who seek God will pray: *I have sought You with all my heart; don't let me wander from Your commands. I have treasured Your word in my heart so that I may not sin against You* (vss 10-11). It is by taking daily delight in His word, *as much as in all riches* (vs 14) that our fellowship with the Lord is assured. The psalmist continues: *I will not forget Your word* (vs 16). This kind of forgetting is more than a momentary memory lapse. It is drifting away from God as a result of becoming so involved in other interests that His word is neglected.

Daily we need to pray: *Help me stay on the path of Your commands, for I take pleasure in it. Turn my heart to Your decrees and not to material gain* (119:18,27,33-36). Because of this, I have something to sing about regardless of circumstances (vs 54). The child of God can also say with the psalmist: *Before I was afflicted I went astray, but now I keep Your word. . . . It was good for me to be afflicted so that I could learn Your statutes* (vss 67,71).

Though he had been afflicted, the psalmist did not find fault with God, nor did he doubt the Lord's wisdom and justice. For many, it is in times like these that we painfully recognize that we have made wrong choices which led to unwholesome consequences. This is when we recognize that the Bible is priceless, for it alone reveals life's true values and prepares us for eternity. *I rejoice over Your promise like one who finds vast treasure* (Psalms 119:162).

Thought for Today: Spiritual growth is dependent on the time we spend with the Lord letting Him speak to us from His word.

In Today's Reading

Prayer for deliverance from lying lips; sustaining power; prayer for peace of Jerusalem; blessing of trusting God.

All male Jews who were physically able and ceremonially clean were required by the law of God to go to Jerusalem three times each year (Exodus 23:14-17; Deuteronomy 16:16).

With confidence in the Lord's protection on the journeys, the Israelite worshiper could sing: *My help comes from the LORD. . . . The LORD will protect your coming and going . . . forever* (Psalms 121:2,5,8).

The psalms were sung as they traveled toward Jerusalem to participate in the festivals, sacrifices, and worship. Even though some may have traveled from one to three weeks to arrive in Jerusalem, these were to be journeys of great joy. They sang with assurance that the Lord would protect their homes and possessions during their absence. *Indeed, the Protector of Israel does not slumber or sleep* (121:4). The psalmist said: *I . . . put my hope* (trust) *in His word. . . with Him is redemption in abundance* (130:5-7). The Israelites were taught to trust in the Lord for provisions and protection, as well as for forgiveness of sins.

We are moving toward the end of our opportunity to build up the kingdom of God. David was inspired to foresee that glorious time when the Messiah would reign in Jerusalem: *Pray for the peace of Jerusalem. . . . For . . . our God . . . will seek your good* (122:6-9).

This prophecy foretells the perfect reign of the Prince of Peace: *Many peoples will . . . say, Come, let us go . . . to the house of the God of Jacob. He will teach us . . . His ways so that we may walk in His paths. For instruction will go out of Zion and the word of the LORD from Jerusalem* (Isaiah 2:3).

Centuries have passed, but the day will soon arrive when Israel's throne will be occupied by a descendant of David – the promised Messiah, the virgin-born Son of God, Jesus Christ.

Blessed be the God and Father of our Lord Jesus Christ, who has blessed us with every spiritual blessing . . . to be holy and blameless in His sight. . . . In Him we have redemption through His blood, the forgiveness of our trespasses (Ephesians 1:3-4,7).

Thought for Today: Being satisfied is the key to praising the Lord.

In Today's Reading

A prayer for God's blessing; joy of unity; exhortation to praise the Lord; God's enduring mercy; God's word magnified.

The psalmist reminds us of *how good and pleasant it is when brothers can live together! It is like fine oil* (anointing oil) *on the head . . . running down Aaron's beard, onto his robes* (consecrating the whole body) (Psalms 133:1-2; Exodus 30:25,30; Leviticus 8:12). The holy anointing oil that was poured upon the head of Aaron, the first high priest, is a foreshadowing of the anointing, indwelling, and outflowing of the Holy Spirit upon believers today. The oil poured out symbolized the Holy Spirit who, in love, covers as well as permeates the lives of those who have submitted themselves to Him.

All Christians have the same indwelling Holy Spirit. Therefore, we should express the oneness of believers in a spirit of love, without partiality, regardless of race, nationality, education, or wealth.

The key to true unity is to *do nothing out of rivalry or conceit, but in humility consider others as more important than yourselves* (Philippians 2:3). Our fallen nature is ever prone to distort unwelcome encounters with others and our emotions can create a crisis out of unimportant incidents. Added to this, we all too often selfishly demand our own rights and blame our frustrations on others. Pride, self-will, and an independent spirit are the great enemies of the Spirit-filled life. It is Christlike to accept personal offense with patience rather than to react to someone's rudeness. We need to recognize that people's bad attitudes are often momentary frustrations caused by previous conflicts, sorrows, sufferings, or bad news. God permits difficult people to come into our lives to give us an opportunity to express His love and patience toward them, just as our Lord has made known His love and mercy toward us.

The unity of believers can be compared to a great orchestra with many instruments creating beautiful harmony. To maintain that harmony, we must stay in tune with the Master Conductor. *For as many of you as have been baptized into Christ have put on Christ. There is no Jew or Greek, slave or free, male or female; for you are all one in Christ Jesus* (Galatians 3:27-28).

Thought for Today: All Christians are members of the Body of Christ.

In Today's Reading

The all-seeing providence of God; David's prayer for deliverance from Saul; comfort in prayer; prayer for mercy in judgment.

Our Creator inspired David to write: *LORD. . . . You are aware of all my ways* (from the time I was conceived unto this very day). . . . *This extraordinary knowledge is beyond me* (beyond my understanding). . . . *For it was You who created my inward parts* (formed my inward spirit and heart); *You knit* (fashioned) *me together in my mother's womb . . . when I was formed in the depths of the earth. Your eyes saw me when I was formless* (139:1-16).God reveals that, at conception, David became a person, a living soul. Although, as an unborn infant, he was hidden from human view, as if buried in the earth, his body was no mystery to his Creator, who was skillfully preparing him for his God-ordained destiny on earth.

God led Isaiah the prophet to write: *The LORD called me from the womb; from the body of my mother He mentioned my name. . . . in the shadow of His hand He hid me. . . . And now the LORD says, He who formed me from the womb to be His servant . . . I will also appoint you as a light for the nations.* Note that Isaiah knew that the Lord had prepared him to be His prophet while he was being *formed* long before his birth (Isaiah 49:1-6).

God also revealed to Jeremiah: *I chose you before I formed you in the womb; I set you apart before you were born. I appointed you a prophet to the nations* (Jeremiah 1:5).

If the mothers of David, Isaiah, or Jeremiah had aborted them, they would have murdered these great men of God. Today's records would have just shown three more unnamed fetuses.

The Holy Spirit inspired the beloved physician Luke to write what the Angel Gabriel announced to the virgin Mary: *You will conceive and give birth to a son, and you will call His name JESUS* (Luke 1:31). Note that the Lord Jesus Christ was announced as a Person at conception. *Jesus said, Leave the children alone, and don't try to keep them from coming to Me* (Matthew 19:14).

Thought for Today: *The one who finds Me finds life* (Proverbs 8:35).

In Today's Reading

David's praise for God's mercy and goodness; benefits of trusting in God; all creation to praise the Lord; triumph in the God of Israel.

The psalmist begins and ends each of the last five psalms saying: *Hallelujah!* (meaning Praise the Lord) – literally – an expression of how great our God is. *I will praise the LORD all my life; I will sing to the LORD as long as I live. . . .* We *praise the LORD* that we can look to Him for our needs. *Happy is the one whose help is the God of Jacob, whose hope is in the LORD his God, the Maker of heaven and earth, the sea and everything in them. He remains faithful forever. . . . Hallelujah* (Psalms 146:1-2,5-6,10).

The psalmist continues by saying: *Hallelujah! . . . He heals the brokenhearted and binds up their wounds. . . . He sends His command throughout the earth; His word runs swiftly* (147:1,3,15). *Let them praise the name of the LORD, for His name alone is exalted* (148:13).

The fact is, the more we are determined to truly put Christ first in our lives, the more we will experience interruptions which demand our time and attention. When this happens, we are tempted to seek what is best for "our" kingdom rather than seeking first His *kingdom* (Matthew 6:33). Many times, even "good things" keep us from "the best" that God would give us. However, it may also be a test of our faithfulness, to see if, like Job, we can say: *He knows the way I have taken. When He has tried me, I will come forth as gold* (Job 23:10).

Throughout the book of Psalms, we are made aware that nothing comes into our lives by accident. In His wisdom and love, everything God permits or causes is to develop His highest good in and for us.

These closing psalms assure us we have a loving, heavenly Father who wants the best for His children. To make this possible, He has provided His word as the one true guide that reveals how we can live to please Him. God has also provided His church where we can sing praises to Him, share our testimonies with others who love Him, and receive instruction and inspiration from our spiritual leaders. We were never meant to be self-sufficient, independent loners (Ephesians 4:16).

The book of Psalms concludes by proclaiming: *Let everything that breathes praise the LORD. Hallelujah!* (Psalms 150:6).

Thought for Today: Trusting in the Lord's unsearchable ways is better than hoping in man's predictable, fallible ways.

Introduction To The Book Of Proverbs

Solomon *uttered 3,000 proverbs, and his songs were 1,005* (I Kings 4:32), but the wisdom revealed was inspired of God. Solomon also collected many of the proverbs written by others (Proverbs 25:1; 30:1; 31:1).

The book of Proverbs begins by stating its purpose: *For gaining wisdom and being instructed* (1:2), and then makes it clear that *the fear of the LORD is the beginning of knowledge; fools despise wisdom and instruction* (1:7). Godly wisdom is an attribute of our Creator, and we need His wisdom to enjoy life to the fullest.

Our Lord quoted frequently from Proverbs. He often said positively what Proverbs say negatively. Compare Proverbs 4:19 with John 12:35; Proverbs 5:23 with John 8:24; Proverbs 8:35 with John 6:47; Proverbs 14:31 with Matthew 25:31-46; Proverbs 18:21 with Matthew 12:37; and Proverbs 23:7 with Matthew 12:34.

The Proverbs focus primarily on the daily conduct of the "wise." Worldly achievements are worthless vanity compared to the eternal values that are gained by keeping the commandments of God (Proverbs 2:1-4). God gives His people wisdom for daily direction. Wisdom is more than knowledge; it is a distinct representation and application of Christ in all areas of our lives (see 8:12-36).

Every word of God is pure; He is a shield to those who take refuge in Him (30:5) and *anyone who turns his ear away from hearing the law – even his prayer is detestable* (28:9).

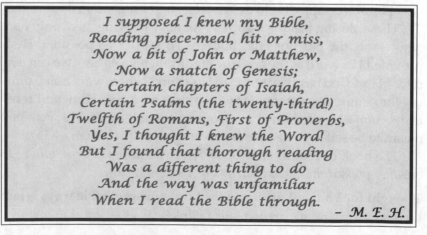

I supposed I knew my Bible,
Reading piece-meal, hit or miss,
Now a bit of John or Matthew,
Now a snatch of Genesis;
Certain chapters of Isaiah,
Certain Psalms (the twenty-third!)
Twelfth of Romans, First of Proverbs,
Yes, I thought I knew the Word!
But I found that thorough reading
Was a different thing to do
And the way was unfamiliar
When I read the Bible through.

– M. E. H.

In Today's Reading

Fear of God is the beginning of wisdom; necessity of searching for wisdom; importance of trusting in the Lord.

Accept my words and store up (take to heart) *my commands within you, listening closely to wisdom and directing your heart to understanding; furthermore . . . if you seek it like* (you would) *silver and search for it like hidden treasure, then you will understand the fear of the LORD and discover the knowledge of God* (Proverbs 2:1-5). *Accept . . . listening closely . . . directing your heart . . . lift your voice . . . seek it . . . search for it* (wisdom) *like* (you would) *hidden treasure.* This means a lifetime of earnest, daily, progressive, spiritual achievement.

God is saying: "Take My word seriously," for it alone can provide you with true spiritual wisdom that will guide you to *understand righteousness, justice, and integrity – every good path. For wisdom will enter your heart, and knowledge will delight your soul. Discretion will watch over you, and understanding will guard you* (2:9-11).

In contrast, some spend little or no time reading the Bible, even though the apostle Paul urged: *Be diligent to present yourself approved to God, a worker who doesn't need to be ashamed, correctly teaching the word of truth* (II Timothy 2:15). How few ever pray for spiritual achievements that they may accomplish the purpose for which God created them. Discerning Christians will put their goals in line with God's purposes and *seek first the kingdom of God and His righteousness* (Matthew 6:33) and make all secular goals secondary. *Our citizenship is in heaven, from which we also eagerly wait for a Savior, the Lord Jesus Christ* (Philippians 3:20).

The choice of whom we will serve is of utmost importance, for it affects everything else in life. The intense energy by which worldly success is pursued should also apply to a Christian's desire for achievements of eternal value.

One of life's most sobering thoughts is that *the Son of Man* (will soon) *. . . come with His angels in the glory of His Father, and then He will reward each according to what he has done* (Matthew 16:27).

Thought for Today: Read God's word with an intense desire to accept His wisdom and reproof in order to mature spiritually.

In Today's Reading

The power of wisdom to protect from evil; the seven most hated sins; the necessity of keeping God's commandments.

Believers in both the Old and New Testaments are likened to the bride of Christ, thus it follows that sexual gratification other than within God-ordained marriage of a man and woman is spiritual adultery against God. Sexual sins are so deceptive and destructive that more space is given in Proverbs to warnings of their wickedness than any other sin. Sexual sin defiles the body which is the temple of the Holy Spirit (I Corinthians 6:19). The warnings in Proverbs are in chapter 5; 6:23-35; all of chapter 7; 9:13-18; and 22:14. God reveals that the only sure way of safety is found when *wisdom . . . delights your soul. . . . It will rescue you from a forbidden woman, from a stranger* (who seduces) *with her flattering talk* (Proverbs 2:10-11,16-19). Indulging in a sinful relationship provides momentary physical pleasure; but *the one who commits adultery lacks sense; whoever does so destroys himself* (6:32).

God is warning that disastrous results are inevitable: *He follows her impulsively like an ox going to the slaughter, like a deer bounding toward a trap* (7:22). Some assume that adultery or fornication is acceptable when it occurs between consenting adults; but God says: *Do not be deceived: no sexually immoral people, idolaters, adulterers, male prostitutes, homosexuals . . . will inherit God's kingdom* (I Corinthians 6:9-10) .

Satan can only tempt us. Sin begins as we dwell upon the temptation. Therefore, we must take *every thought captive to the obedience of Christ* (II Corinthians 10:5).

Anyone who has been drawn into sexual sins should pray for forgiveness, for *the one who conceals his sins will not prosper, but whoever confesses and renounces them will find mercy* (Proverbs 28:13). *For by one offering He has perfected forever those who are sanctified. . . . He adds: I will never again remember their sins and their lawless acts. Now where there is forgiveness of these, there is no longer an offering for sin* (Hebrews 10:14,17-18).

Thought for Today: We are cautioned that as a man *thinks within himself, so he is* (Proverbs 23:7).

In Today's Reading

Benefits of wisdom; wise and foolish contrasted.

Nothing in life is more to be treasured, more priceless, than knowing the word of God, for He has said: *All the words of my mouth are righteous; none of them are deceptive or perverse. All of them are clear to the perceptive, and right to those who discover knowledge. Accept my instruction instead of silver, and knowledge rather than pure gold. For wisdom is better than precious stones, and nothing desirable can compare with it* (Prov. 8:8-11).

Is it any surprise that Satan seeks above all else to keep Christians from reading what God has written, the only sure way of knowing right from wrong? When our first considerations are love, loyalty, and service to the Lord, they lead to our obedience of His word.

The fear of the LORD is the beginning of wisdom, and the knowledge of the Holy One is understanding (9:10). This wisdom and understanding covers every aspect of life: physical, moral, spiritual, financial, and social well-being. *To fear the LORD is to hate evil. I hate arrogant pride, evil conduct, and perverse speech. I possess good advice and competence; I have understanding and strength. . . . I love those who love me* (wisdom), *and those who search for me* (earnestly) *find me. . . . And now, my sons, listen to me; those who keep my ways are happy. . . . For the one who finds me finds life and obtains favor from the LORD, but the one who sins against me harms himself; all who hate me love death* (8:13-14,17,32,35-36).

The basic difference between the wise man and the fool is in the use each makes of his time, talents, and material possessions. When we rely on God (His word) it will result in loving obedience to Him regarding our time, talents, and possessions (3:5-6).

We all are on one of two roads in our journey through life. The road taken followed by the wise is narrower and more difficult, but it brings happiness, satisfaction, peace, and eternal life; however, the broad road of the fool inevitably leads to vanity and ultimately into the eternal lake of fire. *Death and Hades were thrown into the lake of fire. This is the second death, the lake of fire* (Revelation 20:14).

Thought for Today: Failure to give is motivated by selfishness.

In Today's Reading

Moral virtues; pitfalls of evil.

God, in His infinite wisdom, declares: *The one who will not use the rod* (fails to discipline) *hates his son, but the one who loves him disciplines him diligently* (meaning that he doesn't put it off) (Proverbs 13:24).

The greatest contribution we can make to our children's future is to teach them obedience and respect – first, to Christ as their personal Savior and Lord of their lives, then to their parents and all who are in authority, including schoolteachers and law enforcement officers. This obedience should extend to the laws of the government. As a prerequisite to teaching a child submission to authority, it is vital that parents consistently show submission to authority by their own example.

The rod is the symbol of authority that God has committed to parents for training their children. To apply the rod means to exercise authority. The rod must be administered firmly yet lovingly. Using the rod of authority does not mean that parents should release their bottled-up frustrations by shouting demands, slapping faces, or severely spanking. These are examples of mental and physical abuse. We must not expect adult maturity from our children. They need the same loving-kindness and patience from us that we desire from our heavenly Father. Even mature Christians are prone to forget how many times the Lord, with long-suffering love, has forgiven our failures through the years.

Biblical discipline follows the example of our loving Father in heaven, who corrects and disciplines everyone whom He loves (Hebrews 12:6). The psalmist expressed it this way: *Before I was afflicted I went astray, but now I keep* (obey) *Your word* (Psalms 119:67).

We can develop our children's respect for God-ordained authority and, at the same time, provide them with an assurance of both our love and God's love for them. It is important to spend time with our children, especially reading the Bible and praying with them to develop a concern for the things of God (Deuteronomy 6:2-9; Proverbs 22:6).

Children, obey your parents in the Lord (as His representatives), *because this is right. Honor your father and mother—which is the first commandment with a promise* (Ephesians 6:1-2; also Exodus 20:12).

Thought for Today: Prayerfully think before you act or speak.

In Today's Reading

The values of pleasing the Lord and choosing wisdom.

No one is naturally humble. The human heart is permeated with pride passed down from Adam; only the indwelling Christ can develop true humility in our lives. This will manifest itself in kindness toward the unkind, long-suffering toward those who annoy us, and love toward the unlovely. How inconsistent it is to think that we have "humbly given ourselves to Christ" when we snub or react harshly to anyone.

The Lord leads us to see the end result of pride and false humility: *Pride comes before destruction, and an arrogant spirit before a fall. Better to be lowly of spirit with the humble than to divide plunder with the proud* (Proverbs 16:18-19).

It is natural to think of ourselves as humble, especially when we are alone in prayer. But humility, or a lack of it, is apparent by our attitude when we are with someone who irritates us. If our replies are expressed in an unkind way, either outwardly in our words or actions or inwardly in our thoughts, then our "humility" is not real; it is a mere mask for our pride. Knowing the destructive power of pride, let us look upon people who seem difficult to love as those chosen by God to provide us with the opportunity to cleanse ourselves of self-righteousness by expressing Christlike humility and the love of God.

Humble people will feel no jealousy or envy when they are ignored while others are praised. God reminds us: *Do nothing out of rivalry or conceit, but in humility consider others as more important than yourselves* (Philippians 2:3).

Humility allows us to assume a Christlike nature rather than to selfishly center our thoughts and actions on personal achievements and recognition.We also are warned: *Be in agreement with one another. Do not be proud; instead, associate with the humble. Do not be wise in your own estimation* (thinking you are more important than other people) (Romans 12:16). To be Christlike is to give equal consideration to all people, regardless of their race, position, abilities, or wealth, for *God doesn't show favoritism* (Acts 10:34).

Thought for Today: Avoid worldy-minded associations.

In Today's Reading

Deception of wine; sovereignty of God over kings of the earth; moral virtues rewarded.

Alcohol is amazingly deceptive. The insidious "occasional" drink, in moderation, seems harmless. It even gives the appearance of making life more enjoyable.

But many a "social" drinker eventually discovers that he has exchanged a meaningful life for a degrading existence. Brilliant people who were once successful and influential have been reduced to uselessness because of alcohol. And, strange as it may seem, in their own minds they are convinced that they can take it or leave it and stop drinking at any time. God has warned that *wine is a mocker, beer is a brawler, and whoever staggers because of them is not wise* (Proverbs 20:1).

Pity the person who tries to escape the pressures of life and relax with a "little" drink. No words can express the pitiful results of continued use of alcohol. The warning from God of alcohol's poisoning effects is clear: *In the end it bites like a snake and stings like a viper* (23:32).

Alcohol takes control both chemically and emotionally, with both physical and psychological effects. Once a person is "hooked," dependence upon it robs him of good judgment and, eventually, may destroy his life as well as that of others. Alcohol produces unavoidable, irreversible, and far-reaching physical and emotional wounds.

The longer the victim of intoxication continues indulging in alcohol, the more insensible he becomes to the consequences of his behavior. Gradually, millions have allowed themselves to be in direct violation of the word of God. The only release from these tragic consequences is the mercy and love of God. When a person truly repents and turns to Christ and allows Him to be Savior and Lord of his life, the Holy Spirit becomes a source of influence: *Don't get drunk with wine . . . but be filled with the* (His) *Spirit* (Ephesians 5:18).

Let us walk with decency . . . not in carousing and drunkenness; not in sexual impurity and promiscuity. . . . But put on the Lord Jesus Christ, and make no plans to satisfy the fleshly desires (Romans 13:13-14).

Thought for Today: Play it safe – *Stay away from every form of evil* (I Thessalonians 5:22).

In Today's Reading

Moral, ethical, and spiritual teachings; the excellence of wisdom; comparisons, warnings, and instructions with that of evil men.

It seems normal to stand up for our rights – to fight back against those who treat us unjustly or to get even by inflicting suffering upon those who offend us. But, it is a serious sin to be delighted when an enemy suffers and seems to reap what we think he deserves. It is even more serious to harbor a secret hatred and a desire to bring about his downfall: *Don't gloat when your enemy falls, and don't let your heart rejoice when he stumbles, or the LORD will see, be displeased, and turn His wrath away from him* (Proverbs 24:17-18).

Attitudes of bitterness, revenge, hatred, or ill will toward anyone are self-destructive and are indications that we are not living nearly as close to Christ as we may think: *We must not love* (merely) *in word or speech, but in deed and truth* (I John 3:15,18). We are not to regard anyone as an enemy, since we were all created in the image of God and Christ died to save all of us without an exception. Let us pray that those whom we might consider "enemies" may become disciples of Christ.

No one is justified in taking revenge; we are definitely not qualified to be judge, jury, or executioner. We dare not assume the position of God, who said: *Friends, do not avenge yourselves; instead, leave room for His wrath. For it is written: Vengeance belongs to Me; I will repay, says the Lord* (Romans 12:19; Deuteronomy 32:35; Hebrews 10:30). If we are unjustly treated, we should pray for our offender. All thoughts of hatred and revenge were suggested by Satan; but the indwelling Holy Spirit enables the Christian to reject them and be merciful and forgiving rather than hateful toward a wrongdoer.

Our reaction to the unkind behavior of our offenders reveals whether we are controlled by the Holy Spirit or by our old sinful nature. *Blessed are the gentle, because they will inherit the earth. . . . Blessed are those who are persecuted for righteousness, because the kingdom of heaven is theirs* (Matthew 5:5,10).

Thought for Today: To love the unlovely is an expression of Christ's love.

In Today's Reading

Advice to the wise; Agur's confession of his faith; the words of King Lemuel; praise of a good wife.

If we love someone, we want to be with them and to know what pleases them to develop a lasting relationship. We also want to know what they dislike to avoid actions that would displease them. Surely, this is also an important consideration in our relationship with our Lord.

God said: *A discerning son keeps the law. . . . Anyone who turns his ear away from hearing the law—even his prayer is detestable* (unacceptable to God) (Proverbs 28:7,9). Why would God be interested in what we have to say when we are not interested in reading His Guide for successful living? If we want God to listen to us when we pray, then it is important to read all His qualifications for acceptable prayer.

John reminded believers: *We have confidence before God, and can receive whatever we ask from Him because we keep His commands and do what is pleasing in His sight* (I John 3:21-22). But, we can't keep all His commandments if we don't read all of His word to know what they are.

Strange as it may seem, some talk of "biblical principles," but see no need to read all of the Bible in order to know "biblical principles." They pray for solutions to life's problems, but fail to go to the one place where God provides the answers to them.

Why is there such widespread failure among Christians to read all of the word of God? Is it because they assume that their own "good judgment" can take the place of the wisdom of our Creator?

Jeremiah exposed the popular preachers of his day, saying: *See, the word of the LORD has become offensive to them—they find no pleasure in it* (Jeremiah 6:10). The Lord further declared through His prophet: *They have paid no attention to My word. . . . they have rejected it* (6:19). Throughout history, God has rejected His people when they refused to accept His guidance. Without a doubt, God was heartbroken when He said to Hosea: *My people are destroyed for lack of knowledge!* (Hosea 4:6).

Jesus emphasized the necessity of obedience to His word, saying: *If you keep My commandments you will remain in My love, just as I have kept My Father's commandments and remain in His love* (John 15:10).

Thought for Today: Christ is not just the world's Savior in the sweet by and by, but also in the sinful here and now.

Introduction To The Book Of Ecclesiastes

Solomon listed 27 achievements in his life saying: *I denied myself nothing of all that my eyes desired. I did not refuse my heart any joy* (physical pleasure) (Ecclesiastes 2:10). During that time, he completely ignored the word of God by amassing horses, wealth, and wives (Deuteronomy 17:16-17).

Solomon repeatedly used the expression: *Everything is futile* (vanity) (Ecclesiastes 1:2). The word *futile* refers to what is of no lasting value. By the end of his 40-year reign, the people had been oppressed with excessive taxes for his massive building projects for so long that they were at the point of rebellion.

After living his life in vain, Solomon conceded that a man is a fool who thinks he can achieve fulfillment in life by amassing material possessions, because he always wants more (5:10-20; 6:1-9). Solomon described himself when he wrote: *A poor youth who is wise is better than an old king who is foolish and no longer pays attention to warnings* (4:13).

Ecclesiastes is a confession of the worthlessness of all earthly treasures and the impossibility of finding satisfaction apart from God. All is indeed futile if Christ is not enthroned in our hearts.

After a lifetime of searching for satisfaction through wealth, women, and possessions, Solomon eventually recognized that man's true contentment lies only in full obedience to God. He concluded by saying: *Remember your Creator* (you are His property) *in the days of your youth: while the evil days are still in the future, and the years have not arrived that will cause you to say, I have no delight in them* (12:1).

Live out Thy life, Oh Christ, each day
In this poor body made of clay,
Reveal again, through me, dear Lord
The mighty power of Thine own Word.

– M. E. H.

In Today's Reading

The vanity (emptiness) of living for pleasure and material gain; a reason for everything; varied proverbs of wisdom.

It would be easy to become excited over the achievements of Solomon. He wrote: *I built houses for myself while planting vineyards for myself. I made gardens and parks for myself and planted in them every kind of fruit tree. I built irrigation pools for myself from which to irrigate my grove of freshly budding trees. I bought male slaves and slave girls and owned slaves born in my house. My personal property included many herds and flocks, more than all who lived before me in Jerusalem had owned. I collected for myself silver and gold. . . . I secured . . . human luxuries. . . . I became great and surpassed all who lived before me in Jerusalem. . . . I denied myself nothing of all that my eyes desired* (Ecclesiastes 2:4-10).

Solomon eventually concluded: *I turned to all my accomplishments that my hands had accomplished and the struggle that I had struggled to accomplish. See! Everything is futile and a chasing after the wind. Nothing produces profit under the sun* (2:11,17). Solomon was rightly troubled when he said *I hated life because everything is futile and a chasing after the wind*. People today are still trying to gain fulfillment with earthly pursuits while ignoring the will of God.

When he began his reign, we are told that *Solomon loved the LORD, walking in the statutes of his father David* (I Kings 3:3). But, as he set his heart on material projects, wealth, and women, his priorities became distorted and gradually pushed God out of his life. Solomon's life reminds us of many whom God has tested with material success, but their wealth added nothing to God's kingdom when it could have been used to let the world know that God loves them.

Life is short and no one can relive one minute. Each of us needs to ask: "What is the purpose of my brief life?"

Near the close of this sad book, Solomon wisely said: *The person who obeys his command will not experience anything evil* (Ecclesiastes 8:5).

Thought for Today: Possessions and pleasures are no substitute for the Person to whom we owe our supreme devotion – the Lord Jesus.

In Today's Reading

Caution against hasty vows; the emptiness of riches; wisdom and goodness upheld; respect for rulers.

When Solomon began his reign, he *loved the* LORD, *walking in the statutes of his father David, he also used to sacrifice . . . at the high places* (1 Kings 3:3). But, as the years passed, he searched for satisfaction everywhere except from the Lord and His word (Psalms 119:97-98). Following years of an extravagant lifestyle, Solomon observed that both rich and poor were equally obsessed with such vanities.

Solomon's thoughts then turned from the secular to the religious life and noted that many attended the house of God with thoughtlessness and hypocrisy, offering insincere prayers and making vows that were never kept. The Holy Spirit, speaking through him, warned: *Guard your steps* (your own purpose for being there) *when you go to the house of God. Draw near to listen* (and obey) *rather than to offer the sacrifice as fools do* (insincere worship) (Ecclesiastes 5:1). It is an insult to God, as well as self-destructive since God does not overlook the actions of fools. *Do not speak too quickly with your lips* (5:2).

In any gathering of worshipers, there may be those who express the right words of praise and prayer and even give generous offerings but have come with motives other than to worship the Lord.

True worship requires a heart-inspired obedience to the word of God: "Draw near to hear and obey" (see 5:1). Since the Scriptures also reveal *that you are God's sanctuary and that the Spirit of God lives in you* (I Corinthians 13:16). When we assemble to worship, we open our hearts to adore, praise, and exalt the Lord. Jesus defined worship when He said: *God is Spirit, and those who worship Him must worship in spirit and truth* (John 4:24).

The place where we worship the Lord may be a magnificent cathedral, a thatched hut, a disciple's home, a hillside, or a cave. There is no place where God is not with His children (John 14:16; Hebrews13:5). Because of His abiding presence we should always praise Him even when in prison. *About midnight Paul and Silas were praying and singing hymns to God, and the prisoners were listening to them* (Acts 16:25).

Thought for Today: Do not envy the wealth of evildoers – it is only temporary.

In Today's Reading

Struggles of the righteous and the wicked; wisdom better than strength; the wise versus the foolish; the Creator to be remembered.

Solomon was famous for his wisdom, but could be misunderstood when he said: *Rejoice, young man, while you are young, and let your heart be glad in the days of your youth. Follow the ways of your heart and the vision of your eyes* (Ecclesiastes 11:9). Not continuing his message would imply he was encouraging youth to let passion and pleasure go unchecked. But he continued: *Know that for all of these things God will bring you to judgment.*

Solomon spent his lifetime searching for pleasure from every worldly source, but used the word *futility* over 30 times in the book of Ecclesiastes and concluded that ignoring the word of God was *futility of futilities* (12:8). Before finishing his message, Solomon restated the basis for true wisdom: *Remember your Creator* (since you are His property) *in the days of your youth: while the evil days are still in the future, and the years have not arrived that will cause you to say, I have no delight in them. . . . When all has been heard, the conclusion of the matter is this: fear God and obey His commandments* (the only true Guide to Life) (12:1,13). Since all of us are part of the purposes of God, all else in life should be seen as opportunities to advance the kingdom of God.

Satisfaction in life results from giving one's time, talents, and resources to fulfill the will of God. This is the only true source of happiness, peace of mind, and genuine enjoyment in life.

Therefore, it is foolish to seek riches, security, power, popularity, or fleeting goals in life merely for self-satisfaction. It is also vanity to give way to *the lust of the flesh* (craving for sensual gratification), *the lust of the eyes* (greed for more), *and the pride in one's lifestyle* (one's own achievements and material possessions) (I John 2:16).

If anyone among you thinks he is wise in this age (in what the world calls wisdom), *he must become* (recognize that as such his wisdom is) *foolish so that he can become wise* (by turning to the source of true wisdom). *For the wisdom of this world is foolishness with God* (I Corinthians 3:18-19).

Thought for Today: Genuine enjoyment in life is to be like Jesus.

Introduction To The Book Of Song Of Songs

Jewish rabbis regard this book as an illustration of the marriage relationship between God and Israel as His wife (see Isaiah 54:4; Jeremiah 2:2; Ezekiel 16:8-14; Hosea 2:16-20). Many Christian leaders believe that it expresses the love that exists between Christ and His church. It expresses the longing of the Christian for the presence of the heavenly Bridegroom and the precious union of the bride with Jesus Christ, the Bridegroom, our King of kings (Revelation 19:7-9,16; 21:9). This beautiful love story also expresses the love of a marriage relationship planned by the Creator.

There are many difficulties in the spiritual interpretation of some of these passages, just as there are some difficulties in the interpretation of the church as the Bride of Christ and He as our Bridegroom.

The importance of this Song is recognized in two ways. First, the Creator who controls the king's heart led the compilers of Scripture to include *Solomon's Finest Song* (Song Of Songs 1:1); and second, the Lord Himself said through Paul: *All Scripture is inspired by God and is profitable for teaching, for rebuking, for correcting, for training in righteousness* (II Timothy 3:16). Because God inspired this book to be written, we should seek to know Him better through it.

Song of Songs is about a king's love for a maiden and her desire for everyone to admire him. It illustrates the relationship between Christ and those who will not be satisfied with anyone's love but His.

Cast thy bread upon the waters
With a steadfast faith sublime,
All which in His Name one scatters
Will return to him in time.

E'en if some give no reception
God's own Truth is not denied
But, in spite of their rejection
God is truly glorified.

Nothing lost in any service
Rendered to our gracious Lord
Whether it seem glad or grievous
There will be a full reward.

– M. E. H.

In Today's Reading

Virtues of married love – symbolic of Christ's love for the church.

This poem describes the wholesome enjoyment of married love between a man and a woman. It expresses the delight of the bridegroom in the bride and of the bride in her husband. The bride describes her wonderful memories as her bridegroom tarries. The whole narrative has a dreamlike quality. The circumstances are vague and not such as occur in ordinary life. The longing, the wondering, and the searching represent the images of dreams. The bride was asleep on her bed, but her thoughts were continually about her absent bridegroom. *In my bed at night I sought the one I love; I sought him, but did not find him* (Song of Songs 3:1).

Every believer is assured that *my love is mine and I am his* (2:16), for He has entered into our very lives and our love relationship continues to grow and deepen as we spend time listening to Him speak as we read His word. We become a different person by virtue of our relationship with the coming Bridegroom. He is my life: *and I no longer live, but Christ lives in me* (Galatians 2:20).

Sometimes we enjoy a very close sense of the presence of Christ. But, all too often, His presence seems far away. Yet our love for Him continues to grow as we wait expectantly for that first glimpse of Him. This will take place when we die and He welcomes us home or when He returns in all His splendor as King. *For now we see indistinctly* (understand only a little about God and eternity), *as in a mirror, but then face to face* (when we see Jesus, all will be clear). *Now I know in part* (imperfectly), *but then I will know* (understand) *fully, as I am fully known* (and understood by God) (I Corinthians 13:12).

As the Bride, we wait with great anticipation for His return when we too can say: *He brought me to the banquet hall, and he looked on me with love* (Song of Songs 2:4).

Your heart must not be troubled. Believe in God; believe also in Me. . . . If I go away and prepare a place for you, I will come back and receive you to Myself, so that where I am you may be also (John 14:1,3).

Thought for Today: Be prepared for the Lord's return.

Introduction To The Book Of Isaiah

Isaiah's ministry extended about 60 years during the reigns of Judah's kings Uzziah (Azariah), Jotham, Ahaz, and Hezekiah (II Kings 14:21; Isaiah 1:1; II Chronicles 26:22; 32:20-23). This was during the same period of time that Micah was also prophesying in Judah, while Jonah, Amos, and Hosea were prophets to Israel. The ten-tribe northern kingdom had existed about 200 years before it was defeated and its people taken captive by Sennacherib, the ruthless Assyrian monarch.

The book of Isaiah is addressed to the entire world: *Listen, heavens, and pay attention, earth, for the LORD has spoken* (Isaiah 1:2). We also learn that God uses the nations of the world as His instruments for working out His perfect will in history. The message throughout the book is: *Hear the word of the LORD* (1:10). The Lord appealed, through Isaiah, for sinners to *come, let us discuss this, says the LORD. Though your sins are like scarlet, they will be as white as snow* (1:18). It was an appeal: *House of Jacob, come and let us walk in the LORD's light* (2:5) and a warning of judgment upon those who reject His word (2:6 – 3:26). A severe warning of six woes is pronounced upon the faithless (2:12; 5:8,11,18,20-22). A new vision of the glorious King is described: *In the year that King Uzziah died, I saw the LORD seated on a high and lofty throne, and His robe filled the temple. . . . my eyes have seen the King, the LORD of hosts* (6:1,5). The book of Isaiah closes with God's promises of comfort and peace for His children, as well as a warning that eternal punishment awaits those who reject Him (66:24).

Jesus Christ is the Supreme theme of this book. Isaiah prophesied the birth of Christ and His deity (7:14; 9:6-7), His ministry (42:1-7; 61:1-2), His sufferings and death (52:1-3; 53:5-12), and His coming reign following the great tribulation and triumph over the antichrist (2:11; 9:7; 25:1-27:13; 42:4-7; 49:5-6; 52:13; 63:1-6). Isaiah frequently refers to God as *the Holy One of Israel* (1:4; 5:19,24; 10:20; 12:6; 17:7; 29:19,23; 30:11-12,15; 31:1; 37:23; 40:25; 41:14,16,20; 43:3,14-15; 45:11; 47:4; 48:17; 49:7; 54:5; 55:5; 60:9,14).

Visions of *the Day of the LORD* are prominent (2:11-12,17,20; 3:7,18; 4:1-2; 5:30; 28:5; 29:18; 30:23; 31:7) with special attention given to it (10:20; 11:10-11; 12:1,4; 13:6,9,13; 14:3; 17:4,7,9; 19:16,18-19,21,23-24; 22:5,12,20,25; 23:15).

Partial List of Names and Titles of Christ in Isaiah

Angel of His Presence	63:9
Arm of the Lord	51:9-10
Banner for the Peoples	11:10
Boy	7:16
Branch of Jesse	11:1
Branch of the LORD	4:2
Channels of Water	32:2
Child	9:6
Chosen One of the Lord	42:1
Commander & Leader	55:4
Counselor	9:6
Covenant of the People	42:6
Creator of Israel	43:15
Crown/Diadem	28:5
Eliakim	22:20
Eternal Father	9:6
Everlasting Rock	26.4
Everlasting Light	60:20
Glorious One	33:21
Glory of the Lord	40:5
God of Israel, Savior	45:15
God of All the Earth	54:5
Great Light	9:2
Heritage of Jacob	58:14
Highway/Roadway/Pathway	35:8
Holy, Holy, Holy	6:3
Holy One of Israel	41:14; 49:7
Husband	54:5
Immanuel	7:14
Israel	49:3
Lord	40:3
King in His Beauty	33:17
King Lord of Hosts	6:5
Lawgiver	33:22
Light to the Nations	42:6
Lord God [Jehovah]	40:10
Lord [Jehovah] of Hosts	6:3; 54:5
Lord, your Holy One	43:15
Lord, your Redeemer	43:14
Man of Pains	53:3
Mighty God	9:6
Mighty One of Jacob	49:26
Mighty to Save	63:1
My Chosen, in Whom I Myself Delight	42:1
My Messenger	42:19
My Servant	49:3
Place to Hide; to Find Cover	32:2
Polished Arrow	49:2
Precious CornerStone	28:16
Prince of Peace	9:6
Redeemer	59:20; 60:16
Refuge from the Rain	25:4
Righteous Servant	53:11
Rock of Israel	30:29
Rock toTrip Over	8:14
Root of Jesse	11:10
Salvation of the Daughter of Zion	62:11
Sanctuary	8:14
Savior	19:20
Servant	42:1,19
Servant of Rulers	49:7
Shade from the Heat	25:4
Shadow of a Massive Rock	32:2
Sharp Sword	49:2
Shoot and Branch	11:1
Son given	9:6
Stone	28:16
Stone Laid in Zion	28:16
Stone to Stumble Over	8:14
Stronghold for the Poor	25:4
Sure Foundation	28:16
Tested Stone	28:16
Witness to the Peoples	55:4
Wonderful	9:6

In Today's Reading

The nation's sin; Isaiah's exhortation for repentance; coming of Christ's kingdom; Jerusalem's glorious future.

The Lord chose the Israelites to take His written word to all nations. It must have been with deep sorrow that God led Isaiah to say: *Listen . . . the LORD has spoken: I have raised children and brought them up, but they have rebelled against Me. The ox knows its owner, and the donkey its master's feed-trough, but Israel does not know. . . . they have despised the Holy One of Israel; they have turned their backs on Him* (Isaiah 1:2-4). *If you* (continue to) *refuse and rebel, you will be devoured by the sword. For the mouth of the LORD has spoken* (1:20).

Like our heavenly Father, it must have been heartbreaking for king David, the great prophet Samuel, and godly king Josiah of Judah, all of whom had children that were rebellious and did not obey the word of God. He has provided His written word which, through the guidance of the indwelling Holy Spirit, will teach us how to experience the joy of forgiveness and deliverance from guilt and condemnation of sin.

Many godly parents are heartbroken when they see their children turning from the Lord. They too feel the sorrow of our heavenly Father over children who are uncommitted to Him, to reading the Bible or to regular worship in a local church. Whether or not our children succeed or fail in their earthly goals, by comparison, it is of little eternal consequence, for only spiritual achievements bring true success.

God graciously said: *Come, let us discuss this . . . Though your sins are like scarlet, they will be as white as snow; though they are as red as crimson, they will be like wool* (1:18). Isaiah was called to comfort those who were faithful to the Holy One (1:9). He prophesied of a coming King who would reign in righteousness and peace. When the Messiah comes, *many people will come and say, Come, let us go up to the mountain of the LORD, to the house of the God of Jacob. He will teach us about His ways so that we may walk in His paths. For instruction will go out of Zion and the word of the LORD from Jerusalem* (Isaiah 2:3).

Thought for Today: Continued disobedience blinds one's eyes and hardens one's heart to the will of God.

In Today's Reading

God's judgment upon sinners; Isaiah's vision of God's holiness; his message for king Ahaz; Christ's birth and kingdom foretold.

The prophet Isaiah foretold the judgment of God against Judah for five specific sins. First, selfishness and greed: *Woe to those who add house to house and join field to field until there is no more room* (Isaiah 5:8). Second, drunkenness: *Woe to those who rise early in the morning in pursuit of beer, who linger into the evening, inflamed by wine* (5:11). Third, refusing to recognize themselves as sinners and parading their sins before God: *Woe to those who drag wickedness with cords of deceit* (5:18). Fourth, insincerity, self-deception, and hypocrisy: *Woe to those who call evil good and good evil* (5:20). And fifth, pride, the basis of all sin: *Woe to those who are wise in their own opinion and clever in their own sight* (5:21).

Ahaz, king of Judah, was facing war. The prophet appealed to him, saying: *Ask for a sign from the LORD* (7:11). Although Ahaz refused, Isaiah spoke a glorious prophecy of the true King of kings who was yet to come: *The virgin will conceive, have a son, and name him Immanuel* (7:14). Seven hundred years later, the Angel Gabriel confirmed to the Virgin Mary: *The Holy Spirit will come upon you, and the power of the Most High will overshadow you. Therefore the holy child to be born will be called the Son of God* (Luke 1:35). To deny the virgin birth and question either the deity or the humanity of Jesus of Nazareth is to miss the significance that Jesus was both holy God and sinless man.

The prophet Isaiah received another glorious vision of the eternal King of kings of whom he foretold: *For a child will be born for us, a son will be given to us, and the government will be on His shoulders. He will be named Wonderful Counselor, Mighty God, Eternal Father, Prince of Peace* (9:6). Jesus was a *Wonderful Counselor* in His life on earth, *Wonderful Counselor* in providing eternal life to all believers by dying on the cross for our sins, and *Wonderful Counselor* in His triumph over death. He alone is the *Wonderful Counselor*, the Revealer of Truth: *He was with God in the beginning. . . . All things were created through Him, and apart from Him not one thing was created that has been created* (John 1:2-3).

Thought for Today: To their eternal loss, self-righteous people assume they are "good enough" without the Savior.

In Today's Reading

Assyria to be broken; promise of Israel's restoration; Christ, the Branch; thanksgiving for God's mercies; Babylon's doom predicted; Israel to be preserved.

Concerning Christ's return to earth and His glorious millennial reign, Isaiah foretold: *The land will be as full of the knowledge of the LORD as the sea is filled with water. . . . On that day the root of Jesse will stand as a banner for the people. The nations will seek Him, and His resting place will be glorious* (Isaiah 11:9-10). The promise, made through Isaiah, of the Ruler who would come from Jesse, is far-reaching and anticipates the new heavens and the new earth that are yet to be. *And on that day you will say: Give thanks to the LORD; proclaim His name! Celebrate His deeds among the peoples. Declare that His name is exalted. . . . Sing to the LORD, for He has done glorious things. Let this be known throughout the earth. . . . Cry out and sing, citizen of Zion, for the Holy One of Israel is among you in* (His) *greatness* (Isaiah 12:4-6).

Isaiah the prophet also looked beyond the defeat of Assyria to the future when Babylon would carry the people of Judah into captivity. Surprisingly, about 180 years before it took place, he also foretold Babylon's defeat and destruction. Isaiah foretold that *Babylon, the jewel of the kingdoms, the glory of the pride of the Chaldeans, will be like Sodom and Gomorrah when God overthrew them* (13:19-20). In striking contrast, Isaiah prophesied Israel's future restoration: *For the LORD will have compassion on Jacob and will choose Israel again. He will settle them on their own land. The foreigner will join them and be united with the house of Jacob. . . . The nations will escort Israel and bring it to its homeland* (14:1-2).

Until that day, let us say with Isaiah: *Indeed, God is my salvation. . . . the LORD, is my strength and my song . . . You will joyfully draw water from the springs of salvation . . . and on that day you will say: Give thanks to the LORD; proclaim His name! Celebrate His deeds among the peoples. Declare that His name is exalted. . . . Sing to the LORD, for He has done glorious things. Let this be known throughout the earth* (Isaiah 12:2-6).

Thought for Today: Our Lord's love is inexhaustible.

In Today's Reading

Moab's ruin foretold; Syria (Aram) and Israel threatened; God's judgments; Egypt to worship the Lord; captivity of Egypt foretold.

The prophet Isaiah was led to turn his thoughts from the glorious future reign of the King of Peace to proclaim the judgment of God. First it was pronounced upon the idolatrous northern kingdom, saying: *The fortress disappears from Ephraim.* He then included Judah, saying: *On that day the splendor of Jacob will fade. . . . there will be desolation. . . . For you have forgotten the God of your salvation* (Isaiah 17:3-4,9-10).

The fortress . . . of *Ephraim* refers to the ten-tribe kingdom, a symbol of wealth, power, and self-glory, which would be ruthlessly destroyed by Assyria. Perhaps just as surprising, he prophesied that Judah, the splendor *of Jacob,* will fade, a reminder that the kingdom of Judah and the holy city of God would gradually be destroyed because they too had become involved in worldly pursuits and gradually neglected the word of God. Our attention is focused on the futility of depending upon worldly possessions for security and the admonition from David: *If riches increase, set not your heart upon them* (Psalms 62:10).

Nothing hides the will of God from man's view as deceptively as success and pride. Perhaps this is why our Savior said: *Don't collect for yourselves treasures on earth, where moth and rust destroy and where thieves break in and steal* (Matthew 6:19). Wealth can weaken faith, as James pointed out, saying: *Listen, my dear brothers: Didn't God choose the poor in this world to be rich in faith and heirs of the kingdom that He has promised to those who love Him?* (James 2:5). Wealth often leads to an endless pursuit of more and more "things." This, in turn, often leads to covetousness, which is idolatry (Colossians 3:5).

Our Lord warns: *Watch out and be on guard against all greed, because one's life is not in the abundance of his possessions* (Luke 12:15).

The Lord is able to speak to each of us personally as to how He would have us invest in transforming lives and fulfilling His great commission. Paul wrote to Timothy: *Instruct those who are rich in the present age not to be arrogant or to set their hope on the uncertainty of wealth, but on God, who richly provides us with all things to enjoy* (I Timothy 6:17).

Thought for Today: Be vigilant and ever prepared for Jesus' return.

In Today's Reading

Prophecy about Jerusalem; Tyre to be destroyed; God's judgment upon the earth; Isaiah glorifies God; God's dominion over Judah.

The day of the LORD is coming – cruel, with rage and burning anger – to make the earth a desolation and to destroy the sinners on it (Isaiah 13:9). This prophecy was first directed to Judah, then to Israel, then to the surrounding gentile nations, and finally to all the world: *He will destroy death forever. The Lord GOD will wipe away the tears from every face and remove His people's disgrace from the whole earth. . . . On that day it will be said, Look, this is our God; we have waited for Him, and He has saved us. Let us rejoice and be glad in His salvation. . . . You will keep in perfect peace the mind that is dependent on You . . . Trust in the LORD forever, because the LORD, is an everlasting rock!* (25:8-9; 26:3-4).

Just as surely as many of the prophecies were fulfilled in ancient history, this one about the Messiah will be fully and gloriously realized. Soon Jesus will return as Christ the King: *For a child will be born for us, a son will be given to us, and the government will be on His shoulders. He will be named Wonderful Counselor, Mighty God, Eternal Father, Prince of Peace* (9:6) and He will give eternal freedom to both Jew and gentile who have received Him as Lord of their lives. Until then we are not left alone. Jesus has imparted His indwelling Holy Spirit and has assured every believer: *You are from God, little children, and you have conquered them* (spirits of antichrist), *because the One who is in you is greater than the one who is in the world* (I John 4:4). It is no longer necessary to live in slavery to Satan and our fleshly passions because we can *be strengthened by the Lord and by His vast strength. Put on the full armor of God so that you can stand against the tactics of the Devil* (Ephesians 6:10-11).

His word provides a simple revealing test: *Do you not know . . . you are slaves of that one you obey – either of sin leading to death or of obedience leading to righteousness? But thank God that, although you used to be slaves of sin, you obeyed from the heart . . . and having been liberated from sin, you became enslaved to righteousness* (Romans 6:16-18).

Thought for Today: Suffering, hardships, and handicaps have helped many come to know God's will for their lives.

In Today's Reading

Judgment of Ephraim; Jerusalem warned; Israel rebuked for its alliance with Egypt; future destiny assured.

The magnificent and beautiful northern kingdom of Israel was enjoying great prosperity when the Lord led Isaiah to prophesy their captivity by Assyria, proclaiming: *Woe to the majestic crown of Ephraim's drunkards, and to the fading flower of its beautiful splendor, which is on the summit above the rich valley. Woe to those overcome with wine. Look, the LORD has a strong and mighty one – like a devastating hail storm, like a storm with strong flooding waters. He will bring it across the land with His hand. The majestic crown of Ephraim's drunkards will be trampled underfoot* (Isaiah 28:1-3).

The people of Samaria, the capital of the northern kingdom, were enjoying the luxury of summer and winter homes, ivory palaces, and a wealth of gardens.

With a heavy heart, Isaiah warned them that all would soon be destroyed because they had rejected the word of God and turned to idols.

Samaria's *beauty* was likened to *a fading flower*; but, far more horrifying, the prophet foretold: *Ephraim will be trampled underfoot* – helpless to withstand the fierce and cruel Assyrian army. Like most worldly-minded people today, they did not believe judgment could happen to them.

Isaiah appealed to the people to repent of their sins, return to the Lord, and be obedient to His word.

Times and circumstances change; but the fact remains the same – everyone who has not received Christ as their Savior has unknowingly made *a covenant with death* (28:15,18).

Today there is still hope for *the Lord does not delay His promise, as some understand delay, but is patient with you, not wanting any to perish, but all to come to repentance* (II Peter 3:9). *Nevertheless, God's solid foundation stands firm, having this inscription: The Lord knows those who are His, and Everyone who names the name of the Lord must turn away from unrighteousness* (II Timothy 2:19).

Thought for Today: When it seems there is no hope, is it because we are relying on human strength instead of the promises of God's strength?

In Today's Reading

Righteous King foretold; judgment upon nations; Jerusalem threatened; Hezekiah's prayer; destruction of the Assyrians.

About twenty-two years passed after King Shalmaneser of Assyria and his son Sargon invaded and destroyed the northern kingdom of Israel. This ended more than 200 years of the Israelites rejecting the word of God. *In the fourteenth year of King Hezekiah, Sennacherib king of Assyria advanced upon all the fortified cities of Judah and captured them* (Isaiah 36:1). He defeated 46 of the towns and villages of the small southern kingdom of Judah in one military campaign. He carried away into captivity about 200,000 of its inhabitants, but he was not able to conquer Jerusalem. At that time, all of western Asia was under Assyria's control, including Babylonia, Media, Armenia, Syria (Aram), Phoenicia, Philistia, Edom, and most of the promised land.

Eventually, the king of Assyria demanded unconditional surrender. *Thus says the king: Don't let Hezekiah deceive you, for he can't deliver you. Don't let Hezekiah make you trust in the LORD, saying, The LORD will surely deliver us! . . . Don't listen to Hezekiah* (36:14-16).

Upon hearing this demand, Hezekiah immediately *took the letter . . . and read it. Then he went up to the house of the LORD and spread it out before the LORD. And Hezekiah prayed to the LORD: O LORD of hosts, God of Israel, who sits among the cherubim, You are God, You alone, of all the kingdoms of the earth. You Yourself made the heavens and the earth. . . . hear all the words of Sennacherib, which he has sent to mock the living God. . . . O LORD our God, save us from his hand, that all the kingdoms of the earth may know that You are the LORD, You alone* (37:14-17,20).

Isaiah sent word to Hezekiah, saying: *The LORD God of Israel says: Because you prayed to Me concerning Sennacherib king of Assyria. . . . I will defend this city to deliver it* (37:21,35). That night, *the Angel of the LORD went out and struck down . . . the Assyrians* (37:36).

It is important that we honor the Lord in our prayers just as Hezekiah did. The Lord is still saying: *Call to Me and I will answer you and tell you great and mysterious things you do not know* (Jeremiah 33:3).

Thought for Today: You can depend on God's promises; they cannot fail.

In Today's Reading

Hezekiah's life lengthened; Babylonian captivity foretold; comfort for God's people; song of praise to the Lord.

About 13 years had passed since Isaiah brought Hezekiah, king of Judah, the exciting news that the little nation of Judah would be miraculously saved from the "invincible" armies of the Assyrian Empire.

In those days Hezekiah became sick to the point of death. So the prophet Isaiah said, The LORD says: Set your house in order, for you are about to die; you will not recover (Isaiah 38:1; II Kings 20:1; II Chronicles 32:24-26).

With intense weeping, *Hezekiah turned his face to the wall and prayed to the LORD. He said, O LORD . . . please remember how I have walked before You in truth and with a whole heart, and have done what is good in Your sight." And Hezekiah wept bitterly* (Isaiah 38:2-3). When Hezekiah said he had lived before the Lord *in truth and with a perfect heart* (compare 38:17), he meant that he had served the Lord faithfully and had not departed from the Lord's commandments.

Isaiah heard the voice of God say: *Go and tell Hezekiah, the LORD . . . says: I have heard your prayer; I have seen your tears. Look, I am going to add 15 years to your life* (38:5).

We should never hesitate to pray, regardless of how hopeless our circumstances may appear. However, this does not mean that God always answers every prayer in the way we want or according to our timing.

Since we often fall short of our desire to be like Jesus, many find it easy to accept the condemnation of Satan that we are too unworthy for God to answer our prayers. Although it is right to assess our faults and confess our sins, it also magnifies the grace of God to recognize the good in our lives just as Hezekiah did. We can also remind the Lord of our sincere endeavor to live a God-honoring life, which is only produced by the inner working of the Holy Spirit.

He saved us—not by works of righteousness that we had done, but according to His mercy, through the washing of regeneration and renewal by the Holy Spirit (Titus 3:5).

Thought for Today: Trusting in anything or anyone but the Lord for your eternal salvation is deception and will result in eternal death.

In Today's Reading

God's care for Israel; folly of idolatry; Jerusalem and the temple to be rebuilt; God's purpose for Cyrus; power of the Lord and weakness of idols.

When Isaiah was a prophet in Jerusalem, the people felt very secure since it was the City of God where His temple stood. Therefore, Isaiah's prophecy concerning the "ruins" of Jerusalem was shocking. God had said through him: *Who says to Jerusalem, She will be inhabited, and to the cities of Judah, They will be built, and I will restore her ruins* (Isaiah 44:26). Isaiah foretold both the fall and the rebuilding of the temple while it was still standing, the city walls were in perfect condition, and the nation was enjoying freedom, prosperity, and security.

At that time, Babylon, the capital city of the Chaldean dynasty, was surrounded by massive walls about 300 feet high and wide enough for chariots to ride atop it two abreast. The Babylonians were certain that no one could ever invade their great city. However, Isaiah correctly foretold that a man named Cyrus would conquer Babylon. This prophecy was given 150 years before it took place. *Who says to Cyrus, My shepherd, he will fulfill all My pleasure, saying to Jerusalem, She will be built, and of the temple, Its foundation will be laid. Thus says the LORD to His anointed, to Cyrus whom I have taken by his right hand, to subdue nations before . . . him . . . and the gates will not be shut* (44:27-28; 45:1-3).

Only God could have given Isaiah such remarkable details concerning the defeat of Babylon: *Babylon . . . will be like Sodom* (13:19). At the end of Judah's 70 years of captivity, this was fulfilled exactly as foretold by the prophet. Even when men may think they are in control of this world, God is working out His master plan for the ages. This fact should eliminate any question regarding His loving concern and care for His followers. God has a perfect plan for our lives and it is of utmost importance that we read His word daily in order to fulfill His will. Only then can we become the person He wants us to be in order to accomplish the purpose for which He created us.

It is a fact that *a king's heart is a water channel in the LORD's hand: He directs it wherever He chooses* (Proverbs 21:1).

Thought for Today: God is not limited; He will keep His word.

In Today's Reading

Judgment on Babylon; Israel rebuked; Christ, a Light to the gentiles; restoration of Israel; suffering of the Lord's Servant.

We expect judgment upon the ungodly, or upon the backslider, but many do not see why difficult things happen to sincere Christians.

The prophet Isaiah reminds us to maintain our faith, regardless of the circumstances, saying: *Who among you fears the LORD . . . who walks in darkness and has no light? Let him trust in the name of the LORD; let him lean on his God* (Isaiah 50:10). God can bring blessings out of brokenness and triumph out of tragedy just as He did for Job. These experiences are a test of faith as well as the means of developing greater faith. God twice said Job was the most perfect man on earth, yet he suffered. However, Job's faith remained strong because he knew that God was in control of his life. He testified confidently even while he was suffering intensely, saying: *Yet He knows the way I have taken. When He has tried me, I will come forth as gold* (Job 23:10). Each of us will face testing from the Lord as well as temptation from the forces of evil; so be not dismayed if one day your whole world has crumbled and it seems that the Lord has abandoned you. In a message to His people who were oppressed and suffering as captives in Babylon, God said: *I am He who comforts you. Who are you that you should fear man who dies, or a mere mortal* (Isaiah 51:12-13).

The Lord's assurance to the sufferer is also for us. *Brothers, take the prophets who spoke in the Lord's name as an example of suffering and patience* (James 5:10). To doubt the loving concern and wisdom of God to care for his children is to assume that He is unable to keep His word. Furthermore, such an attitude would mean that Satan has more power to defeat us than God has to defend us. When trial after trial confronts us, remember that the sovereign God is working out His perfect plan for our lives. *As you share in the sufferings of the Messiah rejoice, so that you may also rejoice with great joy at the revelation of His glory* (I Peter 4:13). *If we endure, we will also reign with Him* (II Timothy 2:12).

Express confidence that *the God of all grace, who called you to His eternal glory in Christ Jesus, will personally restore, establish, strengthen, and support you after you have suffered a little* (I Peter 5:10).

Thought for Today: Regardless of circumstances, God is in control.

In Today's Reading

Christ to bear our grief, suffering, and sin; the Lord's everlasting love for Israel; everyone a sinner; a call to faith and repentance.

God revealed to Isaiah that the Messiah, the King of kings, would first be *My servant* . . . (then) *He will be high and lifted up and greatly exalted* (Isaiah 52:13). Jesus our Lord, in humility and meekness, did not assert His rights and set up His rightful kingdom by force.

Jesus first came as the *Servant* (of God), as the Suffering Savior, but He will soon return highly *exalted and extolled* as the King of kings. The Jews were looking for a warrior-king, like David, to deliver them from the oppression of Rome. Isaiah foretold: *For He grew up like a young plant before Him, and like a root out of dry ground. He had no form or splendor that we should look at Him, no appearance that we should desire Him* (53:2). *Dry ground* illustrates the spiritual condition of the religious world without Jesus. He alone provides eternal life for all who confess their guilt, repent of their sins and seek to obey His word. That's why it's important to read it. Even then, all of us, from time to time, fall short of what God desires us to be. But Jesus continues to make intercession for us with the Father. *If we confess our sins, He is faithful and righteous to forgive us our sins and to cleanse us from all unrighteousness* (I John 1:9).

Surely our sicknesses He Himself bore, and our pains He carried (Isaiah 53:4). This means emotional and spiritual, as well as physical needs of every kind. *He was pierced through because of our transgressions, crushed because of our iniquities; the punishment for our well-being was upon Him, and by His wounds we are healed* (53:5). His death on the cross provided the means to end the enmity between sinful man and the Righteous Creator God. This means that all repentant believers, Jew and Gentile alike, receive eternal life through the death of the sinless Son of God when they receive Jesus as their Savior and Lord. *There is no other name under heaven given to people by which we must be saved* (Acts 4:12).

Daily we should praise Jesus for who He really is – the Great God of Creation and the Savior who will soon return to rule the world. *On His robe and on His thigh He has a name written: KING OF KINGS AND LORD OF LORDS* (Revelation 19:16).

Thought for Today: Praise Him today for His amazing grace.

In Today's Reading

True fasting; sin, confession, and redemption; future glory of Jerusalem; the day of vengeance; God's loving-kindness to Israel.

During Isaiah's time, the Israelite leaders complained to God: *Why have we fasted, but You have not seen? We have afflicted ourselves, but You have not noticed!* The Lord answered: *Look, on the day of your fasting you do as you please* (continue to seek selfish interests) *and oppress* (exploit) *all your workers. . . . You fast for* (continue your) *contention and strife and to strike someone with a wicked fist* (personal conflicts) (Isaiah 58:3-4).

Even more serious was their hypocrisy, fasting to be seen by others: *Will the fast that I choose be like this, a day for a person to afflict himself? To bow his head like a bulrush, and spread out sackcloth and ashes* (to impress others with pretended humility) (58:5). Through Isaiah, God reminded the Israelites that acceptable fasting will include compassion for those who are suffering: *To loosen the bonds of wickedness . . . to set the oppressed free and . . . to share your bread with the hungry, and bring the homeless poor into your house; when you see the naked, to cover him, and not hide yourself from your own flesh?* (never neglect your responsibility to your own family) (58:6-7).

Isaiah continued: *Remove the yoke from your midst, the finger-pointing and speaking of evil* (58:9). If what we do for someone (or for the Lord) is meant to impose (or implies) a *yoke* of bondage upon them (expecting special favors in return), our prayers and fasting will not be acceptable to God. Our prayers are effective when our attitudes and our relationship with others are in harmony with the will of God.

Often being a Christian is thought of as the sum total of things we don't do. But being a Christian is first and foremost to *let your light shine before men, so that they may see your good works and give glory to your Father in heaven* (Matthew 5:16).

The indwelling Holy Spirit leads us to respond in compassion to the needs of others. *And the King will answer them, I assure you: Whatever you did for one of the least of these brothers of Mine, you did for Me* (Matthew 25:40).

Thought for Today: Graciously submit to God's arrangements in your life, and under no circumstances grieve the Holy Spirit.

In Today's Reading

Our righteousness as filthy rags; prayer for God's presence; rebelliousness punished.

Most of the northern kingdom of Israel was defeated and carried away captive by the Assyrians during the reign of wicked King Pekah (Isaiah 7:1; II Kings 15:27-29). Having witnessed the destruction of the northern kingdom before he came to the throne, undoubtedly godly King Hezekiah of the southern kingdom was greatly encouraged by the prophet Isaiah.

Sadly, after Hezekiah's death, his son Manasseh became one of the most wicked kings in Judah's history. During this time Isaiah's faith remained unshakable.

The apostle Paul quoted from Isaiah 64:4 to encourage the Corinthian church: *As it is written: What no eye has seen and no ear has heard, and what has never come into a man's heart, is what God prepared for those who love Him* (I Corinthians 2:9). But the Israelites did not love the Lord. Isaiah mournfully confessed: *There is no one who calls on Your name, who rouses himself to take hold of You; for You have hidden Your face from us, and melted us away because of our iniquity* (Isaiah 64:7). The word of God, as proclaimed by Isaiah, had been ignored and now God spoke through him these pitiful words: *I spread out My hands all day long to a rebellious people, who walk in a way that is not good, following their own thoughts* (65:2). The Lord continued: *So I Myself will choose their ill-treatment, and I will bring upon them what they dread. Because I called, but no one answered; I spoke, but they did not hear; they did evil in My sight, and chose that in which I did not delight* (66:4). At any time, in any place, we may cry out to our loving God. While we have time to call upon His name we should determine to make His will the priority in our lives.

To the small minority who remain faithful, Isaiah is saying: *Hear the word of the LORD, you who tremble at His word: Your brothers who hate you, who exclude you for My name's sake . . . will be ashamed. . . . For thus says the LORD: I am extending peace to her like a river* (Isaiah 66:5,12).

Thought for Today: Sin breaks our fellowship with the Lord and keeps us from receiving His true peace and wisdom.

Introduction To The Book Of Jeremiah

Jeremiah prophesied during the last 40 years of the small southern kingdom of Judah. This was about 100 years after the Assyrians destroyed the northern kingdom of Israel.

His public ministry began in the 13th year of the reign of godly King Josiah (Jeremiah 1:2), who ruled for 31 years (II Chronicles 34:1).

Jeremiah continued his ministry through the reigns of the last four kings of Judah, all of whom were wicked: Jehoahaz (Shallum), Jehoiakim (Eliakim), Jehoiachin (Coniah, Jeconiah), and Mattaniah (Zedekiah) and with the exiles in Egypt. He was unpopular during those difficult times because he faithfully declared God's word to an unrepentant people.

As the years passed, the Assyrian empire weakened and eventually was overthrown by the Babylonians.

After Nebuchadnezzar defeated Egypt in the battle at Carchemish, the key city of northern Syria (Aram), the kingdom of Judah was then brought under his control. Seven years later, in the eleventh year of Zedekiah's reign, Jerusalem and the temple were destroyed by Nebuchadnezzar and his Babylonian armies who then controlled all of the Near East (II Kings 25:2-21).

The events in this book are not arranged in chronological order but by similar subjects to let us see more clearly the tragic results of sin.

It was at a time when God declared: *From the least to the greatest . . . everyone is gaining profit unjustly. From prophet to priest, everyone is deceptive* (Jeremiah 6:13). *The prophets prophesy falsely, and the priests rule by their own authority. My people love it like this* (5:31). This led to their defeat and this prophecy which was intended to encourage the captives: *When 70 years for Babylon are complete. . . . I will restore the fortunes of My people Israel and Judah, says the LORD. I will restore them back to the land I gave to their fathers and they will possess it* (29:10; 30:3).

The God of mercy also promised: *I will rebuild you again, so that you may be rebuilt. . . . this is the covenant I will make with the house of Israel after those days, says the LORD; I will place My law within them and write it on their heart. I will be their God, and they will be My people* (31:4,33).

The book of Jeremiah closed with a prophecy against the gentile (heathen) nations and the inevitable fall of Jerusalem (46:1 – 52:34).

In Today's Reading

Jeremiah's call; his message to sinful Judah; present apostasy, resulting in idolatry; Judah entreated to repent.

God revealed to Jeremiah that He has a plan and purpose for each of us even before our birth: *The word of the LORD came to me as follows . . . I chose you before I formed you in the womb; I set you apart before you were born. I appointed you a prophet to the nations* (Jeremiah 1:4-5).

Just think! God *knew you* and had a plan for your life even before the day you were born. Through Jeremiah's revelation concerning the origin of human life, it is revealed that our birth is not our real beginning nor will our death be our end. Like Jeremiah, we need to focus on the right thing to do. God is the Giver of life! As believers, let us hold in honor the sanctity of all human life.

The Holy Spirit led King David to write: *I will praise You because I am unique in remarkable ways. Your works are wonderful, and I know this very well. . . . My bones were not hidden from You when I was made in secret, when I was formed in the depths of the earth* (Psalms 139:14-15). Both the mother and father have the biblical responsibility to recognize that every unborn child, from the day of conception, belongs to its Creator God. Both parents are responsible as stewards of God to teach their children to know, love, and be obedient to God.

To the apostle Paul, God revealed that *He chose us in Him, before the foundation of the world, to be holy and blameless in His sight. . . . In Him we were also made His inheritance. . . . I pray that the eyes of your heart may be enlightened so you may know what is the hope of His calling, what are the glorious riches of His inheritance among the saints* (Ephesians 1:4, 11,18). You are special. God had a wonderful plan for you long before you were born. He has chosen each of us for His sacred purpose, but He has given us the freedom to choose whom we will serve. Jesus stated an often overlooked fact when He said that *no one can be a slave of two masters, since either he will hate one and love the other, or be devoted to one and despise the other* (Matthew 6:24).

Thought for Today: The word of God reveals the difference between truth and error; without reading it, we have no way to know the facts.

In Today's Reading

God's call to Israel; Jeremiah's lamentations for Judah; spiritual and civil corruption; destruction of Judah.

The prophet Jeremiah began his public ministry about the 13th year of the reign of King Josiah of Judah (Jeremiah 1:2). Jeremiah exposed the worldly, compromising lifestyle of the Israelites when he called them a *foolish and senseless people. They have eyes, but they do not see. They have ears, but they do not hear. . . . But this people has a stubborn and rebellious heart. They have turned aside and they have gone away. . . .To whom can I speak and give such warning that they will hear? Look, their ear is uncircumcised, so they cannot listen. . . . See, the word of the LORD has become offensive to them – they find no pleasure in it* (5:21,23; 6:10; compare Luke 8:10). Josiah's grandfather Manasseh and Amon his father were wicked kings who led the people to forsake God and encouraged worship of false gods.

However, Amon's son Josiah, *did what was right in the Lord's eyes and walked in all the ways of his forefather David; he did not turn aside to the right or the left* (II Kings 22:2). No doubt Jeremiah was a great encouragement and influence to Josiah. In the 18th year of his reign, Josiah began repairing the temple and restoring worship of the one true God (II Chronicles 34:8). He then initiated a Passover festival unequaled in Israel's history (II Kings 23:22).

Following Josiah's death (23:30-32), the nation reverted to the evil ways of Manasseh and Amon. With deep concern, we see a parallel between the false gods, immorality, and sins that led to the fall of Judah and the growth of false religions, moral decline, and sexual deviation in America today.

A true Christian desires to worship only the Lord with other believers where there is reading and studying of the word of God. The apostle Paul was lead by the Holy Spirit to warn us: *The time will come when they will not tolerate sound doctrine, but according to their own desires, will accumulate teachers for themselves because they have an itch to hear something new. . . . They will turn away from hearing the truth and will turn aside to myths* (II Timothy 4:3-4).

Thought for Today: The more we read the Bible, the more the Lord's ways become our ways, and His thoughts our thoughts.

In Today's Reading

Plea for repentance; punishment for Judah's rebellion; mourning over the people's sins; idols will perish.

All adult men who were physically able were required by the law to attend three major festivals annually in Jerusalem. These occasions were to be joyful celebrations of praise to God for His provision and protection. But, this time Jeremiah did not give the crowd a warm welcome; instead, he pronounced a harsh condemnation: *Hear the word of the LORD, all you who enter through these gates to worship the LORD. . . . Do you steal, murder, commit adultery, swear falsely . . . then come and stand before Me in this house called by My name and insist, We are safe! – thus free to continue doing all these abominations?* (Jeremiah 7:1-2, 9-10).

They were also indifferent to the command God had given about the pagan inhabitants when they first entered Canaan: *You must not make a covenant with them or their gods* (Exodus 23:31-32).

The people considered Jeremiah's preaching far too narrow-minded and would not tolerate this prophet of God. They responded: *We are wise;the law of the LORD is with us* (Jeremiah 8:8). The physical presence of the Scriptures and the temple gave them a false sense of security. The prophet reminded them: *The wise . . . have rejected the word of the LORD, so what wisdom do they really have? Therefore, I will give their wives to other men, their fields to new occupiers. For from the least to the greatest, everyone looks for ill-gotten gain. From prophet to priest, everyone deals falsely* (8:9-11). They were confident that God would never allow them to be destroyed since He had made a covenant with them as His chosen people. But, in reality, the covenants of God have conditions to live by and do not give His people license to sin or ignore His word.

Then, as now, people ignorantly assume that each person should have the freedom to worship whomever or whatever one chooses according to his own conscience while ignoring the rights of our Creator. But Jesus said: *I am the way, the truth, and the life. No one comes to the Father except through Me* (John 14:6).Jesus also reminds those who say they are Christians while still living sinful lives: *Why do you call me Lord, Lord, and don't do the things I say* (Luke 6:46)?

Thought for Today: The best of religious accomplishments are never a substitute for godly living.

In Today's Reading

Jeremiah's proclamation of God's covenant; plot against Jeremiah; Jeremiah's complaint; ruined belt (girdle); filled bottles; famine.

All Israelites were called to be holy and to serve the Lord and, in return, God would provide for all their needs. But many of the people had forsaken the Lord to worship idols and live sinful lives. To illustrate their failure, the Lord directed Jeremiah to: *Go, buy yourself a linen belt and put it around your waist, but do not get it wet* (to wash it) (Jeremiah 13:1). Hebrew men wore tunics, long, loose, gown-like garments. To hold the tunic close to the body while walking or working, they wore a sash-like belt around the waist called a "belt, band, or girdle." The belt of white linen worn by priests represented the close relationship of the Israelites to Jehovah.

Jeremiah reports that, eventually, *the word of the LORD came to me a second time, saying, Take the belt that you bought and are wearing around your waist, and go at once to the Euphrates River and hide it in a rocky crevice. So I went and hid it by the Euphrates, just as the LORD commanded me. A long time later the LORD said to me, Go . . . to the Euphrates and retrieve the belt that I commanded you to hide there. So I went to the Euphrates and dug up and retrieved the belt from the place where I had hidden it, but the belt was ruined, of no use whatsoever* (13:3-7). *Ruined* meant the belt was rotten and unfit for a priest of God to wear. Consequently, *this is what the LORD says. . . . These evil people, who refuse to listen to Me, who walk according to the stubbornness of their own hearts . . . they will be like this belt, good for nothing* (13:9-10).

Like the Israelites, some today are intent on satisfying their self-interests with no desire to serve or obey the Lord. Unfortunately, many will discover too late that they have forfeited their God-given opportunities to truly enjoy life with the assurance of eternal life.

For just as a belt clings to one's waist, so I fastened the whole house of Israel and of Judah to Me, says the LORD, that they might be My people, for My . . . honor, but they would not obey (Jeremiah 13:11).

Thought for Today: Wholeheartedly living for the Lord provides the assurance that *all things work together for . . . good* (Romans 8:28).

In Today's Reading

Jeremiah's prayer; signs of Judah's captivity; Sabbath regulations; lesson from the potter; God's absolute power over the nations.

The LORD *said. . . . Surely I will intercede for you in a time of trouble, a time of distress with the enemy* (Jeremiah 15:11). But, when the Israelites rejected God and His word as their way of life, they forfeited the privilege of His protection and suffered irreparable spiritual and physical loss.

Jeremiah was sent to the potter's house to understand the Israelites' problems and their final outcome.

God spoke to Jeremiah: *Arise, go down to the potter's house. There I will reveal My words to you. So I went down to the potter's house . . . he was, working . . . at the wheel. But the jar that he was making of clay became distorted in the hand of the potter, so he made it into another jar, as it seemed right for him to do* (18:2-4). Then the Lord said: *Can I not, O house of Israel, treat you like this potter? . . . Just like clay in the hand of the potter, so are you in My hand. . . . if that nation about which I have spoken turns from its evil, then I will withhold the harm that I had planned to bring upon it. . . . But if it does evil before Me,not obeying My voice, then I will repeal the good I had said I would do to it* (18:6,8,10).

When *the vessel* (His chosen people) *was distorted in the hand of the potter,* it was the hardness within the clay itself and not the work of the Potter that made the vessel worthless. Israel had rejected the will of God and *was distorted* (hardened) by sin. Consequently *the vessel,* Israel, was broken by Babylon, the instrument of God, and taken into captivity. After 70 years of captivity (Jeremiah 25:11), God made the *clay* into *another vessel* to illustrate the few Jews who returned to Jerusalem to rebuild the temple and worship Him.

We are like earthen vessels and God has a special plan for each of us to be a vessel for His use even though we too are distorted by sin. When we yield ourself to the Master Potter, with loving hands He will mold us again into *another vessel,* prepared to contain and express the Presence of Christ Himself. *Therefore if anyone is in Christ, there is a new creation; old things have passed away, and look, new things have come* (II Corinthians 5:17).

Thought for Today: It is for God's glory that we were created.

In Today's Reading

Jeremiah imprisoned; smitten by Pashur; Jeremiah's grief; destruction of Jerusalem foretold; the way of life or death.

During the last days of the kingdom of Judah, Jeremiah courageously faced the chief governor of the high priest and said: *The LORD says . . . both yourself and those you love . . . will fall by the sword . . . of the king of Babylon. . . . As for you, Pashhur, and all who reside in your house, you will go into captivity. You will go to Babylon. There you will die* (Jeremiah 20:4,6). Jeremiah faithfully foretold a message from God, who said: *I will announce My judgments against them for all the evil they did when they forsook Me to burn incense to other gods and worship the works of their own hands* (1:16).

Soon the people of Judah learned of the defeat of Assyria and then of Egypt. With Nebuchadnezzar's victory in the battle at Carchemish, Babylon emerged as the new dominant world power. This confirmed what Isaiah had foretold about 100 years earlier (Isaiah 39:6-7).

Even after being fully informed of the results of rejecting the word of God, the religious leaders not only would not repent, but began a campaign to discredit Jeremiah before the king and the nation.

Jeremiah sat alone in prison and was momentarily discouraged when he said: *If I say, I will not mention Him, nor speak any longer in His name, His message becomes a fire burning in my heart, shut up in my bones. I become tired of holding it in, and I cannot prevail* (Jeremiah 20:9).

Jeremiah may have thought that he had failed to communicate to the people the importance of obeying the word of God. Most spiritual leaders have at some time felt that they failed in fulfilling their God-given responsibility. But, far beyond all his own expectations, Jeremiah has been an inspiration to millions of believers all over the world.

No one who is devoted to teaching the word of God and who lives by it is a failure in the Lord's eyes. Jesus promised: *I assure you: Anyone who hears My word and believes Him who sent Me has eternal life and will not come under judgment, but has passed from death to life* (John 5:24).

Thought for Today: Pray like Jesus: *Not My will, but Yours, be done* (Luke 22:42).

In Today's Reading

Future restoration; Christ's rule promised; lying prophets; good and bad figs; judgment on Babylon foretold.

Only a few months remained before the Babylonians' destruction of the kingdom of Judah. It was now too late to pray for Jerusalem or the temple to be saved from destruction.The last king, Zedekiah, would have his eyes gouged out and be taken to Babylon in chains (II Kings 25:7). These prophecies are all horrifying reminders that sin and suffering are inseparable and that judgment is inevitable whenever the word of God is disregarded.

Jeremiah's message now turned from the coming judgment to comfort. To illustrate, the Lord showed him *one basket* (of) *very good figs, like early figs; but the other basket contained very bad figs, that were inedible* (Jeremiah 24:2). *This is what the God of Israel says, Like these good figs, so I consider good the exiles from Judah whom I sent away from this place to the land of the Babylonians. . . . I will fix My attention on them for their good and will return them to this land* (24:5-6). There were three fig harvests – June, August, and November. The first figs, in June, were considered a great delicacy (Isaiah 28:4; Hosea 9:10; Micah 7:1). Thus the Lord was lovingly sending the chosen "good figs" into captivity to correct them "for their own good."

Even while the armies of Babylon were besieging Jerusalem, Jeremiah assured those who were faithful to God's word: *The time indeed is coming, says the LORD, when I will raise up a legitimate branch of David. He will reign wisely as king and act with justice and righteousness in the land. . . . In His days Judah will be saved, and Israel will dwell securely. This is the name by which He will be called: The LORD Our Righteousness* (Jeremiah 23:5-6; 33:16).

By our natural birth, *there is no one righteous, not even one. . . . For all have sinned and fall short of the glory of God* (Romans 3:10,23). When we receive Christ as our Savior He becomes *the LORD Our Righteousness.* The Holy Spirit led the apostle Paul to write: *He made the One who did not know sin to be sin for us, so that we might become the righteousness of God in Him* (II Corinthians 5:21).

Thought for Today: Live as the righteousness of God in Christ.

In Today's Reading

Jeremiah's arrest; Judah's subjection to Nebuchadnezzar foretold; Hananiah's false prophecy; his death.

During the early part of Zedekiah's reign, God commanded Jeremiah to make a yoke and put it on his own neck, symbolizing the coming captivityof the kingdom of Judah. *So now I have placed all these lands under the authority of My servant Nebuchadnezzar, king of Babylon. Even the wild animals I have given him to serve him* (Jeremiah 27:6).

Jeremiah proclaimed that, because of their sin, God had appointed Nebuchadnezzar as ruler over all the nations (27:2-11; compare Daniel 2:37-38). *Then the priests and prophets said to the officials and all the people, This man deserves the death sentence, for he has prophesied against this city as you yourselves have heard* (Jeremiah 26:11).

When the Israelites were defeated by Nebuchadnezzar and scattered throughout the earth, it began *the times of the Gentiles* (Luke 21:24). We are near the close of that final generation when *the times of the Gentiles are fulfilled*. God, in His sovereign power, has caused the Jews to return to Jerusalem and once again become a nation before the second coming of the Messiah-King Jesus.

Let us faithfully and diligently tell others how they can be prepared for His return. Failure to do so will result in eternal damnation for all who do not receive Christ as Savior.

Jeremiah would rather have died than be silent about the need to hear the word of God.

It is this same Spirit that led the apostle Paul to say: *I am ready not only to be bound, but also to die in Jerusalem* (Acts 21:13). And it is the same self-sacrificing Spirit that leads Christians today to willingly reject self-interests that interfere with doing or saying what they know needs to be made known.

The Lord's slave must . . . be gentle . . . instructing his opponents with gentleness. Perhaps God will grant them repentance to know the truth (II Timothy 2:24-25).

Thought for Today: Speak boldly for the Lord; it will influence others.

In Today's Reading

Letter to captives in Babylon; Jews' deliverance foretold; full restoration of all things foretold.

The prophets of God warned the Israelites that because of idol worship and their disregard for the word of God they would be scattered throughout the world; and yet, *I will be with you, says the LORD, to save you! For I will bring destruction on all the nations where I have scattered you, but on you I will not bring destruction. I will discipline you only as you deserve, but will not leave you entirely unpunished* (Jeremiah 30:11).

Destruction of the powerful kingdoms of Assyria and Babylon did take place. These two powerful world empires were destroyed just as the Lord foretold through Jeremiah. Jeremiah also prophesied the destruction of Jerusalem and the captivity of the small kingdom of Judah. *This is what the LORD says: Look, I will restore the fortunes of Jacob's tents, and show compassion on his dwellings. Every city will be rebuilt on its mound* (30:18).

The Lord also revealed to Jeremiah that, at a future time, there would be a new covenant: *I will place My law within them and write it on their heart. I will be their God, and they will be My people* (31:33).

During their Babylonian captivity, through Jeremiah the Lord taught the people to *seek the peace of the city where I have sent you into exile. Pray to the LORD on its behalf, for when it has peace, you will have peace* (29:7). This means they were to pray for, and be a blessing to, their captors; and the Israelites, in turn, would be blessed. We are reminded of the self-destruction of hate, of holding a grudge, or of seeking revenge when mistreated or faced with opposition.

Pity the person who, even though physically free, remains dissatisfied with his circumstances and is waiting for a time when he can enjoy living. Perhaps he is waiting until he has a promotion or a better home, or for retirement. But he is always waiting for release from his present situation. Even more serious is the person who has been offended and has quit attending church. Often he is engulfed in bitter resentment and has made himself a prisoner of his own miserable attitude.

Instead of feeling sorry for ourselves, Jesus said: *Blessed are you when they . . . persecute you. Be glad and rejoice, because your reward is great in heaven* (Matthew 5:11-12).

Thought for Today: Every reader of the Bible will be richly rewarded.

In Today's Reading

Jeremiah imprisoned, then buys a field at Anathoth; return to Jerusalem promised; Christ, the Branch of Righteousness, promised.

Jeremiah prophesied that the ungodliness of the Israelites would result in the destruction of their nation by the Babylonian Empire. *At that time, the army of the king of Babylon was besieging Jerusalem, and Jeremiah the prophet was imprisoned in the court of the guard that was in the king of Judah's palace* (Jeremiah 32:2). Yet, under such adverse circumstances when the destruction of the nation was imminent, the Lord had told Jeremiah: *Buy the field with silver and assemble witnesses—but the city has now been delivered over to the Babylonians!* (32:25). Without hesitation Jeremiah paid for the land, took receipts, registered the purchase, then handed over the documents in the presence of many witnesses (32:9-12).

This business transaction would have seemed inconsistent to those who had heard Jeremiah's repeated warnings of approaching destruction and captivity. But, Jeremiah had also proclaimed that the people would be restored to the land, and this purchase of land was evidence of his faith that the Sovereign God was in control of Israel's destiny.

Although Jeremiah could not see how God could accomplish this prophecy, his faith was in the unfailing word of God, who also said: *I am the LORD. . . . Is anything too difficult for Me?* (32:27).

God gave Jeremiah a fresh assurance concerning the future by saying: *I am about to gather them from all the lands where I have banished them in My wrath, rage, and great fury, and I will return them to this place and settle them in safety* (32:37). How wonderful to know that, in the midst of the most difficult circumstances, we can rest assured that God is merciful and will protect and provide for the needs for His faithful servants. The Lord's invitation still is: *Call to Me and I will answer you and tell you great and mysterious things you do not know* (33:3).

Our faith in the word of God can be measured by the influence we allow it to have upon our conduct. We should ask ourselves: "Does my faith affect my everyday conduct by what is taught in the Bible or is it just traditional 'religion'?" *For just as the body without the spirit is dead, so also faith without works is dead* (James 2:26).

Thought for Today: What occupies your thoughts most is a revelation of who or what is your god.

In Today's Reading

Jeremiah's warning to Zedekiah; obedience of the Rechabites; scroll read by Jehudi and destroyed by King Jehoiakim.

Four years after the Egyptians conquered Judah and appointed Jehoiakim as its king, Nebuchadnezzar defeated the Egyptians, invaded Jerusalem, and appointed Jehoiakim as his servant-king. Unlike his godly father Josiah, he was a ruthless ruler.

In the third year of the reign of Jehoiakim king of Judah, Nebuchadnezzar . . . came to Jerusalem and laid siege to it. . . . Jehoiakim remained as puppet king (Daniel 1:1-2). But, Nebuchadnezzar *ordered . . . his court officials, to bring some of the Israelites from the royal family and the nobility. . . . Among them were Daniel, Hananiah, Mishael, and Azariah from Judah* (1:3,6).

During that time, Jeremiah instructed his secretary Baruch to record the judgment of God on *a scroll, and write on it all the words I have spoken to you about Israel, Judah, and all the nations* (Jeremiah 36:2).

Jeremiah instructed Baruch . . . you must go and read from the scroll the words of the LORD that you wrote at my dictation and do so in the hearing of the people at the temple of the LORD. . . . of all . . . who are coming from their cities. Perhaps their cry for mercy, will reach the LORD, and each one will turn from his evil way, for the anger and fury that the LORD has spoken against this people is great (36:5-7). The princes (leaders) were terrified by the prophet's words, and immediately informed the king who *sent Jehudi to get the scroll. . . . Jehudi then read it in the hearing of the king* (36:21).

After *Jehudi had read three or four leaves* of the scroll, Jehoiakim flew into a rage, snatched it from Jehudi, *cut the scroll with a penknife and threw the columns into the blazing fireplace until the entire scroll was burned up in the fireplace* (36:23). That was all he could do. Even as a king it was beyond his power to destroy the truth that the scroll contained.

Like Jehoiakim, some today seal their fate by refusing to even read the truth that God considers necessary to lead them to fulfill His will. History records many Bible burnings; but what is the difference between burning it or not reading it.

I assure you. . . . My word will never pass away (Matthew 24:34-35).

Thought for Today: Those who seek counsel from the Lord through His word will never be deceived.

In Today's Reading

Jeremiah imprisoned in a dungeon; his counsel rejected; Jerusalem destroyed; Jeremiah set free; Ishmael's plan to assassinate Gedaliah.

During the 11th year of Zedekiah's evil reign, the armies of Nebuchadnezzar surrounded Jerusalem and Zedekiah frantically said to Jeremiah: *Inquire of the LORD for us; for Nebuchadnezzar . . . is making war against us* (Jeremiah 21:2). But the answer from the Lord was firm: *I have set My face against this city . . . the king of Babylon . . . will destroy it by fire* (21:10). Zedekiah, *along with . . . the people of the land, did not obey the words of the LORD that He spoke through Jeremiah the prophet* (37:2).

Believing that Egypt would protect his kingdom, Zedekiah sent his officials to Egypt to make an alliance. It also seemed wise to show "good will" to the prophet; so, *King Zedekiah sent . . . the priest, to Jeremiah . . . requesting* (him to) *pray to the LORD our God for us!* (37:3). Instead of praying, Jeremiah replied: *This is what the LORD says: Don't deceive yourselves . . . the Babylonians will . . . . burn this city down* (37:9-10).

When the Chaldean army retreated from Jerusalem, the Israelites believed their alliance with Egypt was successful without the prayers of the prophet. Yet Zedekiah was uneasy. He secretly removed Jeremiah from prison *and received him . . . in his house privately asking him: Is there a word from the LORD? Jeremiah responded, Yes . . . You'll be handed over to the king of Babylon* (37:17).

The fortified city of Jerusalem held out for nearly a year and a half. During this time the people suffered the horrors of famine and pestilence. When Zedekiah finally attempted to escape the city at night, he was captured near Jericho, where Joshua had victoriously begun the conquest of the promised land (39:5).

Some, like Zedekiah, allow friends or self-will, rather than the Lord, to influence their decisions. This blinded and imprisoned (39:7) king is an example of the consequences of those who refuse to seek the Lord's forgiveness for their sins. *Regarding them: the god of this age has blinded the minds of the unbelievers* (II Corinthians 4:4).

Thought for Today: A person who rejects the Lord and His word is blindly moving toward his own destruction.

In Today's Reading

Gedaliah's assassination; Jeremiah taken to Egypt; desolation of Judah because of idolatry.

God used Nebuchadnezzar to chastise his rebellious people and fulfill His prophecy of the destruction of Jerusalem. *The king of Babylon . . . appointed Gedaliah . . . over the land and . . . he put him in charge* (of the people) . . . *who had not been exiled to Babylon* (Jeremiah 40:7).

Gedaliah set up his government at Mizpah, about five miles northwest of the ruins of Jerusalem. Gedaliah then held a banquet in honor of Ishmael at Mizpah. Ishmael was a leader of an anti-Babylonian nationalist party. At this event Ishmael and his ten companions murdered Gedaliah (II Kings 25:25; Jeremiah 40:7 – 41:18). The Israelites who were in the area evidently expected Nebuchadnezzar to retaliate. They escaped into Egypt and even forced Jeremiah to go with them.

In Egypt he watched the Israelites sink further into sin as they worshiped the Egyptian goddess Ashtoreth. They *answered Jeremiah saying . . . As for the word you spoke to us in the name of the LORD, we're not going to listen to you! . . . Rather, we'll . . . burn incense to the queen of heaven and offer drink offerings to her just as we, our fathers . . . and our officials did in Judah's cities . . . when we had enough food and good things, and saw no calamity. . . . But from the time we ceased to burn incense to the queen of heaven and to offer her drink offerings, we have lacked everything* (44:15-19).

Some would say that the godly prophet Jeremiah surely deserved better treatment for his loyalty to the Lord. Though distressed over the unbelief of his people, Jeremiah had nothing to fear, for he knew his life was in the hands of his God. Jeremiah did not compromise but remained loyal to God regardless of the consequences. Surely we too can say with God's servant, the apostle Paul: *I also consider everything to be a loss in view of the surpassing value of knowing Christ Jesus my Lord. Because of Him I have suffered the loss of all things and consider them filth, so that I may gain Christ* (Philippians 3:8).

Thought for Today: Shed God's Light on someone's path today.

In Today's Reading

Jeremiah's message to Baruch; judgment against Egypt, Philistia, and Moab.

Among all the prophecies of Jeremiah, the Lord included a personal message to just one man, Baruch, Jeremiah's discontented assistant. *Thus says the LORD . . . Baruch: You have said, Woe unto me, because the LORD has added misery to my pain! I am worn out with groaning and have found no rest* (Jeremiah 45:2-3). Perhaps he had hoped that his service as a scribe would be a means to achieving personal ambitions, recognition, or other self-serving goals.

Baruch's grandfather Maaseiah had been governor of Jerusalem during Josiah's reign (32:12; II Chronicles 34:8). Did Baruch secretly think he was "overqualified" to be a mere scribe to an unpopular prophet?

Instead of rewards, or even words of sympathy, Baruch received a strong rebuke from the Lord: *Should you seek great things for yourself? Stop doing it* (Jeremiah 45:5).

Baruch expressed no heartfelt grief about the impending destruction of Jerusalem and the temple of God and the pitiful slavery of the people, as foretold by Jeremiah. Instead, he only expressed sorrow over his own lack of personal fulfillment.

Although Baruch was recording the word of God spoken through Jeremiah, he did not have the spiritual concern or insight of Jeremiah, whose desire was for the people to repent of their sins and avoid destruction. What a privilege Baruch had as a coworker in Jeremiah's ministry.

Our time and talents are precious treasures invested in us by the Lord to accomplish His will through us. True fulfillment comes only when we recognize that God has arranged the circumstances in our lives.

Baruch is typical of those who are dissatisfied and often frustrated with their circumstances or position of less esteem than they think they deserve, or are even frustrated with their spouses. They fail to realize that *godliness with contentment is a great gain* (I Timothy 6:6).

Thought for Today: *Look at the birds of the sky: they don't sow or reap or gather into barns, yet your heavenly Father feeds them* (Matthew 6:26).

In Today's Reading

Judgments against Ammon, Edom, Damascus, Kedar, Hazor, Elam, and Babylon foretold; redemption of Israel promised.

Jeremiah prophesied that the Ammonites, descendants of Lot who were historically hostile to the Israelites, would be destroyed (II Chronicles 20:1-3; II Kings 24:1-2; Jeremiah 27:3-6). *That city will become a devastated mound, and its villages will be burned* (49:2). The Lord then turned to Moab, also descendants of Lot, saying: *I am about to bring terror against you, says the LORD, the God of Hosts. . . . You will be banished* (49:5).

Next, our attention is turned to Edom, a nation that descended from Jacob's twin brother Esau. Edom had always been a jealous enemy of Jacob's descendants and had joined Nebuchadnezzar in plundering the city of Jerusalem and even expanded their territory into southern Judah, inhabiting an area later called Idumea. Because of their actions toward Israel, Edom's fate was accurately foretold by the prophet: *I will strip Esau bare. . . . He will exist no longer* (49:10-12).

Finally, judgment was pronounced upon Babylon, the empire that appeared to be invincible. But Jeremiah said: *The word the LORD spoke concerning Babylon . . . the land of the Chaldeans. . . . a nation will invade her . . . it will make her land desolate* (50:1-3).

Following these prophecies of destruction, the release of Israel from captivity is foretold. We note that the Israelites will eventually demonstrate genuine repentance and accept their Messiah, Jesus, *in an everlasting covenant that will never be forgotten* (50:4-5).

We can expect the forces of evil to discourage us in an effort to destroy our faith in God. Keep your eyes on the coming King. There is never a valid reason to allow the pressures and problems of life to depress us. When Satan attempts to bombard you with gloom, lift up your voice and say aloud with the psalmist: *My lips will glorify You because Your faithful love is better than life* (Psalms 63:3).

God is not glorified by our fears, doubts, or frustrations. *Give thanks in everything, for this is God's will for you in Christ Jesus* (I Thessalonians 5:18).

Thought for Today: God will hear the prayer of any repentant sinner.

In Today's Reading

Judgment of Babylon; fall of Jerusalem; captivity of Judah.

The spectacular empire of the Chaldeans surpassed anything the world had ever known. Babylon, the capital, appeared invincible with walls over 300 feet high and wide enough for chariots to ride two abreast. The empire was enjoying absolute rule over all the nations when Jeremiah declared that *suddenly Babylon fell. . . . your end has come. . . . an uninhabited wasteland* (Jeremiah 51:8-62).

As foretold by the prophet, the Babylonian capital "suddenly fell." This was on the night that Belshazzar, the king, saw the *the hand* (that) *appeared and began writing on . . . the king's wall* (Daniel 5:1,5-9).

The conquering king of the Persian empire urged the Jews to go to Jerusalem and rebuild the temple. Most of the older generation that was taken captive to Babylonia had died. The new generation was prospering under the new Persian rule and, consequently, felt no desire to leave.

The unwillingness of the majority of the Jews to forsake the luxuries of Babylon for the poverty and hardships they would experience in returning to Jerusalem has a modern-day parallel. How accurately this describes some who love the pleasures of the world rather than responding to the call of Christ, who said: *If anyone wants to come with Me, he must deny himself, take up his cross, and follow Me* (Matthew 16:24).

"Would-be followers" can be contrasted with Matthew, who had a very prestigious position and influence with the government. But Matthew knew there was something more important than living to serve self, and immediately decided to deny himself and be a follower of Jesus.

Is it possible to *deny . . . self and take up his cross,* and yet devote one's time, tithes, and talents to personal pleasures on the Lord's Day? Jesus never said: "Please" or tried to convince anyone to *deny himself, take up his cross, and follow* Him (16:24). We cheat ourselves when we give less than our best to the Lord.

Followers of Christ will keep their eyes on the coming King. *This is why I tell you: Don't worry about your life. . . . But seek first* (inwardly and outwardly, morally and spiritually) *the kingdom of God and His righteousness* (Matthew 6:25,33).

Thought for Today: We live in the world, but not by its standards.

Introduction To The Book Of Lamentations

The book of Lamentations is an expression of deep sorrow over the sins of the people that eventually resulted in the destruction of the temple and the kingdom of Judah. Jeremiah knew the inevitable consequences of disobedience. *Jerusalem has sinned grievously. . . . because of the sins of her prophets and the guilt of her priests* (Lamentations 1:8; 4:13).

Jerusalem was the only place on earth where acceptable sacrifices could be made to God. This fact gave the people a false sense of security since Jerusalem was *the city of the great King* (Psalms 48:2). But, ignoring the word of God resulted in sin, and the people of Jerusalem were subjected to the horrors of deprivation, disease, suffering, starvation, and finally the destruction of their sacred temple (Lamentations 2:19-22; 4:8-10).

Not what I do, Lord, nor what I say,
But what I am, Lord, matters today.
Busy with nothing we fill up the years,
Hurrying, worrying, gathering tears.

Why can't I learn, Lord, that power is within,
Why can't I see, Lord, the waste of my sin?
If I could be, Lord, growing in soul,
Seeing each day, Lord, more clearly the goal.

If I could live, Lord, discerning thy face,
Ever more strongly held by thy grace;
So take and mold, Lord, this heart of mine,
Till it shall be, Lord, like unto thine!

– M. E. H.

In Today's Reading

Jeremiah's lamentation over Jerusalem's destruction.

The holy city of Jerusalem *has become like a widow. . . . A princess over the provinces has become like a vassal. She weeps uncontrollably in the night, tears on her cheeks. She has none to offer her comfort from among all her lovers. All her friends have betrayed her; they have become her enemies. Judah has gone into captivity following affliction and cruel bondage* (Lamentations 1:1-3). Jeremiah tells us why Jerusalem was reduced to such deplorable destruction: *The LORD has afflicted her because of her many rebellions* (1:5).

Devastated by famine, dying of starvation, and its few remaining inhabitants dragged off by enemies to a foreign land, all that once was so precious was now a pitiful heap of ruins.

To illustrate the Israelites' pitiful suffering and sorrow, the prophet Jeremiah compared the once wealthy, secure, and proud Jerusalem to a widow who had lost her husband. The loving Lord was the generous Provider and powerful Protector of Israel, and they had rejected Him. As a widow, Jerusalem was now alone, weeping in the night, with no one to comfort her: *Jerusalem has sinned grievously; therefore, she has become an object of scorn* (1:8). The houses were burned and the palace demolished; but more tragic, the glorious temple of God was destroyed. The covenant of God with Israel required willing obedience to His word.

The only other nation founded upon God and His word is the United States of America. It is recognized throughout the world as a Christian nation, and its currency tells the world: "In God We Trust." But, God cannot ignore the sins of an individual or of a nation.

Spiritual neglect eventually leads to loss of liberty. It is a fact that sin deceives and blinds our eyes to reality. Even enemies are often seen as friends, but they soon reveal their true nature and destroy true happiness.

Jesus said to the Jews who had believed Him, If you continue in My word, you really are My disciples. You will know the truth, and the truth will set you free (John 8:31-32).

Thought for Today: *I will say to the LORD, My refuge and my fortress, my God, in whom I trust* (Psalms 91:2).

In Today's Reading

God's mercy; punishment of Zion; the faithful grieve over their disaster and confess their sins.

The prophet Jeremiah was one of the greatest prophets in biblical history, and few have suffered so much public humiliation, rejection, and hostility. For more than 40 years, he warned the Israelites to believe Moses and follow the law or face the judgment of God. Eventually they faced the inevitable destruction of their glorious temple and Jerusalem, the city of God.

God does not permit suffering just for the sake of punishment. It always has a twofold purpose: first as judgment upon sin, but second to allow the offenders the opportunity to repent and commit their lives to God. We can truly praise the Lord that He forgives us of all our sins. Jeremiah the prophet assures us: *Even if He torments, He will show compassion, according to His abundant faithful love* (Lamentations 3:32).

Through the destruction of the temple came a realization of the awfulness of sin and the consequences of disregarding God's word. Added to that was assuming God's covenant promise would continue while the people's covenant responsibility was being ignored. The prophet could plead: *Let us explore our ways and examine them, that we may return to the LORD* (3:40). Jeremiah called for confession of sin, repentance, and obedience to God's word.

The once-powerful kingdom of Judah was subjected to every form of public humiliation. Its people had to beg for bread from foreigners, to pay for water, to helplessly stand by and watch their children taken as slaves into heavy, forced labor, and to know that these heathen soldiers had *raped . . . virgins in the cities of Judah* (5:11). *The crown has fallen from our head. Woe to us, for we have sinned* (5:16).

The righteous always suffer in the midst of a wicked nation; but, for the Christian, suffering opens our eyes to the true values of life. *For they disciplined us for a short time based on what seemed good to them, but He does it for our benefit, so that we can share His holiness* (Hebrews 12:10).

Thought for Today: God's word imparts insight into true values.

Introduction To The Book Of Ezekiel

Ezekiel lived in Jerusalem during the great reformation period that followed the discovery of the law in the temple. This was during the reign of Josiah, the last godly king of Judah (II Kings 22:8-20; 23:1-29). After Josiah's death, the people chose as their king his fourth son Jehoahaz, who was also known as Shallum (23:30-34; I Chronicles 3:15, Jeremiah 22:10-12). Just three months later, Pharaoh-nechoh took him in chains to Egypt, and set up Josiah's second son Eliakim as king over Judah (II Kings 23:31-34; II Chronicles 36:1-4). Pharaoh changed Eliakim's name to Jehoiakim (II Kings 23:34-36). He was subject to Pharaoh-nechoh for about four years (Jeremiah 46:2).

Having defeated Egypt, in the same year Nebuchadnezzar entered Jerusalem, stripped the capital and the temple of its treasures and most of its golden vessels, and took many of the young royalty of Judah as captives to Babylon. Among them were Daniel and his three friends (Daniel 1:1-3,6; Ezekiel 33:21).

Nebuchadnezzar left Jehoiakim to be his puppet ruler. He was followed by his 18-year-old son Jehoiachin (also known as Jeconiah and Coniah). He followed his father's evil policies (II Kings 24:8-9). After only three months, Jehoiachin was also taken captive to Babylon, along with Ezekiel and ten thousand influential statesmen and craftsmen; *except* (for) *the poorest people of the land, nobody remained* (II Kings 24:8-16).

Nebuchadnezzar then appointed Mattaniah, who was the third son of Josiah to govern Judah, and renamed him Zedekiah (24:17; I Chronicles 3:15). About 10 years later, Zedekiah also rebelled against Nebuchadnezzar, who once again attacked Jerusalem, broke down its walls and, this time, he destroyed the temple built by Solomon (II Kings 24:18 – 25:21; II Chronicles 36:11-21).

Ezekiel's captivity began about eight years after Daniel was taken to Babylon. Ezekiel was placed at Tel-Abib near the Chebar River, an irrigation canal which routed water from the Euphrates in a large semicircle through the countryside until it rejoined the Euphrates.

Ezekiel prophesied for 22 years (Ezekiel 1:2; 29:17). The key thought in this book is the heart cry of our Creator: *They will know that I am the LORD their God* (28:26; 39:22; 39:28).

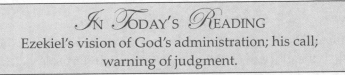

In Today's Reading

Ezekiel's vision of God's administration; his call; warning of judgment.

As a captive of Nebuchadnezzar and far from the promised land, Ezekiel could not offer sacrifices to God according to the law. But, to Ezekiel's great joy, *the word of the LORD came. . . . The hand of the LORD was upon him there* (Ezekiel 1:3).

Ezekiel's first vision appeared as *a whirlwind coming from the north, a great cloud with fire flashing back and forth, and brightness all around it . . . from the center of the fire . . . came the form of four living creatures. . . . they had human form* (1:4-5). The cherubim (angelic beings) were fulfilling the perfect will of God.

Each of the four cherubim had wings and hands and four different faces. These heavenly beings typified Jesus Christ, as seen in the four gospels. The lion represents the ruler of the animal kingdom and symbolizes the royalty and supreme majesty of Jesus Christ the King, as presented in Matthew. The ox represents the most valuable domesticated animal and represents strength and patient service as the servant of God, symbolic of Jesus Christ, as presented in Mark. The face of man represents the humanity of Christ as perfect, fully human, and fully divine, as presented in Luke. The eagle is admired for its superior ability to swiftly rise into the heavens above all enemies on earth and represents the deity of Jesus, as revealed in John. The swiftness of the eagle also represents Christ, who is quick to bring protection, provision, or judgment. Since the cherubim faced all directions simultaneously, they were prepared to instantly obey the will of God in any direction of flight.

The cherubim stood beside the wheel within a wheel (1:16) in which one wheel was revolving north-south and the other east-west, so there was no need to turn the wheel in any direction. *They didn't turn as they moved – each one would go straight forward* (1:9,12,17).

The Lord is prepared to protect and direct the lives of His people. Not only did He deliver them from Babylon and idol worship, but He provided them with His word as guidance for their greatest need. *For the Son of Man has come to seek and to save the lost* (Luke 19:10).

Thought for Today: Regardless of how difficult our circumstances, let us trust the Lord for a good outcome.

In Today's Reading

Famine, pestilence, and sword; remnant to be spared; vision of the glory of God; vision of slaying in Jerusalem.

Fourteen years after Nebuchadnezzar's initial conquest of the kingdom of Judah, life in Jerusalem seemed to have returned to normal. Consequently, the people would not believe Ezekiel, who was in Babylon, when he prophesied concerning Jerusalem: *Your altars will become desolate and. . . . cities will be laid waste* (Ezekiel 6:4-6). Even the Israelites who were captive in Babylon were sure that God would protect Jerusalem and the only temple on earth where His presence dwelt.

But Ezekiel continued to warn: *Whoever is in the city, famine and pestilence will devour him* (7:15). What a horrifying prophecy!

Fourteen months after his first vision (1:1-2), Ezekiel reported: *The Spirit lifted me up . . . brought me to Jerusalem* (8:1-5).

The prophet then saw in his vision *the great abominations which . . . Israel is doing . . . terrible abominations . . . there were women sitting there weeping for Tammuz* (the Babylonian god of fertility) . . . *men with their backs to the LORD's temple. . . . prostrating themselves eastward toward the sun.* As a result of their disobedience to the word of God, the Israelites had filled *the land with violence* (8:6,9-14,16-17).

The people would not believe his second vision that showed the reason for the coming horrifying judgment upon Judah and Jerusalem. Just as Ezekiel had prophesied: *Their silver and their gold won't be able to deliver them in the day of the LORD's wrath* (7:19). How typical this is of our generation with its overemphasis on materialism, success, and sex.

Wealth was never meant to be selfishly accumulated or to be lavished on ourselves. God entrusts people with wealth *so that in every way, always having everything you need, you may excel in every good work* (II Corinthians 9:8). The attitude of the heart is all important since both rich and poor can lust after more possessions.

The Holy Spirit warns: *Those who want to be rich fall into temptation, a trap, and many foolish and harmful desires, which plunge people into ruin and destruction* (I Timothy 6:9).

Thought for Today: *Godliness with contentment is a great gain* (I Timothy 6:6).

In Today's Reading

Glory of the Lord leaving the temple; judgment upon lying leaders; the promise of Israel's restoration and renewal; captivity near.

Ezekiel's vision revealed the dispatching of seven men, one to spare the faithful minority and six to slay the idolatrous majority. *One man . . . clothed in linen* marked the foreheads of all who remained faithful to the Lord (Ezekiel 9:2-7). *Then the glory of the LORD moved away from the threshold of the temple and stood above the cherubim. The cherubim lifted their wings and rose. . . . They stood at the entrance of the eastern gate of the house of the LORD* (10:18-19).

Ezekiel observed the leaders of Jerusalem who, it seemed, were being blessed and called upon to remain in charge as the favored people, while so many others had been taken captive. But, in reality, many of the deprived captives in Babylon eventually learned, through suffering, to repent of their pagan idolatry and trust in the Lord God of Israel. God promised a great future to those who turned to Him. As Ezekiel prepared to leave the temple, he saw the presence of the Lord, which had rested just above the mercy seat of the ark of the covenant in the holy of holies, slowly leaving the place where He had once chosen to dwell.

As *the glory of the LORD rose up from the midst of the city* (11:23), it reluctantly left *the city among all the tribes of Israel where the LORD had chosen to put His name* (I Kings 14:21). It appears the Israelites were so involved in their faithless religious activities that they were not even aware that God had forsaken them.

The Lord again gave Ezekiel a prophecy that reached far into the future: *I will put a new spirit within them; I will remove the heart of stone from their flesh . . . so that they may walk by My statutes and keep My judgments and perform them. And they will be My people,and I will be their God* (Ezekiel 11:19-20). The apostle Paul wrote: *There is one body and one Spirit, just as you were called to one hope at your calling; one Lord, one faith, one baptism, one God and Father of all, who is above all and through all and in all. . . . And He personally gave some to be apostles, some prophets, some evangelists, some pastors and teachers, for the training of the saints in the work of ministry, to build up the body of Christ* (Ephesians 4:4-6,11-12).

Thought for Today: True satisfaction and purpose in life are found only in Christ – never in material things.

In Today's Reading

Judgment pronounced upon elders of Israel and Jerusalem; parable of the vine; promises of future blessings under new covenant.

The Israelites were under the control of Nebuchadnezzar, who had taken thousands of them captive. Once again, certain *elders of Israel* (Ezekiel 14:1) came to consult Ezekiel, as if they desired to know the will of God. But the Lord revealed their hypocrisy to Ezekiel, saying: *These men have set up their idols upon their hearts. . . . the Lord GOD says: Repent and turn away from your idols, and turn your faces from all your abominations. . . . Then they will be My people and I will be their God* (14:3,6-8,11).

Although the Israelites regularly offered sacrifices to God, they also hypocritically worshiped the popular idols of other nations.

Consequently, the Israelites found themselves under the control of a pagan nation. To illustrate their one purpose as the people of God, the Lord presented the question to Ezekiel: *How is the wood of the vine* (the grapevine which was often used by God to illustrate His people) *better than any wood. . . of the forest? Can wood be taken from it to make something useful? . . . Look, it is put into the fire for fuel* (Ezekiel 15:2-4; Genesis 49:22; Deuteronomy 32:32; Psalms 80:8-11; Isaiah 5:1-7; Jeremiah 2:21; Hosea 10:1). Every Israelite knew that the grapevine was valued only for its fruit and was worthless for making lumber for houses.

Ezekiel spoke of the vine as representing Israel, chosen of God to let the world know there was only one true God, who would bless all who honored Him by keeping His word. But the vine had failed to produce fruit; consequently, the only alternative was for it to be uprooted and *put into the fire* (Ezekiel 15:4,7).

The righteous judgment of God upon those in Jerusalem had to be consistent with the great privileges they had willfully forsaken. The same is true today. *No sexually immoral or impure or greedy person, who is an idolater, has an inheritance in the kingdom of the Messiah and of God. Let no one deceive you with empty arguments, for because of these things God's wrath is coming on the disobedient* (Ephesians 5:5-6).

Thought for Today: Consider your priorities today. Are they wrapped up in the things of the world or committed to serving the Lord?

In Today's Reading

Parable of the eagles; judgment upon bad conduct; blessings for good conduct; sorrow over the leaders of Israel.

Ezekiel was given a parable: *The great eagle* (Nebuchadnezzar) *with great wings . . . And a full plumage of many colors, came to Lebanon* (symbolic of Jerusalem, as many of the houses were built of the cedars of Lebanon), *and took the top* (the king) *of the cedar* (tree): *Its topmost shoot he plucked off, and brought it . . . into a city of traders* (Ezekiel 17:1-4).

This vision illustrates the vast extent of Nebuchadnezzar's dominion. The eagle's feathers represent the great number of conquered nations. Removing *the top* represents the removal of Judah's king (17:12). *The topmost shoot* symbolized Jehoiachin, the youthful king of Judah, and *a city of traders* (Babylon), where he would be taken by Nebuchadnezzar. Eventually, there was *a vine, spreading and low in height* (Zedekiah) *with its branches turned toward it* (Nebuchadnezzar) (17:6).

But there was another great eagle (the Egyptian king) *. . . And look! This vine* (Zedekiah) *sent its roots toward him* (17:7). *This is what the Lord GOD says: Will it flourish? Won't he* (Nebuchadnezzar) *tear off its roots* (the kingdom of Judah) (17:9). The purpose of this important prophecy to Zedekiah was to warn him not to betray his oath to Nebuchadnezzar by forming an alliance with Egypt. *When you make a vow to God, don't delay fulfilling it, because He does not delight in fools. Fulfill what you vow! . . . Never let your mouth bring guilt upon you* (Ecclesiastes 5:4-6).

However, in the ninth year of his reign, King Zedekiah made a military treaty with Egypt. As a consequence, Nebuchadnezzar besieged Jerusalem and the people suffered many months of famine and pestilence before the city and temple were utterly destroyed.

Nebuchadnezzar's invasion of Judah could have been averted if Zedekiah had honorably kept his vow. We too are obligated to keep promises made in the name of God, even when they are made with the unsaved (Joshua 9:19-20; II Samuel 21:1-3; Psalms 15:4.) There are always consequences when we break our promises, whether it be a marriage vow or a business transaction. *If a man makes a vow to the LORD . . . He must do exactly what he promised* (Numbers 30:2).

Thought for Today: All who love the Lord keep His commandments.

In Today's Reading

God's refusal to be consulted by the elders; history of rebellious Israel; its defeat by Babylon and scattering among the heathen.

The king and the religious leaders of Judah had expressed growing hatred for Jeremiah because of his messages of judgment against them. The revelations and visions given by God to Ezekiel in Babylon were also ignored. There comes a time when God says: *They will call me, but I won't answer* (Proverbs 1:28). It was now too late to pray for God to spare Jerusalem from destruction. However, Ezekiel records: *Certain of the elders of Israel came to inquire of the LORD, and they sat before me* (Ezekiel 20:1).

Then God gave Ezekiel the following message for the elders: *I will not be inquired of by you . . . . I chose Israel. . . . But they rebelled against Me. . . . They had rejected My judgments . . . for their heart went after their idols* (20:3,5,8,16). Following this, Ezekiel received a horrifying message from the Lord for Israel: *I am against you. I will take My sword and . . . put it into the hand of* (Nebuchadnezzar) *the killer* (21:3,11).

Ezekiel's prophecy of the sharpened sword revealed impending doom as Nebuchadnezzar turned to destroy Jerusalem. Nebuchadnezzar, no doubt, congratulated himself on his splendid triumph in Judah when, in fact, he was only serving the King of kings, unknowingly being used to fulfill God's judgment upon His rebellious people. *The lot is cast into the lap, but its every decision is from the LORD* (Proverbs 16:33).

King Zedekiah, the *wicked prince of Israel* (Ezekiel 21:25), and the people would soon be captured. Jerusalem and the temple would be destroyed to fulfill Ezekiel's prophecy: *This . . . will be no more until He comes to whom it rightfully belongs* (21:27).

No other king has been anointed to sit on the throne of David in Israel for the past 2500 years. In the time of Jesus, an Edomite named Herod was merely a puppet king appointed by Rome to govern over only the Jews of Judea. Israel will continue to exist without a king until the return of Jesus Christ as *King of kings, and the Lord of lords* (I Timothy 6:15).

Thought for Today: God is full of compassion toward all who hear His call, repent, and turn to Him "today" – tomorrow could be too late.

In Today's Reading

Sins of Israel enumerated; abominations of two sisters; parable of the boiling pot; death of Ezekiel's wife.

On the very day that God revealed to Ezekiel that his precious wife, *the delight of your eyes,* was to die, God also said: *But you shall not lament, nor shall you weep, nor shall your tears flow* (Ezekiel 24:16). Ezekiel was told by the Lord that, after his wife's death, he was to refrain from all the conventional signs of mourning for the dead. It was not that he was to be insensitive to the death of his wife. But, his own grief was to give way to the far greater heartbreak over the death of his nation and the destruction of the temple which took place the same day his wife died. *For this is what the Lord GOD says . . . they* (Nebuchadnezzar's army) *will kill their sons and their daughters . . . . you will bear the consequences for your idolatrous sins* (23:46-47,49).

News of Ezekiel's unusual reaction to his wife's death must have spread quickly, for the people asked: *Tell us what these things mean to us?* (24:19). Then came the tragic news from Ezekiel: *This is what the Lord GOD says: I am about to profane* (destroy) *My sanctuary, the pride of your power. . . and your sons and your daughters whom you left behind* (in Jerusalem) *will fall by the sword. . . . When it* (the news of the destruction of the temple) *happens, then you will know* (be convinced) *that I am the Lord GOD,* who has confirmed His word (24:21-24).

Eventually, a messenger who escaped the devastation of Jerusalem arrived in Babylon to report the city's destruction (33:21). Just as they had been forewarned by Jeremiah in Jerusalem and by Ezekiel in Babylonia, the Israelites' acceptance of false gods and indifference to the word of God had brought about the destruction of Jerusalem and the death of their own sons and daughters.

Often we see worldly-minded people grieving over material losses, but showing little concern for their own or their children's eternal welfare. Jesus said that we are not to be preoccupied with earthly things, not even our daily needs: *For the gentile world eagerly seeks all these things, and your Father knows that you need them. But seek His kingdom, and these things will be provided for you* (Luke 12:30-31).

Thought for Today: Allow Christ to truly be Lord of your life.

In Today's Reading

Gentile nations judged; judgment on Tyre's king and the fate of Satan who inspired him; future regathering of Israel.

Tyre was one of the richest cities of the world. Its wealth was not gained from war, like that of Babylon, but from trade. Its fleet of ships was the greatest of all nations. Ezekiel prophesied: *The word of the LORD came to me . . . I am against you, O Tyre* (proud queen of the seas) (Ezekiel 26:1,3). God foretold that it would be fully destroyed, not only because of its immoral idolatry, but also because of its jealousy toward the chosen city of God. Tyre was rejoicing over the downfall of Jerusalem because its competition no longer existed, saying: *I will be filled* (prosper)! *She* (Jerusalem) *lies in ruins!* (26:2).

The detailed prophecy of Ezekiel concerning the destruction of Tyre leaves no doubt that only God, who rules over every detail on earth, would be able to say: *They will destroy the walls of Tyre and demolish her towers. I will scrape her soil from her, and I will turn her into a bare rock. She* (her island capital) *will become a place to spread nets in the midst of the sea, for I have spoken. . . . you will never be rebuilt* (26:4-5,14).

Nebuchadnezzar besieged Tyre for 13 years and fully destroyed the mainland city. During that long siege, the city's administration and much of its wealth was moved to the offshore island section of the city. More than two centuries later, Alexander the Great besieged Tyre, which was then just an island city nearly half a mile from the mainland. Since Alexander had no fleet, his men used the stones from the walls of the ancient mainland city to build a causeway to reach the island and destroy it exactly as prophesied: *You will exist no more* (26:20-21). Tyre was never again a world power.

Tyre should be a warning to the person who rejoices when his competition goes bankrupt or to the "Christian" who resents the success of his "rivals" in the church or in the marketplace: *Now the works* (practices) *of the flesh are obvious . . . strife, jealousy, outbursts of anger, selfish ambitions . . . envy . . . and anything similar, about which I tell you in advance . . . that those who practice such things will not inherit the kingdom of God* (Galatians 5:19-21).

Thought for Today: In the midst of temptation, determine in your heart that you will remain faithful to God.

In Today's Reading

Egypt's defeat by Babylon foretold; Assyria's fall – warning to Egypt; lamentation (great sorrow) over Egypt's fall.

The prophecy concerning Egypt came to Ezekiel about a year after the siege of Jerusalem began. He foretold the end of Pharaoh as a ruler and of Egypt as a great nation and said: *Son of man, set your face against Pharaoh, king of Egypt, and prophesy against him and against all Egypt. . . . because they have been a staff of reed to the house of Israel . . . . I am about to bring a sword against you, and I will cut off from you man and beast. The land of Egypt will be a desolate ruin. . . . for forty years* (Ezekiel 29:2-11).

Egypt would no longer be a great power of the world. But it would not be destroyed, as Babylon would be. Ezekiel also foretold: *At the end of forty years I will gather the Egyptians . . . and bring them back . . . There they will be a lowly kingdom . . . . It . . . will never again lift itself up above the nations. I will make them small, so that they won't rule over the nations* (29:13-15). Egypt has remained a *lowly* nation over the centuries. It stands as a witness to the supreme authority of God.

At the time of the Exodus, the ten plagues forced the Egyptians to acknowledge that their own gods were powerless against the one true God. This should have taught Egypt, and particularly Israel, to reject their idols and worship the one true God of creation.

Judgment upon Israel, Judah, Tyre, Sidon, Egypt, and other nations was to cause them to realize *that I am the LORD* (29:9). This phrase is mentioned 66 times in this book alone to point out the absolute accuracy and importance of the word of God and His sovereignty over creation.

A future time of redemption and restoration was also foretold: *In that day I will cause a horn to sprout for the house of Israel* (29:21; Psalms 92:10). The horn is a symbol of power and strength (I Samuel 2:10). As prophesied, the people of God, both Jew and Gentile, have a future destiny of glory with Jesus of Nazareth as the Messiah/King of kings.

At the name of Jesus every knee should bow – of those who are in heaven and on earth and under the earth – and every tongue should confess that Jesus Christ is Lord, to the glory of God the Father (Philippians 2:10-11).

Thought for Today: Pride robs the Lord of His glory. The Lord endows glory to the humble.

In Today's Reading

Jerusalem's destruction; justice of God's dealing; reproof of the false shepherds; destruction of Edom; restoration of Israel foretold.

Ezekiel was called *a watchman* (prophet) *for the house of Israel;* (and God said to Him) *when you hear a message from My mouth, you shall warn them for Me* (Ezekiel 33:7). The Israelites remaining in Jerusalem, as well as the captives in Babylon, disregarded Ezekiel's warnings that God would destroy them if they refused to repent of their sinful ways.

Now in the twelfth year of our exile (in Babylon) . . . *a survivor from Jerusalem came to me and reported: The city has been taken!* (33:21).

The majority of the Jews in Babylon complained that the horrifying death of their kindred in Jerusalem and the destruction of their homeland were inconsistent with the promises of God's protection, saying: *The way of the LORD isn't fair* (33:17). The Lord responded: *When a righteous person turns from his righteousness and commits iniquity, he will die in it. But when a wicked person turns from his wickedness and does what is just and right, he himself will live by them* (33:18-19).

As foretold by Ezekiel, the inevitable judgment had taken place. Then the Lord told him to say: *Lift up your eyes to your idols . . . you have committed abominations. . . . Then they will know that I am the LORD, when I make the land an utter desolation on account of all their abominations which they committed* (33:25-29). This all was fulfilled as prophesied by Ezekiel on the day of his wife's death (24:18,25-26).

Ezekiel's message proclaimed holiness as the Israelites' responsibility in their covenant relationship with God. This was rejected by those unwilling to forsake their sins. Living a godly life is equally unpopular to the majority today. God will judge all who love the world – *the lust of the flesh* (physical gratification), *the lust of the eyes* (covetousness), *and the pride in one's lifestyle* (worldly goals that have priority in one's life) (I John 2:15-17). Like the Israelites, many people today dwell only on the love of God while ignoring His perfect holiness, righteousness, and justice. *Just as you offered the parts of yourselves as slaves to moral im-purity, and to greater and greater lawlessness, so now offer them as slaves to righteousness, which results in sanctification* (holiness, purity). . . . *For the end of those things is death* (Romans 6:19,21).

Thought for Today: Sinful conduct cannot bring lasting satisfaction.

In Today's

Valley of the dry bones; prophecy against Gog; vision of a restored Israel.

After Nebuchadnezzar destroyed Jerusalem in 586 BC, most of the Israelites who remained were scattered throughout Babylonia among exiles from many heathen nations. Since their temple and city were destroyed, hope for the restoration of their homeland was abandoned.

It was at this time of national hopelessness that Ezekiel was given a new vision and said: *The hand of the LORD was upon me, and He brought me out by the Spirit of the LORD and set me down in the middle of a valley; it was full of bones* (Ezekiel 37:1; compare 37:3,9; 39:11). The bones were *dry* and bleached, having been there for some time. *Then He said to me, Son of man, can these bones live? I replied, O Lord GOD, only You know. He said to me, Prophesy to these bones and say to them: Dry bones, hear the word of the LORD! This is what the Lord GOD says to these bones: Look, I will cause breath to enter you, and you shall live* (37:3-5).

As a nation, Israel was literally and spiritually dead and without hope of restoration. However, like the dry bones, it was not buried. Ezekiel continued to prophesy: *There was a noise, a rattling sound, and the bones came together, bone to its bone* (37:7). Ezekiel proclaimed the word of God, *and the breath* (Spirit) *came into them and they lived. They stood up on their feet, an exceedingly great army* (37:10). Although the Israelites were saying: *Our hope has perished; we are cut off* from the land of promise (37:11), this army foretold the future restoration of Israel.

Ezekiel then was commanded to proclaim the good news: *I will put My Spirit within you, and you shall live . . . on your own land* (37:13-14). After more than 2500 years, the Israelites do exist as a nation within the promised land and God will soon fulfill His promise to David. Israel's Messiah King, Jesus Christ, will rule the world from Jerusalem.

Dry bones also describe our sinful human nature apart from the transforming power of the Holy Spirit. Eternal life is made possible when we confess and repent of our sins and allow Jesus to be Lord of our lives. *For by grace you are saved through faith, and this is not from yourselves; it is God's gift — not from works, so that no one can boast* (Ephesians 2:8-9).

Thought for Today: Jesus is coming soon! Are you ready?

In Today's Reading
Vision of the future temple.

A few years after the vision of dry bones, Ezekiel received another vision: *In the twenty-fifth year of our exile . . . in the fourteenth year after the city had been captured, on that very day the hand of the LORD was upon me . . . In visions of God He brought me to the land of Israel and set me down on a very high mountain* (Ezekiel 40:1-2). This new vision looked far into the future, where Ezekiel beheld a glorious temple, far more magnificent than the temple built by Solomon.

The measurements of the grounds and the many details concerning the building and its unusual architectural design are recorded; but no instruction was given to Ezekiel regarding who would build it or when it would be built. In striking contrast, God gave Moses detailed instructions for building the tabernacle and even the names of the craftsmen who were to build it in the wilderness (Exodus 25:9; 31:1-11). David also gave detailed instructions to Solomon concerning the temple.

No direction was given to Zerubbabel, in the messages of the prophets Haggai, Zechariah, Ezra, Nehemiah, or any other inspired writer, or anyone since that time, to build this spectacular temple.

Since AD 70, when the Romans destroyed Herod's temple, almost 2000 years have passed, with no recovery of the bronze altar, bronze basin, pure gold lampstand, table of the Presence, or gold altar. The ark of the covenant, representing the presence of God, disappeared in 586 BC when Nebuchadnezzar destroyed Jerusalem.

The form of worship with the altar and the priests offering sacrifices for the sins of the people all foreshadowed Jesus Christ, His atonement for our sins, and our relationship with Him through His sacrifice on the cross. Through the Romans, God removed the opportunity for the Jews to offer any of the redemptive sacrifices. These laws were *imposed until the time of restoration. Now the Messiah has appeared, high priest of. . . . the greater and more perfect tabernacle. . . . He entered the holy of holies once for all . . . by His own blood, having obtained eternal redemption* (Hebrews 9:10-12; compare John 4:21-24; Galatians 3:23-25; Colossians 2:17).

Thought for Today: We always seek after what our hearts treasure most – whether it is the Lord or the things of the world – it can't be both.

In Today's Reading

Vision of God's glory filling the temple; ordinances for the priests; land for the sanctuary and the city described.

In a vision, Ezekiel had witnessed the departure of *the glory of the LORD* from the magnificent, but now destroyed, temple built by Solomon (Ezekiel 10:4,18-19; 11:22-23). Israel had chosen to ignore God's word and had actually worshiped idols, the sun, and all sorts of creatures in the temple that had been dedicated to God alone (8:5-17).

Now, the Israelites had only memories of their once-glorious kingdom and were slaves in a heathen land. Ezekiel now received a vision of a future temple far greater than Solomon's, and the glory of the Lord would return to dwell in it. Ezekiel was *led . . . to the gate facing east. And there the glory of the God of Israel was coming from the east. His voice was like the sound of mighty waters and the earth shone with His glory! The glory of the LORD entered the house by way of the gate that faced east. . . . Then the Spirit lifted me up and brought me to the inner court and the glory of the LORD filled the temple* (43:1-2,4-5).

In this vision, the Lord of Glory entered His new temple by the very way through which He had departed from the old temple (compare 10:19 and 11:22-23). The Eastern Gate led straight to the temple entrance of the eternal King, who said: *I will dwell in the midst of the children of Israel forever. The house of Israel will no longer defile My holy name* (43:7). The emphasis of this vision is the importance of holiness in the lives of the people of God.

The physical temple foreshadowed the life and ministry of Christ. There will be no need for types or symbols because God the Father and Jesus Christ, whom they represented, will be present. Our chief concern should not be with when or how Ezekiel's temple will be built, or even when and how all the supernatural prophecies will be fulfilled. Our foremost concern should be that our body, mind, and spirit be holy. *You are God's sanctuary . . . and the Spirit of God lives in you. If anyone ruins God's sanctuary, God will ruin him; for God's sanctuary is holy, and that is what you are* (I Corinthians 3:16-17).

Thought for Today: Determine that today others will see Christ in you.

In Today's Reading

Worship of the prince; river flowing from the temple; boundaries and divisions of the land; gates of Jerusalem.

The first part of Ezekiel's final vision from God described the *temple* (Ezekiel 40 – 43); the second part described the worship and the character of the worshipers (44 – 46); and the final part tells us that *water was flowing from under the threshold of the temple eastward* (47:1). The further the water flowed, the deeper it became. Among other things, this symbolizes our continued walk with the Lord for, as we experience more and more the all-sufficiency of His provision, we come to realize that His abundant supply for all of our needs is unlimited.

The description of the land and the city are very different from either ancient or present-day, geographical Israel and Jerusalem. This is a vision anticipating the glorious future that all believers in Jesus as the Messiah will experience. All who love Him will enjoy the new promised land during the millennial reign of our Lord and Savior Jesus Christ.

Ezekiel was led by his guide to the front of the temple. The water apparently emerged from under the eastern gate as a small stream that flowed *one thousand cubits,* a little less than one-third of a mile (47:2-3). The prophet's guide *led me through the water,* and Ezekiel found that it was ankle-deep. The same process was repeated at a second and at a third distance, each measuring *one thousand cubits.* At these locations the water was found to be *knee-deep* and then *waist-deep* (47:4). At a fourth distance of *one thousand cubits* (47:5), the water had become *a river* that could not be passed through because of its depth.

The water provides life for the trees which bear wholesome fruit (47:9,12). This is what the Holy Spirit does in the lives of those who yield to Him. We begin to experience His gracious supply as a small stream which flows out from Christ the Fountainhead and which continues to increase in preciousness as we daily walk in the light of His word.

Our loving Father has provided His people with *the river of living water, sparkling like crystal, flowing from the throne of God and of the Lamb. . . . Whoever desires should take the living water as a gift* (Rev. 22:1-2,17).

Thought for Today: The living water is available to all who *thirst for righteousness* (Matthew 5:6).

Introduction To The Book Of Daniel

The first chapter of Daniel is written in Hebrew, but chapters 2 – 7 are in Aramaic, the common language of the Israelites during their stay in Babylon. Chapters 1 – 7 describe Daniel and some of his fellow exiles who remained faithful to God despite life-threatening pressures. These *Israelites from the royal family and the nobility* (Daniel 1:3) were among the first captives taken to Babylon (1:1-17).

In chapters 8 – 12, Daniel writes in Hebrew concerning future events. Daniel's ministry covered the entire period of Judah's Babylonian captivity. He served as an official in the courts of the Chaldean and Medo-Persian dynasties. He wrote during a time when the Jews were suffering great sorrow over the loss of life and of all their possessions in Jerusalem. The book of Daniel gave comfort to the exiles and assurance of Israel's eventual triumph over its enemies. His writings were undoubtedly the basis for the wise men who hundreds of years later entered Jerusalem, saying: *Where is He who has been born King of the Jews? For we saw His star in the east and have come to worship Him* (Matthew 2:2).

Only Daniel could interpret the meaning of the giant image in Nebuchadnezzar's dream in chapter 2. This was the way that God used to move him into a position of administrative prominence. Nebuchadnezzar's dream image in chapter 2 and the first of Daniel's visions in chapter 7 both give similar outlines of the empires of Babylon, Medo-Persia, Greece, and Rome. These are the nations that would successively rule the world from the time of Nebuchadnezzar *until the times of the Gentiles are fulfilled* (Luke 21:24). Near the end of this present age, the antichrist will make *war with the holy ones* (Daniel 7:21). Then Jesus Christ will return and establish His kingdom *that will never be destroyed* (2:44). The stone cut without hands, which ultimately *became a great mountain and filled the whole earth* (2:34-35), refers to Jesus.

This book reveals the sovereign control of God over all individuals as well as world governments. Soon His kingdom will fill the whole earth (2:35). Although it is far easier to get excited over details of future events, obedience is clearly the central theme of this great book. Jesus quoted Daniel when He spoke of the *abomination that causes desolation* (Matthew 24:15; Mark 13:14; compare Daniel 9:27; 11:31; 12:11) and of the *great tribulation* (Matthew 24:21; compare Daniel 12:1).

Two Views Of Governments That Rule During "The Times Of The Gentiles"

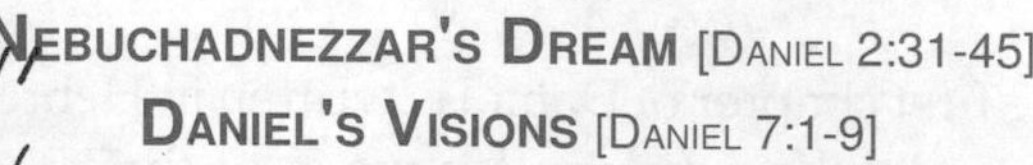

A stone broke off without a hand touching it, struck the statue on its feet . . . and crushed [them] [2:34,44-45]

The World's Point Of View

A dazzling giant to be admired and achieved at any price: *The lust of the flesh, the lust of the eyes, and the pride in one's lifestyle* [I John 2:15-17].

From God's Point Of View

The world system is full of pride, selfishness, greed, and cruelty, but is only temporary: *The world with its lust is passing away, but the one who does God's will remains forever* [I John 2:15-17].

Nebuchadnezzar's Dream [Daniel 2:31-45]

Daniel's Visions [Daniel 7:1-9]

Babylon is represented by the *head of pure gold* [7:4; see also 2:31-32,37-38; 7:17]. The head of gold in Nebuchadnezzar's dream was seen in Daniel's vision as a lion with eagle's wings. Both the head of gold and the lion represent Nebuchadnezzar, the king who conquered Israel, which represents the earthly Kingdom of God.

Medo-Persia is represented in Nebuchadnezzar's dream by the *chest and arms of silver* [7:5; see also 2:32,39; 7:17; 8:3-8; 11:1-2]. But, in Daniel's vision, they were seen as a bear with three ribs in its mouth. The bear was Medo-Persia.

Greece is represented in Nebuchadnezzar's dream by the *stomach and thighs of bronze* [7:6; see also 2:32, 39; 7:17; 8:5-8,21-22; 11:3-20]. In Daniel's vision, the stomach and thighs of bronze were seen instead as a leopard with four wings of a bird on its back. Like a leopard, Greece was swift in conquering the known world under the youthful Alexander the Great. In Daniel's second vision, he saw a ram and a he-goat [8:5-8]. The one-horned goat [Greece] trampled the ram [Medo-Persia] to pieces. After his death, Alexander's kingdom was divided among his four generals, represented by the four heads of the leopard.

Rome is represented by the *legs of iron* [7:7:8; see also 2:33,40-44; 7:23-24], which Daniel interpreted from Nebuchadnezzar's dream [2:33,40-43]. They were the two great divisions of Rome. They are seen in Daniel's vision as a dreadful beast with iron teeth, ten big horns and one little horn. After defeating Greece, Rome [the beast] was the fourth great empire to rule the world.

Revived from Rome [The New World Order] [10 toes *partly iron and partly fired clay*] [7:7:8; see also 2:33,40-44; 7:7-8, 23-24] -- This confederacy will consist of 10 kings. In his intent to destroy Christianity and rule the world, one day soon the antichrist [the little horn of 7:24] will defeat three of the ten kingdoms of this confederation. Ultimately, the New World Order, under the antichrist, will be destroyed by Jesus Christ [the Stone of 2:45] who will then set up His 1000 year earthly kingdom for Israel and all of His true followers.

In Today's Reading

Daniel rejects king's food; Nebuchadnezzar's dream interpreted by Daniel; Shadrach, Meshach, and Abednego saved out of fiery furnace.

Soon after their capture, Daniel and other selected Israelite captives were assigned new names which would identify them as citizens of Babylon. This was an attempt to remove their identities as children of God. The king's intent was that these select men be taught to think and live like Babylonians. Daniel means "God is my Judge," but his Babylonian name Belteshazzar means "Prince of Baal." As Daniel heard his name called day after day, it was intended to remind him that the comfort, self-esteem, and high position he enjoyed in his new society were all the results of his being the "Prince of Baal."

Nebuchadnezzar had dreams that disturbed him. . . . The king gave orders to . . . the . . . Chaldeans to tell the king his dreams. . . . The Chaldeans answered the king, No one on earth can disclose what the king requests (Daniel 2:1-2,10). But, after Daniel and his friends prayed, he said to the king: *There is a God in heaven who reveals mysteries, and He has let King Nebuchadnezzar know what will happen in future days* (2:18,28).

Daniel revealed to Nebuchadnezzar that the giant image in his dream represented kingdoms that would rule the world. Nebuchadnezzar was represented by the *head . . . of pure gold* (2:32). *Its chest and arms were silver* symbolizing the Medo-Persian Empire, which would become the next dominating world power. The Grecian Empire, represented by *its stomach and thighs were bronze* came next. The fourth empire, *its legs were iron, and its feet were partly iron and partly fired clay* (2:33), depicted the Roman Empire. It will be revived as a one-world government ruled by the antichrist, who will be destroyed at the return of Christ whose kingdom *will never be destroyed* (2:44).

Babylon and Jerusalem symbolize two diverse loyalties of which Scripture speaks – two gates, two ways, and two masters. Are we living according to God's word or the ways of this world? As Jesus said: *No one can be a slave of two masters, since . . . he will . . . be devoted to one and despise the other. You cannot be slaves of God and of money* (Matthew 6:24).

Thought for Today: Jesus holds today and all your tomorrows.

In Today's Reading

Nebuchadnezzar's second dream and Daniel's interpretation; Belshazzar's feast; Daniel in the lions' den.

Belshazzar was the last king to rule Babylon; he reigned near the end of the 70-year-long Jewish exile. On the night that the Medo-Persian army invaded Babylon to defeat and execute Belshazzar, he was celebrating a great feast with *a thousand of his nobles and drank wine . . . from the gold vessels that had been taken from the temple . . . in Jerusalem . . . and praised their gods made of gold and silver* (Daniel 5:1,3-4).

Suddenly the *fingers of a man's hand* (5:5) appeared and wrote on the wall. Belshazzar panicked *and his knees knocked together* (5:6). His astrologers and soothsayers could not interpret the message. In desperation, Belshazzar summoned Daniel, who appears to have been ignored by this king for perhaps ten years. Daniel boldly proclaimed: *This is the interpretation . . . God has numbered the days of your kingdom and brought it to an end* (5:23,26). That night *Darius the Mede received* (seized) *the kingdom* (5:31).

Darius decided to set 120 satraps (princes) *over the kingdom to rule over the whole realm. . . . Daniel distinguished himself above the 120 administrators* (6:1,3). In an effort to destroy him, they said to the king: *All the administrators . . . have agreed . . . that for 30 days, anyone who petitions any god or man except you the king, will be thrown into the lions' den. Therefore, O king, establish the edict . . . that it cannot be changed* (6:7-8).

Daniel could have reasoned that since he was not asked to worship an idol, why not cooperate or just pray in secret?

The document was signed. Daniel went into his house, opened the windows . . . and three times a day he knelt down on his knees, prayed, and gave thanks to his God, just as he had done before (6:10). We need to ask ourselves: "If a similar decree were issued today, would it make a difference if we were told that we could not read the word of God or could not attend church on the Lord's day?" Yes, Daniel ended up in the den of lions but, he could vigorously testify to the king: *My God sent His angel and shut the lions' mouths. They haven't hurt me* (Daniel 6:22).

Thought for Today: Pride blinds the mind to the will of God.

In Today's Reading

Daniel's vision of the beasts; vision of the ram and goat; Daniel's prayer for his people; vision of 70 weeks.

All the grandeur of Nebuchadnezzar's dream is later seen as selfish ambition and savage power by Daniel, who said: *In my vision . . . suddenly the four winds of heaven* (political and social forces) *stirred up the great sea* (Daniel 7:2). The *four winds* represented forces of selfish ambition and greed which blew in defiance of God and His elect. The great sea is humanity with its fierce competition and illustrates godless instability. *Four beasts* (nations of the world) *came up from the sea* (in succession) (7:3).

They correspond to the kingdoms of Babylon, Medo-Persia, Greece, and Rome. The first beast *was like a lion, but had eagle's wings* (7:4). The head of the great image was gold, so the lion represented the king among animals. *Behold another beast, a second, that looked like a bear* (7:5), represented the Medo-Persian Empire which conquered Babylon.

The third beast, *like a leopard with four wings of a bird on its back,* represented the Grecian Empire. The *four wings* illustrate the speed with which Alexander the Great conquered the ancient world. *It also had four heads* (7:6).

The fourth beast was *different from all the beasts before it, and it had ten horns*. This final beast was *frightening and dreadful, and incredibly strong, with large iron teeth. It devoured and crushed, and it trampled with its feet whatever was left* (7:7). This reveals ruthless expansion.The *ten horns* (7:24) correspond to the ten toes *on the feet* of Nebuchadnezzar's *colossal statue* and represent a confederation of ten world rulers.

Daniel stated: *While I was considering the horns, there was another horn . . . with . . . eyes like a man's, and it had a mouth that spoke arrogantly* (7:8, 23). This represents the antichrist who *will speak words against the Most High and oppress the holy ones of the Most High* (7:25).

The antichrist destroys everything that stands in his way in order to achieve his goal of world domination (I John 2:18-22; 4:3; II John 7). However, in the midst of extreme persecution, the stone (Jesus Christ) broke in pieces the giant image. We await the day with the apostle Paul *when He* (Christ) *comes to be glorified by His saints and to be admired by all those who have believed* (II Thessalonians 1:10).

Thought for Today: Satisfaction is living for Jesus.

In Today's Reading

Heavenly messenger detained; prophecy of kingdoms from Daniel to antichrist; great tribulation.

The kingdom of God and the kingdoms of this world are portrayed by Daniel as being in a constant state of conflict that eventually erupts into open hostility. Daniel recorded that, during the period of the Roman Empire, terrible persecution would take place.

Jesus speaks of an *abomination that causes desolation* that has yet to come (Mark 13:14). The most wicked of all antichrists is foretold: *The king . . . will exalt and magnify himself above every god, and he will say outrageous things against the God of gods. He will be successful until the time of wrath is completed, because what has been decreed will be accomplished* (Daniel 11:36).

There have been *many antichrists*, as the apostle John foretold (I John 2:18), and the driving force of all antichrists is to destroy the kingdom of God. *There will be a time of distress like no other since nations began. . . . But at that time your people will escape – all who are found written in the book. . . . Many will roam far and wide, and knowledge will increase* (Daniel 12:1,4). Knowledge has increased in our generation faster and far beyond that of all history. However, having rejected the Creator God, many still *roam far and wide* while they seek knowledge.

Daniel said: *I heard but did not understand. So I said, My lord, what will be the outcome of these things? He said, Daniel, go, for the words are secret and sealed until the appointed time* (12:8-9). Daniel admitted that there was much in his prophecy that he did not understand but he had the utmost assurance that God controls the future and that His people will reign with Him forever. A great peace of mind can rest within the hearts of the people of God, and *many will be purified, cleansed, and refined, but the wicked will act wickedly; none of the wicked will understand, but the wise will understand* (12:10). These closing chapters of Daniel's prophecy remind us to be prepared for the soon coming of Christ, when He shall reign and rule over all the world. *Since all these things are to be destroyed in this way, it is clear what sort of people you should be in holy conduct and godliness* (II Peter 3:11).

Thought for Today: There is no need to fear since our Creator loves us.

Introduction To The Book Of Hosea

Hosea lived in the northern kingdom of Israel and prophesied for about 50 years during the reigns of *Uzziah, Jotham, Ahaz, and Hezekiah, kings of Judah, and . . . Jeroboam son of Joash, king of Israel* (Hosea 1:1).

It appears that, during Hosea's ministry, the northern kingdom was experiencing material prosperity and an expansion of its territory. This was primarily due to the decline of Syria (Aram) and Moab, which resulted in the northern kingdom gaining control of the major east-west trade routes in the region. In the meantime, the golden calf worship centers, erected many years earlier in the cities of Bethel and Dan, had prepared the way for the immoral worship of Baal and Ashtoreth and Israel's spiritual corruption and decline (I Kings 12:28-32; also Hosea 2:13; 10:5-6; 13:2).

The Assyrian invasion took place while Hezekiah was king of Judah (Isaiah 36). Hosea fled to Judah after witnessing the destruction of the kingdom of Israel. He endured much pain and suffering and deep humiliation because of his unfaithful wife, Gomer. This illustrated how Israel had broken her covenant relationship with God, just as a wife who chooses other lovers is unfaithful to her mate in the marriage covenant (Hosea 2:7-13). Hosea's forgiving love toward his unfaithful wife and the res-toration of their marriage was an example to Israel of how God, in His mercy, would restore His blessings upon the nation, if only they would return to Him (2:8,15-16; 10:12; 11:8-9; 12:6; 14:1,4). The ten-tribe nation of Israel is called "Ephraim" more than 35 times because they were the largest tribe.

Some Christians have forsaken God and, like Israel, are guilty of spiritual hypocrisy (4:1-2), widespread adultery (4:2,11; 7:4), false dealings (10:4; 12:7), idolatry (4:12-13; 8:5; 10:1,5; 13:2), drunkenness (4:11; 7:5), and ignoring the word of God (4:4,10; 8:14). The history of Israel should serve as a warning to all of us.

Key Thought: *My people are destroyed for lack of knowledge! Because you have rejected knowledge, I will reject you from serving as My priest. Since you have forgotten the law of your God, I, on My part, will forget your children* ***(Hosea 4:6).***

In Today's Reading

Israel compared to an unfaithful wife; judgment upon adulterous Israel; Jehovah's withdrawal from His people; repentance urged.

Jeroboam II was king near the end of the northern kingdom's existence. He was followed by the brief reigns of Zachariah, Shallum, Menahem, Pekahiah, Pekah, and Hoshea. During that time, Hosea, Obadiah, Jonah, Amos, and, possibly, Joel were prophets.

Jeroboam II followed the evil example of Jeroboam I, the first king of the ten tribes of Israel which separated from the united kingdom following Solomon's death (I Kings 11:26-40; 12:2-20).

The moral and spiritual level of the Israelites had now become so low as to embrace sodomites (male cult prostitutes) and *all the abominations of the nations that the LORD had dispossessed* (from Canaan) (I Kings 14:24). Not one of the 19 kings of the northern kingdom of Israel attempted to lead the people to worship in Jerusalem as God had instructed Moses. It was under these circumstances that *the word of the LORD . . . came to Hosea . . . during the reign of . . . Jeroboam . . . king of Israel. . . . I will no longer have pity on the house of Israel that I should forgive them* (Hosea 1:1-6).

The Lord spoke against the people through Hosea, saying: *There is no integrity, no faithful love, and no knowledge of God in the land! Cursing, lying, murder, stealing, and adultery are rampant* (4:1-2). God revealed the consequences of their sin, saying: *My people are destroyed for lack of knowledge! Because you have rejected knowledge, I will reject you from serving as My priest. Since you have forgotten the law of your God, I, on My part, will forget your children* (4:6).

Israel's kings as well as their political and religious leadership refused to see the importance of obedience to the word of God. In His day, Jesus prayed: *This is eternal life: that they may know You, the only true God, and the One You have sent – Jesus Christ . . . . I have given them Your word. The world hated them . . . protect them from the evil one . . . . Sanctify them by the truth; Your word is truth* (John 17:3,14-15,17).

Thought for Today: True love for the Lord is expressed through us when we forgive those who offend us.

In Today's Reading

Israel's sin rebuked and captivity foretold;
Israel's immediate ruin but ultimate blessing.

The northern kingdom of Israel did *not return to the LORD their God or seek Him . . . Ephraim* (symbolic of the northern kingdom) *has become like a silly, senseless dove.They call to Egypt; they go to Assyria* (Hosea 7:10-11) for national security rather than trust the Lord according to His word. Nothing could have been more foolish than to seek help from Egypt, which had once cruelly enslaved them, or to make friends with ungodly Assyria, which would soon destroy them.

Israel's leaders had *gone up to Assyria . . . Israel has forgotten his Maker . . . they have . . . corrupted themselves . . . their glory will fly away like a bird . . . they will become wanderers among the nations* (8:9,14; 9:9,11,17). The Lord gave a heartrending plea for Israel to return to Him before they were destroyed: *It is time to seek the LORD until He comes to rain righteousness on you* (10:12). Feel God's heartbreak as He says: *I led them with . . . ropes of love* (11:4). He lovingly pleaded: *Return, Israel, to the LORD your God, for you have stumbled in your guilt* (14:1).

Israel had foolishly put its trust in other nations and false gods (5:13; 7:11; 8:9-10) and in its own strength (12:8), rather than in the One who is the only true Savior. Still, we see the willingness of the Lord to show mercy, as He always does to any repentant sinner, when He said: *I will heal their infidelity, I will love them freely* (14:4). The final words of the prophet Hosea before the Israelites were conquered by the Assyrians are a reminder to all of us: *Let whoever is wise understand these things and whoever is insightful recognize them, for the ways of the LORD are right, and the righteous walk in them, but the rebellious stumble in them* (14:9).

When we repent, turn from our sins, receive Jesus as our Savior, and let the indwelling Holy Spirit control our lives, we are freed from the power of Satan, sin, and spiritual death. *If we say, We have fellowship with Him, and walk in darkness, we are lying and are not practicing the truth. . . . I am writing you these things so that you may not sin. But if anyone does sin, we have an advocate with the Father – Jesus Christ the righteous One. He Himself is the propitiation* (atonement) *for our sins, and not only for ours, but also for those of the whole world* (I John 1:6; 2:1-2).

Thought for Today: Those who rejoice in the Lord can rejoice in tribulation.

Introduction To The Book Of Joel

The future end-time *day of the LORD* is mentioned five times in this book (Joel 1:15; 2:1,11,31; 3:14) and Judah is mentioned six times (3:1,6,8,18-20). But, since the ten-tribed northern kingdom is not mentioned, we assume that it had already been destroyed by the Assyrians and that Jerusalem was soon to face a similar destruction by the Babylonians.

Joel prophesied a warning to Jerusalem, of a coming national disaster, a result of the nation's departure from the word of God. Joel likened it to an invasion of locusts sweeping through the country, devouring the crops, stripping every leaf from the trees, and leading to a severe famine. He foretold of a *nation . . . powerful and beyond counting* (1:6). *It has devastated My grapevines and splintered My fig trees. It has stripped off their bark and thrown it away; their branches have turned white . . . cut off from the house of the LORD* (1:7,9). The invaders are *a great and mighty people* (2:2). As with most prophecies, there was a local application as well as a future one. Joel stated that *such as never existed in ages past nor will again in the years of coming generations* (2:2). That nation would invade the land and leave *behind them . . . a desert wasteland; there is no escape from them* (2:3). Because of the impending doom, the Lord appealed to the nation to repent: *return to Me with all your heart* (2:12). To ignore the Lord's appeal, they would face the invasion that would inevitably come (2:20) and destroy the nation of Judah.

The prophet also foretold of that future *day of the LORD* (2:11) when God would pour out His *Spirit on all humanity* (2:28). We are now living in the *last days,* which began on the day of Pentecost when *they were all filled with the Holy Spirit* (Acts 2:4,17). Peter then openly declared: *This is what was spoken through the prophet Joel* (2:16).

Joel's prophecy foretells the time of the Lord's judgment, saying: *I will gather all the nations and take them down to the valley of Jehoshaphat* (Joel 3:2). Many scholars believe that this *valley* is located on the eastern side of Jerusalem, known as the Kidron Valley, as well as the *valley of verdict* (decision) (3:14). Soon, the nations that oppose the kingdom of God will assemble for war; but it will be their final day of judgment. Jesus, the Prince of Peace, will bring an end to all wars and begin His glorious reign of peace: *Jerusalem will be holy, and foreigners will never overrun it again . . . for the LORD dwells in Zion* (3:17,21).

In Today's Reading

Plague of locusts; Joel's call to repentance; day of the Lord; the Holy Spirit; restoration of Israel; judgment on nations.

Joel warned of the impending destruction of Jerusalem. In mercy, *the word of the LORD . . . came to Joel . . . . Blow a horn in Zion! Sound the battle cry on My holy mountain* (Joel 1:1; 2:1). The trumpet was often used for religious purposes to call the congregation together, to announce solemn days and festivals, and by watchmen to warn of approaching danger (Numbers 10:1-10). In this instance, the trumpet was used to warn of a great enemy army. But, the sins of the enemies from within Israel were even more serious. *The day of the LORD is coming. . . . A day of darkness and gloom . . . there is no escape from them. . . . Even now . . . return to Me with all your heart, with fasting, weeping, and lamenting* (Joel 2:1-12).

The one indispensable condition for forgiveness and acceptance by the Lord is genuine repentance. True repentance is threefold. First, it is a sorrow for one's sin against God, as well as against others; second, it is a turning to the Lord, asking His forgiveness for all sins; and third, it is forsaking sin to live a life pleasing to Jesus Christ as Savior and Lord.

Peter preached the prophetic meaning of Joel's words, saying: *Whoever calls on the name of the Lord will be saved* (Acts 2:21). He concluded his message by saying: *Repent . . . and be baptized, each of you, in the name of Jesus the Messiah for the forgiveness of your sins, and you will receive the gift of the Holy Spirit. For the promise is for you and for your children, and for all who are far off* (2:38-39). We are among those *who are far off*; and the invitation and promise issued by Peter is still open to all.

The prophet Joel also foretold of the final *day of the LORD* that is yet to take place: *Alas for the day! For the day of the LORD is near and will come as devastation from the Almighty* (Joel 1:15). It will bring to a close the miserable rule of sinful mankind and finally usher in the glorious reign of Jesus, the righteous King of Peace.

Jesus spoke of that time triumphantly: *They will see the Son of Man coming on the clouds of heaven with power and great glory* (Matthew 24:30).

Thought for Today: The Holy Spirit works in our lives to the extent that we yield to His will as revealed in His word.

Introduction To The Book Of Amos

Amos was not a priest, nor was he trained in the prophetic schools; he was merely a shepherd and a caretaker of sycamore (fig) trees near the small mountain village of Tekoa. But, in obedience to the word of God, he became a prophet (Amos 1:1; 7:14). Tekoa was located about 10 miles south of Jerusalem, in the area known as the wilderness of Judea, in the southern kingdom of Judah. However, God called Amos to preach in the northern kingdom of Israel (1:1; 3:9; 7:7-17). In obedience to this call, Amos traveled north about 22 miles to Bethel, the southern location of Israel's two golden calf worship centers. He then boldly denounced their religious idolatry and social evils (2:6-8; 3:9-10; 4:1-5).

The prophecy of Amos seems to have been proclaimed *in the* (city) *gate* (5:10,12,15), a city's center of business and administration and the site where the elders judged the people (Jeremiah 17:19; 19:2-3). It was at this place that the Lord spoke through Amos, saying: *Seek Me . . . the LORD . . . that you may live* (Amos 5:4,6,14). If they continued to disregard God's word, they were told the destruction of the kingdom would be inevitable: *She* (Israel) *has fallen* (5:1-6). During this time, Uzziah was king of Judah, Jeroboam II was king of Israel, and the prophets Micah, Isaiah, Hosea, and Jonah were prominent. Both kingdoms were prospering materially and militarily (II Chronicles 26:1-16; II Kings 14:23,25), but their prosperity and success only led to more immorality and injustice.

Nothing looked more unlikely to be fulfilled than the warnings of this country herdsman; but, according to the prophetic word of God, about 30 years later, in 722 BC, the northern kingdom of Israel was invaded and destroyed by the Assyrians.

Does thy sacrifice seem useless
As you humbly serve the Lord?
Yes, to one who is most faithless
And ignores His Holy Word.

But to one who really knows Him
And His mighty Word of power
Nothing his sight of faith can dim
Even in the trying hour.

- M. E. H.

In Today's Reading

Judgments pronounced on Judah, Israel, and surrounding nations; Jehovah's sorrow over Israel's future captivity.

Amos was only a farm laborer from the village of Tekoa in Judah, but he was willing to speak for God against sin even beyond the borders of the southern kingdom. He delivered his prophecy of impending judgment in Bethel, the site of one of the two false worship centers and one of several residences of King Jeroboam II in the northern kingdom of Israel. This took place at a time when the northern kingdom was prospering and expanding its boundaries. Since the people of Israel were proud of their prosperity, it must have seemed ridiculous to hear this "outsider" shout: *Hear this word the LORD has spoken against you, Israelites . . . I will punish you for all your sins. . . . A foe will surround the land; he will tear away your strongholds, and your citadels will be plundered* (Amos 3:1-2,11). Because of their sins, destruction was inevitable. But, Amos' message concerning the judgment of God was ignored (2:6-8; 5:11-12).

Amaziah, the non-Levitical paid priest of King Jeroboam II, was quick to get word to the king about this disagreeable prophet from the southern kingdom. He interpreted the words of Amos to mean that Jeroboam would die by the sword; but the prophet had only stated what God had said: *I will rise against the house of Jeroboam with a sword. . . . Amaziah said to Amos, Go, seer! Flee to the land of Judah* (7:9-12). The prophecy was fulfilled when Zachariah, Jeroboam's son, was assassinated by Shallum after reigning only six months. Shallum took his place, but he only reigned for one month before he, in turn, was murdered by Menahem (II Kings 15:8-10,13-14).

God often uses ordinary people like Amos to proclaim His message. It is not what we possess in talents, or how popular we may be, but how obedient we are that qualifies us to be used by the Lord.

Consider your calling: not many are wise from a human perspective, not many powerful, not many of noble birth. Instead . . . God has chosen the world's insignificant . . . things . . . viewed as nothing . . . so that no one can boast in His Presence (I Corinthians 1:26-29).

Thought for Today: The Holy Spirit will provide His strength in anyone who willingly yields to Him.

Introduction To The Book Of Obadiah

Obadiah is the shortest book in the Old Testament. His twofold subject is the punishment of God upon Edom and the ultimate establishment of the kingdom of God on earth.

The territory of Edom extended south, below the Dead Sea, and along the Arabah (a desert plain). The land of Edom was also called Mount Seir because of the rugged range of mountains that dominated it, chief of which was Mount Seir. The mountains jutted upward about 3500 feet above the desert floor and more than 4500 feet above sea level. Edom's capital was the illustrious red-rock city of Sela, or Petra, which was situated securely in the midst of limestone mountain peaks. It was considered very secure because of the narrow passageway through the rocky mountain that led into Petra. Edom's fortified cities were located on an important caravan route between Egypt, in the south, and Syria (Aram), Assyria, and others, in the north.

The prophet foretold the destruction of the Edomites, who had followed their ancestor Esau's example of disregarding godly values and of intense hatred toward the Israelites. The Edomites had aided Nebuchadnezzar in destroying Jerusalem when they should have shown compassion and protected the Israelites, since both were descendants of Abraham and Isaac (Obadiah 1:10; Deuteronomy 23:7). Obadiah warned of the certain and impartial judgment of God on all who oppose Him and His people.

Tomorrow he promised his conscience,
Tomorrow I mean to believe.
Tomorrow I'll live as I ought to;
Tomorrow my Savior receive.

Tomorrow, tomorrow, tomorrow
Thus day after day it went on.
Tomorrow, tomorrow, tomorrow
Till youth like a vision had gone.

Till age in its passion had written
The message of fate on his brow,
And forth from the shadows of death
Came that pitiful syllable, now.

– M. E. H.

In Today's Reading

Woe pronounced upon sin; the grasshoppers; fire; plumbline; basket of summer fruit; famine of God's word.

The Edomites had been hostile to the Israelites for centuries because Esau (Edom) hated his brother Jacob (Israel) for his loss of the family birthright. The prophet Obadiah foretold the eventual triumph of Israel, as well as the complete destruction of Edom: *Because of the violence done to your brother Jacob, you will be covered with shame and destroyed forever . . . for the LORD has spoken* (Obadiah 1:10,18).

Esau had moved to Mount Seir where the Edomites, his descendants, felt secure in their mountain fortress. Their self-sufficiency and disinterest in God led them to ignore Obadiah's warning.

The Edomites conspired with Ammon and Moab against Judah and took Israelite captives. They also raided Judah in the days of King Ahaz to take even more captives to be their slaves (II Kings 8:20-22; II Chronicles 20:1-2, 22-23; 21:8-9,16-17; 28:16-17; Joel 3:3-8; Amos 1:6,9). When Jerusalem was destroyed by the Babylonian army, some of the Jewish escapees tried to flee out of the land; but, the Edomites took advantage of the fleeing Israelites and blocked roads, robbed them, and delivered the refugees to the Babylonians (Obadiah 1:12-14). Because of their treachery, God foretold that Edom would be utterly destroyed (1:9-10,18).

About four years after the fall of Jerusalem, Nebuchadnezzar's army swept through Ammon, Moab, and Edom. Edomite refugees fled to the western area of their country south of Judea. They then made incursions north into Judea, taking part of that land. This territory became known as Idumaea, from which came Herod, the Roman-appointed puppet king who sought to kill the child Jesus. Eventually, the Edomites disappeared from history, just as Obadiah had foretold. Unlike the prophecy against the Edomites, Obadiah foretold that Judah would recover and one day would *occupy their territorial possessions* (1:15-17).

The absolute justice of God and assurance of His faithfulness encourage us to know that the principles of right and wrong never change. Jesus expressed the inevitable spiritual law of God's kingdom: *Just as you want others to do for you, do the same for them* (Luke 6:31).

Thought for Today: When we give God the credit, pride for accomplishments does not exist.

Introduction To The Book Of Jonah

Jonah was a prominent prophet in the northern kingdom of Israel during the prosperous but evil reign of King Jeroboam II. Jonah foretold the great military success of Jeroboam over the Syrians (II Kings 14:25).

The book of Jonah is the historical account of the prophet's mission to Nineveh, the capital of Assyria and Israel's great enemy. Because of its great wickedness, at first Jonah failed to comply when God commanded him to prophesy its coming destruction. But, after a series of dramatic events, he reluctantly obeyed. Then he was unhappy when the king and the people of Nineveh repented and God, in His great mercy, withdrew His judgment from them. This book reveals that *God doesn't show favoritism* (Acts 10:34). His compassion extends toward all who repent, turn from their sins, and worship Him.

The book of Jonah reveals that God is concerned about Gentiles, as well as Jews, for both are eternally lost apart from faith in Jesus Christ, who proclaimed: *I am the way, the truth, and the life. No one comes to the Father except through Me* (John 14:6).

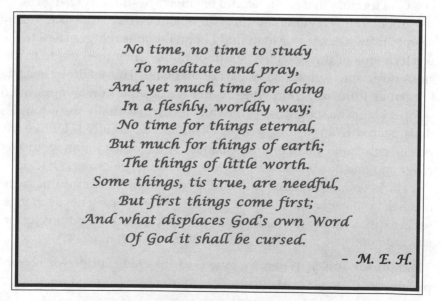

No time, no time to study
To meditate and pray,
And yet much time for doing
In a fleshly, worldly way;
No time for things eternal,
But much for things of earth;
The things of little worth.
Some things, tis true, are needful,
But first things come first;
And what displaces God's own Word
Of God it shall be cursed.

– M. E. H.

In Today's Reading

Jonah's effort to avoid God's will; His second commission; Nineveh repents; Jonah's displeasure.

The Lord directed Jonah: *Go to the great city of Nineveh and preach against it, because their wickedness has come up before Me. However, Jonah got up to flee to Tarshish away from the LORD's presence* (Jonah 1:2-3). Jonah was probably delighted with the good news that the judgment of God would soon fall upon Nineveh. Jonah could not believe the mercy and love of God would include even Israel's enemies. So, he decided not to be a missionary to Nineveh. He must have felt blessed by God when he discovered a ship sailing to Tarshish, the most remote of the Phoenician trading places, on the day he arrived in Joppa.

For a while, events seemed to favor Jonah's "vacation plan" and gave him such peace of mind that he was soon *into a deep sleep* on the ship (1:5). However, favorable circumstances in avoiding the will of God are only temporary and they never lead to a pleasant end. The sailors were filled with fear when a great storm arose. Upon hearing that Jonah was fleeing from God, he was thrown overboard, only to be swallowed by a big fish. After three days of soul searching, a repentant Jonah was vomited onto dry land by the great fish. He then became the greatest evangelist of his day, and saw the entire city of Nineveh repent of its wickedness. God could have chosen another prophet and let Jonah sink to the bottom of the sea, but God was merciful, demonstrating His love toward both the prophet and the repentant people in Nineveh. The willingness of God to forgive the greatest of sinners who repent was made known when Nineveh's king and his people repented and were spared from the destruction prophesied by Jonah.

Jesus confirmed the historic truth concerning Jonah, saying: *For as Jonah was in the belly of the great fish three days and three nights, so the Son of Man will be in the heart of the earth three days and three nights. The men of Nineveh will stand up at the judgment with this generation and condemn it, because they repented at Jonah's proclamation; and look – something greater than Jonah is here!* (Matthew 12:40-41).

Thought for Today: The one thing gained by ignoring God is trouble.

Introduction To The Book Of Micah

Micah was just a countryman who lived in a small village in Judea, about 25 miles southwest of Jerusalem near Gath (Micah 1:14). He prophesied during the reigns of kings Jotham, Ahaz, and Hezekiah of Judah. At the same time, Isaiah was a prominent prophet in Jerusalem. Micah exposed the sins of both the kingdoms of Judah and Israel, and boldly proclaimed the destruction of Israel (1:6-7), as well as of Jerusalem and the temple (3:12). He also foretold Judah's restoration. Undoubtedly, Hezekiah found the prophecies of Isaiah and Micah about the Israelites' promised restoration of great comfort (Isaiah 1:1; 62:1-12; Jeremiah 26:18; Micah 1:1; 7:11-20). Micah also gave a remarkable prophecy, not only that the Messiah would be born in *Bethlehem,* but also concerning His eternal existence (5:2).

Micah closes with a message of hope declaring the ultimate fulfillment of the covenant blessing God had promised to Abraham (7:20). Micah's prophecy confirms that God requires obedience to His word: *He has told you, O man, what is good* (a reference to Deuteronomy 10:12); *And what does the LORD require of you other than to act justly, to love faithfulness, and to walk humbly with your God?* (Micah 6:8).

"God's Holy Word has surely been
Inspired of God and not of men;
No power of eloquence of men
Could ere conceive God's wondrous plan.
Withstanding all the tests of time,
It stands unchanged, unique, sublime;
Proving to every tongue and race,
God's wisdom, mercy, love and grace.
So hammer on, ye hostile hands;
Your hammers break, God's anvil stands."

– M. E. H.

In Today's Reading

Impending judgment against Israel and Judah; future deliverance of a remnant; birth of Christ foretold; Lord's judgment and mercy.

Except for David, all the kings of Judah had been born in Jerusalem – the city of God. But, 700 years before Jesus was born, the prophet Micah was led to prophesy: *You, Bethlehem Ephrathah, so small to be among the clans of Judah, from you One will come on My behalf to be ruler over Israel. His origins are from antiquity, from ancient times* (Micah 5:2).

At the God-appointed time, *a decree went out from Caesar Augustus that the whole empire should be registered . . . . Joseph also went up from the town of Nazareth in Galilee, to Judea, to the city of David, which is called Bethlehem* (Luke 2:1,4). As a descendant of King David, Joseph had to go to David's hometown of Bethlehem to register. In issuing his command from Rome, Caesar could only have thought of his kingdom. However, the Sovereign God, who determines history, used the heathen emperor's authority to bring about the fulfillment of Micah's prophecy.

Perhaps the most significant statement of Micah's prophecy is: *Whose origins are from antiquity, from ancient times*. This clearly proclaims the deity and eternal existence of the Redeemer King. He could not be the Savior of mankind and suffer for the sins of the world if He had inherited a sinful nature like everyone else. Because of this, Jesus, the Son of God, was born of the virgin Mary without a human father. The angel Gabriel announced to Mary: *You will conceive and give birth to a son, and you will call His name JESUS. He will be great and will be called the Son of the Most High. . . . and His kingdom will have no end. Mary asked the angel, How can this be, since I have not been intimate with a man? The angel replied to her: The Holy Spirit will come upon you, and . . . overshadow you. Therefore the holy child to be born will be called the Son of God* (Luke 1:31-35).

Jesus never ceased being the Eternal God. However, *He emptied Himself by assuming the form of a slave, taking on the likeness of men* (Philippians 2:7). As descendants of Adam, we have inherited his sinful nature since *through one man's disobedience the many were made sinners, so also through the one man's obedience* (Jesus) *the many will be made righteous* (Romans 5:17-19).

Thought for Today: Wise men seek Jesus regardless of what others do.

Introduction To The Books Of Nahum & Habakkuk

Nahum probably lived just before the defeat of Assyria, possibly during the same period as Zephaniah. Both prophesied after Isaiah, toward the end of the reign of Judah's wicked King Jehoiakim, a godless king who led his nation down the path to destruction (II Kings 23:34 – 24:5; Jeremiah 22:17). Both prophets foretold the destruction of Nineveh, as a result of its cruelties, oppressions, adulteries, and witchcraft (Nahum 1:1,8; Zephaniah 2:13-15). Its destruction had been delayed about 150 years because of its repentance following Jonah's message of judgment (Jonah 3:5-10). Eventually, the people reverted to their wicked ways.

It appeared very unlikely that the powerful capital of the Assyrian Empire would ever cease to control the world because its heavily-fortified walls were surrounded by a moat.

The Assyrian Empire destroyed the northern kingdom of Israel in 722 BC but it was, in turn, conquered by the Babylonians within 50 years of Nahum's prophecy. As Nahum foretold, Assyria is extinct.

Habakkuk lived during the time Nebuchadnezzar was conquering the world. He probably prophesied in Judah during the later years of Josiah's rule and into the reign of King Jehoiakim. Unlike his godly father Josiah, Jehoiakim *did what was evil in the LORD's eyes* (II Kings 23:37). Habakkuk cried out against the moral corruption of idolatrous Judah that prevailed in his day. He foretold that God would permit the ruthless Babylonians to bring judgment upon Judah. During those horrifying experiences, *the righteous one will live by his faith,* became the watchword of the faithful (Habakkuk 2:4; Romans 1:17; Galatians 3:11; Hebrews 10:38).

Habakkuk encourages all believers to accept by faith every situation trusting that righteousness and justice will ultimately triumph according to the righteous judgment of the one true God.

My only hope, my only plea --
The Blood of Jesus shed for me;
His righteousness -- my only claim --
I come, dear Lord, in Jesus' Name.

- M. E. H.

In Today's Reading

Prophecy and fulfillment of Nineveh's destruction; vision of coming woes; Habakkuk's prayer.

About 150 years had passed since the revival of Jonah's day, when all of Nineveh repented and fasted (Jonah 3:5,10). As the years passed, the Ninevites failed to teach their children about the one true God who had spared their lives. They had long since returned to their sinful behavior. The time had now come for God to judge this wicked people. Oppressed by Assyria, the prophet Nahum foretold freedom to Judah, if they remained faithful to God. He appealed to them: *Judah, fulfill your vows. For the wicked one will never again march through you; he will be entirely wiped out* (Nahum 1:15).

Assyria was probably the most brutal of all the ancient heathen nations, and its capital Nineveh had enriched itself by wars. Through Nahum, God forewarned: *Woe to the bloodthirsty city, totally deceitful, full of plunder. . . . Nineveh is devastated . . . . the sword will cut you down* (3:1,7,15). Nineveh was destroyed exactly as foretold. That once-mighty city still lies in ruins as a witness to the word of God.

Habakkuk foretold the coming judgment that God would bring upon His idol-worshiping people in Judah by using Babylon to punish them. He also foretold the judgment of God upon Babylon for its destruction of Judah: *My Holy One . . . LORD, You appointed them* (the Babylonians) *for execution of justice; O Rock, You destined them to punish us* (Habakkuk 1:12; compare Romans 5:3; II Corinthians 4:17; Hebrews 2:10; 12:10-11).

In the midst of numerous, perplexing injustices where evil seems to triumph, since we do not know all the facts, we dare not express doubt in the *Holy One* (Habakkuk 1:12) by asking: "Why?" God is just as uncompromising toward sin today as He was then. Yet the Lord always forgives even the most sinful person who truly repents and turns to Him. All mankind will one day realize that the justice and mercy of *the LORD is good . . . He cares for those who take refuge in Him* (Nahum 1:7). *By . . . faith,* we expectantly look forward to a day when *the earth will be filled with the knowledge of the LORD's glory* (Habakkuk 2:4,14; compare Romans 1:17; Galatians 3:11; Hebrews 10:38; 11:1-6).

Thought for Today: Religious activity is no substitute for godly living.

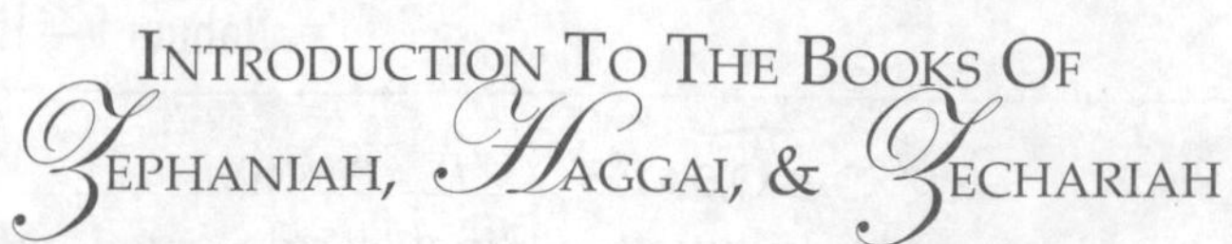

Introduction To The Books Of Zephaniah, Haggai, & Zechariah

Zephaniah, the only prophet of royal lineage, probably influenced his kinsman King Josiah in his godly reformation, which began in the 8th year of his reign in Judah (II Chronicles 34:3-7).

Zephaniah foretold the fall of Jerusalem perhaps 35 years before it took place (Zephaniah 1:4-13). He warned that *a day of wrath, a day of trouble and . . . desolation was imminent because they have sinned against the LORD* (1:15,17). The prophet then appealed to Judah to repent: *Seek the LORD, all you humble of the earth, who carry out what He commands* (2:3). In God's time, He would graciously restore the nation.

Zephaniah also prophesied that Christ would come in power and glory. Known as *the great day of the LORD* (1:7,14), it is referred to more than 15 times in these three chapters. The *day of the LORD* will be *a day of wrath* (1:15,18) upon all evildoers; but it will be a blessed "homecoming" for the faithful (3:14,17).

Zephaniah, Nahum, Habakkuk, and Jeremiah prophesied at the same time. The period of Israel's history in which they lived is recorded in the books of Ezra, Nehemiah, and Esther. They were among the last prophets who spoke for God before the 70-year Babylonian captivity.

Both Haggai and Zechariah were born in Babylon during the exile and went to Jerusalem some time after King Cyrus of Medo-Persia gave the decree to return and rebuild the temple. Haggai and Zechariah began preaching in Jerusalem about 14 years after the decree.

Zechariah joined Haggai in encouraging the Jews to give first priority to their spiritual responsibility to rebuild the temple: *So the elders of the Jews went on successfully with the building under the prophesying of Haggai the prophet and Zechariah. They finished the building according to the command of the God of Israel* (Ezra 6:14) in about four years. It was the preaching of the word of God that turned the Israelites from an attitude of indifference toward spiritual needs to a willingness to carry out the will of the Lord. The turning point in anyone's life is the moment he realizes the power of God's word.

The *Angel of the LORD* (Zechariah 1:11-12; 3:1,5-6; 12:8) is prominent in this book. Zechariah foretold more about Christ than any other prophet except Isaiah. (Note 3:8; 9:9,16; 11:11-13; 12:10; 13:1,6.) The second coming of Christ is foretold in 6:12 and 14:3-21.

In Today's Reading

The Lord's judgment; future destruction of the gentile nations; the people urged to rebuild the temple; unfaithfulness reproved.

The Israelites who had returned from Persia with Zerubbabel started to rebuild the temple in Jerusalem with great enthusiasm. But, there was great opposition by Samaritan enemies. They also began building their own homes and working long hours in the fields, which contributed to their failure to put God first in their lives. No doubt, many "legitimate excuses" were given as to why the construction of the temple ceased.

As the people built their homes and developed their businesses, time to rebuild the temple looked hopeless. Zerubbabel must have been discouraged as he thought of how much there was to do, how few willing workers there were, and how threatening the opposition was. While the Israelites continued to hope for better times, about 14 years passed and nothing more was accomplished for the Lord.

Then God moved upon the prophet Haggai to proclaim *the word of the LORD*. Two months later, Zechariah also began proclaiming *the word of the LORD* (Ezra 5:1; Haggai 1:3-11).

Haggai first announced: *This is what the LORD of Hosts says: These people say, The time has not yet come . . . for the house of the LORD to be rebuilt. The word of the LORD came through Haggai . . . Is it time for you . . . to live in your paneled houses, while this house* (of the Lord) *lies in ruins? Think carefully . . . You have planted much but harvested little* (1:2-6).

Upon hearing *the word of the LORD*, the people renewed their interest in building the temple, the one place designated by God for His people to worship Him. This time they ignored the threats of their enemies and *the elders of the Jews went on successfully with the building* (Ezra 6:14); and the temple was completed in just four years.

Without *the word of the LORD* as a standard, we subsequently fall prey to deception. Reading the word of God renews our love for His word and imparts spiritual strength needed to put Him first in our lives.

I will not leave you as orphans; I am coming to you. . . . the Counselor, the Holy Spirit, whom the Father will send in My name, will teach you all things and remind you of everything I have told you (John 14:18,26).

Thought for Today: Today, let us speak to someone about the Lord.

In Today's Reading

High priest resisted; Zechariah's visions of the lampstand, flying scroll, four chariots; disobedience resulting in captivity.

Zechariah foretold the glorious promise of the presence of God and inspired the Israelites to *shout for joy and be glad . . . for I am coming to dwell among you, declares the LORD* (Zechariah 2:10).

Zechariah prophesied the restoration of the Jewish nation as well as declaring: *Many nations* (Gentiles) *will join themselves to the LORD on that day and become My people. I will dwell among you* (2:11).

Usually we come to the end of our resources and lose confidence in our own abilities before we learn to trust in the Lord. It was at just such a time that an angel said to Zechariah: *This is the word of the LORD to Zerubbabel: Not by strength or by might, but by My Spirit, says the LORD of Hosts. What are you, great mountain* (of human obstacles such as Syria (Aram), Babylonia, and Egypt)? *Before Zerubbabel you will become a plain* (4:6-7).

Zerubbabel, governor of Judah (Haggai 1:1), was told to rebuild the temple. Joshua (not Joshua of conquest) was the high priest (3:1). These two are types of our Lord as both king and priest (Matthew 2:2; Hebrews 5:1-10).

The work of God is not accomplished *by strength,* nor *by might,* meaning our human power, zeal, or finances; *but by My Spirit, says the LORD of Hosts*. The indwelling presence of the Holy Spirit is indispensable in living a true Christian life. *Yes, He . . . will sit on His throne and rule. There will also be a priest on His throne, and there will be peaceful counsel between the two of them. . . . People who are far off will come and build the LORD's temple, and you will know that the LORD of Hosts has sent Me to you. This will happen when you fully obey the LORD your God* (Zechariah 6:13,15).

Zechariah foretold the rejection of Jesus, His second coming and millennial reign. After His resurrection, Jesus said to His disciples: *believe in your hearts all that the prophets have spoken! . . . beginning with Moses and all the Prophets, He interpreted for them in all the Scriptures the things concerning Himself* (Luke 24:13-27).

Thought for Today: The Lord Jesus will return *to be admired by all those who have believed* (II Thessalonians 1:10).

In Today's Reading

Restoration of Jerusalem promised; judgment on neighboring nations; Zion's future King and Jerusalem's future deliverance.

Although his prophetic message was fulfilled centuries later, in great anticipation Zechariah proclaimed: *Rejoice greatly! . . . Shout in triumph, Daughter Jerusalem! See, your King is coming to you; He is righteous and victorious, humble and riding on a . . . colt, the foal of a donkey* (Zechariah 9:9). This prophecy was fulfilled as Jesus entered Jerusalem during the last week before His crucifixion. *A very large crowd. . . . kept shouting, Hosanna to the Son of David! Blessed is He who comes in the name of the Lord! Hosanna in the highest heaven!* (Matthew 21:8-9). The cry of *Hosanna* by the people (meaning "save us") was rejected by the jealous religious leaders who, instead, insisted that He be crucified (Mark 15:13).

Zechariah also foretold details concerning Judas, Jesus' betrayer, and his transactions with the religious leaders, saying: *Then I said to them, If it seems right to you, give me my wages; but if not, keep [them]. So they weighed my wages, 30 pieces of silver* (just as prophesied) (Zechariah 11:12). Jesus, the true King of kings, was rejected and betrayed for a mere *30 pieces of silver* just as prophesied (Exodus 21:32; compare Matthew 26:15). Israel will soon recognize its Messiah as Zechariah foretold: *Then I will pour out the Spirit of grace and supplication on the house of David and the residents of Jerusalem, so that they will look at Me whom they pierced. They will mourn . . . and weep bitterly for Him as one weeps for a firstborn* (Zechariah 12:10; compare Romans 11:26-27).

Zechariah foretold the end of this present sinful and chaotic age: *A day of the LORD is about to come. . . . I will gather all the nations against Jerusalem for battle. . . . Then the LORD will go out to fight against those nations. . . . On that day His feet will stand on the Mount of Olives, which lies to the east of Jerusalem. . . . The LORD will become king over all the earth. On that day He will be the only LORD* (Zechariah 14:1-4,9).

We are all prone to waste time speculating on future events and forget what Jesus said to His disciples when they asked: *Lord, at this time are You restoring the kingdom to Israel? He said to them, It is not for you to know times or periods that the Father has set . . . But . . . be My witnesses in Jerusalem, in all Judea and Samaria, and to the ends of the earth* (Acts 1:6-8).

Thought for Today: Where God guides He provides.

Introduction To The Book Of Malachi

It is unknown at what time Malachi prophesied. But, it is certain that Malachi's desire was for the Israelites to renew their covenant relationship with God. A spirit of worldliness prevailed among the Israelites just as it does in our communities today. Malachi pointed out the sins that separated the Israelites from experiencing the blessings of God and appealed to them to repent (Malachi 3:7).

In chapter 1, Malachi first pleaded with Israel to return in full repentance to the Lord who loved them. Then, in chapter 2, he appealed to the priests, pointing out their hypocrisy. And, in chapter 3, he prophesied the coming Messiah probably 400 years before the Christian era: *See, I am about to send my messenger* (John the Baptist)*, and he will clear the way before Me. And . . . the LORD whom you seek . . . shall come* (3:1). Finally, like other prophets before him, Malachi foretold *the coming of the great and terrible day of the LORD* (4:5), when *all the arrogant and every doer of wickedness* will be destroyed. *But for you who fear My name* (Son of God) *Sun of righteousness will rise with healing in its* (His) *wings* (4:1-2).

Perhaps you've often wondered why
Sore trials came your way,
Or murmured when dark clouds of grief
Obscured the light of day.

God says the trial of your faith
More precious is than gold;
And He'll reward His servants true
With blessings manifold.

So trust in Him, His Word is sure
And infinite His Love;
Oh, child of God, press on in faith –
Your Father reigns Above.

– M. E. H.

In Today's Reading

The Lord's love for Jacob; the sins of the priests; Israel's unfaithfulness rebuked; the day of the Lord and final judgment.

The first generation of Israelites that returned to Jerusalem with Zerubbabel to rebuild the temple was dead, and the following generations had lost sight of the purpose God had for them as His people.

Malachi declared that God may not always be fully understood, but He will only be questioned by those who reject or neglect His word: *If you don't take this warning to heart to give honor to My name, says the LORD of Hosts, I will send the curse upon you* (Malachi 2:2).

Malachi left no room for excuses when he declared that the Israelites were thieves. He boldly asked: *Should a man rob God? Yet you are robbing Me. . . . In the tithe and the contribution* (3:8). He then pronounced the inevitable judgment of God: *Even though you are suffering the effects of the curse, nevertheless the whole nation of you continues to rob Me* (3:9).

The people were *suffering the effects of the curse* because the tithes belonged to God for the spiritual needs of the people and the support of the priesthood. They failed to *honor the LORD with . . . the first produce of your entire harvest* (Proverbs 3:9; Exodus 22:29; II Chronicles 31:5).

Returning one-tenth of all our income to God expresses our faith that all we are and have belongs to the Lord and tithing demonstrates our love and gratitude to Him as our Savior and Lord.

More than 500 years before the law was given, tithing was introduced by Abraham, *the father of all who believe* (Romans 4:11), who brought *a tenth of everything . . . to a priest of God Most High* (Genesis 14:18,20). To refuse to return *to God the things that are God's* (Matthew 22:21) is to keep for ourselves what God has said is for proclaiming the gospel of Christ. Is it greed, selfishness, indifference, or just a refusal to be obedient to what the word of God clearly states? The seriousness of this sin can be seen in the severity of the famine they were experiencing: *You are suffering the effects of the curse* (Malachi 3:9).

The Christian is to give *as he has decided in his heart – not out of regret or out of necessity, for God loves a cheerful giver* (II Corinthians 9:7).

Thought for Today: Faith is demonstrated by obedience to the will of God.

Introduction To The Book Of Matthew

The gospel of Matthew was written by a Jew who was also known as Levi (Mark 2:14; Luke 5:27). Matthew presents Jesus as the fulfillment of all Messianic prophecy. In the opening sentence, we read: *The historical record of Jesus Christ, the Son of David, the Son of Abraham* (Matthew 1:1).

Matthew identifies Jesus as the prophesied Messiah-King. *Son of Abraham* associates Him with the covenant that God had made with Abraham, saying: *All the peoples on earth will be blessed through you* (Genesis 12:3; 17:7; II Samuel 7:8-17). *All the peoples on earth* includes both Jew and Gentile.

Since the focus of Old Testament Scripture is on the coming of the promised Messiah and His kingdom, Matthew used the phrase *kingdom of heaven* more than 30 times, *Son of David* 10 times, and *that it might be fulfilled which was spoken* 16 times. As confirmation of the Messiahship of Jesus, the Holy Spirit led Matthew to record more than 20 of His miracles. Matthew has 60 references to Christ Jesus and records seven parables of Jesus that begin with the phrase: *The kingdom of heaven is like* (Matthew 13:24,31,33,44-45,47,52; 20:1; 22:2; 25:1,14).

The Sanhedrin kept complete genealogical archives of the descendants of Abraham and David. These enemies of Christ never questioned Jesus' ancestry. Both Joseph's and Mary's genealogies are the same from Abraham to David. Then Joseph's genealogy follows through Solomon while Mary's traces from Nathan, another of David's sons.

To remove all doubt as to who Jesus is, Matthew records that when Jesus was baptized *there came a voice from heaven: This is My beloved Son. I take delight in Him!* (3:17). Sometime later, Matthew also records the spectacular transfiguration of Christ during His conversation with Moses and Elijah, when *a voice from the cloud said: This is My beloved Son. . . . Listen to Him!* (17:2-5). This completed Jesus' Galilean ministry. He traveled south toward Jerusalem where He then would be *crucified, and . . . be resurrected on the third day* (20:19).

It was on the Mount of Olives (28:16; Luke 24:50), 40 days after His resurrection, that Jesus told His disciples: *Go . . . make disciples of all nations, baptizing them in the name of the Father and of the Son and of the Holy Spirit, teaching them to observe everything I have commanded you* (Matthew 28:19-20).

In Today's Reading

Ancestry of Jesus; His birth; wise men; flight into Egypt; ministry of John; baptism of Jesus; temptation by Satan; first apostles called.

The birth of Jesus Christ came about this way: After His mother Mary had been engaged to Joseph, before they came together, she was found to be with child by the Holy Spirit (Matthew 1:18).

The amazing *wise men from the east,* perhaps from Babylon, were led by a star *to Jerusalem,* where they inquired: *Where is He who has been born King of the Jews? For we saw His star in the east and have come to worship Him* (2:1-2). It is probable that these men had studied the prophecies of Daniel who, during the captivity, gave detailed explanation of the number of years before the Messiah would be born (Daniel 9:25-26).

It took the *wise men* some length of time after the birth of Christ to arrive in Bethlehem since we read: *Entering the house, they saw the child with Mary His mother, and falling to their knees, they worshiped Him* (Matthew 2:11). Finding the newborn King in *the house* as a *young child* rather than a babe in the manger indicates several months or more had passed after the birth of Jesus in a Bethlehem manger.

The *wise men* had *come to worship Him* (2:2). Their worship included three gifts (2:11). First, they offered *gold,* the most fitting gift for *the King of kings, and the Lord of lords* (I Timothy 6:15). Then, they offered *frankincense,* a sweet perfume used on the altar of incense in the temple, symbolic of prayer ascending to God. It was a fitting gift for a priest, for this King would also be our *High Priest* (Hebrews 4:14) who *intercedes for us* (Romans 8:34) before God. They also offered *myrrh,* which signified that He was destined to die; myrrh was often used as a burial spice (John 19:39).

In the providence of God, their gifts also provided adequate resources for Joseph and Mary's journey and stay in Egypt. Mary and Joseph remained in Egypt *until Herod's death, so that what was spoken by the Lord through the prophet might be fulfilled: Out of Egypt I called My Son* (Matthew 2:15; Hosea 11:1). Then they *settled . . . in Nazareth* (where Jesus lived until He was about 30 years old) (Matthew 2:23).

Thought for Today: It takes genuine love and dedication to willingly sacrifice time and treasure to the Lord.

In Today's Reading

Sermon on the Mount; the Beatitudes; believers likened to salt and light; Jesus' teaching on the law, divorce, oaths, giving, fasting.

Following His baptism in the Jordan River, *Jesus was led up by the Spirit into the wilderness to be tempted by the Devil. And after He had fasted 40 days and 40 nights, He was hungry. Then the tempter* (Satan) *approached Him and said, If You are the Son of God, tell these stones to become bread* (Matthew 4:1-3). The word *tempt* carries the thought "to test." Such testing is a necessary part of our lives for it reveals our true character. First, the Devil suggested an easy, self-serving way in which Jesus might achieve His goal: *If* (since) *You are the Son of God, tell these stones to become bread,* meaning: "Surely You can use Your abilities to satisfy Your hunger (lust of the flesh)." But Jesus, knowing obedience to the word of God must be the basis for all decisions, quoted Scripture saying: *It is written: Man must not live on bread alone, but on every word that comes from the mouth of God* (4:4; Deuteronomy 8:3). The abilities that God has bestowed upon us are meant to be used for His honor and glory, but many are seduced by Satan's deception to use them to satisfy self.

Satan's second temptation came in *the holy city . . . on the pinnacle of the temple* (Matthew 4:5). Satan suggested that Jesus should leap down into the midst of the people and present Himself as a super-human Messiah (pride of life). Satan quoted Scripture to support this temptation, saying: *He will give His angels orders concerning you . . . so that you will not strike your foot against a stone* (Psalms 91:11-12). The Devil frequently appears very religious by quoting Scripture, but only the portion which fits his scheme. Jesus responded: *You must not tempt the Lord your God* (Matthew 4:7).

In Satan's final attempt to seduce Jesus to sin, he *showed Him all the kingdoms of the world. . . . And he said . . . I will give You all these things if You will fall down and worship me* (4:8-9). The Devil suggested an easy way in which Jesus might avoid all the pain and suffering of the cross and yet rule *all the kingdoms of the world*. Jesus' reply was: *You must worship the Lord your God. . . . serve Him only* (4:10). Jesus is our example: *Just as the Father taught Me . . . I always do what pleases Him* (John 8:28-29).

Thought for Today: The poor in spirit are rich in God.

Old Testament Quoted by Christ – Partial List

Matthew	Old Testament Passage	Occasion
4:4	Deut. 8:3	40-Day Temptation
4:7	Deut. 6:16	
4:10	Deut. 6:13	
5:21	Ex. 20:13; Deut. 5:17	Sermon on the Mount
5:27	Ex. 20:14; Deut. 5:18	
5:31	Deut. 24:1	
5:33	Lev. 19:12; Num. 30:2; Deut. 23:21	
5:38	Ex. 21:24; Lev. 24:20; Deut. 19:21	
5:43	Lev. 19:18; Deut. 23:6; 25:19	
9:13	Hos. 6:6	Response to His Critics
11:10	Mal. 3:1	Concerning John
12:7	Hos. 6:6	Response to His Critics
13:14-15	Isa. 6:9-10	Why Speaks in Parables
15:4	Ex. 20:12; 21:17; Lev. 20:9; Deut. 5:16	Response to His Critics
15:7-9	Isa. 29:13	Response to His Critics
19:4-5	Gen. 1:27; 2:24	Sacredness of Marriage; Response to His Critics
21:16	Psa. 8:2	Triumphal Entry
21:42,44	Psa. 118:22-23	"Builders" Rejected
27:46	Psa. 22:1	On the Cross

Mark	Old Testament Passage	Occasion
7:6-7	Isa 29:13	Sermon on the Mount
7:10	Ex. 20:12; 21:17; Lev. 20:9; Deut. 5:16	
10:16	Gen. 1:27	Response to His Critics
10:7-8	Gen. 2:24	Response to His Critics
12:29-30	Deut. 6:4-5	Response to His Critics
12:36	Psa. 110:1	Teaching Concerning David's Son

Luke	Old Testament Passage	Occasion
4:4	Deut. 8:3	40-Day Temptation
4:8	Deut. 6:13	
4:12	Deut. 6:16	
4:18-19	Isa. 61:1-2	Nazareth Synagogue
7:27	Mal. 3:1	Concerning John
19:46	Isa. 56:7	The Temple Cleansing
23:46	Psa. 31:5	On the Cross

John	Old Testament Passage	Occasion
6:45	Isa. 54:13	Response to His Critics
8:17	Deut. 17:6	Response to His Critics
10:34	Psa. 82:6	Response to His Critics
15:25	Psa. 35:19; 69:4	Last Supper

In Today's Reading

Conclusion of the Sermon on the Mount; preaching and miracles of Jesus; call of Matthew.

Jesus warned: *Beware of false prophets . . . in sheep's clothing* (Matthew 7:15). Teaching is false when it offers eternal life without discipleship or when it says good works qualify a person for heaven. To clarify the difference between true prophets and false prophets, our Lord said: *Not everyone who says to Me, Lord, Lord! will enter the kingdom of heaven, but the one who does the will of My Father in heaven. On that day many will say to Me, Lord, Lord, didn't we prophesy in Your name, drive out demons in Your name, and do many miracles in Your name? Then I will announce to them, I never knew you!* (7:21-23). The evidence of being a true Christian is more than doing great things; it is desiring to be obedient to the Lord Jesus Christ.

Our Lord spoke a parable: *Therefore, everyone who hears these words of Mine and acts on them will be like a sensible man who built his house on the rock. The rain fell, the rivers rose, and the winds blew and pounded that house. Yet it didn't collapse, because its foundation was on the rock. But everyone who hears these words of Mine and doesn't act on them will be like a foolish man who built his house on the sand. The rain fell, the rivers rose, the winds blew and pounded that house, and it collapsed. And its collapse was great!* (7:24-27).

Obedience is twofold: first, one *hears these words of Mine,* then acts on *these words of Mine*. The wise and the foolish are both giving much thought and labor to their activities – one to laying up treasures in heaven, but the other to achieving human goals. When our desire is to please Christ, His word will be our supreme rule of life and lead us to avoid the snares of self-will, pride, and greed. Through His word alone, guided by the Holy Spirit, we are enabled to live accountable to our Creator.

It is impossible to relive the wasted years, but it is possible to turn from sinking sand to build upon the eternal rock. *No one can lay any other foundation than what has been laid - that is, Jesus Christ. If anyone builds on the foundation . . . each one's work will become obvious . . . because it will be revealed by fire; the fire will test the quality of each one's work* (I Corinthians 3:11-13).

Thought for Today: Having the mind of Christ purifies our thoughts.

In Today's Reading

Mission of the 12 apostles; John the Baptist's questions; Jesus pronounces judgment on unrepentant cities; great invitation.

Jesus *said to His disciples, the harvest is abundant, but the workers are few. Therefore, pray to the Lord of the harvest to send out workers into His harvest* (Matthew 9:36-38). In answer to this prayer, Jesus chose just 12 ordinary men whom he taught, saying: *I am sending you out like sheep among wolves. Therefore be as shrewd as serpents and harmless as doves* (10:16-17). Wolves are the natural enemy of sheep. Although "wolves" (false prophets) in human form sometimes appear to be *sheep* (7:15), beneath their surface, the hostility against Christ and His word is apparent. Like Satan (4:5-6), they only quote the few verses that support their agenda.

The Christian is given a "sheep-like" nature, symbolic of innocence, not cowardice. Sheep, by their very nature, are in need of a shepherd or they will wander off and easily become prey. Still worse, if one wanders, the entire flock may follow aimlessly. There is never safety in numbers for sheep; a shepherd is always necessary. *All of us like sheep* (Isaiah 53:6) need the *Good Shepherd* (John 10:11,14) to be our Overseer.

With Christ, the Christian can stand boldly in the face of the fiercest enemy. He assured us: *Don't fear those who kill the body but are not able to kill the soul; but rather, fear Him who is able to destroy both soul and body in hell* (Matthew 10:28). The Christian has no reason to expect kindness from a hostile world when his Master faced fierce enemies in His earthly walk. Christian persecution, often in the form of pressure to compromise, always tests one's sincerity. Times of peace too often cause the *sheep* to be indifferent and lukewarm. But, during persecution, the *sheep* discover they must depend on the Shepherd.

Later, Jesus said that *the kingdom of heaven has been suffering* (enduring) *violence, and the violent have been seizing it by force* (11:12). The kingdom will be entered by men and women who will not be intimidated or stopped by friends, peer pressure, or fierce opposition.

Our responsibility is to be like the apostle Paul: *When we are reviled, we bless; when we are persecuted, we endure it; when we are slandered, we entreat* (I Corinthians 4:12-13).

Thought for Today: The meek are patient when faced with difficulties.

In Today's Reading

Jesus, Lord of the Sabbath; controversy with Pharisees; unpardonable sin; Christ's death and resurrection foretold; His true kin.

Jesus was confronted by the Pharisees who criticized His disciples by saying: *Look, Your disciples are doing what is not lawful to do on the Sabbath!* (Matthew 12:2). Jesus responded: *But I tell you that something greater than the temple is here! . . . For the Son of Man is Lord of the Sabbath* (12:6-8). The Old Testament worship system foreshadowed the life and redemptive ministry of Jesus Christ as well as His church.

Israel was commanded to keep the last day of the week, the Sabbath, as a day of rest to commemorate God's work of creation in six days.

Most Christians assemble to collectively worship the Lord Jesus Christ on the first day of the week because He rose from the grave on *the first day of the week* (Mark 16:9). In this way they honor Him as Lord of their lives by putting Him first in every week. The Sabbath day of rest has its counterpart in the new covenant: *So that He* (Christ) *might come to have first place in everything. Therefore don't let anyone judge you in regard to food and drink or in the matter of a festival or a new moon* ***or a Sabbath day.*** *These are a shadow of what was to come* (Colossians 1:18; 2:16-17). The Sabbath, as well as all Jewish worship days, which were also Sabbaths, were a *shadow of things to come*. The early church recognized this and, in commemoration of Christ's resurrection, *on the first day of the week, we assembled to break bread* (Acts 20:7). A few years later, Paul was led to write: *On the first day of the week, each of you is to set something aside and save to the extent that he prospers, so that no collections will need to be made when I come* (I Corinthians 16:2).

The Passover commemorating Israel's freedom from Egyptian bondage was replaced in Christ's final Passover, when He instituted the Lord's Supper. As Jesus and the apostles were eating the Passover meal, *Jesus took bread, blessed and broke it, gave it to the disciples, and said, Take, eat; this is My body. Then He took a cup, and after giving thanks, He gave it to them and said, Drink from it, all of you. For this is My blood of the covenant, which is shed for many for the forgiveness of sins* (Matthew 26:26-28).

Thought for Today: Pity the foolish ones who question the validity of any part of God's holy Scriptures!

In Today's Reading

Jesus' parables; execution of John the Baptist; feeding of 5,000; Jesus walks on the water.

Matthew recorded seven prophetic parables of Jesus concerning *the secrets* (truths that had not been revealed in the past) *of the kingdom of heaven* (Matthew 13:11). In the first parable, Jesus described four kinds of responses from those who hear His word. The true disciple of Christ is represented by the *good ground* that received seed, which in turn brings forth fruit even to *100* times (13:8-23). His second parable was of *weeds* that grew in the same field with wheat but produced no fruit (13:24-30). The *weeds* (darnel) look identical to wheat as it grows. In its young stages, only the expert can tell the difference. But when *weeds* reach maturity, the head reveals its lack of value. In this parable, the Master said: *Let both grow together until the harvest* (13:30). Jesus explained that *the field is the world; and the good seed—these are the sons of the kingdom* (13:38), who produce fruitful lives.

The *weeds* represent those who outwardly appear to be converts to Christ but who have never truly received Jesus as Savior and Lord of their lives. They may fool the church world but not Christ. Eventually, *the Son of Man will send out His angels, and they will gather from His kingdom . . . those guilty of lawlessness. They will throw them into the blazing furnace where there will be weeping and gnashing of teeth* (13:41-42).

In His fourth parable, Jesus compared *the kingdom of heaven* with *yeast that a woman took and mixed into three measures of flour until it spread through all of it* (13:33). Leaven is not seen in the bread. It works invisibly, yet its results are visible and transform the loaf.

Again, the kingdom of heaven is like a merchant in search of fine pearls. When he found one priceless pearl, he went and sold everything he had, and bought it (13:45-46). This illustrates Christ and His kingdom as *one priceless pearl*. All else in life fades into insignificance compared to eternal life with Him. *What will it benefit a man if he gains the whole world yet loses his life? Or what will a man give in exchange for his life?* (Matthew 16:26).

Thought for Today: Our faith is strengthened as we obey God's word – the *source* of faith.

In Today's Reading

Scribes and Pharisees rebuked; 4,000 fed; the leaven; Peter's confession; transfiguration; the disciples' unbelief.

Caesarea Philippi is located near the northern border of the promised land. It is just 50 miles southwest of Damascus on the southwestern slopes of Mount Hermon. Its waters are one of the four sources of the River Jordan and it was also a major site of many pagan shrines. Here, in the midst of numerous idol worshipers, Jesus said: *I will build My church* (Matthew 16:18). The word *church* means "called out ones," a fellowship of those who have received Jesus Christ as their Savior and Lord and who, consequently, no longer live like the world.

Following the preaching of Peter on the day of Pentecost, *those who accepted his message were baptized. . . . And every day the Lord added those being saved to them* (Acts 2:41,47). In the New Testament, a church existed as soon as believers in Jesus Christ associated themselves together to worship the one true God (Ephesians 3:10; I Peter 2:9). *They devoted themselves to the apostles' teaching, to fellowship, to the breaking of bread, and to prayers* (Acts 2:42).

In the book of Acts, the church fellowship was very significant and also provided a channel for service (4:32-35). Later, the apostle Paul organized a large-scale offering from the various churches founded by him to meet the needs of the persecuted and poverty-stricken church in Jerusalem (Romans 15:25-26; I Corinthians 16:1; II Corinthians 8:1-2). A sense of mutual obligation was recognized and fulfilled as these Christians were reminded of their oneness in Christ with believers in other localities.

Paul encouraged Timothy to give attention to the public reading of the Old Testament Scriptures, as well as his own letters, at public worship (Colossians 4:16; I Timothy 4:11-13; Philemon 1:2).

The apostle Paul encouraged the church at Ephesus: *Speaking to one another in psalms, hymns, and spiritual songs, singing and making music to the Lord in your heart* (Ephesians 5:19-21).

Thought for Today: Our worship is never in vain when we desire to worship our wonderful Lord.

In Today's Reading

Humility; the lost sheep; forgiveness; marriage and divorce; rich young ruler; workers in the vineyard; two blind men healed.

Peter asked a far more important question than he realized when he said to Jesus: *Lord, how many times could my brother sin against me and I forgive him? As many as seven times? I tell you, not as many as seven, Jesus said to him, but 70 times seven* (Matthew 18:21-22).

Peter thought he was being generous in choosing *seven*. This was twice as many times as required by the traditions of the scribes, plus one more, for a total of *seven times*. For us to fail to forgive everyone of their sins against us while, at the same time, expecting Christ to forgive us of all our sins against Him for a lifetime violates the teaching of the Lord Jesus. It is, therefore, a serious thing to hear Him say: *But if you don't forgive people, your Father will not forgive your wrongdoing* (6:15).

The Lord gives an illustration of a servant who owed *ten thousand talents* (meaning an infinite amount of money) to his king. The amount was impossible to repay even in a lifetime. But, *the slave fell down on his face before him and said, Be patient with me, and I will pay you everything! Then the master of that slave had compassion, released him, and forgave him the loan. But that slave went out and found one of his fellow slaves who owed him 100 denarii* – about 3 month's wages, mere pennies when compared to 10,000 talents. *He grabbed him, started choking him, and said, Pay what you owe! At this, his fellow slave fell down and began begging him, Be patient with me, and I will pay you back. But he wasn't willing. On the contrary, he went and threw him into prison.* When his lord was made aware of what took place, he *got angry and handed him over to the jailers until he could pay everything that was owed. So My heavenly Father will also do to you if each of you does not forgive his brother from his heart* (18:24-35).

When the love of God controls our hearts, we find it much easier to forgive others than to demand our own rights, hold grudges, or exact our dues. *If anyone has caused pain. . . . forgive and comfort him. . . . For what I have forgiven . . . it is for you in the presence of Christ, so that we may not be taken advantage of by Satan* (II Corinthians 2:5-11).

Thought for Today: Live for the Lord and enjoy the peace of God now and eternity later.

In Today's Reading

Jesus' triumphal entry; temple cleansed; fig tree cursed; authority of Jesus questioned; parables; taxes; the greatest commandment.

On the Monday preceding His crucifixion, and just one day after His triumphant entry into Jerusalem, *Jesus went into* (the courts of) *the temple complex and drove out all those buying and selling. . . . And He said to them, It is written, My House will be called a house of prayer. But you are making it a den of thieves!* (Matthew 21:12-13; see Isaiah 56:7).

The chief priests were outraged and dispatched a delegation to interrupt Jesus *as He was teaching* and demanded: *By what authority are You doing these things?* (Matthew 21:23). They were referring to His accepting all the hosannas and praises that the multitude had given Him as the Messiah, the Son of David, and they demanded who gave Him authority to dismiss their money changers. For these reasons they conspired to kill Him (see Mark 11:18).

The temple belonged to God who was standing in their midst but they refused to recognize Him. The cleansing of the temple illustrated the cleansing that Christ alone brings into our lives through His atoning blood.

After pronouncing His judgment upon the temple activities, Jesus *spoke to them in parables: The kingdom of heaven may be compared to a king who gave a wedding banquet for his son. He sent out his slaves to summon those invited to the banquet. . . . But they paid no attention . . . Then he told his slaves, The banquet is ready . . . go to where the roads exit the city and invite everyone you find . . . But when the king came in to view the guests, he saw a man there who was not dressed for a wedding. So he said to . . . the attendants . . . Throw him into the outer darkness, where there will be weeping and gnashing of teeth* (Matthew 22:1-13).

Because eternal separation from God is so final and so terrifying, Jesus said more about the torments of eternal hell than all the writers of the New Testament combined. In this parable, Jesus exposes all who assume they are good enough for heaven. The apostle Paul said: *For there are also many rebellious people, idle talkers and deceivers. . . . They profess to know God, but they deny Him by their works. They are detestable, disobedient, and disqualified for any good work* (Titus 1:10,16).

Thought for Today: True humility before God is lived before men.

In Today's Reading

Hypocrisy denounced; destruction of the temple foretold; signs of Christ's return.

Following the cleansing of the temple and the denouncing of the religious leaders as hypocrites, the Lord sat with His disciples on the Mount of Olives and foretold: *Many false prophets will rise up and deceive many. And because lawlessness will multiply, the love of many will grow cold. But the one who endures to the end, this one will be delivered. This good news of the kingdom will be proclaimed in all the world as a testimony to all nations. And then the end will come. . . . Heaven and earth will pass away, but My words will never pass away* (Matthew 24:11-14,35). *False prophets* oppose the authority of Christ. Like the Pharisees of old, the false prophets today substitute contemporary opinions for the authority of God's word.

On the Mount of Olives, just three days before His crucifixion, our Lord foretold the destruction of the temple that would take place about 40 years after His resurrection. He also spoke of His future return from heaven, saying: *Now concerning that day and hour no one knows – neither the angels in heaven, nor the Son – except the Father only* (24:36). He also warned: *Therefore be alert, since you don't know what day your Lord is coming. . . . This is why you also should get ready, because the Son of Man is coming at an hour you do not expect* (24:42,44). Jesus made no attempt to detail the soon destruction of Jerusalem, nor the more distant end of the age. But these words from the King emphasized the importance of being prepared by speaking of two servants. The *wicked slave* is one who may not be guilty of committing gross sins, but one who simply gets involved in personal activities that crowd out his opportunities of service to his master. *Who then is a faithful and sensible slave, whom his master has put in charge of his household, to give them food at the proper time? Blessed is that slave whom his master, when he comes, will find working* (Matthew 24:45-46).

Thought for Today: God is more concerned about the inward condition of the heart than with the outward keeping of rules and regulations.

In Today's Reading

Parables; plot to kill Jesus; Jesus anointed; Lord's Supper; Christ's agony and prayer; Judas' betrayal; Jesus' trial; Peter's denial.

Jesus represented Himself in a parable saying: *It is just like a man going on a journey. He called his own slaves and turned over his possessions to them. To one he gave five talents; to another, two; and to another, one— to each according to his own ability. Then he went on a journey* (Matthew 25:14-15). *His slaves* were responsible for *his possessions*. These did not belong to them but remained the property of the master; they were to be his managers (stewards). These *possessions* represent our opportunities and abilities that God expects us to use for His kingdom.

The servant who received *five talents* recognized that what he had received belonged to his master, for on the day of judgment he said: *Master, you gave me five talents. Look, I've earned five more talents* (25:20).

In the same way, the man with two earned two more (25:17). He was not expected to gain five since he had been given according to his ability. Both faithfully doubled their talents and both were equally commended. God gave us a free will. We can choose to ignore our opportunities to serve Him, withhold our tithes, and desecrate the Lord's day; but, without an exception, *each of us will give an account of himself to God* (Romans 14:12). *You are not your own, for you were bought at a price; therefore glorify God in your body* (I Corinthians 6:19-20).

The third servant received *one talent*. He put forth no effort for his master. Instead, he *went off, dug a hole in the ground, and hid his master's money* (Matthew 25:18). His effort for "earthly security" was inexcusable. He tried to excuse himself like the person today who shows great diligence working in the secular world, but says: "I'm too busy now. I'll serve the Lord at some more convenient time, or after I retire."

The consequences of neglecting the opportunities to serve his master were irreversible; there was no second chance to relive his life. The master declared: *Throw this good-for-nothing slave into the outer darkness. In that place there will be weeping and gnashing of teeth* (Matthew 25:30; compare 8:12; 22:13; 24:51).

Thought for Today: Christians receive and enjoy a spiritual experience as they help others.

In Today's Reading

Judas' suicide; Jesus before Pilate; Jesus' crucifixion, burial, and resurrection; Great Commission.

Though Jesus had repeatedly told the disciples what was to take place, they finally realized that His life did not end with His crucifixion. His resurrection gave them the key to understanding that their King and His kingdom were both eternal. *Then Jesus came near and said to them, All authority has been given to Me in heaven and on earth. Go, therefore, and make disciples of all nations, baptizing them in the name of the Father and of the Son and of the Holy Spirit, teaching them to observe everything I have commanded you* (Matthew 28:16-20).

When Christians are baptized *in the name of the Father and of the Son and of the Holy Spirit,* we proclaim the fullness of the Godhead. Thus, by public baptism, we confess to the world that God is our heavenly *Father*. The phrase *and of the Son* is our witness to the world that Jesus is now Savior and Lord of our lives. Upon our confession, *the Holy Spirit* becomes our indwelling Sanctifier, Comforter, and Guide throughout life (John 14:26; 16:13). This confirms the Trinity of the Godhead and proclaims One God expressed in Three Persons.

Being *born again* (3:3,7) by His Spirit is a supernatural experience which changes the heart and transforms the life to one of daily worship and service to the Lord. This does not mean that we will reach perfection in this life; but let us say with Paul: *forgetting what is behind and reaching forward to what is ahead, I pursue as my goal the prize promised by God's heavenly call in Christ Jesus* (Philippians 3:13-14).

Submitting to the rule of Christ over our lives is of utmost importance. He has provided just one book and His Holy Spirit to tell us how to live and what He expects us to do. We are commissioned by Jesus to teach all of His word, the Bible, throughout the world. *This good news of the kingdom will be proclaimed in all the . . . nations. And then the end will come* (Matthew 24:14). Soon Christ will return; *then comes the end, when He hands over the kingdom to God the Father, when He abolishes all rule and all authority and power* (I Corinthians 15:24).

Thought for Today: "If God is your partner, you had better have BIG Plans" – D.L. Moody.

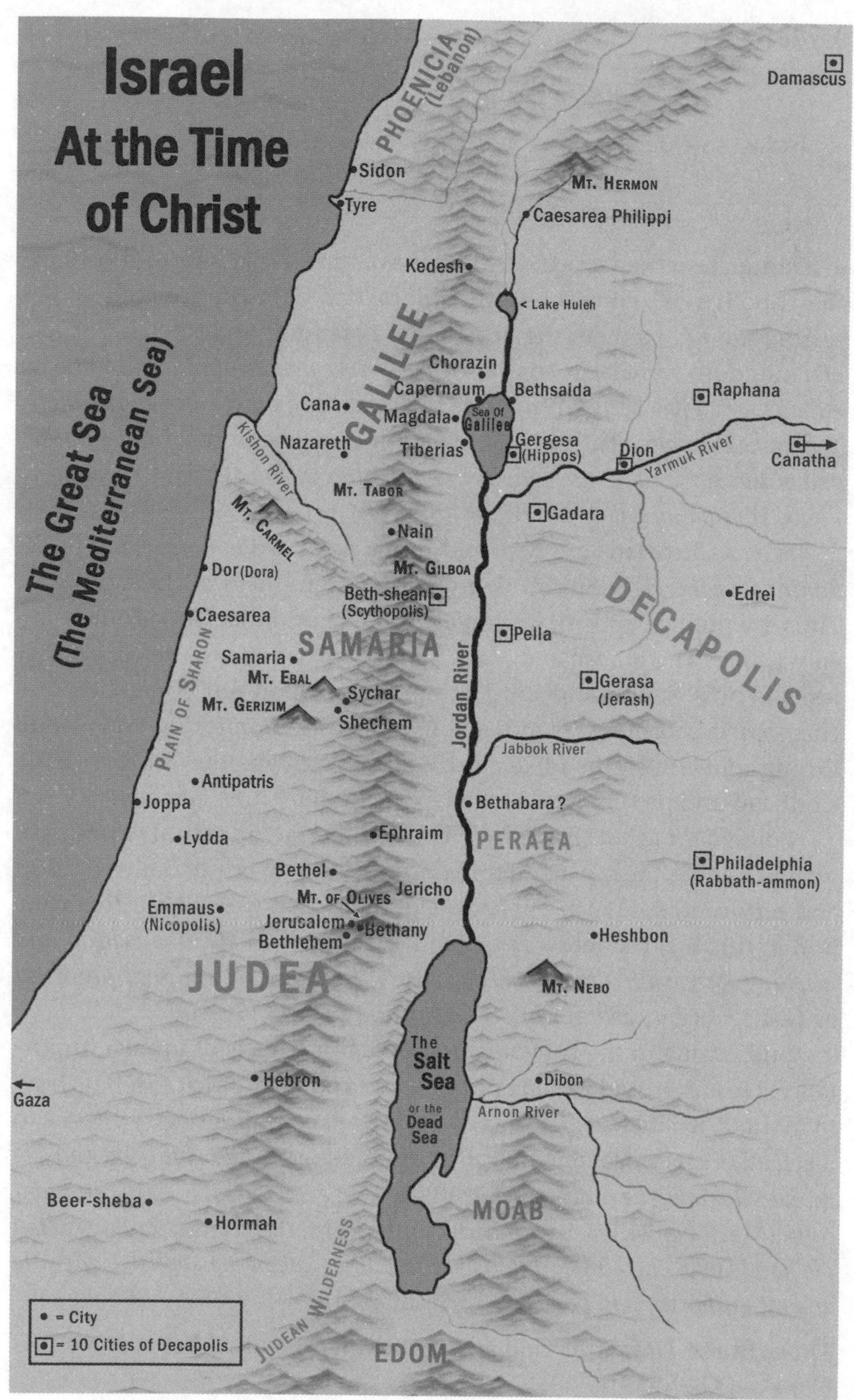

Israel
At the Time of Christ
Damascus
PHOENICIA (Lebanon)
Sidon
Tyre
Mt. Hermon
Caesarea Philippi
Kedesh
Lake Huleh
GALILEE
Chorazin
Capernaum
Bethsaida
Cana
Magdala
Sea Of Galilee
Raphana
Nazareth
Tiberias
Gergesa (Hippos)
Dion
Yarmuk River
Canatha
Kishon River
Mt. Tabor
Gadara
The Great Sea (The Mediterranean Sea)
Mt. Carmel
Nain
Dor (Dora)
Mt. Gilboa
Beth-shean (Scythopolis)
DECAPOLIS
Edrei
Caesarea
Pella
SAMARIA
Samaria
Jordan River
Mt. Ebal
Gerasa (Jerash)
Sychar
Mt. Gerizim
Shechem
Plain of Sharon
Jabbok River
Antipatris
Joppa
Bethabara?
Lydda
Ephraim
PERAEA
Philadelphia (Rabbath-ammon)
Bethel
Mt. of Olives
Jericho
Emmaus (Nicopolis)
Jerusalem
Bethany
Bethlehem
Heshbon
JUDEA
Mt. Nebo
The Salt Sea or the Dead Sea
Hebron
Dibon
Gaza
Arnon River
Beer-sheba
Hormah
MOAB
Judean Wilderness
• = City
= 10 Cities of Decapolis
EDOM

Introduction To The Book Of Mark

The Holy Spirit directed Mark to emphasize the deity of Jesus as the perfect Servant of God as well as the Son of God. The expression *Son of God* occurs five times in this book (Mark 1:1; 3:11; 5:7; 14:61; 15:39). The first verse reads: *The beginning of the gospel of Jesus Christ, the Son of God* (1:1). To confirm Jesus as *the Son of God,* Mark records 20 of His miracles, demonstrating Jesus' authority over demons, nature, disease, and death (1:21-28; 1:29-31; 1:32-34; 1:40-45; 2:3-12; 3:1-6; 4:35-41; 5:1-20; 5:25-34; 5:22-24,35-43; 6:34-44; 6:45-52; 6:53-56; 7:24-30; 7:31-37; 8:1-9; 8:22-26; 9:14-29; 10:46-52; 11:12-14,20-26). His servanthood is portrayed in such passages as: *For even the Son of Man did not come to be served, but to serve, and to give His life – a ransom for many* (10:45). The Holy Spirit also led Mark to record nine parables (2:21; 2:22; 4:1-20; 4:21; 4:26-29; 4:30-32; 12:1-12; 13:28-31; 13:32-37).

The humanity of Jesus is pointed out by telling how He felt and acted as a Man – His sorrow (3:5); seeking to be alone (1:35; 6:30-32); fatigue (4:38; 7:34; 8:12; 14:36); composure (4:38-40; 15:5); compassion (6:34; 8:2); love (10:21); anger and displeasure (3:5; 7:34; 8:12; 10:14). No other gospel describes Jesus taking *a child . . . in His arms* (9:36) or . . . *sleeping on the cushion* in a ship during *a fierce windstorm* (4:37-38).

Mark portrayed Jesus as a Man of action, always busy doing and working, with such terms as *immediately* (at once), *as soon as, instantly* and *right away,* which are used over 40 times.

Mark also declares Jesus as *Teacher* (Rabbi) 15 times (4:38; 5:35; 9:5, 17,38; 10:17,20,35; 11:21; 12:14,19,32; 13:1; 14:14,45).

In contrast to Mark, Matthew provided no explanation of Jewish customs because he was appealing to Jews. But Mark was appealing to gentiles so he explained many Jewish customs and teachings which non-Jewish readers might not be familiar with (Mark 2:18; 7:3-4; 14:12; 15:42), Judean geographic names and plants (1:13; 11:13; 13:3), and the value of Jewish coins in Roman money (12:42).

In Today's Reading

Ministry of John the Baptist; baptism and temptation of Jesus; His Galilean ministry; twelve apostles chosen; the unpardonable sin.

God had directed Moses to *command the Israelites to send away from the camp anyone who is afflicted with a skin disease . . . so they will not defile their camps where I am living among them* (Numbers 5:2-3). No disease occupies so much space in the Scriptures as leprosy. It first appears as just a white, then a pink spot. As it slowly progresses it becomes dreadful, loathsome, and fatal in its effects. It illustrates how insignificant sin may first appear, but, if continued, its consequence is devastating.

A leper loses the ability to feel pain. Still worse, as leprosy progresses, fingers and toes decay and fall off. For centuries, lepers were incurable – they were the untouchables of society.

One of these pitiful outcasts boldly made his way to Jesus – *begged on his knees before Him, saying, If You are willing, You can make me clean.* When the leper said: *If You are willing, You can make me clean* (Mark 1:40), he had no doubt that Jesus could heal him. But he doubted His willingness since leprosy was much worse than a hopeless disease; he was ceremonially unclean. It was not "could He?" but "would He?" *Moved with compassion, Jesus reached out His hand and touched him. I am willing, He told him. Be made clean* (1:40-41). Matthew records that this leper *knelt before Him* (Matthew 8:2), and Luke said that he *fell on his face* before Him (Luke 5:12). Only Mark tells us that Jesus was *moved with compassion* and His loving hand reached out to this defiled leper and *touched him*. *Jesus* was *moved with compassion,* the deepest of human emotions and the truest expression of the loving heart of Jesus.

Although Jesus' touch expressed compassion, the true power was in His word: *Be made clean* (Mark 1:41; Luke 5:13). Today Jesus says: *You are . . . clean because of the word I have spoken to you* (John 15:3). Faith in God comes through His word (Romans 10:17). Once saved, like the cleansed leper who *began to proclaim it widely* (Mark 1:45), you too will express your deep gratitude for what Jesus has done for you.

It is important to remember: *The Lord . . . is patient . . . not wanting any to perish, but all to come to repentance* (II Peter 3:9).

Thought for Today: The greater the outward pressures, the more time we must give to unhurried prayer.

In Today's Reading

Jesus' parables; the storm stilled; a legion of demons cast out; Jairus' daughter raised.

Jesus described in a parable four kinds of responses from those who hear His word saying: *Consider the sower who went out to sow* (Mark 4:1-3). Some respond with self-destroying indifference, representing seed that *fell along the path, and the birds came and ate it up* (4:4). The indifferent hearer's heart is open to the pleasures of self-interest, but callously closed to the word of God. *Satan comes and takes away the word sown in them* (4:15).

Others who hear His word are like the seed that *fell on rocky ground* (4:5). At first they seem receptive, but they soon lose interest. *These are the ones . . . when they hear the word, immediately . . . receive it with joy. But they have no root in themselves; they are short-lived* (4:16-17). "Stony places" illustrate solid rock beneath a shallow covering of soil. These "converts" appear promising and full of life; but, when they are faced with the loss of a friend or a job, or even a correction from the word of God, *they stumble immediately*, and quit because there is no real commitment.

Still other "converts" are like seed *sown among thorns; these are the ones who hear the word, but the worries of this age, the pleasure of wealth, and the desires for other things enter in and choke the word, and it becomes unfruitful* (4:18-19). They seem to recognize the true worth of Christ and eternal life, but have never made a break from their past. *The worries of this age, the pleasure of wealth, and the desires for other things enter in and choke the word,* gradually take control of their hearts, and the word of God and spiritual desires are eventually crowded out.

However, the parable goes on to say: *But the ones sown on good ground are those who hear the word, welcome it, and produce . . . 30, 60, and 100 times what was sown* (4:20). By faith, these few break up their rocky ground – the areas in their lives that were never yielded to God. And they root out the weeds and thorns of mixed motives that destroy spiritual effectiveness.

Jesus has said to all: *I am the vine; you are the branches. The one who remains in Me and I in him produces much fruit* (John 15:5).

Thought for Today: It is not *what* a person possesses that is important, but *who* possesses him.

In Today's Reading

Apostles sent out; John the Baptist beheaded; 5,000 fed; Jesus walks on water; rebuke of the Pharisees; faith of Syrophoenician woman.

For many generations, the law had been explained by the scribes and the Pharisees, who were the two largest religious groups of their day. They believed in the one true God, but they gave more attention to *the tradition of the elders* (the interpretation of the law by earlier scribes) (Mark 7:3; Matthew 15:2) than to the Scriptures. They believed that Jesus' disciples were defiled because they did not ceremonially wash before eating as prescribed in *the tradition of the elders* (Mark 7:5). It should have been a wake-up call to these self-righteous leaders to hear Jesus say: *Isaiah prophesied correctly about you hypocrites, as it is written: This people honors Me with their lips, but their heart is far from Me. They worship Me in vain* (empty show), *teaching as doctrines the commands of men. . . . You revoke God's word by your tradition* (7:6-8,13; see Isaiah 29:13; Ezekiel 33:31).

Later, He said to His disciples: *Nothing going into a man from the outside can defile him. . . . For from within, out of people's hearts, come evil thoughts, sexual immoralities, thefts, murders, adulteries, greed, evil actions, deceit, lewdness, stinginess, blasphemy, pride, and foolishness. All these evil things come from within and defile a man* (Mark 7:18-23).

We deceive ourselves if we believe there is no harm in continued sinful thoughts so long as they are never verbalized or physically carried out. The Holy Spirit led the apostle Paul to write: *The mind-set of the flesh is hostile to God because it does not submit itself to God's law* (Romans 8:7).

Christians have a responsibility – and the ability through the Holy Spirit – to be overcomers: *since the weapons of our warfare are not fleshly, but are powerful through God for the demolition of strongholds. We demolish arguments and every high-minded thing that is raised up against the knowledge of God, taking every thought captive to the obedience of Christ* (II Corinthians 10:4-5). A true commitment to the word of God will produce inward changes in our hearts that will also affect all that we say and do. The true Christian has a genuine desire to please his Lord. *I say then, walk by the Spirit and you will not carry out the desire of the flesh* (Galatians 5:16).

Thought for Today: Our unspoken thoughts express the true desires of our hearts.

In Today's Reading

Feeding 4,000; leaven explained; healing a blind man; Peter's confession of faith; death and resurrection foretold; transfiguration; disciples unable to heal boy; dispute over who is greatest.

Jesus and His disciples had been in the famous idol-worshiping town of *Caesarea Philippi* (Mark 8:27 – 9:2). It was here that Jesus *asked His disciples, who do people say that I am? And they answered Him, John the Baptist; others, Elijah; still others, one of the prophets. But you, He asked them again, who do you say that I am? Peter answered Him, You are the Messiah!* (God's Anointed) (8:27-29).

A short time later, Jesus invited the people to follow Him, but with certain qualifications, saying: *If anyone wants to be My follower, he must deny himself, take up his cross, and follow Me. For whoever wants to save his life* (for worldly ambitions) *will lose it, but whoever loses his life because of Me and the gospel will save it. For what does it benefit a man to gain the whole world yet lose his life? What can a man give in exchange for his life? For whoever is ashamed of Me and of My words in this adulterous and sinful generation, the Son of Man will also be ashamed of him* (8:34-38).

It was in this region that Jesus and three of His disciples went up on a *high mountain. . . . He was transformed in front of them . . . Elijah appeared to them with Moses, and they were talking with Jesus* (9:2-4). Moses and Elijah were now in the presence of their Messiah.

At this momentous event, they spoke of *His death; which He was about to* fulfill *in Jerusalem* (Luke 9:31). Moses representing the law and Elijah, the prophets, joined Jesus to honor Him prior to His suffering, death on the cross, and physical resurrection. Peter made the mistake of suggesting they *make three tabernacles: one for* Jesus, *one for Moses, and one for Elijah – because he did not know what he should say* (Mark 9:5-6). Jesus Christ is the Only Begotten Son of God. He alone is worthy of our worship and obedience (see Revelation 4:9-11). Nothing, or no one, can replace or equal personal communion with Him as our Lord.

Following Peter's *three tabernacles* suggestion, *a voice came from the cloud: This is My Beloved Son;* (He is the final authority) *listen to Him!* (obey Him) (Mark 9:7).

Thought for Today: The worship, love, and loyalty that is due Christ is not to be shared with anyone else.

In Today's Reading

Jesus on divorce; children blessed; rich young ruler; blind Bartimaeus healed; triumphal entry; cleansing the temple.

The Pharisees asked Jesus: *Is it lawful for a man to divorce his wife?* He answered: *From the beginning of creation God made them male and female. For this reason a man will leave his father and mother and be joined to his wife, and the two will become one flesh. So they are no longer two, but one flesh. Therefore what God has joined together, man must not separate* (Mark 10:2,6-9; Genesis 1:27; 2:24).

God created the world and put Adam in charge. He created woman to be Adam's helpmate. Among other things, a helpmate is a working partner who gives support, being *kind and compassionate to one another, forgiving one another, just as God also forgave you in Christ* (Ephesians 4:32).

The foremost responsibility rests with the husband, who is to love his wife, *just as also Christ loved the church and gave Himself for her* (5:25). Although numerous imperfections exist in the church, Jesus does not give up on the church and seek some other means of uniting people to follow Him. Furthermore, Jesus doesn't force anyone to be in submission to Him. The husband's conduct and compassion need to be like that of Christ for His church. Christ sets the example and leads the way in compassion, kindness, and forgiveness. *We love because He first loved us* (I John 4:19).

When a man is in submission to Christ, he prepares the way for his wife to desire to be in submission to her husband: *Now as the church submits to Christ, so wives should submit to their husbands in everything* (Ephesians 5:24). It is imperative that a wife feel secure in her husband's love. Therefore, it is his responsibility to let her know that she is very important to him.

Jesus said: *The Gentiles* (the unsaved world) *dominate them* (lord it over them). The nature of the unsaved is to control whoever they can. *But it* (that attitude) *must not be like that among you. . . . For even the Son of Man did not come to be served, but to serve* (help others), *and to give His life – a ransom for many* (Mark 10:42-45).

Thought for Today: A person can become a slave to the one he hates by allowing bitter thoughts about that person to dominate his mind.

In Today's Reading

Wicked tenant farmers; paying taxes to Caesar; the resurrection; greatest commandment; widow's offering; signs of the end.

Jesus was questioned by a scribe, who asked: *Which commandment is the most important of all?* (Mark 12:28). Jesus answered him by quoting Deuteronomy 6:4-5. *This is the most important . . . Hear, O Israel! The Lord our God is one Lord. And you shall love the Lord your God with all your heart, with all your soul, with all your mind, and with all your strength* (Mark 12:29-30). Jesus then quoted Leviticus 19:18, saying: *The second is: You shall love your neighbor as yourself. There is no other commandment greater than these* (Mark 12:31).

The Hebrew word *Elohenu* is translated in English as *our God*. However, God chose to use the plural form, *Elohim*, meaning *Gods*, 2500 times in reference to Himself as the self-existent, one true God. This, then, is what the sacred proclamation to Israel literally says: *Hear, O Israel; The Lord our Gods is one Lord*. Furthermore, the Hebrew word for *One* is also a solemn declaration that the Lord is a plurality in unity. *One* (*echad*) is a word which expresses *one* in the collective sense. It signifies a compound unity – not an absolute unity. For example, God said: *Man . . . and . . . wife . . . shall be one flesh* (Genesis 2:24). Even with numerous children, they are still called *one* family. The *one tabernacle* (Exodus 36:13) included many individual parts. However, there is a Hebrew word for *one* in the sense of an absolute one and it is used elsewhere in Scripture. It is the word *yacheed* and this word is never used to express the Godhead, although it is used many times in Scripture.

This truth exposes the ignorance of all who refuse to recognize Jesus as the one true God, the Creator of all things. The Holy Spirit guided the apostle Paul to write: *By Him everything was created, in heaven and on earth* (Colossians 1:16). Those who reject Jesus as God and the Holy Spirit as the One who will *guide you into all the truth* (John 16:13) are, in fact, rejecting the revelation of God Himself as God the Father, God the Son, and God the Holy Spirit. Jesus said: *The Father and I are one* (John 10:30; see also 5:18; 12:45; 14:9-11,20).

Thought for Today: Pray today for those in authority.

In Today's Reading

Jesus' last Passover; Gethsemane; Peter's denial; Jesus before Pilate; Jesus' crucifixion, burial, resurrection, and ascension.

When He raised Lazarus from the dead, the Sanhedrin determined that Jesus must die (John 11:53). However, His popularity made them fearful to openly arrest Him (Luke 22:2).

Simon, a leper who had been healed by Jesus, lived in Bethany. Just a few days before Jesus was crucified, Simon invited Him and the apostles to his home for supper. As they sat eating, *a woman came with an alabaster jar of pure and expensive fragrant oil . . . she broke the jar and poured it on His head* (Mark 14:3; see also Matthew 26:6-13; John 12:1-8).

This *oil of nard* was valued at *300 denarii* – almost a year's wages for a common laborer (Matthew 20:2; Mark 14:5). John records that Judas spoke up, saying: *Why wasn't this fragrant oil sold . . . and given to the poor? He didn't say this because he cared about the poor, but because he was a thief. He was in charge of the money-bag* (the treasurer) *and would steal part of . . . it* (John 12:5-6). To Judas, anything that was poured out upon Jesus was wasted; he coveted the money that the ointment was worth. Jesus replied: *Why are you bothering her? . . . She has done what she could; she has anointed My body in advance for burial* (Mark 14:6,8).

The lost opportunity to sell the ointment and pocket the money, coupled with the strong rebuke from Jesus and the great honor He bestowed upon Mary, probably embittered Judas, and he *went to the chief priests to hand Him over to them* (14:10; also Luke 22:3-4). Judas' real reason for being one of the 12 apostles became clear when he said to the chief priests: *What are you willing to give me if I hand Him over to you?* (Matthew 26:15). *When they heard this, they were glad and promised to give him silver* (Mark 14:11). All this had been foretold by the prophet 700 years before: *I said to them . . . give me my wages . . . So they weighed my wages, 30 pieces of silver* (Zechariah 11:12). Every person must make the personal choice whether to accept or reject Jesus as Savior and Lord of their lives.

The question asked by Pilate must still be answered: *What should I do then with Jesus, who is called Messiah?* (Matthew 27:22).

Thought for Today: What you decide to do with Jesus determines your eternal destiny.

Introduction To The Book Of Luke

Luke was a Gentile who addressed this book, as well as the book of Acts, to Theophilus, which means "friend of God." He proclaimed a universal gospel to everyone who desires to be called a "friend of God" when he recorded the message of the angel: *Do not be afraid, for you see, I announce to you good news of great joy that will be for all people* (Luke 2:10). Luke revealed that the purpose for Jesus leaving heaven was *to seek and to save the lost* (Luke 1:47,68; 2:11,38; 19:10; 24:21). Luke was not one of the 12 apostles, but he was closely associated with Paul in his missionary journeys and was known as *the loved physician* (Colossians 4:14).

The perfect humanity of Jesus is revealed as Luke presents Jesus as the Son of Man. The phrase *Son of Man* is mentioned at least 26 times in this book. Luke also proclaimed the full deity of Jesus as the virgin-born Son of God as he traced the genealogy of Jesus through His mother Mary back to the creation of the first man, Adam. Through the actual, physical genealogy of Mary, Christ is linked with all mankind.

No other gospel gives as many details of the human aspects of Jesus as did Luke, who told us about the parents and the birth of John the Baptist, the cousin of Jesus, and the details of the journey of Mary and Joseph to Bethlehem where Jesus was born (Luke 2:1-7). Only Luke records that Jesus was *laid . . . in a manger* (2:7); was presented for circumcision in the temple (2:21-24); conversed with the teachers (rabbinic scholars) at the age of twelve (2:42-46); and He *increased in wisdom and stature, and in favor with God and with people* (2:52).

Luke also reveals the human dependence of Jesus upon the heavenly Father in prayer (3:21; 5:16; 6:12; 9:16,18,28-29; 10:21; 11:1; 22:17,19; 23:46; 24:30). This points out the vital importance for all of His followers to realize how dependent upon God we are to accomplish His will through prayer. Only Luke records the disciples asking: *Lord, teach us to pray* (11:1), or Jesus teaching: *The need for them to pray always and not become discouraged* (lose heart and give up) (18:1). The parable of the unjust judge and the widow (18:2-8), and the parable of the midnight appeal: *Friend, lend me three loaves* (11:5-13) are only in Luke. All teach the importance of continuing to pray until the need is met.

In Today's Reading

Virgin birth of Jesus foretold; Mary's visit to Elizabeth; Mary's praise to God; birth of John the Baptist.

Jesus would have been born with the sinful nature of Adam if Joseph had been His biological father. This would have made Jesus a sinner like all mankind and, thus, unable to be the sinless substitute for our sins. But Gabriel, the angelic messenger of good news, came to Mary and said: *Rejoice, favored woman! The Lord is with you. . . . Listen: You will conceive and give birth to a son, and you will call His name Jesus. He will be great and will be called the Son of the Most High, and the Lord God will give Him the throne of His father David. . . . The Holy Spirit will come upon you, and the power of the Most High will overshadow you. Therefore the holy child to be born will be called the Son of God* (Luke 1:28,31-32,35).

Luke records that Mary *was deeply troubled by* the angel's saying (1:29). Joseph also was troubled when he learned Mary was pregnant and contemplated ending his legal engagement to her. *An angel of the Lord suddenly appeared to him in a dream, saying, Joseph, son of David, don't be afraid to take Mary as your wife, because what has been conceived in her is by the Holy Spirit. She will give birth to a son, and you are to name Him Jesus, because He will save His people from their sins* (Matthew 1:20-21). How comforting this must have been to Mary. Instead of living under suspicion, there was a miraculous confirmation to Joseph of her virginity.

The prophet Isaiah 700 years before had foretold: *The virgin will conceive, have a son, and name him Immanuel* (God is with us). . . . *The government will be on His shoulders. He will be named Wonderful Counselor, Mighty God, Eternal Father, Prince of Peace* (Isaiah 7:14; 9:6). Jesus' birth revealed His unique nature as both God and man.

The prophet Micah foretold that the Messiah, whose *origins are from antiquity, from ancient times* (Micah 5:2), would be born in Bethlehem of Judah. This small town, about six miles south of Jerusalem, was called the City of David, for that is where David was born and grew up.

Zachariah was filled with the Holy Spirit and prophesied: Blessed is the Lord, the God of Israel, because He has visited and provided redemption for His people (Luke 1:67-75).

Thought for Today: *We observed His glory . . . full of grace and truth* (John 1:14).

In Today's Reading

Jesus' birth; shepherds' adoration; Simeon's and Anna's prophecies; Jesus in the temple; John the Baptist; baptism of Jesus; Jesus' genealogy.

Passover brought Mary and Joseph to Jerusalem. In the busy preparation for returning home, Mary and Joseph, *assuming He* (Jesus) *was in the traveling party, they went a day's journey. Then they began looking for Him among their relatives and friends. When they did not find Him, they returned to Jerusalem to search for Him. After three days, they found Him in the temple complex sitting among the teachers* (of the law), *listening to them and asking them questions* (Luke 2:44-46).

After finding Him in the temple, Mary said: *Son, why have You treated us like this? Your father and I have been anxiously searching for You* (2:48). Jesus calmly explained to Mary His reason for being in the temple, saying: *Why were you searching for Me? . . . Didn't you know that I must be involved in My Father's interests?* (2:49). Jesus made it very clear who His real Father was. Devotion to His Father's interests drew Him to the temple; but His submission to the will of His Father also caused Him to return to Nazareth where He *was obedient to them* (2:51).

In this age of rebellion, many young people are not disciplined to be in subjection to their parents or to anyone else. Honoring and obeying God-ordained parental authority *is the first commandment with a promise* (Ephesians 6:2). Parents who are in submission to God have a responsibility to spiritually train by personal example, through daily devotions, and by regular attendance in a Bible-teaching church on the Lord's day. Pity the parents who rebel against restrictions which are placed on them on the job, at church, or in the community. Such people may even think they have a right to be independent of God-ordained authority, yet still expect their children to be obedient to authorities.

Everyone must submit to the governing authorities, for there is no authority except from God . . . the one who resists the authority is opposing God's command, and those who oppose it will bring judgment on themselves (Romans 13:1-2).

Thought for Today: The certainty that all of God's word will be fulfilled is the foundation of our Christian faith.

In Today's Reading

Temptation of Jesus; His teachings; healings; the miraculous catch of fish; other miracles; the call of Matthew.

Some think they can worship God just as well while on the lake fishing or at home resting. In contrast, Jesus recognized the need to honor God by regularly attending worship services. We read that He was *teaching in their synagogues* while in Galilee (Luke 4:15). *He came to Nazareth, where He had been brought up. As usual, He entered the synagogue on the Sabbath day* (4:16). Jesus was invited to speak. *The scroll of the prophet Isaiah was given to Him, and . . . He found the place where it was written: The Spirit of the Lord* (God) *is upon Me* (the Messiah), *because He has anointed Me to preach good news to the poor. He has sent Me to proclaim freedom to the captives and recovery of sight to the blind, to set free the oppressed, to proclaim the year of the Lord's favor. He then rolled up the scroll, gave it back to the attendant, and sat down* (4:17-20; Isaiah 61:1-2).

The words Jesus read contained a clear mention of the three Persons of the Trinity: *The Spirit of the Lord* (the Holy Spirit) *is upon Me; He* (the Father) *has anointed Me*; and *He has sent Me* (the Anointed One).

The people were amazed, *and the eyes of everyone in the synagogue were fixed on Him. He began by saying to them, Today this Scripture has been fulfilled in your hearing* (Luke 4:20-21). They marveled at His *gracious words* (4:22), but knew He clearly referred to Himself as the Messiah who had been foretold by Isaiah. You can imagine how startled they were when Jesus said that He (the local carpenter) whom they assumed to be *the son of Joseph* (Luke 3:23) was their Messiah.

The congregation listening to Jesus was so infuriated that they disrupted the worship service, seized Jesus, and attempted to put Him to death by pushing Him over a rocky precipice. *But He passed right through the crowd and went on His way* (4:28-30).

How easy it is to miss God's best. In contrast, the Jews in Berea *welcomed the message with eagerness and examined the Scriptures daily to see if these things were so* (Acts 17:11).

Thought for Today: Just think! You have the privilege to work for God.

In Today's Reading

Jesus and the Sabbath; 12 apostles chosen; Sermon on the Mount; healing and miracles; John the Baptist's question; Jesus anointed.

We all have sinned beyond our ability to count, and we are deeply grateful that our heavenly Father forgives us. If we are truly grateful, we will approach everyone who sins against us with the same mercy and compassion that we receive from the Lord. Knowing how natural it is to be hypocritical, Jesus said: *Why do you look at the speck in your brother's eye, but don't notice the log in your own eye? . . . Hypocrite! First take the log out of your eye, and then you will see clearly to take out the speck in your brother's eye* (Luke 6:41-42).

It is our responsibility to recognize *the speck* for what it is, but we must first consider our own *log*. Only then are we qualified to examine our attitude toward the sinner, as well as *the speck* (sin in his life).

Such a heart of compassion and concern contrasts with those who overlook their own faults and failures, but who rarely miss an opportunity to gossip about someone else's conduct. We are prone to imply evil motives to others' actions, and even exaggerate them. We tend to judge ourselves by our good intentions, but others by their mistakes. Thankfully, God is a merciful God who fully forgives us when we repent of our sins. But His mercy also makes a vital demand upon us – we must extend that same mercy to others.

Criticism is often an act of self-righteousness to build one's own self-esteem by putting others down.

It is easy to jump to conclusions without hearing or caring about all the facts. We have an amazing ability to misjudge the thoughts and actions of others. Judgmental people thrive on faultfinding and always find something wrong with everything that is said or done by another whom they would love to belittle. It is this self-righteousness that Jesus spoke of when He said: *First take the log out of your eye*. Then the love of Christ can be expressed through us. If anyone *is caught in any wrongdoing, you who are spiritual should restore such a person with a gentle spirit* (Galatians 6:1).

Thought for Today: It is unjust to criticize anyone – even those whose efforts fall short of what we expect.

In Today's Reading

Jesus' teachings; more miracles; 12 apostles sent forth; 5,000 fed; Peter's confession; transfiguration of Christ.

Jesus put the sincerity of would-be disciples to the test when *someone said to Him, I will follow You wherever You go. Jesus told him, Foxes have dens, and birds of the sky have nests, but the Son of Man has no place to lay His head* (Luke 9:57-58). The *foxes* illustrate the clever ones and the *birds of the sky* illustrate the worldly. Jesus pointed out to this man that if he chose to follow Him he could expect hardships. Jesus was also saying that He was not attached to earthly possessions, nor could His followers expect any guarantee of earthly resources.

Another also said, I will follow You, Lord, but first let me go and say good-bye to those at my house. But Jesus said to him, No one who puts his hand to the plow and looks back (to the things left behind or to other attractions) *is fit for the kingdom of God* (9:61-62). Our Lord did not welcome volunteers who were only willing to join Him on their own terms; serving Christ is a lifetime commitment. Love dictated the uncompromising requirement of following Him. He was not in the midst of a membership drive, nor counting converts to prove His success.

Self-seekers and compromisers are often misled, believing there will be a more convenient time when they can choose to follow the Lord. Their excuses reveal divided hearts. Some lack the "single eye" of devotion to Christ where, by comparison, all else in this world is of little importance. Others fail to put Christ first in their daily decisions and, yet, all who do will discover that the satisfaction of self-denial far exceeds fleeting earthly rewards. Each of us needs to consider whether there is someone in our life, or something in our heart, that keeps us from giving first place to Christ, His word, and His will.

Jesus warned: *The kingdom of God is near. I assure you . . . Heaven and earth will pass away, but My words will never pass away. Be on your guard, so that your minds are not dulled from . . . worries of life, or that day will come on you unexpectedly* (Luke 21:31-34).

Thought for Today: Worldly ambitions fade into insignificance when we devote ourselves to knowing the Lord by reading His word.

In Today's Reading

Seventy sent out; Good Samaritan; Martha and Mary; teaching on prayer; Pharisees denounced.

An official interpreter of both the Mosaic law and the traditions of the elders *stood up to test Him* (Jesus), *saying, Teacher, what must I do to inherit eternal life?* (Luke 10:25). And Jesus said to him: *What is written in the law?* He said: *You shall love the Lord your God with all your heart, with all your soul, with all your strength, and with all your mind; and your neighbor as yourself.* And Jesus said to him, *You've answered correctly. . . . Do this and you will live. But wanting to justify himself, he asked Jesus, And who is my neighbor?* (10:26-29; Deuter-onomy 6:5; Leviticus 19:18).

Jesus illustrated the answer by saying: *A man was going down from Jerusalem to Jericho and fell into the hands of robbers. They stripped him, beat him up, and fled, leaving him half dead. A priest happened to be going down that road. When he saw him, he passed by on the other side. In the same way, a Levite, when he arrived at the place and saw him, passed by on the other side. But a Samaritan, while traveling, came up to him; and when he saw the man, he had compassion. . . . bandaged his wounds . . . brought him to an inn, and took care of him. . . . Which of these three do you think proved to be a neighbor to the man who fell into the hands of the robbers?* And he said: *The one who showed mercy to him. . . . Then Jesus told him, Go and do the same* (Luke 10:30-37).

My *neighbor* is anyone who needs my compassion and whom I have the opportunity to help, no matter what his position, race, or religion may be. We are simply to enter into the feelings of another's sufferings or misfortunes as God has done for us. Whatever is mine belongs to God and whatever belongs to God should be shared with my neighbor because my neighbor was also created in the image of God.

All of us need to be reminded of our Lord's answer to the lawyer. *What must I do to inherit eternal life?* Jesus reminded him that the evidence of eternal life within us is loving God *with all your heart, with all your soul . . . and with all your mind; and your neighbor as yourself* (Luke 10:27).

Thought for Today: It is one thing to serve God, but quite another thing to show compassion to those who are less fortunate than we are.

In Today's Reading

Warnings against greed, hypocrisy; parables, healings, and teachings.

The Lord illustrated the deceptive danger of covetousness by saying: *A rich man's land was very productive. He thought to himself, What should I do, since I don't have anywhere to store my crops? . . . I'll tear down my barns and build bigger ones, and store all . . . my goods there. Then I'll say to myself, You have many goods stored up for many years. Take it easy; eat, drink, and enjoy yourself. But God said to him, You fool! This very night your life is demanded of you. And the things you have prepared—whose will they be?* (Luke 12:16-20). By hard work in the highly-respected occupation of farming, this man had become wealthy. There is no hint that he had gained his wealth by dishonest methods. His soul-destroying sin was that he spent his lifetime in self-gratification. God called him a *fool,* and then added: *That's how it is with the one who stores up treasure for himself and is not rich toward God* (12:20-21).

We Christians should not allow material desires to distract us from doing the will of God. We are not to worry about future needs. As important as food, clothing, and shelter are to maintaining life, our first concern should be to: *Seek first the kingdom of God and His righteousness* (Matthew 6:33). Keeping our priorities right, we prepare ourselves to be all that our Lord wants us to be in order to accomplish the purpose for which He created us.

How we use our time and talents is an expression of our Christian faith. Christ taught that life is truly fulfilling by loving, serving, and giving to extend the good news to a lost world. Regardless of how much or how little talent, ability, or possessions we may have or acquire, as good stewards we should prayerfully consider what Jesus would have us do with them.

Now you, man of God, run from these things; but pursue righteousness, godliness, faith, love, endurance, and gentleness. Fight the good fight for the faith; take hold of eternal life, to which you were called and have made a good confession before many witnesses (I Timothy 6:11-12).

Thought for Today: If we are truly concerned about God's interests, He will take care of ours.

In Today's Reading

Humility; more parables; prodigal son; rich man and Lazarus.

Our Lord illustrates two alternatives in life. The first is that of a self-centered prodigal son who demanded freedom from his father's authority, and then *traveled to a distant country, where he squandered his estate in foolish living. After he had spent everything, a severe famine struck that country, and he had nothing. Then he went to work for one of the citizens of that country, who sent him into his fields to feed pigs. He longed to eat his fill from the carob pods the pigs were eating, and no one would give him any. But when he came to his senses, he said, How many of my father's hired hands have more than enough food, and here I am dying of hunger! I'll get up, go to my father, and say to him, Father, I have sinned against heaven and in your sight* (Luke 15:13-18). The word "prodigal" means a waster; he had *wasted* his father's substance. As he struggled with a sense of emptiness and the shame of a wasted life, he finally came to his senses and humbly returned to his father saying: *Father, I have sinned against heaven and in your sight* (15:21). The second lifestyle was after he had repented: *Because this son of mine was dead and is alive again; he was lost and is found! . . . they began to celebrate* (15:24).

Just as the prodigal son discovered his father's compassion and love were far greater than he had realized, every repentant sinner will discover that the heavenly Father is waiting with great love and compassion to forgive all who come to Him. Forgiveness will not restore or reverse the result of wasted years. It is an inevitable and irreversible law of the universe that *whatever a man sows he will also reap* (Galatians 6:7).

The foremost purpose of our brief lives on earth is to prepare for eternity with God. We also are to provide spiritual food for those who have no other way of obtaining it. Earthly pleasures should never be our priorities. All mankind, rich or poor, has one thing in common – physical death will open the door to either eternal life or eternal hell. *Therefore pay even more attention to what we have heard. . . . How will we escape if we neglect such a great salvation?* (Hebrews 2:1,3).

Thought for Today: Have you "wasted" your life like the prodigal? Return to the Father; He is lovingly waiting to welcome you.

In Today's Reading

Forgiveness; 10 lepers; Christ's return foretold; rich young ruler; Christ's death and resurrection foretold; healing of a blind beggar.

In a lifetime, no one question could be of greater importance than that of a wealthy young man who ran to Jesus and knelt before Him asking: *Good Teacher, what must I do to inherit eternal life?* (Luke 18:18-27; also Matthew 19:16-30; Mark 10:17-31). Since he knelt before Jesus, he clearly understood that Jesus was the Messiah and that, beyond this physical life, there was an eternity, a real personal existence. His question concerning eternal life indicates that he was a Pharisee, for an afterlife was one of their major doctrinal convictions, as opposed to the Sadducees who did not believe in life after death. All three of the gospels mention his great wealth.

Luke records that this young man was *a ruler* – perhaps a member of the Sanhedrin, well-versed in the law, and very "religious." He was no hypocrite. Jesus did not question his integrity when *he said, I have kept all these* (the commandments) *from my youth* (Luke 18:21). In response to his most vital question: *What must I do,* Jesus told him: *You still lack one thing: sell all that you have and distribute it to the poor, and you will have treasure in heaven. Then come, follow Me. After he heard this, he became extremely sad, because he was very rich* (18:22-23). This young ruler was unwilling to give up the pleasant life or his proud position that he loved so much, as well as the influence, prestige, and financial securities that his wealth provided. His response revealed, through the things he refused to give to the poor, that he was also covetous. He was religious but eternally lost.

Note carefully that the question was not: "What shall I believe or confess or pray?"; but: *What must I do to inherit eternal life?*

This should not be twisted to mean that eternal life can be earned by self-effort or sacrificial giving. It can only come from Him who loved us *and has set us free from our sins by His blood* (Revelation 1:5).

Thought for Today: *Think about Him in all your ways, and He will guide you on the right paths* (Proverbs 3:6).

In Today's Reading

Jesus and Zacchaeus; triumphal entry; cleansing the temple; parable of wicked tenants; paying taxes; the resurrection; Jesus' authority.

The investigative committee from the Sanhedrin pretended to be interested in following Jesus. The Pharisees conspired against Jesus with the cooperation of the nonreligious political party called the Herodians, a group which urged Israel's submission to Rome (Matthew 22:16). These opposite-thinking groups of people hypocritically said to Jesus: *Teacher, we know that You speak and teach correctly, and You don't show partiality, but teach the way of God in truth. Is it lawful for us to pay taxes to Caesar or not?* (Luke 20:21-22). Since the majority of Jews deeply resented paying taxes to the Roman government, this "committee" was sure the crowd would quickly turn against Jesus if He said: "Yes." And the Pharisees could also say He was not the Messiah of Israel if He taught subjection to a gentile government. But if He said: "No," the Herodian party would then accuse Him of conspiracy against the Roman government and Pilate would have Him arrested for treason.

Detecting their craftiness, He said to them, Show Me a denarius – a Roman coin that was an accepted currency among the Jews. Then Jesus asked: *Whose image and inscription does it have?* They answered *Caesar's. . . . Well then, He told them, give back to Caesar the things that are Caesar's.* But the rest of His comment came as a stinging rebuke to their hypocrisy when He added: *And to God the things that are God's* (20:23-25). While the image upon a coin is representative of governmental authority, we must also submit to a higher authority because we are created *in the image of God* (Genesis 1:26-27). This means that the words of Jesus are still just as true for us today.

Some misguided citizens accept the benefits of government, but avoid paying taxes. They ignore the two reasons for paying them. Christians are to pay required taxes and obey the law, but they also pay them as a requirement to please God. We simply cannot ignore His clear command to: *Submit to every human institution because of the Lord, whether to the Emperor as the supreme authority, or to governors as those sent out by him to punish those who do evil* (I Peter 2:13-14).

Thought for Today: Oh, to hear Jesus say, "Well done!"

In Today's Reading

The widow's offering; signs of the end; Jesus' last Passover; the Lord's Supper; prayer in the garden; Jesus' arrest; Peter's denial.

The Israelites' annual Passover meal was a reminder that the blood of an innocent lamb had made it possible for them to be redeemed from death and set free from Pharaoh and Egyptian slavery.

On the night of the Passover preceding His crucifixion, Jesus *took bread, gave thanks, broke it, gave it to them, and said, This is My body, which is given for you. Do this in remembrance of Me. In the same way He also took the cup after supper and said, This cup is the new covenant in My blood, which is shed for you* (Luke 22:19-20). At this Passover, our Lord identified Himself with the Sacrificial Passover Lamb.

The Lord's Supper instituted that night is a reminder that Jesus' death on the cross delivered us from Satan, our pharaoh, and set us free from the condemnation for our sins to receive eternal life. It is so sacred that our Lord further reveals its importance through Paul who wrote: *On the night when He was betrayed, the Lord Jesus took bread, gave thanks, broke it, and said, This is My body. . . . Do this. . . . in remembrance of Me* (I Corinthians 11:23-25). It is of the utmost importance that we consider carefully that our Lord said: *Do this. . . . in remembrance of Me*. He did not make a suggestion but a command. Jesus reminded all followers: *Why do you call Me, Lord, Lord, and don't do the things I say? . . . If anyone loves Me, he will keep My word* (Luke 6:46; John 14:23).

The Lord wanted us to know that His death on the cross made the difference for us between eternity in *the lake of fire* (Revelation 20:14) and eternity in heaven with Him. The Lord's Supper is a continuing reminder there is forgiveness for all who, by faith, accept His atoning sacrifice as the only means of receiving eternal life. It is also a reminder that our self-centered preoccupation with material possessions tends to direct our attention to things that have no eternal value. Attitudes of ill will toward others, revenge, and lust suppress the resurrection life of Christ within each of us. The Lord's table is a reminder that we *were bought at a price* (His sacred blood). . . . *each person should remain with God in whatever situation he was called* (I Corinthians 7:23-24).

Thought for Today: When we truly love the Lord, we will express forgiving love in our hearts toward all offenders.

In Today's Reading

Jesus before Pilate and Herod; His crucifixion and resurrection; ministry of the risen Christ; His commission; His ascension.

Some of the women who were followers of Jesus watched as He died on the cross, and then watched as the body of their beloved Lord was hastily laid in the rock-hewn tomb of Joseph of Arimathea. *It was preparation day, and the Sabbath was about to begin. The women. . . . returned and prepared spices and perfumes. And they rested on the Sabbath according to the commandment* (Luke 23:54-56). *On the first day of the week, very early in the morning* (24:1), on their way to the tomb, these women wondered: *Who will roll away the stone from the entrance to the tomb? . . . the stone . . . was very large* (Mark 16:3-4). They soon discovered that their concern had already been cared for.

Matthew recorded the terror experienced by the Roman guards who had been assigned to watch the sealed tomb, when *an angel of the Lord . . . rolled back the stone and was sitting on it* (Matthew 28:2,4). Later the women came to the tomb to complete the burial procedures. *They went in but did not find the body of the Lord Jesus. . . . suddenly two men stood by them in dazzling clothes. . . . Why are you looking for the living among the dead? asked the men. He is not here, but He has been resurrected! Remember how He spoke to you when He was still in Galilee, saying, The Son of Man must be betrayed into the hands of sinful men, be crucified, and rise* (from death) *on the third day?* (Luke 24:3-7). The message was clear – He had fulfilled His word. Excitedly, the women rushed to the disciples to relate their thrilling discovery.

These women had no thought of deserting their Lord in death, even though a hostile crowd had crucified Him. Our genuine love for the Lord Jesus and His word will overcome temptations to draw back when we face opposition and it is demonstrated when we serve Him.

Neither the women, nor the doubting apostles, were expecting such a glorious experience on that resurrection morning. God always has better things in store for us than we think possible. God *is able to do above and beyond all that we ask or think – according to the power that works in you – to Him be glory in the church and in Christ Jesus* (Ephesians 3:20-21).

Thought for Today: God is merciful to all who ask.

Introduction To The Book Of John

The Holy Spirit guided the apostle John to reveal the true nature and purpose of Jesus Christ, both as perfect Man and as deity, one with God the Father in the creation of all things. The gospel of John begins by declaring: *In the beginning* (before all time) *was the Word* (Jesus Christ)*; and the Word was with God, and the Word was God. . . . and apart from Him not one thing was created that has been created* (John 1:1,3).

God further revealed Himself when *the Word* (Jesus) *became flesh and took up residence among us. We observed His glory, the glory as the only Son from the Father, full of grace and truth* (1:14).

John revealed Jesus as the prophesied, sinless *Lamb of God, who takes away the sin of the world* (1:29; Isaiah 53:7). The religious leaders *began trying all the more to kill Him:* (because) (1) *He was even calling God His own Father, making Himself equal with God* (John 5:18); (2) in knowing *everything* (vs 20); (3) in judging, *the Father . . . has given all judgment to the Son* (vs 22); (4) in receiving honor *just as they honor the Father* (vs 23); (5) in imparting *eternal life* (vss 24-25); (6) in being self-existent, *as the Father has life in Himself, so also He has granted to the Son to have life in Himself* (vs 26); and (7) in resurrecting, *the Son gives life to whomever He wishes* (vss 21,28-29).

Jesus said: *The Father and I are One. . . . The one who has seen Me has seen the Father* (10:30; 14:9). He also spoke of *that glory* which He had with the Father *before the world existed* (17:5). Jesus also revealed Himself as the eternal *I AM* of the Old Testament (Exodus 3:14) with eight *I am* statements: *I am the bread of life* (John 6:35); *Before Abraham was* (existed), *I am* (8:58); *I am the light of the world* (8:12); *I am the door. If anyone enters by Me, he will be saved* (10:7-9); *I am the good shepherd* (10:11); *I am the resurrection and the life* (11:25); *I am the way, the truth, and the life. No one comes to the Father except through Me* (14:6); and *I am the true vine* (the source of all true fruitfulness). . . . *If anyone does not remain in Me, he is thrown aside like a branch. . . . They . . . throw them into the fire* (15:1-2,6).

Jesus said to His followers: *Remain in Me. . . . keep My commandments* (15:4,7,10). *If you continue in My word* (live in accordance with it), *you really are My disciples. You will know the truth, and the truth will set you free* (from Satan and sin) (8:31-32). The purpose of John is clear. *These are written so that you may believe Jesus is the Messiah, the Son of God, and by believing you may have life in His name* (20:31).

In Today's Reading

Deity of Christ; John the Baptist; the Lamb of God; first miracle in Cana; cleansing of the temple; Nicodemus.

There was a man from the Pharisees named Nicodemus, a ruler of the Jews. . . . (who) *came to Him at night and said, Rabbi, we know that You have come from God* (John 3:1-2). This prominent rabbi probably wanted an uninterrupted conversation with Jesus, so he chose to see Him at night. He was a member of the Sanhedrin, the council which controlled the religious life of Israel, yet he confessed to Jesus: *Rabbi, we know that You have come from God* (3:2).

Jesus said to Nicodemus: *Unless someone is born of water and the Spirit, he cannot enter the kingdom of God. Whatever is born of the flesh is flesh, and whatever is born of the Spirit is spirit. . . . you must be born again* (3:5-7). To illustrate how essential it is to be "born again," Jesus reminded him of when the Israelites, near the end of their 40 years of wilderness wandering, again complained about their circumstances. So, the Lord sent fiery snakes among them. Thousands of people died. When the people cried out to God, He commanded Moses to make a snake of bronze and lift it up on a pole. The people could only be healed by turning their eyes and looking up at the bronze snake. Jesus then said: *As Moses lifted up the serpent in the wilderness, so the Son of Man must be lifted up, so that everyone who believes in Him will have eternal life* (3:14-15). *Anyone who believes in Him is not judged, but anyone who does not believe is already judged, because he has not believed in the name of the only Son of God* (3:18). The snake was made of bronze because it is the biblical symbol of judgment.

The one who is *born again* loves the things he once ignored, and he now hates the things he once desired. When we were born the first time, we received the sinful nature of our parents, which was inherited from Adam. We are *born again* into the family of God and receive His divine nature: *Walk as children of light – for the fruit of the light results in all goodness, righteousness, and truth – discerning what is pleasing to the Lord* (Ephesians 5:8-10).

Thought for Today: The most insignificant person by the world's standards is precious in the eyes of God.

In Today's Reading

Jesus and the Samaritan woman; miracles of healing; Jesus answers the Jews.

The sheep gate where lambs were bought for sacrifice was located at the northeast area of the temple court in Jerusalem. Nearby was a pool that was called Bethesda. At this pool *lay a multitude* of the physically disabled. It was believed that the first to enter the pool of water after an angel troubled the water would be cured (John 5:3-4).

In this crowd of helpless people was *one man . . . who had been sick for 38 years* (5:5). What chance was there that anyone would ever care if he were healed? We are reminded that Jesus sees everyone and equally cares for all, desiring that they will all recognize Him as Savior and Lord. They may be popular athletes, intellectual leaders such as Nicodemus, pitiful prostitutes like the woman at the well, or any needy persons.

The sheep gate illustrates Jesus, *the Lamb of God, who takes away the sin of the world* (1:29). The pool called *Bethesda* means "house of mercy or grace." It is only through the compassion of Christ that any lost sinner, without exception, can find mercy through accepting His sacrifice on the cross for our sins.

Bethesda had *five colonnades* (5:2). In the Bible *five* always implies "grace." It was with five loaves that the Lord Jesus fed the hungry multitude. The fifth clause in the Lord's prayer is: *Give us today our daily breud* (Matthew 6:11). When this man expressed his hopelessness, Jesus looked beyond the man's problem, asked him to do something about it, and said: *Get up . . . pick up your bedroll and walk! Instantly the man got well, picked up his bedroll, and started to walk* (John 5:7-9).

Like this man, you and I once were spiritually helpless. We should be eternally grateful that Jesus did not pass us by but asked us if we wanted to be well. The apostle Paul reminds us that we once were *children under wrath* (Ephesians 2:3), but we have been cleansed from our sins and given a new nature with the privilege to *put on the new man . . . created according to God's likeness in righteousness and purity of the truth* (Ephesians 4:24).

Thought for Today: Temporal "satisfactions" may "quench our thirst" momentarily, but they will never truly satisfy.

In Today's Reading

Feeding 5,000; Jesus, the bread of life; Festival of Tabernacles; Jesus forgives the adulteress; Jesus, the light of the world.

Jesus entered *the temple complex again, and all the people were coming to Him. He sat down and began to teach them* (John 8:2). Jesus was rudely interrupted by *the scribes and the Pharisees* (who) *brought a woman. . . . Teacher, they said to Him, this woman was caught in the act of committing adultery. In the law Moses commanded us to stone such women. So what do you say?* (8:3-5). They brought this woman to Jesus, not because they were shocked at her conduct or grieved that the holy law of God had been broken, but *that they might . . . accuse Him* (8:6). Had He said: "Let her go," they could accuse Him of compromising with sin and breaking the Mosaic law. If He said: "Stone her," He would break Roman law and be accountable to Rome and His followers would have questioned His compassion and forgiveness of sinners.

Jesus brought conviction to each one of her accusers when He said: *The one without sin among you should be the first to throw a stone at her* (8:7). *When they heard this, they left one by one, starting with the older men* (who had the most sin to hide and the most reputation to protect). *. . . He was left, with the woman in the center* (8:9). Then Jesus said to her: *Woman, where are they? Has no one condemned you? No one, Lord, she answered. Neither do I condemn you, said Jesus. Go, and from now on do not sin any more* (8:10-11). Following this cruel interruption by these hypocritical religious leaders, Jesus resumed His teaching, saying: *I am the light of the world. Anyone who follows Me will never walk in the darkness, but will have the light of life* (8:12).

It is possible to "follow the light of the world" for the wrong motives. During times when some face death, financial reverses, or diseases, they may "appear" to sincerely follow Jesus. Let health return, or let there be a change of circumstances, and often these once-zealous professors of faith return to their self-centered ways. Such people are only temporarily "reformed" and not "transformed." In striking contrast with the hypocrites are those who, regardless of circumstance, remain faithful to Jesus. *Whoever keeps His word, truly in him the love of God is perfected. This is how we know we are in Him* (I John 2:5).

Thought for Today: To know what is right, and not live it, is sin.

In Today's Reading

Healing the man born blind; Jesus, the Good Shepherd; religious leaders desire to stone Jesus.

Jesus identified Himself with the prophecy of Ezekiel. He said: *I am the good shepherd. The good shepherd lays down his life for the sheep. The hired man . . . leaves them and runs away when he sees a wolf coming. The wolf then snatches and scatters them. . . . I am the good shepherd. . . . I lay down My life for the sheep* (John 10:11-15).

The religious authorities in Israel were known as the shepherds of Israel; but they were false, self-centered prophets, as Ezekiel had foretold: *Ah, shepherds of Israel, who have been tending yourselves! Shouldn't the shepherds tend the flock?* (Ezekiel 34:2). Ezekiel then revealed the true shepherd: *Then I will appoint over them a single shepherd and he will tend them – My servant, David. . . . And I, the LORD, will be their God and My servant David will be a prince in their midst. . . . I will make a covenant of peace with them* (34:23-25).

The Holy Spirit led the apostle Paul to write: *Now may the God of peace, who brought up from the dead our Lord Jesus – the great Shepherd of the sheep – with the blood of the everlasting covenant, equip you with all that is good to do His will, working in us what is pleasing in His sight, through Jesus Christ, to whom be glory for ever and ever* (Hebrews 13:20-21). The apostle Peter foretold: *When the chief Shepherd appears, you will receive the unfading crown of glory* (I Peter 5:4). *They will never follow a stranger* (John 10:5).

Jesus also said: *I give them eternal life, and they will never perish. . . No one will snatch them out of My hand. My Father, who has given them to Me, is greater than all* (10:28-29). Here Jesus reveals Himself as both coequal and coeternal with God the Father. How comforting it is to be assured that we have Jesus the Good Shepherd caring for us.

One of the distinguishing marks of the Christian is a recognition of the need for guidance and a desire to follow the Shepherd. *The sheep follow him because they recognize his voice. They will never follow a stranger; instead they will run away from him* (John 10:4-5).

Thought for Today: Christians, like sheep, need to stay near the Shepherd in order to be protected from the deceptions of the world.

In Today's Reading

Raising of Lazarus; Pharisees' plot to kill Jesus; Mary's anointing of Jesus' feet; triumphal entry; Jesus' answer to the Greeks.

Throughout the years of Jesus' ministry, we see Him withdrawing Himself from public notice, often into the wilderness, and even charging *the disciples . . . to tell no one that He was the Messiah* (Matthew 16:20). When He raised the daughter of Jairus, He *gave them strict orders that no one should know about* it (Mark 5:43). When they came down from the Mount of Transfiguration, He gave orders to His disciples *to tell no one what they had seen* (9:9). The reason for this can be seen when the 5,000 who were miraculously fed by two fish and five loaves of bread planned *to make Him king, He withdrew . . . to the mountain by Himself* (John 6:15). When His unbelieving brethren urged: *Show Yourself to the world,* He answered: *My time has not yet arrived* (7:4,6).

Now Jerusalem was crowded with worshipers who had come from Judea, Samaria, Galilee, and from as far away as Greece. They came early in order that they might be ceremonially qualified to partake of the feast: *The Jewish Passover was near, and . . . many went up to Jerusalem from the country to purify themselves* (11:55-56) as well as to see Jesus.

As Jesus made His public entry into Jerusalem, the religious leaders were overwhelmed by the immense crowd that followed Him and they were heard to say: *Look – the world has gone after Him!* (12:19). Jesus openly and rightly accepted the acclaim of the multitude that He was their Messiah.

The prophet had foretold almost 500 years earlier: *Rejoice greatly, Daughter Zion! Shout in triumph, Daughter Jerusalem! See, your King is coming to you . . . humble and riding on a donkey, on a colt, the foal of a donkey* (Zechariah 9:9). Israel's true king now officially presented Himself to the nation as fulfilling that prophecy. *Many did believe in Him even among the rulers, but because of the Pharisees they did not confess Him, so they would not be banned from the synagogue. For they loved praise from men more than praise from God* (John 12:42-43).

Thought for Today: We should live so others can see Christ living in us.

In Today's Reading

Jesus washes the disciples' feet; Jesus foretells His betrayal, His death and second coming; Holy Spirit promised.

One of the most comforting thoughts that Jesus left with us is: *Your heart must not be troubled. Believe in God; believe also in Me. . . I am going away to prepare a place for you. . . . I will come back and receive you to Myself. . . . Peace I leave with you. . . . I do not give to you as the world gives. Your heart must not be troubled or fearful* (John 14:1-3,27).

After Judas had departed, these precious promises were given to the eleven disciples on the last night before Jesus was crucified. At that moment, their hearts were "fearful and troubled" because He had said He was leaving them. They were convinced that Jesus was the Messiah. Along with the multitudes, they too had shouted: *Hosanna! Blessed is . . . the King of Israel!* (12:13). But recently, Jesus had said: *Now My soul is troubled. What should I say – Father, save Me from this hour?* (12:27). He also had said that He must *suffer many things from the elders, chief priests, and scribes,* and *be killed* (Matthew 16:21). The apostles were troubled that one of their own number would betray Jesus (John 13:21-22).

The picture is much clearer to us 2000 years later, as we read the full story. However, like the disciples, occasionally, each of us is faced with fears of what tomorrow may bring. We need to remember that the Lord knows how to take care of our tomorrows. We too can have the utmost confidence in our Lord's comforting words: *Your heart must not be troubled. Believe in God; believe also in Me* (14:1).

When we are facing financial loss, divorce, disease, handicaps, or other "things" that happen to those who love the Lord, we should remember that He said: *Your heart must not be troubled* (14:1).

Every disappointment offers an opportunity to overcome stress, fear, and depression, and to develop our patience as well as our faith in God.

Dear friends, when the fiery ordeal arises among you to test you, don't be surprised by it, as if something unusual were happening to you. Instead, as you share in the sufferings of the Messiah rejoice (I Peter 4:12-13).

Thought for Today: We need to be thankful for the ministry of the Holy Spirit in and through us!

In Today's Reading

Jesus' prayer of intercession; His betrayal and arrest; Peter's denial; Jesus before high priests; Jesus condemned; Barabbas released.

After the Passover meal, Jesus began praying: *Father, the hour has come. Glorify Your Son. . . . I have glorified You on the earth. . . . I have revealed Your name to the men You gave Me . . . and they have kept Your word* (John 17:1,4-6). All true believers are also united in glorifying the *Father,* Christ our Lord and keeping His word.

Jesus continued praying for all who would ever believe on Him. *May they be one just as We are one* (17:22). Jesus and the eleven disciples then went to the Mount of Olives. Jesus knew that Judas would soon arrive with the religious leaders who would lead the hostile mob and Roman military to crucify Him. Just moments later, all of Jesus' followers forsook Him. Satan is the *accuser of our brothers* (Revelation 12:10); but the love of God looks past our mistakes. It is comforting to know that Jesus sees far more in His followers than we see in ourselves or in each other.

The difference between the weakest of Jesus' disciples and the worldly, unsaved person is this: *The words that You gave to Me, I have given to them. They have received them and have known for certain that I came from You. They have believed that You sent Me* (John 17:8). Notice the order: *The words You gave to Me, I have given to them,* and: *They have received them.* This emphasizes that *faith comes from what is heard, and what is heard comes through the message about Christ* (Romans 10:17). Faith and spiritual discernment are imparted as we daily meditate upon the word of God. As the psalmist recorded: *All who follow His instructions have good insight* (Psalms 111:10).

Jesus also prayed that the heavenly Father would *protect them by Your name that You have given Me* (John 17:11). How comforting to know that His prayer included everyone of us as He prayed: *I have given them Your word. . . . They are not of the world, just as I* (Jesus) *am not of the world. Sanctify them by Your truth. . . . I pray not only for these, but also for those who believe in Me through their message* (John 17:14,16-20).

Thought for Today: We receive the joy of the Lord as we share His love.

Post-Resurrection Appearances of Christ

Who Sees Him	Where	When	Reference
Mary Magdalene, Mary the mother of James & Salome	At the tomb	Early Sunday morning	Matt. 28:1-10 Mark 16:1-8;
Mary Magdalene	In the garden	Early Sunday morning	Mark 16:9-11; John 20:11-18
Two disciples	Road to Emmaus	Midday Sunday	Luke 24:13-32; Mark 16:12-13
Peter	Jerusalem	Sunday	Luke 24:34; I Cor. 15:5
Ten Apostles	Upper room	Sunday evening	Luke 24:36-43; John 20:19-23
Eleven Apostles	Upper room	One week later	Mark 16:14 John 20:24-29; I Cor. 15:5
Seven Apostles	Fishing in Galilee	Dawn	John 21:1-14
Eleven Apostles . . . disciples/ 500 followers	Galilee	Much later	Matt. 28:16-20; Mark 16:15-18; John 21:1-24; I Cor. 15:6
Disciples, principle women, Jesus' brothers, & others	Mount of Olives	40 days after the resurrection	Luke 24:46-53; Acts 1:3-14
Saul of Tarsus	Road to Damascus	Midday, years later	Acts 9:1-9; I Cor.15:8
James		Much later	I Cor. 15:7

In Today's Reading

Christ's crucifixion, burial, resurrection, and appearances to His disciples; Peter's allegiance reaffirmed.

Judas led the mob and the Roman soldiers to arrest Jesus. After Jesus' arrest, *they led Him to Annas. . . the father-in-law of Caiaphas, who was high priest that year* (John 18:13).

According to the word of God, the *high priest* was to be a direct descendant of Aaron and retain his office until death (Exodus 40:15; Numbers 35:25). However, Rome appointed a new *high priest* every year. Annas was *high priest* through Aaronic succession but was deposed by Rome. He was succeeded by his son-in-law Caiaphas who was the "official" *high priest* according to Rome. But, Annas continued to have great influence and was still considered the high priest by many.

Jesus, the prophesied *Lamb of God, who takes away the sin of the world* (John 1:29), was led to both the Jewish and then the gentile-appointed high priests. With Caiaphas were the scribes, the elders, the chief priests *and the whole Sanhedrin* (Matthew 26:57,59). In response to the question by the high priest regarding His deity, Jesus said: *In the future you will see the Son of Man seated at the right hand of the Power, and coming on the clouds of heaven* (26:64). Understanding that Jesus was claiming to be the Messiah, Caiaphas ripped his robe of authority and shouted: *Why do we still need witnesses? . . . you've heard the blasphemy!* (26:65). *After tying Him up, they led Him away and handed Him over to Pilate, the governor* (27:2).

Pilate knew Jesus was innocent of any criminal offense and said: *I find no grounds for charging Him* (John 18:38). But the religious leaders with loud voices cried out violently: *Crucify! Crucify! . . . He must die, because He made Himself the Son of God. . . . If you release this man, you are not Caesar's friend* (19:6-12). Pilate had to choose between Jesus "the Son of God" and the angry crowd; he chose the religious authorities. When a person compromises what is right for fear of losing prestige or anything else, he has taken the first step on the road to eternal hell. Jesus said: *No servant can be the slave of two masters* (Luke 16:13).

Thought for Today: Every Christian has a personal "world" to which he is responsible to show and tell of God's saving power.

Introduction To The Book Of Acts

The book of Acts is a continuation of the gospel of Luke. It includes over 10 recorded appearances of Christ during the 40 days following His physical resurrection. His parting words to His disciples before *He was taken up. . . . into heaven* are of utmost importance: *You will receive power when the Holy Spirit has come upon you, and you will be My witnesses . . . to the ends of the earth. After He had said this, He was taken up as they were watching, and a cloud received Him out of their sight* (Acts 1:8-11).

Throughout the first 30 years of the church, as recorded in Acts, on every occasion following a confession of Jesus as Lord and Savior, a believer was baptized (Matthew 28:18-20; Mark 16:16; Acts 2:38,41; 8:12-13,36,38; 9:18; 10:47-48; 16:15,33; 18:8; 19:5).

The first 12 chapters of this book focus on the apostle Peter and the first church in Jerusalem and conclude with his remarkable experiences among gentiles in Samaria who became believers in Jesus as their Savior.

Beginning with the stoning death of Stephen, intense persecution began against the church (7:59 – 8:4). Saul of Tarsus was one of the chief leaders of this persecution of all who accepted Jesus as the prophesied Messiah (the Anointed One). These believers would later be called Christians. After his remarkable conversion, Saul dedicated his life to Christ for worldwide evangelism and became known as the apostle Paul. He made his headquarters in Antioch of Syria (Aram), a gentile city, which became the center of world evangelism. Acts 13:1 through 21:26 describe the events of Paul's three missionary journeys.

From Acts 21:27 to the end of the book, we have details of Paul's arrest and his transfer to Rome to appear before Emperor Nero. The book ends with Paul still under house arrest after two years in Rome (28:30). Prominent throughout this book is "the word," which refers to the recorded Scriptures (11:16; 18:11; 19:10), also referred to as "message" or "preaching" (2:41; 4:4,29,31; 8:4,14,25; 10:36-37,44; 11:1,19; 12:24; 13:5, 7,26,44,46,48-49; 14:3,25; 15:7,35-36; 16:6,32; 17:11,13; 19:20; 20:32). The Holy Spirit is referred to more than 40 times as He fills, guides, and sustains Christians and prayer is mentioned over 30 times. This book demonstrates how vital the word of God, prayer, and the Holy Spirit are in the life of every believer and in the collective body of Christ, His church.

In Today's Reading

Ascension of Christ; promise of the Lord's return; Matthias chosen to replace Judas; coming of the Holy Spirit at Pentecost; Peter's sermon.

The Festival of Unleavened Bread portrayed the sinless Savior and was celebrated in conjunction with the Passover. The lamb without blemish also portrayed Jesus, the perfect Lamb of God.

The third festival of Passover week was Firstfruits. It was always on the Sunday after the regular Sabbath following the Passover observance. It was on Firstfruits that Jesus arose: *Now Christ has been raised from the dead, the firstfruits of those who have fallen asleep* (I Corinthians 15:20).

The second major festival for which every male was to appear annually before God was 50 days later, *the day after the seventh Sabbath* following Firstfruits (Leviticus 23:15-16). It was the Festival of the Harvest and celebrated the first ingathering of the crops.

After the miracle in the upper room, this festival became known to Christians as Pentecost from the Greek word for fifty. Pentecost was the first great harvest of souls after Christ sent the Holy Spirit. On that day, being filled with the Holy Spirit and quoting the prophetic Scriptures (Joel 2:28-32; Psalms 16:8-11; 41:9; 109:8), Peter boldly proclaimed *that God has made this Jesus, whom you crucified, both Lord and Messiah!* (Acts 2:36). Then the crowd said to Peter: *Brothers, what must we do? Repent, Peter said to them, and be baptized, each of you, in the name of Jesus the Messiah for the forgiveness of your sins, and you will receive the gift of the Holy Spirit. For the promise* (of the Holy Spirit) *is for you and for your children, and for all who are far off* (future generations of Jews and Gentiles), *as many as the Lord our God will call* (Acts 2:37-39).

The required offering on Pentecost consisted of two loaves of leavened bread (Leviticus 23:17). The loaves which represented both Jewish and Gentile believers included leaven, symbolizing sin, since everyone except Jesus has sinned. The two loaves of ground grain mixed with oil and leaven were then baked. The separate identities of the grains consolidated into a oneness, symbolic of all believers who lose their individual identities in Christ. The apostle Paul later declared: *Here there is not Greek and Jew . . . but Christ is all and in all* (Colossians 3:11).

Thought for Today: We all can help others know the Lord.

In Today's Reading

Peter and John imprisoned; believers share their possessions; Ananias and Sapphira; seven helpers chosen; Stephen's arrest.

Loyalty to the Lord and a love for one another permeated the first church. *Now the multitude . . . who believed were of one heart and soul, and no one said that any of his possessions was his own, but instead they held everything in common . . . all those who owned lands or houses sold them, brought the proceeds of the things that were sold, and laid them at the apostles' feet. This was then distributed to each person as anyone had a need. . . . Barnabas . . . a Levite . . . sold a field he owned, brought the money, and laid it at the apostles' feet* (Acts 4:32,34-37). No one was required to sell his property or to share his wealth. Barnabas' voluntary sacrifice undoubtedly brought great encouragement to the congregation because most Jews who confessed Jesus as the Messiah probably would have lost their jobs.

Ananias and his wife Sapphira also sold a piece of property, but they gave only a part of the proceeds to the church while implying they were giving everything just as Barnabas had done (5:1-2). The property was theirs to dispose of as they chose; and, even after they had sold it, the money was theirs to do with as they pleased. All giving was voluntary (5:4). Since the "generous gift" of Ananias and Sapphira resulted in their deaths, we need to consider how this may affect us.

The problem today is even more serious, not because Christians keep part of the proceeds of a sale, but because many refuse to give even a tithe (10%) of their income, the minimum that God requires. Tithing is not an option; it is a debt. God rightfully owns all that He created, but He only requires us to return to Him one-tenth of what He has entrusted to us, thereby acknowledging that we are stewards (managers) of His property. This principle was demonstrated by Abraham about 500 years before the law was given (Genesis 14:20; Hebrews 7:1-2). Later, the law stated: *Every tithe of the land, whether grain from the soil or fruit from the trees, belongs to the LORD; it is holy to the LORD* (Leviticus 27:30).

The Holy Spirit also directed Paul to write to the Corinthians: *The person who sows generously will also reap generously* (II Corinthians 9:6).

Thought for Today: Nothing is impossible. Put your trust in God.

In Today's Reading

Stephen's speech; his martyrdom; Saul's persecution of Christians; Simon, the sorcerer; Philip and the Ethiopian.

Stephen was a deacon in the church at Jerusalem, a man *of good reputation, full of the Spirit and wisdom* (Acts 6:3). Stephen knew the Old Testament Scriptures well and his faith was unshakable as he faced the anger of the religious authorities. He boldly reminded them: *You are always resisting the Holy Spirit; as your forefathers did, so do you. Which of the prophets did your fathers not persecute? They even killed those who announced beforehand the coming of the Righteous One, whose betrayers and murderers you have now become* (7:51-56).

Stephen could have avoided death by saying nothing, but he made it clear to the hostile crowd that they were responsible for crucifying Jesus, *the Righteous One*. With the same hatred which had demanded the crucifixion of Christ, the authorities now dragged Stephen *out of the city and began to stone him*. As he was dying, *he . . . cried out with a loud voice, Lord, do not charge them with this sin!* (7:57-60). Saul of Tarsus stood by watching. Stephen's faith and forgiving attitude in the face of death was the same as his Savior's on the cross and it surely must have made a powerful impression on those who witnessed Stephen's love toward his murderers.

In the same spirit of love, we too need to pray for those who despitefully treat us. Those who seem to be our enemies may someday be saved if we express the love of Christ to them as Stephen did.

On that day a severe persecution broke out against the church in Jerusalem (8:1). Instead of discouraging believers, persecution resulted in a great missionary movement. Philip, who was also a deacon in the first church, was led by the Holy Spirit to meet an Ethiopian official on his way home. As he read the book of Isaiah, God led Philip to explain to the Ethiopian how the prophecy of Isaiah 53:7-8 had been fulfilled in Jesus of Nazareth. On learning that Jesus was the Savior, the Ethiopian asked to be *baptized. . . . Philip said, If you believe with all your heart you may. And he replied, I believe that Jesus Christ is the Son of God. . . . and he baptized him. . . . and the eunuch . . . went on his way rejoicing* (Acts 8:36-39).

Thought for Today: Christ desires to control all your thoughts today.

In Today's Reading

Conversion of Saul; Dorcas raised from the dead; visions of Peter and Cornelius; Gentiles receive the Holy Spirit.

Saul of Tarsus was a sincere Pharisee determined to stamp out the followers of Jesus whom he considered religious blasphemers worthy of death. So he obtained letters from the high priest to go about 133 miles to Damascus in Syria (Aram) to arrest Christians who had fled from Jerusalem, that, *if he found any who belonged to the Way* (followers of Jesus), *either men or women, he might bring them as prisoners to Jerusalem* (Acts 9:2), where they could be tried for heresy and put to death.

As he neared Damascus, *a light from heaven suddenly flashed around him. Falling to the ground, he heard a voice saying to him, Saul, Saul, why are you persecuting Me? Who are You, Lord? he said. I am Jesus, whom you are persecuting, He replied* (9:3-5). About the same time, the Lord spoke to Ananias, a disciple of Christ who lived in Damascus, saying to him: *Get up and go to the street called Straight . . . ask for a man from Tarsus named Saul, since he is praying there* (9:11).

Ananias replied that he had *heard . . . how much harm he* (Saul) *has done to Your saints in Jerusalem. . . . But the Lord said . . . Go! For this man is My chosen instrument to carry My name before the Gentiles. . . . I will certainly show him how much he must suffer for My name! So Ananias . . . placed his hands on him and said, Brother Saul, the Lord Jesus . . . has sent me so* (that) *you may regain your sight and be filled with the Holy Spirit. . . . and he* (Paul) *regained his sight. . . . and was baptized* (9:13-18).

Peter also had a vision; it caused him to realize *that God doesn't show favoritism* (10:34). Speaking to Gentiles at the home of Cornelius, Peter said: *All the prophets testify about Him* (Jesus) *that through His name everyone who believes in Him will receive forgiveness of sins. While Peter was still speaking these words, the Holy Spirit came down on all those who heard the message* (10:43-44). After they were filled with the Holy Spirit, Peter said: *Can anyone withhold water and prevent these from being baptized, who have received the Holy Spirit just as we have? And he commanded them to be baptized in the name of Jesus Christ* (10:47-48).

We were all baptized by one Spirit into one body (I Corinthians 12:13).

Thought for Today: Live for God and He will give you His best.

In Today's Reading

Peter's report to the Jerusalem church; death of James; Peter's imprisonment and deliverance; death of Herod; Paul's first missionary journey.

Saul of Tarsus was born a Jew, but he was also a Roman citizen by birth in the town of Cilicia. His family, it seems, had considerable wealth and standing. Following the prescribed study of the Scriptures in Tarsus, Saul was selected for further rabbinic studies in Jerusalem as a student of the famous Rabbi Gamaliel (Acts 9:11; 16:37-38; 21:39; 22:3,25,29). Paul told the Galatian Christians: *I was extremely zealous for the traditions* (the Jewish interpretations of the law) *of my ancestors* (Galatians 1:14).

After his acceptance of Jesus as the Messiah, he then changed his Hebrew name of Saul to his Roman (Gentile) name Paul. On his first missionary journey, Paul *and his companions set sail . . . . from Perga and reached Antioch in Pisidia. On the Sabbath day they went into the synagogue and sat down. After the reading of the Law and the Prophets* (Acts 13:13-15) they were invited to speak. Pisidian Antioch was within a Roman province of Galatia in what is now Turkey. It was here that Paul gave a message about the atoning death and resurrection of Jesus Christ. Paul chose certain prophetic Scriptures to prove that Jesus was Christ – the Messiah. He began with a review of how *the God of . . . Israel chose our forefathers . . . . raised up David as their king. . . . From this man's descendants, according to the promise, God brought the Savior, Jesus, to Israel. . . . their rulers . . . . asked Pilate to have Him killed. When they had fulfilled all that had been written about Him* (by the prophets),*they took Him down from the tree and put Him in a tomb. But God raised Him from the dead* (13:17, 22-23,27-30).

It is through Christ's death and resurrection that we are able to receive eternal life. But being saved and *justified from everything* is far more than just choosing a better way of life. First it is a realization of the awfulness of sin as an offense against God, having real sorrow for that sin and a sincere desire to be delivered from sin. This is followed by a daily decision to avoid and resist sin through the power of the Holy Spirit. Paul declared: *Everyone who believes in Him is justified from everything, which you could not be justified from through the law of Moses* (13:39).

Thought for Today: Share what Jesus means to you with someone today.

Apostle Paul's First & Second Missionary Journeys

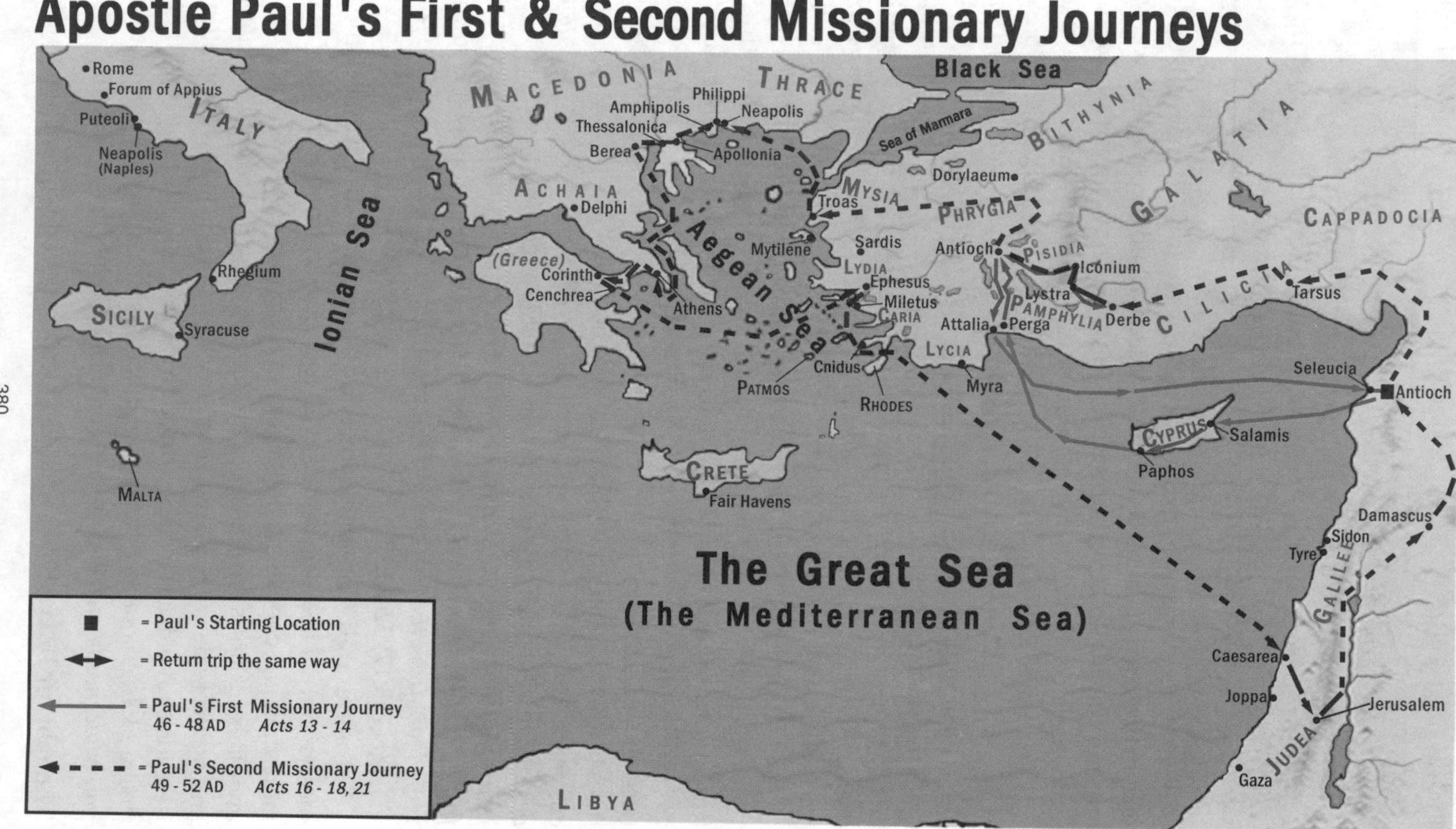

In Today's Reading

Paul and Barnabas at Iconium; stoning of Paul at Lystra; his return to Antioch; Paul's journey with Silas; Paul's Macedonian vision; conversion of Lydia; conversion of the Philippian jailer.

Almost everywhere Paul and Barnabas traveled, *an attempt was made . . . to assault and stone them* (Acts 14:5). In Iconium, about 90 miles east of Pisidian Antioch, violent opposition erupted when Paul told them that Jesus was the Messiah (Savior) foretold by the prophets. At Lystra, Paul's attention was drawn to a crippled man. *After observing him closely and seeing that he had faith to be healed, Paul said in a loud voice, Stand up straight on your feet. And he jumped up and started to walk around* (14:9-10). Upon seeing this miraculous healing, the people who worshiped false gods were convinced that *the gods have come down to us in the form of men* (14:11). Paul and Barnabas strongly objected to being made objects of idolatrous worship.

Following this event, *some Jews* (who had come to Lystra) *came from Antioch and Iconium, and when they had won over the crowds and stoned Paul, they dragged him out of the city, thinking he was dead. After the disciples surrounded him, he got up and went into the town. The next day he left with Barnabas for Derbe* (14:19-20).

Later, Paul made a brief reference to his sufferings for Christ (9:16), saying: *It is necessary to pass through many troubles on our way into the kingdom of God* (14:22). Whenever there is a true spiritual awakening and people are being saved, without exception, Satan will seek to disrupt, discourage, and destroy its effect. So, we too should not be surprised that, following our best efforts to serve the Lord, Satan will seek to discourage us through hardships and even disappointments from those from whom we expected encouragement. The man God chose to write more of our New Testament than any other writer, the apostle Paul wrote: *On frequent journeys, I faced dangers . . . among false brothers . . . often without food, cold, and lacking clothing* (II Corinthians 11:26-27). But he also wrote: *In any and all circumstances, I have learned the secret of being content . . . whether in abundance or in need. I am able to do all things through Him who strengthens me* (Philippians 4:12-13).

Thought for Today: Failure to be guided into all truth is the consequence of not reading all the truth.

In Today's Reading

Jewish opposition; Paul and Silas in Berea; Paul on Mars Hill, at Corinth, at Ephesus; Priscilla and Aquila; the silversmiths.

The apostle Paul and his coworker Silas were brutally beaten by a mob in Philippi and then thrown into prison. Through God's intervention, they were released the next day. Paul was no quitter; *they saw and encouraged the brothers, and departed. . . . to Thessalonica* (Acts 16:40 – 17:1). Wherever he went, Paul always attended the synagogue. *On three Sabbath days* (he) *reasoned with them from the Scriptures* (Old Testament), *explaining and showing that the Messiah had to suffer and rise from the dead, and saying: This is the Messiah, Jesus, whom I am proclaiming to you. Then some of them were persuaded* (17:2-4). When the unbelieving religious leaders became aware of these conversions, they were outraged and started a riot. After the riot, Paul left at night and traveled southwest to Berea. *On arrival, they went into the synagogue of the Jews. The people here were more open-minded than those in Thessalonica, since they welcomed the message with eagerness and examined the Scriptures daily to see if these things were so. Consequently, many of them believed* (17:10-12). Confessing Jesus as their Messiah was a monumental decision that would affect all aspects of their lives – family, friends, and business associates. Their dedication to the truth should encourage everyone, regardless of religious training, to study all the Scriptures with a sincere desire to know the truth it reveals.

Our Creator has allotted each of us with only one lifetime to prepare for our eternal destiny. We have a dual responsibility – to become the person He wants us to be in order to accomplish the purposes for which He created us. Think how tragic it will be for those who fail to fulfill the will of God, wasting their few short years achieving material, social, and financial goals for self-gratification. God has provided one perfect guide – the Bible – and He expects us to read it or suffer the consequences.

Having overlooked the times of ignorance, God now commands all people everywhere to repent, because He has set a day on which He is going to judge the world in righteousness (Acts 17:30-31).

Thought for Today: Praise the Lord! His ways are always best.

In Today's Reading

Paul's mission to Macedonia and Greece; raising of Eutychus from death; message to the Ephesian elders; seized in the temple.

The apostle Paul met with the Ephesian elders at Miletus, saying: *I am on my way to Jerusalem, bound in my spirit, not knowing what I will encounter there, except that in town after town the Holy Spirit testifies to me that chains and afflictions are waiting for me. But I count my life of no value to myself, so that I may finish my course and the ministry I received from the Lord Jesus, to testify to the gospel of God's grace* (Acts 20:22-24).

The indwelling Holy Spirit will strengthen us to withstand our trials and temptations as He did for Paul. Jesus promised: *I will ask the Father, and He will give you another Counselor* (Helper, Friend, Comforter) *to be with you forever* (John 14:16). We have not been left alone, but are *strengthened with power through His Spirit in the inner man* (Ephesians 3:16). With the assurance of the indwelling Holy Spirit, we can face life with certainty concerning our future. This enables us to enjoy a deep, inward peace, because we do not fear tomorrow. We have an inner contentment that *surpasses every thought* (Philippians 4:7) – one that outward circumstances cannot affect. Because God is within us and since God is love, we can respond with a love for others that sweeps away all prejudice, jealousy, hate, and envy. No opposition can rob us of the peace God bestows when we permit Christ the King to reign over our emotions.

Though we have not always permitted Christ to rule our emotions, we can say: "Though I'm not what I ought to be, I'm not what I used to be; but, thanks to Christ, I'm becoming what I was intended to be."

Spiritual growth takes place as we give, not just material things, but what people need most, our love, forgiveness, and understanding. In doing this, we are becoming more like Jesus. Paul never denounced the Roman Emperor Nero, but prayed for him. Even in his chains he wrote: *I urge that petitions, prayers, intercessions, and thanksgivings be made for everyone, for kings and all those who are in authority, so that we may lead a tranquil and quiet life in all godliness and dignity. This is good, and it pleases God our Savior, who wants everyone to be saved and to come to the knowledge of the truth* (I Timothy 2:1-4).

Thought for Today: *This is the day the LORD has made; let us rejoice and be glad in it* (Psalms 118:24).

In Today's Reading

Paul before religious rulers; Jews vow to kill Paul;
Paul sent to Felix; Paul before Festus; his appeal to Caesar.

When the apostle Paul arrived in Jerusalem, the religious leaders *stirred up the whole crowd* with false accusations: *This is the man who teaches . . . against . . . our law* (Acts 21:27-28). In response, an angry mob seized Paul and tried to kill him, but he was rescued from their violence by Roman soldiers. He was then allowed to speak in his own defense to the Jews. When Paul mentioned his commission by Jesus to go to the Gentiles, they immediately considered him a traitor to their religion, and angrily shouted: *Wipe this person off the earth – it's a disgrace for him to live* (22:22).

When the Sanhedrin authorities failed to convict Paul, the religious zealots decided to take the law into their own hands and murder him (23:12-15). *But the son of Paul's sister* overheard their wicked plan to murder Paul and told the Roman captain, who then had Paul secretly transferred by night to Felix, the Roman governor of Judea at Caesarea (23:16-24).

During his several years' confinement in Caesarea, Paul was tried before three powerful rulers of the Roman Empire who listened to what he had to say about his faith in Jesus Christ. He faithfully *spoke about righteousness, self-control, and the judgment to come* (24:25). Each of his judges had a different reaction as Paul spoke of the *judgment to come.* His first judge Felix *became afraid* and so heard him from time to time. Later, his second judge Festus exposed his indifference when he *exclaimed in a loud voice, You're out of your mind, Paul!* And, for whatever he may have meant, his third judge Agrippa said: *Are you going to persuade me to become a Christian so easily?* (26:24,28). Whether Agrippa's words were sincere, or sarcastic, as some think, is not important – the outcome was the same. As far as we know, none of these men received Christ as Lord and Savior of their lives and, consequently, all were eternally lost.

There is only one convenient time to repent and receive Christ as Savior and Lord: *Look, now is the day of salvation* (II Corinthians 6:2).

Thought for Today: Christ gave His all for us; let's give Him our all that He might live His life through us.

In Today's Reading

Paul's defense before Agrippa; his voyage to Rome; storm at sea; shipwreck at Melita (Malta); Paul at Rome.

When Saul of Tarsus confessed his faith in Jesus Christ as the risen Savior and Messiah, Festus, the new Roman governor of Judea, *exclaimed in a loud voice, You're out of your mind, Paul! . . . But Paul replied, I'm not out of my mind. . . . I'm speaking words of truth* (Acts 26:24-25).

Since Paul, as a Roman citizen, had appealed his case to Caesar, Festus placed him in the custody of *a centurion* (officer) *named Julius, of the Imperial Regiment* (27:1). Julius was to take Paul safely to Rome to stand trial before Nero, the Roman Emperor. They set sail and, after a brief docking at Sidon, continued along the northern coast of Cyprus. Stormy winds kept them from making much progress. On reaching *Fair Havens* in Crete (27:8), Paul urged them to stay there during the winter months, warning: *I can see that this voyage is headed toward damage and heavy loss,* but the majority of the people on board urged Julius to continue on to *Phoenix, a harbor on Crete . . . to winter there* (27:10-12).

Shortly afterwards, furious hurricane winds beat upon them. After two stormy weeks, their ship began to sink off the coast of Melita. *Paul stood up among them and said. . . . take courage, because there will be no loss of any of your lives, but only of the ship. For this night an angel of the God I belong to and serve stood by me, saying, Don't be afraid, Paul. You must stand before Caesar. And, look! God has graciously given you all those who are sailing with you* (27:21-24). This is a reminder that one's judgment is only as good as his source of information.

Our life's voyage, like Paul's, may also be filled with violent storms. We may also experience physical, financial, or emotional "shipwreck" and *all hope that we would be saved* may appear gone (27:20). But there will come a day when the tempests we have weathered will seem insignificant compared to what God has accomplished through our faithfulness. Paul could confidently say: *Because of Christ, I am pleased in weaknesses . . . in persecutions, and in pressures. For when I am weak, then I am strong* (II Corinthians 12:10).

Thought for Today: There is no guarantee you can accept Christ tomorrow because you may not have a tomorrow.

Introduction To The Book Of Romans

The Christian life is progressively explained in the book of Romans:

Chapters 1 – 3 establish three facts: 1. *God's wrath is revealed from heaven against all godlessness* (Romans 1:18); 2. *Both Jews and Gentiles are all under sin;* 3. *No flesh will be justified in His* (God's) *sight by the works of the law* (3:9-11,20).

Chapters 4 – 5 explain that a righteous God has provided the way for all people to be forgiven of all sin: *Jesus our Lord . . . was delivered up for our trespasses and raised for our justification. Therefore . . . we have peace with God through our Lord Jesus Christ* (4:24-25; 5:1).

Chapter 6 provides the meaning and importance of believer's baptism: *All of us who were baptized into Christ Jesus were . . . buried with Him by baptism into death . . . just as Christ was raised from the dead . . . so we too may walk in a new way of life* (6:3-4).

Chapters 7 – 8 reveal the conflict that exists between the believer's new spiritual nature and the old fleshly nature: *Now if Christ is in you, the body is dead because of sin, but the Spirit is life because of righteousness. . . . So then, brothers, we are not obligated to the flesh to live according to the flesh, for if you live according to the flesh, you are going to die. But if by the Spirit you put to death the* (sinful) *deeds of the body, you will live* (8:10,12-13).

Chapters 9 – 11 declare a universal gospel to all mankind: *There is no distinction between Jew and Greek, since the same Lord of all is rich to all who call on Him. For everyone who calls on the name of the Lord will be saved* (10:12-13).

Chapters 12 – 16 contain guidelines for spiritual growth and insight: (1) *Present your bodies as a living sacrifice;* (2) *Do not be conformed to this age;* (3) *Be transformed by the renewing of your mind, so that you may discern what is the good, pleasing, and perfect will of God* (12:1-2).

Paul emphasizes how important the Old Testament is to a true understanding of the Christian life: *For whatever was written before was written for our instruction* (15:4).

In Today's Reading

Paul's desire to visit the Christians in Rome; both Jews and Gentiles under condemnation; righteousness through faith.

We usually think of *God's wrath* (Romans 1:18) as something that will take place in the future when Satan and all unbelievers in Christ will be cast into the eternal *lake of fire* (Revelation 20:10,15). However, *God's wrath is . . . against all godlessness and unrighteousness of people who . . . suppress* (hinder) *the truth . . . God has shown it to them. . . . As a result, people are without excuse. . . .though they knew God, they did not glorify Him as God or show gratitude. . . . their senseless minds were darkened. Claiming to be wise, they became fools and exchanged the glory of the immortal God for images. . . . Therefore God delivered them over in the cravings of their hearts to sexual impurity, so that their bodies were degraded among themselves* (they committed sexual perversion) (Romans 1:18-27). Three times we read: *God delivered them over* to their degrading passions (1:24,26,28). Again, Christ has said: *The cowards, unbelievers, vile, murderers, sexually immoral . . . will be in the lake that burns with fire* (Revelation 21:8). The Bible views sex as a gift from God which can bring happiness and fulfillment only within the marriage relationship of one man with one woman.

There is a disturbing and growing ignorance of the Bible, the only book which reveals sin for what it is – rebellion against God, who alone has the right to set the standard for righteousness.

There is a growing tendency to neglect the church and to use the Lord's day and His tithe for self-centered pleasures. Instead of proclaiming the moral absolutes of the word of God, there are some who view sex as no more than a physical appetite to be satisfied. Doing so results in worldly compromise and situation ethics, where everyone chooses to define sin for himself.

There is no victory over sexual perversion until it is seen for what it really is, not as sickness or alternative lifestyle, but as sin. The good news is that, *when we were in the flesh, the sinful passions operated through the law in every part of us and bore fruit for death. But now we have been released from the law, since we have died to what held us, so that we may serve in the new way of the Spirit and not in the old letter of the law* (Romans 7:5-6).

Thought for Today: God desires to take care of your life. Trust Him.

In Today's Reading

Salvation, righteousness through Jesus Christ; sin through Adam; Christians under grace, not law; baptism explained.

The more we understand the horrible suffering and death of Jesus and the glory and power of His resurrection, the more we will desire to *walk in a new way of life*, daily manifesting the life of Christ. *Therefore we were buried with Him by baptism into death, in order that, just as Christ was raised from the dead by the glory of the Father, so we too may walk in a new way of life. For if we have been joined with Him in the likeness of His death, we will certainly also be in the likeness of His resurrection. For we know that our old self was crucified with Him in order that sin's dominion over the body may be abolished, so that we may no longer be enslaved to sin* (Romans 6:4-6).

To commit ourselves to only the *likeness of His death*, of bearing the cross, and of self-denial, would produce a very dismal view of following Christ. It is the glorious indwelling power of His physical resurrection that not only freed us from sin's control but also encourages and strengthens us to *walk in a new way of life*. Followers of Christ accept the fact that sin is no longer to be our master and that we are *dead to sin* (6:11). This does not mean we no longer sin, but that we are enabled to overcome sin!

Therefore do not let sin reign in your mortal body, so that you obey its desires. . . . But as those who are alive from the dead, offer yourselves to God (6:12-13). Our old "natural" man is still capable of yielding to the sinful desires of the flesh. But, Christ has made it possible for us to experience the reality of being *more than victorious through Him* (8:37).

His life in us makes the difference: *Do you not know that if you offer yourselves to someone as obedient slaves, you are slaves of that one you obey – either of sin leading to death or of obedience leading to righteousness?* (6:16). *You have your fruit, which results in sanctification – and the end is eternal life!* (Romans 6:22).

Thought for Today: The disciples were not theologians, just common people (as most of us are), who needed a simple, easy-to-understand plan of how Jesus wanted them to live. He did not disappoint them.

In Today's Reading

Law of life in the Spirit; suffering versus future glory; Israel's failure because of unbelief; a means of mercy to Gentiles.

Through the convicting and illuminating power of the Holy Spirit, we are led to see how deceptive and destructive sin really is (John 16:8-11). Only when a person recognizes that he is a lost sinner, unable to save himself and living in rebellion against his Creator God, will there be a *godly grief* that leads to *repentance* and *salvation* (II Corinthians 7:10).

When we accept Christ as our personal Savior, we receive the spiritual nature of God and sincerely desire that *the law's requirement would be accomplished in us who do not walk according to the flesh* (worldly ways) *but according to the Spirit. For those whose lives are according to the flesh think about* (desire) *the things of the flesh. . . . For the mind-set of the flesh is hostile to God because it does not submit itself to God's law* (Romans 8:4-5,7). Consequently, *if you live according to the flesh, you are going to die. But if by the Spirit you put to death the deeds of the body, you will live* (8:13).

True repentance results in a change of our heart attitude. This change should manifest itself in our becoming involved in a local church when physically able. Sadly, some people join a church, attend worship services, give generously, and assume that their good works are sufficient for entrance into heaven. But, they are only expressing *the form of religion but denying its power* (II Timothy 3:5). God is concerned first with what we are, then with what we do for Him.

Set your minds on what is above, not on what is on the earth. . . . Therefore, put to death whatever in you is worldly: sexual immorality, impurity, lust, evil desire, and greed, which is idolatry. Because of these, God's wrath comes on the disobedient, and you once walked in these things when you were living in them. But now you must also put away all the following: anger, wrath, malice, slander, and filthy language from your mouth. Do not lie to one another, since you have put off the old man with his practices and have put on the new man, who is being renewed in knowledge according to the image of his Creator (Colossians 3:2,5-10).

Thought for Today: Christ has made it possible for us to experience the reality of being *more than victorious* through Him (Romans 8:37).

In Today's Reading

Israel still to be saved; duties of a Christian in personal life, in the church, in society, toward government.

When we become Christians, we receive a new nature – the nature of God. The indwelling Holy Spirit enables us to let Christ control our lives instead of our old master Satan.

Therefore, it is only reasonable that we should live each day manifesting Christ's resurrection life, free from Satan's control. The apostle Paul wrote: *present your bodies as a living sacrifice, holy and pleasing to God; this is your spiritual worship. Do not be conformed to this age, but be transformed by the renewing of your mind, so that you may discern what is the good, pleasing, and perfect will of God* (Romans 12:1-2).

As we prayerfully read through the Bible, God's word becomes our spiritual food, our source of strength and spiritual insight to accomplish His will. Just as physical food is assimilated into our bodies to provide good health and physical strength, so the indwelling Holy Spirit strengthens our spiritual lives through His word that we might be healthy in our spiritual lives. The Holy Spirit alone can *guide you into all the truth* (John 16:13). However, He will not guide us into *all the truth* if we refuse to read *all the truth* from Genesis through Revelation. The word of God displaces our former way of thinking and His will becomes our purpose, which, in turn, changes our outward actions.

We daily live in the midst of many voices calling for our attention. We will always be tempted to satisfy our self-serving, fleshly desires. We also need to daily be on guard against allowing "good things," or even "good people," to occupy our time and keep us from the best God has for us. Life is far too short to allow material possessions and the desire for worldly accomplishments to dominate our lives. Our opportunities to serve the Lord and to be prepared to meet Him will soon end. *Pay careful attention, then, to how you walk – not as unwise people but as wise – making the most of the time, because the days are evil* (Ephesians 5:15-16).

Thought for Today: When we are controlled by the indwelling Holy Spirit, we are pleasing to God.

In Today's Reading

Law of love concerning doubtful things; Jewish and Gentile believers share the same salvation; Paul's desire to visit Rome; personal greeting.

Even now, the resurrected Christ is making intercession on our behalf because of our weaknesses and temptations (Hebrews 7:25).

Not one person in history has lived without sin, except Jesus. Since we do not know the hearts of anyone, we are warned: *Who are you to criticize another's servant? Before his own Lord he stands or falls. And stand he will! For the Lord is able to make him stand* (Romans 14:4).

We who (think we) *are* (morally and spiritually) *strong have an obligation to bear the weaknesses of those without strength, and not to please ourselves. Each one of us must* (make it a practice to) *please his neighbor for his good, in order to build him up* (to encourage rather than criticize). *For even the Messiah did not please Himself* (15:1-3). The greatest example is Jesus Christ, who unselfishly took all our sins upon Himself, suffering insult, persecution, and a cruel physical death on the cross for our sake. His personal sacrifice expressed the Christian way to deal with other people for their good and God's glory.

The "stronger" brother will put aside his spiritual pride and lovingly consider how to strengthen his brother without passing judgment, so as not to give Satan a foothold through division or self-righteousness.

When we allow Christ to be Lord of our lives, it results in a sincere, compassionate concern for others, not only for a weaker brother or sister in Christ, but for the lost as well. Spiritual discernment leads us to be understanding of others and their situations. The admonition *to bear the weaknesses* of others requires active involvement and not indifference on the part of more mature Christians.

God judges sin and makes it clear that we must *rebuke, correct, and encourage with great patience and teaching* (warning, urging, and encouraging the sinner to be obedient to the word of God) (II Timothy 4:2). Our compassionate Lord is also saying to those who represent Him: *Be merciful, just as your Father also is merciful* (Luke 6:36).

Thought for Today: Giving – not getting – is the key to our receiving blessings from God.

Apostle Paul's Third Missionary Journey & Trip to Rome

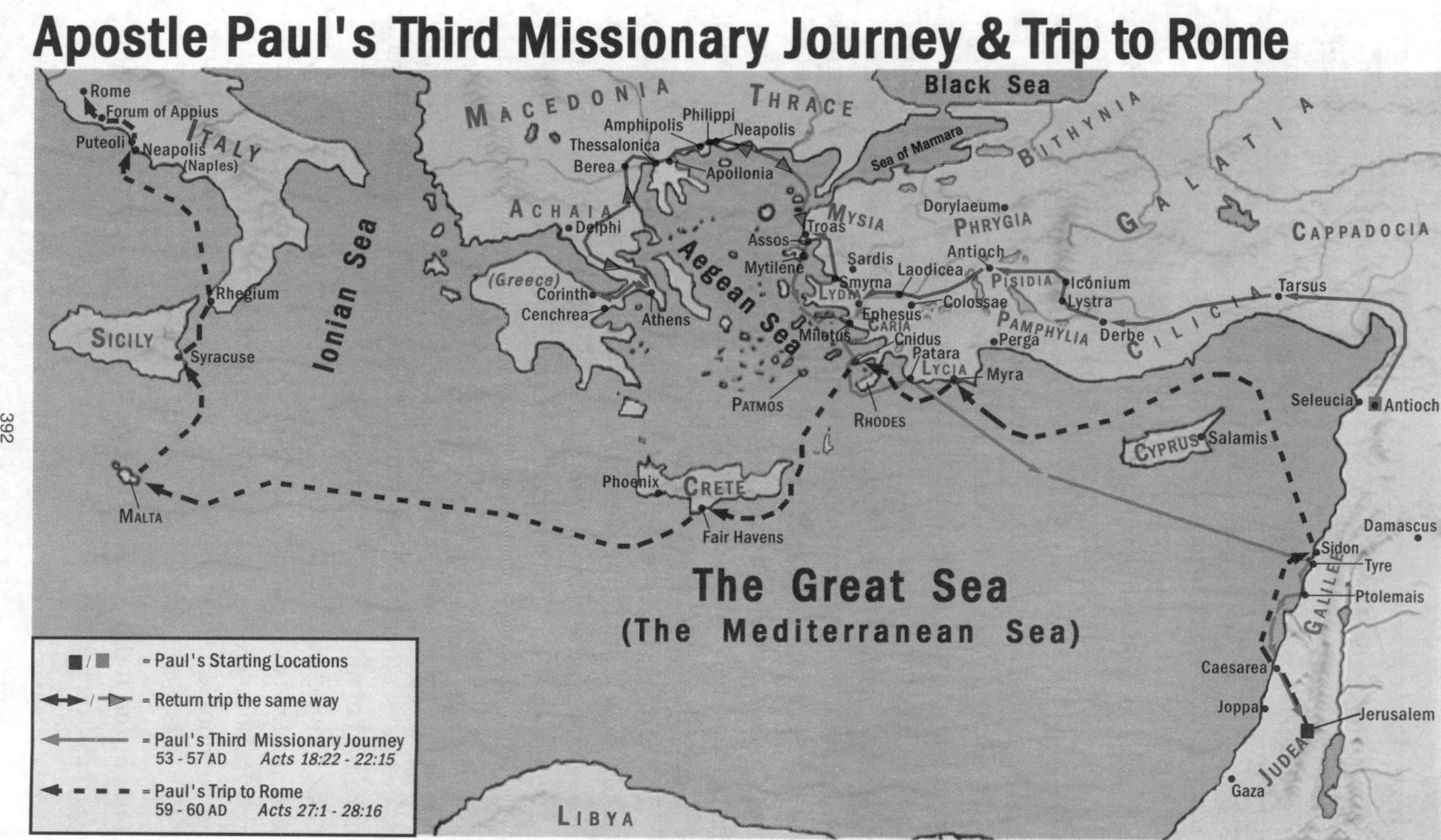

Introduction To The Books Of I & II Corinthians

There was little apparent acceptance of Jesus as the promised Messiah and Savior from sin in Athens (Acts 17:17,23,30-34). On the hill overlooking Corinth was the temple to Aphrodite, the Greek goddess of erotic love, where male and female prostitutes took part in sexually immoral acts as part of their religious rituals.

After preaching on the Areopagus (Mars Hill), the apostle Paul departed for Corinth, located about 50 miles to the west. He stayed in Corinth a year and one half (18:11,18). During that time, he supported himself through his profession of tent making. He also worked with Aquila and Priscilla, who had a church in their home (I Corinthians 16:19). They were a Jewish couple who had fled Rome because of Emperor Claudius' edict forcing all Jews to leave (Acts 18:1-3).

Corinth was a very immoral and wealthy city with a population estimated at more than 400,000. It controlled all of the east/west commerce on the sea, as well as north/south land travel. It was the capital of the Roman province of Achaia and was one of the most prominent cities in Greece. Paul concluded his second missionary journey by making a brief stop in Ephesus (18:18-19).

On his third missionary journey, Paul returned to Ephesus (I Corinthians 16:8), where he received disturbing reports concerning problems in the Corinthian church (1:11; 5:1; 7:1; 11:18). It was divided into four factions (1:10 – 4:21) and some members were openly living immoral lives (5:1-13). Responding out of great concern and love, Paul was directed by the Holy Spirit to explain how everything we do should be *for God's glory* (10:31). He gave a detailed explanation of the Lord's Supper (11:23-34); set forth the nine gifts of the Holy Spirit in chapters 12 – 14; and, in chapter 13, gave us the incomparable definition of love. The best explanation of the resurrection of Christ follows in chapter 15.

The primary purpose of II Corinthians was to commend the disciplinary action taken by the church against the sins of its members.

During the years that followed Paul's departure, there seems to have been a clique that developed within the church which was antagonistic toward his leadership and questioned his credentials, saying: *His physical presence is weak, and his public speaking is despicable* (II Corinthians 10:10). A major theme of II Corinthians is the ministry of reconciliation.

In Today's Reading

Grace and faithfulness of God; problems at Corinth; Christians, as temples of God; authority of apostles.

The church at Corinth was divided over who was the most important spiritual leader. Some preferred Paul, others Apollos, and still others Peter. *So, what is Apollos? And what is Paul? They are servants through whom you believed, and each has the role the Lord has given. I planted, Apollos watered, but God gave the growth. So then neither the one who plants nor the one who waters is anything, but only God who gives the growth. Now . . . each will receive his own reward according to his own labor* (I Corinthians 3:5-8). Because they were all servants of God, who enabled them to minister to His people, all praise should have gone to God. This illustrates how all of us need each other, as together we can fulfill His will in the body of Christ through our prayers, tithes, gifts, talents, and witnessing to others. No one should feel either indispensable or inadequate.

Our foremost concern should be: "Am I doing all I should with the opportunities that God has given me to use my time, talents, and possessions to glorify Him?" It takes every Christian to make up the body of Christ, which is the church. Everyone, without exception, is needed: *We who are many are one body, for all of us share that one bread* (10:17), and *we are God's co-workers* (3:9).

A body has many parts, each with different functions, but each part and function is necessary for the health, strength, and usefulness of the whole body. *The purpose is that none of you will be inflated with pride in favor of one person over another. For who makes you so superior? What do you have that you didn't receive? If, in fact, you did receive it, why do you boast as if you hadn't received it?* (4:6-7).

All praise should be given to the Lord, who alone qualified us for His service. This leaves no room for envying another person's ability or usefulness. Jealousy dishonors Christ and destroys the spirit of unity. *My brothers, hold your faith in our glorious Lord Jesus Christ without showing favoritism* (James 2:1).

Thought for Today: We should not boast – nor complain – about the gifts or abilities God has bestowed on us or on others.

In Today's Reading

Immorality and other sins condemned;
guidelines for marriage and Christian conduct.

The Bible makes a distinction between Christian and pagan lifestyles. It was reported to Paul that immorality existed in some of the members in the church at Corinth. Although it was apparently common knowledge, no one was doing anything about it. One member was committing fornication or adultery with *his father's wife* (I Corinthians 5:1), which would mean that he had an ongoing sexual relationship with his stepmother. Whether his father was still alive is not indicated. Paul admonished them to immediately excommunicate the offending member: *In the name of our Lord Jesus . . . along with my spirit and with the power of our Lord Jesus, turn that one over to Satan for the destruction of the flesh, so that his spirit may be saved in the Day of the Lord* (5:4-5).

It is vital that we be sensitive as to how our lives affect our witness in the world. In addition to that, the consequence of how our lives affect the church, our families, and our Christian friends is equally important. Still more serious is how our lives affect our relationship with God.

When leaders of a church body allow obvious ongoing sin among its members, it encourages a sinner to excuse his own sin, and continue his immoral lifestyle. Consequently, the decision to say or do nothing, merely in the interest of "harmony," is in opposition to what the Holy Spirit led Paul to write: *I am writing you not to associate with anyone who bears the name of brother who is sexually immoral or greedy, an idolater or a reviler, a drunkard or a swindler. Do not even eat with such a person. . . . Put away the evil person from among yourselves* (5:11-13).

Because of the inevitable result of sin, Paul again said: *Do not be deceived: no sexually immoral people, idolaters, adulterers, male prostitutes, homosexuals, thieves, greedy people, drunkards, revilers, or swindlers will inherit God's kingdom. Some of you were like this* (6:9-11). The key word here is WERE because all who received Christ as Savior and Lord of their lives should have forsaken their sins. *For God loved the world in this way: He gave His only Son, so that everyone who believes in Him will not perish but have eternal life* (John 3:16).

Thought for Today: To reject the Bible is to reject God Himself.

In Today's Reading

Guidelines for worship; the Lord's Supper; spiritual gifts; charity (love), the greatest gift.

Surprising as it may seem to the world, from God's point of view it is more important to be known for your loving-kindness, thoughtfulness, and being considerate of others than being a famous evangelist, preacher, or teacher. *If I speak the languages of men and of angels, but do not have love, I am a sounding gong or a clanging cymbal* – just a big noise (I Corinthians 13:1).

It is also more important to be known for one's love, as God loves, than to be the most prominent prophetic speaker in the world. Paul went on to reveal this God-given ability to love: *If I have the gift of prophecy, and understand all mysteries and all knowledge, and if I have all faith, so that I can move mountains, but do not have love, I am nothing* – nothing but a hindrance (13:2).

Love is patient; love is kind (13:4). It is not *conceited,* with inflated ideas of its own importance, meaning it does not insist on its own way and is never rude to anyone. Neither is it self-seeking, quick to take offense, or resentful. Love does not think evil of anyone. This God-kind of love is very patient – never envious or boastful.

Another dimension of love is that it *does not act improperly; is not selfish . . . does not keep a record of wrongs* (13:5), meaning it is tactful, charitable, and willing to forgive. Love has a way of making us more concerned for the feelings and rights of others and less preoccupied with self-seeking. The love of God keeps us from always trying to grab the best for ourselves or taking advantage of another.

Love has a way of keeping us from listening to people who are anxious to pass on the latest gossip about the faults and failures of another brother or sister in Christ.

Love *bears all things . . . endures all things* (13:7) without getting frustrated or angry. *Love never ends* (13:8), regardless of whether it is for friends, difficult people, or strangers. *Everyone who loves has been born of God and knows God. . . . because God* (His nature) *is love* (I John 4:7-8).

Thought for Today: When you love the Lord, love for others will be its natural overflow.

In Today's Reading

Spiritual gifts; resurrection of Christ; collection for the Jerusalem saints.

The physical resurrection of Jesus Christ is indispensable to our Christian faith. If He did not physically rise then He did not conquer death, and we have no hope beyond the grave. It is a triumphant fact *that Christ died for our sins according to the Scriptures, that He was buried, that He was raised on the third day according to the Scriptures* (I Corinthians 15:3-4). For the Christian, death is not the end of life, but only the beginning of a magnificent, eternal future with our wonderful Lord. *We will all be changed, in a moment, in the twinkling of an eye, at the last trumpet. For the trumpet will sound, and the dead* (in Christ) *will be raised incorruptible, and we will be changed* (15:51-52).

Paul concluded his glorious thoughts on the return of the Lord Jesus by saying: *Therefore, my dear brothers, be steadfast, immovable, always abounding in the Lord's work, knowing that your labor in the Lord is not in vain* (it is always profitable) (15:58).

Our Savior has assured us that *a time is coming when all who are in the graves will hear His voice and come out – those who have done good things, to the resurrection of life, but those who have done wicked things, to the resurrection of judgment* (John 5:28-29). We have the utmost confidence that, *if the Spirit of Him who raised Jesus from the dead lives in you, then He who raised Christ* (Jesus) *from the dead will also bring your mortal bodies to life through His Spirit who lives in you* (Romans 8:11).

Our twofold purpose for living is to become the person that God planned for us to be so that we may accomplish our Lord's will for us on earth and be prepared for the triumphant splendor of heaven. Concerning eternal life, Paul wrote: *Listen! I am telling you a mystery: We will not all fall asleep, but we will all be changed, in a moment, in the twinkling of an eye, at the last trumpet. For the trumpet will sound, and the dead will be raised incorruptible, and we will be changed.... Thanks be to God, who gives us the victory through our Lord Jesus Christ! Therefore, my dear brothers, be steadfast, immovable, always abounding in the Lord's work, knowing that your labor in the Lord is not in vain* (I Corinthians 15:51-52,57-58).

Thought for Today: Because Jesus died and rose again, Christians too will live for all eternity with Him. What a precious assurance!

In Today's Reading

Forgiveness of those who repent; Lordship of Christ;
Christian suffering.

Earthen vessels (clay pots) have very little value of their own. Their essential worth depends upon what they contain. If they are left empty, they have no purpose for existence. However, if they are filled with gold, their value increases dramatically. The body of a Christian is compared to an ordinary clay pot and the precious treasure it contains is *Christ in you, the hope of glory* (Colossians 1:27). *We have this treasure in clay jars* (II Corinthians 4:7) and are precious to God as dispensers of His life-producing word. But, at the same time Paul reveals this glorious truth, he also describes experiences common to all children of God: *We are pressured in every way but not crushed; we are perplexed but not in despair; we are persecuted but not abandoned; we are struck down but not destroyed. We always carry the death of Jesus in our body, so that the life of Jesus may also be revealed in our body* (4:8-10).

Since the Holy Spirit dwells in every born again Christian, we have the privilege of expressing His characteristics during every trial and suffering. We can face trials and suffering with the confidence that our Lord lovingly provides His best for our eternal good.

Trials and troubles, in whatever form, are necessary for spiritual growth; without them, we would not exercise our faith or develop spiritual insight and strength (Acts 14:22; I Peter 1:6-7). Just as it was necessary for Jesus to die, we too must die to self-love and become willing partakers of His sufferings.

For our momentary light afflication (distress of the passing hour) *is producing for us* (preparing and achieving) *an absolutely incomparable eternal weight of glory. So we do not focus on what is seen, but on what is unseen; for what is seen is temporary* (brief and earthly), *but what is unseen is eternal* (II Corinthians 4:17-18).

Thought for Today: We are called to *share in the sufferings of the Messiah* (I Peter 4:13).

In Today's Reading

Living by faith; ministry of reconciliation; believers not to be unequally joined with unbelievers; Paul's ministry; the grace of giving.

No one would deny that we are living in a day of deception and compromise and, unfortunately, Christians are tempted to search for satisfaction through what the world has to offer. To provide answers for this problem, Paul earnestly asked five questions that deserve our prayerful consideration because they have eternal consequences for us: *Do not be mismatched with unbelievers. For what partnership is there between righteousness and lawlessness? Or what fellowship does light have with darkness? What agreement does Christ have with Belial* (Satan)*? Or what does a believer have in common with an unbeliever? And what agreement does God's sanctuary have with idols? For we are the sanctuary of the living God* (II Corinthians 6:14-16).

Since there is a real danger of being caught up with world views that press upon us daily, James was led to warn us that *whoever wants to be the world's friend becomes God's enemy* (James 4:4). This is important to remember, since the believer and the unbeliever each have a different master. Paul was led to write: *If you have been raised with the Messiah, seek what is above, where the Messiah is, seated at the right hand of God. Set your minds on what is above, not on what is on the earth* (Colossians 3:1-2).

The believer should also be separated in heart and practice from the world which crucified Jesus and still hates Him today. The Christian call is to *come out from among them* (unbelievers) *and be separate, says the Lord; do not touch any unclean thing, and I will welcome you. I will be a Father to you, and you will be sons and daughters to Me, says the Lord Almighty* (II Corinthians 6:17-18). To *come out from* means, among other things, that we should avoid becoming involved with unbelieving friends or joining in activities that keep us from being our best for Christ and His church.

Paul went on to say: *Since we have such promises, we should wash ourselves clean from every impurity of the flesh and spirit, making our sanctification complete in the fear of God* (II Corinthians 7:1).

Thought for Today: It is only by the grace of God that we *are* anything or can *do* anything of eternal value.

In Today's Reading

Paul's spiritual authority; warning against false teachers; Paul's suffering; his thorn in the flesh; his plans to visit Corinth.

Paul faced rejection from hostile enemies of Christ and believers as well. He recalls: *Five times I received from the Jews 40 lashes minus one. Three times I was beaten with rods. Once I was stoned. Three times I was shipwrecked. I have spent a night and a day in the depths of the sea. On frequent journeys, I faced dangers from rivers, dangers from robbers, dangers from my own people, dangers from the Gentiles, dangers in the city, dangers in the open country, dangers on the sea, and dangers among false brothers; labor and hardship, many sleepless nights, hunger and thirst, often without food, cold, and lacking clothing. Not to mention other things, there is the daily pressure on me: my care for all the churches* (II Corinthians 11:24-28).

After his conversion, Paul lived with one purpose in life: To *preach the gospel to the regions beyond* (in lands never before reached) (10:16).

We too have the high calling to reach out in love to all nations with the good news of eternal life. Surely everyone should have the opportunity of hearing, at least once, that at death everyone is destined to either eternal death in the lake of fire or eternal life in heaven. Even though one's life and good works are very commendable, our Creator Jesus Christ said: *I am the way, the truth, and the life. No one comes to the Father except through Me* (John 14:6). Have you ever thought what it means for your friends or loved ones to die without being saved?

The dividing line between the sheep and the goats, the weeds and the wheat, the saved and the lost rests upon one fact; Jesus assured us that, *if anyone keeps My word, he will never see death – ever!* (8:51).

It is of utmost importance that we consider our priorities. Do they bring us closer to the Lord and His purpose for our lives or take us further away from Him? *When the Son of Man comes. . . . All the nations will be gathered before Him, and He will separate them . . . just as a shepherd separates the sheep from the goats. . . . Then the King will say to those on His right, Come . . . inherit the kingdom prepared for you from the foundation of the world* (Matthew 25:31-34).

Thought for Today: *Rejoice. . . . be encouraged . . . be at peace, and the God of love and peace will be with you* (II Corinthians 13:11).

Introduction To The Book Of Galatians

The apostle Paul wrote this letter *to the churches of Galatia* (Galatians 1:2) to refute the false teaching regarding salvation. This included Pisidian Antioch, Iconium, Lystra, and Derbe, all in different districts within the Roman province of Galatia.

False teachers were persuading some believers that keeping the ceremonial laws given to Moses was essential for both Jew and Gentile to become Christians. *Those who want to make a good showing in the flesh are the ones who would compel you to be circumcised – but only to avoid being persecuted for the cross of Christ. For even the circumcised don't* (can't) *keep the law* (6:12-13).

Only a smile, yes, only a smile
That a woman o'er-burdened with grief
Expected from you, 'twould have given relief
For her heart ached sore the while.
But weary and cheerless she went her way
Because, as it happened, that very day
You were out of touch with your Lord.

Only a word, yes, only a word
That the Spirit's small voice whispered, "Speak."
But the workers passed on, unblessed and weak,
Whom you were meant to have stirred
To courage, devotion, and love anew
Because, when the message came to you,
You were out of touch with your Lord.

Only a day, yes, only a day
But ah! could you guess my friend,
Where the influence reaches and where it will end
Of the hours you have frittered away?
The Master's command is, "Abide in Me."
And fruitless and vain will your service be
If you are out of touch with your Lord.

– M. E. H.

In Today's Reading

Only one gospel; Paul's rebuke of Peter; justification by faith, not law; the law, our guide to Christ.

This letter forever settles the fact that there is but one way to avoid eternal hell and to be assured of eternal life in heaven for either Jew or Gentile. *Grace to you and peace from God the Father and our Lord Jesus Christ, who gave Himself for our sins to rescue us from this present evil age, according to the will of our God and Father. . . . we know that no one is justified by the works of the law but by faith in Jesus Christ. . . . and not by the works of the law, because by the works of the law no human being will be justified. But if, while seeking to be justified by Christ, we ourselves are also found to be sinners, is Christ then a promoter of sin? Absolutely not!* (Galatians 1:3-4; 2:16-17). The law, given by God to Moses, was threefold: ceremonial, judicial, and moral. The laws foreshadowed Christ who fulfilled all the law. This means that Christians possess the nature of Christ and thereby are enabled to live by His law of love.

James set the record straight when he wrote: *Carry out the royal law prescribed in Scripture, You shall love your neighbor as yourself* (James 2:8). The laws of God illustrate His loving nature. We have a choice in that we can accept God's way and live according to His law of love or we can rebel against Him. But, we cannot change what He is or what He has said.

The farmer learns the laws of the seasons and becomes governed by them. He plants his crop when it should be planted; and because of this, he will reap when he should be reaping. For him to rebel and plant out of season does not change the laws of God, and crop failure is inevitable. When we express selfishness and sin, we disregard the laws that reveal the nature of God by which He operates the universe. We are like the farmer who plants out of season.

Now, we are led and empowered by the indwelling God the Holy Spirit. *Don't fear those who kill the body, and after that can do nothing more. But I will show you the One to fear: Fear Him who, after He has killed, has authority to throw into hell* (Luke 12:4-5).

Thought for Today: We fear men so much because we fear God so little.

In Today's Reading

The two covenants of law and promise; liberty of the gospel; fruit of the Spirit.

Sixteen sins are listed: *Now the works of the flesh are obvious: sexual immorality, moral impurity, promiscuity, idolatry, sorcery, hatreds, strife, jealousy, outbursts of anger, selfish ambitions, dissensions, factions, envy, drunkenness, carousing, and anything similar, about which I tell you in advance – as I told you before – that those who practice such things will not inherit the kingdom of God* (Galatians 5:19-21).

Sexual immorality, which includes adultery and fornication, heads the list. These sins include intercourse between any unmarried man and woman, as well as the vile perversions of sex, such as homosexuality, sodomy, and lesbianism. Sexual sin is one of the most deceptive sins of our day and destroys God-ordained marriage relationships.

However, *the works of the flesh* also include everything that defiles our mind, body, or spirit, such as illicit magazines and TV programs, impure movies, immoral jokes, evil thoughts, or indecency.

Idolatry includes not only the worship of anything or anyone other than God Himself but whatever determines our conduct. The object of idolatry could include an occupation, a person, or personal pleasure. Though these may not be evil in themselves, if they occupy the time and the loyalty which only God deserves, they actually are idols.

Not to be overlooked is *sorcery,* which includes horoscopes, palm reading, hypnotism, and other acts of the occult.

Also on the list are *hatreds, strife, jealousy, outbursts of anger, selfish ambitions, dissensions, factions* (5:20). *Strife and factions* include rivalry or discord, while *jealousy* includes the obsession to excel above others at any cost. These all begin with selfish attitudes.

Thanks be to God that *those who belong to Christ Jesus have crucified the flesh with its passions and desires* (5:24). We are no longer enslaved to these works of the flesh, but are endowed with the Holy Spirit and can bear His fruit, which is *love, joy, peace, patience, kindness, goodness, faith, gentleness, self-control* (Galatians 5:22-23).

Thought for Today: Perhaps the failure we see in another person's life is a reflection of the hidden sin of self-righteousness in our own hearts.

Introduction To The Book Of Ephesians

Beginning his third missionary journey, Paul returned to Ephesus and stayed there for about two years, preaching and teaching (Acts 19:1,8-10;20:31). During this time, a great number of people renounced the false worship of Diana and became Christians. Paul focuses attention on how God makes us alive in Christ Jesus. He reminds us: *You were dead in your trespasses and sins in which you previously walked according to this worldly age, according to . . . the spirit now working in the disobedient. . . . carrying out the inclinations of our flesh and thoughts, and by nature we were children under wrath* (Ephesians 2:1-3). But now, *you are being renewed in the spirit of your minds; you put on the new man, the one created according to God's likeness in righteousness and purity of the truth* (4:23-24).

In contrast to those who walk in the newness of life in Christ are those who *walk as the Gentiles* (unbelieving world) *walk, in the futility of their thoughts. They are darkened in their understanding, excluded from the life of God, because of the ignorance that is in them and because of the hardness of their hearts* (4:17-18). We are warned that *no sexually immoral or impure or greedy person, who is an idolater, has an inheritance in the kingdom of the Messiah and of God* (5:5).

Ephesians teaches us to prepare for spiritual warfare, to *put on the full armor of God so that you can stand against the tactics of the Devil. For our battle is not against flesh and blood, but against the rulers, against the authorities, against the world powers of this darkness, against the spiritual forces of evil in the heavens. This is why you must take up the full armor of God, so that you may be able to resist in the evil day, and having prepared everything, to take your stand. Stand, therefore, with truth like a belt around your waist, righteousness like armor on your chest, and your feet sandaled with the readiness of the gospel of peace. In every situation take the shield of faith, and with it you will be able to extinguish the flaming arrows of the evil one. Take the helmet of salvation, and the sword of the Spirit, which is God's word* (6:11-17). The book of Ephesians leads us to see how powerful the word of God is in overcoming *the tactics of the Devil* (6:11). It not only is our protection from evil; it is our offensive weapon – and the one Jesus used against the Devil. *Man must not live on bread alone, but on every word that comes from the mouth of God* (Matthew 4:4).

In Today's Reading

Spiritual blessings in Christ; prayers of Paul; unity of believers; Paul's mission to the Gentiles.

The God who created all mankind has chosen us to be His children. In fact, *He chose us in Him, before the foundation of the world, to be holy and blameless in His sight. . . . In Him we have redemption through His blood, the forgiveness of our trespasses, according to the riches of His grace* (Ephesians 1:4,7). No person or power can cheat us out of God's very best for our lives as we daily read and study His word with a desire to do His will, and then pray and depend upon the Holy Spirit to guide our lives.

Before Christ came to earth, only the Jews had a covenant relationship with God: *At that time you were without the Messiah, excluded from the citizenship of Israel, and foreigners to the covenants of the promise, with no hope and without God in the world* (2:12). Jews and Gentiles alike who receive Christ as Savior and Lord have a covenant relationship with God: *Through Him we both have access by one Spirit to the Father* (2:18). In A.D. 70, God used the Roman general Titus to destroy the temple, the altar of sacrifice, and the functions of the high priest. These merely foreshadowed the Messiah who became the only means through which a worshiper may be accepted.

Only through Jesus Christ is it possible to approach the one true holy God in prayer at anytime, day or night for *we have boldness, access, and confidence through faith in Him* (3:12).

Is it any surprise that Satan will deceptively seek to keep us too busy doing good things in his effort to keep us from reading God's word in order to make our prayers effective. Because of our love for the Lord, the true believer looks forward to a daily dialog of prayer (talking to God) and reading His word (God talking to us). *I pray that . . . the Messiah may dwell in your hearts through faith. I pray that you, being rooted and firmly established in love, may be able to . . . know the Messiah's love that surpasses knowledge, so you may be filled with all the fullness of God* (Ephesians 3:16-19).

Thought for Today: Prayer is a powerful force that goes beyond our limited human wisdom and strength.

In Today's Reading

Exhortations on unity; spiritual gifts; the importance of holiness; walk in love; marriage, symbolic of the church; duties of children; armor of God.

When we let the love of Christ flow through us and manifest His loving-kindness to everyone without discrimination, then we enjoy His bountiful blessings. The Lord says to give up all thoughts of resentment and ill will without exception. *All bitterness* (resentment), *anger and wrath* (quarreling), *insult and slander must be removed from you, along with all wickedness* (desire to inflict suffering on another) (Ephe-sians 4:31). Instead, *be kind and compassionate to one another, forgiving one another, just as God also forgave you in Christ* (4:32).

Anger and wrath are often demonstrated in an outburst of abusive language as a reaction against someone who disagrees with our views.

Even more serious is the sin of *slander* which is one of the seven sins that God hates the most (Proverbs 6:16-19).

The presence of any of these evils destroys our peace of mind, grieves the Holy Spirit, and affects our relationship with God. If we allow the Holy Spirit to rule our lives, feelings of anger are overcome. Sadly, when some people are offended they decide not to forgive.

Instead of thoughts of bitterness, revenge, and anger, we should pray for those who wrong us as Stephen prayed while he was being stoned to death: *He knelt down and cried out with a loud voice, Lord, do not charge them with this sin!* (Acts 7:60).

Every Christian is a representative of the Lord Jesus Christ and is responsible for, as well as capable of, responding with the love of God toward those who, by their words, attitudes, or actions, are unlovely. We are to be *diligently keeping the unity of the Spirit with the peace that binds us. . . . But speaking the truth in love, let us grow in every way into Him who is the head – Christ. From Him the whole body, fitted and knit together by every supporting ligament, promotes the growth of the body for building up itself in love by the proper working of each individual part* (Ephesians 4:3,15-16).

Thought for Today: Those who love the Lord keep His commandments.

Continued on page 411

VICTORY OVER SATAN ASSURED

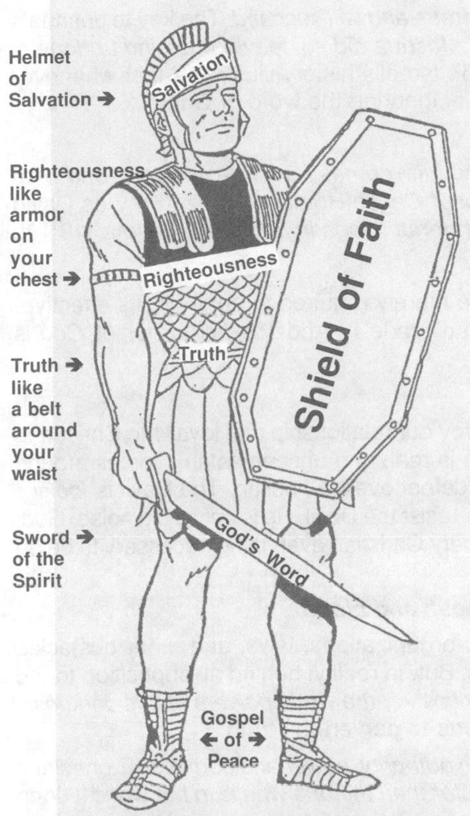

Pray at all times . . . for all the saints
[Ephesians 6:18]

Be strengthened by the Lord and by His vast strength. Put on the full armor of God so that you can [successfully] stand against [all] the tactics [strategies, strength, and deceits] of the Devil. For our battle is not against flesh and blood, but against the rulers, against the authorities, against the world powers of this darkness, against the spiritual forces of evil in the heavens. This is why you must take up the full armor of God, so that you may be able to resist in the evil day [when you are tempted] [Ephesians 6:10-13].

Jesus' victory over Satan during His 40 days in the wilderness was accomplished as He quoted Scripture. And He reminds us that *man must not live [victoriously] on bread alone [physical needs that supply physical strength], but on every word that comes from the mouth of God* [Matthew 4:4]. "Every word" begins in Genesis.

Every piece of the *armor of God* illustrates the word of God. Never is there a time when the Christian soldier can put aside his *armor* and say: "The battle is won." We are to *fight the good fight for the faith* [I Timothy 6:12], and *faith comes from what is heard [read], and what is heard comes through the message about Christ* [Romans 10:17]. *The word of God is living and effective . . . a judge of the ideas and thoughts of the heart* [Hebrews 4:12]. *It is God [through His word] who is working among you both the willing and the working for His good purpose* [Philippians 2:13].

We overcome in the great conflict with worldliness as the soldier of Christ when we *put on the full armor of God* [Ephesians 6:11]. Furthermore, there are no alternatives, no substitutes. College degrees, theology, and psychology are all powerless to prepare the soldier for spiritual warfare. It is futile to put on only half the *armor*, for Satan and his *tactics* are sure to aim his *flaming arrows* at the most vulnerable spot [6:16]. We're all inclined to fortify ourselves against certain selected sins and neglect the areas in which we think of ourselves as most secure. But the Lord warns: *Whoever thinks he stands must be careful not to fall!* [I Corinthians 10:12]. God knows all the enemy forces that we face, and He knows our weaknesses and has provided full protection and complete armor for us to be victorious -- *more than victorious through Him who loved us* [Romans 8:37].

Verse 10: *Be strengthened by the Lord*

These are the same words that God spoke to Joshua: *Be strong.* Joshua was able to conquer the kings in the promised land in just seven years. His secret of strength is pointed out in Joshua 1:8: *This book of the law must not depart from your mouth; you must recite it day and night, so that you may keep observing all that is written in it. For then you will make your way prosperous and will succeed.* The key to Joshua's conquest of the promised land is evident: *Joshua did so, leaving nothing undone of all that the LORD had commanded* [11:15]. Israel's history illustrates that whenever there were failures, it was a direct result of ignoring the word of God.

By His vast strength

To be overcome by sin is a faith failure, and *faith comes from what is heard, and what is heard comes through the message about Christ* [Romans 10:17]. Pray as David did: *Open my eyes so that I may see wonderful things in Your law* [Psalms 119:18].

Verse 11: *Put on the full armor of God*

We cannot provide our *armor*, but we are merely required to put it on. Its effectiveness depends entirely upon the One who made it. And *the full armor of God* is essential for a victorious Christian life.

Stand against the tactics of the Devil

The purpose of Satan [the Devil] is to destroy our relationship and loyalty to Christ and make us ineffective as His soldiers. Satan is real, and unseen satanic forces around us are seeking to discourage and then to defeat every Christian. The Devil is *looking for anyone he can devour* [I Peter 5:8]. But, resist the Devil. He is only a big noise. God, through His word, has made available to every Christian everything necessary to be an overcomer.

Verse 12: *For our battle is not against flesh and blood*

Our conflict may appear to be with men, organizations, laws, and other obstacles that seek to hinder our Christian activities. But, in reality, behind all opposition to the gospel is Satan – *the rulers . . . the authorities . . . the world powers of this darkness.* This darkness is the result of satanic efforts to pervert the truth.

He [Christ] (is) *. . . far above every ruler and authority, power and dominion* [Ephesians 1:20-21] and *the One who is in you is greater than the one who is in the world* [I John 4:4]. The normal Christian life is one of continual victory over satanic assaults. In the natural man, there is a desire for *the lust of the flesh, the lust of the eyes, and the pride in one's lifestyle* [I John 2:15-17]. However, *if you live according to the flesh, you are going to die. But if by the Spirit you put to death the deeds of the body, you will live* (Romans 8:13).

Verse 13: *Take up the full armor of God, so that you may be able to resist in the evil day*

The evil day of temptation will come but at a time when we least expect it.

and having prepared everything, to take your stand

Our reason for failure is *friendship with the world . . . So whoever wants to be the world's friend becomes God's enemy* [James 4:4]. Jesus said: *No one can be a slave of two masters* [Matthew 6:24]. We must decide who and what we are living for. James wrote: *An indecisive man is unstable in all his ways* [James 1:8]. And Paul wrote: *Therefore, my dear brothers, be steadfast, immovable, always abounding in the Lord's work, knowing that your labor in the Lord is not in vain* [I Corinthians 15:58].

Verse 14: *With truth like a belt around your waist*

The *belt* was often made of linen, wide enough for several folds that could carry valuables around the waist. Such is the word of God, wrapped around us, encompassing our life, involving our whole being, preparing us to be effective.

The words *with truth* have a twofold meaning. One: it denotes the whole truth of God's word in order to know His will and to accomplish His purposes.

The second meaning is personal integrity – honesty, sincerity, devotion, and determination – the opposite of hypocrisy, indifference, half-heartedness or selfish motives.

Truth is our belt holding our valuables. Nothing short of God's truth is sufficient as we move into action against the *tactics of the Devil.*

Righteousness like armor on your chest

The *armor on [the] chest [the breastplate]* of the Roman soldier was worn to protect his heart -- the source of physical life. The *armor* of the Christian is here called *righteousness. Righteousness* is an attribute of *the Lord, our righteousness* [Jeremiah 23:6; 33:16].

The *armor on [the] chest [breastplate]* covers the heart, the motives, the desires of our inmost being. Jesus prayed: *Sanctify them by the truth: Your word is truth* [John 17:17]. His ultimate desire for every Christian is that He might *make [us] holy, cleansing [us] in the washing of water by the word. . . . holy and blameless* [Ephesians 5:26-27].

Verse 15: *Your feet sandaled with the readiness of the gospel of peace*

The *feet* must be protected to *run with endurance the race* [Heb. 12:1]. To be *sandaled* has reference to the military sandals – a symbol *of the gospel of peace*. The *gospel of peace* keeps us moving forward in the never ending goal to win lost souls for Christ.

Verse 16: *Take the shield of faith*

The Roman soldier's *shield* was a large, oblong instrument covering most of his body. But it was his responsibility to hold it. The *shield* becomes our overall protection. *This is the victory that has conquered the world: our faith* [I John 5:4-5]. *Without faith it is impossible to please God* [Hebrews 11:6]. This *shield of faith* affirms our faith in the Bible as the infallible word of God. We believe in God the Father; Christ, our Redeemer; and the Holy Spirit to *guide [us] into all the truth* [John 16:13].

You will be able to extinguish the flaming arrows of the evil one

Flaming arrows were tipped with flammable materials, like a fire brand, and shot through the air. They were intended to cripple or put out of service the enemy. The *flaming arrows* are temptations of covetousness, lust, immortality, pride, love of money, revenge, hate, bitterness, and strife that will cripple the Christian and put him out of commission as an active, effective soldier of Jesus Christ.

Verse 17: *Take the helmet of salvation*

The helmet is the head covering. It is *the helmet* that protected the head and allowed the Roman soldier to hold his head high and face the enemy. And it is *salvation* – the new birth experience – *born of . . . [His] Spirit* [John 3:5] – that causes us to look up in faith, knowing that our *salvation* is *not by works of righteousness that we had done, but according to His mercy [He saved us]* [Titus 3:5].

Furthermore, having accepted Christ as our Savior, as did the believers who listened to Peter on the day of Pentecost, we gladly *accepted His message [and] were baptized* [Acts 2:41]. His word not only has the solution for gaining eternal life, but gives direction to overcome all of life's problems.

And the sword of the Spirit

The sword of the Spirit is the word of God. That word makes us aware of the *tactics of the Devil*. It is the soldier's weapon of offense against unbelief, covetousness, pride, hatred, and worldliness. The secret to spiritual effectiveness is determined by how much of God's word is a living reality in our lives. We need to ask ourselves: "How big is our *sword*?" Is it the size of a toothpick – a few verses here and there?

Just as the good soldier does not make up his mind whether or not to fight or in which direction to move, so the good soldier of Christ must be familiar with and trained to use his *sword* under the authority of the Holy Spirit.

This same indwelling Holy Spirit *will guide you into all truth* [John 16:13]. But He cannot guide us into the truth that we have refused to read. There is no substitute for the word of God. That is why the Holy Spirit led David to write: *I will . . . give thanks to Your name for. . . . You have exalted Your name and Your promise [Your word] above everything else* [Psalms 138:2]. Only the word of God is said to be the source of our new birth, being *born again* [I Peter 1:23; James 1:18]. Only the word of God is said to be the source of our spiritual growth. *Desire the unadulterated spiritual milk [of the word], so that you may grow by it* [I Peter 2:2].

The church world has a thousand imitation swords -- one for every problem. You name it and someone has written a book about it. One of the greatest victories of Satan is keeping Christians busy reading "good" books that keep them from reading THE BOOK. The Bible was created for your profit, for *all Scripture . . . is profitable* [II Timothy 3:16].

Verse 18: *Pray at all times in the Spirit, and stay alert in this, with all perseverance and intercession*

It becomes evident that the Christian soldier is not left defenseless. *The weapons of our warfare are not fleshly, but powerful through God for the demolition of strongholds* [II Corinthians 10:4]. As God's word becomes our way of life, our prayers are answered. Satan will do everything in his power to distract us from reading God's word, living God's word, and praying according to God's word. *Anyone who turns his ear away from hearing the law [God's word] – even his prayer is detestable* [Proverbs 28:9].

The Christian's *warfare* never ends. It's 365 days of every year. There is no leave of absence, no vacation, no time off. It is a continual fight against *the lust of the flesh, the lust of the eyes, and the pride in one's lifestyle* [I John 2:16].

for all the saints

The Christian soldier is a volunteer in the King of kings' army -- not for self-interests -- but *for all the saints*. It is of utmost importance that we pray for the leadership, pastors, evangelists, missionaries, our church, and heads of ministries. But it is of equal importance to pray for the weakest saint -- the one who may have offended us. Difficulty in forgiving others indicates an inadequate view of our need of forgiveness from God. Jesus warned: *If you [from your heart] don't forgive people [everyone], your Father will not forgive your wrongdoing* [Matthew 6:15; compare 18:21-35].

This points out the importance of heartfelt earnestness in prayer. When Jesus prayed: *I pray for them. . . . You have given Me, because they are Yours. . . . that they may have My joy completed in them. I have given them Your word. . . . They are not of the world, just as I am not of the world. . . . Sanctify them by the truth; Your word is truth. Just as You sent Me into the world, I also have sent them into the world. . . . May they all be one. . . . That the love with which You have loved Me may be in them, and that I may be in them* [John 17:9,13-14,16-18,21,26]. Oh, how we need to recognize the importance of heartfelt praying *for ALL the saints*!

Art thou abiding in the Vine
In fellowship serene,
His precious Word, thy daily Bread
With naught thy Lord between?

Doth thy heart yearn new heights to gain,
Yea! new depths to explore,
To mount on eagles' wings superb
In Faith and love to soar?

My Child, if thou wouldst e'er abound
In Jesus Christ, thy Lord,
Then truly thou must e'er abide
In God's own Holy Word.

– M. E. H.

Continued from page 406

Introduction To The Book Of Philippians

The apostle Paul was in Troas, in Asia Minor, on his second missionary journey when he received the call, in a vision, to carry the good news into Macedonia, *to Philippi, a Roman colony, which is a leading city of that district of Macedonia. We* (Paul and probably Luke) *stayed in that city for a number of days* (Acts 16:12). The church that grew out of his stay was the first one Paul established within Europe.

As he wrote this letter, Paul was a prisoner in the custody of the Roman Emperor Nero, but he called himself *the prisoner of Christ Jesus*. Paul knew who was in control of his life (Ephesians 3:1; 4:1; II Timothy 1:8; Philemon 1:1,9). He assured the Philippians that Christ is the never-failing source of strength during adverse circumstances, saying: *I am able to do all things through Him who strengthens me* (Philippians 4:13). The key thought is: *Rejoice in the Lord always. I will say it again: Rejoice!* (4:4). *Joy* and *rejoice* occur about 15 times in Philippians (1:4,18,25-26; 2:17-18,28; 3:1,3; 4:1,4,10).

In Today's Reading

Paul's prayer for the Philippians; the privilege of suffering for Christ; unity gained by humility; exhortation to rejoice in the Lord.

The apostle Paul first preached in Europe at Philippi. On the Sabbath, he went to a place of prayer by a river where he met Lydia, a businesswoman from Thyatira who was saved along with a few others, and a church was planted. At a later date, as a missionary prisoner at Rome, Paul wrote to his converts: *My eager expectation and hope is that . . . Christ will be highly honored in my body. . . . For me, living is Christ and dying is gain* (Philippians 1:20-21).

His imprisonment in Rome gave him the opportunity to share the good news about Jesus with the elite guard of the Roman Empire. This was a great opportunity. As there was a change of guard three or four times a day, Paul wrote to the Philippians: *Now I want you to know, brothers, that what has happened to me has actually resulted in the advancement of the gospel, so that it has become known throughout the whole imperial guard, and to everyone else, that my imprisonment is for Christ* (1:12-13).

Paul encouraged the church: *Hold firmly the message of life. Then I can boast in the day of Christ that I didn't run in vain or labor for nothing* (2:16). Our occupation in life may be politics, the military, business, education, manual labor, or homemaking, but our primary concern should always be *that I didn't run in vain or labor for nothing.*

We all have a natural desire for physical comforts, security, and material things. However, in making our decisions, our first loyalty should be to Christ. In Him, there is a storehouse of spiritual wealth and peace that makes all earthly possessions eternally worthless.

Paul had renounced a prominent career for a life of unceasing hardships and persecutions which was destined to end in a violent death. Knowing what the future held, he still said: *In view of the surpassing value of knowing Christ Jesus my Lord. . . . I have suffered the loss of all things and consider them filth, so that I may gain Christ. . . . My goal is to know Him and the power of His resurrection and the fellowship of His sufferings, being conformed to His death* (Philippians 3:8,10).

Thought for Today: Happiness cannot result from an act of sin.

Introduction To The Book Of Colossians

The city of Colossae was located in the Roman province of Asia Minor on the east/west trade route that ran from Ephesus to Tarsus, and then to Aram (Syria). In this brief letter, Paul focused on the fundamental doctrines of our faith in God. *He has rescued us from the domain of darkness and transferred us into the kingdom of the Son He loves, in whom we have redemption, the forgiveness of sins* (Colossians 1:13-14).

Paul also combated false teachings by confirming the deity of Christ and His supremacy over all things. *By Him everything was created, in heaven and on earth, the visible and the invisible, whether thrones or dominions or rulers or authorities – all things have been created through Him and for Him. He is before all things, and by Him all things hold together. He is also the head of the body, the church; He is the beginning, the firstborn from the dead, so that He might come to have first place in everything* (Colossians 1:16-18).

We all have sinned against the Lord
And stand condemned by His own Word,
No prayer or plea of ours could win
God's free forgiveness for all sin

But Jesus came and took our place
That He might save us by His grace;
He bore our sins – so great and wide –
That we, through Him, be justified.

And as we plead Christ's work complete
Upon the Cross – where He did meet
Each claim of God's most righteous Law –
God wipes away each sin and flaw.

He speaks His peace within the heart
And bids all guilt and fear depart,
Counts, us accepted in His Son
And sees the life of faith begun.

May we, in gratitude and love,
Seek e'er those things that are Above
And let Christ live His life anew
Through all who love His will to do.

– *M. E. H.*

In Today's Reading

The supremacy of Christ; reconciliation in Christ; warning against false teaching; the new life in Christ; Christian virtues.

As we continue reading God's word with a desire to please Him in all of our decisions, the Holy Spirit guides us into a deeper revelation of His will and His ways. There is no limit to the understanding, strength, and endurance that are made available to every Christian. Christ alone, through His word, can reveal and meet all of our spiritual needs. To help us grasp the importance of this, Paul wrote: *We haven't stopped praying for you. We are asking that you may be filled with the knowledge of His will in* ***all*** *wisdom and spiritual understanding, so that you may walk worthy of the Lord, fully pleasing to Him, bearing fruit in every good work and growing in the knowledge of God. May you be strengthened with* ***all*** *power, according to His glorious might, for* ***all*** *endurance and patience, with joy giving thanks to the Father, who has enabled you to share in the saints' inheritance in the light* (Colossians 1:9-12). Notice how often the word *all* is used – *all wisdom . . . all power. . . all endurance . . . all patience.*

What follows is the practical expression of the new life in Christ. *Having been buried with Him in baptism, you were also raised with Him through faith in the working of God, who raised Him from the dead. . . . when you were dead in trespasses and in the uncircumcision of your flesh, He made you alive with Him and forgave us all our trespasses* (2:12-13). As evidence of this new life as Christians, Paul encouraged the new believers: *Therefore, put to death whatever in you is worldly: sexual immorality, impurity, lust, evil desire, and greed, which is idolatry. Because of these, God's wrath comes on the disobedient* (3:5-6).

The Christian's strength in fulfilling God's will is the result of letting *the message about the Messiah dwell richly among you, teaching and admonishing one another in all wisdom, and singing psalms, hymns, and spiritual songs, with gratitude in your hearts to God. And whatever you do, in word or in deed, do everything in the name of the Lord Jesus, giving thanks to God the Father through Him* (3:16-17).

Thought for Today: The prayers of the upright are the Lord's delight.

Introduction To The Books Of I & II Thessalonians

After being beaten and jailed in Philippi along with Silas and then miraculously delivered, the apostle Paul arrived in Thessalonica on his second missionary journey (Acts 17:1). This was the capital city of Macedonia (northern Greece) and a prosperous seaport and commercial center. Some Jews, and many Greeks, accepted Jesus during this time and a church was established. *This is why we constantly thank God, because when you received the message about God that you heard from us, you welcomed it not as a human message, but as it truly is, the message of God, which also works effectively in you believers* (I Thessalonians 2:13).

Forced to leave Thessalonica because of violent opposition to his message, Paul journeyed to Berea, where he was well received. But, within a short time, fanatical Jews came from Thessalonica and again fiercely opposed him. He then went on to Athens, where he faced the coldness of the intellectuals and had little success (Acts 17:15-17; I Thessalonians 3:1). From there he went to Corinth (Acts 18:1). In his first letter to the Thessalonians, Paul earnestly urged them to prepare for Christ's return and prayed: *Now may the God of peace Himself sanctify you completely. And may your spirit, soul, and body be kept sound and blameless for the coming of our Lord Jesus Christ* (I Thessalonians 5:23).

In II Thessalonians, Paul foretold that, before Christ returns, evil and wickedness will become more intense under the control of *the man of lawlessness,* the antichrist (II Thessalonians 2:3). At that time there will be intense opposition to the truth of God. He also warned that false teaching will cause a great falling away from the faith. *Don't let anyone deceive you in any way. For that day will not come unless the apostasy comes . . . and the man of lawlessness is revealed, the son of destruction. . . . working, with all kinds of false miracles, signs, and wonders, and with every unrighteous deception among those who are perishing. . . . because they did not accept the love of the truth in order to be saved* (2:3,9-10). The return of Christ is referred to more than 20 times in the 8 short chapters of these two letters.

In Today's Reading

Paul's preaching; his appeal for purity; coming Day of the Lord.

The certainty of the believer's eternal life with Christ is based on the physical resurrection of Jesus Christ (see I Corinthians 15:20-23). The apostle Paul wrote: *Since we believe that Jesus died and rose again, in the same way God will bring with Him those who have fallen asleep through Jesus. For we say this to you by a revelation from the Lord: We who are still alive at the Lord's coming will certainly have no advantage over those who have fallen asleep. For the Lord Himself will descend from heaven with a shout, with the archangel's voice, and with the trumpet of God, and the dead in Christ will rise first. Then we who are still alive will be caught up together with them in the clouds to meet the Lord in the air; and so we will always be with the Lord. Therefore encourage one another with these words* (I Thessalonians 4:14-18).

The physical return of Christ to earth will be the greatest event since His ascension, when *He was taken up as they* (His disciples) *were watching, and a cloud received Him out of their sight* (Acts 1:9). His return was confirmed at the time of His ascension by two witnesses from heaven: *This Jesus, who has been taken from you into heaven, will come in the same way that you have seen Him going into heaven* (1:11).

We can comfort fellow Christians whose loved ones have been called home to be with the Lord with the assurance that soon they will have a joyous reunion – not only with Christ, but also with all their redeemed loved ones.

There are no words to describe the wonderful, glorious, thrilling return of our Lord Jesus Christ. All of history is reduced to just two ages: the present age that began with Adam, and the age to come. *For you yourselves know very well that the Day of the Lord will come just like a thief in the night* (I Thessalonians 5:2). All history is moving toward the appointed *Day of the Lord.* This is the joyous anticipation of every Christian who is faithfully preparing and waiting for the triumphant return of our Redeemer.

Because of this assurance of Christ's return, *encourage one another and build each other up as you are already doing* (I Thessalonians 5:11).

Thought for Today: Security is found in Christ – not material things.

In Today's Reading

Encouragement in persecution; instruction concerning the Day of the Lord; commandment to work.

It grieves our hearts to realize that the vast majority of mankind is blindly rushing toward an eternal lake of fire, ignorant of the horrors of their impending doom and judgment. *This will take place at the revelation of the Lord Jesus from heaven with His powerful angels, taking vengeance with flaming fire on those who don't know God and on those who don't obey the gospel of our Lord Jesus. These will pay the penalty of everlasting destruction, away from the Lord's presence and from His glo-rious strength* (II Thessalonians 1:7-9).

To be sure, much of the world has its heart set on gaining more and more of life's luxuries and on increasing its income level compared to the year before. So they work harder, or get a part-time job, to pay for things they cannot afford. Their fears and frustrations continue to grow as the result of their inability to cope adequately with situations they can't change. This drive has, at times, led to physical and emotional exhaustion, depression, and what some call "burnout."

At times, we are all tempted to be influenced by this spirit of the world that deceives many *with every unrighteous deception among those who are perishing. They perish because they did not accept the love of the truth in order to be saved. For this reason God sends them a strong delusion so that they will believe what is false, so that all will be condemned – those who did not believe the truth but enjoyed unrighteousness* (2:10-12). We need to remind ourselves that we are in a daily spiritual battle against satanic forces.

Without exception, those who choose to invest their lives in serving Christ receive true satisfaction beyond words to explain. This means regularly reading the whole counsel of God to be fully prepared, not merely for a future event, but for present-day living and the ministry of God's word in the use of our time, talents, and possessions.

The apostle John tells us: *These are written so that you may believe Jesus is the Messiah, the Son of God, and by believing you may have life in His name* (John 20:31).

Thought for Today: Jesus Christ is coming soon! It could be today.

Introduction To The Books Of I & II Timothy

In his two letters to Timothy, Paul emphasized that knowing the Scriptures was vital, both for worshiping the Lord and for living to please Him. Then Paul stressed that an important qualification of elders and deacons was to be *a good servant of Christ Jesus, nourished by the words of the faith and of the good teaching that you have followed. . . . If anyone teaches other doctrine and does not agree with the sound teaching of our Lord Jesus Christ and with the teaching that promotes godliness, he is conceited, understanding nothing* (I Timothy 4:6; 6:3-4).

In this first letter, Paul clearly states: *There is one God and one mediator between God and man, a man, Christ Jesus* (2:5). Paul admonished Timothy to remain faithful to Christ and His word.

Shortly before his martyrdom in Rome, Paul wrote his second letter to Timothy, which also was the last letter that he wrote (II Timothy 4:6-7). Paul again urged his beloved Timothy to *be strong in the grace that is in Christ Jesus* (2:1). He warned that failure to thoroughly study all the Scriptures would ultimately result in facing God *ashamed*. He encouraged Timothy to *be diligent to present yourself approved to God, a worker who doesn't need to be ashamed, correctly teaching the word of truth* (2:15). God's word alone provides godly wisdom to instruct you *for salvation* and to know and do God's perfect will (3:15). Knowing all the Scriptures is the only safeguard against deceptions which result from a mixture of truth and error. Paul declared the all-sufficiency of the Scriptures to reveal answers to all of life's problems.

Essential Truth: *All Scripture is inspired by God and is profitable for teaching, for rebuking, for correcting, for training in righteousness, so that the man of God may be complete, equipped for every good work.*

(II Timothy 3:16-17)

In Today's Reading

Warning against false doctrine; thankfulness for mercy; qualifications of church leaders; instructions about the widows and the elderly; the good fight of faith.

The Roman emperor Nero was ruthlessly persecuting Christians and committing many of them to death at the time Paul wrote this letter to Timothy. Yet, Paul emphasized the importance of Christians praying for those who were in authority over them, regardless of their conduct. He wrote: *First of all, then, I urge that petitions, prayers, intercessions, and thanksgivings be made for everyone, for kings and all those who are in authority, so that we may lead a tranquil and quiet life in all godliness and dignity* (I Timothy 2:1-2).

As we pray for world leaders, as well as our local officials, we can be sure our prayers will have an effect upon their actions, whether the men themselves are godly or evil, for *a king's heart is a water channel in the LORD's hand: He directs it wherever He chooses* (Proverbs 21:1).

When Peter and the other apostles were commanded by the religious authorities to stop telling others that Jesus was the Savior of the world, as faithful Christians, *Peter and the apostles replied: We must obey God rather than men* (Acts 5:29).

Christians should faithfully witness to the truth as revealed by Christ and His word, even when it could mean imprisonment or death. Later, Peter also emphasized the responsibility of Christians to be law-abiding citizens, writing: *Submit to every human institution because of the Lord, whether to the Emperor as the supreme authority, or to governors as those sent out by him to punish those who do evil and to praise those who do good* (I Peter 2:13-14).

No one is ever justified in responding to corrupt government with force or by not paying taxes. It is Satan who instigates rebellion, violence, and riots.

Praise God! We can be changed through the power of Christ revealed in His word. *We too were once foolish, disobedient, deceived, captives of various passions and pleasures, living in malice and envy, hateful, detesting one another. But . . . God . . . saved us* (Titus 3:3-4).

Thought for Today: Just think! Every Christian can enjoy the peace of God – regardless of circumstances.

In Today's Reading

Exhortations to Timothy; the coming apostasy; steadfastness in the Scriptures; the charge to preach.

There was no hesitancy in Paul's conviction that he was *an apostle of Christ Jesus. . . . who has saved us and called us with a holy calling, not according to our works, but according to His own purpose . . . before time began* (II Timothy 1:1,9).

The name *Jesus* and the title *Christ* were used six times in the first two verses of chapter 1. In verse 10, we see the word *Savior,* which reminds us of His mission to *save the lost* (Matthew 18:11). The good news of the gospel of Jesus Christ is that He imparts eternal life to all who will receive Him by faith. Everything that we may do in a humanitarian way to help others is incidental to the supreme purpose for which Jesus Christ came – *for the Son of Man has come to seek and to save the lost* (Luke 19:10). Satan seeks to get us involved in "good" activities that have no relevance to eternal spiritual goals.

The Christian life may involve us *in suffering for the gospel, relying on the power of God, who has saved us and called us with a holy calling. . . . This has now been made evident through the appearing of our Savior Christ Jesus, who has abolished death and has brought life and immortality to light through the gospel* (II Timothy 1:8-10).

To deny Christ takes on many forms. Our lifestyle could be a form of denying Him. If, in the midst of a lost world, we remain silent in the presence of gross sin, we deny Him. To not do what we should in reaching the lost world with His word is perhaps the most serious denial of all. We have been forewarned: *The time will come when they will not tolerate sound doctrine, but according to their own desires, will accumulate teachers for themselves. . . . They will turn away from hearing the truth and will turn aside to myths* (4:3-4).

A compromised Christianity supports human greed and lust for comfort, wealth, leisure, and material possessions. What a striking contrast this is to the "good soldier" who "endures hardness" (suffers hardships) and of whom Paul wrote: *To please the recruiter, no one serving as a soldier gets entangled in the concerns of everyday life* (II Timothy 2:4).

Thought for Today: The *will* of God does not lead where the *grace* of God does not provide.

Introduction To The Books Of Titus & Philemon

Paul had left Titus on the island of Crete and this letter was sent to instruct him *to set right what was left undone and, as I directed you, to appoint elders in every town* (Titus 1:5). The Holy Spirit, through Paul, clearly set forth qualifications for an elder (bishop, minister) (1:6-9).

From prison in Rome, Paul wrote his letter to Philemon, who may have been an influential Christian in Colossae and possibly one of Paul's converts.

It appears that Onesimus, a slave that belonged to Philemon, had run away and later became a convert to Jesus Christ through Paul's teachings in Rome. It is assumed that, after becoming a Christian, Onesimus agreed to return to his master in Colossae. This beautiful letter urged Philemon to receive Onesimus, not as a runaway slave, but as a beloved brother in the Lord, just as he would have received Paul himself (Philemon 1:16-17).

God is our Refuge and our Strength
In every time of need,
In life - throughout its breadth and length -
His Spirit e'er doth lead.

The ground of 'faith that will abide'
Is knowledge of His Word;
With which obedience is allied -
In blessed, full accord.

His Angels, ministering spirits are
Encamped around His own -
To guard from dangers, near and far;
- They ne'er are left alone.

So, rest in Him, poor weary heart
Whatever may betide,
His fullest grace He will impart
As we in Him abide.

- M. E. H.

In Today's Reading

The qualifications of church officers; a warning against false teachers; Christian conduct; Paul's appeal for Onesimus.

The churches on the island of Crete needed qualified spiritual leadership. Paul instructed Titus: *The reason I left you in Crete was to set right what was left undone and, as I directed you, to appoint elders in every town: someone who is blameless, the husband of one wife, having faithful children not accused of wildness or rebellion. For an overseer, as God's manager, must be blameless, not arrogant, not quick tempered, not addicted to wine, not a bully, not greedy for money, but hospitable, loving what is good, sensible, righteous, holy, self-controlled, holding to the faithful message as taught, so that he will be able both to encourage with sound teaching and to refute those who contradict it. . . . An overseer, therefore, must be above reproach, the husband of one wife, self-controlled, sensible, respectable, hospitable, an able teacher, not addicted to wine, not a bully but gentle, not quarrelsome, not greedy – one who manages his own household competently, having his children under control with all dignity* (Titus 1:5-9; I Timothy 3:2-5).

The church belongs to Christ. His specific qualifications for spiritual leaders cannot be disregarded; alternative options are unacceptable. Paul's letter to Titus warns that leaders must be blameless in their personal lives and true to all Scripture (Titus 1:6-9).

Paul gave instruction that older men and women should teach the younger men and women, instructing them to forsake evil passions and worldly ambitions, and to live honorably before the Lord *while we wait for . . . the appearing . . . of our great God and Savior, Jesus Christ. He gave Himself for us to redeem us from all lawlessness and to cleanse for Himself a special people, eager to do good works* (2:13-14).

Christ has created all mankind equally precious to Him. Therefore, everyone, rich or poor, weak or strong, regardless of race or nationality, should be treated with equal respect and consideration.

For there is no distinction between Jew and Greek, since the same Lord of all is rich to all who call on Him. For everyone who calls on the name of the Lord will be saved (Romans 10:12-13).

Thought for Today: No one can have feelings of superiority or look upon another as an inferior and be right with God.

Introduction To The Book Of Hebrews

Though the authorship of this book is uncertain, many Bible scholars assume that Paul wrote it while *in his own rented house* in Rome (Acts 28:30). However, the true Author of every book in the Bible is the Holy Spirit.

There are about 30 direct quotations and 50 allusions to the Old Testament in the book of Hebrews.

The superiority of Christ is the major theme in the first five chapters. *Long ago God spoke to the fathers by the prophets at different times and in different ways. In these last days, He has spoken to us by His Son, whom He has appointed heir of all things and through whom He made the universe. . . . So He became higher in rank than the angels, just as the name He inherited is superior to theirs. . . . We must therefore pay even more attention to what we have heard, so that we will not drift away* (Hebrews 1:1-2,4; 2:1; see 3:3; 7:21-27). The Ten Commandments were written on tablets of stone, but Christ's covenant is written upon our hearts (8:10).

The infallible *word of God is living and effective and sharper than any two-edged sword, penetrating as far as to divide soul, spirit, joints, and marrow; it is a judge of the ideas and thoughts of the heart* (4:12).

The word *better* (superior) is one of the key words in Hebrews. *A better hope is introduced, through which we draw near to God. . . . Jesus has now obtained a superior ministry, and to that degree He is the mediator of a better covenant, which has been legally enacted on better promises* (7:19; 8:6).

The old covenant, with its endless animal sacrifices, is in striking contrast to the new covenant which required only one sacrifice, the perfect Lamb of God (Revelation 5:6,12; 13:8). Christ's own sinless blood cleanses us from all our sins (Hebrews 9:12; 10:1-29).

For the Hebrews to worship God under the old covenant, it was necessary for the blood of innocent animals to be offered daily for sin committed in ignorance (Leviticus 4:1-3). However, no offering was provided for deliberate or willful sins (Numbers 15:30). Under the new covenant, we read: *For if we deliberately sin after receiving the knowledge of the truth, there no longer remains a sacrifice for sins, but a terrifying expectation of judgment* (Hebrews 10:26-27; compare Romans 6:1-2).

In Today's Reading

Why Christ assumed a human body; Christ's superiority to angels and Moses; salvation; Christ, our High Priest.

It was angels who delivered Lot out of Sodom (Genesis 19:13-16); who ministered to Jesus following His 40-day fast (Matthew 4:11); and who delivered Peter from prison (Acts 12:11). But, even more comforting to us is to know that angels are *ministering spirits sent out to serve those who are going to inherit salvation* (Hebrews 1:14), including you and me.

The importance of the angels is insignificant compared to the superiority of Christ: *For to which of the angels did He ever say, You are My Son. . . . Therefore He had to be like His brothers in every way, so that He could become a merciful and faithful high priest in service to God, to make propitiation* (atonement) *for the sins of the people* (Hebrews 1:5; 2:17).

Consider the honors conferred upon Moses. Through Moses, the whole Levitical order, the tabernacle, and the worship system were instituted. But Christ is far superior, inasmuch as He is God Himself: *Jesus is considered worthy of more glory than Moses, just as the builder has more honor than the house* (3:3). Moses delivered Israel from Egypt; but Christ delivered all who receive Him by faith from eternal hell and separation from God. Even when it seems that Satan has devastated our lives, God, who created and rules the universe, is making the works of Satan and the wrath of men to serve Him and further His ultimate will for each one of us.

The full revelation and manifestation of the love of God is seen only through Christ, our High Priest. *Forever and ever . . . the scepter of Your kingdom is a scepter of justice. You have loved righteousness and hated lawlessness. . . . For we do not have a high priest who is unable to sympathize with our weaknesses, but One who has been tested in every way as we are, yet without sin. Therefore let us approach the throne of grace . . . that we may receive . . . grace to help us at the proper time* (Hebrews 1:8-9; 4:15-16).

Thought for Today: When Christ, the Prince of Peace rules our hearts, we will not insist on having things our way.

In Today's Reading

Christ, the High Priest; appeal to believe; priestly order of Melchizedek; Aaronic priesthood inferior to Christ's priesthood.

Our greatest need is to *receive mercy*. God is absolutely holy, and as such, He cannot be in the presence of sin. By nature, we are inclined to evil and, consequently, have no rightful claim to His mercy. How we ought to continuously praise Him *that we may receive mercy and find grace to help us at the proper time* (Hebrews 4:16). Yes, our needs for mercy are numerous. Daily we are tempted with satanic thoughts and our moral weakness within often causes us to fall short of what we know through His word is right.

For every high priest taken from men is appointed in service to God for the people, to offer both gifts and sacrifices for sins. He is able to deal gently with those who are ignorant and are going astray, since he himself is also subject to weakness. Because of this, he must make a sin offering for himself as well as for the people. No one takes this honor on himself; instead, a person is called by God, just as Aaron was. In the same way, the Messiah did not exalt Himself to become a high priest, but the One who said to Him, You are My Son . . . You are a priest forever. . . . He became the source of eternal salvation to all who obey Him (5:1-6,9).

When John the Baptist *saw Jesus coming toward him* (he) *said, Here is the Lamb of God, who takes away the sin of the world!* (John 1:29). There was no need for Jesus to make a sin offering for Himself, as was required of Aaron, because Jesus was and is the sinless Son of God. He is now seated at *the right hand of the throne of the Majesty in the heavens* (Hebrews 8:1).

Regardless of the circumstances, let us remember that His unlimited *mercy* and forgiving love are always available (4:16).

But I will sing of Your strength and will joyfully proclaim Your faithful love in the morning (Psalms 59:16).

Thought for Today: We can no more attain a worthwhile purpose in life apart from God than the clay can become a useful vessel apart from the potter.

In Today's Reading

The new covenant; the perfect sacrifice of Christ compared to temporary sacrifices under the law; an appeal to remain faithful.

The tabernacle worship system for Israel was revealed by God to Moses on Mount Sinai. It consisted of numerous sacrifices which could not cleanse from sin, but only "cover" it temporarily. However, every detail of this vast worship system was symbolic of the future sacrifice of Christ on the cross. He replaced Israel's high priest, priests, and all of the sacrificial tabernacle worship. God foretold through His prophet: *I will make a new covenant with the house of Israel, and with the house of Judah* (Jeremiah 31:31; compare Hebrews 8:6-13).

In the old covenant worship, the *blood of goats and calves* (9:12, 19), which were innocent animals, were sacrificed daily for worshipers' sins. But Christ, who is God become Man, shed His own blood and entered, not an earthly holy of holies, *for the Messiah* (Jesus) *did not enter a sanctuary made with hands* (only a model of the true one) *but into heaven itself, that He might now appear in the presence of God for us* (9:24). The confession of our faith is a public acknowledgment that we have renounced the world and its lusts to remain loyal to our Lord and Savior Jesus Christ.

The Holy Spirit signified that the old covenant looked forward to a *greater and more perfect tabernacle.* The words *more perfect tabernacle* (9:10-11) refer to the humanity of Jesus, since its contents, as well as the tabernacle itself, symbolized Christ, His life, ministry, and death, as did all of the sacrifices. Animal sacrifices are no longer acceptable because *the Messiah* (Jesus) *has appeared, high priest of the good things that have come. In the greater and more perfect tabernacle not made with hands (that is, not of this creation), He entered the holy of holies once for all, not by the blood of goats and calves, but by His own blood, having obtained eternal redemption* (Hebrews 9:11-12).

Thought for Today: Yes, God is all-wise, all-powerful, and ever-present. How could we fear the future?

In Today's Reading

Worthy fruits of faith, patience, godliness; warning against disobedience; service well-pleasing to God.

The history of the people of God confirms that many endured adverse circumstances and suffering, yet remained faithful and fulfilled His will. In the "Faith Hall of Fame" we are given a review of some of them. *Abraham, when he was tested, offered up Isaac. . . . He considered God to be able even to raise someone from the dead, from which he also got him back as an illustration. By faith Isaac blessed Jacob and Esau concerning things to come. By faith Jacob, when he was dying, blessed each of the sons of Joseph. . . . By faith Joseph, as he was nearing the end of his life, mentioned the exodus of the sons of Israel. . . . By faith Moses, after he was born, was hidden by his parents . . . and they didn't fear the king's edict. By faith Moses . . . refused to be called the son of Pharaoh's daughter and chose to suffer with the people of God rather than to enjoy the short-lived pleasure of sin. For he considered reproach for the sake of the Messiah to be greater wealth than the treasures of Egypt* (Hebrews 11:17-26). The Old Testament men and women listed in Chapter 11 lived godly lives.

This reminds us of how much more Jesus our Savior has made available to us through the indwelling of the Holy Spirit and the full knowledge of thc will of God through His written word. Surely, we too can *lay aside every weight and the sin that so easily ensnares us, and run with endurance the race that lies before us* (12:1). The Christian life demands self-denial, discipline, and wholehearted love for God and His word. These characteristics distinguish the Christian from the self-indulgence practiced by the world. Each of us must decide for himself, by a prayerful reading of the Scriptures and self-examination, if there are worldly hindrances to our spiritual lives that need to be eliminated.

The race of which Paul writes is a life of faithfulness and obedience to the word of God. The runners who win the race of life are *keeping* (their) *eyes on Jesus, the source and perfecter of* (their) *faith, who for the joy that lay before Him endured a cross and despised the shame, and has sat down at the right hand of God's throne* (Hebrews 12:2).

Thought for Today: *Let your heart keep My commands; for they will bring you . . . a full life* (Proverbs 3:1-2).

Introduction To The Book Of James

The author of this book identifies himself as *James, a slave of God and of the Lord Jesus Christ: To the 12 tribes in the Dispersion. Greetings* (James 1:1).

He was not one of the twelve apostles (Matthew 10:2-4), but appears to be the first presiding elder over the Jerusalem church (Acts 12:17). Paul spoke of him as *James, the Lord's brother* (Galatians 1:19).

James often quotes the Old Testament Scriptures, then proceeds to apply them to Christian living (James 2:8,23; 4:5-6), and he warns *that friendship with the world* makes one *God's enemy* (4:4).

James presents a series of practical tests whereby we may recognize the genuineness of our faith (2:14,17-18,20,22,24,26; 5:15). He admonished each believer *to keep oneself unstained by the world* (1:27).

James reminds us that we have become spiritual children of God by His word of truth *which is able to save you. . . . By His own choice, He gave us a new birth by the message of truth so that we would be the firstfruits of His creatures. . . . Therefore, ridding yourselves of all moral filth and evil excess, humbly receive the implanted word, which is able to save you. But be doers of the word and not hearers only, deceiving yourselves* (1:21,18,21-22).

James explains the great power of prayer by reminding us of Elijah. *The intense prayer of the righteous is very powerful. Elijah was a man with a nature like ours; yet he prayed earnestly that it would not rain, and for three years and six months it did not rain on the land. Then he prayed again, and the sky gave rain and the land produced its fruit* (James 5:16-18).

Essential Truth: *But the wisdom from above is first pure, then peace-loving, gentle, compliant, full of mercy and good fruits, without favoritism and hypocrisy. And the fruit of righteousness is sown in peace by those who make peace.*

(James 3:17-18)

In Today's Reading

Christians to rejoice in trials; heeding the word of God; faith that works; dangers of the tongue; worldliness and pride; warning to the rich; power of prayer.

Most of us are prone to tell others about all our sufferings and sorrows with a "Woe is me" attitude of despair, seeking sympathy from our listeners. But James may surprise you because he wrote: *Consider it a great joy, my brothers, whenever you experience various trials, knowing that the testing of your faith produces endurance. But endurance must do its complete work, so that you may be mature and complete, lacking nothing* (James 1:2-4). How prone we are to blame anyone but ourselves for our failures, or even to blame God. However, James also reminds us: *Blessed is a man who endures trial, because when he passes the test he will receive the crown of life that He* (the Lord) *has promised to those who love Him. No one undergoing a trial should say, I am being tempted by God. For God is not tempted by evil, and He Himself doesn't tempt anyone* (1:12-13). Trials in life may seem to be wasted time, but they are a great benefit to those who remain teachable and faithful to the Lord. The psalmist wrote: *If Your instruction had not been my delight, I would have died in my affliction* (Psalms 119:92).

From time to time, some of our unhappiness comes through our disobedience to the Lord's word. James points out that *each person is tempted when he is drawn away and enticed by his own evil desires. Then after desire has conceived, it gives birth to sin, and when sin is fully grown, it gives birth to death* (James 1:14-15).

All of us need to be reminded to *draw near to God, and He will draw near to you* (4:8). Pity the poor soul who believes that it is only the Devil who is giving him a hard time and, consequently, feels frustrated and distressed. All trials and assaults by Satan are under the permission of God and should prompt us to praise the Lord since the results are in His hands. We don't need to fear what may happen. *In every situation take the shield of faith, and with it you will be able to extinguish the flaming arrows of the evil one* (Ephesians 6:16).

Thought for Today: Sinful things blight our lives, but so do good things that take the place of prayer or Bible reading.

Introduction To The Books Of I & II Peter

In writing these two letters, Peter obeyed two specific commands given to him by the Lord Jesus Himself. *I have prayed for you, that your faith may not fail. And you, when you have turned back, strengthen your brothers* (Luke 22:32). Then *He asked him the third time, Simon, son of John, do you love Me? Peter was grieved that He asked him the third time, Do you love Me? He said, Lord, You know everything! You know that I love You. Feed My sheep, Jesus said* (John 21:17).

Peter called himself *an apostle of Jesus Christ. . . . a fellow elder and witness to the sufferings of the Messiah, and also a participant in the glory about to be revealed* (I Peter 1:1; 5:1). He also mentioned that he was sending this letter from Babylon (5:13). In this first letter, he was writing to encourage the Christians who had fled their homeland because of persecution and had become *the temporary residents of the Dispersion in the provinces of Pontus, Galatia, Cappadocia, Asia, and Bithynia* (1:1).

Throughout the past 2,000 years, Christians have been subjected to much suffering: *You were called to this, because Christ also suffered for you, leaving you an example, so that you should follow in His steps* (2:21).

The highlight of the first book is the importance of the word of God as the only guide for our life in Christ: *Since you have been born again – not of perishable seed but of imperishable – through the living and enduring word of God* (1:23). We are to, *like newborn infants, desire the unadulterated spiritual milk, so that you may grow by it in your salvation* (2:2).

In the interval between the two letters, an even more critical situation of false teaching confronted the church. Peter warned in his second book: *Therefore, brothers, make every effort to confirm your calling and election, because if you do these things you will never stumble . . . . But there were also false prophets among the people, just as there will be false teachers among you. They will secretly bring in destructive heresies, even denying the Master who bought them, and will bring swift destruction on themselves. Many will follow their unrestrained ways, and because of them the way of truth will be blasphemed* (II Peter 1:10; 2:1-2).

In Today's Reading

Call to Christian dedication; proper use of Christian liberty; the example of Christ's suffering.

Peter refers to Christians as *set apart by the Spirit for obedience and for the sprinkling with the blood of Jesus Christ* (I Peter 1:2). "Sprinkling" alludes to the blood which was sprinkled on the altar as a symbol of the people's obedience to God, as well as on the people as a symbol of God's acceptance of them (Exodus 24:1-11).

As Christians, we look forward to *an inheritance that is imperishable, uncorrupted, and unfading, kept in heaven for you, who are being protected by God's power through faith for a salvation that is ready to be revealed in the last time* (I Peter 1:4-5). However, during our brief lifetime in this world, Peter urged us *as aliens and temporary residents to abstain from fleshly desires that war against you* (2:11).

Peter reminded us of the deception of sin, saying: *As obedient children, do not be conformed to the desires of your former ignorance but, as the One who called you is holy, you also are to be holy in all your conduct. . . . By obedience to the truth, having purified yourselves for sincere love of the brothers, love one another earnestly from a pure heart, since you have been born again – not of perishable seed but of imperishable – through the living and enduring word of God. . . . But the word of the Lord endures forever* (1:14-15,22-23,25).

Since the Bible is our source of guidance and strength, Peter urged all believers: *Like newborn infants, desire the unadulterated spiritual milk, so that you may grow by it in your salvation* (2:2). Though Peter directs his words to new converts, he points out that the nourishment of the word is essential if we are to live *as obedient children*. This could only mean our surrender to His authority since it is always in our very best interest. Peter also describes Christians as *a spiritual house for a holy priesthood, to offer spiritual sacrifices acceptable to God through Jesus Christ* (2:5). Each of us is a sacred temple for the indwelling Holy Spirit. In addition, we have been chosen to be *a people for His possession, so that you may proclaim the praises of the One who called you out of darkness into His marvelous light* (I Peter 2:9).

Thought for Today: Can others see a difference between your life as a Christian and your former life as an unbeliever?

In Today's Reading

Duties of husbands and wives; suffering and reward; duties of the elders.

There is just one source of spiritual knowledge and strength. The Holy Spirit led the apostle to write: *If anyone speaks, his speech should be like the oracles* (utterances) *of God; if anyone serves, his service should be from the strength God provides, so that in everything God may be glorified through Jesus Christ. To Him belong the glory and the power forever and ever. Amen!* (I Peter 4:11). In contrast to the word of God are the opinions, reasonings, culture, or traditions of men. We must not minimize, modify, or ignore the only guide to life that our Creator has given as the standard by which we must live.

The last recorded words that Jesus spoke personally to Peter were on the shores of the Sea of Galilee, when Jesus asked three times: *Simon, son of John, do you love Me? Peter was grieved that He asked him the third time, Do you love Me? He said, Lord, You know everything! You know that I love You. Feed My sheep, Jesus said* (John 21:15-17). Peter fulfilled that commission by passing the word along to all of us. Caring, defending, guiding, and numerous other duties are needed to care for believers; but *feed My sheep* means to teach them all of His word, from Genesis to Revelation. All of us can be involved. Some write, edit, print, and others support the distribution of the teaching ministries for Jesus, who commanded us as well: *Feed My sheep*.

The underlying principle of most worldly endeavors is: "How much is in it for me?" This spirit of greed, pride, and power has so permeated everything in our age that even the church is not free from the danger of self-serving ambition. The apostle Paul charged Timothy: *Before God and Christ Jesus, who is going to judge the living and the dead, and by His appearing and His kingdom, I solemnly charge you: proclaim the message; persist in it whether convenient or not; rebuke, correct, and encourage with great patience and teaching* (II Timothy 4:1-2).

Thought for Today: Christian growth is evident when one finds satisfaction in helping others discover spiritual values.

In Today's Reading

God's manifold graces; false teachers; certainty of Christ's return.

This second letter begins with one significant thought – God *has given us everything required for life and godliness, through the knowledge of Him who called us by His own glory and goodness* (II Peter 1:3). Peter's key thought is that a life of godliness is made possible by appropriating the *very great and precious promises, so that through them you may share in the divine nature, escaping the corruption that is in the world because of evil desires. For this very reason, make every effort to supplement your faith with goodness, goodness with knowledge, knowledge with self-control, self-control with endurance, endurance with godliness, godliness with brotherly affection, and brotherly affection with love. For if these qualities are yours they will keep you from being useless or unfruitful in the knowledge of our Lord Jesus Christ. The person who lacks these things is blind and shortsighted, and has forgotten the cleansing from his past sins* (1:4-9).

Since the first concern of God is for His children's moral and spiritual health, whatever is contrary to this in their lives necessarily brings about His loving discipline and correction. His holiness and His wrath against sin are inseparable. *Our momentary light affliction is producing for us an absolutely incomparable eternal weight of glory* (II Corinthians 4:17). God has given us the freedom to choose to let "affliction" work for us or against us. *Therefore, dear friends, since you have been forewarned, be on your guard, so that you are not led away by the error of the im-moral and fall from your own stability. But grow in the grace and knowledge of our Lord and Savior Jesus Christ. To Him be the glory both now and to the day of eternity* (II Peter 3:17-18).

The ultimate goal for the Christian is becoming more Christlike. *For you know that you were redeemed from your empty way of life inherited from the fathers, not with perishable things, like silver or gold, but with the precious blood of Christ. . . . By obedience to the truth, having purified yourselves for sincere love of the brothers, love one another earnestly from a pure heart, since you have been born again – not of perishable seed but of imperishable – through the living and enduring word of God* (I Peter 1:18-19,22-23).

Thought for Today: The Lord forgives all who desire to live for Him.

Introduction To The Book Of I John

The writer of this book did not identify himself. However, many believe him to be John, the apostle *whom Jesus loved* (John 13:23). The Holy Spirit's first and main theme is *the word.*

John said that he and others had seen with their own eyes *what was from the beginning, what we have heard . . . what we have observed, and have touched with our hands, concerning the Word of life. . . . The one who says, I have come to know Him, without keeping His commands, is a liar, and the truth is not in him. But whoever keeps His word, truly in him the love of God is perfected. This is how we know we are in Him* (I John 1:1; 2:4-5).

As a second theme, he exposes the "professing Christians" who continue to pursue *the lust of the flesh, the lust of the eyes, and the pride in one's lifestyle* (2:16).

In theme number three, we are reminded that love is the distinguishing characteristic of a Christian. The word *love* appears about 46 times in these five short chapters. The indwelling love of God causes a remarkable transformation in the lives of Christians. It imparts a desire to live in full obedience to the will of God, as revealed in His word. *We know that when He appears, we will be like Him, because we will see Him as He is. And everyone who has this hope in Him purifies himself just as He is pure* (3:2-3).

In a fourth theme, we are warned against false teaching: *Test the spirits to determine if they are from God, because many false prophets have gone out into the world. . . . They are from the world. Therefore what they say is from the world, and the world listens to them* (4:1,5).

A fifth theme is: *I have written these things to you who believe in the name of the Son of God, so that you may know that you have eternal life* (5:13). Assurance of salvation and eternal life are prominent as seen by the vast number of references to the born again followers of Christ (2:3,5,29; 3:14,19,24; 4:13,16; 5:15,18-20). *We know that everyone who has been born of God does not sin, but the One who is born of God keeps him, and the evil one does not touch him. We know that we are of God, and the whole world is under the sway of the evil one. . . . guard yourselves from idols* (5:18-19,21).

In Today's Reading

Fellowship with God; reality of and remedy for sin; danger of antichrists; children of God and righteousness; loving one another.

Most of us know someone whom we admire and respect. Often we pattern our lives after that person. Our heavenly Father has provided us with the incomparable Role Model in all of history – Jesus Christ. Let us follow His example, even as John wrote: *If we say, We have fellowship with Him, and walk in darkness, we are lying and are not practicing the truth. But if we walk in the light as He Himself is in the light, we have fellowship with one another* (I John 1:6-7).

There are some who have a relationship with Christ, but still *walk in the darkness* of the world. The darkness of the natural mind is always more concerned about one's self, one's well-being and one's successes. But, the spiritually minded who *walk in the light as He . . . is in the light,* are first and foremost concerned that Christ be *exalted* in their attitude and conversation with others.

A characteristic of "darkness" is a desire to be noticed, a feeling of supremacy by drawing attention to self and seeking to dominate conversations. With others, it appears in the form of impatience, a sensitive spirit that's easily offended, a disposition to resent and retaliate when contradicted, or a desire to criticize.

A jealous disposition, a secret spirit of envy, or a disposition to speak of the faults and failings of others rather than their virtues are also characteristics of "darkness" and expose one's pride. Some walk in "darkness" with a spirit of discouragement and self-pity, and a determination to convey that spirit to everyone who will listen.

Then there are those who are so preoccupied with their own self-image and their ambitions that they are indifferent to reaching a lost world with the good news that Jesus died to save them.

Pity the person who feels he has no need to pray: *Search me, God, and know my heart; test me and know my concerns. See if there is any offensive way in me; lead me in the everlasting way* (Psalms 139:23-24).

Thought for Today: Those who harbor hatred do far more damage to themselves than they do to those whom they hate.

In Today's Reading

How to test the spirits; an appeal to brotherly love; the witness of the Spirit.

The apostle John speaks of many antichrists: *Children, it is the last hour. And as you have heard, Antichrist is coming, even now many antichrists have come. We know from this that it is the last hour* (I John 2:18). While John warned of all those who are anti-Christ (against Christ), there is coming a day when one unique person will be known as the Antichrist. As such, he will openly oppose God and all biblical, spiritual, and moral principles. *Don't let anyone deceive you in any way. For that day will not come unless the apostasy comes first and the man of lawlessness is revealed, the son of destruction* (II Thessalonians 2:3). Because of this, John counseled: *Dear friends, do not believe every spirit, but test the spirits to determine if they are from God, because many false prophets have gone out into the world* (I John 4:1).

False prophets are deceiving multitudes today because they are usually popular, friendly, and courteous. But how does one *test the spirits*? John explained: *This is how you know the Spirit of God: Every spirit who confesses that Jesus Christ has come in the flesh is from God. But every spirit who does not confess Jesus is not from God* (4:2-3). Deception today is widespread and often difficult to discern.

If Jesus is less than fully God and yet fully Man, what hope have we of salvation? A good man, however good, could not atone for our sins. Only Jesus, fully God and fully Man, in His perfect life as a sinless Man wholly dependent upon God the Father and becoming the final blood sacrifice in our stead, could save our souls from the curse of sin.

Our assurance of eternal life does not rest on our feelings, which change with circumstances, nor on our ability to detect enemy spirits, but only on our assurance *that the Father has sent the Son as Savior of the world. Whoever confesses that Jesus is the Son of God – God remains in him and he in God. And we have come to know and to believe the love that God has for us. God is love, and the one who remains in love remains in God, and God remains in him* (I John 4:14-16).

Thought for Today: The sincerity of our love for Christ can be measured by the kindness that we show to others.

Introduction To The Books Of II & III John & Jude

The writer of **II John** referred to himself as *the Elder*, and the letter is addressed from *the Elder: To the elect lady and her children, whom I love in truth – and not only I, but also all who have come to know the truth* (II John 1:1). While some believe the letter was addressed to an individual, others believe that, since persecution was so intense at the time the book was written, the author was actually writing to the church, or the bride of Christ, and its members, whom he addressed as *children, whom I love in truth*. He goes on to say: *I was very glad to find some of your childen walking in truth, in keeping with a command we have received from the Father* (1:1,4). The writer emphasized the importance of teaching the word of God. The word *truth* is used five times in the first four verses of II John. Believers are urged to examine their traditions, opinions, beliefs, and motives as they read the letter, to make sure they are living according to the truth of the word of God.

In **III John**, the word *truth* is used 6 times in its 14 verses. We are introduced to three people: Demetrius, whom John praises; Gaius, a generous helper and colaborer in the work of the Lord; and Diotrephes, a man with exceptional abilities but who was a hindrance to the ministry. We need to remember that no one can be neutral in regard to the gospel; these men are examples of many today who are either helping or hindering the ministry of Christ.

Jude identifies himself as *Jude, a slave of Jesus Christ, and a brother of James: To those who are the called, loved by God the Father and kept by Jesus Christ* (Jude 1:1). Jude was not the Judas of John 14:22, but is considered to have been the Judas of Matthew 13:55 and Mark 6:3.

Because of growing pressures and persecution, Jude encouraged his readers to stand fast and *to contend for the faith that was delivered to the saints once for all* (Jude 1:3). Jude's letter is devoted to exposing the fearful, deadly consequences of believing false doctrines and false teachers. *Certain men, who were designated for this judgment long ago, have come in by stealth; they are ungodly, turning the grace of our God into promiscuity and denying our only Master and Lord, Jesus Christ* (1:4), meaning that, since salvation is by grace and not of works, they taught that Christians could continue to sin. The apostle Paul had written against such apostasy: *How can we who died to sin still live in it?* (Romans 6:2).

In Today's Reading

The commandment to love; warning against deceivers; Diotrephes rebuked; judgment on false teachers.

In his brief but very important letter to all believers, Jude wrote: *I found it necessary to write and exhort you to contend for the faith that was delivered to the saints once for all. For certain men . . . have come in by stealth; they are ungodly, turning the grace of our God into promiscuity and denying our only Master and Lord, Jesus Christ. . . . Woe to them!* (Jude 1:3-4,11). To *contend* implies not only the necessity of knowing that *all Scripture is inspired by God* (II Timothy 3:16), since it alone is the final word on all doctrine, but that we must also speak out against every form of religious deception.

There is a superficial and deceptive unity being promoted today by many who have joined hands with religions that reject Christ as the Only God and Savior. Such religions also deny either the total deity or the total humanity of Jesus. Many assume there is but one god who is called by various names such as Allah or Buddha. They conclude that all religions are equally acceptable. Others say that as long as you are sincere, it doesn't matter what you believe. But Jesus said: *No one comes to the Father except through Me* (John 14:6). Luke proclaimed: *There is salvation in no one else, for there is no other name under heaven given to people by which we must be saved* (Acts 4:12).

Jude warns that deceivers will be judged. *In the same way, Sodom and Gomorrah and the cities around them committed sexual immorality . . . and serve as an example by undergoing the punishment of eternal fire* (Jude 1:7). *Woe to them! For they have traveled in the way of Cain, have abandoned themselves to the error of Balaam for profit, and have perished in Korah's rebellion* (1:11; Numbers 16:1-3,31-35).

Jude closes by saying: *Now to Him who is able to protect you from stumbling and to make you stand in the presence of His glory, blameless and with great joy, to the only God our Savior, through Jesus Christ our Lord, be glory, majesty, power, and authority before all time, now, and forever. Amen* (Jude 1:24-25).

Thought for Today: Knowing God's word is the only safeguard against being deceived by false teachings.

Introduction To The Book Of Revelation

The aged apostle John was imprisoned on Patmos (Revelation 1:9), a small, rocky island about ten miles long and six miles wide, which lies about 35 miles off the southwest coast of Asia Minor (modern-day Turkey). During this imprisonment, John received *the revelation of Jesus Christ that God gave Him to show His slaves what must quickly take place* (1:1). John is told to *write on a scroll what you see and send it to the seven churches: Ephesus, Smyrna, Pergamum, Thyatira, Sardis, Philadelphia, and Laodicea* (1:11). . . . *from Jesus Christ, the faithful witness, the firstborn from the dead and the ruler of the kings of the earth* (1:5; also 1:18; 2:8). This final message of Christ to His church is exceedingly important. These seven churches point out the dangers that still confront Christians today. In addition, we learn the importance of being an "overcomer" and the glorious future that the Lord has prepared for us. As we read through this book, we will recognize the progression of the plan of God as the events of prophecy unfold.

More than 300 symbolic terms throughout the book of Revelation describe numerous events concerning Christ and His church. His ultimate, glorious, and eternal reign is the outstanding theme and promise. The symbols can be understood by referring to their use in over 500 references in the Old Testament. However, there is danger of becoming fascinated by the details of future events and failing to see that Revelation is the unveiling of the Person and purpose of Jesus Christ, who must be the center of all things. The key phrase is the book's first five words: *The revelation of Jesus Christ*. We find the sacrificial title of Christ as *the Lamb* 28 times in Revelation. Four aspects of Christ as *the Lamb* are seen in Revelation: In chapters 4 – 5, the worship of *the Lamb* is celebrated; in chapters 6 – 18, the wrath of *the Lamb* is detailed; the second coming and Armaggedon are revealed and the wedding of *the Lamb* and the great white throne judgment are observed in chapters 19 – 20; and, in chapters 21 – 22, the wife of *the Lamb* is described.

The last glorious event involving Christ on earth was His ascension, and the next great event will be His soon return.

We *hear the words of this prophecy and keep what is written in it, because the time is near!* (Revelation 1:3).

In Today's Reading

Greetings to the seven churches; a vision of the Son of Man; His messages to the churches.

Seven churches of Asia Minor each received a letter dictated by Christ and recorded by John while he was on the island of Patmos. Since the character and conduct of churches and Christians is the same in every generation, the messages are just as vital for us today.

Words of praise were given to the church at Ephesus for its sound doctrine. However, Christ said: *You have abandoned the love you had at first* (Revelation 2:4).

Losing devotion to Christ usually happens gradually. Some become so much involved in business, leisure activities or even church responsibilities that worship of Christ becomes a mere formality. The charge is most serious: *Remember then how far you have fallen* and *repent* (2:5). Twice in one verse Jesus said: *Repent.*

The letter sent to the church at Smyrna mentioned that they were suffering: *I know your tribulation and poverty, yet you are rich* (2:9). This church appeared destitute of the comforts of life. Some would be cast into prison, others would suffer persecution. But because of their loyal devotion, the Lord promised: *Be faithful until death, and I will give you the crown of life* (2:9-10).

The letter Jesus Christ sent to the church at Pergamum said they lived *where Satan's throne is! And you . . . . did not deny your faith in Me* (2:13). However, some *hold to the teaching of Balaam, who taught Balak to place a stumbling block in front of the sons of Israel . . . to commit sexual immorality* (2:14). *Repent! Otherwise, I will . . . fight against them with the sword of My mouth* (2:16). False prophets like Balaam seem to have one thing in common; they are motivated by money. Others today say they have a "special revelation of the truth" that must be the guide to biblical interpretation. In Paul's letter to the Galatians, he warned of the dangers of *a gospel other than what we have preached to you. . . . if anyone preaches to you a gospel contrary to what you received, a curse be on him!* (Galatians 1:8-9).

Thought for Today: Our present burdens may often seem heavy, but the Lord always enables us to bear them.

In Today's Reading

Our Lord's messages to the churches at Sardis and Philadelphia; disapproval of the church at Laodicea; the sealed book.

The church in Sardis had no Nicolaitans, Balaams, or Jezebels. They could boast that there were no false teachers, nor was false doctrine being taught; but there was an equally serious evil. What a fearful revelation when the King who knows all things announces: *To . . . the church in Sardis write . . . I know your works; you have a reputation for being alive, but you are dead. Be alert and strengthen what remains, which is about to die, for I have not found your works complete before my God . . . repent* (Revelation 3:1-3).

A few people in Sardis . . . have not defiled their clothes, and they will walk with Me in white. . . . the victor . . . I will never erase his name from the book of life (Revelation 3:4-5). Jesus had also said: *If you keep My commandments you will remain in My love* (John 15:10).

In Philadelphia, Jesus commended them for their faithfulness, saying: *Look, I have placed before you an open door that no one is able to close; because you have limited strength, have kept My word, and have not denied My name. . . . I will also keep you from the hour of testing that is going to come over the whole world* (Revelation 3:8,10).

The majority of church members in Laodicea probably congratulated themselves on being moderate and broad-minded. They could pity the zealous Christians in other churches who provoked the anger of their neighbors who worshiped false gods. The Laodicean believers could also pride themselves on their ability to compromise and make friends with those who hated Christ. But Jesus severely condemned this church: *So, because you are lukewarm, and neither hot nor cold, I am going to vomit you out of My mouth* (3:16-17). Our Lord appealed to them: *Be committed and repent* (3:18-19). This means pay the price for true faith. Compromise is both self-deceiving and self-destructive.

The King of kings and Lord of His church is still knocking on doors of men's hearts with the same words of encouragement: *I will give him the right to sit with Me on My throne, just as I also won the victory and sat down with My Father on His throne* (Revelation 3:21).

Thought for Today: A Christian can lay up treasures in heaven which no one on earth can steal.

In Today's Reading

The seven seals; 144,000 sealed; the numberless multitude; four trumpets sounded.

The exile of John on Patmos and the suffering taking place in Smyrna (Revelation 2:8-10) are examples of the persecution that was intensifying against Christians throughout the Roman Empire.

However, we are thrilled to read one of the greatest promises of the Bible: *After this I looked, and there was a vast multitude from every nation, tribe, people and language, which no one could number, standing before the throne and before the Lamb. They were robed in white with palm branches in their hands. And they cried out in a loud voice: Salvation belongs to our God, who is seated on the throne, and to the Lamb!* (7:9-10). This multitude had overcome Satan and are, at last, in the presence of their Lord and Savior. This revelation has strengthened the faith of many Christians who have faced fierce opposition from a hostile world.

Each generation of believers discovers that the opposition is strong, the wicked numerous, and the deceptions so subtle that, in our human strength and wisdom, we would easily lose heart or be led astray. Down through the ages, those who have had their hearts set upon living for Jesus have always been a small minority. As Jesus foretold: *How narrow is the gate and difficult the road that leads to life; and few find it* (Matthew 7:14). However, the total population of heaven will be *a . . . multitude . . . which no one could number*. These faithful Christians may not have had much of earth's pleasures but life is exceedingly short compared to eternity. The trials we face now will seem insignificant compared to the glorious privilege of being in the presence of the King of kings throughout the ages.

God deserves our highest praise for what He is in Himself, and for His great love in giving us eternal life. *The Lamb who is at the center of the throne will shepherd them; He will guide them to springs of living waters, and God will wipe away every tear from their eyes* (Revelation 7:17).

Thought for Today: Every day "Praise the Lord" for who He is and what He has done for you!

In Today's Reading

Fifth and sixth trumpets; the angel and the little scroll; the two witnesses; the seventh trumpet.

A voice from heaven directed the apostle John to go, *take the scroll that lies open in the hand of the angel who is standing on the sea and on the land. So I went to the angel and asked him to give me the . . . scroll. He said to me, Take and eat it; it will be bitter in your stomach, but it will be as sweet as honey in your mouth. Then I took the little scroll from the angel's hand and ate it. It was as sweet as honey in my mouth, but when I ate it, my stomach became bitter. And I was told, You must prophesy again about many people, nations, languages, and kings* (Revelation 10:8-11).

John is first given a *little scroll* symbolic of God's word. Once it was digested, he was qualified to tell the world that the *little scroll* has a message that is exceedingly sweet to those who have received Christ as Savior; but the same scroll has an exceedingly bitter message to all who reject Him as Lord of their lives. The act of eating all of it speaks of understanding and appropriating all the Scriptures into our lives (compare Ezekiel 2:8-9; 3:1-3).

Jesus then said: *I will empower my two witnesses, and they will prophesy for 1,260 days, dressed in sackcloth* (Revelation 11:3). They will face overwhelming opposition. *When they finish their testimony, the beast that comes up out of the abyss will make war with them, conquer them, and kill them* (11:5-8). These *two witnesses* of Christ cannot be martyred until they have *finished their testimony*. Then, and only then, the enemies of God *will make war with them, conquer them, and kill them. . . . Those who live on the earth will gloat over them and celebrate and send gifts to one another, because these two prophets tormented those who live on the earth* (11:7,10). Regardless of how fearful our future may appear, we can enjoy the peace of God, knowing that everything is under His absolute control. *The seventh angel blew his trumpet, and there were loud voices in heaven saying: The kingdom of the world has become the kingdom of our Lord and of His Messiah, and He will reign forever and ever!* (Revelation 11:15).

Thought for Today: Praise the Lord! Our God reigns! Our work for the Lord cannot end until He allows it.

In Today's Reading

The sun-clad woman; the dragon; a baby boy; the blood of the Lamb; the beasts.

A great sign appeared in heaven: a woman clothed with the sun, with the moon under her feet, and a crown of 12 stars on her head. She was pregnant and cried out in labor and agony to give birth. Then another sign appeared in heaven: There was a . . . fiery red dragon having seven heads and 10 horns, and on his heads were seven diadems. . . . And the dragon stood in front of the woman who was about to give birth, so that when she did give birth he might devour her child. But she gave birth to a Son – a male who is going to shepherd all nations with an iron scepter – and her child was caught up to God and to His throne (Revelation 12:1-5). This is reference to the birth and ascension of Jesus Christ.

The great dragon . . . the ancient serpent, who is called the Devil and Satan, the one who deceives the whole world (12:9), is always in opposition to the people of God. Satan is given four designations here: *Dragon* portrays his monstrous character as the enemy of God; *Serpent* points out his deception as in the Garden of Eden; *Devil* reminds us that he is a slanderer, and *Satan* means adversary. *Your adversary the Devil is . . . looking for anyone he can devour* (meaning to defeat or discourage) (I Peter 5:8). His most effective means of defeating a Christian are the "good" things that appeal to our human nature. We seek success on earth and happiness through material things. But, only as we surrender to His will do satisfying blessings become our way of life. This is illustrated in *the woman* (who) *fled into the wilderness, where she had a place prepared by God, to be fed there* (Revelation 12:6). The trial of the remnant of God occurs in *a wilderness,* which also appears to be a desert-like moral condition of this world ruled by the *great fiery red dragon* (Satan) (12:3). But, there is a precious peace in the desert – leaving the results in the hands of our Creator. God is never defeated.

They conquered him by the blood of the Lamb and by the word of their testimony, for they did not love their lives in the face of death (Revelation 12:11).

Thought for Today: Satan thrives on the biblical ignorance of saints.

The 7 Churches of Asia
(Revelation Chapters 2 & 3)

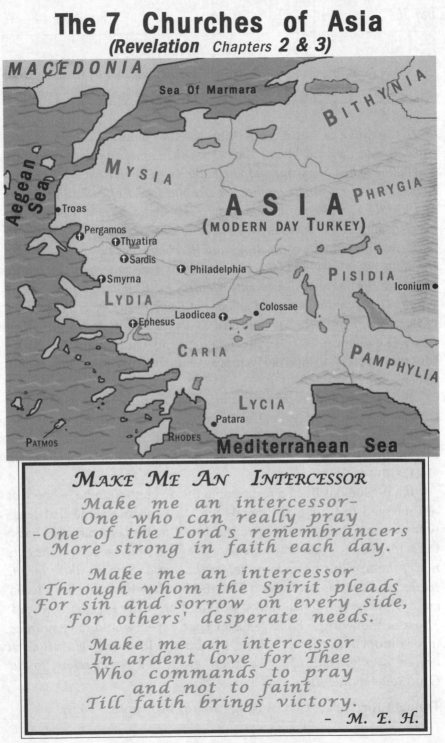

Make Me An Intercessor

Make me an intercessor-
One who can really pray
-One of the Lord's remembrancers
More strong in faith each day.

Make me an intercessor
Through whom the Spirit pleads
For sin and sorrow on every side,
For others' desperate needs.

Make me an intercessor
In ardent love for Thee
Who commands to pray
and not to faint
Till faith brings victory.

\- M. E. H.

In Today's Reading

The Lamb; messages of the three angels; harvest of the earth; preparation for the seven vials (bowls) of wrath.

In the midst of world chaos, John is led to report good news: *Then I looked, and there on Mount Zion stood the Lamb, and with Him were 144,000 who had His name and His Father's name written on their foreheads. I heard a sound from heaven like the sound of cascading waters and like the rumbling of loud thunder. The sound I heard was also like harpists playing on their harps. They sang a new song before the throne and before the four living creatures and the elders, but no one could learn the song except the 144,000 who had been redeemed from the earth. These are the ones not defiled with women, for they have kept their virginity. These are the ones who follow the Lamb wherever He goes. They were redeemed from the human race as the firstfruits for God and the Lamb* (Revelation 14:1-4). *The Lamb* is the triumphant Christ on Mount Zion, the location of His temple. His sheep, whom Satan cannot deceive, are the undefiled.

Here is the endurance of the saints, who keep the commandments of God and the faith in Jesus. Then I heard a voice from heaven saying, Write: Blessed are the dead who die in the Lord from now on. Yes, says the Spirit, let them rest from their labors, for their works follow them! (14:12-13).

If a person has lived a respectable life, even though he or she was not devoted to Christ, at funerals we all want to assume that Jesus will welcome them into heaven. But to *die in the Lord* can only mean those for whom Jesus prayed: *They have kept Your word. . . . They are not of the world, just as I am not of the world. Sanctify them by the truth; Your word is truth* (John 17:6,16-17). They have taken up Jesus' cross of daily self-denial (Luke 9:23) and are truly serving the Lord. Those of the world who have never been saved would have nothing in common with those praising the Lord with *a vast multitude in heaven, saying: Hallelujah! Salvation, glory, and power belong to our God* (Revelation 19:1).

Thought for Today: God's loving care for us is unlimited.

In Today's Reading

Babylon, the mother of abominations; the doom of Babylon predicted; fall of Babylon.

The apostle John reports that *he carried me away in the Spirit to a desert. I saw a woman sitting on a scarlet beast that was covered with blasphemous names, having seven heads and 10 horns. . . . She had a gold cup in her hand filled with everything vile and with the impurities of her prostitution. On her forehead a cryptic name was written: BABLYON THE GREAT THE MOTHER OF PROSTITUTES AND OF THE VILE THINGS OF THE EARTH* (Revelation 17:3-5). Old Testament Babylon became the most magnificent capital city of the ancient world, and its king Nebuchadnezzar controlled the then-known world. During his conquests, he destroyed the kingdom of Judah, as well as the temple of God and the holy city of Jerusalem.

BABYLON THE GREAT THE MOTHER OF PROSTITUTES, seated on the *beast,* illustrates the political and religious God-defying forces that one day soon will control the world. This apostate ecumenical federation of churches and world religions will give full support to the one-world political and economic system called the *scarlet beast,* which will be ruled by the antichrist.

The *woman* and the *beast* represent the close alliance that exists between the world government called the beast and the harlot Babylon who pretends to be the true church.

This false church will promote the "equality of all religions." Eventually, together they will fiercely oppose Jesus Christ as *the only way* to obtain eternal life. The message of this ecumenical superchurch will be based on social issues, humanitarian objectives, and lifeless formalism, and will appeal to the majority of people.

The forces of the world *will make war against the Lamb, but the Lamb will conquer them because He is Lord of lords and King of kings. Those with Him are called and elect and faithful* (Revelation 17:14).

Daily we face the forces of Satan – lust, hate, and envy. In the midst of this chaotic universe, Jesus said: *Blessed are the peacemakers, because they will be called sons of God* (Matthew 5:9).

Thought for Today: Praise the Lord, Jesus of Nazareth, the King of Peace will soon return.

In Today's Reading

Marriage supper of the Lamb; rider on the white horse; Satan bound and doomed; great white throne judgment.

I saw heaven opened, and there was a white horse! Its rider is called Faithful and True, and in righteousness He judges and makes war (Revelation 19:11). *Then I saw the beast, the kings of the earth, and their armies gathered together to wage war against the rider on the horse and against His army* (19:19).

Another scene takes place before *a great white throne and One seated on it. Earth and heaven fled from His presence, and no place was found for them. I also saw the dead, the great and the small, standing before the throne, and books were opened. Another book was opened, which is the book of life, and the dead were judged according to their works by what was written in the books. Then the sea gave up its dead, and Death and Hades gave up their dead; all were judged according to their works. Death and Hades were thrown into the lake of fire. This is the second death. . . . And anyone not found written in the book of life was thrown into the lake of fire* (20:11-15). This is the final destination of Satan and all who reject Christ as Savior and Lord. God will not push His way into one's life. Repentance is a redemptive experience which leads to forgiveness. It buries the past under the blessed hope of tomorrow *and the appearing of the glory of our great God and our Savior, Jesus Christ* (Titus 2:13).

Think how joyous it will be for those who do repent and accept Jesus Christ as Savior and Lord of their lives, to see again their loved ones and all the saints of the ages: Abraham, Jacob, Joseph, David, and Paul. However, first, and best of all, we will meet Jesus, our wonderful Redeemer. *A voice came from the throne, saying: Praise our God, all you His servants, you who fear Him, both small and great! Then I heard something like the voice of a vast multitude, like the sound of cascading waters, and like the rumbling of loud thunder, saying: Hallelujah – because our Lord God, the Almighty, has begun to reign! Let us be glad, rejoice, and give Him glory, because the marriage of the Lamb has come, and His wife has prepared herself* (Revelation 19:5-7).

Thought for Today: Satan distorts the facts, but the word of God reveals the truth.

In Today's Reading

The new heaven and the new earth;
the heavenly Jerusalem; Christ's coming.

We are not left with uncertainty as to what lies beyond the grave. One day, *when the 1000 years are completed* (Revelation 20:7,11-13), all true followers of Christ will dwell in *a new heaven and a new earth, for the first heaven and the first earth had passed away, and the sea existed no longer. I also saw the Holy City, new Jerusalem, coming down out of heaven from God, prepared like a bride adorned for her husband. Then I heard a loud voice from the throne: Look! God's dwelling is with men, and He will live with them. They will be His people, and God Himself will be with them and be their God* (21:1-3).

The struggles of this life, and our war against sin, will soon end. Then *He will wipe away every tear from their eyes. Death will exist no longer; grief, crying, and pain will exist no longer, because the previous things have passed away* (21:4).

Just think! There will be no more crying, no physical distress, and no suffering; and no condemnation will press on our consciences. There will be no fear of evil; *nothing profane will ever enter it: no one who does what is vile or false, but only those written in the Lamb's book of life* (21:27) will be there. Oh! the joy that awaits us in its full realization. Praise His wonderful Name! We soon will be welcomed home by our wonderful Lord!

In our glorious, future, eternal home *nothing profane* can enter. *Therefore dear friends, since we have such promises, we should wash ourselves clean from every impurity of the flesh and spirit, making our sanctification complete in the fear of God* (II Corinthians 7:1). . . . *and every high-minded thing that is raised up against the knowledge of God, taking every thought captive to the obedience of Christ* (10:5).

We close this glorious revelation of Jesus Christ, having completed the reading of the entire God-given guide to life, and we hear Jesus say: *Yes, I am coming quickly. Amen! Come, Lord Jesus!* Our heartfelt response to our Savior is: *Come, Lord Jesus!* For our readers, our prayer is that *the grace of the Lord Jesus be with all the saints. Amen* (Revelation 22:20-21).

Thought for Today: Death promotes Christians into everlasting life.

Daily Topical Reference Index

(PARTIAL LIST)

Note: Numbers refer to days rather than pages